Sanford D. Horwitt

LET THEM CALL ME REBEL

Sanford D. Horwitt was born in Milwaukee, Wisconsin. He received his bachelor's and doctoral degrees at Northwestern University and later taught at the University of Illinois. In Washington, D.C., he served as speechwriter and legislative aide to U.S. Representative Abner J. Mikva, and currently works as a writer and policy adviser for national public interest and advocacy organizations. He and his wife have two children and live in Arlington, Virginia. *Let Them Call Me Rebel* is his first book.

LET THEM CALL ME REBEL

LET THEM CALL ME REBEL

 Saul Alinsky—
His Life and Legacy

Sanford D. Horwitt

Vintage Books
A Division of Random House, Inc.
New York

FIRST VINTAGE BOOKS EDITION, APRIL 1992

Copyright © 1989 by Sanford D. Horwitt

All rights reserved under International and Pan-American Copyright Conventions. Published in the United States by Vintage Books, a division of Random House, Inc., New York, and simultaneously in Canada by Random House of Canada Limited, Toronto. Originally published in hardcover by Alfred A. Knopf, Inc., New York, in 1989.

Library of Congress Cataloging-in-Publication Data
Horwitt, Sanford D.
    Let them call me rebel: Saul Alinsky, his life and legacy /
Sanford D. Horwitt.—1st Vintage Books ed.
        p.   cm.
    Originally published: New York: Knopf: Distributed by Random
House, 1989.
    Includes bibliographical references and index.
    ISBN 0-679-73418-X
    1. Alinsky, Saul David, 1909-1972.   2. Radicals—United States—
Biography.   3. Social reformers—United States—Biography.
4. Community organization—United States—History—20th century.
I. Title.
HN90.R3H615   1992
303.48'4'092—dc20   91-50701
                            CIP

Manufactured in the United States of America
10 9 8 7 6 5 4 3 2 1

To

my mother

Mary Horwitt

and

Joan, Dusty, and

Jeffrey

Let them call me rebel and welcome,
I feel no concern from it; but I should
suffer the misery of devils, were I to
make a whore of my soul. . . .

—THOMAS PAINE,
as quoted by Saul Alinsky in
the epigraphs to his books
Reveille for Radicals and
Rules for Radicals

CONTENTS

24 pages of illustrations will be

found following page   334

ACKNOWLEDGMENTS

Eight years is a long time to have spent researching and writing a book, but exploring the life of Saul Alinsky and meeting so many of the people who were part of his world has been a great privilege. I treasure the many evenings I spent with Rachel and Ralph Helstein in Chicago; the memorable day in Toronto in Jane Jacobs's backyard, where I was treated to wonderful stories and great thoughts; the morning in Mill Valley with Gordon Sherman, that gentle man of uncommon courage and integrity; the times spent with Nicholas von Hoffman, whose wit, wisdom, and generosity I enjoyed and appreciate. And I cherish my new friendships with Jack Egan and Fred Ross, whose contributions to the cause of social justice are unending and profound. All these men and women share a deep devotion to democratic ideals, and each in his or her own way has been an inspiration to me as well as to many others.

Another great inspiration has been my friend Frank Haiman at Northwestern University, who by personal example and scholarship has taught several generations of students the value of freedom of thought and speech in a democratic society. Also at Northwestern, John McKnight, director of Community Studies at the Center for Urban Affairs, has been a good friend and intellectual resource, and I am grateful to him and the Center for their support.

I am also indebted to George Todd, former director of the Wieboldt Foundation, for his extraordinary kindness and personal interest in this project. Grants from the Wieboldt Foundation, the Woods Charitable Fund, the Joyce Foundation, and the Chicago Resource Center helped to defray some of the travel and research costs. Similarly, I want to thank the New World Foundation in New York and its former president, David Ramage.

I might never have thought seriously about writing this book had it not been for the urging and encouragement of my sister-in-law, Washington *Post* reporter Margaret Engel. Since then, there have been other helping hands, including the many people who gave generously of their time and whose names appear in the pages of this book. But I would also like to thank some people who have helped in other ways, including Mary Ann Bamberger, assistant librarian of special collections at the University of Illinois at Chicago, and Archie Motley, curator of manuscripts at the Chicago Historical Society. Their expertise and guidance were invaluable resources.

On my many forays into Chicago, my home-away-from-home was at Mim and Dick Lyon's house, and I will be forever grateful for their love and hospitality. Other friends in Chicago and elsewhere whom I can only begin to thank for their help are: Zoe Gratsias, Betty Steele, Ellen Warren, Wade Nelson, Jerry Watson, Allison Engel, Jerry Esrig, Dick Meltzer, Carl Tjerandsen, Robert Slayton, Peggy Roach, Bernard Doering, and Jimmy Epstein.

A friend who read the final manuscript and liked it said: "You must have had a good editor." The truth is that I had a *great* editor, Elisabeth Sifton, and I thank her for a superb job. I am also grateful to her assistant, Jenna Laslocky, for her help and good cheer. And I appreciate Carol Mann's efforts in getting this book off the ground and headed in Elisabeth Sifton's direction.

During this long odyssey my wife, Joan, and my sons, Dusty and Jeffrey, have been forever understanding and helpful, and in many ways this is their book too.

Finally, I'd like to thank Saul Alinsky's family, friends, and associates who shared their recollections with me and provided access to correspondence and other important information. All of this was done with "no strings attached"—I suspect that everybody who cooperated did so with the expectation, or hope, that I would be fair and reasonably accurate in my interpretations. I have done my best, and take full responsibility for the results.

S.D.H.

INTRODUCTION

I remember distinctly the first time I "met" Saul Alinsky: it was early in the afternoon, I was in the university library reading an interview with him published in *Harper's* magazine, and before I had finished Alinsky had leaped from the pages, ten feet tall, the most fascinating person I had ever encountered. I was no less impressed when I met him in person a month later at a ten-day retreat near Monterey, California, where he propounded his theories on social change, or on several subsequent occasions in Chicago in the late 1960s and early '70s.

Young graduate students of twenty years ago were not the only ones thus affected. Many political journalists were similarly attracted by Alinsky's uniqueness—Jules Witcover even described him as the most interesting person he had ever known in public life. Alinsky's friend the renowned Thomist scholar Jacques Maritain called him "one of the truly great men of our century."

Saul Alinsky first burst upon the national scene in 1945 with a best-selling book, *Reveille for Radicals,* a passionate account of how he had established "People's Organizations" in industrial slums, most notably in the notorious Back of the Yards in Chicago, the old immigrant stockyards community that had been the setting for Upton Sinclair's muckraking masterpiece, *The Jungle.* In short order, Alinsky took a phrase from the dull vocabulary of social work—"community organization"—and turned it into something controversial, important, even romantic. "We the people will work out our own destiny" was the rallying cry and motto of The Back of the Yards Neighborhood Council which Alinsky, together with Joseph Meegan, organized in the summer of 1939. During the next four decades, he and his lieutenants taught people in other communities throughout the country how to organize to better their lives and working conditions; everywhere they went they won fame for their efforts to help poor people and others help themselves. Indeed, Alinsky had invented a new political form, and in the 1960s, his star rose to new heights amid the turmoil of that decade. Alinsky-style community organization came to suggest David-

and-Goliath struggles marked by colorful, confrontational tactics: dumping a mound of garbage in front of a tavern owned by the wife of an alderman, to protest his unresponsiveness to complaints of inadequate garbage pickup, or dispatching black tenants of a run-down tenement to picket the white suburban home of the slumlord who has refused to make necessary repairs. He also pioneered the use of stockholdings by churches and others to help promote socially responsible policies on the part of corporations. Alinsky's urban populism was immensely attractive and successful, but how it evolved—and out of what amalgam of elements—is a story as complex and idiosyncratic as the man himself.

Saul Alinsky was a character, 'most everybody who knew him agreed. But even his close friends were often not quite sure which character he was. Was that the real Saul Alinsky who enjoyed flaunting a bagful of personal oddities and foibles, or was that only a character whom the real Saul Alinsky enjoyed playing? Sometimes it seemed as though the mask and the face might be one and the same.

There is in Alinsky a hint of Randall McMurphy, the heroic figure of Ken Kesey's best-selling 1960s novel, *One Flew Over the Cuckoo's Nest* (a nonconformist's bible, as one critic called it). McMurphy is bold, raucous, shrewd, and, above all, fearless. He challenges and defies Big Nurse, the poised, powerful, oppressive symbol of Authority who runs a mental ward in a state hospital for The Combine, the secret power center that controls society. It is her job to keep the "mentally ill"—the misfits and malcontents—under control. But by standing up to Big Nurse, McMurphy demonstrates that the establishment can be beaten and in the process rallies the patients in the ward to overcome their fears and fight for their freedom and dignity. There is an echo here not only of Alinsky's fearlessness, ribaldry, and anti-establishment instincts, but of his prodding and agitating of the downtrodden urban poor: not only can they beat City Hall, but they must, they will, and they'll have a ball doing it!

And yet Saul Alinsky was in many respects far removed from a northwestern lumberjack like McMurphy. While Alinsky was certainly intuitive and shrewd, nervy and aggressive, he was also reflective, interested in ideas, even intellectual, an urbanized Russian Jew educated in the University of Chicago's renowned sociology department.

Throughout Alinsky's life there was confusion about where to place him and his concepts on the political spectrum, more confusion than one would have expected of a man who had been a friend and supporter of the great labor leader John L. Lewis and the industrial labor movement in the 1930s, a self-professed radical in the 1940s, and an outspoken advocate of racial integration and civil rights in the 1950s and 1960s. But other symbols and ideas are associated with Alinsky, too: he had a powerful ally in the Catholic Church; he insisted that power—not reason—was fundamental to the achievement of social change; he often adopted an anti-intellectual pose and used or encouraged tactics that violated normal canons of good taste and civility. Such behavior made many conventional liberals uncomfortable, even hostile, while to others further to the left, Alinsky's disavowal of a class analysis made him and the importance of his work suspect.

But at the height of his career Alinsky was the center of press attention—and a hero to many journalists, among others—not only because he was working in the explosive urban scene with considerable effectiveness but also because he was doing it with flair and style. Alinsky could be counted on for a good one-liner, or a zinger deflating some pompous politician, or controversial broadsides that few others would deliver on the record. And he always made good copy. At a time when he was working closely with a number of Catholic clergy, he blasted the reactionary cardinal of Los Angeles as "an unchristian, prehistoric muttonhead." When he came to Rochester, New York, invited by white churches and the black community to build a community organization after the bloody race riot there in 1964, he infuriated executives of the Rochester-based Eastman Kodak firm with the line that "Kodak's only contribution to race relations was the invention of color film." A fan of his own mischief-making, Alinsky later recalled with delight the community uproar in Rochester that greeted his suggestion as to what might be the only way for poor blacks to get the attention of the smug, self-righteous establishment: they should purchase a large bloc of tickets to a performance of the Rochester symphony—but, just before arriving, they would all get together for a huge baked-bean dinner so that at the symphony, Alinsky deadpanned, their presence could not be ignored.

College student activists in the 1960s and '70s sought out Alinsky for advice about tactics and strategy. On one such occasion, in the spring of 1972, at Tulane University's annual week-long series of events featuring leading public figures, students asked Alinsky to help plan a protest of a scheduled speech by George Bush, then U.S. representative to the United Nations—a speech likely to include a defense of the Nixon administration's Vietnam War policies. The students told Alinsky they were thinking about picketing or disrupting Bush's address. That's the wrong approach, he rejoined, not very creative—and besides, causing a disruption might get them thrown out of school. He told them, instead, to go to hear the speech dressed as members of the Ku Klux Klan, and whenever Bush said something in defense of the Vietnam War, they should cheer and wave placards reading "The KKK Supports Bush." And that is what the students did, with very successful, attention-getting results.

NO QUICK summing up or concluding paragraph can capture the complexity of this fascinating character whose life suggests, among other things, that one can be heroic without being saintly. The larger significance of his life lies in his persistent experimentation with a set of ideas and methods aimed at addressing a number of the country's historic, enduring problems, especially those having to do with race, poverty, and political inequality.

Alinsky was a true believer in the possibilities of American democracy as a means to social justice. He saw it as a great political game among competing interests, a game in which there were few fixed boundaries and where the rules could be changed to help make losers into winners and vice versa. He loved to play the game and had a special flair for it. During a lifetime of action and experimentation, he created a set of new tactics and strategies for playing the game—and, most important, excited the imagination of a succeeding generation of players to carry on. Alinsky's influence, relevance, and legacy live on in no small part because he effectively advanced the great American radical ideal that democracy is for ordinary people.

LET THEM CALL ME REBEL

Sarah's Son

In the early 1950s Saul Alinsky wrote a play with a friend, Robert Shayon. The play was a comedy about labor-union politics of the 1930s. The backdrop was a power struggle between the President of the United States and the president of a large federation of unions—Franklin D. Roosevelt and John L. Lewis thinly disguised—and the protagonist was Socrates McGuinness, a not so thinly disguised portrait of Alinsky, who is introduced midway through the first act:

> Socrates is a lean, tall rangy man of forty-five. He has had an excellent education. He is brilliant, intellectual and cultured. On the other hand, his twenty years in the labor movement have given him a rugged, colloquial simplicity which makes him equally at home in a drawing room, on a picket line, or in a bar-room brawl. Brooks Brothers have never left him. He wears a banker's gray, rather rumpled, single-breasted suit.

Modesty was not an Alinsky virtue. Of course, he took a certain amount of dramatic license in creating McGuinness, and the result was a composite of the real and the imagined, but to a considerable extent, Alinsky did that in real life, too, for he had a lively imagination. He liked to tell stories, but he was not a liar.

In fact, Alinsky was an unusually good storyteller; he savored the fun of a good yarn. His friends and associates eagerly collected and traded Alinsky's stories and, of course, he was the star of many of them. One set of stories had to do with his association with colorful, exotic crime figures—members of the Capone mob or promising young mobsters from the tough Italian street gangs on the West Side of Chicago in the 1930s. One story, which Alinsky recounted in an interview in 1971, nearly thirty-five years after the fact, went this way:

> [I was] investigating a gang of Italian kids who called themselves the 42 Mob. They were held responsible by the D.A. for about 80 percent of the auto thefts in Chicago at the time, and they were just graduating into the outer fringes of the big-time rackets. It was even tougher to get in with them than with the Capone mob, believe me. Those kids were really suspicious and they were tough, too, with hair-trigger tempers. I finally got my chance when one of the gang's leaders, a kid named Thomas Massina, or Little Dumas, as he called himself, was shot and killed in a drugstore stick-up. The minute I heard about it, I went over to the Massina home, hoping to get in good with Dumas' friends. But they were as leery as ever. By a stroke of luck, though, I heard Mrs. Massina, Dumas' mother, weeping and wailing, repeating the same thing over and over in Italian. I asked one of the kids what she was saying and he said she was bemoaning the fact that she didn't have any pictures of Dumas since he was a baby, nothing to remember him by. So I left right away, picked up a photographer friend of mine and rushed down to the morgue. I showed my credentials and the attendant took us in to the icebox, where Dumas was laid out on a slab. We took a photograph, opening his eyes first, then rushed back to the studio to develop it. We carefully retouched it to eliminate all the bullet holes, and then had it hand-tinted. The next morning, I went back to the wake and presented the photograph to Mrs. Massina. "Dumas gave this to me just last week," I said, "and I'd like you to have it." She cried and thanked me, and pretty soon word of the incident spread throughout the gang. "That Alinsky, he's an all-right motherfucker," the kids would say, and from that moment on they began to trust me.

This is a preposterous story, one might think, invented long after the fact. Yet, in the late 1930s, Alinsky and a colleague wrote a description of how they had gained the trust of West Side gang members. One of the episodes they described had to do with the shooting death of Little Dumas.

> The authors visited Thomas' mother and noticed that in her grief she would occasionally sob that she did not even possess a picture of her dead son. The authors arranged to have a police photographer take a picture of Thomas in the morgue. The picture (touched up) was then presented to Mrs. Massina. . . . News of this action spread throughout

the community. It was regarded by the community as a kind, considerate act to a grief stricken mother (who had the sympathy of the community) and it secured the writers the descriptive title of "regular guys."

Alinsky's friends over the years learned not to dismiss his apparently farfetched stories too quickly, even when their normal level of credulity was being pushed. He had a great deal of nerve, he was disdainful of many of the rituals of polite, conventional behavior, and he loved to be mischievous. As the years rolled by and the Alinsky stories accumulated, the line between fact and fiction often blurred. With the passage of time, it also seemed to matter less what part of a story had been literally true or merely, in Eric Hoffer's apt phrase, "the truth imagined." The passage of time, however, never did obscure the roots of Saul Alinsky's extraordinary personality, at least not among those who knew the Alinsky family.

BETWEEN 1840 AND 1900, Chicago's population grew from 4,000 to 1.7 million. German, Irish, and Polish immigrants came in waves to a city that rapidly became a major railroad and commercial center. Immigration to Chicago, and to the United States in general, in the last half of the nineteenth century was spurred by natural calamities, such as the Irish potato famine, and by political ones. For Russian Jews, the brutal pogroms of 1881 following the assassination of Alexander II were, indeed, a calamity. For the next several decades, there was a mass exodus of Eastern European Jews, many of whom came to the United States. Many of those arrived in New York and stayed; others eventually headed west. By 1897, one Russian-Jewish immigrant, Benjamin Alinsky, had left New York and moved to the teeming Maxwell Street area of Chicago, a short distance south of the city's downtown area.

Benjamin was in his late twenties when he arrived in Chicago and took up residence as a tailor at 263 Maxwell Street. He came to Chicago with a wife, a woman whom he had met in New York. They had three children—Harry, Max, and Kay—before they separated. The children stayed with Benjamin. As his tailoring business prospered, Benjamin Alinsky moved to new quarters on the edge of the Maxwell Street area, on Hastings Street, and remarried. In January 1909, Benjamin and Sarah Tannenbaum Alinsky had their first son, Saul David.

Many years later, Saul Alinsky painted a somewhat selective account of "growing up in the slums"—which, in intended effect, was probably

supposed to be the urban-poor, Jewish-ghetto equivalent of the Abraham
Lincoln log-cabin legend. For example, Alinsky said, "I was born in one
of the worst slums in Chicago. . . . We were poor—my parents were
Russian immigrants, Jewish and very orthodox. . . . [My mother] was only
seventeen when she had me. As a kid I remember living in back of a store.
My idea of luxury was to live in an apartment where I could use the
bathroom without one of my parents banging on the door for me to get
out because a customer wanted to get in."

It is true that Sarah Alinsky was quite young when Saul was born, and
about twenty years younger than her husband, whom she probably met
when she went to work for him as a seamstress. They were both Orthodox
Jews, as were the vast majority of the immigrants who lived in the Maxwell
Street area. Life was not easy for those packed into this small, rectangular
Jewish ghetto. At the turn of the century, by one estimate, if the city of
Chicago had had the population density of Maxwell Street, it would have
housed the entire population of the Western Hemisphere. Sweatshops were
everywhere, and almost always in tenement houses. It is possible that this
early memory of Saul's was of living behind his father's shop on Hastings
Street. But few immigrants stayed in the Maxwell Street ghetto if they
could help it, and by 1910 Jews started to move en masse farther west, to
the Douglas Park–Lawndale area. In 1915, when Saul had just turned six,
the Alinskys moved to Douglas Park, too, where his father bought a new,
nine-flat apartment building on the corner of Thirteenth and Springfield.
Living in a poor, overcrowded ghetto was, at the most, an experience
confined to Saul's earliest childhood.

It was not the personal experience of grinding poverty that made the
deepest impression on young Saul Alinsky. For, through his elementary
and high school years, Sollie, as he was known in school and to his friends,
lived in this mostly pleasant neighborhood of Douglas Park, near the
center of Jewish cultural life on the West Side: several blocks east was
Independence Boulevard, where wealthier Jewish families lived and where
some of the largest synagogues were built; two blocks west was the dividing
line between Jewish Douglas Park and a largely Polish neighborhood. Saul
remembered invading gangs of Polish boys crossing Crawford Avenue
"and storming into our neighborhood and we'd get up on the roofs with
piles of bricks and pans of boiling water and slingshots, just like a medieval
siege. I had an air rifle myself. There'd be a bloody battle for blocks around
and some people on both sides had real guns, so sometimes there'd be
fatalities." Gangs of Jewish boys would retaliate by invading the Polish
territory, and if the numbers were against them and they needed help, they
might go to Davey Miller's pool hall on Twelfth Street, where the older,
bigger guys hung out.

The fact that Benjamin Alinsky was able to buy the light-yellow brick apartment building in 1915 was not exactly a rarity, but it was not commonplace either. Affluence and heightened social status among West Side Jews were mostly confined to Independence and Douglas boulevards. On the other hand, most of the apartment buildings in Douglas Park were modest two- or three-flats. It was an achievement of sorts, therefore, even for a man already well into his forties to have his own nine-flat, to own a little real estate.

In most other respects, however, Benjamin Alinsky was a man of few accomplishments and noticeable limitations. He is remembered in the neighborhood as an unattractive man, not so much in his features as in his bearing and image. He was heavy and disheveled—neighbors called him a *shlub*. He worked long hours in his tailor shop and went to the synagogue regularly. Orthodox Jews interested in cultural or political activities could join a variety of clubs and organizations—the more progressive-minded joined the socialist Workmen's Circle—but Benjamin Alinsky had few such interests. Indeed, in spite of some financial success, he appears to have been a withdrawn, passive man who would never become Americanized enough to operate confidently in a wider sphere.

Sollie Alinsky was Sarah's son; it could not have been any other way. It was not merely that Benjamin was ineffectual and, having already raised three children, uninterested. It was simply that Sarah Alinsky—even as a very young woman—was a force to be reckoned with under any circumstances.

Sarah was the third oldest of six children—four boys and two girls—whose parents lived in a small town in Belorussia. The oldest child, Sam, was the first to emigrate to the United States, and in the early 1900s he arranged for the others to come, too. They remained a reasonably close-knit family, except for Sarah, who didn't get along well with any of them. "She wasn't very close to the brothers," recalls Sarah's nephew Walter Frank. "And the brothers didn't think much of Sarah."

After Sarah was divorced from Benjamin in 1922, she took at least three other husbands, divorcing one and outliving the other two. She also outlived Saul. Sarah, a survivor but on her terms, was demanding, self-centered, and manipulative. Her coarse energy and drive were expressed in an Old World Yiddish style. Yes, Sarah Alinsky was a Jewish mother, but that familiar generalization covers a broad spectrum of characteristics. There were meddlers and there were meddlers. There were cajolers and there were cajolers. Sarah Alinsky was an extremist, a brassy scourge who was not always interested in taking prisoners. Kay, youngest of Benjamin's children from his first marriage, lived for a while with her father and Sarah, but she remembers being forced out by Sarah's attacks and tirades.

Toward Sollie, Sarah was protective—a tendency intensified by the death from either influenza or diphtheria of a younger, second son, Ablim. Sollie became not merely the only son but the only surviving child of a doomed marriage. Sarah, in turn, became forever vigilant. When the other ten- and eleven-year-olds on the Alinsky block would play a version of stickball in the street or in the passageway between the Alinskys' apartment building and the Blumenthals' three-flat, Sollie (a few of the kids also called him "Cottonhead" because of his thick, curly hair) would often stand off to the side watching, safely removed from the action. If, by chance, Sarah's son was picked on, she could appear in a flash, throwing her arms around him and screaming, "Everybody hits my Sollie. Those who dig graves will fall in themselves."

When he was thirteen, Saul was bar-mitzvahed. Soon thereafter, his parents were divorced and Benjamin escaped to California, where his other children, now adults, had migrated. Prior to the divorce, there had been rumors on Springfield Avenue of an affair between Sarah and a deliveryman from a cleaning store. But while Sarah was nobody's favorite neighbor, Benjamin Alinsky was such a hapless figure—by now into his fifties and clearly a mismatch for Sarah—that this alleged affair provoked no dramatic reprobation.

Despite the family turmoil, Saul was able to do reasonably well in school. His first eight grades were at Bryant School, a short walk to the west, in the Polish territory just over the Crawford (later Pulaski) Avenue dividing line, though it drew most of its students from Douglas Park and was 90 percent Jewish. In the fall of 1922, Saul entered Marshall High School, also heavily Jewish. (In that same year a Hebrew Club was organized there.) Marshall was a large school that was getting bigger, and Saul's freshman class of 750 had to be split into morning and afternoon shifts. A little more than half of the class enrolled in either a two-year or a four-year commercial course, while the remainder, including Saul, took the general course.

As a freshman Saul received grades of "fair" or "good," but his grades improved during the four years and as a senior he earned an "excellent" in English, civics, and European history, and a "superior" in U.S. history. The most significant episodes during this time, however, happened outside the classroom. When Saul was fourteen he severely injured his hip playing football with friends. Decades later, he still talked of his long hospital stay, of being immobilized in a cast, and of his uncertainty as to whether he would walk again without crutches. Only a few years after he recovered, he wrote in a college term paper of his despondency while confined in a cast: "Life . . . was stretched out before me as black, hopeless." At least on one occasion, he even had brief thoughts of suicide. Later, though, he told family members that his nearly yearlong incapacitation provided a chance for extensive reading, a habit he maintained into adulthood.

The other significant episodes involved Saul's visits to his father in California. It is unclear whether Benjamin or Sarah insisted on these visits—or whether they were nothing more than a convention to be fulfilled. In any event, Saul's nonrelationship with Benjamin continued. About those California trips, Saul remembered: "I didn't see much of my father except to say, 'Hello,' and three months later to say, 'Goodbye.' Out there I lived alone." Except, according to his testimony, when he had a brief fling with an "older" woman: "I was shacked up with an old bag of twenty-two. When you are sixteen or seventeen, twenty-two is really an old bag." Whatever adventurous cast Saul tried in retrospect to put on his summer visits to his father, the reality almost certainly included loneliness and embarrassment. Although it was typical for American children of Russian-Jewish immigrants to be ill at ease with their parents' Old World ways, Saul's disrespect for his father was an extreme case. Still, he said, "I don't think I ever hated the old man; I never really knew him and what little I did know just didn't interest me." But the estrangement between the two was virtually complete by the time Saul was thirty. When Benjamin died in 1952, he left an estate of $30,000. To Saul, he left $50.

As distant as Saul was from his father, the emotional ties to his mother were strong and enduring. Sarah, with her unfocused aggression and overpowering style, left her indelible imprint on her only son. Saul's widow, Irene, felt that if you knew the mother, you knew the son. And throughout the years, there was a consensus among Saul's friends about Sarah. Many different people used many of the same words to describe her—not so much her nature as her style, since that was paramount. And one phrase was used more often than any other to sum her up, to explain what it was like to have the experience—some would say misfortune—of dealing with her. "Sarah Alinsky," they would say in Yiddish in the old West Side neighborhood, *"iz a plotka fuhrer."* Sarah was, indeed, a troublemaker. It was her style. For her son, it would be a profession.

2

Helene and the University of Chicago

When Saul Alinsky entered the University of Chicago in the fall of 1926, the university was not yet four decades old and its architectural center-piece, the Rockefeller Memorial Chapel, was two years away from comple-tion. But in its short history the university had already begun to make its mark. Backed by John D. Rockefeller's money, its first president, William Rainey Harper, had recruited the presidents of seven other colleges to join the fledgling Chicago faculty. In the early years, the likes of John Dewey, Thorstein Veblen, and George Herbert Mead gave it genuine scholarly luster. Through most of the 1920s, the Law School had a reputation of the first rank, and the Sociology Department was often called the world's finest. The University of Chicago by the mid-1920s may not have rated with Harvard and Yale, but it was considered perhaps the best school in the Midwest.

The student body that Alinsky joined in 1926 had a sizable Jewish minority. The poorer Jewish students, those who could not afford the $270-a-year tuition, often started at another Chicago area school—perhaps one of the night schools, or even the Central YMCA College—and then transferred. That Alinsky went directly to Chicago from high school was a measure of his relative financial security. Kay Alinsky, Saul's half sister, claims that their father paid for Saul's tuition and that it was a source of resentment for her and her older brothers because it was far more financial help than he had given them. Nonetheless, few students from Chicago at the university were actually wealthy or even comfortably affluent. Children from well-to-do families most likely went away to college. Those who could not afford to go away chose either Northwestern or Chicago, and since the former was thought of as a North Shore party school, Chicago was the first choice of the brighter, more serious students.

In spite of the University of Chicago's solid academic reputation, the pre-Depression period was not one of great intellectual fervor for under-graduates on campus. There was, for example, little serious political activity, little interest in making waves on social issues. The Liberal Club had just seven student members in 1929. The faculty, with a rare exception such as Robert Lovett, had no radical orientation. The campus atmosphere was to change dramatically under the leadership of "boy wonder" Robert Maynard Hutchins, who became university president at the age of twenty-nine in Alinsky's senior year, and then from the politicizing effects of the Depression. But in the fall of 1926, the campus was a generally tranquil, apolitical place, a reflection of the larger society.

As an undergraduate, Saul Alinsky had two significant experiences. One was his discovery of the university's famed sociologists, and the other was meeting an attractive girl from Elkins Park in Philadelphia named Helene Simon. Both these discoveries came later in Alinsky's undergraduate years. In his first two years, he simply struggled. By the end of his freshman year, during which he flunked an American history course and received no grade above a C, Alinsky was on academic probation. The next year saw only modest improvement, and he remained on probation. For a boy who had done well in high school, this mediocre performance must have been a blow to both his confidence and his self-image. Apart from his classes, Alinsky took no active part in organized campus life. He is identified with no activities in his class yearbook and he belonged to none of the Jewish fraternities that might have been open to him. He was, for most of his undergraduate days, something of a loner. That is not to suggest that Alinsky was generally withdrawn. Far from it. For on an interpersonal basis, outside of a formal institutional or organizational setting, he was outgoing, interesting, opinionated, glib, sharp-tongued, profane. What he was not, above almost all else, was an organization man.

Returning from summer vacation in September 1928, Alinsky began his junior year in E. W. Burgess's social pathology course, the first in which he received an A. Ernest Watson Burgess and Robert Ezra Park were giants in America's first Sociology Department. Their jointly authored textbook, *Introduction to the Science of Sociology* (1921), was a landmark in the field; according to one scholar, "the direction and content of American sociology after 1921 was mainly set by the Park and Burgess text." Park and Burgess shared an office in the department, and while Park was generally regarded as intellectually the stronger of the two, Burgess was highly respected for his pioneering empirical studies and for his prodigious capacity for work. He had a reputation for working fourteen- to sixteen-hour days, six or seven days a week, fifty-two weeks a year. He never married, living much of his life with a spinster sister. While extraordinarily conscientious about his work and his students, Burgess was also excruciatingly dull as a lecturer. He was, according to one of his colleagues, "the most unobtrusive, self-effacing kind of person you could imagine." Ernest Burgess and Saul Alinsky had personalities that were polar opposites, but for the first time as a college student, Saul found somebody whose questions and sociological analysis stimulated his own intellect.

Park, Burgess, Ellsworth Faris, and W. F. Ogburn were the senior members of the department by the late 1920s. They were the second generation. The Sociology Department had been organized in 1892 under the chairmanship of Albion Small. A primary concern of the first two generations at Chicago was to develop a new science of social behavior. This demanded, among other things, a conscious effort at objectivity and scholarly detachment. Sociology was not to be confused, for example, with social work. Nor would serious sociologists follow the example of E. A. Ross, at the University of Wisconsin, whose sociological research was merely part of a larger interest in social reform.

Yet to a significant extent, these men, Park and Burgess in particular, were reformers—though not in the political arena, which would have been incompatible with their role as social scientists and with their own scholarly temperaments. The liveliest discussions and disagreements within the department in the late 1920s were not about politics but about the relative merits of the case-study method versus the statistical approach. At a faculty–graduate student picnic during the height of the controversy, a softball game was played by a team of case-study practitioners against a team of statistical advocates. Much of the reforming zeal of the Chicago sociologists was directed toward a new understanding of the city or, more precisely, of American industrial cities like Chicago with large, recently arrived immigrant populations. Park, Burgess, and the others were interested in concepts that could explain the ecological structure of the city. Park, for instance, spoke of cities as composed of "natural areas"—that is, slums, business districts, etc.—which occurred in similar patterns in any city of a given type. "[These natural areas] are the products of forces that are constantly at work to effect an orderly distribution of populations and functions within the urban complex," he wrote. "They are 'natural' because they are not planned, and because the order that they display is not the result of design, but rather a manifestation of tendencies that city plans seek—though not always successfully—to control and correct."

The Burgess zonal hypothesis was a graphic display of the ecological tendencies in all larger industrial cities. A map could be constructed of various zones, beginning with a central business zone, followed by an industrial and slum zone, then a zone farther from the center where newly arrived immigrants lived, and so forth to the edge of the city. Such analyses by Burgess and his colleagues, which identified demographic characteristics unique to each area or zone, helped to counteract, for example, the nineteenth-century argument of the eugenics movement that slums were populated by the genetically inferior. The Chicago sociologists argued that social disorganization, not heredity, was the cause of disease, crime, and other characteristics of slum life. Thus, when members of an immigrant group became acculturated and prosperous enough to move out of a slum neighborhood, social disorganization and its consequences did not follow them to the new neighborhood. This recurring pattern, Park and Burgess argued, showed that it was the slum area itself, and not the particular group living there, with which behavior pathologies were associated.

Park had acknowledged in his famous paper on the city in 1915 that the modern industrial urban complex was shaped by more than ecological factors. "The fact is . . . that the city is rooted in the habits and customs of the people who inhabit it. The consequence is that the city possesses a moral as well as a physical organization, and these two mutually interact in characteristic ways to mold and modify one another." Yet the primary perspective on the city for Park and Burgess was ecological. While such a perspective would lead to progressive, community-based approaches to combat crime and juvenile delinquency, it did not necessarily encourage an analysis or a more radical program which might focus on existing economic and power arrangements that prolonged slum life for a newly arrived immigrant group or that made slums inevitable.

Many of these Chicago sociologists who were so fascinated by the city came from small-town, rural backgrounds. Several had fathers who were ministers, and one, Faris, had himself been a missionary in the Belgian Congo before turning to an academic career. Thus, the rough-and-tumble quality of Chicago had an almost exotic appeal. This was the city of Al Capone, of machine guns and machine politics, of the infamous 1919 race riot, of immigrant slums and Gold Coast wealth. Chicago became a fertile laboratory for Park and Burgess and for their students. It was common practice for both undergraduate and graduate students to be sent into neighborhoods to observe behavior, collect data, and write reports on a broad range of urban life, including the offbeat world of dance halls, skid rows, and rooming houses.

One of Alinsky's first field-study assignments for Burgess's course was to visit Chicago's public dance halls. Many sociology students were involved in various aspects of the dance-hall project, which included a detailed plotting or mapping of dance-hall locations and a study of how these correlated with the public transportation system, the types of people who

frequented a particular hall, and so forth. Dance halls were a popular
meeting place for young men and women in the 1920s. Although their
image was on the whole more savory than that of taxi-dance establishments, managements were often concerned with stratagems to keep trouble
to a minimum. On a return visit as a participant-observer to the Dreamland
Ballroom, Alinsky wrote in his report for Burgess:

> The most striking change . . . was the fact that the orchestra had been
> moved from the center of the floor to the side. This may sound trivial
> to the reader but it is very significant. When the orchestra was in the
> center of the ballroom, [there] was a circling, milling mob of dancing
> and very much immoral dancing at the center of the milling mob,
> which was the most congested area on the floor. [Now] I noticed a
> decrease of "dirty" dancing due to this change and a general improve-
> ment throughout the ballroom.

Part of Alinsky's job as a participant-observer, as it was for many of
the other sociology students, was to ingratiate himself or win the trust of
the dance-hall crowd so that he could conduct interviews and compile
personal histories. At the Merry Garden Ballroom on the North Side, for
example, he coaxed a reticent publicity manager to open up by becoming
a sympathetic audience for the manager's complaint that his ballroom
didn't receive the acclaim that the Aragon did. Young Saul was good at
this schmoozing, and at projecting a certain kind of credibility in the
fractious world of Chicago dance halls and, later, with street gangs on the
tough West Side.

Alinsky flourished in this environment on the edges of conventional
culture because, at the simplest level, he looked and sounded as if he
belonged. With a cigarette dangling from the corner of his mouth, he could
speak easily in the language of the street and could strike a pose that, if
it did not quite suggest toughness, effectively passed for surliness. Where
the pose ended and the real Saul Alinsky began was not always clear. What
was clearer, however, was that he was finally attracted to an academic
pursuit that allowed him to draw on his strengths. In the process, he was
also beginning to develop a sociological perspective, a more sophisticated
understanding of the relationships among Chicago's institutions and
people.

From the early field-work experiences with Burgess had come
Alinsky's first taste of success in the classroom at Chicago. There would
be more courses with Burgess in Alinsky's last year and a half as an
undergraduate, leading eventually to graduate work and a budding career

in another of Burgess's special interests—the study of crime and juvenile delinquency in urban areas.

ELKINS PARK, in northeastern Philadelphia, had very little in common with the Douglas Park neighborhood in Chicago where Saul Alinsky grew up. Elkins was an area of considerable affluence and even wealth, where, as in the nearby suburbs, handsome big houses stood on rolling, terraced acreage. There were swimming pools, flower gardens, and carefully arranged shrubbery commonly tended by hired gardeners. Many families had several full-time servants—cooks and maids and, occasionally, chauffeurs. In the 1920s, this was where the elite German Jews of Philadelphia lived and where immigrant Polish or Russian Jews—the Alinskys of the world—most certainly did not live.

Helene Simon was the youngest of three children. In 1906, several years before she was born, and when Saul's father was still living in Chicago's Maxwell Street ghetto, the Simons moved from an inner section of Philadelphia out to Elkins Park, where they bought a large Victorian house on the largest plot in the area, set off by box hedges in symmetrical design, an orchard, and a large formal garden (where, years later, Helene and Saul would be married).

Helene's father was a wholesaler in the liquor business. When Helene first started school, her parents sent her to Oaklane Country Day, an expensive private school that had been started by some parents who thought public education wasn't good enough for their children. Before her high school years, however, Helene's father suffered serious financial losses in real estate and she left Oaklane and went to the public school. Nonetheless, if the Simons were not considered wealthy by the standards of the wealthiest German Jews, they had a comfortable life and a daughter who was bright, athletic, and popular.

Helene Simon was fair-skinned, with blue eyes and blondish hair. She had a slight tendency toward plumpness, with strong shoulders and arms, in the manner of girl swimmers—she was, in fact, an exceptional swimmer, and good at other sports, too, such as field hockey and basketball. But water sports were her specialty. Every summer she would go to a camp in Maine, Camp Acamac. German-Jewish girls from all over the United States went to Acamac. Helene went with her good friend from Melrose Park, near where Helene lived, Bertha Heimerdinger. They were friendly athletic rivals, sometimes as the opposing captains of water-sports teams.

Helene followed Bertha to the University of Chicago, arriving in the fall of 1927. They roomed together at Foster Hall, across from the president's house, during Helene's first year. It wasn't until several years later that Helene met Saul, probably in a sociology class. Very quickly, they started going together. Mary Maize Stinson, who became a close friend of Helene's at the university, remembered them "mooning and loving. They would go walking in the rain and never knew it was raining, it was that kind of love affair."

Helene was an almost perfect counterpoint to Saul. Open, friendly, and unassuming, she had an attractive wholesomeness about her, without any hint of blandness, and a sense of humor that ranged to irreverence without becoming antagonistic. She was an economics major, but when somebody asked her what her major was, she would reply, "Ec-o-nom-ics," dragging out the word in mock seriousness, suggesting how unlikely she thought it was for her to be studying something so weighty and ponderous. Although there was little that was outwardly unconventional about Helene, she did have a certain independence that had something to do with her growing relationship with Saul and, finally, the marriage. For at the University of Chicago in the 1920s as elsewhere, sharp social distinctions were made not only between Jewish and Gentile students but also between German Jews and the sons and daughters of Eastern European Jewish immigrants.

Anti-Semitism was a fact of social life on college campuses, and the University of Chicago was little different. Mary Maize Stinson once invited Helene and Saul to one of her Quadrangle Club dances—such clubs took the place of national sororities at Chicago—but she was told that Jews were not allowed, and Mary Maize herself was almost run out of the club for her terrible transgression. The practices and attitudes of German-Jewish students toward the Alinskys on campus could be nearly as exclusionary. The most prestigious Jewish fraternity, Zeta Beta Tau, was German-Jewish, and informal relationships and friendships among Jewish students were similarly segregated. So Helene's interest in Saul was atypical, and made even more so by Saul's personal qualities. This was, after all, Sarah's son, who, like his mother, often came across as abrasive and self-centered.

But there was more to Saul than what casual acquaintances saw on the surface. One of Helene's friends remembers Saul as "the most lovable, tenderhearted guy, with a heart of gold underneath that brusque exterior. I was suffering from a horrible love affair, but Saul would take my hand, take me out to the lakefront, and I can remember time after time sitting there with him until dawn, him trying to comfort me." Only a few of his fellow students got to know that side of Saul. Helene, with her warmth and kindness, no doubt made it easier for Saul to be more than a gruff young man.

Still, when they decided to get married a year after Helene graduated, her family was anything but pleased. Saul Alinsky was hardly their idea of a suitable son-in-law. At one point, someone in the family suggested that he change his name to Saul Allen. Others were hostile because they felt that Saul was contemptuous of them and their friends, of their wealth and country-club pretensions. Then there was the matter of Saul's manners and social graces, or his lack thereof. Without question, Saul's linguistic fare was a new experience at the dinner table in Elkins Park. It was typical of Saul, in the most genteel of settings, to spice his conversation with the kind of words his host would regard as gutter language. It was also typical of him to pronounce his host's food or drink unfit for human consumption if he disliked it. One day, at the house of a wealthy Simon family relative, Saul took a sip of coffee, proclaimed it awful, and announced he was driving over to a restaurant in Jenkintown to get a better cup of coffee.

In spite of everything, Helene and Saul were married on a beautiful June day in 1932 on the steps leading to the Simons' formal garden. It was a small wedding, celebrated by the local senior rabbi amidst the Simon family's Philadelphia relatives and a few close friends. Saul's mother, Sarah, was not at the wedding. It is not clear why, whether because of illness or because of a disagreement, but her absence may have assured that the wedding ceremony came off without a hitch.

Back in Chicago, Helene and Saul took an apartment in Hyde Park. The Depression and the growing turbulence of the 1930s were to politicize both of them. As a social worker, Helene won the admiration of labor-movement radicals for her leadership in organizing other social workers. But, above all, she was devoted to Saul. Her easy and genuine love for him, her unqualified support and encouragement, made life immeasurably richer for a young man with an uncertain future and an unhappy past. Although he may never have said so in so many words, Saul Alinsky considered himself to be a very fortunate young man.

3

Prison Bug Ward
and Other Stories

Long before Scarface Al Capone and the beer wars of the 1920s made Chicago internationally infamous for its crime and corruption, the city had an open, flourishing vice industry. Politicians and gangsters worked out mutually satisfying arrangements. Services such as gambling and prostitution were provided to satisfied customers. Some church leaders, respectable civic types, and reformers were left unsatisfied by these cozy arrangements, and periodically these forces would spring into action, as they did in 1909, when they were able to stop an annual underworld orgy, the New Year's Day Ball of the 1st Ward, sponsored by the colorful Hinky Dink and Bathhouse John (who were also known as Aldermen Michael Kenna and John Coughlin). Such triumphs of morals over market forces tended to be short-lived, however. By the start of the 1920s and Prohibition, Chicago already had a well-developed network of gangsters, politicians, and police who enjoyed the fruits of expanding vice operations.

Even by Chicago standards, however, the magnitude of criminal activity soon after Prohibition took effect in 1920 was unprecedented. Before, rivalries among gangs for control of territory and specific vice operations had flared into open warfare. But with Prohibition, and especially in Chicago with the bootlegging of beer and booze, the stakes became infinitely higher, the gangs larger, and open warfare an everyday occurrence. Between 1922 and 1926, 250 gangsters were murdered by other gangsters. There were also battles between gangsters and police, including one in the adjacent suburb of Cicero on election day in 1924, when the Torrio-Capone gang, whose control of beer supplies in Cicero was being challenged by rival forces, took to the streets, beating and even kidnapping voters and election workers until the polls closed. The climax of the day's violence came when Capone gunmen and police had a shoot-out in front of a polling place. When it was over, one man had been shot dead, Frank Capone, Scarface Al's brother.

In 1926, an assistant state's attorney, one William McSwiggin, was machine-gunned to death along with two gangster companions. (Al Capone, when asked about his possible role in the shooting of McSwiggin, replied with the kind of logic Chicago could understand: "Of course, I didn't kill him. Why should I? I liked the kid. Only the day before he got killed he was up to my place and when he went home I gave him a bottle of 'scotch' for his old man. I paid McSwiggin and I paid him plenty, and I got what I was paying for.") The failure of the coroner's jury and six grand juries to fix blame for the shootings acted as a catalyst, albeit a modest one, for civic action. Members of the Illinois bar and other civic leaders, alarmed about the general breakdown in law and order that the grand juries' investigations seemed to confirm, announced their sponsorship of a comprehensive study of the crime problem. The result was *The Illinois Crime Survey,* a massive, 1,100-page document printed in early 1929. Most of the survey focused on problems within the criminal-justice system, on corruption, law-enforcement inefficiencies, and deterrence. Another part of the survey, however, had a distinctly different orientation. Those chapters, written by several disciples of E. W. Burgess, reflected the theories of the University of Chicago sociologists. The Burgess disciples argued that there was a direct connection between social disorganization and juvenile delinquency and, ultimately, between delinquency and the gangs that were terrorizing Chicago.

All of this—the prevalence of crime in Chicago and the Chicago sociologists' intellectual interest in the causes of urban crime—was an important context for Saul Alinsky in 1929. In the spring, he had taken Burgess's course "The Study of Organized Crime." In the fall, however, he transferred briefly to the Law School. (It was possible then for a student to enter law school after his junior year.) Alinsky stayed for only two quarters, returning to sociology in time to receive his undergraduate degree in the spring of 1930. He began graduate work in the fall. Whatever reservations he might have had about doing graduate work were offset by his winning a graduate fellowship in criminology.

As a graduate student, Alinsky spent an unusually large amount of course time in fieldwork. Although he passed a French exam—one of two languages required for a Ph.D.—the rest of his graduate study was short on many of the core subjects required for the degree, such as theory and statistics. Perhaps he intended to pick up those courses after his fieldwork or perhaps he was never fully committed to getting a Ph.D. In any event, in 1930 and 1931, his priorities were fieldwork experiences with gangs, especially the teenage Italian gangs on the West Side and the Capone gang.

Alinsky's own account of how he won acceptance by Capone's associates, given many years after the fact, had a ring of self-promotion, portraying him as exceptionally clever, imaginative, and brazen. Nevertheless, the fact that Alinsky *was* all of those things gives his account a measure of plausibility.

In 1930, he was apparently thinking about doing a study of the Capone gang for his dissertation. It was common for sociology students at Chicago to do fieldwork in the general area of crime, with an emphasis on developing contacts and firsthand accounts. One student in particular, John Landesco, had done a book-length study of organized crime in Chicago several years earlier that was first published as part of *The Illinois Crime Survey*. Landesco's work included much material on the Torrio-Capone operation. Alinsky, however, claimed that he set off on his own to meet members of the Capone gang:

> My reception was pretty chilly at first. I went over to the old Lexington Hotel, which was the gang's headquarters, and I hung around the lobby and the restaurant. I'd spot one of the mobsters whose picture I'd seen in the papers and go up to him and say, "I'm Saul Alinsky, I'm studying criminology, do you mind if I hang around with you?" And he'd look me over and say, "Get lost, punk." This happened again and again, and I began to feel I'd never get anywhere. Then one night I was sitting in the restaurant and at the next table was Big Ed Stash, a professional assassin who was the Capone mob's top executioner. He was drinking with a bunch of his pals and he was saying, "Hey, you guys, did I ever tell you about the time I picked up that redhead in Detroit?" and he was cut off by a chorus of moans. "My God," one guy said, "do we have to hear that one again?" I saw Big Ed's face fall. . . . And I reached over and plucked his sleeve. "Mr. Stash," I said, "I'd love to hear that story." His face lit up. "You would, kid?" He slapped me on the shoulder. "Here, pull up a chair." . . . And that's how it started.

According to Alinsky, his introduction to Stash led to his meeting other Capone men, including Frank Nitti, "the Enforcer," who was de facto head of the gang after Al Capone went to jail in 1931. In fact, Alinsky used to say that Nitti "took me under his wing. I called him the Professor and I became his student." As for any reluctance that Nitti and the others might have had about letting an outsider hang around, Alinsky said,

"What harm could I do them? Even if I told what I'd learned, nobody would listen. They had Chicago tied up tight as a drum; they owned the city, from the cop on the beat right up to the mayor." Looking back on that period, Alinsky belittled Hollywood's version of gallant FBI men riding into town and cleaning it up. "Forget all that Eliot Ness shit," he once said by way of explaining how things really were. "The only real opposition to the mob came from other gangsters, like Bugs Moran or Roger Touhy. The federal government could try to nail 'em on an occasional income-tax rap, but inside Chicago they couldn't touch their power. Capone *was* the establishment."

What did Alinsky remember learning from Professor Nitti?

> Once, when I was looking over their records, I noticed an item listing a $7,500 payment for an out-of-town killer. I called Nitti over and I said, "Look, Mr. Nitti, I don't understand this. You've got at least twenty killers on your payroll. Why waste that much money to bring somebody in from St. Louis?" Frank was really shocked by my ignorance. "Look, kid," he said patiently, "sometimes our guys might know the guy they're hitting, they may have been to his house for dinner, taken his kids to the ball game, been the best man at his wedding, gotten drunk together. But you call in a guy from out of town, all you've got to do is tell him, 'Look, there's this guy in a dark coat on State and Randolph; our boy in the car will point him out; just go up and give him three in the belly and fade into the crowd.' So that's a job and he's a professional, he does it. But one of *our* boys goes up, the guy turns to face him and it's a friend, right away he knows that when he pulls the trigger there's gonna be a widow, kids without a father, funerals, weeping—Christ, it'd be a murder." . . . That was the reason they used out-of-town killers. This is what sociologists call a "primary relationship." They spend lecture after lecture and all kinds of assigned reading explaining it. Professor Nitti taught me the whole thing in five minutes.

It is difficult to judge how much embellishment or exaggeration there is in these recollections. Alinsky said that he saw Nitti and others in the gang over a two-year period; he never did see Capone himself. Still, there is no question that he began to meet many young criminals and underworld characters, though he did not then publish anything that directly cited his experiences with the Capone gang. Indeed, Stanley Kaplan, who was a contemporary of Alinsky's at the University of Chicago, recalls a memorable night when he, Alinsky, and their mutual friend Jerry Sampson made the rounds of mobster-run speakeasies, courtesy of Alinsky's underworld connections. "Saul was talking about some prominent hoodlum—I remember his first name was Joe—and Saul said this man trusted him, and he was going to have one of his lieutenants take us to all of his beer joints, but we had to be very careful because these were all hoodlum-operated." Kaplan, who did not know Alinsky well but had sized him up as a name-dropper and blowhard, was skeptical. But at the appointed hour, Kaplan recalls, the three of them were picked up by Joe's man, a large gentleman "with a very large dose of 'dees' and 'doses,' very hard-boiled. He took us around to one joint after another. We started out around nine at night and ended up at dawn." Decades later, incidents still occurred that suggested Alinsky knew Chicago mobsters in high places, or at least that he knew how to get to them. In the 1950s, for instance, his mother's third husband, who owned a North Side drugstore, was being pressured by an allegedly mob-dominated local labor union that had launched a drive to organize Chicago's drugstore workers. When pickets went up in front of his store, he called Sarah's son, who told him he'd see what he could do. Within days, the pickets disappeared.

During the same period when Alinsky was seeing Nitti and his henchmen, he was also spending time on the West Side winning the trust of a tough crowd of fifteen-to-seventeen-year-olds sometimes called the Sholto Street gang by Alinsky's colleagues. The near West Side of Chicago was well known as a home base for young hoodlums. A decade before, the area gave Chicago the 42 Gang, a wild car-stealing outfit whose members graduated—if they were not killed or jailed for long stretches—into the adult world of big-time crime. It was in the same West Side area of high delinquency rates that Clifford Shaw was now working in the early 1930s. Shaw, and his associate and collaborator, Henry McKay, had been graduate students in sociology at the University of Chicago a few years before, when Shaw had also worked in the Illinois prison system as a parole and probation officer. This early exposure to the problems of crime and punishment and especially the theoretical influence of Professors Park and Burgess led Shaw to publish several landmark books in American criminology. One was *The Jack Roller: A Delinquent Boy's Own Story* (1930). The jack roller, a term for someone who beat up and robbed drunks and derelicts, was in this case a Polish boy who lived in a slum neighborhood on the South Side. The book was an autobiography, or, as Burgess called such first-person accounts, a life history. When Alinsky had studied public dance halls as an undergraduate, Burgess encouraged him to get dance-hall habitués to write their life histories, to have the subject in his own words describe and, to some extent, analyze his life experiences. Shaw's jack roller's account provided a unique insight into the interplay between his acts of delinquency and his social environment. *The Jack Roller* became a piece of the "evidence" for Shaw and an emerging school of American criminologists that crime and delinquency were not merely—or largely—explained by individual pathologies. Rather than looking at young criminals primarily as sick or defective individuals, criminologists should look to the social setting that spawns and supports acts of delinquency.

Burgess and Shaw placed great importance on obtaining life histories. It was first necessary, of course, for someone like Shaw to win the trust of street-smart and suspicious delinquents, as he had done with the jack roller. Not all of Shaw's street workers were successful at this, especially those who were a little square and easily dismissed by young gang members. It was not an easy or quick assignment to carry out; it required style, even a certain charisma. It was just the kind of assignment that a young Saul Alinsky would enjoy.

In December 1931, while still a graduate student, Alinsky began to work for Clifford Shaw at the Institute for Juvenile Research (IJR), located just west of downtown and only a few blocks from Hull House, the famous settlement house founded by Jane Addams and Ellen Starr in 1889 to help immigrants cope with their new surroundings. Addams, who shared the 1931 Nobel Peace Prize, believed in the importance of trained social workers and in government programs to help the poor. The IJR was a state agency, part of the Illinois Division of the State Criminologist. A major activity within the IJR was a child-guidance clinic staffed with psychiatrists and social workers. A separate Department of Research Sociology within the IJR had been created in 1926, probably through Burgess's efforts. Shaw became its director and used the department as his base for conducting empirical studies on delinquency in Chicago.

Among Alinsky's early assignments from Shaw was that of establishing a relationship with one of the teenage Italian gangs on the West Side and getting the life histories of the gang members. Early on this assignment he visited the house where the Taccio family lived on South Sholto Street and asked to see Felix (the Cat), one of three Taccio boys. Felix recalls that he was skeptical at first:

> I says, "Who's this guy? I don't even know him." So he said listen, and then explained himself. He says, "Chips sent me." Chips at that time was doing time at St. Charles [School for Boys]. I said, "What's his full name?" And he told me, and he started talking. So I said, well, it must be true, because if he knew the guy's name, nickname and full name, he must know him. But we were a little skeptical until later on, then we got the word that he was all right.

Alinsky invested an extraordinary amount of time and energy in the Sholto Street gang. He soon got to know other members—Chickenman, Rags, Step-and-a-Half (so called because he had a limp), Stiff, Hank, and Nick, who was Felix's younger brother. And over a nearly ten-year period he became good friends with many of them. Between 1931 and 1933, he saw many of the boys almost every day. He also got to know the community, talking with parents, priests, and shopkeepers and writing reports of these encounters for Shaw and the IJR staff. One of the boys in the neighborhood at that time recalls that "Saul knew everybody. He knew just as many people as we did. They knew that he was helping the kids. Let's say he was one of the family, that's how close we were."

For the boys, Alinsky was someone they could respect and even admire. Only six or seven years older than they were, Saul had style. He would drive up to Felix's house in a little Ford convertible (probably given to him by his mother when he graduated from college). When the boys first spotted him wearing a tam, they kidded him for looking a bit like a dandy; he countered, a bit defensively, by saying he only wore it when the car top was down to keep the wind from blowing his hair. Alinsky was also old enough to be a source of practical, worldly-wise advice, and he did not hesitate to play that role. When he first took the boys out to lunch at a neighborhood delicatessen, he instructed them that when you order in a restaurant, you don't say, "I would like" such and such, or "May I"; rather, you say, "I'll have" that sandwich. The boys appreciated the subtle distinction, the aggressiveness, and the philosophy that he who pays the freight should call the shot. Alinsky's generosity was also appreciated. He often took the boys out to lunch—Gold's for corned beef; Spino's or Tufano's for spaghetti. Sometimes he would give the boys money to set up a spread at one of their houses for the whole gang. Of course, being generous was part of Alinsky's job of winning the trust and friendship of the boys. Shaw, too, got to know the boys he studied: the boy who was the jack roller became a lifelong friend. Alinsky's friendships with many members of the Sholto Street gang went well beyond the requirements of his job. It was not only that the boys thought Saul was a good guy whom they could trust. There was also plenty in the boys' lives that Alinsky could identify with—the broken homes; the Old World parents who didn't understand; the sense of being on a low rung far down the social ladder.

Soon after his first meetings with them, Alinsky told the boys straight out that he wanted to know how their gang worked. If there was an early quid pro quo, it was that Alinsky (and Shaw and the others at the IJR) could be helpful when it came to relaying information to gang members who were doing time at St. Charles or providing a little help when one of the boys got hauled into court. But the relationship, built heavily on trust and friendship, evolved over a long period of time. Later, after the New Deal was launched, some of the boys got Works Progress Administration jobs through Alinsky at the IJR or at a recreation center. (By then, Clifford Shaw had developed an anti-delinquency program, and WPA jobs were a part of it.)

When Alinsky first started working with Shaw, one of his primary assignments was to get each gang member to sit down periodically to write his life history. Up to this point in his research, Shaw had gathered accounts of individual delinquents and now he wanted to focus on the group nature of delinquency. So every so often, Saul would hand one of the boys a piece of paper and ask him to write about some aspect of their collective life—to describe when he first started stealing eggs with his friends or when he and his friends had their first encounter with the police.

The life histories were to make up a major part of *Companions in Crime,* a book that Shaw and Alinsky intended to write together. The life histories of the Sholto boys revealed a chronology of delinquency: simple acts of truancy or bumming as early as the third or fourth grade; then the first thefts—often with an older brother or friend—of fruit on Maxwell Street or of lead pipes taken out of school buildings and sold for nine cents a pound. By the mid-teenage years, there were car thefts, holdups, and, on one occasion, a shoot-out with police that left one gang member dead.

Alinsky was enormously successful in getting the boys to write detailed, graphic accounts of the gang's activities. In *Companions in Crime,* their life histories were intended to illustrate the influence of the group on delinquent behavior. But there was another dimension to this study, which had also been an earlier concern of Shaw and the other Chicago sociologists. At virtually the same time that he published the book on the jack roller, Shaw was making statistical studies of delinquency concentrations in various areas of Chicago, studies based largely on the theories of Park and Burgess that in a city like Chicago one could identify a natural growth pattern with distinct, concentric zones. A transitional zone, for example, the next one out from the central business district, was characterized by old, deteriorated housing, a low-income population made up largely of immigrants, and, among other slumlike conditions, a relatively high rate of juvenile delinquency. Using census data and various school and court records, Shaw showed that the highest rates of delinquency were—and had been for a long time—in the transitional zone. In Chicago, that included a section around the central business district (the near West Side, where Alinsky was working), as well as sections adjacent to large industrial areas such as the Union Stock Yards and the South Chicago steel mills.

For the Chicago sociologists, social disorganization was a key concept for understanding the dynamics of the high delinquency areas. W. I. Thomas had done important caı ly work on the concept at Chicago before 1920, and Burgess continued from there. What Burgess—and his disciple Shaw—found was, first, that there were definable "delinquency areas" and, second, that they would maintain a high rate of delinquency even when one particular national immigrant group was replaced by a different one. This made it very clear that genetic makeup could not account for high delinquency rates. Rather, Burgess and Shaw argued, the social process of disorganization in that kind of area explained the persistently high delinquency.

In these areas, according to Burgess and Shaw, mostly immigrant families, many of them from rural backgrounds, were thrown into an unfamiliar urban setting. The culture they brought with them no longer sufficed; they could not organize their new life on it. One consequence was that their children, at least the kind with whom Shaw and Alinsky were working, found themselves growing up in an amoral world with no organized ways of behavior. Alinsky's delinquent boys felt, for example, that their parents were, as Alinsky described it in a draft of *Companions in Crime,* "living" in Italy while residing in Chicago. Alinsky wrote: "Since the boys rejected the parents and the 'Old World' attitudes identified with them, they had no difficulty in giving up the family ideologically."

But it was not only the Old World character of the parents, the fact that they spoke little if any English and the boys little if any Italian. Many of these boys also had at least one parent who died at an early age or a father who was a heavy drinker and unsteady provider. But individual parental failings could not explain the crisis either. As Alinsky reported:

> Family traditions, religion, cultural drives, stabilizing neighborhood factors, all were wanting. Instead, there was all about the boy an atmosphere of chaos—familial, cultural and sociological—which bred in him solely a desire to get as much pleasure out of life as possible. Truly this is a purely hedonistic code, but the boys had no other drives, because of the disintegrated society about them. Delinquency, a pattern acceptable in the "area," personified by the flashy hoodlums with thick bankrolls, fast cars, and numerous women, offered the most attractive outlet. The boys accepted the pattern, stabilized it in the form of a gang, each in terms of his own personality. The bright, aggressive boy became a leader, the passive, a follower. The one with the reflective mind was the planner of activities, or the "Peacemaker."

Clifford Shaw's empirical research and growing contacts among teenage gangs led him quite naturally to develop an experimental anti-delinquency program. He was inspired by what he believed was a key insight—namely, that traditional anti-delinquency efforts had failed because they had not come to grips with the basic problem of social disorganization. He picked three areas with high delinquency rates in which to test his controversial, pioneering program. Alinsky became one of Shaw's staff and worked with delinquents when this Chicago Area Project began to evolve informally. But before the Area Project was officially incorporated in 1934, Alinsky had already been detached to another unit of the Illinois Division of the State Criminologist. He spent a major portion of the next three years, 1933–35, at the Illinois State Penitentiary at Joliet, a commuter's drive southwest of Chicago, as a staff sociologist and member of the parole classification board.

The path to Joliet was one that others at the Institute for Juvenile Research traveled, and that movement reflected Ernest Burgess's influence. Burgess's interest in the problem of crime included doing research on prisons, especially on the probation and parole system, and he wanted to develop a scientific approach for predicting which prisoners were good risks for parole. Burgess and two others directed a study in which twenty-one key factors in a prisoner's background were identified as important predictors of parole success. Under the reform administration of Illinois governor Henry Horner, Illinois became the first of many states to use the prediction criteria for its parole decisions.

Alinsky was detached from the Institute for Juvenile Research in 1933 to go to Joliet. The cycling of IJR staff through the prison system was often part of a career pattern. Front-line experience within prisons was appropriate training for young criminologists. Alinsky, who ended his graduate studies in the spring of 1932, when he married, was now thinking about career possibilities in criminology. With the backing of Burgess and Shaw, he had important sponsors.

Alinsky was twenty-four when he started at Joliet, which had a reputation as a particularly tough, troubled institution. There had been a recent string of riots at the Joliet prison, including the Washington's Birthday Massacre in 1931, which started because the inmates believed that prison officials had intentionally shot and killed three men trying to escape, even though the officials had advance knowledge of the escape plans and could have stopped it earlier. Alinsky's primary job at Joliet was to interview inmates and assess their prospects for parole. He could also recommend transfers to another prison. Many of his interviewees were young men from Chicago, not much older than the gang members he had been working with on the West Side. His first published article, "A Sociological Technique in Clinical Criminology," drew on his experience with these interviews and described how an interviewer could win the trust of an inmate:

> The usage of delinquent vocabularies characteristic of the inmate's community is of great value in the establishing of closer rapport. To illustrate, if the question, "Have you ever been chased by the police while you were in a stolen car and have the police shoot at you" is phrased "Have you ever been in a hot short and got lammed by the heat and have them toss slugs at you," a warmer and more responsive answer usually results. Furthermore, the usage of delinquent terminology may serve as a criterion in analyses of degree of development of delinquent attitudes.

Joliet housed more than aging delinquents, however. One of the big-name, big-time inmates who was convicted while Alinsky was working at Joliet was Roger (the Terrible) Touhy. Touhy was one of the three or four leading gangsters in Chicago, along with Al Capone and Bugs Moran, his turf the Northwest Side of the city, extending into suburban Cook County. In 1931, Capone became intent upon infiltrating Touhy's preserve. Big Al sent two emissaries to convince Touhy to step aside so that the Capone mob could fill the suburbs with taxi-dance halls, gambling houses, and brothels. As one of Al's emissaries informed Touhy in a classic phrase, "Al says this is virgin territory out here for whorehouses."

Touhy's cooperation was slow in coming, and Capone's patience wore thin, so he had Touhy's partner, Matt Kolb, kidnapped. Kolb was released only after Touhy paid a $50,000 ransom. But not long after that two gunmen shot and killed Kolb in a suburban speakeasy. The progression of events reached a climax in 1933 when Touhy and three others were convicted and sentenced to prison for ninety-nine years for kidnapping another underworld character. Touhy insisted that he was innocent, a victim of a Capone frame-up. Nonetheless, Touhy was sent to Joliet to begin his sentence, and Alinsky wrote in his personal journal a few years later of the circumstances that brought Touhy to Joliet and his own confrontation with Roger the Terrible:

> Roger Touhy, Basil Banghart, Gus Schaeffer and Pollynose Kator . . . were convicted for the kidnapping of another slightly soiled gentleman named Jake (The Barber) Factor. . . . Basil Banghart [was] at the time of his conviction known as Public Enemy No. 1 by the

Federal Bureau of Investigation. . . . Gus Schaeffer, a slow-thinking, stolid, loyal gunman, served as Touhy's personal bodyguard, and Pollynose Kator [was a] man who ate, slept, drank and thought of only blood—the kind of blood that spurts out of the holes of 45-calibre slugs. It was Kator who after committing a murder on the northwest side of the city, read that a housewife had seen a car slow up in front of her house, the door opened and a body had come tumbling out. The housewife . . . told the newspaper men that she felt she could identify the car and driver if she ever saw them again. There was little doubt that Kator was the driver of the car, and there was no doubt that the housewife would never identify either the car or Pollynose Kator—at least there was no doubt at 10 o'clock the next morning when she opened the door and a sawed-off shotgun blasted into her face.

When Touhy first went to Joliet, Alinsky was supposed to review his case and background and decide whether he was an incorrigible. The decision would determine whether Touhy served his time at Joliet or at the Stateville prison. "The difference between the old prison at Joliet and the new prison at Stateville was comparable to the difference between a modern apartment house and an old convict ship," Alinsky wrote. "The prison cells in Joliet are so narrow that if one prisoner wants to walk up and down in his cell the other one has to lie in his bunk. There is no plumbing; the bucket system is used, and the odor of the cell block makes the unaccustomed visitor stop and sway." Since Touhy had had no prior convictions before the Factor kidnapping, he was, as Alinsky noted, literally a first offender. But everybody knew Touhy's background as a gangster, so Alinsky classified him as an incorrigible, which condemned Touhy to the old Joliet prison.

Touhy was not happy with the decision when he came to Alinsky's office. According to Alinsky's reconstruction of the conversation, Touhy said, "Alinsky, you're sending me to Stateville on Monday. Today is Friday. Tomorrow morning there will be an envelope in your mailbox containing $20,000 in small bills." To which Alinsky replied, "Today is Friday. Friday of next week, Friday of the week after, and every Friday for the next ninety-nine years you're going to be in the old prison." Touhy stared at Alinsky, got up, and left. The next day, however, Alinsky was informed that Pollynose Kator wanted to see him. Kator came into Alinsky's office, and after the guards left the room, he walked over to Alinsky and said, "Alinsky, our boys outside have checked on you, and we know that you drive down to the prison from Chicago every morning, and we know every road you take. . . . Now the boss is going to the new prison. I'm telling you, the boss has got to be in the new prison next week. There are ways and ways of reaching people and if we can't reach you by next week you're going to be reached in such a way that you'll never know you were reached." As Kator finished, Alinsky got out of his chair and pushed the buzzer that brought in his secretary. He asked Kator to repeat his threat. Kator said, "I haven't been threatening you. I don't know what you're talking about." Alinsky then dictated to his secretary the threat that Kator had made. He turned to Kator and said, "Look, Pollynose, if you guys are out to get me, you're going to get me—there's no way I can stop it. But I've got friends in this prison, and within two hours from the time I'm gotten, you and Touhy and the rest of your boys are going to be shot trying to escape. You know what I mean?" In Alinsky's version, Kator and Touhy apparently got his message. But somebody else—somebody in the governor's office, Alinsky heard—got $50,000 for arranging Touhy's transfer to Stateville.

The Joliet prison was a tough, grim place, but also a fascinating institution. If its brutality and degradation did not overwhelm one, one could occasionally discover brighter facets of the human condition. Alinsky's fascination was with the possibility that one man's courage and imagination could transform the witch's brew of sadistic prison guards, filth, and despair. This is one of the themes in *Prison Bug Ward,* a fictionalized account he wrote of his prison experiences.

The book-length manuscript, never published, was written with a reformer's pen. In the preface to *Prison Bug Ward* (the inmates' pejorative for a prison's psychiatric unit), Alinsky warns that what is to come "is not pleasant reading. There is much in it that is revolting, much that is shocking, and all of it valuable source material to those students who are devoting their lives to the study and help of their fellow men." Whatever Alinsky's writing lacked in subtlety and artistry was offset by his forcefulness and, of course, by the rightness of the cause: society, through its prisons, can be as barbaric and maliciously cruel as the worst criminals. Alinsky's most moving passages were based on his recognition of this truth. The extreme brutality of Joliet eventually leads Alinsky's protagonist, a hardened convict named Jerry, to come to the aid of some of the most defenseless and victimized inmates and, in the process, discover his own humanity.

Alinsky's inmates avoid the bug ward at all costs. It is worse than the hole, the solitary cell that was used as temporary punishment. The bug ward is the end of the line, the final assault. In dialogue between two inmates, one explains to the other:

"You're all washed up once you hit the bug ward. You can't win there. They ask you a lot of questions that no one can answer, and when you don't answer them they say you're nuts. The bug doctor will want to know if you're fruit or something and if you get sore, it goes against you. He'll make cracks that sound screwy and if you laugh he'll say it indicates you're goofy; and if you don't laugh he'll say it's because you ain't got no sense of humor. . . ."

"Yes," agrees Tony, "and I hear they keep a lot of jigs working there that sap hell out of you every chance they get."

"Sure they do. They got a buddy of mine up there about three years ago and beat him silly. There wasn't nothing wrong with him when he went up there except that he was feeling a little bit blue. His old lady had died and then about the same time he got a notice that his broad wanted to divorce him. It kind of got him down and he told the chaplain about it. He must have mentioned it to the bug doctor. Anyway the croaker calls him up there to examine him and keeps him there. A few weeks later one of the X-ray guys told me they had him down that day for a head picture and that he had a fresh skull fracture. I tried to find out what it's all about, but nobody would say anything except that he fell out of bed. He was sent to the state nut house, and I guess he's still there. He was a good guy and they drove him batty, the bastards."

Prison Bug Ward was, in a sense, a variation of the first-person life histories that delinquents wrote for Clifford Shaw. As Alinsky explained, his book was going to portray "the convict's side, his views, and his attitude. . . . The convict's side of the picture has been sorely needed . . . [and] it will furnish a viewpoint which has been hitherto lacking." But Alinsky was not inclined to sentimentality. While he portrayed the convicts sympathetically as the victimized underdogs of prison society, he also saw them as flawed, even vicious and demented underdogs. What turns a bad situation into a morally indefensible system is the cowardice and stupidity of the authorities, the prison officials who have the power to do better but, instead, settle for the bug ward. Alinsky wrote:

Theoretically, the ward was under the direct supervision of the psy-chiatrist, the bug doctor. Actually it was governed by a sadistic guard . . . who was assisted by three attendants, all heavyweights selected for their posts because of their proficiency as boxers! An ardent hater of politics and politicians, the bug doctor spent much of his time grousing, in undertones, about the difficulties of doing good profes-sional work in an institution controlled by political hirelings. He seemed unaware that it was just these politicians who had placed within his hands complete control of his department.

Alinsky claimed that each of his "criticism[s] of psychiatry as it is practiced today in our penal institutions . . . is a driving argument or really a plea" for a better, more humane and effective psychiatry. Nonetheless, over a period of years Alinsky vacillated in his attitude toward psychiatry. On the one hand, there was nothing in his own makeup or in the orientation of his work with Clifford Shaw that would have elevated psychiatry to a front-line solution or a primary concern. On the other hand, intellectuals of Alinsky's generation held psychiatry in high regard, and one in particular, a brilliant young psychiatrist named Max Gitelson, was a close friend whom Alinsky greatly respected. Gitelson, a Hyde Park neighbor on the staff of the Institute for Juvenile Research, drove with Saul one day each week to the Joliet prison. They would leave early in the morning, spend the day working at the prison, and drive back late at night. They exchanged ideas and theories, and Gitelson opened Saul to the practical possibilities of an enlightened psychiatry.

Even so, in *Prison Bug Ward,* Alinsky's young psychiatrist who is hired to take over the bug ward, while professionally competent, humane, and most certainly well intentioned, is doomed by his innocence and political naïveté—until, that is, his path crosses fortuitously with Jerry's, the hardened but street-savvy criminal. Jerry is an operator; Jerry knows instinctively the political psychology of institutions. He knows how to use bureaucratic inertia to his advantage, knows how to coax or push men into action, knows that while the young psychiatrist is motivated by abstractions—by his ideal of professionalism, for instance—the inmates respond to concrete rewards or punishments. So he persuades a handful of inmates by cutting a bargain: they will steal badly needed supplies for the bug ward from other prison departments, and in exchange the new psychiatrist will get them job transfers to the ward, where they will have better food and hot showers.

The real Jerry—described by Alinsky in the preface as a habitual bank robber who "found himself" in the prison bug ward—was someone Alinsky not only admired but identified with:

A mind of extremely clear logic which could immediately cut problems to their primary elements. His impatience with routine, seemingly stupid obstacles, created a number of bitter antagonisms against him. Jerry [was] not the most tactful of persons. His piercing, humorous cynicisms . . . made many of us so-called honest, law-abiding, sane persons squirm . . . [but] I doubt that much of the good that has come [to the Detention Hospital] could have been achieved without . . . Jerry. As I close three years of daily work in the state prisons, I cannot help but look back upon my association with Jerry as the richest memory of this experience. . . . To Jerry, who now lies free in a potter's field grave outside the penitentiary, I am deeply grateful.

4

A New Hero

By 1935, twenty-six-year-old Saul Alinsky seemed to be on his way to a career as a criminologist. He had done a splendid job working with delinquents on the streets of the near West Side. He clearly enjoyed the kids, and also the fact that the kids liked him and looked up to him. He enjoyed using his wits and charm to build relationships. The fluid situation on the West Side streets called for a lot of individual free-lancing on Alinsky's part. Working at Joliet prison, however, was very different and much less satisfying. Alinsky's job was sharply circumscribed, the prison system was rigidly bureaucratic, and the prisons themselves—especially Joliet—ranged from depressing to barbaric. If young Saul Alinsky was going to pursue a career in criminology, it was highly unlikely that it would be in penology.

Alinsky's salary of $105 a month was not very much, even by Depression standards. For Alinsky, however, there was another attraction to the work. It was a sign of his general prowess, perhaps even his masculinity, that he functioned effectively and with a certain panache in an often dangerous, unconventional subculture. It was important to him that his public identity reflect this insider status, the fact that he rubbed shoulders with a tough crowd. Alinsky's professional reputation among his Hyde Park friends, for instance, was shaped by his accounts of exotic underworld characters in Chicago and in the Joliet prison. Though he did not quite flaunt his unusual contacts and experiences, he did nothing to discourage an impression that he had access to a dangerous and exciting world.

Alinsky told vivid stories, for instance, about how the prisoners at Joliet would indulge their sexual impulses. He was completely sympathetic with that, and scornful of prison officials whose most creative and enlightened response was severe punishment. Or Alinsky might tell a story about giving fifty bucks to two of his delinquent friends from the West Side and sending them off to a whorehouse after they had traveled with him to a conference of criminologists to explain the evils of incarceration.

Sometimes Alinsky would take an associate on a tour of the West Side to visit the young Italian gang members. On one such occasion, he took Marian Despres, a fellow Hyde Parker then doing psychological testing at the Institute for Juvenile Research, to several of the gang members' homes, and at each stop Alinsky was welcomed as an old friend. For Despres, it was a different, unfamiliar world. At one house, some of the boys were angry: in a gang shag the week before, a Polish girl with whom they'd had a sexual encounter had gotten them all infected and they were angry at her. Alinsky was accepted within this world; the boys and their families liked and trusted him. Alinsky was, in the style of Clifford Shaw's street workers, accepting and not moralistic or overtly judgmental of the West Side subculture. On this particular day, since it was the noon hour, Alinsky and his guest were obliged to eat lunch at each of the three or four homes they visited. By the time they were finished, they had enjoyed multiple servings of spaghetti and hot sausage and lots of wine. Marian Despres staggered contentedly back to her office that afternoon at the IJR, having her own colorful stories to tell that night in Hyde Park about Alinsky and his West Side friends.

Alinsky also had stories to tell about the famous inmates at Joliet, such as Roger Touhy and Nathan Leopold, who for a time was assigned to work with Alinsky in the diagnostic clinic. It was from Touhy that Alinsky claimed he got the material for one of his more memorable stories, about the assassination attempt on President-elect Franklin Roosevelt in Miami in February 1933.

According to Alinsky, it all began with Chicago mayor Anton Cermak. After Cermak was elected on a Chicago-style "reform" ticket in 1931, he called Capone. Referring to Capone's arrangements with the previous mayor, Big Bill Thompson, the new mayor proclaimed that City Hall's percentage of Capone's profits had to be increased. "The Big Boy told Cermak he couldn't do it. Profits weren't big enough," Touhy recounted to Alinsky. After further negotiations hit a dead end, Cermak called Touhy and made him a simple offer: "Roger, how would you like to run this town?" When Touhy expressed reservations based on the most practical of considerations—"The Big Boy's got too many boys in his mob"— Cermak had an answer that iced the deal. In exchange for a percentage of the take that Cermak deemed suitable, the mayor volunteered the services of the Chicago Police Department to assist Touhy's boys with the Capone mob. Cermak said, "Between your boys and my police department, you ought to be able to handle them."

And so, in the months that followed, a lot of Capone's gangsters were regularly found in ditches. In fact, some Chicagoans began to think that Cermak was actually cleaning up the Capone gang. Finally, Capone sent word to Mayor Cermak that enough was enough, and if he did not back off, he'd be knocked off. Then, the day that Cermak went to the Illinois Central Station to board the Seminole for his trip to Florida, the Chicago police picked up and removed from the same train one of Capone's boys, Machine Gun Jack McGurn, who was dressed as a golfer and carrying a golf bag containing three tommy guns. What Cermak and his police did not know, however, was that another Capone mobster was stalking the mayor.

So, on a fateful February day in Miami, Cermak stepped forward to shake hands with Roosevelt at a rally in a waterfront park. Suddenly, a political fanatic, Giuseppe Zangara, who was trying to kill Roosevelt, started shooting. As the shots rang out, Cermak was seriously wounded; he died three weeks later. The generally accepted explanation was that Zangara's bullets had killed Cermak. Not so, Touhy told Alinsky. What really happened was that Capone's mobster, who was in the crowd still stalking the mayor, took advantage of the confusion as Zangara started blasting away. He pulled his own gun and shot Cermak. When Alinsky doubted Touhy's version, the latter supposedly said:

> You don't believe me, huh? Well, if you're such a smart doc, give me the answer to this one. . . . In any kind of murder case they produce the bullet that killed the guy and match it up with the gun . . . but in the trial of that screwball they didn't come up with the slug . . . did you notice, and you know why? Because Zangara was popping a 38 calibre gun and the slug that knocked off Cermak was a 45 calibre slug, and you can't even put a 45 calibre slug into a 38 calibre gun, let alone shoot it—and even you, Doc, know that.

This was such a good story that if Alinsky harbored any doubts about its veracity, he never let on, and over the years he often repeated it to friends. This kind of storytelling was an important source of Alinsky's charm, and the charm sweetened his persuasiveness. He could develop a friendly, useful relationship with a stubborn, dull, narrow-minded prison official, for instance, while another young staff sociologist would be frozen out. He was admired for such accomplishments, but since he was not modest about them, his co-workers often gave their admiration grudgingly.

In Hyde Park, Alinsky was also known as somebody who got around and who cultivated an unusual number of diverse relationships. Sol Kolbrin, an acquaintance who got a job with Clifford Shaw through Alinsky's intervention, was constantly amazed at the scope of Alinsky's associations. When he and Alinsky walked into one of the cigar stores on Fifty-fifth Street that served as a front for a horse betting parlor, it seemed as if Alinsky knew everybody, including the guys who were running the place. While placing a bet, Alinsky would kibitz with them about mutual friends, some of whom were doing a little time at Joliet.

Alinsky was something of a public person in Hyde Park. Restless, he seemed to be out in the neighborhood every night doing something. That "something," as the 1930s unfolded, was increasingly tied to the politics of the Depression and the gathering storm clouds over Europe.

SAUL ALINSKY, like so many others in the 1930s, became politicized by the events and conditions of the Depression. During his undergraduate days, Alinsky had shared in the general lack of interest in politics at the University of Chicago and was never part of the small minority of students who participated in organized political activities. Had he first entered the University of Chicago in 1933 or 1934, his political interests might have been quite different. Certainly the campus activities would have been: there were now communist cells, Trotskyites, a large and active socialist club— the campus had become a hotbed of political debate, most of it on the left.

The debates continued off campus in the brick homes and apartment buildings of Hyde Park. On Blackstone, just past Fifty-fifth Street, Helene and Saul Alinsky lived in a comfortable five-room apartment with a fireplace, across the hall from Fran and Max Gitelson. Marian and Leon Despres also lived in the building, and the young couples would often get together for dinner, to see a movie, and to talk and argue politics.

It is easy to understand that, once activated, Saul Alinsky's politics would be left-of-center. It was not only that his closest friends, such as fellow grad student and co-worker Jerry Sampson, were already involved in progressive causes; there were also the influences of his sociological training and work with delinquents and his own childhood experiences. He had been closer to the bottom than to the top of his social world. His family had not been poor, but they were poorly thought of—his father a graceless embarrassment, his mother a shrew and troublemaker. At the university, where the Gentile fraternities and clubs and the relatively well-to-do German-Jewish elite embodied social acceptability in their respective spheres, Saul Alinsky was an outsider. When he married, he was tolerated by his wife's affluent family and relatives only to accommodate her love for him. To the extent that Depression politics was, broadly speaking, a contest between the privileged and the disadvantaged, rich and poor, insiders and outsiders, right and left, there was no question as to which side young Saul Alinsky would identify with. It was not so easy to forecast, however, exactly where on the political spectrum Alinsky might land. That depended on an interplay of events, friendships, and Alinsky's own strong personality.

In 1935, two political developments, one abroad and the other at home, affected Saul Alinsky's political thinking and activities. These two developments—a sharp shift in tactics by the Soviet Union and the emergence in the United States of a militant industrial-labor-union movement—were, at their core, unrelated. And yet, it was typical of the turbulent politics of the time that the interests and motives of one set of forces could become intertwined with those of another.

The important political development that occurred in Moscow, in the summer of 1935, was a prime example of the many flip-flops in the Communist Party line during the 1930s. The Russians, growing increasingly concerned about their own vulnerability to Hitler and fascism, and after joining the League of Nations in 1934 and concluding the Franco-Russian Alliance in early 1935, dropped their official stance of bitter opposition to Roosevelt and the New Deal. The immediate priority now was to defeat fascism, explained the prominent Bulgarian communist Georgi Dimitrov, who had himself survived the Nazis and in August 1935 joined other party leaders in Moscow at the Seventh World Congress of the Communist International. In his speech at the Congress, "The Tasks of the Communist International in the Fight for the Unity of the Working Class Against Fascism," Dimitrov said that it was indeed obvious that "the most reactionary circles of American finance capital, which are attacking Roosevelt, represent first and foremost the very force which is stimulating and organizing the fascist movement in the United States." Thus, Dimitrov proposed the organization of a united front of all anti-fascist forces in the United States.

This sharp U-turn in Soviet policy soon had consequences in the United States, where membership in the American Communist Party increased, albeit moderately. Perhaps more significantly, many on the non-communist American left began to work openly with the communists in the mid-1930s. These people saw the Soviet Union as an important anti-fascist force, though many of them were wary of or even hostile toward communists. But with Hitler on the move, and with a civil war in Spain, many American leftists answered the call for a united front.

The united-front strategy would have appealed to Saul Alinsky on several levels. First, it gave a high priority to stopping Hitler, whom, Alinsky said, he "hated with a passion." Second, it included a measure of political realism: the intention of the united-front strategy was, by placing pragmatism over ideological concerns, to build a new political coalition. Although Alinsky had not been enthusiastic about some of Roosevelt's politics, he could appreciate the President's personal popularity. And though he criticized the early New Deal for not being fully committed to sweeping, fundamental change, he could understand the popularity of its more progressive thrusts. In essence, it was simply more important to stop Hitler and the forces of fascism than to dwell on Roosevelt's shortcomings and lack of commitment. Finally, organizing a united front would produce action, movement, even excitement in rallying the forces of good against evil.

Alinsky was enchanted with the action and adventure of the mid-1930s. When the civil war began in Spain in 1936, for instance, he was excited by the volunteers from Chicago and elsewhere who were going to fight alongside the Spanish Loyalists against the forces of General Franco and fascism. It was not something that Alinsky would do—he was too practical for that kind of adventure—but he did raise money for the International Brigade. He also liked what the Stalinists were doing in Spain, recalls Leon Despres, who was at the time a member of the Socialist Party and strongly anti-communist. "I don't think he ever remotely thought of joining the Communist Party [but] emotionally he aligned very strongly with it," said Despres. In fact, it would be accurate to say that Alinsky was more radical in his inclinations, convictions, rhetoric, and wishes than in his actions, which took a more pragmatic form.

Alinsky was never a member of the party or a communist. He was too independent and combative to surrender his intellect to dogma. But the communists did not give up on him, Alinsky believed. "The definition of myself in the higher circles of the Communist Party was quite interesting," Alinsky wrote in the early 1940s. "They felt that I was doing a united front job . . . and that while I was a rank individualist, fundamentally I was a liberal and maybe through a period of time I could be educated and possibly recruited."

If Alinsky was an unlikely party convert, he had nevertheless some interest in developing class consciousness. In the fall of 1937, he presented a paper at the annual congress of the American Prison Association in New York: "The Philosophical Implications of the Individualistic Approach in Criminology." This rather theoretical and historical paper raises more questions than it answers about the ideological direction in which Alinsky was headed. On the one hand, it suggested a flirtation with Marxism but, on the other hand, held out the hope that reformist solutions were still possible. His starting point was that mainstream American criminology was culture-bound. Criminologists had been providing seemingly "objective" explanations of criminal behavior when, in truth, their so-called objectivity followed inevitably from the implicit values and assumptions of the "individualistic, competitive social order of our present times." That they saw events through a cultural filter was not unique to them: "Prior to the transition of world society into capitalism," Alinsky wrote, "crime had been regarded as behavior inspired by the devil. During the feudal era the supernatural taboos and sanctions of the church wrapped the religious cloak of mysticism about human behavior."

Alinsky traced the switch to individualism to "that period when the capitalistic state was marching forward rapidly. . . . Capitalism was striving for a free open market. This meant the abolition of the feudal states with 'divine rights' and rule by a hereditary class of nobility. Capitalism had to smash this feudal caste system in order to live. The antithesis of this hereditary caste system was the so-called 'free individual' or the philosophy of individual determinism . . . [which] may be regarded as the keynote of a capitalistic society."

Individual determinism led early criminologists to explain criminality as a function of biology; heredity explained why some individuals were born criminals. "The social order generally was absolved from responsibility," said Alinsky. Modern psychiatry carried this absolution to its next step by introducing, among other concepts, "psychopathy as the successor to mental deficiency in the attempt to understand criminal behavior. The fashion shifted to the 'psychopathic personality' and the latter became the chief theme of the individualistic symphony," he charged. But psychiatry gives only lip service to the importance of economics and culture, Alinsky argued, because its most powerful theories are rooted in biology and thus it shares "the common denominator of all individualistic approaches: individual determinism." From the English Marxist John Strachey's *The Coming Struggle for Power,* Alinsky borrowed the observation that "Dr. Freud remains, for all of his great intellectual powers, the last major thinker of the European capitalist class, unable to step outside of his class limitations."

Alinsky was not prepared to suggest that capitalism must be replaced. After venturing into deeper philosophical waters, he retreated to where the currents were safer and more familiar, arguing that the Chicago sociologists' ecological studies had demonstrated clearly that social disorganization, not individual pathologies, was the proper concept, untainted by culture bias, for understanding juvenile delinquency and criminal behavior generally. But what was the *cause* of social disorganization? Economic factors, said Alinsky. "The delinquent sequence can be roughly stated as follows: Delinquency areas are due to social disorganization which, in turn, [is] largely the result of economic defects in our social order. The effects of competition in social disorganization cannot be ignored."

Clifford Shaw's earliest ecological studies, carried out before the Depression, were modestly optimistic when it came to economic considerations. Yes, competitive forces put urban immigrant groups and other minorities at the bottom of the heap, but many or most of these people—Shaw was a little vague on the numbers—could work their way up and out to greener pastures. As long as the country and its economy grew, the nastier side effects of the capitalistic order were mitigated. The Depression, however, threw this progressivism into reverse. Now, in 1937, Alinsky urged his colleagues to reexamine their culture-bound assumptions in light of "the present chaos and threatening collapse of the capitalistic system."

Where would such a reexamination lead? Was Alinsky prepared to go beyond the theories of the Chicago sociologists, to move from sociological analysis to political advocacy? And if so, what form would his advocacy take? There were only strong hints, nothing to suggest with certainty that Alinsky had chosen one course over all others.

OF GREATER CONSEQUENCE to domestic politics than the call for a united front—and eventually of far greater consequence to Saul Alinsky—was the rapid emergence of the Committee for Industrial Organization under the leadership of the remarkable John L. Lewis.

In mid-October 1935, the American Federation of Labor assembled at its convention in Atlantic City. The convention came at a time of increasing resentment and frustration on the part of the radical activists in the unorganized mass-production industries, such as automobiles, steel, and rubber, concerning the old-guard AF of L leadership. The AF of L was, they felt, asleep at the wheel. In the first two years of the New Deal, there had been more defeats than victories in the organizing of workers, more company unions than strong independent ones. If the ultimate obstacle to the labor radicals' dream of "organizing the unorganized" was the opposition of a General Motors or a U.S. Steel, the immediate obstacle was often the leadership of the AF of L.

The AF of L was predominantly a federation of individual craft unions—carpenters, machinists, plumbers, and others. The few exceptions included industrial unions, such as in mining and textiles, where all work-

ers in the same industry, regardless of their specialized job or craft, belonged to one large union. Craft unions were a throwback to the days
before mass production dominated the largest industries. The timid, un-
creative AF of L leadership was, for various reasons, in no hurry to change.
The individual craft unions—within the auto industry, for example—
guarded their jurisdictions jealously. In addition, there was an arrogance
toward the less skilled production workers, expressed well in one AF of L
leader's crack that mass-production workers were "the rubbish at labor's
door." The self-interest of the AF of L leadership was, of course, threatened by the prospect of enrolling a new, different, and potentially far larger
constituency in its ranks. They were scarcely eager to provide money and
other resources to young organizers in autos and steel or to offer the
legitimacy of unrestricted charters. Their foot-dragging and rationalizations were surely a main cause for a sorry set of numbers: in mid-1934 a
smaller proportion of the nonagricultural work force in America belonged
to labor unions than had in 1922.

It was not as though opportunities to organize did not exist after
Roosevelt took office in 1933. There was strong support for labor among
Roosevelt's brain trust, and economic as well as political conditions were
also favorable. One labor leader in particular wanted to seize the moment:
the president of the United Mine Workers of America, John L. Lewis.

"John L."—brilliant, an egotist of nearly unrivaled dimensions, colorful and complex—had been a Coolidge and Hoover Republican in the
1920s, an anti-communist, and the president of a union on the verge of
bankruptcy. Even before the Depression hit, Lewis had experienced the
extreme vagaries and economic crises of the coal industry. He viewed the
larger economic troubles of the Depression as additional and definitive
evidence that the federal government must play a central role in stabilizing
and planning the economy. Thus, Lewis and his advisers were actively
involved in the discussions that led to the Roosevelt administration's proposals for the National Industrial Recovery Act (NIRA).

As passed by Congress in June 1933, the NIRA was a trade-off:
business got antitrust exemptions to allow for the allocation of markets and
the stabilization of prices, while labor got a foot in the door—not its Magna
Carta but an opportunity—with the federal government's recognition of
the right of workers to organize unions and bargain collectively. Lewis
grabbed the opportunity, risked the slim resources of the UMW treasury
on an all-out organizing drive, and won. By the fall of 1933, Lewis had won
for his miners an unprecedented contract covering all the major soft-coal-
producing districts. With more victories to come, he succeeded in revitalizing the UMW. John L. Lewis quickly became—along with Franklin D.

Roosevelt—a hero not only to mine workers but to workers in other industries, many of whom were still unorganized.

At what point John L. started to become Saul Alinsky's hero is not exactly clear—perhaps early in 1933 when Lewis was helping the Roosevelt administration sell the labor provisions of the NIRA and, in the typical Lewisian rhetoric of vilification, labeled corporate opposition as the "rapac[ious] . . . robber barons of American industry." Or perhaps it was the next year, 1934, when Lewis came up against the stubborn, hostile opposition of the Alabama coal operators. At a federal hearing that had been called at Lewis's urging, John L. first demolished the coal operators' argument that lower pay for Negro miners was justified because Negroes in the South had a more modest style of living. Lewis showed that it was racial discrimination, not a preferred lifestyle, that determined their living standards and that discrimination forced Negro miners to pay more for housing than white miners did. Later at the same hearing, Lewis let fly with the kind of lethal ridicule from which his target often never recovered. The lawyer for the operators, Forney Johnston, had apparently gone overboard in his oratorical zeal, implying before a heretofore drowsy audience that, if push came to shove, Alabama's operators could declare war on the United States. No doubt savoring a delicious opening, Lewis intoned: "If they think [that they can declare war] and care to resort to that method to maintain their arrogant position, the United Mine Workers of America is ready . . . to furnish the President . . . with 20 army divisions to help make the Alabama operators comply with the law of the United States." With the audience now aroused, Lewis added a tidy final wallop: "I assume Mr. Johnston . . . was somewhat inebriated by the exuberance of his own verbosity."

Although Lewis had been riding a new, progressive wave in the period leading up to the AF of L convention in 1935, Alinsky, like many young leftists in labor, may not yet have been completely captivated. After all, this was the same John L. Lewis who had been part of the old-guard leadership of the AF of L in the 1920s. It was Lewis, for instance, who, after Samuel Gompers died in 1924, had outmaneuvered his opponents within the Federation and installed his own man, William Green, as AF of L president.

One of the more common practices that Lewis shared with his AF of L brethren in the 1920s was a frequent indulgence in Red-baiting. Going after communists, real or imagined, served a variety of political needs. It was always an efficient way to demonstrate patriotism and to distinguish oneself and one's union from the Red menace. Lewis spoke on one occasion, for instance, of "the three times the Bolshevik leaders have attempted armed insurrection and revolt in the United States . . . during the steel strike of 1919, in the 'outlaw' switchmen's strike of 1920, and in the railroad and coal strikes of 1922." Not least, Red-baiting also served to blunt opposition within one's own union. Lewis, in fact, had had opposition in some UMW locals. As late as 1933, in another political context, when Lewis was working with the Roosevelt administration to gain congressional approval of the NIRA, he continued to play off of the communist threat, positioning the NIRA supporters on the political middle ground between the greedy "robber barons of American industry" and "the lustful rage of the communists, who would lay waste to our traditions and our institutions with fire and sword."

But as the delegates began to assemble in Atlantic City in mid-October 1935, there was growing hope, even expectation, among some on the labor left that Lewis would provide the crucial leadership to "organize the unorganized" in the mass-production industries. There was talk, the labor radical Len De Caux remembers, of "a new Lewis." At his Atlantic City hotel, Lewis met privately with many of the labor leftists, and the word started to get around that Lewis was ready to lead, regardless if that meant working with industrial-union activists on the left or right.

Historians would later debate whether Lewis had already planned a full-scale organizing campaign as early as 1933 with the passage of Section 7a, the clause in the landmark National Industrial Recovery Act guaranteeing workers the right to "organize unions of their own choosing" and bargain collectively with their employers. Certainly Lewis had been steadily moving, if not galloping, in that direction. At various AF of L meetings, he had tried to prod the executive council leadership but with little success. The old-guard AF of L strategy was to deflect with half-measures or simple procrastination the pressure mounting from workers in auto, steel, and other basic industries.

Perhaps Lewis had privately given up any hope of organizing under the banner of the AF of L before the October convention began. With notable exceptions such as Sidney Hillman of the Amalgamated Clothing Workers, he no doubt saw himself as a giant in a land of pygmies. He once said, for example, of William Green—when someone asked Lewis to meet with Green face to face to "explore each other's minds"—that "I have done a lot of exploring in Bill's mind—and I give you my word there is nothing there." In any event, the stage was set for what would become a historic turning point in the history of the American labor movement. Day after day at the convention, the old-guard leaders, who controlled a decisive plurality of delegate votes, reaffirmed their intransigence. All efforts by the Lewis forces to have the AF of L initiate a massive organizing campaign in the basic industries were systematically defeated. As the convention neared its conclusion, with tempers short on both sides, an incident suddenly developed. It was the kind of incident—or opportunity—for which John L. Lewis may have been looking.

William L. (Big Bill) Hutcheson, the powerful, autocratic president of the Carpenters Union, called for a point of order to silence a delegate from the insurgent Rubber Workers. Lewis suddenly hollered at Hutcheson: "This thing of raising points of order all the time on minor delegates is rather small potatoes." Hutcheson, who weighed about three hundred pounds, bellowed that he grew up on small potatoes, that's how he got to be so big. Heated words flew back and forth. Hutcheson called Lewis a bastard. In a flash, Lewis was moving toward Hutcheson, leaping over a row of chairs and throwing a right-handed haymaker into Hutcheson's face. According to one newspaper account, as a bloodied Hutcheson was helped from the convention hall, "Lewis casually adjusted his tie and collar, relit his cigar, and sauntered slowly through the crowded aisles to the rostrum."

BEFORE 1935 was over, the Committee for Industrial Organization opened a small office in Washington, and by the middle of 1936, perhaps the greatest mass movement in the history of the United States was underway, led by John L. Lewis. Saul Alinsky's personal relationship with Lewis was still several years off. But from afar, Alinsky was swept up by the excitement, the incredible string of CIO victories, and the brilliant, powerful leadership of Lewis in 1936 and 1937.

John L. Lewis was the great general in American labor's finest hours. He often provided the strategic difference between victory and defeat. The successful sit-down strike by auto workers at General Motors' Flint, Michigan, plant in 1936–37 might have ended in violent tragedy without his timely, audacious chess moves with GM and the governor of Michigan; instead, it ended with GM accepting the United Automobile Workers as sole bargaining agent for workers in all GM plants. After the success at Flint, there was the stunning revelation that Lewis had privately and personally negotiated a collective bargaining agreement with Myron C. Taylor, chief executive officer of U.S. Steel. It was the kind of historic breakthrough which only Lewis was capable of achieving.

In addition to his valuable strategic contributions, Lewis was important, too, for his ability to use the public stage to articulate the attitudes and feelings of millions of American workers—workers who were treated as second-class citizens economically, socially, and intellectually. A man who had the respect and admiration of workers and whose commanding presence and intellect made him a match for any corporate opponent was an awesomely potent leader. Lewis made possible the revolution that the CIO seemed to represent by the fall of 1937. For in less than two years the CIO claimed an organized membership of 3.4 million, divided into thirty-two national unions and more than five hundred locals. It was widely considered to be the most important progressive force in the country.

Interestingly, Helene Alinsky, president of her social workers' union in Chicago, was directly involved with the labor movement and the CIO before Saul was. While Lewis and chants of "CIO! CIO! CIO!" were sweeping across the country, Alinsky had only recently extricated himself from the job at Joliet prison, and it was another year before he was sent by his boss, Clifford Shaw, to Chicago's Back of the Yards neighborhood, where the CIO was fighting an organizing battle with the country's giant meat-packing houses, the ones made infamous around the turn of the century by Upton Sinclair's muckraking classic *The Jungle*.

5

The Area Project

When Saul Alinsky ended his three years at Joliet prison in late 1936 and returned to work with Clifford Shaw at the Institute for Juvenile Research, it is possible that he did not leave his job completely voluntarily. One story that Alinsky told to friends was that he was kicked out because he physically attacked a prison guard in an angry rage. Seeing the guard, a burly two-hundred-pounder, giving an unmerciful beating to a young, scrawny inmate, Alinsky jumped on the guard's back, slammed him down, and beat his head on the floor repeatedly. Alinsky said he might have killed the guard if someone hadn't pulled him off. The incident, Alinsky told friends, forced an internal investigation of sadistic behavior by prison guards—but also forced Alinsky's exile from the prison system.

Alinsky was in any case probably ready to leave. Joliet was not a fertile ground for inquisitive academic criminologists, let alone freewheeling young men with reformist tendencies. Although the Illinois criminal-justice system had a patina of progressiveness, enlightened outsiders rarely penetrated its bureaucracy and decision-making apparatus. When they tried to capitalize on spasmodic public outrage at prison conditions, they sometimes won a temporary victory, but new ideas or new people were quickly pigeonholed. That turned out to be the case with the Illinois Division of the State Criminologist, the unit in which Alinsky worked. Created during a burst of reform in 1917, the unit soon found its role highly restricted. In a recent historical study of the Joliet and Stateville prisons, one scholar has noted that "it [was] a telling commentary on the [entrenched bureaucracy's] ability to isolate and restrict intellectual roles that men of the caliber of . . . Saul Alinsky . . . could be present at the Stateville/Joliet prisons and have no impact whatsoever on the day-to-day operations." Frustrated and bored by the repetitive cycle of interviewing inmates and filing reports, Alinsky was probably ready to return to the streets of Chicago.

Back in Chicago, Alinsky resumed work with Shaw on the manuscript of their book, *Companions in Crime*, and spent time with the delinquents on the West Side. He also had an active speaking schedule as Shaw's staff assistant, giving lectures on delinquency to civic groups and social workers in Chicago. One of these lectures, to the Council of Social Agencies in November 1938, was on the Chicago Area Project, an outgrowth of Shaw's earlier statistical analyses of delinquency and the in-depth life histories of delinquents he compiled. This logical next step in delinquency prevention came at a time of growing public concern with gangs and crime and an equally strong sense that traditional anti-crime efforts had failed.

Shaw, too, had become a strong critic of the criminology establishment, especially in relation to theories on juvenile delinquency. The design or conceptual framework of his Area Project was, in no small part, a reaction against the professionals who dominated much of the dialogue and treatment of delinquency—physicians, psychiatrists, psychologists, and social workers who tended to see delinquency as a quasi-medical problem, who saw chiefly "individuals" who had been "diagnosed" as "delinquent" and who therefore should receive the appropriate "treatment," be it incarceration, counseling, or other therapy. The preeminence of the professional in such a relationship was taken for granted, and it was symptomatic of a broader presumption that the relationship between the upper classes and the immigrant classes in areas of high delinquency was, above all, a relationship between superiors and inferiors, with all wisdom flowing from the former to the latter.

Shaw rejected both the emphasis on the individual and the preeminent role of the professional. His early studies had showed that only a small percentage of delinquents were feebleminded or psychopathic. In the main, delinquency was not "caused" by an individual's mental deficiencies or by ethnicity or race; nor was it cured by punishment through incarceration. In fact, delinquents who were imprisoned for long periods probably learned more about becoming adult criminals.

Shaw was convinced that he knew what *did* cause delinquency: "the social milieu." The areas or neighborhoods of Chicago that had the highest delinquency rates also had the highest rates of tuberculosis and infant mortality; the greatest physical deterioration; populations that seemed demoralized; and community attitudes that tended to tolerate delinquent behavior. Alinsky alluded to this last factor in one of his reports while working with the Sholto gang on the West Side: ". . . the attitudes in this community toward stealing, as such, are not those of immediate disapproval. In so far as the delinquent act does not affect the individual who is observing it, he is quite willing to allow the delinquent to escape attention. This is in great contrast to the situation in the so-called better neighborhoods in Chicago where a person observing a delinquency feels compelled to report it to the authorities." Shaw believed that social disorganization—the failure of institutions within a community to provide social controls—was a root cause of most delinquency, and that delinquency rates might be reduced if local institutions were strengthened or if new ones were created.

But what about poverty? It was more than coincidental that the areas with high delinquency rates were also among the poorest in Chicago. Was not grinding poverty a reason that people were forced to live in substandard housing? Did not the energy required to eke out a living preclude active participation in strengthening institutions, whether one's own family or communal institutions? Shaw was not oblivious to these important questions, but the implications were larger than he was interested in exploring at that point, for ultimately they were questions about "the system," about economics. Shaw was a sociologist by training and a practical man by nature. He had developed a sociological perspective and certain sociological tools. He was interested in using those tools. Exactly what he could build and how significant it would be were at the beginning unclear. That is why he called the Area Project a "great experiment."

It began by trial and error. Shaw assigned staff from the Institute of Juvenile Research to work with teenage gangs in three areas of Chicago with high delinquency rates: on the West Side, where Alinsky established a relationship with the Sholto gang; on the near North Side, also a largely Italian area; and in Russell Square in South Chicago, a primarily Polish area adjacent to the steel mills. It was in the last that Shaw's new approach seemed to develop most quickly.

One of Saul Alinsky's first assignments from Shaw in 1932 was to go to Russell Square to establish relationships with the Polish teenage gang members there. So he split his time between them and the Italian kids on the West Side. The initial contacts at Russell Square were made in a variety of ways. Sometimes Alinsky or another young street worker—Alinsky was only twenty-three when he first went to Russell Square—would simply hang out where kids congregated. One conversation would lead to another or one pickup softball game would lead to another softball game until, through patience and personality, Alinsky and other street workers had the beginnings of trusting relationships.

But that was not all. About a year before Alinsky appeared on the scene, Shaw had dispatched another staff person, E. A. Conover, to get a firsthand sense of Russell Square, to survey its institutions and leaders. Shaw's staff had already compiled a demographic profile of the community from census data and the records of the Juvenile Court of Cook County. Conover, who was experienced in running recreational programs for youth and who had contacts among social agencies, had already established a presence in Russell Square and had identified a number of youth gangs and "natural leaders" before Alinsky came on the scene. Alinsky could use his association with Conover as an entrée to some of the teenage gangs.

From the start, Clifford Shaw's method of working with delinquents was controversial. Partly this was due to the nonjudgmental, accepting relationship that he wanted his workers to have with delinquents. Many social workers were highly critical of him for his alleged tolerance of "criminal" behavior. And it was true that Alinsky and the others were not particularly interested in reporting their delinquents to the police for the burglaries or even the rapes they heard about. They were more interested in establishing a bond of trust. Typically, they did not coerce, threaten, or resort to homilies; they were careful not to project a self-righteous "you had better shape up or else" attitude. Rather, they would persuade by suggestion, indirectly by the example of their own life and conduct, or by challenging their delinquent friends to consider alternatives. Perhaps most importantly, they were simply available. They tried to be with their boys after school and in the evenings, when trouble was most likely to occur. They spent endless hours as "curbstone counselors," listening to a boy's problem, sharing a good story, and being a friend.

Alinsky, for instance, worked with one Russell Square gang that he nicknamed, with their approval, the University Juniors. He often took them to Hyde Park, where they might sit in on a University of Chicago class, visit the library, and end the day with dinner at Alinsky's apartment. Alinsky also devised true-and-false tests on various subjects which appealed to the boys' competitive instincts. Alinsky was trying to inspire an interest in education, in a neighborhood where only a small minority went as far as high school and a minuscule number to college.

Another controversial aspect of Shaw's approach was that he assigned the professional social worker a supportive rather than a commanding role. Although Alinsky and others on Shaw's staff filled in as curbstone counselors for delinquent-prone youth, Shaw's preference was to have local people in the area take on this key task—ideally, former delinquents who as law-abiding young adults now offered a positive model of more acceptable, conventional behavior. They were the people, Shaw believed, with whom the teenagers would most easily identify and whose values and ideas would be most credible and persuasive. A main function for Shaw's staff was to identify, encourage, and train these indigenous counselors. From the traditional view, this was at best romantic, at worst dangerous. The Chicago social worker Hasseltine Byrd Taylor came to regard the Area Project as an attempt to "fight the devil with fire," and the use of indigenous leaders as "questionable and fraught with danger to the community. To expect good results from the use of such means is to expect the impossible."

The one-to-one work with juveniles was, in a sense, part of a two-pronged effort. The other part had to do with the issue of social disorganization. Shaw had viewed the Russell Square area as a good place to test his theories, not only because of its high delinquency rates but also because it looked manageable from several other perspectives: it was relatively small and compact, stretching only seven blocks from north to south, from Seventy-ninth to Eighty-sixth Street, and not much more from west to east, beginning at the Illinois Central rail yards and ending at the Carnegie-Illinois Steel plant; second, it was homogeneous, perhaps 75 percent Polish and mostly Catholic, with a sizable number of families that had at least one person who worked in the steel mills. These and other factors gave the area a clear definition; an important part of the self-identity of local residents came from living in Russell Square—or "the Bush," as the neighborhood was also called because of the prevalence of wild shrubs there. If part of Shaw's answer to the problem of social disorganization was to create a consensus in a given community that new social controls were needed, then an existing common ground seemed to be an important asset.

The most important institution in Russell Square was the Catholic church, St. Michael's. The big organizational breakthrough for Shaw's staff came when they were introduced to Dr. A. S. Mioduski, a leader in both the church and the community. Jim McDonald, another of Shaw's staff in the area, met Mioduski, a chiropodist, through two of the doctor's children, who played at a local park. McDonald's "excuse" for his first meeting with Mioduski was to ask him if he could help distribute to local kids three hundred free tickets for a Chicago White Sox baseball game. McDonald took advantage of the meeting to explain what he was doing in Russell Square, that the Area Project "was not interested in setting up another recreational agency in the community . . . [but that] we are interested in developing a neighborhood committee to sponsor activities for the children."

Mioduski, who thought that he and the nuns at St. Michael's could, indeed, pass out free White Sox tickets to the kids, was interested in what McDonald had said. He emphasized that the support of St. Michael's pastor, John Lange, was essential because 90 percent of the community belonged to that parish and followed Lange's lead on community matters. Mioduski agreed to arrange a meeting with the pastor for McDonald and Shaw.

At the meeting, Shaw emphasized the difference between the philosophy of his Area Project and the typical settlement house that was "superimposed upon the community by individuals residing in communities of higher economic level, who were quite strange to the neighborhood and its problems." Shaw's staff had become aware of the dislike Lange had for Neighborhood House, the nearby Baptist-controlled settlement. At one point, Lange's suspicion that Conover, Shaw's first staff man in Russell Square, had developed friendly ties with Neighborhood House may have prompted Shaw to bring in McDonald and shift Conover to a less central role. Shaw also listened carefully when Lange told him about the difficult financial situation of the parish. Picking up on this, Shaw made a proposal: the Area Project would pay for the entire cost—$350, as it turned out—of refurbishing a number of rooms in the church basement, constructing a boxing ring, and purchasing games and equipment to create a new St. Michael's Boys Club.

It was possible to interpret Shaw's charitable proposal as contrary to the essence of his self-help philosophy. But Shaw, who found ways to make his ideology and practical needs coexist, was eager to get things moving in Russell Square. From his perspective, there was now an implicit quid pro quo. In exchange for his money and the benefit to Father Lange of having closer ties to the children of his parishioners, Shaw expected Lange's and Mioduski's help in establishing a formal community organization that would set policy and generally preside over a delinquency-prevention program. Soon after Shaw agreed to fund the start of the Boys Club, his staff man, McDonald, went to Mioduski and asked him for names of others in the area who could head up a Russell Square Community Committee (RSCC).

More than a year after the Boys Club was started, the RSCC finally became a reality. Its board of directors over the years would be made up of some of the community's "natural leaders." These leaders tended to be of relatively high economic and social status—a foreman at the steel mill, a druggist, an owner of a small business, an attorney, grocers, and physicians. But it was the volunteers, grouped into committees and subcommittees under the direction of a small full-time staff, who gave the RSCC its energy and effectiveness. For instance, they ran many of the recreational programs at the Boys Club and carried out the fund-raising drives. As poor as the neighborhood was, most of the budget for the RSCC eventually came from an array of local efforts—bazaars, fairs, smokers, door-to-door solicitations. And since much of the money went to the Boys Club, Father Lange did not see this fund-raising as unfriendly competition. Indeed, the people of Russell Square, the Area Project, and the St. Michael's Boys Club were one and the same.

But Shaw and his staff were interested in much more. In Shaw's scheme, the actual recreational activities, while useful for keeping kids busy, providing an energy release, and allowing for subtle surveillance, were nevertheless only a means to a more ambitious end. That end was to involve people, especially the adults of Russell Square, in a range of activities to improve the community—and an important part of the "improvement" would be the citizen participation itself. When the people realized they could change local conditions, Shaw theorized, they would then feel more responsible for doing something about the problems that plagued them. Thus, Shaw's staff encouraged one RSCC committee to consider the problem of physical deterioration and to clean up neighborhood eyesores. Another RSCC project focused on improved sanitation. That campaign was organized block by block, with representatives on each block responsible for taking orders for new garbage cans (sold at cost by the RSCC). In this kind of campaign, there was social pressure on families to conform, just as there had been a similar kind of community pressure exerted on tavern owners to change their ways and to keep shoeshine boys and other neighborhood kids out of their places.

Although there is no record of Alinsky's speech in the fall of 1938 to the Council of Social Agencies, it would not be surprising if speaker and audience reflected the hostility between the Area Project people and Chicago's traditional social-work establishment. The hostility not only concerned differing philosophies and the threat which the philosophy of the Area Project posed to the preeminence and power of social work, but also came because Shaw's people felt vastly superior and did not try to hide it. There was a swagger to their style. They wore their populism on their sleeves. In Russell Square and in the two Italian areas where Shaw's people were also working, the enemies to be conquered were not only delinquency, apathy, and social disorganization but also those interlopers from the world of the downtown professional social-work agencies and the Gold Coast benefactors of the settlement houses.

By now the private social agencies were alarmed that the Area Project was, in the words of one agency leader, "becoming a Frankenstein on the scene." The community committees organized by Shaw's staff were into everything: it seemed that they had defined delinquency prevention so broadly that even citizenship classes for immigrants fell within their reach—or, as the social-work critics might have put it, "within their grab."

The Area Project's community committees showed little respect for traditional social-service boundaries—one set of workers for child welfare,
another for housing, and so on—and thus the very idea of "expertise," the
raison d'être of professionalism, was under attack. One establishment
leader from the YMCA charged that Shaw's people were playing the "role
of agitators—stirring up the community against private agencies."

There was an irony in these accusations: although Shaw's methods
sharply diverged from the conventional, his goals did not; his staff was
interested in enabling low-income immigrant communities to have the
same kind of social controls and attitudes toward delinquency problems
that existed in middle-class communities. For all of the genuine populist
spirit among Shaw's workers, their overall community-betterment agenda
and the politics of the community committees were safely conventional. In
the Russell Square area, for example, the RSCC had nothing to do with
labor-union activity in the steel mills. Nor did the RSCC show much
interest in flexing its muscles vis-à-vis the local political organization.
Thus, while in one sense the RSCC was "a big deal" in Russell Square,
highly visible and actively supported by many people, its role was in
another sense narrow and limited, identified mostly with the St. Michael's
Boys Club.

By the late 1930s, if Clifford Shaw was confident that he knew the
causes of delinquency, he was nevertheless a little less certain about his
prescribed solution. Or, to put it another way, Shaw thought that the Area
Project was conceptually sound as far as it went, but did it go far enough
to make a real difference? More than five years after he had started the
Area Project, Shaw was forced to conclude that the jury was still out. On
the one hand, he thought he had seen enough good signs to suggest that
he and the Area Project were headed in the right direction. He liked to talk
about the good signs: the acceptance of his organizers by community
residents; the residents' willingness to become involved in youth programs;
a growing awareness that community problems could be effectively addressed by the collective effort of the people themselves; early fragmentary
statistics that delinquent rates in one Area Project community had declined. On the other hand, Shaw now talked less frequently about a more
difficult, even troubling set of fundamental questions concerning the economic and political realities. "It should be emphasized that the socio-
economic conditions which are probably responsible for delinquency in the
areas in which the Area Project is operating, are the product of influences
which are city-wide in their scope. It is not known, therefore, just how far
the reorganization of life in local areas can be achieved without reorienting
the social and economic life of the city itself. It is possible that the political

and civic reorganizations of the city as a whole, so greatly desired by public spirited citizens, may best be achieved by starting with reconstruction of community life in specific areas."

Shaw seemed to be saying—or perhaps hoping—that the limited changes brought about by the Area Project might somehow lead to greater reform, although somebody else, not Clifford Shaw, would have to take on that reform role. In the meantime, he started to explore the possibilities of moving the Area Project staff into another community: the Back of the Yards, Chicago's legendary slum. Shaw must have had doubts that his philosophy, which seemed to require a homogeneous population with the potential for reaching a consensus, could be successful in this famously difficult neighborhood. When Shaw sent Saul Alinsky into Upton Sinclair's "jungle," there were good reasons to predict that Alinsky would come out with the Area Project's first failure.

6

Life in the Jungle

Chicago was—and still is—a colorful mosaic of well-defined, even famous neighborhoods. There was the Jewish immigrant ghetto where Alinsky's father lived when he first came to Chicago, the Maxwell Street neighborhood. There was Hyde Park, where the University of Chicago had become internationally known in the 1930s for its controversial Great Books program under the leadership of Robert Maynard Hutchins and Mortimer Adler. There was the Gold Coast, stretching north from downtown along the Lake Michigan shoreline, where many of Chicago's wealthy lived— great wealth derived from retailing, steel, and meat-packing. And the large meat-packing plants and the Union Stock Yards, located a half dozen miles southwest of downtown, made their own industrial neighborhood famous.

In many respects, the growth of the Chicago stockyards and packing-houses and the adjacent neighborhood represented a familiar scenario in early American industrial life. As the country started to grow in the last quarter of the nineteenth century, new industrial centers sprouted. Immigrants in these new industries worked long, hard hours; the working conditions were poor and so was the pay. Housing, often put up quickly and cheaply, was not very good even when new, and it deteriorated rapidly thereafter. Not surprisingly, the first wave of immigrants moved out of these industrial areas as soon as they could afford to, only to be replaced by more recently arrived ethnic groups.

The meat-packing industry in Chicago and its adjacent neighborhood followed the familiar scenario. But early in the twentieth century, Upton Sinclair's blockbuster exposé *The Jungle* gave the stockyards area a special niche in American popular culture. His graphic portrayal of the filthy, unsanitary conditions in the packinghouses and slaughterhouses and the human suffering in the immigrant neighborhood shocked the country. The book, published in 1906 and an immediate best-seller in the United States and England that was also translated into seventeen languages, showed Chicago's slaughterhouses as perhaps the nadir of industrial slum life, a place where the bosses made little distinction between four-legged and two-legged animals.

The Jungle quickly triggered federal legislation—the Pure Food and Drug Act and the Meat Inspection Act—designed to clean up the packinghouses and reassure a horrified public. But the public's hunger for reform was too easily satisfied. The other abuses revealed by Sinclair—the plight of the workers and the living conditions of their families in the neighborhood—were not effectively addressed.

Three decades after Sinclair wrote his book, the jungle was little changed. Indeed, the public image of Chicago's stockyards area also included touches of drama and celebrity. "Hog butcher to the world," Carl Sandburg's memorable appellation, conveyed a certain swashbuckling romanticism. But it was romantic only from afar, since the overpowering sensation as one drew near to the intersection of Forty-seventh and Ashland, the heart of the Back of the Yards, was a horrifically putrid stench of thousands of animal carcasses in various stages of slaughter and decay—a stench that accumulated from the penned hogs and cattle, from the fertilizer plants, and from the rendering vats. That was reality, and reality also emerged from the smokestacks of the packinghouses to form a heavy grayness that hung over the Back of the Yards for as long as most could remember.

The Back of the Yards—so called because the neighborhood was located behind the Union Stock Yards—was not an address that helped to get a resident a job downtown or a young man a date with a girl he met at a North Side dance hall. After all, if he wasn't a thief and if he had anything on the ball, why was he living in the Back of the Yards? Why was he living near the four-block stretch of city dumps on Damen Avenue, where the meat-packers burned their waste, producing a perpetually smoldering fire? Why would anybody want to live near Bubbly Creek—the south branch of the Chicago River—which had become a communal sewer for more of the packers' waste? One time it became so clogged with organic matter that it caught fire, but usually—and this is how Bubbly Creek got its name—there was merely a vile blanket of foamy, gaseous bubbles that bobbed and popped on the surface. Why would anybody want to live in a smelly neighborhood, in a ramshackle frame house overcrowded beyond the legal limit with family and boarders and with a yard toilet out back?

There were many important occasions when a person would rather lie than admit that he lived in Packingtown, which was another name for the neighborhood. In that respect, the Back of the Yards was similar to Russell Square in South Chicago, where many felt stigmatized. But when Clifford Shaw decided to try his Area Project concepts in the stockyards community, he was moving into a vastly larger, more complex, and—although he may not have realized it at the time—politically explosive situation. Compared with what he had done earlier in Russell Square and elsewhere in Chicago, Shaw was now making a leap from the low minor leagues to the big time.

Shaw first started to test the waters in the Back of the Yards because several Polish leaders who were active in civic affairs asked him to consider starting delinquency-prevention programs in other areas of the city with sizable Polish populations. In July and August 1938, Shaw sent John Brown of the Area Project staff, who had worked for him in Russell Square, into the Back of the Yards.

From census data and other published materials, Brown first drew a profile of the neighborhood. Nearly 75 percent of the heads of families were foreign-born, and of them more than half were Polish. He made an inventory of the schools and churches—nine of fourteen were Catholic—and the private social agencies and local businesses. Most of this was intended as a cursory sketch, providing not much more information or insight than the impressions that most Chicagoans already had of the Back of the Yards as a grimy, poor, heavily Polish and Catholic neighborhood.

On the other hand, what attracted Brown's serious attention during his two months of prowling around the Back of the Yards were the juveniles and the parks and playgrounds where many of them hung out. Brown, who was thorough and conscientious like most of Shaw's workers when it came to digging into the world of the delinquent, kept a diary of his contacts with the youth gangs. One of his observations was that delinquency-prone youths spent a lot of time at one or two of the neighborhood's large parks, such as Davis Square Park. The boys in the Rams Athletic Club, for example, played softball and went swimming at Davis Square. But after they finished and left the park, they would steal from fruit trucks passing through an alley or shoplift at the nearby Goldblatt's department store. Brown learned about this by spending time with kids from the Rams, the Beeps, and other clubs and gangs. His main adult contacts were among the personnel who ran the parks and playgrounds and those who operated the local Mary McDowell Settlement House.

Shaw assigned Saul Alinsky to the Back of the Yards to continue the work that Brown had started. This was a time of both great despair and great hope in the stockyards community. The despair was a consequence of the Depression. After a period of economic recovery during the mid-1930s, there was a "Second Depression" in 1938. Unemployment in the Back of the Yards was now heading toward 20 percent. Old World pride had a lot to do with the fact that only a portion of the unemployed went on relief. As the historian Robert A. Slayton recounts, families survived on potatoes, sauerkraut, and bread—often stale bread softened with tap water and covered with sugar or mustard. Those afflicted with tuberculosis often did not survive, especially during the cold winters, when the last piece of coal went into the furnace at dinnertime and by midnight you could see your breath.

The great, even passionate hope in the Back of the Yards was found among some young men and a few women in an office at Forty-seventh and Marshfield, Chicago headquarters of the CIO's Packinghouse Workers Organizing Committee (PWOC). Packing was Chicago's second-largest industry, after steel. As head of the CIO, John L. Lewis had assigned one of his men, Van Bittner, to lead the national campaign to organize Armour, Swift, Wilson, Cudahy, and the rest of the meat-packing industry. But in Chicago, the center of the industry, the primary leader of the all-important organizing campaign was Herb March.

March was among Alinsky's earliest contacts in the Back of the Yards. While John Brown would seek out park directors and settlement-house workers, Alinsky would seek out March. March and other union leaders were also interested in trying to help the young people in the neighborhood, in part because such help would generate goodwill for the union in the Back of the Yards. So there was an overlap of interests between March and Alinsky, but there was also another reason Alinsky was interested in meeting March—his, Alinsky's, enthusiasm for the CIO generally and for what March and the PWOC were trying to do in Chicago.

Herb March was just a few years younger than Alinsky. Both had been caught up in politics, although by the fall of 1938 March's involvement had been more direct, deeper, and more radical. The son of working-class parents in New York, March was a precocious fifteen-year-old when he started at the Brooklyn branch of City College. He listened to the street-corner speeches of politicians and radicals, and while still a teenager started to attend the meetings of the Young Workers League. He dropped out of college after a year to go to work but lost his job shortly after the stock-market crash in 1929. By then, the Young Workers League had become the Young Communist League (YCL) and March was a member.

For the next several years, March honed his youthful yet considerable talents as a public speaker and organizer for the YCL in the unemployed movement—first in New York, where in 1930 he helped organize a big demonstration of unemployed around the slogan "Work or Wages." After that March went to Kansas City, where he was in charge of a seven-state district for the YCL, again working with unemployed councils on issues of jobs and relief benefits.

After March married, he and his wife wanted to start a family, so they moved to Chicago, where they thought it might be a little easier to find work. In 1933, March went to work in the Armour plant for 32.5¢ an hour. When the National Recovery Act went into effect a short time later, his hourly pay zoomed to a still less than astronomical 42.5¢. March lived about two miles from Armour, and to save the streetcar fare of seven cents, he would often walk home after work.

March, still a Marxist, was interested in organizing the packinghouse workers; by the fall of 1938, the workers had won some important organizing skirmishes though not yet the war. Armour, the giant of the industry, steadfastly refused to recognize the PWOC or to sign a collective-bargaining agreement. But March had won a tremendous following: the bright young New York boy had become a genuinely charismatic leader. He was extremely handsome—a lean, well-proportioned five-feet-eleven with dark hair and dark eyes—and a powerful and effective speaker with great range, exceptionally good both at street-corner rallies and at dissecting tactical alternatives at labor council meetings. Many thought of Herb March not merely as very bright but as brilliant, a man of great integrity and principle who was also effective.

Alinsky asked a mutual friend to introduce him to March, to let March know that Alinsky was okay, that he could be trusted. The two men got along well together from the start. They respected each other and quickly developed a friendly relationship. Alinsky was broadly sympathetic with March's politics, but he was especially attracted to the exciting progressive force that the PWOC had come to be in the jungle. Uppermost in Alinsky's mind, March recalls, was his interest in developing united-front organizations to oppose fascism. March appreciated Alinsky's pragmatic approach, in which he avoided overt partisan political stands; his style, his preference not to be labeled lest the label reduce his effectiveness with various people or groups; and his ideas about youth programs and about drawing together diverse elements in the community. The stockyards were littered with failed labor organizing campaigns dating back to the 1880s, and the failures had occurred in part because the meat-packers were able to drive a wedge between the organizers and the community by playing on ethnic rivalries and on the hostility of the Catholic churches to labor radicals and communists. If Alinsky could come up with something to promote unity, March was interested.

From the beginning in the Back of the Yards, there had been unity only within each nationality group. Everywhere else there had been disunity, division, and discord. That was still true even now, long after the Poles had replaced the Irish and the Germans as the largest nationality group in the Back of the Yards. By the late 1930s, Poles accounted for about 40 percent of the neighborhood, and the next-largest group was the Lithuanians; they and the Poles generally hated each other. Much the same feelings existed between Slovaks and Bohemians, the next-largest groups. It was often said that each group brought with it from the old country all of its historic animosities toward other nationalities.

Even among the Poles, there were cleavages and a pecking order that were not always appreciated or understood by outsiders. There were three Roman Catholic Polish parishes in the Back of the Yards, the first dating from around the time of the meat-packing strike of 1886, when the companies had imported scab labor from Poland; as more Poles came to Chicago, a second and then a third church were built. Within the Catholic Church, these were called national churches, which meant that the parishioners were all of the same nationality and the activities were conducted in the mother tongue. Each ethnic group in the Back of the Yards had its own national church. Among the three Polish parishes, St. John of God was the most prestigious. It was located toward the south boundary of the neighborhood, farther from the stockyards than the other two, and in a relatively expensive and desirable section of the neighborhood. The least prestigious Polish church was Sacred Heart: not only was it located in the poorest part of the neighborhood but its parishioners had come from the lowest strata of Polish society; these were the *goral,* the mountain people of Poland, who were thought of as the equivalent of American hillbillies.

The Polish parishes and the other national churches created their own separate worlds. Each national church—the Irish, Lithuanian, Slovak, Bohemian, German, and Mexican—had its own grammar school. Each parish had its own sodalities and Holy Name Societies—the clubs where women and men gathered to socialize and to work on church projects—and its own athletic club. The commitment to one's parish was near-total. Anybody, including the Archbishop of Chicago, who tried to break this traditional pattern had a battle on his hands. George Cardinal Mundelein, Chicago's relatively progressive archbishop in the 1930s, tried to Americanize Chicago's national parishes in the belief that this would reduce nativist hostility and give the Church the best chance of holding on to the second and third generations of the immigrant families. But in the Back of the Yards there was fierce resistance to Mundelein's orders. Many of the priests had been there years before Mundelein came to Chicago and would be there years after he died—Father Karabasz was the pastor at Sacred

Heart for forty-four years; Father Cholewinski was the pastor at another Polish church, St. Joseph's, for fifty-five years; and the Bohemian pastor at St. Cyril's, Father Bobal, retired after sixty-three years. The pastors in the Back of the Yards had their own power bases, and nobody from downtown was going to push them around without a fight.

The Old World antagonisms and the inward-looking preoccupation of each parish were formidable obstacles for labor organizers. But the Depression and then the excitement of the CIO started to change things. Prolonged unemployment was devastating to the families in the Back of the Yards, many of whom had lost their savings when all four local banks went bust in 1932. There had been terrible scenes outside the banks, with desperate people crying and begging for their money. The economic suffering in the neighborhood had reached a magnitude that overwhelmed the old tried-and-true support system of the church, of friends in the parish, of Catholic Charities. Even those who were lucky enough to get work at Armour or Swift were hardly making enough money to make ends meet. Thus, by late 1936, the contagion of the CIO had spread to the packinghouses. In May 1937, the PWOC, some of whose core activists were veterans of failed organizing efforts in the 1920s, held a rally in Chicago that attracted an enthusiastic crowd of more than two thousand packinghouse workers. Suddenly, the passion was there, but so was the legacy of ethnic rivalries, disunity, and defeat, a legacy that ran deep and that no labor organizer could ignore. That is why Herb March was interested in Saul Alinsky's ideas about an anti-delinquency program that might help to unify the community.

At about the time when March and Alinsky began to talk, a small group of women who, like Herb March's wife, Jane, were staunch union members or supporters, were moving ahead with their own youth program and would soon organize the Packingtown Youth Committee. These were mostly women in their twenties from the local YWCA and the Mary McDowell Settlement House as well as from the union. Many of the young people in the Back of the Yards were unemployed and, beyond a few local parks, there were few recreational opportunities for them. The women came up with a plan designed not only to create jobs and develop new recreational outlets but also to help unite the community. They had the official support of the PWOC, which meant a few dollars from each of the PWOC locals for expenses and the union credential when they talked to neighborhood people. The plan as it evolved was to ask the National Youth Administration in Washington to authorize the construction of a large playground and ballpark on vacant railroad property, a construction job that would provide NYA jobs for unemployed kids in the neighborhood.

To drum up support, the young women made the rounds of the sodalities, clubs, and sports teams and talked to as many of the priests as would see them. At each meeting, the young women would explain that there might be a way to bring jobs into the neighborhood. Would you please come to a conference in a few weeks, they would ask, where we can all talk about how we might be able to do it?

The women succeeded beyond their best hopes in rallying interest in their cause. They were more successful than Saul Alinsky might have guessed, too. As the time for the conference drew near, one of the women, who had heard about Alinsky's work with delinquents and thought that he would be interested in what they were doing, arranged to meet with him. She planned to ask him to be one of the two or three speakers at the upcoming conference. Vicki Starr met Alinsky at the Jucus restaurant in the Back of the Yards. They talked about delinquency in Chicago, and Alinsky showed her maps with shaded areas indicating where the highest delinquency rates were and recounted his own work with gangs. Vicki Starr was impressed. "I figured this man could really talk and would make a real contribution to the conference. He could talk about crime and how kids needed places to play. I asked him to be a speaker, and he turned us down."

Starr was angry; she had expected Alinsky to accept. Why had he refused? Starr wasn't sure. Alinsky himself was vague, Starr recalls. "He didn't feel like it," she remembers him implying. Maybe he thought the conference wasn't going to amount to much, or perhaps he did not want to be too closely identified publicly with the young communists, like Starr, who were among the leaders of the women's group. Undoubtedly there were those who saw Starr and her friends as "a bunch of Reds," as she puts it. Although by 1938 more and more workers were joining the PWOC, the union was looked upon by many in the neighborhood, Starr says, "as a radical Red organization." Still, so many of the different ethnic groups and parishes were represented at the Packingtown Youth Conference, twenty-six in all, and there was such a sense of purpose and accomplishment at it, that word quickly spread about how successful the conference had been. An eyewitness to that success, standing at the back of the room, watching and listening but never speaking, was Saul Alinsky.

One of the people in the neighborhood who had helped the young women, who put them in contact with the groups and clubs that used Davis Square Park, was Joe Meegan, the park's director. John Brown—Alinsky's colleague from the Area Project, who had spent time at Davis Square and met Meegan in the summer of 1938—described Davis Square in his reports as a center of community activity, especially for young people, and he also mentioned Meegan. So when Alinsky came calling at Davis Square in the fall of 1938, he already knew something about the young, energetic Irishman.

Meegan was a lanky man, over six feet, with blond hair and fair skin, and he looked younger than his twenty-seven years. He had grown up in St. Cecilia's parish in Fuller Park, east of the Back of the Yards; his immigrant father had worked for fourteen years in the stockyards for a dollar a day, until he became the janitor at St. Cecilia's, where he stayed for forty-four years. As a boy, Joe Meegan spent a lot of time playing at Fuller Park—he also went there twice a week to use the showers because, until the day when one of his three brothers became a priest, there was no shower at the Meegan house.

Joe Meegan worked his way through De Paul University in Chicago, and became a teacher at St. Philip's in 1932. By 1936, he was close to getting married. His wife-to-be's father was a Democratic precinct captain and he helped to arrange a contact for Joe with another Democratic politico at St. Cecilia's. The result was a job in the Park District. In the spring of 1937, Joe became director of the newly renovated Davis Square Park, with its ten acres of athletic fields and a large field house with meeting rooms.

Alinsky and Meegan hit it off reasonably well. They were nearly the same age, both had been working with young people, both cared about the poverty and suffering in the neighborhood, both distrusted social workers, and both liked to talk and plot and plan. But Alinsky's first encounters were not mere social visits. A key part of his job was to size up Meegan, to size up the priests, the assistant pastors, the businessmen, because it was central to Clifford Shaw's approach in his Chicago Area Project experiment to identify indigenous leaders and to persuade as many of them as possible to organize a community committee. Shaw and his staff had done this successfully before—but always in an ethnically homogeneous area.

Perhaps Shaw had thought initially, when the Polish civic leaders in Chicago had approached him, that a Polish pastor and parish in the Back of the Yards could somehow be the focus of a Back of the Yards community committee, as Father Lange at St. Michael's had been in Russell Square. Alinsky probably decided very early that this was impossible. First, the Poles had natural enemies, especially the Lithuanians. Second, there was no Polish pastor who had either the charm or the interest to transcend the ethnic divisions. Father Cholewinski, for example, the priest at St. Joseph's, was a cantankerous, difficult old man. When he was a kid, the story was told, he was so troublesome and disagreeable that he was finally given an ultimatum: either go to jail or go to the seminary—and that's how he became a priest. The pastor at Sacred Heart was a decent, caring man but very quiet and not inclined toward a public role. Using any one parish or pastor as the focal point was likely to have extremely negative if not disastrous consequences. So Alinsky went in another direction, toward Joe Meegan and the relatively neutral turf of Davis Square Park.

In the Back of the Yards, the closest thing to a consensus on ethnicity was the feelings about the Irish: nobody liked or trusted the Irish. To everyone else, the Irish were haughty, arrogant, and patronizing, not to mention double-dealing and dishonest. They were also powerful. The Irish had been the first immigrants in the stockyards, and although by now most had moved to better working-class neighborhoods, there was still a strong Irish presence in the Back of the Yards: they still worked in the yards and packinghouses, often at the best jobs, and, most important symbolically and practically, they controlled the local political machinery.

Thus, on the one hand, the Irish were resented in the Back of the Yards because of their self-importance and because they dominated the positions of leadership, power, and prestige. On the other hand, these very same factors were also sources of respect, albeit grudging. Say what you will about the Irish, the attitude in the Back of the Yards seemed to be, but they do know how to get things done. And young Joe Meegan, at Davis Square, was a specimen of that familiar type of Irishman, the ward politician.

Joe Meegan was an Irish charmer. He genuinely liked people, liked to say nice, upbeat things to them. He was also good at insinuating friendship. ("How are you today, mother?" Meegan would cheerfully greet almost any neighborhood woman over forty.) He came to know the birthdays and anniversaries of a prodigious number of people, and came to rival the professional politicians in his attendance record at baptisms, weddings, and wakes. If there was any hint of unctuousness in his style, it was more than offset by his energy and hard work. In his two years at Davis Square, he had cleaned up the place and started a free-lunch program with surplus foods (he got the Palmer House hotel to send him dishes) and put on free Halloween and Christmas parties for children underwritten by donations from local merchants (who were told by Meegan that these kinds of activities might help reduce vandalism and delinquency in the neighborhood). Joe Meegan was not only a hard worker but also something of an entrepreneur.

By the end of 1938, Saul Alinsky had probably decided that Joe Meegan was the best bet, at least to begin with, to lead an effort to form a community committee in the Back of the Yards. Being Irish and having his home parish outside the neighborhood, Meegan escaped some of the worst of the ethnic hostilities; as director of Davis Square Park, he was nonetheless part of the neighborhood, perceived as someone trying to do good things, especially for young people. And, of course, there was Davis Square Park itself, with its meeting rooms and its convenient location.

THE FIRST SIX MONTHS of 1939 passed swiftly for Saul Alinsky. He and Meegan were meeting regularly, often late into the night at a neighborhood tavern or at Meegan's house, to plan their next moves for launching the community committee. Within the Back of the Yards, the big public drama was the Packinghouse Workers' organizing crusade. There was a sense of movement and even of excitement as the Packinghouse Workers stepped up their demands on Armour, but also a sense of foreboding, a fear that perhaps the contending forces were on an irreversible, dangerous, and violent collision course. Those fears suddenly seemed all too justified when somebody shot at Herb March.

7

Organizing the
Back of the Yards

"Like a great battleship bracing herself for a plunge into stormy seas, Chicago watches her Packingtown and the workers and managers of her greatest industry. A titanic conflict, to make or break the CIO unions in the stock yards, may begin today, tomorrow or in a fortnight. Chicago remembers the Memorial Day riots and remembering looks today with fear and horror at the yards." Those were the melodramatic lead sentences of a long news story in one Chicago paper in mid-July 1939, and they probably captured the feelings of most people in the Back of the Yards.

In that embattled neighborhood, the conflict and violence had heated up the cold Chicago winter. In December 1938, Herb March was driving from his home to the union hall after lunch. When he got to the busy intersection of Fifty-first and Ashland, another car suddenly screeched alongside his '32 Dodge and tried to force him to the curb. When March glanced out his side window, he found himself looking down the barrels of what appeared to be two .45 automatics. He quickly hit the brake and gas pedals successively, so that his car was jerking and rocking back and forth as two gunmen, standing on the running board of their car, opened fire. March hit a parked car and came to a stop; he got out and dove for the sidewalk as the gunmen continued shooting.

Miraculously, he escaped with only a broken nose. But his bullet-ridden car was soon picked up by his friends and put on display, while word spread throughout the plants that somebody had tried to kill March. As workers went home that day, March recalls, a steady pilgrimage came to see the car. "The shooting resulted in terrific indignation among the workers," March says.

Throughout the rest of the winter and into the spring of 1939, the struggle between the packing companies and the PWOC, punctuated by more bursts of violence, dominated the Back of the Yards. In March, Joe Meegan and Alinsky had pulled together their first meeting at Davis Square Park. The local newspaper gave a brief account:

> The [Back of the Yards] Neighborhood Council, made up of representatives from church and social groups from this district, met for the first time on Monday evening at Davis Square for the purpose of discussing problems that face residents of the Back of the Yards community.
>
> Unemployment, education, delinquency, housing and health were introduced as issues to be taken up in greater detail by the council at future meetings.
>
> Joe Meegan, director of Davis Square Park, who conducted the meeting, emphasized that the council is to be representative of the people who actually live in the district and that it is to be open to all church and nationality groups.

Alinsky and Meegan spent the next four months organizing and preparing for their first full-scale public meeting. It was clear that their agenda was going to be much broader than jobs and recreation for young people. Alinsky was faithful to the approach that had evolved in the Area Project, where "delinquency prevention" was defined so broadly as to include virtually all community problems that might have contributed to social disorganization and slum conditions. Yet the Area Project retained its identity as a delinquency-prevention program. From the outset, Alinsky had something more in mind that was not only programmatically broader but distinctly more political. Another important difference was that Alinsky envisioned the neighborhood council as made up of representatives of specific groups in the Back of the Yards. This was not Clifford Shaw's approach: the members of the Area Project's community committees served as individuals, not as representatives of groups or clubs. What Alinsky and Meegan had in mind was closer to a labor-union model, in which delegates from each local serve as representatives on a central council of delegates.

It is virtually impossible to separate the roles of Alinsky and Meegan at this juncture. Alinsky had the concept and modified the strategy as they went along; Meegan had the contacts in the community and the lines of communication, although Alinsky soon developed credibility of his own with a wide assortment of people. From the beginning, Alinsky probably felt that he had recruited Meegan as the front man, and this later became a sensitive point between them, for in Meegan's view they were equals who had equally divided up the work of organizing the Council.

Of the major organizational categories or groupings in the Back of the Yards—churches, fraternal and athletic clubs, local businesses, labor unions—the most important to the success of a broadly representative Neighborhood Council was the churches. Had Alinsky and Meegan tried to organize among the national parishes a decade or so earlier, their words would have probably fallen on deaf ears. But an important new development was an infusion of young neighborhood priests, a result of Archbishop Mundelein's effort to Americanize the diocesan clergy and to invigorate its intellectual quality. One of Mundelein's major projects after he became Archbishop of Chicago in 1915 was to construct a seminary northwest of Chicago, St. Mary's of the Lake, where all the priests for the Chicago diocese were to be educated. (Appropriately, the seminary's architecture was American Colonial, including a chapel that was a reproduction of a Puritan meetinghouse in Lyme, Connecticut, and an archbishop's residence that was a replica of George Washington's house at Mount Vernon.)

These young priests soon dotted the parishes in the Back of the Yards. They came with far less of the Old World rigidities, especially when it came to relationships with Catholics of different nationalities. Many of them also saw links between their theological tradition and the politics of the 1930s. Most relevant to the situation in the stockyards was Pope Leo XIII's encyclical of 1891. With European socialists threatening to win over workers exploited by laissez-faire capitalism, Pope Leo's encyclical had attempted a middle course by providing a Catholic rationale for the worker's right to organize to secure a wage "to maintain himself, his wife, and children in reasonable comfort."

It was not only the modern outlook and the more cooperative spirit of the new priests that made them potentially valuable allies. They also had a great deal of time. The seminary was producing an abundance of young clergy, and some of the larger churches in the Back of the Yards now had four or five assistants. Rarely did they feel overworked. With time on their hands, many were receptive to a visit from Alinsky or Meegan.

The most important churchman for Alinsky and Meegan—indeed, the most magnetic and popular Catholic in the city—was Chicago's auxiliary bishop, Bernard J. Sheil. The founder of the Catholic Youth Organization, Sheil was a beloved figure in Chicago's working-class neighborhoods for his sponsorship of athletic programs and for his spirit and enthusiasm generally. Nationally, Sheil had won a following among liberal Catholics and non-Catholics for his outspoken, courageous support of the labor movement, the New Deal, anti-discrimination policies, and other progressive causes on which most ranking Catholic clerics either didn't speak out or took the other side. Sheil had a fondness for battle, as was demonstrated in his attacks on the demagogic ravings of the right-wing radio priest Charles E. Coughlin. He had an appreciation for the grand gesture or dramatic event, staging the finals of his CYO boxing tournament at Chicago Stadium, jammed to the rafters with everybody from Gold Coast socialites to Al Capone's boys from the "Bloody 20th" Ward. Benny Sheil had guts, he had a flair. Not surprisingly, he and Saul Alinsky were to find that they had much in common.

By coincidence, Joe Meegan's brother, Peter, a priest, was now serving as Bishop Sheil's secretary. Through Joe and his brother, Saul Alinsky met Sheil. It was not long before word spread that Bishop Sheil was going to be honorary chairman of the new neighborhood council. Sheil's imprimatur gave Alinsky and Meegan's organizing campaign added visibility and luster. It also provided some additional safety—a clerical covering—for any young priest who was sympathetic to the idea of a community-wide council but might have been wary of the consequences of straying beyond traditional parish duties.

As it was, Alinsky and Meegan did not win the active participation of any of the senior pastors. At St. Joseph's, one of the three Polish parishes, the cantankerous old pastor was actively hostile and forbade his assistants to get involved. At St. John of God, also a Polish nationalist hotbed, the pastor showed little interest. Only at Sacred Heart was there the promise of substantial participation from both parishioners and assistant pastors.

Traditional standoffishness was only one reason for the Polish churches' reluctance to join. Another reason was their rivalry with the mostly Irish church St. Rose of Lima. All the Catholic churches in the Back of the Yards were national, ethnic churches except one: Rose of Lima was a so-called territorial church; all Catholics living within its boundaries were eligible to join it. Earlier in the 1930s, after most of the Irish had moved out of the neighborhood and attendance at the church had fallen off, there had been talk that Rose of Lima would close. Not only did it stay open, but its pastor, with the support of Mundelein, actively tried to raid the Polish parishes. This was part of the archbishop's retaliation against the Polish pastors who had refused to go along with his program to Americanize the churches. The priests at Rose of Lima were encouraged to be especially friendly to the neighborhood Poles. "Stand out in front of the church and smile at them," Mundelein was said to have told them. Other blandishments, such as a cut-rate fifteen-dollar fee for weddings and a superior athletic program, had indeed won over a number of young Poles.

Rose of Lima's participation in the formative stages of the Council might have been an additional reason why two of the Polish churches failed to join in. On the other hand, Alinsky enjoyed playing rivals off against each other, warning a priest at a Polish church, for instance, that if his church didn't get involved, Rose of Lima (or some other parish) was going to get an advantage. Sometimes that threat worked, but not with two of the Polish churches in the spring of 1939.

Nevertheless, Alinsky and Meegan did an extraordinary job of pulling together a large part of the Back of the Yards. A week before the Council's scheduled July 14 unveiling at Davis Square Park, Meegan announced in the neighborhood newspaper that more than a hundred organizations had already agreed to send representatives. The executive board of the Council was also announced: four priests, one each from a Polish, Lithuanian, Slovak, and Irish parish; four men and a woman from church-related clubs, including one at the German Catholic church; three businessmen; the leader of an athletic club; a man from the Packingtown Youth Committee; the local police captain; and Herb March of the PWOC.

Had the emergence of the Back of the Yards Neighborhood Council come at a more ordinary time, it might not have attracted or warranted great attention. After all, however unprecedented it was to pull together priests and other diverse elements for a common cause, the Council had not yet done anything. But this was not an ordinary time. The very week-end that began with the Council's Friday-night meeting was a historic one in Chicago. The increasingly bitter struggle between the PWOC and the packers was heading for a possible showdown, and on Sunday night, CIO president John L. Lewis was coming to town to speak at a PWOC mass rally of delegates from throughout the country and to give the go-ahead for a national strike against the Big Four packers: Armour, Swift, Cudahy, and Wilson.

It was in this context that a newspaper story appeared on July 14, the day of the Council's meeting, in the Chicago *Daily News,* the first time one of the major downtown papers ran a story about the Council and, there-fore, the first time that most Chicagoans learned of it. "Something new in community organization" was about to happen in the Back of the Yards, the story began, and in the second paragraph the reporter quickly added that "the council is the conception and individual project of Saul D. Alinsky. . . . The residents of the district, according to Alinsky's findings, are almost completely stockyard workers and Catholics, and on this basis the sociologist has enlisted churchmen and the C.I.O. leaders to form the main pillars of the neighborhood council."

Although the newspaper went on to report that the Council meeting was going to include discussion sections "on child welfare, housing, health and unemployment," the clear emphasis was on the link between the Council and the PWOC:

> Either by accident or design, the formation of the back-of-the-yards council coincides with the culmination of an organizing drive by the C.I.O. in the stockyards. . . . In some sections it is expected—and hoped—that the neighborhood council will be a crystalizing agent for public opinion in the event of a stockyards strike by the C.I.O., regarded in informed circles as a certainty for August in view of the refusal of the Big Four packers to engage in conference with the C.I.O. for national collective bargaining agreements.

There is little question that Saul Alinsky was the source for the *Daily News* story. He was eager to have the Council identified with the organizing drive of the PWOC, for that is where his real interest and enthusiasm lay. He had been swept up in the excitement of the tremendous victories of Lewis and the CIO in 1936–37, and when Shaw assigned him to the Back of the Yards in 1938, as the PWOC organizing drive was rolling ahead, Alinsky soon realized how he could become part of the action. He used his job with Shaw to organize a Neighborhood Council that—on the eve of the most dramatic labor event in Chicago since the Memorial Day massacre—was publicly identified as a means to consolidate community support behind the PWOC. This is not what Clifford Shaw had in mind, for he steered clear of political controversy. He could not have been very happy with the *Daily News* story. Though Alinsky took care not to be identified in it as being on Shaw's staff (he was identified ambiguously as "a University of Chicago sociologist, now attached to the Rockefeller Foundation," which was a funding source for Shaw), Shaw was probably not mollified by Alinsky's effort to put a distance between himself and the Area Project.

Shaw had reason to be concerned about how Alinsky positioned the Council. In Chicago, as elsewhere, the CIO was regarded by conservative detractors as a dangerous, radical force. The terms "radical" and "communist" were often used interchangeably when opponents were attacking the motives of the CIO and its leaders. The reactionary Chicago *Tribune* gave a good example of this when it editorialized in July 1939 that "the [meatpacking] strike, if it comes, . . . will be another of John Lewis' Red C.I.O. revolutions. He wants to take the meat industry as he took G.M. and steel."

Calling the CIO "radical/communist" was often a simple tactical device on the part of pro-business forces to discredit the CIO, especially in the eyes of Catholics. In Chicago, the response among Catholic clergy to Red-baiting, or to the fact that communists were involved in the CIO, was mixed. Archbishop Mundelein was not known to use the Chicago *Tribune* style of rhetoric when speaking of the CIO; in the neighborhoods, the priests' attitudes varied from parish to parish. In the Back of the Yards, just after World War I, some priests actively opposed Communist-led labor organizing drives, but by the summer of 1939 the older ones were more indifferent than hostile. Herb March and the other PWOC organizers, however, wanted more than indifference or passivity from the local churches. They wanted active support to shore up the workers' enthusiasm and to combat the packers' Red-baiting. That is exactly what Alinsky had in mind when he finessed a story in the *Daily News* that said that the Council "has enlisted churchmen and C.I.O. leaders to form [its] main pillars." In fact, in the neighborhood, the image was somewhat different, having less to do with church-union "pillars" than with the Council's agenda of child welfare and health and housing—local concerns that were separate from the CIO drive.

Alinsky's plant in the *Daily News* made for a good story; it was provocative and timely, especially with Lewis coming to town on Sunday to throw down the gauntlet to the packers. And it was timely for another reason. Not only was Bishop Sheil going to be the honored speaker at Friday night's meeting of the Back of the Yards Neighborhood Council (BYNC), but it had also been announced that he had agreed to appear on Sunday night with Lewis at the PWOC rally. This had been engineered by Alinsky, recalls PWOC national director Don Harris. It was a simple yet brilliant idea.

Tension had been mounting in Chicago in the days leading up to the weekend of July 14. There was a rumor (it is reported as a fact in a biography of Sheil) that the bishop was shot at while eating in a restaurant. Stories circulated in the stockyards that Sheil was being advised to cancel his appearance with Lewis—to plead sickness and leave for a trip to Florida "for his health." But Sheil had a pugnacious side, and as the threats mounted, the likelihood of his appearance probably increased.

Sheil had already done much to give the BYNC a quick dose of legitimacy and prominence. He had announced two weeks before that he had asked it to head the official welcoming committee for a delegation of Irish boxers who were coming to Chicago for a tournament with CYO champion boxers at Soldier Field. These boxing tournaments were highly visible, well-attended civic events, and Sheil delighted in the hoopla that surrounded them. This time, the fledgling BYNC was going to be a major part of it: welcoming ceremonies at Davis Square Park; speeches by Sheil and Mayor Kelly; a giant parade through the Back of the Yards neighbor-hood; fireworks and music. Joe Meegan, as its executive, took the occasion of Sheil's announcement to orate: "Our organization here is working to improve housing, health and recreation facilities . . . just as I am sure these boys must work to better their families' conditions in Ireland. I am told they come from working sections of Ireland, and we from one of Chicago's largest industrial sections intend to extend to them the heartiest . . . welcome."

Sheil's appearance at the first BYNC meeting helped to bring out 350 people and make it a rousing success. The bishop, outlining the important work that needed to be done, anticipated the resolutions that were adopted later in the evening—committing the Council to develop a recreation facility at Forty-seventh and Damen, to implement child-nutrition and disease-prevention programs, and, most dramatically and significantly, to urge Armour to avert the impending strike by negotiating a settlement with the PWOC.

Herb March could not have been happier. Not only was the BYNC, with its church, business, and social clubs, closing ranks behind his union, but a mighty symbol of the Catholic Church itself, the beloved Bishop Sheil, was saying to the world—but more importantly, saying to the Catholic packinghouse workers—that the PWOC was a legitimate instrument and expression of the workers' needs.

When the meeting ended, Herb March and other BYNC delegates stepped out of the Davis Square field house into the warm air of the July night. March started driving home, still savoring the night's success as he turned left onto Fifty-eighth Street. Suddenly, another car's lights hit, and tires screeched once again. All at once, March heard the shot of a gun, felt bits of glass against his face and a sharp blow to his shoulder. He ducked down on the front seat, pulled on the emergency brake, and quickly reached into the glove compartment for the .45 automatic he had started to carry after the last shooting. But by the time he got up from the seat and looked out the window, all he could see were taillights a half-block away.

March's gunshot wound turned out not to be serious, but it heightened the sense of danger and excitement surrounding Sheil's appearance with Lewis. It was one thing for Sheil to be generally supportive of liberal causes—and that was bad enough in the eyes of conservative Catholics of the corporate class. It was worse still that he was generally pro-labor, pro-working-class, and all too often strayed from the arena of religion and charity into that of protest and politics. This time, however, Sheil had gone too far. The prospect of Sheil sharing a platform with the devil incarnate,

Lewis, was too much. The image of Sheil embracing Lewis—literally and symbolically—before 10,000 cheering packinghouse workers was all too powerful. One newspaper headline read: "Sheil defies threats; talks at CIO rally today." (He was now receiving telephone threats hourly.) When Sheil finally made his way to the Chicago Coliseum on Sunday night, he went in a borrowed bulletproof car, it was rumored, and with a large police escort. "A scene unprecedented in the social history of Chicago," one news account trumpeted, "with men representing every shade of the many hued left-wing labor movement in America."

In the past, Sheil's attractive, buoyant personality and his CYO successes had helped to drain the venom from the anger generated by his liberalism. This time was different. Benny Sheil, not only a courageous man but an ambitious one, wanted to be Archbishop of Chicago one day. But in the view of his many friends, the moment he stepped on the stage of the Chicago Coliseum and greeted Lewis with a long, warm handshake, his chance to become the head of the largest Catholic diocese in the world was gone forever.

The Chicago *Tribune* reported that "Bishop Sheil's appearance as a speaker marked a departure from Roman Catholic policy in Chicago. Usually the bishops have avoided active participation in controversial and economic movements." But the event had significance beyond Chicago, and *Time* magazine captured some of it with a story entitled "Meat and the Bishop," filed by its bureau chief in Chicago, Sidney James, a Catholic admirer of Sheil. The entire CIO received an important boost from Sheil's signal that the Lewis-led industrial-union movement fell within the bounds of traditional Catholic teaching and deserved Catholic support, James wrote. Sheil's appearance and his application of a papal encyclical to support the cause of the packinghouse workers "was making not only Chicago, but U.S. history."

Although Sheil and Lewis dominated the headlines of the important July 14 weekend, it was Saul Alinsky who had perhaps won the most. Alinsky had cleverly maneuvered the BYNC into the mainstream of action during the weekend and, in the process, became identified in Chicago as the one who had conceived of "something new in community organization." This also further isolated the packers politically by changing their relationship with the Catholic Church—or at least it was Alinsky's machinations that changed the popular perceptions of that relationship. For nearly a half century in the Back of the Yards, church spires and packinghouse smokestacks had shared the skyline, each in their own place. After the July 14 weekend, the skyline somehow looked different. The spires and smokestacks now competed for space rather than shared it. As a political architect, Alinsky had done a masterful job. For this, he won widespread respect in the Back of the Yards. He also enhanced one important relationship and started another.

Perhaps nobody appreciated Alinsky's behind-the-scenes work more than Benny Sheil. Sheil enjoyed the limelight, enjoyed championing the cause of the underdog, enjoyed being embroiled in controversy. Alinsky had put him in a position where he was able to enjoy all this and more. Not surprisingly, after the successful weekend Sheil and Alinsky became increasingly friendly, and it was a friendship that would be of enormous benefit to Alinsky. Also not surprisingly, Lewis enjoyed his visit to Chicago and an opportunity to receive the blessing of a prominent Catholic bishop—a happening rare enough to be both memorable and impressive. It is not certain when and how the word about Alinsky was passed along to Lewis, only that their meeting in Chicago was the beginning of another important relationship for Alinsky.

All in all, it had been an extraordinary weekend. The BYNC had got off to an auspicious start. The PWOC seemed to have gained new strength and momentum. Alinsky had emerged as a promising young figure, but would he continue to work with Shaw on delinquency prevention or might he hitch up with the PWOC or CIO? When he and Helene went down to the Smokies for a vacation in late August, there was a chance, perhaps, to get a better view of the future from a high mountain peak.

8

New Friends
in High Places

At a time when political identities seemed distinct and discrete, the political identity of the Back of the Yards Neighborhood Council seemed varied, even muddled. Looking at the Council for its political coloration was like looking at a kaleidoscope: the colors changed as the angle of vision changed.

Was the Council merely or primarily an appendage of the radical Packinghouse Workers Organizing Committee? That might have been a reasonable judgment from the perspective of Armour, the Chicago *Tribune,* or other anti-union elements. Or was it a convenient vehicle for Cardinal Mundelein to integrate the tradition-bound ethnic parishes into the larger Catholic community? Or was it essentially a conservative self-help effort? Was it perhaps implicitly rejecting both New Deal philosophy and outside do-gooders generally when it announced at its founding: "For fifty years we have waited for someone to offer a solution—but nothing has happened. Today we know that we ourselves must face and solve these problems. We know what poor housing, disease, unemployment and juvenile delinquency means; and we are sure that if a way out is to be found, we can and must find it."

If there was confusion about the Council's true politics, there was also some confusion about Alinsky's political and professional identity. From afar, it may have seemed that he was on the PWOC payroll. The union organizers, however, while regarding him as a friend, never saw him as a CIO man. He was a sociologist—or was it a criminologist? He was a left liberal—but he had a strong dislike for traditional social work, so what kind of a Jewish left liberal was he anyhow?

Perhaps Herb March understood Alinsky's style and politics in 1939 as well as anybody. On September 1, while the Alinskys were still on vacation in the Smoky Mountains, in a remote area accessible only by packhorse, somebody brought them the news that Hitler had invaded Poland. The next morning Saul and Helene returned to Grand Lake, where, Alinsky recalled later, "I made a beeline for a radio set. Warsaw was being bombed. The German Army was marching into Poland, [and] Chamberlain was wetting his pants."

Alinsky's contempt for Chamberlain and other Allied leaders was the reason for his initial reaction to the signing of the nonaggression pact in August between Germany and the Soviet Union. "At the time of the signing of the nonaggression pact I did not share the wild bitterness and hysteria of my many liberal friends because, while it seemed obvious to me that any agreement with Adolf Hitler carried no good faith, I would have had to stretch my imagination further than it can stretch to find a basis for belief in any good faith in the word of Neville Chamberlain or Georges Bonnet." The Russians had concluded, Alinsky thought, that Britain's leaders would continue to sit on their hands and that the French would sit behind the Maginot Line while Hitler unleashed his fury on Russia. So the Soviet Union moved to redirect Hitler's military power, a not unreasonable move from its perspective, Alinsky thought. He had not thought, however, that the consequences on the battlefield would be so sudden and devastating. He had expected

> from two to four or six years of Soviet-Nazi surface vibrations. I thought of it in terms of years because I could not visualize nor would I have believed that the Nazi blitzkrieg through the Lowlands would have resulted in such a speedy collapse of France as well as the other Lowland nations. However, if that collaboration were to continue, it meant that the Communist Party would change its line completely, and if that were the case, I had better get back to Chicago in one big hurry.

Alinsky was concerned about a possible clash between the communists in the PWOC and the Poles in the Back of the Yards. March recalls a conversation he had with Alinsky during this period:

> Alinsky said to me, "You and I got off the same train when that nonaggression pact was signed." I said, "What do you mean?" He said, "You fellows had moved in a united front against fascism. As far as I'm concerned, the total movement that I'm interested in is fighting for the people in the form of the united front against reac-

tion." We called it fascism at that time. And he said, "I'm still for it but I don't think you guys are." I remember that conversation very distinctly because on a personal level we had a very honest, straightforward, cordial relationship. We had a good deal of respect for one another.

March tried to assure Alinsky that his foreign-policy beliefs were not going to intrude on their collaboration in Chicago.

I told Alinsky, "Look, the Back of the Yards Council has its role to perform and I agree with the concept, and our union will support it as we always have. And as far as these political questions are concerned, they don't belong in there." Alinsky never brought up any political questions in the Council in terms of foreign policy, nor did the union—ever—because as far as we were concerned, we certainly didn't want to clash with that world of politics.

But in the political world of the late 1930s, Saul Alinsky saw the Back of the Yards Neighborhood Council as a bulwark of democracy, as an answer to the forces of reaction at home and abroad. In addition to whatever child-nutrition or delinquency-prevention programs it might develop, it was equally important—perhaps even more important—that it was making a political statement. "This organization," Alinsky had written on the eve of its first meeting, "is founded for the purpose of uniting all of the organizations within the community . . . in order to promote the welfare of all residents . . . regardless of their race, color or creed, so that they may all have the opportunity to find health, happiness and security through the democratic way of life." In his mind—in his very imaginative, theatrical mind—the Council was not merely a little community group that was going to help some kids. No, not at all. It represented nothing short of a defense of "the democratic way of life," a defense against right-wing hate-mongers and the forces of fascism at home and abroad. Part of Alinsky would have dearly loved to be in Spain, fighting the glorious fight with the Loyalists against Franco. There would have been great stories to tell about those adventures! As it was, he often spoke in bellicose metaphors in the early days of organizing the BYNC. If PWOC communists dared to infiltrate the BYNC with the new party line after the German-Soviet non-aggression pact, then "in that case there would be war," Alinsky said, "and it would not be war against some half-dizzy liberal of the kind they knew well how to fight, but it would be my kind of war, because I would make it that way."

Alinsky's boldness, especially his verbal boldness, was his hallmark in the Back of the Yards. (Interestingly, he thought that his being a Jew was not a negative factor in this Catholic community but rather, if anything, a small benefit in that it placed him outside the old ethnic and parish conflicts.) He said and did things that others couldn't bring themselves to do. Alinsky's abrasiveness might rub the older priests the wrong way; but the younger ones, who were pro-union and receptive to new ideas about improving the dismal conditions in the Back of the Yards, responded to him and came to appreciate his audaciousness and theatrics—indeed, he did and said things they could enjoy vicariously.

And Alinsky was audacious. Soon after the founding of the Council on July 14, Alinsky and Meegan started the hard work of mobilizing the supporters they had won over. All their initial efforts had been essentially a numbers game: sign up as many church groups, clubs, and priests as possible to show that the Council had a real constituency—and then get them to the first meeting to show that it was more than a paper organization. Now Alinsky and Meegan sought active support. First they went after the local businessmen. The Council needed an operating budget, and part of it would come from the Ashland Avenue businessmen, they decided. Three businessmen had been recruited for the Council's board of directors, two of whom were known as tightwads who always had an excuse for not contributing to a fund-raising drive. For these and others like them, Alinsky worked out a routine. First, he would go into a store and demand an exorbitant contribution. In the bluntest tones he would tell the owner, "Bill, the Council needs to raise some dough and we've put you down for two hundred bucks." Bill would immediately go into a barely controlled rage, arguing that everybody in the neighborhood always had a hand in his pocket, that business was lousy, and that Alinsky was crazy if he thought he was going to get two hundred bucks. Alinsky would then heat up the argument, telling Bill that his business depended on the community and asking him how he would like it if Alinsky told the next Council meeting that Bill was too cheap to contribute. After ten minutes of escalating threats and counter-threats, Meegan would suddenly appear. Feigning surprise, he would say, "Saul, what are you doing here?" And Alinsky would start to complain that he had asked Bill for a contribution to the Council. Meegan would then interrupt and would plead, in his most earnest, Irish Boy Scout way: "I've known Bill for years, Saul, and I know he'll help out. Bill's a great guy, Saul, so take it easy on him. Bill, you'll give a hundred bucks, won't you? Saul, Bill's always good for a hundred bucks when it's for a good cause, aren't you, Bill? For crying out loud, Saul, don't give him such a hard time. Bill'll give a hundred bucks, and we'll announce it at the next Council meeting. Now, come on, Saul, let's go and let Bill get back to work." And the two of them would leave and walk down Ashland Avenue laughing and replaying their holdup of Bill, and then would replay it again that night when they met at Meegan's house with some of the young priests.

In a variation of the same theme, Alinsky would regale Meegan and the others with another of his exploits, like the time he approached a local store owner for a hundred-dollar ad on the back page of a program for a fund-raising dance.

> "A hundred bucks!" [Alinsky said the guy screamed]. "What the hell do you think I am—nuts? Do you think I'm made of money? Just for that dumb bunch of Polacks out there?"
>
> "Well, let's cut the crap," I said. "I know and you know that you're not a damn bit interested in those people. The only reason you've ever been in the Council has been to promote yourself and your business, and if you want to show off what a great guy you are, okay. If not, I'll talk to Barney about it."

Barney Goldberg and William Lewis were bitter competitors, selling the same kind of merchandise on the same street, and their price wars were at once fierce and comic. As Alinsky described it, whenever Lewis put a dress in the window with a price of $3.55, only twenty minutes later a similar dress would appear in Barney's window at $3.54. Fifteen minutes later, Lewis's dress went down to $3.53, and the test of wills would continue until, Alinsky cracked, it seemed "that only the National Guard could prevent an almost certain case of homicide."

As Alinsky told it, a threat of going to Barney would soften up Lewis.

> "I'll go up from fifteen to thirty bucks," Lewis said.
>
> I said, "There's nothing to go up from since we didn't start from fifteen or fifty—but with a flat hundred."
>
> "A hundred dollars!" he almost screamed. "Take my heart—take my blood! Here, take it."
>
> I said, "I'm not taking anything. It's up to you to take it or leave it," and I started to walk out.
>
> "Well now, look. Be reasonable," he said. "For God's sakes, don't make me pay a hundred dollars."
>
> "I'm not making you pay anything," I said. "Barney is the one who's interested in paying for it. Do you want to buy it or don't you?"
>
> "Why must you always bring Barney into this?" he shrieked.

"Listen, Lewis," I said. "You haven't got a damn bit of use for the people out there and I haven't got a damn bit of use for you. And if you think you are going to exploit them and get all of this phony goodwill that you are getting for nothing, you're crazy. If you want this kind of advertising, you'll pay for it. If you don't want it, okay."

"Well, can't you compromise?"

"Sure, I'll compromise. I'll give you two admission tickets to the dance, at forty cents apiece, for nothing."

Alinsky and Meegan also pressured the co-owners of the neighborhood newspaper into a deal. Aaron Hurwitz and John Haffner ran a small, barely solvent tabloid paper, *The Town of Lake Journal,* its name a throwback to an era when the neighborhood was called Town of Lake. One day Alinsky and Meegan called the two newspaper owners in for a talk. They hadn't decided exactly what they were going to say, except that they wanted to use the paper to publicize the Council's activities. After a few initial pleasantries, Alinsky announced matter-of-factly that the Council was probably going to start its own newspaper and that he just wanted to be a nice guy and let Hurwitz and Haffner know about it. The two owners, both mild-mannered, pleasant men in their forties, were stunned. It probably didn't take them more than a few seconds to envision the end of their already shaky journalistic enterprise. If Hurwitz and Haffner were not great newspaper publishers, they were even worse chess players. They quickly took Alinsky's opening gambit, skipped over any intermediate moves, and pleaded desperation. Anything Alinsky and Meegan wanted was fine with them. If they wanted to become partners, that was fine. Anything was fine, but please don't start another paper. Alinsky told them he wanted to settle the matter then and there but he and Meegan needed a few minutes to talk it over. With that, Alinsky and Meegan went into another room to figure out what they *did* want. Their bluff—they had no real interest in or intention of starting their own newspaper—had worked so well that they had been caught unprepared by the instant capitulation. When they emerged, they made an offer that Hurwitz and Haffner were happy to accept. No, Alinsky and Meegan said, they didn't want to become partners, but they did want two things: they wanted the Council's activities to be promoted and described as though it were the Council's newspaper; and they wanted the name of the paper changed to *The Back of the Yards Journal,* a name that would remind people of the Council and, in any event, was more up-to-date than *Town of Lake.* In exchange, they promised to round up more advertising from local businessmen.

Hurwitz and Haffner took the deal, and an episode that occurred later illustrates not only how Alinsky executed his end of the bargain but also his sense of priorities. The episode involved Sidney Lens, a young radical union activist in Chicago. Lens had been fired from one job because of his organizing activities and then took another one at Meyer Bros., a department store on Ashland Avenue in the Back of the Yards, where he was put in charge of the lunch-counter fountain. Being a compulsively committed unionist, he started organizing the workers at Meyer Bros. History soon repeated itself, and Lens was fired again. He set up a one-man picket line in front of the department store but made little progress. Lens then met with Alinsky and a small group of priests. He asked them if the Council would support him and his organizing drive by starting a boycott of Meyer Bros. Since Alinsky and the Council had the reputation of being staunchly supportive of the packinghouse workers, Lens was surprised when Alinsky, acerbic and unsympathetic, did not embrace his noble cause. Alinsky grumbled that some of the Council members would have to talk about it. That was the last Lens heard from them. A week or two later, however, Meyer Bros. bought an exceptionally large, two-page advertisement in *The Back of the Yards Journal.*

To the businessmen and others in the Back of the Yards, Alinsky was the iron fist inside the velvet glove of democracy. His tough-mindedness and sharp tongue were real, but to an important extent, the democracy was real, too. Or perhaps it would be more accurate to say that a democratic spirit had begun to evolve. Much was made of the simple but unprecedented fact that representatives of the antagonistic nationality groups had joined hands to form the Council. Much would be made of the dinners the Council sponsored to bring together people from different parishes, and of the fact that young priests would come together periodically to break bread and to break up the old ethnic barriers. A respect for individual differences and a new appreciation of the possibilities of communal action were very much part of an evolving democratic spirit in the Back of the Yards. If this new spirit had not yet penetrated all the various levels of community life, it had at least been absorbed by the people active in the Council.

In the early stages, the Council also had a semblance of a formal democratic structure. Its executive board met regularly in an open community meeting, and its standing committees—four were established at the first Council meeting—were active. Later, the structure was expanded and refined. But in the early months, Alinsky and Meegan largely shaped the Council's direction and program.

And there was a flood of activity, for various reasons most of it centered on young children and youth. Meegan and Alinsky's own experience was in working with juveniles, of course, and since the Council's "office" was in Meegan's office at Davis Square Park, where young people congregated, it was easy to link the Council to programs for kids, which in any case were obviously needed and popular. By the fall of 1939, an Infant Welfare Station was established at Davis Square to provide early medical assistance (the neighborhood had one of Chicago's highest infant-mortality rates), and the Council had begun the process to acquire the vacant land at Forty-seventh and Damen for its recreational center. The Delinquency Committee, whose members believed that delinquents were more likely to come from homes with unemployed parents, developed plans to find jobs for such parents. The Council also pushed for more National Youth Administration jobs. It applied pressure on local businesses to hire more neighborhood young people, especially during the busy holiday seasons. Alinsky and Meegan turned the Council into a job referral agency and insisted that job applicants who came to the Council for help "must have a letter of recommendation from some organization or church within the Back of the Yards Neighborhood Council," thus applying additional pressure on reluctant parishes and clubs not yet in the Council. In exchange for local business cooperation, Alinsky and Meegan saw to it that the Council supported a campaign to "Buy in the Back of the Yards."

SAUL ALINSKY'S WORK in the Back of the Yards impressed a lot of people, including Bishop Sheil and John L. Lewis. The reaction of Alinsky's boss, Clifford Shaw, was almost certainly very different. There is a mystery surrounding the end of the relationship between Shaw and Alinsky. In Shaw's large collection of papers from his days as head of the Chicago Area Project, there is no mention or evidence of Alinsky's work after the fall of 1938; in the 1940s, when Shaw published a list of the various sections of Chicago where the Area Project had established programs, conspicuous by its absence was the Back of the Yards. It is possible that Shaw, who received financial support from more conservative civic and business leaders, changed his mind about pursuing a project in the stock-yards because the community was too divided and especially because of the labor unrest.

What happened? Nobody knows for sure. After Alinsky officially resigned from Shaw's staff in mid-January 1940, neither man said much—indeed, anything—about the other. Even while he was organizing the Council in 1939, Alinsky had been vague regarding his staff assignment from Shaw, and it is possible that he was moonlighting. Since most of his contacts and meetings with Meegan and others occurred late in the day or at night, Alinsky could have been at the office of the Institute for Juvenile Research with Shaw during the day and then in the Back of the Yards later. Or perhaps Shaw allowed Alinsky to continue his activities in the Back of the Yards as an experiment of sorts, while he nonetheless disowned any Area Project sponsorship.

From Alinsky's perspective, it was understandable why he was ready to leave Shaw's operation. He told Meegan after they met that he was not particularly happy with what he was doing. The work with juvenile gangs had become repetitive and no doubt boring, especially for Alinsky, who was easily bored and often impatient. Then there was Shaw himself. As individuals, Shaw and Alinsky had little in common. Shaw had grown up, the fifth of ten children, in a tiny Indiana farm town, Luray, twenty miles south of Muncie. As a young man, he had studied briefly for the ministry and then came to the University of Chicago as a graduate student in sociology in the early 1920s. His ambition and drive had more to do with the development of the Chicago Area Project than did his scholarly work. His associate, Henry McKay, who was quiet and retiring, was the more reflective, research-oriented of the two, compiling and analyzing much of the data that Shaw used in books and other forums to influence American criminology. As something of an empire-builder, Shaw was good at using his staff. Since Alinsky was monumentally unsuited to being used by anybody, it was only a matter of time before the inevitable parting of the ways.

In the fall of 1939, Bishop Sheil told Marshall Field III about Saul Alinsky. The timing of this introduction was significant. Only several years earlier, Field had been known mainly as the polo-playing, socialite grandson of the founder of the huge Field fortune, which had originated with a retailing business in Chicago in the 1860s and 1870s. By the time Alinsky met him, Field, then forty-six years old, had recently acquired a social conscience and appeared to be heading steadily—some thought rapidly—to the left. He would soon be called "a traitor to his class."

Marshall Field III, who had taken up investment banking as a young man although he had no need to work, had voted for Hoover in 1932. He was, however, essentially apolitical. A likable, soft-spoken gentleman, exceptionally handsome and distinguished-looking, he appeared to have few strong beliefs. Although he had voted for Hoover, he did not share the horror of his fellow bankers or of his class generally for the Roosevelt administration.

The transformation of Marshall Field III coincided roughly with the events of the Depression. The Depression did not have much of an effect on Field's large and diverse fortune, but his personal life was sinking, if not plunging, in the early 1930s. A second marriage had fallen apart, his drinking escalated, and, from his new depths of despair, a personal crash seemed possible. At about this point Field began to see a brilliant New York psychiatrist, Gregory Zilboorg.

Neither Field nor his family ever denied that Field's psychoanalysis under Zilboorg was an important episode. But they did not agree with what they felt were grossly exaggerated accounts of Zilboorg's influence on the "new" Marshall Field, the Field who began to emerge as a man with a purpose, a sense of social responsibility, and even a reformer's zeal. To be sure, there were other influences. Field's third marriage, to the recently divorced Ruth Phipps, gave him stability and happiness, and there were new friends, Democrats and liberals, who steered him into support of social causes. The first of these causes was child welfare. Louis S. Weiss, a dynamic New York lawyer, was influential in this regard. So, too, was Justine Wise Polier, daughter of the famous liberal rabbi Stephen Wise. Polier, a Yale Law School graduate, a courageous, pro-labor, persuasive woman who was a friend of Roosevelt's from childhood, was appointed a judge in the Children's Court in New York City by Mayor La Guardia after she had worked on a special project to try to bring a semblance of decency to the horrendously cruel conditions of New York's child-welfare system. Polier, Zilboorg, Weiss, and others with whom Field became friends during the mid-1930s were extraordinary people—strong personalities with superior intellects and devoted, in various ways, to the pursuit of social justice. These people, collectively, were responsible for Marshall Field's transformation.

Field and Bishop Sheil were not intimate friends, but their paths and interests coincided on child-welfare projects. In 1940, for instance, Sheil served on the important United States Committee for the Care of European Children, a war-relief effort that was organized with the help of Eleanor Roosevelt and chaired by Field. In the fall of 1939, Sheil knew Field well enough to arrange a meeting for Alinsky. They met briefly at the Waldorf-Astoria in New York, and Sheil was there, too. Alinsky talked about the Back of the Yards programs for children that had already been launched and, most importantly, about the possibility of re-creating democratic community organizations in other cities. The meeting ended on a friendly note but without any signal from Field that he wanted to get involved. A few days later, however, he asked Alinsky to lunch and pressed him for more details.

In many respects, they made an odd pair. They looked and sounded as though they came from different worlds. Field was patrician, with straight graying hair and the sound of Eton and Cambridge in his voice.

Across the table sat Alinsky, with kinky dark brown hair, thickish lips, wire-rimmed glasses, and the sound of the West Side of Chicago in his voice. And yet they seemed to hit it off. Of course, Field saw Alinsky through the filter of the endorsement of Sheil, whom liberals like Field greatly admired and respected. Nonetheless, there was much about Alinsky's own orientation and style that Field would have appreciated: his work with delinquents and his criticism of the traditional juvenile justice system; his involvement with the labor movement, which Field had come to support; and a tough-minded pragmatism that suggested Alinsky might be able to convert abstract ideals into tangible accomplishments. For Alinsky, the combination of Field's maverick status, prominence, and wealth was made to order. He could identify with the anger and controversy Field had stirred up among his upper-class friends. Alinsky also liked being associated with prominent people, whether they were the Capone mob's Frank Nitti or "Babe" Leopold or Benny Sheil. And Field's wealth and willingness to support a worthy cause could obviously open up new, exciting possibilities. They talked about money and how much it might take to get Alinsky started on his own. Field suggested the creation of a foundation that would offer tax deductions for wealthy contributors. Alinsky had reservations: foundations connoted stuffiness, elitism, and the possibility of cautious, meddling trustees. Field suggested a compromise of sorts: if the contributions were limited, the influence of any single contributor could be limited, too, and Alinsky could work at keeping control of the foundation in his hands. In any event, this foundation was not going to fund somebody else's projects. It was going to be a convenience, a base from which Alinsky would organize democratic community organizations.

By the time Alinsky left New York, Field had promised his support. By February 1940, the Industrial Areas Foundation was incorporated, and Field had provided $15,000, half for Alinsky's salary and half for expenses. The Back of the Yards Neighborhood Council, which had made all of this possible, was still in its infancy, and it would be four more years before it would prove that it had a life beyond infancy. Talk would soon begin— however premature it may have sounded—of a "Back of the Yards Movement." It was the kind of talk Saul Alinsky liked to encourage as he began to travel north and west to spread the spirit of democracy in urban industrial America.

9

The Great John L.
and Presidential Politics

Saul Alinsky officially resigned from Clifford Shaw's staff on January 15, 1940, and moved into a small, two-room office on the seventh floor at 8 South Michigan Avenue in downtown Chicago. As the year unfolded, Alinsky not only worked to multiply the early success of the Back of the Yards in other cities but played a behind-the-scenes role in one of the most dramatic episodes of the 1940 presidential campaign. That episode, which he seized as an opportunity to solidify his relationship with the country's most powerful labor leader, John L. Lewis, also marked a historic turning point for the American labor movement and for the fortunes of the great John L.

As Alinsky was setting up shop in his new Chicago office, Lewis delivered the first of his election-year anti-Roosevelt speeches in Columbus, Ohio. At the Golden Anniversary convention of the United Mine Workers, Lewis called on the union delegates not to endorse any presidential candidate in 1940. Lewis's pronouncement stunned many political observers. After all, Lewis and the UMW had been staunch supporters of the President's reelection in 1936 and had contributed manpower and large sums of money to Roosevelt's landslide victory that year. But there had been an erosion of Lewis's relationship with Roosevelt, and now Lewis was telling his delegates—and the country—that "with conditions now confronting the nation and the dissatisfaction now permeating the minds of people, [Roosevelt's] candidacy would result in ignominious defeat."

The sources of Lewis's disenchantment with Roosevelt were many. Lewis felt that Roosevelt had not provided political support commensurate with labor's—and particularly with his own—support of the President. In Lewis's view, this called into question Roosevelt's true commitment to the industrial-labor-union movement; it also raised doubts about the President's integrity. Lewis had come to believe that Roosevelt could not be trusted, that he was little more than an opportunist and a hypocrite. He claimed, for example, that soon after the 1936 election Roosevelt double-crossed him at a critical juncture of the Flint sit-down strike in 1936–37. (Of this episode, Alinsky later wrote: "Lewis, prior to departing for Detroit, was given assurance by the President that the sit-down strikers could continue sitting, and upon arrival in Detroit discovered not only that the President had instructed Governor Murphy to the contrary but had added the postscript, 'Disregard whatever Mr. Lewis tells you.' ")

Another alleged betrayal by Roosevelt came later in 1937. After a string of major organizing victories, the CIO had run into trouble, particularly in trying to organize Little Steel (meaning all the major steel companies except for U.S. Steel). Violence escalated as Little Steel strikers and the companies clashed repeatedly. Sensing public revulsion with the violence, Roosevelt sought to distance himself from both sides by proclaiming at a news conference that "the majority of the people are saying just one thing, 'A plague on both your houses.' " Lewis made a contemptuous reply, delivered in that strange amalgam of Shakespeare and bombast so typical of him: "It ill behooves one who has supped at labor's table and who has been sheltered in labor's house to curse with equal fervor and fine impartiality both labor and its adversaries when they become locked in deadly embrace."

Lewis and Roosevelt also had growing, bitter differences on foreign policy. Lewis was a staunch anti-interventionist in the period before Pearl Harbor. His isolationist tendencies were based in part on his interpretation of American involvement in World War I, when, he believed, another reform-minded President, Woodrow Wilson, had misled the country and brought it into an unnecessary foreign war. According to the Lewis biographers Melvyn Dubofsky and Warren Van Tine, he believed that once the United States entered World War I, Wilson "then allowed reactionary businessmen and politicians to repress labor and. prosecute radicals in the guise of national security. In 1940, [Lewis feared that] Franklin D. Roosevelt seemed likely to repeat Wilson's mistakes of 1917–1918, to involve the United States in someone else's quarrel, and to terminate the New Deal and domestic reform, as Wilson earlier had gutted the New Freedom."

Most observers would not have predicted, however, that policy disagreements would have led to an irretrievable break between the two leaders. As Alinsky wrote years later, the popular image of Lewis and Roosevelt was of two men working for a common cause:

To the coal miner in the pit, the steel worker in the mill, the packing-house worker in the slaughter houses . . . or the man who worked in New York's dark subway, Franklin Delano Roosevelt was not only the greatest president they had ever known but the greatest friend they had ever had, and John L. Lewis was their great knight in shin-ing armour who was leading them out of the economic jungle to the promised land. . . . In that sense, these two men were almost in-divisible.

Yet this "popular image" obscured the extreme animosity the two men actually had for each other. In his own biography of Lewis published in 1949, Alinsky emphasized the corrosive effects of their mutual hatred, without which they might have maintained a public alliance, however uneasy, in spite of differences over specific tactics and policies. Their antagonism precluded the possibility of resolving at least some of these differences through negotiation, or of achieving any sort of rapprochement.

Until the election year of 1940, Lewis's feelings toward Roosevelt were often subordinated to political realities and to Lewis's own political ambi-tions. Even when he made the speech opposing an unprecedented third term for Roosevelt, his motives were open to several interpretations. Per-haps, some thought, he was trying to establish a bargaining position. Perhaps he was sending a message both to the Democratic Party and to Roosevelt that his support had a price—assurances, for example, that labor would not be shut out of the administration after the election as, in Lewis's view, it had been in 1936, when the trade-union movement did not have its own leaders as Secretary of Labor or in other policy-making positions.

Still another interpretation of what Lewis was up to came from Roose-velt's Labor Secretary, Frances Perkins. Around the time that Lewis gave his speech, she later wrote, he met with the President and in private suggested that widespread opposition to a third term could be effectively countered if he picked Lewis as his vice-presidential running mate. Lewis told Roosevelt, according to the President's account to Perkins, that "a strong labor man would insure full support, not only of all the labor people but of all the liberals who worry about such things as third terms."

Whether or not Lewis made such a proposal to Roosevelt in the winter of 1940—Lewis refused to confirm or deny the story when Alinsky inter-viewed him for his biography—by Labor Day Lewis had repeated his public criticisms of Roosevelt often and with such intensity that a final, formal break was now a distinct possibility, even a probability. What seemed less likely, but had been unthinkable only a short time before, was that Lewis would endorse the Republican nominee, Wendell Willkie. The implications for Lewis, the CIO, and Roosevelt were great. In October 1940, polls showed Willkie gaining ground rapidly. It was by no means a sure thing that the American electorate would award any President a third term.

Several weeks earlier, Saul Alinsky had jumped into the fray. Alinsky's role in this episode of presidential politics and his claim to have arranged a last round of negotiations between Lewis and Roosevelt have been disputed. Dubofsky and Van Tine doubt the veracity of Alinsky's account. But although Alinsky may have exaggerated the importance of his role in arranging a last-chance meeting between Lewis and Roosevelt, evidence suggests that he had access to Lewis during this period and was in a position to help set up such a meeting, two key points that Dubofsky and Van Tine find difficult to accept.

When the board of directors of Alinsky's new Industrial Areas Foundation was established early in 1940, joining Marshall Field and Bishop Sheil on the board was, among others, Kathryn Lewis, John L.'s daughter. Alinsky probably met Kathryn around the same time that he met John L., at the rally for the Packinghouse Workers in the Chicago Coliseum the preceding July, when he had arranged to have Bishop Sheil share the platform with John L. Kathryn was a close, active participant in her father's professional life. This intelligent and capable woman, who was troubled with a severe weight problem, was intensely loyal, committed, and protective of her father's interests, and in turn she was the apple of her father's eye. If Saul Alinsky was looking for one person to help him get to the great John L. Lewis, he could do no better than Kathryn Lewis.

In the fall of 1940, however, with the election drawing near, Lewis occupied a peculiar political position. Although he was still president of the CIO, he had become, to a significant degree, politically isolated. Other CIO leaders supported Roosevelt; some, like Sidney Hillman, leader of the Amalgamated Clothing Workers of America, were among Roosevelt's most active, staunchest allies. Within the CIO, the communists shared Lewis's anti-interventionist, anti-Roosevelt position, albeit for different reasons. But Hillman and other CIO leaders were working to keep most of the CIO behind Roosevelt.

What were Alinsky's politics during this period? His Chicago Hyde Park friend Sidney Hyman remembers Alinsky talking sarcastically about Roosevelt, calling him "the great smiler." By this time many liberals and radicals had become disenchanted with Roosevelt, blaming his political turn to the right and his cuts in federal spending for the new surges in unemployment and the advent of a "Second Depression." By 1940, Alinsky's enthusiasm for Roosevelt's domestic policies may still have been limited. On the other hand, Alinsky could not have shared Lewis's passionate anti-interventionism. Lending support to the Allies' war effort and stopping Hitler were top priorities for Alinsky.

As the campaign headed into the homestretch, the great irony was that Roosevelt and Lewis needed each other. Roosevelt needed solid labor support to win the election. Lewis, who had apparently believed early in the year that Roosevelt would not run for a third term, had painted himself into a political corner. After his continuous criticism of Roosevelt, it was no longer a simple matter of doing an about-face; the great John L. Lewis's diet did not include any swallowing of pride. What, then, to do? He could endorse the Republican, which seemed almost absurd. Nevertheless, if Lewis did come out for Wendell Willkie, would the CIO follow his lead? Most certainly they would, Lewis must have believed. As Alinsky said later: "Lewis, victorious and determined, constantly praised and eulogized by the unions of the C.I.O., was confident that his people would follow." But the thought of endorsing Willkie could not have been very satisfying. Willkie was the candidate of the moneyed interests, although he seemed to represent the views of a more enlightened element of those interests. Furthermore, his foreign policy, an area in which Lewis had strong feelings, was little different from Roosevelt's.

Endorsing neither Willkie nor Roosevelt was not a promising alternative for Lewis either. As Alinsky wrote later, if Lewis angrily refused to support either candidate—a spiteful mocking of Roosevelt's "A plague on both your houses"—he would lose any chance to gain political leverage to influence post-election policies, and the CIO rank and file would vote en masse for Roosevelt without Lewis's gaining any political benefit. Also, Lewis was concerned about the left wing within the CIO, according to Alinsky:

> The Communist Party at that time was following a line of condemning the war in Europe as an 'imperialist war' and attacking Roosevelt as a war monger. On the other side, they attacked Wendell Willkie as a barefoot Wall Street boy. If Lewis came out with a condemnation of both the Republican and Democratic parties, he would be supporting the left wing's position on the election, thereby greatly enhancing their prestige and consolidating the position of all the left-wing leaders in the C.I.O.

Alinsky was sympathetic with Lewis's political predicament. However, he also claimed later, he was torn by the worsening conflict between Roosevelt and Lewis. When Alinsky wrote a new introduction to a reissue of his Lewis biography in 1970, he recalled the events in the fall of 1940 and referred to both Roosevelt and Lewis as "my idols." Perhaps in his memory they both were, but in September 1940 his emotional sympathies were with Lewis.

Alinsky recounts that by mid-September "a last attempt was made to bridge the rapidly increasing gap between Lewis and Roosevelt," in which he and Bishop Sheil were, as he termed it, "the final negotiators." "[A]n arrangement was devised," says Alinsky, "whereby Lewis, expressing complete confidence in the integrity of [the two of us], was willing to enter negotiations with the President. Bishop Sheil got in touch with the President and was informed that the President was fully prepared and eager to try to close the breach and that he definitely wanted Mr. Lewis's support in the campaign." A series of telegrams was exchanged between Sheil and Roosevelt, setting up a confidential, off-the-record meeting between the two of them for September 16. The White House Ushers' Diary shows that Sheil did see Roosevelt at 4 p.m. on that date, although no written record exists of their discussion. Sheil's interest in serving as a negotiator was consistent with his politics and style. It also reflected the immediate concern of many liberals and others on the left that a formal break between Roosevelt and Lewis could hand the election to the Republicans and cause a devastating rupture in the industrial-labor-union movement. Alinsky, too, despite whatever reservations he had about Roosevelt's domestic policies and despite his growing personal ties to Lewis, was also motivated by the larger concern of keeping the left liberal coalition together.

It was easy to understand why Alinsky enlisted Sheil's help. Sheil was a man of national stature, an ardent supporter of the New Deal, and he could have access to Roosevelt. He no doubt had Lewis's respect, especially after the historic gathering of Packinghouse Workers delegates in Chicago in the summer of 1939, when he had shown courage and political friendliness. Also, Lewis appreciated the political importance of the Catholic Church. Len De Caux, a Lewis aide in the CIO, said that "the Catholic Church was important to Lewis, [and] a connection with Sheil was important to him. And if Sheil had come into the picture, Lewis would certainly pay attention to him and go through the motions of trying to effect a reconciliation with Roosevelt [although] he really didn't intend to. I think he made up his mind quite a long way back."

Not only is it not known exactly what was said at the first meeting between Sheil and Roosevelt; it is not clear what role Sheil played afterward. Alinsky wrote—somewhat ambiguously—that "Bishop Sheil not only supervised the arrangements at the White House, but was present when a number of Lewis's statements were made." There is a suggestion here that Lewis had several private meetings with Roosevelt in Sheil's presence in late September or early October, but no specific dates are mentioned. Dubofsky and Van Tine find this highly implausible because, they argue, "Lewis, who insisted consistently throughout his career that trade unionism and religion could not be mixed, would hardly engage in political maneuvers in the company of a Roman Catholic bishop." This inference fails to take into account, however, the unique personal experience Lewis had with Sheil in Chicago and the fact that Sheil was, as a liberal political activist, a highly unusual American Catholic bishop.

The fact that Sheil might have had any role to play whatsoever suggests the degree of estrangement between the Lewis and Roosevelt camps. But by now, no advocates for Roosevelt could be effective with Lewis. Indeed, even access to Lewis was a problem. The great man was in a sulk, or so it seemed. As the election drew near, not even Lewis's closest associates saw much of him. He had retreated to the privacy of his family.

It is likely that Saul Alinsky, after brainstorming with Sheil in Chicago about how they might head off a split that would hurt both Roosevelt and Lewis, then got in touch with Kathryn Lewis. Although Kathryn shared her father's hatred for Roosevelt and was also a member of the America First Committee, she was, above all, concerned with her father's best interests. It is not difficult to imagine Alinsky's argument to Kathryn that there was little to lose and enough to gain to justify a round of negotiations between her father and Roosevelt. Years later, Alinsky claimed that "it will come as a shock to many Lewis critics who have attributed Kathryn Lewis's feelings toward and advice to her father as a factor in the break with Roosevelt to know that this attempt to reunite Lewis and Roosevelt had her ardent support. Kathryn Lewis was determined to avoid the break and fought to maintain negotiations until the end."

The end came at the White House in the President's bedroom on the morning of October 17. Alinsky said that Lewis gave him an account of the meeting that afternoon. According to this account, Roosevelt was in bed when Lewis entered the room.

> "The President seemed to be quite uncomfortable. His face had an unhealthy pallor, and he seemed to be laboring under a great deal of tension. After greeting me, he said, 'John, sit down over here by my side.' I sat down. After a moment's silence, he said, 'John, I want your support.' I said, 'You mean, Mr. President, you want the C.I.O.'s support. If you want the C.I.O.'s support, what assurances can you give the C.I.O.?' The President became irritated and snapped at me,

'Well, what do you mean? Haven't I always been friendly to the C.I.O.?' I didn't answer. He continued and his voice rose angrily. 'Haven't I always been a friend of labor, John?' I said, 'Well, Mr. President, if you are a friend of labor, why is the FBI tapping all my phones, both my home and my office, and why do they have instructions to follow me about?' The President said, 'That's a damn lie.' I got up, looked down at him and said, 'Nobody can call John L. Lewis a liar and least of all Franklin Delano Roosevelt.'" After some uncomfortable small talk, the meeting came to an end. Lewis said: "I stretched out my hand and said, 'Good-by, Mr. President.' The President was quite upset and nervous. I guess I wasn't feeling too good myself. His face became quite hard, and he turned away from me, and even when we shook hands he was looking the other way. I walked out. Roosevelt and I are done."

The election was less than three weeks away as Lewis talked and Alinsky listened on that October afternoon. Apparently Alinsky was stunned by the final reality of the split. "The negotiations that had begun with such high hopes burst like a skyrocket across the sky," Alinsky wrote, "and now there was nothing left, no way to try to bring these two leaders of the working people together again." Alinsky gave Lewis and Roosevelt equal billing—the "two leaders of the working people"—when he wrote this passage nine years after the negotiations fell apart. In the fall of 1940, however, in the remaining days of the presidential election campaign, Alinsky became an active partisan. He helped Lewis when the labor leader made his extraordinary decision to come out for the Republican, Wendell Willkie. Later, Alinsky never mentioned his role in helping Lewis try to defeat Roosevelt, and there is no mention of it in his biography of Lewis. None of Alinsky's friends who first met him after 1940 remember him saying anything about it. In fact, very few people who knew Alinsky at the time of the election knew that he was trying to help Willkie's campaign as an agent of John L. Lewis. One of the few who did was a Chicago businessman named Hermon Dunlop Smith.

Dutch Smith was a vice president of the insurance company Marsh & McClennan. He was forty-two, a graduate of Harvard, and was becoming known in Chicago as one of a small but growing group of younger, "responsible" businessmen—in Smith's case, a man who not only was on his way to becoming rich but also felt a sense of social responsibility. Saul Alinsky met Dutch Smith in late 1939 through a woman who served with Smith on Chicago's Community Fund. Smith recalls that the woman was impressed by what Alinsky had been doing in the Back of the Yards and thought the Community Fund should support such innovative efforts. "She felt that the Community Fund was a charity structure that was run too much by people on Astor Street rather than by people on Madison Street," Smith recalls. "She wanted to break down that barrier." She told Smith about Alinsky. "She said he's unusual, what he's doing is interesting but I'm afraid some of the people on the budget committee would just turn it down flat. Hopefully you will give him a try. So he came in to see me and made quite an impression on me. He was different," Smith says, entertaining and lively, and his idealism had an underpinning of realism and toughness. Smith was so impressed that, as chairman of the Community Fund's budget committee, he saw to it that the Back of the Yards Neighborhood Council received a grant of $3,500. And when Alinsky started the Industrial Areas Foundation months later, Smith accepted an invitation to serve on the board of directors.

Dutch Smith was working for the election of Wendell Willkie when he received a call from Alinsky a few days after Lewis and Roosevelt had their last fateful meeting. Alinsky "called me up and said I want to talk to you and it's very confidential. And he said it is so confidential that I don't want to talk on the telephone. Can you possibly come over here? So I said okay." When Smith got to the Michigan Avenue office, Alinsky told him that Lewis was going to come out for Willkie and that "we"—meaning Lewis and Alinsky, Smith was made to understand—"want to get all of the capital out of this that we can get." Alinsky had approached Smith for his help because, as Smith remembers Alinsky saying bluntly, "you're the only Republican I know."

Alinsky asked Smith to begin raising money quietly for a crash organizing effort that would begin as soon as Lewis made a nationwide radio speech endorsing Willkie that was set for Friday night, October 25. At lunchtime one day, Smith went to solicit funds at the Attic Club, a private businessmen's club hidden away on the twenty-second floor of a La Salle Street office building. The place was filled with Republicans. Smith remembers that "I picked up $10,000 before anybody had their soup. They were delighted to make an extra contribution" if it helped Willkie's chances to defeat Roosevelt.

Before election day, Alinsky took Smith to Cincinnati to meet Lewis, who was there for a speech. The three of them had dinner together in Lewis's hotel suite, before Alinsky and Smith took a night flight back to Chicago. It was one of those meetings that had no specific agenda but was rather intended to establish relationships. Ostensibly, it was a chance for Lewis and Smith to meet each other, to get to know each other personally. From Alinsky's perspective, however, it was another chance to demonstrate to Lewis that he, Alinsky, was himself a shrewd operator who could not only work with some of the communists who were leaders in the Packinghouse Workers Union but also deliver for Lewis a prominent Catholic bishop and, now, a well-connected Republican insurance executive. Indeed, Dutch Smith had the strong impression that Lewis had confidence in young Saul Alinsky.

Ten days before the election, John L. Lewis sat down in front of network radio microphones to speak to an estimated national audience of 25 million. A few Washington insiders and labor leaders thought they knew that Lewis was going to come out for Willkie. For most of the country, however, there was still great suspense. Lewis had shut himself off from the outside world during the week before. Not even his closest aides saw him, including those who would normally have helped him with a major speech. Nobody knew exactly what Lewis was going to say, and even those who thought they did could not be certain what might be produced from within the deep, dark caverns of the Lewis mind. Those in the listening audience who were attracted by the possibility of fiery rhetoric and dramatic surprise were not disappointed.

Lewis fired one poison arrow after another at Roosevelt, accusing him of being a warmonger, a liar, and a man with an insatiable craving for power. "Our forebears paid the price in blood, agony, privation and sorrow, requisite for the building of this republic," Lewis intoned in a deep, ominous voice. "Are we now to cast away that priceless liberty, which is our heritage? Are we to yield to the appetite for power and the vaulting ambitions of a man who plays with the lives of human beings for a pastime?" Lewis's answer was not merely a grave, stentorian no. Nor was his answer merely that he was endorsing Willkie. From the depths of Lewis's hatred for Roosevelt came his answer, an answer whose seismic reverberations were intended by Lewis to be of a magnitude equal to the labor leader's estimate of his own importance.

> It is obvious that President Roosevelt will not be elected for a third term unless he has the overwhelming support of the men and women of labor. If he is, therefore, reelected, it will mean that members of the Congress of Industrial Organizations will have rejected my advice and recommendation. I will accept the result as being the equivalent of a vote of no confidence and will retire as president of the Congress of Industrial Organizations, at its convention in November. This action will save our great movement, composed of millions of men and women, from the embarrassment and handicap of my leadership during the ensuing reign of President Roosevelt.

Not even the political insiders had been ready for this theatrical ultimatum: It's either Roosevelt or me. Sidney Hillman, listening to the speech on the radio with friends in Washington, was astonished. The next morning, Hillman went to the White House and found Roosevelt with Harry Hopkins; both were dispirited. "What now? What does this mean?" Roosevelt asked. Hillman, who thought Roosevelt looked "thoroughly scared," tried to be reassuring. "What are you worried about? It will be all right. So what if John Lewis made a speech for Willkie?" Hillman told them that Lewis could not deliver the CIO vote.

Hillman was right; Lewis was not able to sway much of the CIO leadership or the rank and file, although he tried. Saul Alinsky attempted to help in Chicago. He asked Dutch Smith to provide office space and telephones. "He brought packinghouse workers and steelworkers into my office," Smith remembers, "and my office pretty much fell apart because there were great big black fellows and in those days you didn't have black fellows around. And my office practically became their headquarters." Alinsky was probably working with his friend Hank Johnson, the black assistant national director of the Packinghouse Workers. (In fact, Johnson's boss, Don Harris, feels certain that Johnson, who was very close to Kathryn Lewis, was responsible for bringing Alinsky and Kathryn together.) Johnson was a magnetically attractive leader and outstanding speaker who had a large following among both black and white workers. And Johnson sided with Lewis when the head of the CIO came out for Willkie.

But even someone of Johnson's caliber and stature could not pull many of the packinghouse workers with him. The reason was simple: most workers, in Chicago and elsewhere, never bought the argument that they had to choose between Lewis and Roosevelt. Alinsky was right when he wrote later that workers saw both men as champions of their cause, even if the two had differed on specific issues. Thus, rank-and-file workers could vote for Roosevelt again and still see Lewis as their great union leader. Other CIO leaders, however, who had publicly visible roles and were called on to endorse or repudiate Lewis's support of Willkie, were in a more difficult situation, and many resented Lewis for the trouble he was causing them. Lewis associate Phil Murray, a Roosevelt man, tried to keep quiet. Many of the leaders of the left-wing unions in the CIO, who may have approved of Lewis's opposition to Roosevelt but who were not about to endorse the Republican opponent, tried to avoid talking to Lewis. When Lewis personally asked Mike Quill, the communist leader of the New York Transit Workers, to endorse Willkie, Quill did, but when Lewis's brother sent Quill campaign literature for Willkie, Quill's staff promptly tossed it in the incinerator.

Even Lewis's closest associates did not vote for Willkie. Len De Caux, who was with Lewis the night he made his Willkie speech, remembers that "Katie [Kathryn] was sticking Willkie badges on us that night in the headquarters. We were all supposed to vote for Willkie. I wasn't for Willkie. Lee Pressman wasn't for Willkie. None of Lewis's own mine worker people were personally for Willkie. And I didn't vote for Willkie. I think I didn't vote for either. That stopped me from voting for Roosevelt."

Did Saul Alinsky vote for Wendell Willkie? His Hyde Park friend Sidney Hyman remembers him being "mealymouthed and ambiguous." Hyman heard him "go through a lame drill in support of Willkie . . . as if he wanted to keep himself in the right with all hearkening angels and that would be John L. Lewis. I never heard him say it publicly, but I heard him say it in small circles, trying to persuade somebody and really trying to persuade himself, but being rather cautious about . . . not offending Lewis. I just thought that it was very uncomfortable for him."

It is no wonder that Alinsky did not want to tell many of his friends that he was helping Lewis in the closing days of the presidential election. Lewis's endorsement of Willkie had, at best, little support or respectability on the liberal left. To many, no doubt, it seemed as though Lewis had gone off the deep end, that his hatred for Roosevelt and the supremely large Lewis ego had blinded him from seeing the political world realistically. Even after Roosevelt's reelection and Lewis's resignation as CIO president, Lewis could not admit that he had made a serious miscalculation. Years later, Alinsky told Lewis that he thought Lewis's challenge had been "unnecessary and a wild gamble that was politically pointless." Lewis's answer, which Alinsky saw as only a flimsy rationalization, was that "there was never a momentary doubt in my mind that Mr. Roosevelt was going to be reelected. That was the very reason I deliberately publicly committed myself . . . to the camp of Wendell Willkie. You see . . . I had to get out of the presidency of the CIO if I were to be effective in uniting the divided forces of labor. The CIO presidency placed me in an impossible situation, insofar as I could personally strive to unite the CIO and the AF of L."

ALINSKY'S LOYALTY to Lewis during the turbulent fall of 1940 cemented his friendship with John L. and Kathryn. Both father and daughter demanded total loyalty as a prerequisite for friendship. Saul Alinsky had qualified. Lewis, however, was not a man who had many friendships, and those that he had were not close or intimate. On the contrary, he was a distant man, who was personally close only to members of his immediate

family. He was also a busy, important man and Kathryn, a gatekeeper for
her father, was an important link to John L. So Alinsky's friendship was
defined by the peculiarities of Lewis's personality.

Yet Alinsky enjoyed an almost starry-eyed relationship with Lewis.
They came from totally different backgrounds and out of different experiences, but there was enough overlap in personality, style, and inclination
for Alinsky, nearly thirty years younger than Lewis, to see himself in
Lewis's commanding image. Lewis's great nerve, the pleasure he took in
assuming a defiant stance, his projection of intellectual superiority—these
were characteristics that Alinsky could relate to and appreciate. And when
these Lewisian characteristics were played out in the epic labor organizing
battles during the halcyon days of the CIO, the romantic attraction of a
great movement and its great leader was irresistible to Alinsky.

Saul Alinsky wore his friendship—his public identification—with
John L. Lewis as a badge of honor. Even after Lewis's blunders in the
presidential campaign had diminished his stature, Alinsky remained an
ardent defender and apologist. In August 1940, Alinsky was sitting next to
Carl Sandburg at a going-away dinner party that Bishop Sheil hosted for
Sidney James, the *Time* magazine bureau chief in Chicago who was being
transferred to Los Angeles. Alinsky remembered:

> Suddenly, in the midst of dinner, Mr. Sandburg turned to me and in
> a loud, stentorian voice said, "I understand, Alinsky, that you are a
> friend and strong supporter of John L. Lewis." I nodded and con-
> tinued eating. Then he burst loose: "John L. Lewis is and always has
> been a reptilian, treasonous son of a bitch." I stopped eating and
> stared at him (I was really surprised as all of this came like a bolt out
> of the blue). Sandburg continued: "And you, a person of known
> integrity, supporting that rat—that Benedict Arnold—wait until he
> plants his knife in your back."

Other dinner guests seated nearby chimed in, each taking a whack at Lewis
and his character defects. During the give-and-take, Alinsky recalled the
"sum and essence of my replies": "John L. Lewis may be a devil to the
poets, but he is an angel to the workers—possibly, Mr. Sandburg, their
avenging angel. You say John L. Lewis is ruthless—maybe he is—but he
has fought all of his life against the most ruthless and destructive forces
known to our alleged civilization. It has been, and it is today, a hard
fight—a grim one. The organized labor movement was not built, Mr.
Sandburg, through poems, champagne dinners, or witty columns. It was
built by a ruthless fight against ruthless evils."

Alinsky was especially captivated by Lewis's flair for rhetorically skewering political opponents. Lewis's attitude seemed to be that there was no fun or skill in merely waylaying an adversary; one had to use some imagination. Alinsky, Sidney Hyman remembers, would recount tales of Lewis's imaginative triumphs "as though Saul were savoring them and identifying himself with every nuance of the stories." On one occasion, Alinsky told Hyman that Lewis had used a word he had never heard before to ridicule an opponent, a word Alinsky obviously planned to add to his own arsenal. What was the word? Hyman asked. "Retromingian," Alinsky said with a mischievous grin, setting up Hyman's inevitable question. "You're going to call some guy a retromingian," Hyman said. "What in the hell is that?" And Alinsky replied: "It's a kind of dumb animal that urinates backwards."

Alinsky was also impressed with the great attention that Lewis gave to contests of interpersonal gamesmanship. He was fascinated by Lewis's account of his tactical skirmishes with Roosevelt—how Lewis would cleverly make a public announcement that suggested he had Roosevelt's support, thus leaving the President in the awkward position of having to deny something that he had never intended to support; or how Lewis would speak at length at White House meetings with Roosevelt so that the President could not control the meetings' agenda himself; or how Lewis would invariably try to pin Roosevelt down to a yes or no answer when others, out of politeness, would accept an evasive generalization. These were the kinds of small stratagems that many people might have found merely interesting or amusing. Saul Alinsky found them important as tools for manipulating and controlling events and people. Tactics and power—even at a seemingly mundane level—went hand in hand, and there were few better practitioners to watch and to learn from than John L. Lewis.

It was difficult to foresee immediately after the 1940 election and the CIO convention later in November that Lewis was headed into the wilderness of the labor movement. Much later, Alinsky would write that the rupture between Lewis and Roosevelt "broke the militant surge of . . . labor. . . . Historians will describe it as the great American Tragedy of the labor movement." Nonetheless, as 1940 was winding down, Lewis was still a labor leader to contend with as president of the United Mine Workers. As for Alinsky, he had now added his friendly relationship with Lewis to those with Marshall Field, Bishop Sheil, and Dutch Smith. This was a small but important network of supporters. There was a sense in Chicago among those who knew him that Saul Alinsky was on his way to bigger and better things.

10

"Miracle of Democracy"

The international scene had grown bleaker through the summer and fall of 1940. Nazi Germany's assault was relentless, and there was growing consternation in the United States over the fate of the remaining Western democracies—indeed, of the fate of democracy itself as a viable political idea. Against this backdrop of discouragement and despair, almost any sign of hope for the future came to be welcomed, even encouraged and magnified, by political leaders and by mainstream newspapers and magazines. That was true not only with any optimistic signs in the world arena but with any budding signs of hope in the United States.

Through the late summer and fall of 1940, Saul Alinsky and his work received a flurry of laudatory journalistic attention. A long, flowery editorial in the New York *Herald Tribune,* for example, under the heading "Democracy in the Jungle," recounted Alinsky's recent work in the Back of the Yards in Chicago and suggested that if seemingly intractable slum conditions and ethnic hostilities could be improved through a reinvigorated democratic process, then there was hope for the future. The *Herald Tribune* went on to say that if Alinsky and Bishop Sheil's methods in the Back of the Yards could be employed in other communities around the country, then "in these difficult times, it may well mean the salvation of our way of life."

The *Herald Tribune* editorial appeared just days before Alinsky and the directors of the Industrial Areas Foundation met in New York in late August for the first time. These annual IAF meetings in the 1940s and later were usually held in New York, which was convenient for the two most actively involved directors: Marshall Field, who had one of his homes in the city, and Bishop Sheil, who had a suite at the Waldorf-Astoria (and who enjoyed living the good life). The IAF board consisted of a diverse, seemingly unlikely collection of people. In addition to Field and Sheil, there were Kathryn Lewis; Hermon Dunlop Smith; G. Howland Shaw, an assistant secretary in the State Department; Britton Budd, president of a Chicago area utility, the Public Service Company of Northern Illinois; and another Chicago businessman, Stuyvesant Peabody, of the Peabody Coal Company family. One other person, Judge Theodore Rosen, a prominent jurist and civic leader in Philadelphia, who knew Alinsky through Helene Alinsky's family, was briefly identified as a founding member of the board but died soon after the IAF was started.

The composition of the board largely reflected Bishop Sheil's influence and connections. Not only had Sheil first introduced Alinsky to Marshall Field, but he was probably responsible for bringing in Budd, who was a supporter of Sheil's Catholic Youth Organization, and Howland Shaw, who as a lay Catholic was involved in child-welfare and anti-delinquency projects and who was familiar with the work of the Chicago Area Project. Even Peabody might have been a Sheil recruit, although it is possible that he might have been approached first by Kathryn Lewis or her father.

In addition to a feature story and editorial in the *Herald Tribune,* other press accounts also noted the diversity of Alinsky's board—symbols of labor and capital, New Deal Democrats and Republicans, Catholics, social reformers, hardheaded businessmen. All had been brought together not only because of Sheil and Alinsky, the press accounts suggested, but by a set of values, ideas, and images that was quintessentially American.

In fact, the dominant themes in the major newspaper and magazine treatment of Alinsky's work had to do with "democracy," "unity," and "the American way of life." During the last four months of 1940, stories ran in more than a score of newspapers throughout the country, based often on a long Associated Press feature that focused on these themes. Headlines and subheadlines conveyed a dramatic image of both Alinsky and the Back of the Yards Neighborhood Council: "They Called Him a 'Red,' But Young Sociologist Did the Job"; "Slum Dwellers Improve Lives—Chicago Organization Amazes with Rehabilitation of Hard-Fisted Street Urchins"; "Democracy at Work: Cleaning Up Chicago's 'Packingtown' Slums"; "How Czechs and Poles and Germans and Irish Learned to Work Together."

Much of the press treatment was shaped by Alinsky, either through interviews with him or through an eight-page statement of purpose that he wrote to define the objectives of the Industrial Areas Foundation. This was distributed in the form of a pamphlet with a full-page photograph on the

cover showing an urban industrial scene. "Fundamentally . . . our purpose
[is] to restore the democratic way of life to modern society," it said.
Alinsky's analysis of why there was a need for a restoration—what had
gone wrong, that is—was devoid of any suggestion that perhaps the capitalistic system was flawed. He had hinted at such a possibility in the theoretical paper he delivered to the American Prison Association in 1937, but
times had changed, and so had Alinsky's role.

From being a quasi-academic professional in the world of criminology
and delinquency prevention, Alinsky had moved to the public stage as the
leader of what might be a budding social movement. He was clearly interested in more than provocative theorizing, and yet ideas were still very
important to him. Although by background and temperament Alinsky had
not been cut out to be a scholar, intellectual respectability was important
to him. Intellectual prowess and achievements were the highest values in
the University of Chicago milieu, which included the Hyde Park neighborhood where Alinsky continued to live after his graduate days. Being intellectually competitive there was a sign that Alinsky belonged, that he had
moved up and away from the West Side and his parents' narrow, materialistic definition of success.

Ideas, and the language to express them, were important for another
reason. Alinsky understood that the way in which political acts are explained—the intellectual and rhetorical justification—is as important as
the action itself and, often, a prerequisite for action. Alinsky had seen, for
example, how John L. Lewis had legitimized the CIO during its most
radical, energetic, and menacing period by persuasive argumentation and
by identifying CIO demands with American ideals of fairness and justice.
Similarly, Alinsky's own argumentation sought to place the objectives of
his Industrial Areas Foundation firmly within a familiar-sounding American political tradition.

Alinsky wrote in his statement of purpose, after first acknowledging
that industrial advancement had brought material rewards and other opportunities, that "along with these advantages have arisen forces of so
menacing a character that today they threaten the very foundations upon
which rest the hopes of those committed to the democratic way of life.
These destructive forces are unemployment, deterioration, disease and
delinquency. From the havoc wrought from these forces issue distrust,
bigotry, disorganization and demoralization. Together they constitute significant indexes of a rapidly growing crisis of confusion in our democratic
process. They present a challenge which must be realistically met and
solved if the future of democracy is to be secured."

Much of what followed in Alinsky's statement of purpose was a description of the successes of the Back of the Yards Neighborhood Council. The overall message was that local residents, even in a notorious slum, could pool "all of their efforts and collective skill towards the solution of their common problems." If this sounded Pollyannaish, there were other arguments and insights that struck more authentic chords. There was an insistence that the *process* of problem-solving, the active participation of ordinary people, was at least as important as the solutions or decisions themselves.

> In our modern urban civilization, multitudes of our people have been condemned to urban anonymity—to living the kind of life where many of them neither know nor care for their own neighbors. This course of urban anonymity, of individual divorce from the general social life, is one of eroding destruction to the foundations of democracy. For although we profess that we are citizens of a democracy, and although we may vote once every four years, millions of our people feel deep down in their heart of hearts that there is no place for them—that they do not "count." They have no voice of their own, no organization (which is really their own instead of absentee) to represent them, no way in which they may lay their hand and their heart to the shaping of their own destinies.

Alinsky, in attempting to place his analysis on a larger, historical canvas, quoted Tocqueville's observation in *Democracy in America* that "no one will ever believe that a liberal, wise and energetic government can spring from the suffrages of a subservient people."

Alinsky argued that the newfound united, democratic action in the Back of the Yards symbolized something that was not merely important but *fundamentally* important. It was an argument for which there was a receptive, friendly audience in the press. A columnist in the Chicago *Daily Times* referred to Alinsky's efforts in the Back of the Yards as "the miracle of democracy." Other accounts implied that Alinsky and Sheil had discovered the magic powers of a newly stimulated democratic spirit. In *Time,* for instance, Sheil's friend Sidney James wrote:

> Fifteen months ago, with the bishop's blessing, friendly, chesty, Jewish Sociologist Saul Alinsky set up a Back of the Yards Neighborhood Council. Aim: to reconcile the potentially conflicting interests of business, labor, politics and religion in a crowded, depressed industrial area. Typical Council results to date: C.I.O. leaders helping the Chamber of Commerce in its membership drive; 1,200 hot meals free

each day for undernourished children; a new recreation centre five
blocks square; an infant-welfare station which has cut the infant death
rate from ten in every 100 to four out of 100.

The cheerleading for Alinsky's work that came from establishment
publications had fascinating implications. On the surface, one could see the
stabilizing potential of Alinsky's approach: within a Depression-racked
social order that seemed as if it might still fall apart, Alinsky was pulling
disparate groups together. And there was an impression that Alinsky's
brand of "democracy" was politically safe. It not only played to the myth
of the American melting pot but seemed to suggest that the disgruntled
lower classes could—indeed, should—lift themselves by their own bootstraps. Neither of these impressions, however, was exactly what Alinsky
had in mind.

In fact, Alinsky was attracted not to the melting-pot ideal but rather
to what years later would be called "cultural pluralism." Alinsky recognized that immigrants found great pride, comfort, and strength in their
ethnic heritage, and that there was much that was genuine and healthy
about this identification. He had said as much when he wrote to Howland Shaw from South St. Paul, where the South St. Paul Community
Council had staged a fund-raising festival one evening that featured a
celebration of the community's ethnic diversity. If ethnic pride represented one side of a coin, however, the other side was often represented
by rivalries and hatreds. But Alinsky genuinely believed that "once
people get to know each other as human beings rather than as impersonal symbols representing diverse philosophies and organizations, then a
new set of relationships composed of a genuine understanding and real
sympathy will arise." This kind of assertion simultaneously contains
much truth and much wishful thinking. Clearly, for Alinsky there was
enough truth in it so that he referred to it, with some exaggeration,
as "the cardinal principle" of his work. But this cardinal principle
also had significance for Alinsky personally, for him as an American
Jew.

One of his anecdotes, the kind of tale about ordinary behavior that he
loved to tell because he thought it revealed large truths and principles, had
to do with an anti-Semitic Irish cop who directed traffic at the corner of
Michigan Avenue and Monroe, down the street from Alinsky's office. They
used to exchange greetings when Alinsky passed by on the way to the
parking lot to get his car. One night, Alinsky left the office late and ran
into the cop as he was coming off duty. They stopped to have a glass of
beer and, from then on, would occasionally sit down and talk. On those

occasions, the cop "would expound his own philosophy of what ails the world," Alinsky recounted.

> He was an ardent follower of Father Coughlin. He felt that all of the ills and troubles of our modern world were due to international Jewry. He was positive that all Jews were insidious, dark destructive little devils—that is, all Jews with the exception of myself and Isaac Greenberg, who lived upstairs from him. He frequently plays pinochle with Isaac Greenberg. The Greenberg children play with his children. He knew Isaac's troubles, he shared Isaac's joys. Both he and Isaac were devoted followers of the Chicago White Sox. To him Isaac was a human being. He was a man who had to worry about his rent, meeting his time payments and his insurance installments. Isaac was no international, insidious devil—he was a White Sox fan, and he was just a guy trying to get along.

Alinsky knew, of course, that the end of bigotry was not merely a matter of lining up all of the world's bigots and introducing each to a real-life Isaac Greenberg. The tangle of history, fear, ignorance, and competition—the infectious strains of bigotry—was much too complex for any simple solution. Even in the Back of the Yards, where people had begun to get to know one another "as real people," the progress in human relations came mainly from another direction, Alinsky knew. He touched on this point when he wrote in his statement of purpose: "It should be emphasized that this community solidarity does not rest completely upon any special benevolence on the part of the members of the [Back of the Yards] Council and the organizations for which they speak, but upon the clear recognition that to a large extent they either stand or fall together." A tenuous coalition had been fashioned in the Back of the Yards based on shared self-interests. A community where mutual respect, goodwill, and trust among individuals flourished across ethnic boundaries was, with some exceptions, still mainly a hope in the Back of the Yards.

If an erroneous impression had evolved in the establishment press that tied Alinsky's work to the melting-pot ideal, an even greater inaccuracy was the suggestion that Alinsky's work reaffirmed the legitimacy of the old bootstrap shibboleth. Alinsky was explicit about this when he wrote:

> An understanding of the fashion in which a local community functions within the larger social organism demands a marked departure from the conventional procedures characteristic of that kind of communal organization which proposes that the community elevate itself

by means of its own bootstraps. It means that while the community as a whole is taken as a specific starting point for a program of social construction, the organizational procedures must direct their attention toward those larger socio-economic issues which converge upon that scene to create the plight of the area.

From this followed a left liberal, New Deal agenda. To help alleviate the economic ills of its families, a community organization would support the labor movement, as the Council had in the Back of the Yards. There would be active support for a national housing program and a national health program and, in the process, "the development of a common curiosity regarding the reasons pro and con of national programs."

This last point symbolized one of Alinsky's central concerns in 1940, the idea of citizenship. In its essence, citizenship meant participation to Alinsky; it meant being active rather than passive. It also meant that one questioned authority, took the initiative to address community problems, and developed an understanding of how events and forces in the larger world affected one's own life and community.

In the urban industrial immigrant communities in which Alinsky worked during the 1930s, as well as in the Back of the Yards, the rights and possibilities of citizenship were not familiar concepts and, moreover, in many ways contradicted the Old World culture. Thus, Alinsky paid much attention to "teaching" the possibilities of citizenship. Sidney Hyman, a young aide to Chicago alderman Paul Douglas at the time, remembers Alinsky's sometimes subtle teaching methods and how he would create a dramatic learning experience out of an ordinary event. On one occasion, Alinsky wanted to arouse the interest of the people in the Back of the Yards in the rehabilitation of their housing, Hyman remembers. One day, there was an important softball game scheduled in the neighborhood that would determine a championship. It was going to be a big game, and there had already been a lot of betting by players on both sides. Hyman recalls: "Then the star pitcher for the favored team steps out of his house, steps on a step which is rotten, because the whole place is falling down, and either breaks his wrist or throws his arm out of joint. Suddenly, he can't pitch and his team loses because there's no substitute. Saul seizes on that episode when he senses the disappointment, the bitter disappointment. They've all lost their money, they've lost the championship, and they've lost their pride. And he said, 'Well, it need not have happened.' And they said, 'What do you mean, it need not have happened?' And Saul said, 'That step there could have been fixed. There are ways to get some dough. There are these federal programs for housing.' Saul got them interested, and I remember a couple letters were sent off to Washington and the Housing Authority replied: 'Yes, there is this program, this is the way you go about it.' And the guys who got the letters strutted around the community," Hyman recalls, because "they had gotten a personal, typewritten letter from Washington." Hyman also remembers a follow-up trip to the Chicago City Council when some of the neighborhood people started asking angrily why they hadn't known about the housing program before. Hyman says: "This is how Saul promoted the whole concept of awareness, starting with a softball game, then letting them know what is available, and then: 'You're helping yourself. I'm not telling you; you're telling you. You've made the discovery.' And something happens there. That was some of Saul's real genius, his sense of timing and understanding how others would perceive something. Saul knew that if I grab you by the shoulders and say do this, do that and the other, you're going to resent it. If you make the discovery yourself, you're going to strut because *you* made it."

Alinsky had tried to bring a new language to the Back of the Yards and, consequently, a new set of attitudes as well. The language had the vocabulary of citizenship and democracy: debate and discussion; agendas and bylaws; elected representatives and collective action. These were the means, Alinsky was saying in effect, by which the masses of people in the forlorn industrial areas of America could move into the mainstream of American life. In a sense, it was that simple: Alinsky was advocating a way for outsiders to get inside. "The Industrial Areas Foundation aims to break down the feeling on the part of our people that they are social automatons with no stake in the future, rather than human beings in possession of all the responsibility, strength, and human dignity which constitute the heritage of free citizens in a democracy," he wrote. Alinsky's lofty aspirations and sense of mission were contagious. "If the final results be as successful as its beginnings in the Back of the Yards," the *Herald Tribune* proclaimed enthusiastically, "if it awakens in other communities that sense of joint responsibility for the common welfare that is stirring in Packingtown, the historian of the future may well look back on the formation of the [Industrial Areas] Foundation as a highly significant step in the evolution of American democracy. . . . That the idea will spread seems inevitable."

ALINSKY SET OUT to spread the idea himself by organizing two new community organizations between the late summer of 1940 and the winter of 1941.

The communities that he picked, the Armourdale section in Kansas City, Kansas, and South St. Paul, Minnesota, were similar in many ways to the Back of the Yards. First and foremost, both were stockyards and packinghouse communities; a sizable part of both communities worked in the packinghouses, where there was a strong CIO presence. South St. Paul in particular had a large percentage of residents born in Eastern Europe. Both communities had many of the same social problems that existed in the Back of the Yards—run-down housing, a general appearance of decay and disrepair, delinquency, and high unemployment.

Yet although the similarities to the Back of the Yards were strong, there were also important differences and new challenges facing Alinsky. After all, neither South St. Paul nor Kansas City was familiar turf to Alinsky as Chicago had been. Bishop Sheil, who was crucial to Alinsky's early success in the Back of the Yards, was a national figure, but his power and influence were far greater in Chicago's parishes than elsewhere. Moreover, South St. Paul was somewhat less Catholic than the Back of the Yards, and Kansas City was less Catholic still. Joe Meegan, the park director, had turned out to be the near-perfect contact in the Back of the Yards, and he and Alinsky became near-perfect complements to each other. Without a Meegan, the Back of the Yards Neighborhood Council might not have gotten off the ground so fast or flown so high. It remained to be seen if Alinsky could spot or train other Joe Meegans. Finally, the Back of the Yards was only a short drive from Alinsky's Hyde Park apartment; thus the BYNC's technical consultant—Alinsky's official title on BYNC stationery—did not have far to travel to deal with a political problem or mediate a personality clash or to keep an eye on Meegan. It would not be possible for Alinsky to use the force of his personality as often or as effectively from long range.

When Alinsky first started to visit Kansas City and South St. Paul, he would typically spend a few days at a time, sometimes as much as a week, in each city. On one trip to Armourdale, Alinsky said he saw "seventy to eighty people" in just two days. Initially, he had gotten the names of CIO contacts through his friends in the Packinghouse Workers Union in Chicago. Additional contacts—priests, ministers, and others active in the two communities—came from other Chicago friends. "If you don't think seventy or eighty people in two days is a lot of people, try it sometime," Alinsky wrote in his journal. "Some were convinced in fifteen minutes. Some took an hour and a half." The general message that Alinsky delivered at these early meetings was that the success of the Back of the Yards could be repeated in Armourdale. But he also zeroed in on people's special interests.

When I talked to the Mexicans, the main importance [was the] abolition of the discriminatory practices and unfair prejudices which the
Mexicans had to endure. To the Catholic Church, [a community
council] was presented as an organization which fundamentally concerned the strengthening of the Catholic Church; to the Protestant
Church, the same; to ambitious individuals, a medium for that satisfaction of their own desires for personal aggrandizement; to the
Negroes, an organization dedicated to the abolition of Jim Crow
practices; to the union man, an organization that would develop the
rights of organized labor.

Later, when Alinsky's surrogates had trouble recruiting people for the
Armourdale Neighborhood Council, Alinsky wrote: "They had to learn
two simple things: First, that if they did not wholeheartedly believe in it,
their own waverings and uncertainty would reflect themselves in their
arguments; and, second, that their arguments must be adapted to the
particular people they were talking with."

But Alinsky himself, even in his earliest visits to Armourdale, appealed to something more than narrow self-interest. He also tried to make
people feel as though they were going to be part of a historic, patriotic
mission. "The problems arising in [our industrial] civilization are centered
in the areas populated most densely by the workers," Alinsky told one of
the first group meetings that he spoke to in Armourdale at the Skyline
Community Center. "This is the heart of democracy. The [Industrial
Areas] Foundation believes that unless these antisocial problems are solved
in these localities, a condition will arise inimical to the survival of democracy as a whole." Alinsky's elevation of Armourdale to a first-rank position
in the "fight to save democracy" was hardly the kind of description that
was familiar to longtime residents. "People who lived elsewhere in Kansas
City thought that if you lived in Armourdale, you didn't amount to much,"
says Dollie Martinson, who had grown up there. "Armourdale was in the
bottoms, the river bottoms. They'd say, 'You're just an Armourdale rat;
you're just a flood rat.' "

In fact, ever since the great flood of 1903, there had been talk about
what it would take to restore Armourdale to its "pre-flood glory," a phrase
that probably said more about the current state of semi-squalor than about
romantic memories. If Alinsky's coming did not immediately conjure a
restoration of nineteenth-century grace, it did inspire a wave of interest and
enthusiasm which, in turn, inspired quite a bit of press coverage by the
Kansas City newspapers. Suddenly, in the space of about three months,
there were observable signs of new citizen activity in Armourdale. Com-

mittees were formed along the lines of those of the BYNC: committees on housing, unemployment, recreation, health, and public improvements.

The Armourdale Neighborhood Council was housed temporarily in the Skyline Community Center, which was part of the Skyline Chapel. And the temporary head of the Council was Skyline's Reverend Elmer D. Russell. Russell was one of Alinsky's first mistakes. Perhaps Alinsky had been attracted to him because the Skyline Community Center reminded him of Joe Meegan's Davis Square Park in the Back of the Yards. A community center meant free office space, meeting rooms, a place that people knew and where many of them congregated. But whatever the physical or political advantages in meeting initially at Skyline, they were far outweighed by Alinsky's growing dislike of Russell. He wrote to one of his IAF board members, Howland Shaw:

> You can trust me to pick up in my collection of executive secretaries a lunatic, among others. I thought I had gotten the worse [sic] kind of person to deal with in this Elmer "Gantry" Russell—a slimy, Seventh-Day Adventist, self-ordained minister, who passionately preached morals and just as passionately seduced the maids of his congregation. A man with whom after shaking hands, you instinctively wiped your hand on your trouser leg—a double-crossing, loathsome specie of humanity. As time goes on and as I gain some philosophic insight, I justify him as a necessary product for contrast between good and evil.

The search for good leadership, for people who in addition to other qualities understood tactics and human nature, was a constant concern of Alinsky's and, in the early days in both Armourdale and South St. Paul, an ongoing problem. To Shaw, Alinsky wrote:

> Another problem which has arisen in all of the councils, but not to the extreme degree that is characteristic of Kansas City, is the tactics involved in organization. On one side of the Kansas City situation are two young leaders (a young man and woman named Tom Carroll and Catherine Flynn) who are constantly embittered and discouraged because their conception of a real community organization is one which is a constant campaign about issues—one in which the residents are kept at a fevered pitch and one in which they can daily or weekly see for themselves definite, visible and concrete achievements. On the other extreme is to be found our field representative, Clifford Stover, who thinks in terms of moving at a very slow pace and having few community campaigns.

Alinsky told Shaw that the two young leaders were being unrealistic, that "human beings can maintain a certain emotional pitch for just so long. After that level of emotional fervor is carried beyond a certain point, they are sucked dry of their feeling and will just disintegrate into an 'apathy'— an apathy induced by a maintenance of this high level of emotional frenzy." On the other hand, Alinsky was not satisfied with his phlegmatic field representative either. Stover, who was forty-six when Alinsky hired him in the spring of 1941, had grown up in Armourdale, had been working at the local Griffin Wheel Company as a machinist, and had been involved in the labor movement—when Alinsky hired him, he was state secretary of the Industrial Union Council. But, though Stover had some of the right credentials, he lacked the right personality or an appreciation of the rhythm and nuance of organization.

It was well into 1941 before Alinsky discovered Lloyd Murphy, a robust, warm, and friendly man, about thirty years old, who was a fore-man at Columbia Steel Tank in Armourdale. Murphy, with reddish-blond hair and fair skin, was of average height but weighed well over two hundred pounds. He had a zest for both food and work. Before he began to emerge as a leader of the Council, he had already been active in the Council's cleanup program. Dollie Martinson, a friend of Murphy's, remembers the door-to-door cleanup program: "We got two horses and two carts. We charged twenty-five cents a week to pick up the trash. It was very successful. You'd be surprised how much it improved the area in a short time."

While Murphy and Dollie and Robert Martinson were working on the sanitation committee in the earliest days of the Council, there was also an active employment committee, which, like a similar committee in the Back of the Yards, set up a job-placement service. The public im-provements committee was also especially active. Two thousand people from Armourdale signed petitions, which the Council's executive com-mittee took to the City Commission, demanding that traffic signals be installed at Seventh and Osage. On another issue, a large delegation of Council members descended upon the office of the commission in charge of street cleaning, demanding to know why earlier requests by the Coun-cil for improved service in the Armourdale district had been ignored. Nobody in Armourdale could remember when the community had acted so aggressively.

It is not entirely clear when the rumor started that Alinsky was a communist. Perhaps it began after demands were made on city officials by the Council. Perhaps the meat-packers started to get anxious about the Council, suspicious that it was a front for the Packinghouse Workers Organizing Committee. Perhaps it was a combination of Alinsky's own identification with the CIO, his aggressiveness, and his being a Russian Jew that triggered a Kansas City stereotype of a communist. Whatever the cause, the effect of the rumor, as the Martinsons recall it, was to "[turn] a lot of people off," and attendance at some of the Council meetings seemed to go down.

Who initiated the rumor? That, too, is unclear. However, on October 21, 1940, the special agent in charge of the FBI office in Chicago passed along some information to his counterpart in Kansas City, Missouri. The "information" had originally been sent to the FBI in Chicago by the Assistant Chief of Staff of the U.S. Army's VI Corps area headquarters in Chicago. The Army report stated that "Saul Alinsky appeared before the Skyline Community Center in Kansas City, Kansas. . . . The operators of the center are known to be strictly loyal. Alinsky, a communist, addressed a meeting at this center at which time he urged that the center be reorganized along the lines of a similar Community Center in Chicago, which is reported to be communistically controlled."

The effect of the rumor on Alinsky in Armourdale was only temporary, more troublesome than devastating. On the other hand, the question of his being a communist or not was something he could not ignore, either in Armourdale or in South St. Paul, where he was also a target of Red-baiting.

In South St. Paul, a small community dominated by Swift, Armour, and other meat-packers, Alinsky thought that the packers considered him a subversive. In fact, the Minnesota Bureau of Criminal Apprehension asked the FBI to check reports that Alinsky "may be interested in organizing some type of Communistic or subversive group in the packing area of South St. Paul." Finally, after several months had passed, the FBI concluded, in January 1941, that Alinsky was not a communist, or, in the bureaucratic language of J. Edgar Hoover's agency, that "the investigation . . . did not disclose that he had ever made any remarks or exhibited any acts against the United States Government, or in favor of any foreign government." A follow-up report a month later indicated that another FBI source in Chicago had praised Alinsky's work in the Back of the Yards and thought that Alinsky was a "great benefit to the community" and definitely not a communist. The FBI also noted that "Alinsky said that he would furnish any document of proof showing that he wasn't a communist."

Alinsky reacted to the "communist question" in several ways. One was simply to deny it. Another was to point to the board of directors of the IAF—Marshall Field, Bishop Sheil, G. Howland Shaw, and Dutch Smith—and claim innocence by association. In St. Paul, for example, Alinsky was introduced to Mrs. Peavey F. Hefflefinger, a wealthy Republican matron, and at Alinsky's suggestion she called Dutch Smith in Chicago. "She had a long talk [with him]," Alinsky said, "and [then] felt completely assured about both the character and the objectives of the Industrial Areas Foundation." Alinsky also enjoyed turning the charge of being a communist into a self-serving claim that he was considered dangerous only by people who, for selfish ends, had reason to fear him. In one version of this story, Alinsky was told by an acquaintance in St. Paul that the general superintendent at the Swift plant had said that Alinsky was a dyed-in-the-wool Red. Looking at Alinsky, the acquaintance supposedly said, "You know, from the expression on your face, I could almost swear that you are pleased by what I just said about Mr. Cushman." To which Alinsky said he replied:

> Well, it so happens that you're right. During the past few months I have been getting quite worried because I felt I was getting so respectable. . . . I have been receiving a good many compliments and I was becoming so socially acceptable, even in Who's Who in Chicago, that I really began to have grave doubts as to whether or not I was on the right track. So what you've said has been very reassuring to me, because as long as people like Cushman and his breed of rats define me as dangerous, and dyed-in-the-wool Red, revolutionary, or what have you—so long do I know . . . that I am still on the right track.

Even after the FBI reports cleared Alinsky of the "communist" charge, Alinsky wrote that the packers in South St. Paul were still out to get him and the emerging South St. Paul Community Council. Alinsky wrote in his journal that Fallon Kelly, one of the co-executive secretaries of the Council, came to Chicago on Friday and described developments of that week: "We are having a very tough time with the packers. As you know, South St. Paul is a company town. . . . Now the packers don't like our council and of course it's obvious why they don't. This is the first organization . . . over which they have no control. Besides that, our organization has the CIO in it and they say that the CIO is poison, it's revolutionary, it's communistic and that therefore we are communists by going along."

Fallon Kelly, more than forty years later, agreed with the substance of Alinsky's quotation of him, while not recalling "saying it in those kind of words." But Kelly did remember that some people were being warned not to join the Council. And Alinsky wrote in the spring of 1941 that Kelly said: "Of course, what I tell you must never be repeated. But I have a friend at the bank and he is pretty thick with the packers and he has told me if I wanted to get along I'd better get out of this Community Council. . . .

Now I understand that the packers are going to get their people to stop patronizing Doc Carroll who, incidentally, they say is a pinko anyways and always has been and they are going to drive Carroll out of business. . . . Then take Charlie Burnley. He has been working with the South St. Paul *Reporter* for twenty years and the South St. Paul *Reporter* has been told that if they want advertising and want to stay in business they'd better fire Burnley."

This was the kind of conflict that Alinsky thrived on, for he loved a chance to retaliate, to kick the Big Boys in a tender spot. And if he didn't have an opportunity to land a telling blow, he could be temporarily satisfied by simply outmaneuvering the Big Boys, or by revealing their stupidity and hypocrisy. "When the charges of communism exploded in the faces of the packers," Alinsky wrote during his South St. Paul campaign, "and when they recognized that all of their charges could be disproved, they shifted their ground and began to center their attacks on my personality. From time to time they attempted to prove that I was a liar and a knave." Alinsky recalled that during his first few trips to South St. Paul he mentioned that Swift in Chicago "was a participating agency in the Back of the Yards Neighborhood Council." It may have been true that Swift had made a token contribution to the BYNC, but Swift did not have a significant presence within the Council. Alinsky had no doubt stretched a point to illustrate how unified the Back of the Yards neighborhood had become through the work of the Council. In South St. Paul, a Swift official checked with Swift's Chicago office and was apparently told that what Alinsky had said about Swift was a lie, that Swift in Chicago had nothing whatsoever to do with the BYNC. But Alinsky recalled at the time:

> Unfortunately the Chicago headquarters of Swift and Co. forgot that they had sent a letter to the BYNC endorsing the work and stating that it was a privilege to be a participant in the work of the Council. I had a couple of photostatic copies made of this letter and then, after giving out the impression in South St. Paul that I was fearful of the packers . . . , I lured this attack to new heights. When it reached its crest, I humbly produced the photostatic copy of those letters and there was something of a panic.

These small skirmishes with the packers were not the only satisfying events for Alinsky in South St. Paul. He felt a great sense of accomplishment when the various ethnic groups had been pulled together to make the Council's first community fair a success. To Howland Shaw, he wrote:

My wire from St. Paul was dispatched in one of those bursts of enthusiasm, after seeing how the immigrant groups of this community had not only banded together in an American organization but taken the leadership in the American way of life. Incidentally, the native-born Americans were the followers. Immigrant leaders even conducted the final services on Saturday night, when gold-braided American flags (to be hung in the windows) were presented to mothers of all draftees. The presentations were made by a committee consisting of five immigrants—a Serbian, a Russian, a Rumanian, a Yugoslav and a German. . . . All of the people were dressed in their native costumes and it truly was the most colorful Fair of all three communities, despite the fact that it was the smallest in view of the small population of South St. Paul.

Alinsky also loved to orchestrate and manipulate the new relationships that were being created within the Council. "An observer at a Board of Director's meeting . . . would be somewhat astonished to watch the behavior of the technical consultant," Alinsky wrote, referring to himself. "He would see a group of persons seated around a table and the consultant shuttling around from one person to another, leaning over one and then another, and whispering individually to each board member." What he was doing, Alinsky explained, was more than merely interpreting to each representative the significance to that person's organization of the issue being considered. More important, Alinsky thought, was that each person be made to feel that he had a special role to play. Alinsky would whisper advice to one person, and then whisper the same advice to somebody else, believing that his pose of confidentiality not only made the information seem important but made the person feel important, too.

Much of Alinsky's time was absorbed by a web of organizational rivalries, interpersonal disputes, and jealousies, in which he often tried to be the mediator. At the first community fair in South St. Paul, Alinsky set up a table and chair under a tree off to one side of the fairgrounds.

This tree is now known as the "gripe" tree [Alinsky noted in his journal]. For three nights I had a chair and desk under that tree and spent hours listening to individual complaints or "gripes" from at least thirty or forty individuals. . . . Aldermen were complaining about the aggressiveness and personal insults which they had received from officers of the Community Council. Community Council officers complained about the Veterans of Foreign Wars. Vets complained about the Legionnaires. . . . All the problems were [temporarily] ironed out with the exception of one personality problem.

The problem involved the co-executive secretaries of the South St. Paul Council, Fallon Kelly and Doc Carroll. Kelly, a young Republican attorney, was a junior member of the former law firm of Minnesota governor Harold Stassen. Carroll was older, about fifty, a dentist and an active Democrat. Alinsky had decided to experiment with co-executive secretaries because he was not happy with the way Meegan was often able to dominate the organization in the Back of the Yards. But the division of authority in South St. Paul had not worked very well either. In a letter to a friend, Alinsky wrote: "Both secretaries are very jealous about their own prerogatives and their personal relationships with me. . . . It may surprise you to know that I have never once sent a letter even simply announcing that I plan to arrive in St. Paul on such and such a day to one of them without writing to the other one at the same time, each letter being individually composed and never daring to send a carbon to one."

Alinsky eventually feared he had miscalculated in pushing Carroll as one of the executive secretaries. "I had been warned about Carroll in the very beginning by his own priest who told me that he was so unstable that the parish did not care to place any responsibilities into his hands," Alinsky wrote in his journal. But Alinsky had seen aspects of Carroll that he liked; the dentist was outspoken and pugnacious, and these were qualities that Alinsky knew were important in the early, organizational phases. In addition, he desperately wanted to recruit a Democrat as a balance to the Republican. "A Democrat up in that neck of the woods is almost as rare as a Jew in the Gestapo," Alinsky said, a comparison that was not as much of an exaggeration in 1941 as it may have sounded. South St. Paul's most prominent, influential politicians were Republicans, people like Stassen and Harold Levander, who would become a Minnesota governor, too. Alinsky thought that having a Democrat as one of the Council's leaders would "serve as a check on the strong Republican partisanship that might develop into an attempt to capture the Council."

Alinsky felt he could handle Carroll, in spite of the warnings he was given. Often, however, Carroll refused to listen to Alinsky, and he would react explosively to instructions. When he became ill during the fall of 1941, these leadership and personality problems were temporarily diminished.

Indeed, the first year had been a success in many ways. The first Community Congress, at which bylaws were adopted and permanent officers elected, had drawn two hundred delegates to the school auditorium. Charlie Burnley, who was active in the formation of the Council and also a reporter for the South St. Paul *Daily Reporter,* wrote a friendly front-page story about the Congress having "started South St. Paul marching toward its goal to make democracy work for the benefit of the whole community." The first Congress had launched a wide range of activities, similar to the priorities in Armourdale: a health committee promoted immunization and a new, free blood donors club; recreation programs were planned to curb delinquency. Representatives of the new Council lobbied in the state legislature for enabling legislation to permit the state to receive $15 million in federal funds for low-income housing. The legislation was defeated by three votes, but the Council had approved a resolution to continue to push for new low-income-housing programs.

All in all, Saul Alinsky had reason to feel a growing sense of confidence. More than two years earlier, in Chicago, the Back of the Yards Neighborhood Council had evolved, unplanned, out of a seemingly unique interplay of events and people: labor unrest that was heading swiftly toward a possible violent climax; serious unemployment and poverty; the charismatic presence of Bishop Sheil; a young, energetic park director. By now Alinsky had organized effectively in two other cities. True, Armourdale and South St. Paul were stockyards and packinghouse communities like the Back of the Yards. But they were different in enough respects—not the least of which was the absence of a revered figure like Benny Sheil—so that they had posed a legitimate test as to whether Alinsky's experiment in the Back of the Yards was workable elsewhere.

The early returns were certainly encouraging. Everything was looking up for Alinsky—he was excited about the work and was encouraged further by the recognition he received. Then, on the first Sunday in December, everything changed. The changes for Alinsky were not immediate, and never so dramatic or profound as they were for many Americans who went off to war. But his life and work were affected in many ways as the months gave way to years and the war dragged on longer than most people, including Alinsky, had expected.

11

War Years

Saul Alinsky was nearly thirty-three years old and waiting to receive his Selective Service classification when the Japanese bombed Pearl Harbor. But his age and physical condition made it unlikely that he could ever serve in a combat role—he wore thick glasses because of his nearsightedness and, although he was nearly six feet and solidly built, he walked with a slight limp because his right leg was slightly shorter than the left owing to the hip injury he had suffered as a child. Anyone who saw him approaching from a distance could easily spot his rolling gait. On October 4, Bishop Sheil had written a letter to Alinsky's local draft board—the kind of letter that Alinsky might have asked him to write, or even drafted for him, and that the Bishop would have sent without hesitation. Alinsky was more important to the well-being of the country as executive director of the Industrial Areas Foundation than he would be in the armed forces, Sheil wrote:

> The immediate future demands that the American people have a deep and abiding faith in the American way of life. It is imperative that our people have this faith in democracy in order that America be sustained through the coming grave conflicts, regardless of whether they be of a military, economic, or political nature. . . . [The] outstanding service to the defense program which Mr. Alinsky is rendering in his present occupation far transcends any contribution that he could make in the armed forces.

For his part, Alinsky saw himself very much as a participant in the struggle between good and evil that was being waged on the battlefield in

Europe. Troubled by the pockets of support for Hitler's views on religion and race that he had seen en route to his organizing projects in Kansas City and St. Paul, he warned friends that they were underestimating the size of the American audience sympathetic to Hitler. "Every time I return to Chicago, I am impressed by the complete placidity and cheerful ignorance of the people here with regards to the violent hatreds which are surging through the rural and smaller urban communities," he wrote to a friend in September 1941. "In many places, the situation is so bad that it is impossible to tell people what is happening. They neither have the desire to hear or believe. In certain Wisconsin communities, all that is lacking is the open placing of the swastika on the store fronts. These people are not isolationists. These people are not against involvement in the war. They are definitely pro-Hitler." A hideous, living beast of anti-Semitism was taking shape, he wrote, and "I cannot help but feel almost grief-stricken at the prospects facing my Jewish friends, as well as my own family." In a characteristic peroration of melodrama and bravado, he added: "I do have the personal consolation of realizing that I have so many open enemies amongst the various anti-Semitic groups and have been defined by them as a person to be eliminated as soon as possible, that if they ever do get into power I, at least, won't have to worry about concentration camps."

Alinsky was not drafted into the armed forces, but he did work on projects for the War Manpower Commission. The details of what he did are sketchy. Apparently, he was involved in efforts to maintain worker morale and harmony in key industries, such as in defense plants. Alinsky did some of this work with Hank Johnson, the black union leader, who was his good friend.

By all accounts, Hank Johnson was an extraordinary man. He was born around the turn of the century in Sibio, Texas, a delta town in the Brazos Bottom between the Colorado and Brazos rivers. Johnson's father was active in labor unions and, in part because of that, the Johnson family had several close calls with white lynch mobs. But Southern racism was sometimes modified by social and economic class loyalties. When Johnson was about ten years old, a white neighbor, who belonged to the radical International Workers of the World, as did Johnson's father, warned the family that a lynch mob was coming. The Johnsons escaped, but the warning cost the white neighbor his life. Years later, Hank Johnson not only followed in his father's footsteps in labor-union activities but brought with him a unique understanding of the politics of race as they were played out in union-management struggles.

Hank Johnson and Saul Alinsky had become friends after Johnson was brought in as the assistant national director of the Packinghouse Workers Organizing Committee in 1937. He had already been in Chicago with the CIO the previous year, organizing steelworkers. But the PWOC urgently needed someone like Johnson. The meat-packing industry in Chicago had a history of uneasy race relations that sometimes erupted into ugly, violent episodes. Many southern blacks who had migrated to Chicago during World War I and found jobs at Armour, Swift, and the other large packinghouses were recruited by management, in part to dim union organizing prospects by swelling the war-depleted labor force. When white workers had returned from the war, racial tensions mounted as competition over jobs increased. A riot in Chicago in 1919, which was sparked by a racial incident on a South Side beach, was quickly fueled by other racial antagonisms and hatreds, not the least of which could be traced to relations between black and white workers in the meat-packing plants.

As far back as the 1870s, packinghouse management in Chicago had been adept at defeating unionizing campaigns by pitting one nationality group against another. The divisions between white and black workers were there to be exploited again in the late 1930s. If the PWOC was to be successful this time, there would have to be exceptional leadership.

Hank Johnson was an exceptional leader. As a PWOC organizer, he gained the strong allegiance of black workers, who, because of their numbers and the strategically located jobs they held, were critically important to the organizing campaign. At the big Armour plant, for instance, blacks made up 25 percent or more of the work force. They were heavily represented on the killing floors, and if the killing floors were organized, the union had leverage; it could, if necessary, pull the men out and slow down or even shut down the rest of the slaughtering process.

Johnson also won the respect of many white workers and had a following among them. Partly by learning from his father's biracial union experiences, he knew how to communicate in both black and white worlds. He was also an orator of enormous power and effectiveness. Some thought that he was at least as good as or even better than Herb March, probably the most important PWOC leader in Chicago. The comparison was a compliment to both.

There was much to admire and like about Hank Johnson, who, in addition to his professional talents, was a friendly, warm man with a good mind. Alinsky's friendship with Johnson grew during 1939, when Alinsky was launching the Back of the Yards Neighborhood Council. A prominent passage in the Council's statement of purpose called for uniting all residents of the community "regardless of race, color or creed." No blacks lived in the Back of the Yards, of course, because the neighborhood was, except for a small number of Mexican families, an enclave for Eastern European immigrants and their children. Blacks who worked in the meat-packing plants, at least many of them, lived in a ghetto about a mile east of the stockyards; Wentworth Avenue was the racial dividing line. The Council's call for unity regardless of racial differences was not meant to disturb the racial housing patterns. In those prewar years, it was an uncontested given that blacks simply did not live in the Back of the Yards. Indeed, restrictive covenants in Chicago, as in other cities, kept blacks from buying houses in any white neighborhood. What, then, was the meaning of "regardless of race, color or creed"? Alinsky's intent was to reduce interpersonal and intergroup hostilities, especially the kind that undermined efforts of PWOC organizers to create solidarity among workers. Both the union and the Council were alert to the racial problem, and even when a racial incident seemed minor, they attempted to address it. Herb March remembers, for instance, that "one of our Polish guys was married at St. Rose's and we had some black guys who went there for the wedding, and they were made to feel not welcome. I remember that this incident came up at a union meeting, that because an active union member, a black, had gone to the wedding and was insulted. I don't know whether it was by ushers or priests. We sent a committee to see the people in the parish to discuss it with them." Similarly, when there was a rumor that a black had been given a hard time while riding a bus through the Back of the Yards, the Council dispatched a delegation of young priests to ride the buses to make sure that there were no further incidents. The Council also made certain that this effort on behalf of equality was well publicized.

Johnson and the other union leaders, and Alinsky and the Council, helped to build solidarity among black and white workers. If solidarity on bread-and-butter issues such as wages and job security did not necessarily lead to interracial friendships, nonetheless a shared understanding by blacks and whites that they needed each other did produce a degree of civility, especially in the Back of the Yards. Black packinghouse workers, for example, could go to an evening union meeting at Forty-seventh and Marshfield, in the heart of the Back of the Yards, with a reasonable degree of confidence that they would not be harassed or harmed. Such safe after-dark passage in the stockyards neighborhood could not earlier have been taken for granted.

Alinsky's relations with Hank Johnson became closer when both men worked on John L. Lewis's behalf when Lewis broke with Roosevelt and came out for Wendell Willkie in the fall of 1940. No other ranking PWOC leader followed Lewis's lead, but Johnson was close to the Lewis forces,

and especially to Kathryn. After the 1940 election, Johnson stayed with
Lewis, working out of the United Mine Workers' District 50 in Chicago,
the UMW catchall office for organizing an array of workers in addition to
coal miners.

There is no written account of Alinsky and Johnson's travels to boost
worker morale and harmony during the early war years, only verbal frag-
ments that Alinsky related years later to his family. He evidently relished
these experiences; he told of the racial discrimination that they encountered in restaurants and hotels, and of Johnson's ability to mesmerize an
audience with a stump speech on a plant floor—a skill that Alinsky would
have both admired and envied. Alinsky himself had a persuasive presence
in small, informal groups, an aggressive rhetorical style, and a deep, no-
nonsense voice reminiscent of the late movie actor Lee Marvin. But he was
not an orator like Johnson or Herb March, who could bring a crowd to
their feet at a climactic moment.

Despite his power as a speaker and his energy and drive, Hank Johnson was a very gentle man. He abhorred violence; perhaps he was even
afraid of it. Among some packinghouse workers there had been unkind talk
about his fearfulness, in the aftermath of the Memorial Day Massacre in
1937, when Chicago police shot and killed twelve workers who had gathered along with more than a thousand others for a rally at the Republic
Steel plant. Hank Johnson had not gone to the rally and, especially in light
of the deaths and injuries among his fellow unionists, had been conspicuous
by his absence.

Early in 1944, Johnson was still working out of the UMW's District
50 office, where he had an associate, Arthur Shelton, whom Herb March
remembers as "a little bit of a nutty guy, very much a zealot and a very
rough character. And he had implicit faith in Johnson." In fact, Johnson
had brought Shelton with him when he moved from the steelworkers to
the packinghouse workers, and then again when he left packing and went
with Lewis in 1940. One day, after Shelton had been handling protracted
negotiations at a utility company in northern Indiana, Johnson came to
town, took over the negotiations, and quickly settled one issue after another. It seemed to Shelton that Johnson must have had some private,
prearranged understanding with management, and he went into a rage.
Feeling betrayed and humiliated, he filed a complaint against Johnson
within the UMW. At a hearing in a downtown Chicago office building,
Shelton took the witness stand. After some testimony, the hearing exam-
iner asked Shelton if he had anything else to say. "I just want to make one
other point," Shelton said. Then, according to Ed Heckelbeck, a union
organizer who was there, Shelton "just reached down. He had a briefcase

on the floor." He pulled a gun from the briefcase. Heckelbeck and another organizer in the room, Frank Alsop, broke for the door. Shelton fired and wounded both of them. He then turned, walked toward Johnson, and, at point-blank range, shot and killed him.

Johnson's death stunned Saul Alinsky. And Herb March remembers that "Alinsky chided me" for not showing proper respect for Johnson by going to the funeral, but "I told him I considered Johnson a traitor to the packinghouse workers, and I wasn't about to attend his funeral." Over the next few months, Alinsky tried to help his friend's widow, Gladys, who was having problems collecting her husband's death benefits from the UMW and the insurance company. Alinsky met with Kathryn Lewis on a trip to New York in December 1944 and asked her for help, and in January 1945 he wrote to Gladys Johnson: "I have written [Kathryn] today and put the matter as strongly as possible (and on this issue the horizon is the only limitation of 'possible'). I am bringing the entire matter to a crisis. It is my own opinion . . . that any further delay will not act in your favor. If there is no definite commitment as a result of this letter [to Kathryn] I will then write directly to Mr. Lewis. From then on we will cross each bridge as we find it." Whether or not Alinsky's efforts were instrumental, by the spring of 1945 Gladys Johnson finally received an advance payment from the insurance company.

Johnson's death had not been related to the war effort, but other relationships of Alinsky's were affected by it. The encouraging starts to Alinsky's projects in Kansas City and South St. Paul before Pearl Harbor began to slow as the war effort consumed the time and energy of more people. In the beginning, Alinsky had been effective enough from long range—keeping in touch by telephone and by letter to follow up his periodic visits—but as the early excitement of building a local community organization ran its course and as the war effort consumed local talent, working at long range from Chicago was a serious handicap. Lloyd Murphy, the key leader of Alinsky's fledgling community council in Kansas City, told Alinsky in October 1942 that he was resigning since he no longer had the time or the energy, given the increasingly long hours he was putting in as a supervisor in a defense plant. "I have had great pleasure in watching democracy in action in our community . . . as I have seen all races, colors and creeds united together for one purpose with no malice of any kind, nor prejudice toward each other." Soon after Murphy resigned, Fallon Kelly in South St. Paul also resigned when he went into the Navy. Other men at the second and third tiers of leadership in both councils also went off to defense plants and to the armed services.

Alinsky was unable to find effective surrogates to work in Kansas

City, in South St. Paul, or in Cleveland, where he was considering a new project. Soon after the IAF had been formed in 1940, he had approached Joe Meegan with an offer to come aboard as, in effect, associate director, but Helen Meegan, Joe's attractive, intelligent wife, was adamantly opposed. She thought Joe's natural habitat was the South Side neighborhood of Chicago, and wanted no part of Joe's riding a circuit of unfamiliar industrial slums.

One person who wanted to work with Alinsky was Sidney Hyman. A recent graduate of the University of Chicago, intellectual and idealistic, Hyman would often stop by Alinsky's Michigan Avenue office late in the day after finishing his work at City Hall as an aide to Alderman—later U.S. Senator—Paul Douglas. Hyman was fascinated and inspired by both Alinsky and the work he was doing. He was in awe of Alinsky's outspokenness, which, he thought, was effectively and consciously used as evidence of both fearlessness and integrity. Hyman remembers Alinsky telling him stories. "I would stand there with my mouth agape; he truly had a captive audience." One story, for example, was about Alinsky eating at a local Walgreen drugstore when a man sitting nearby made an anti-Semitic remark. Alinsky grabbed the man by the lapel of his coat with one hand and took a piece of blueberry pie with the other and shoved it into the man's face. Hyman had his own special reason for being enchanted by Alinsky. "I was reared as the son of a rabbi," Hyman says, "and had to be conscious of every one of my movements, of what the community would think. I was always having to control my tongue, mostly for my father's sake. Now here comes Saul, and says any goddamned thing he wants to. How does he survive?" Hyman would wonder in amazement. Conversely, he thought Alinsky liked the idea of having a friend who was an heir to a distinguished man. Back in the old Jewish neighborhood where Alinsky grew up, "the old 24th Ward" as they say in Chicago, a rabbi was an important man. Hyman says, "I gave Saul a certain respectability, being the son of the rabbi, by my high-gloss intellectual Talmudic tradition and all that sort of stuff."

Hyman was also excited about the intellectual assumptions of Alinsky's work. He would tag along with Alinsky on visits to the Back of the Yards that were empirical expeditions for the curious Hyman. Or, on a late winter afternoon, Hyman and Alinsky might walk the streets, exchanging ideas about the potential of the Back of the Yards Neighborhood Council and the other councils Alinsky was building. Hyman recalls thinking that Alinsky was doing "one of the most interesting things to be done at that time." Hyman's sister had worked with Jane Addams at Hull-House, and Hyman saw a sharp, revealing contrast between the assumptions of Addams and Alinsky.

The good Episcopalian ladies with the good-bad conscience did everything for Hull House. These were the so-called hellfare workers, the Lady Bountifuls. Going to work for Jane Addams at Hull-House was a romantic thing to do for a young, sensitive woman. [Their noble purpose was] to help, but it was always the Lady Bountifuls who were *doing* the helping. Now Saul comes along and turns it around and sort of sets the whole Hull-House idea on its head. He says he doesn't want the hellfare worker, he doesn't want the Lady Bountiful; he wants people to help themselves. And *that* became a very romantic idea. A lot of people wanted to get in on that one, just like in an earlier generation a lot of people wanted to get in on the Hull-House idea.

Hyman wanted to be part of Alinsky's experiment, but those plans had to be suspended when he was called into military service early in 1942. Other recruits did not pan out either. Through mutual acquaintances, Alinsky offered jobs to both Jack Conway and Bill Dodds, young men who were organizing for the United Automobile Workers in the Chicago area. Alinsky wanted Conway or Dodds to go to Los Angeles, where the "zoot-suit riots" had recently occurred. The riots had pitted servicemen against Mexican-American "zoot-suiters" (their distinctive dress consisted of tight pants and coats with padded shoulders and wide lapels). The threat of continued violence and instability, in a city with large numbers of servicemen and defense plants, worried civic leaders and government officials. Alinsky was approached about coming to Los Angeles because of the reputation of the Back of the Yards Neighborhood Council for lessening intergroup hostilities, and he was excited about setting up a major project on the West Coast: it not only could head off postwar turmoil among minority groups triggered by the loss of defense-plant jobs, Alinsky wrote to a friend, but could also bring together whites, Negroes, and Mexicans and act "as a pioneer upon a new progressive course worthy of a postwar world." Alinsky said that he

informed the Mayor's Committee for Home Front Unity that we felt reasonably certain of success and would undertake to start simultaneously three projects. One to be in the Negro community, one in the adjacent white war workers' area and one in an adjacent Mexican community. These three projects would start as separate organizations but within a very short time, say six months at the outside, they would be quickly fused into a single organization which would admit to no lines of distinction in terms of nationality or race.

In trying to get the Los Angeles project off the ground, Alinsky did a little bluffing, lying, and stretching of the truth to almost everybody. The style was a hybrid of a friendly, cunning poker player and a crafty salesman. Who was the "we" who told the Mayor's Committee that success was reasonably certain? There was, of course, no "we," which was part of Alinsky's problem. There was as yet nobody except Alinsky to do the job. Alinsky's "vision" of a triracial democratic community organization in Los Angeles was not so much the result of firsthand experience in or in-depth study of Los Angeles; it sprang from the requirements of fundraising. Alinsky had to find the money to pay for staff, travel, and office space. He sent a message to his well-placed friend Sidney James, now *Time* magazine bureau chief in Los Angeles, which he expected James to pass along to the appropriate people. "The pressure on this end to make commitments for work in other cities is getting pretty bad and, frankly, I don't know how much longer we can wait on Los Angeles. There are two other cities, including the entire West Side of Chicago, now bidding for our services," Alinsky wrote somberly, although in truth there was nothing much brewing on the West Side of Chicago and Alinsky was not eager to spend time on the prairie in Omaha, Nebraska, where there was some preliminary interest in organizing a community council. "Candidly," Alinsky fibbed to James, "if it weren't for my grave concern over the Los Angeles situation, which is filled with dynamite, I would not be postponing and stalling on the commitments to other cities. These commitments would completely tie us up for next year so that we would not be able even to consider Los Angeles until '46 or '47, by which time I'm convinced there would be plenty of hell in that town."

Alinsky apparently never got enough financial commitment in Los Angeles to get started. But he did have a few chips to play with, and used one of them when he approached Jack Conway. Conway, who was later to become an important figure under Walter Reuther in the UAW and then in the anti-poverty program during Lyndon Johnson's administration, listened to Alinsky's offer to go out West because, he remembers, Alinsky was "a man with a considerable growing reputation." Alinsky explained to Conway that he wanted a man with some organizing experience to go out to Los Angeles and establish a legitimate base. He had made arrangements with the Northrup Corporation, perhaps with the help of the Los Angeles mayor's office, to give his organizer a job. The job at Northrup, which happened to be a nonunion company, would provide a base of operation, and would give Alinsky's man both an acceptable identity and economic support. "I toyed with [the offer] for a while but decided not to do it," Conway recalls. Not long before, he had returned to Chicago from a stint on the West Coast in Seattle, and his work for the UAW in Chicago was going well. But he also didn't like the setup at Northrup. "I told Saul that I wouldn't be interested in that under any circumstances. I wasn't going to go into a situation in which there was a nonunion environment and have to pledge myself not to be a union organizer, just to stick to being a community organizer."

Bill Dodds had a similar reaction. It was clear that Alinsky's main interest in Los Angeles, in spite of his close ties with the Packinghouse Workers in Chicago and with John L. Lewis, was not to organize new labor unions but rather to work on brown-white race relations. Alinsky didn't see the Los Angeles project as tied into organizing the Northrup plant for the UAW, as Dodds remembers it. "He wouldn't say that it was irrelevant, but it was certainly lower down on his list. The first job was to try to get the workers in the plant who lived in that community interested in their own backyard, and in the troubles that were obviously evident in all kinds of ways, in terms of race relations." In addition, "I also had the feeling that it was at that point a seat-of-the-pants [operation], with very little assurance that there was any end in sight, and I wasn't ready to organize like that." As it turned out, Alinsky's Los Angeles project never got off the ground. It was several years, after the war, before Alinsky returned to Los Angeles to begin a more successful campaign.

IN THE SUMMER of 1941, Saul and Helene became parents. They adopted a baby girl, whom they named Kathryn, after the daughter of John L. Lewis. A second child, a baby boy whom they named Lee David, was adopted nearly four years later. The Alinskys' Hyde Park friends thought it was Helene who wanted to have a family and Helene who pressed for adopting a child when it became clear that she and Saul could not have children of their own. Fran Gitelson, who considered Helene her best friend in the early 1940s, thought that it was Saul who couldn't have children and that he was not anxious to adopt any. "I don't know how much he resisted Helene's wanting to adopt. They were very close and compatible, a very good couple together. They had much pleasure and were very secure in their relationship. [But] I'm not so sure Saul didn't feel like kids would be an intrusion, and at that time he was beginning to travel a lot, and I think it interfered in part with what he wanted to do. He adjusted as best he could, but I never felt him to be terribly fatherly."

Indeed, tending to young children was not Saul's natural inclination; he did not have the patience or the interest. In this as in other respects, he was probably typical of many men during the period, especially men absorbed in a world of power and politics, who took it for granted that "feminine interests" such as child-rearing were, by definition, not things that men concerned themselves with. In personal style, Saul Alinsky shared many of the characteristics of the macho crowd of the CIO—the fondness for a good steak at the Savoy in Kansas City; for good bourbon (although Alinsky did not drink much he enjoyed pointing out to friends when Truman was President that he and Harry both drank Wild Turkey); for good hotels such as the Biltmore in Los Angeles or the Grosvenor in New York. These were not lavish tastes but they were important symbols of success for men like Alinsky, and he was very interested in being successful and being respected.

While Helene became the supportive wife who stayed home and took care of the children during the war years, it was her own radical allegiances that, ironically, prevented Saul from being invited to lecture to law-enforcement personnel on the problems of crime and juvenile delinquency. Throughout the 1940s and even as late as the early 1950s, Alinsky remained active within the professional delinquency-prevention network. His credentials included his college work at the University of Chicago, his association with Clifford Shaw and the Institute for Juvenile Research in Chicago, and his work with the Back of the Yards Neighborhood Council. In the summer of 1944, G. Howland Shaw, Assistant Secretary of State for foreign service personnel and a member of Alinsky's board of directors, recommended to the FBI that Alinsky be invited as an instructor on crime prevention and juvenile delinquency at the FBI's National Academy. An FBI check gave Saul a clean bill of health but reported that Helene was a member of the State, County, and Municipal Workers Union and also, in 1939, a member of the Jackson Park Branch of the American League for Peace and Democracy, "a Communistic type" of organization, the FBI report claimed. Thus, although Helene's membership had ended five years earlier, the FBI concluded that "in view of the affiliation of Alinsky's wife with an allegedly Communistic outfit, it is not recommended that he be invited to speak before the FBI National Academy." Saul probably never knew exactly why Shaw's recommendation was rebuffed.

Alinsky continued to participate in professional meetings and symposia on juvenile delinquency, for the problems of crime and juvenile delinquency remained high on the national agenda. Throughout most of Alinsky's adult life—from his days as a graduate student beginning in 1930, through the war years, and during the postwar period—the problem of juvenile delinquency induced much hand-wringing and rhetoric about the dire implications for the nation's future, about the "survival of democracy as we know it," and other well-intentioned, semi-hysterical warnings and pleadings that something must be done. Indeed, contemporary American history shows that as long as there is a juvenile population, there will be sufficient behavior defined as juvenile delinquency to provide a comfortable living for a sizable number of criminologists, social workers, and camp counselors.

Because juvenile delinquency was perceived as a kind of national enemy, those who were "fighting" it almost automatically had conferred on them a measure of public approval and respect. Such people, especially if they were bright and ambitious, were invited to participate in prestigious forums, as Alinsky was in the 1940s. In 1942—perhaps at the suggestion of G. Howland Shaw, then president of the American Prison Association—Sheldon Glueck, the Harvard criminologist and law professor, invited Alinsky to serve on the Association's Crime Prevention Committee, a committee which Alinsky chaired briefly a few years later. He was also asked to share a platform with Harry Stack Sullivan at the annual meeting of the American Orthopsychiatric Association; he testified in Congress before Senator Claude Pepper's committee investigating juvenile delinquency; and he was asked to lecture occasionally to gatherings of juvenile case and field workers in New York, lectures arranged by one of Alinsky's New York friends, Morris Ploscowe.

During this period, Alinsky was often identified in newspaper stories as a criminologist. Yet, for the most part, he did not identify with either the field or the professionals who populated it, men who had their own professional axes to grind and were concerned with petty matters of career enhancement, he thought. In a letter to Ploscowe, Alinsky noted the people on the editorial board of a new publication, *Crime News and Feature Service*. "A glance at the pusses of the editorial board presented sufficient reason why our work should be overlooked," he wrote, citing the presence of several detractors, including his former boss at the Chicago Area Project, Clifford Shaw. "I assume," he continued sarcastically, "that the reports of the next twelve issues will concern the work of the members of the board. The reason I say twelve is that I note that there are twelve people on it."

Alinsky's readiness to cut up his professional detractors was not only a reflection of his usual combativeness; he also had limited intellectual interest in and respect for criminology, given the narrowness of its boundaries. Most crime and delinquency, he believed, were clearly intertwined with—indeed, usually the result of—poverty, discrimination, and despair. And most of these problems were essentially political problems, the result of unfair and unequal political arrangements. Yet criminology would have little to do with addressing explicitly these fundamental issues.

Saul Alinsky wanted to address the big political and social questions partly because he wanted to have a big impact. He wanted to do it as other men throughout history had done it, with the force of his ideas and the power of his pen. From time to time, he would seek out others who were interested in doing the same. In June 1943, Alinsky wrote a note to a brilliant young sociology professor at the University of Maryland, C. Wright Mills. "I have been told of you by a number of people, including Robert S. Lynd," Alinsky explained by way of introduction, and suggested that on an upcoming trip East, "if it is possible, I would very much like to meet and get to know you." Alinsky and Mills exchanged a number of letters over the next six months, but the relationship never grew beyond that. Mills, who at twenty-seven was seven years younger than Alinsky, had many of the qualities he admired: he had been something of a prodigy as a graduate student and had a growing reputation among sociologists long before the publication of his books *White Collar* and *The Power Elite* brought him to the attention of a wider public. His politics—although more at the level of philosophy than of activism—placed him as an independent leftist: anti-totalitarian, noncommunist, but with an affinity for Marxist ideas, who argued that it was the role of the intellectual in American society to unmask the "lies which sustain irresponsible power." This was bound to be especially appealing to Alinsky, who took great delight in exposing the hypocrisies of the established order.

Mills was not only brilliant but opinionated and arrogant, a contrarian who often seemed to go out of his way to alienate his academic colleagues—all qualities that Alinsky would understand and appreciate, but not qualities likely to make for an enduring friendship between the two of them. Alinsky sent Mills a copy of a paper he had given at the 1937 meeting of the American Prison Association. The paper had been Alinsky's most analytic effort, a critique of the functional relationship between a capitalistic social order and the individualistic approach in American criminology. Mills thought the paper was "really very fine and penetrating." To Alinsky's comment, no doubt delivered with pride, that he, Alinsky, had been attacked for being a radical, he replied: "As far as being attacked as a radical . . . well, you are a radical. 'To be a radical is to grasp a thing by the root. Now the root of man is himself.' K. Marx, which is what I always say."

Mills suggested that Alinsky write something for Dwight Macdonald's new monthly, *Politics,* and later wrote Alinsky with a plan for a book of articles and essays on the sociology of knowledge and communication that would include a piece by Alinsky on criminology. Nothing more came of this discussion, however. Mills must have realized that Alinsky was not particularly good at developing sociological theories or writing abstract formulations, that he was not a scholar. Alinsky would not admit this to himself, however, for he saw scholarship and intellectual achievement, especially in social criticism, as one important avenue to recognition and respect.

Alinsky did not write much in the early 1940s. What little coherent social criticism he attempted was confined to an occasional speech. His style was not abstract or theoretical but concrete and aimed at real people and institutions. Perhaps the best example of this was a speech he gave to the National Conference of Catholic Charities in the fall of 1942. Alinsky traveled with Bishop Sheil to Kansas City, where both were featured speakers. Sheil's speech, which Alinsky might have drafted, was on the relationship between delinquency and racial minority groups. Alinsky spoke on Catholic leadership, or, more to the point, the lack of it. There were few true leaders among Catholic clergy, he bluntly told his audience of Catholic clergy, because there were few "who are completely committed to rendering their services, their abilities and their lives for the benefit of their fellow men." Much of the Church had turned its back on the industrial-labor-union movement, had practiced discrimination by excluding Negroes and Mexicans from many parishes, and had "surrendered to a materialistic civilization." "When the Catholic Church . . . mines for gold instead of for souls it is no longer a church," he charged, setting up the kind of play on words he enjoyed. "You cannot substitute the gold standard for the golden rule," and, moreover, it could be of little comfort that much the same could be said of Jewish and Protestant clergy. Then Alinsky fired a parting salvo:

> [T]he teachings of Christ and the philosophy represented by him . . . [is] one of the most revolutionary doctrines the world has ever witnessed, a doctrine so radical that both by itself as well as in its implications it would make the most left-wing aspect of communism appear conservative. This radical, revolutionary philosophy of Catholicism makes it impossible for one to subscribe to it and yet be a centrist or a right-wing conservative. [Those who have] may be Catholics in name, but they are pagan in soul.

Alinsky was pleased with himself for striking enough provocative chords to create a stir. He sent copies of his speech to John L. Lewis, Marshall Field, Robert Lynd, and nearly two dozen other prominent friends or acquaintances. His New York friend Morris Ploscowe wrote him a congratulatory letter that said exactly what Saul Alinsky wanted to hear: "You have said things in this speech which have needed saying for a long time. Few men that I know would have had the courage to say it, even though they would agree with everything that you said." True, it was Alinsky's natural inclination to climb into the ring and throw verbal punches. Even so, there was much to admire about a man who would not mince words when speaking out on racial discrimination or on the hypocrisy of organized religion.

As the war appeared to be ending, Alinsky finally began to write the book he had been thinking about for a long time. Suddenly, however, a political crisis erupted in Chicago that threatened the survival of the Back of the Yards Neighborhood Council. Alinsky's future was on the line, too, for most of his growing national reputation was synonymous with the perceived success of the Council. If the Council were to fail now, Alinsky's own luster would inevitably be tarnished.

12

Battle for Survival

Saul Alinsky's Back of the Yards Neighborhood Council had two natural enemies in Chicago: the professional social-work establishment and the Kelly-Nash Democratic Party machine. As the Council grew in stature and legitimacy in Chicago in the early 1940s, neither could continue to ignore the competition it represented. Both finally launched attacks.

MUCH OF THE SOCIAL workers' offensive against the BYNC and Alinsky sprang from the same well of self-interest that had fed the professionals' attack on Clifford Shaw and his Chicago Area Project a decade earlier. The social workers felt threatened and offended by "the minimizing of the part that can be played by professional people" in solving problems in lower-class industrial communities. This misleadingly restrained criticism—misleading because it masked the depth of antagonism felt by many in the Chicago social-work establishment—appeared in a confidential report filed by the executive committee of the Division on Education and Recreation of the Council of Social Agencies of Chicago. The report, which ran nine pages, was based largely on the predispositions, suspicions, and impressions of the six committee members and their colleagues, and, to a lesser extent, on a few conversations the committee had with people on the periphery of the BYNC.

This "preliminary" report (it was never followed up with a more substantial, systematic investigation) conceded that, although the BYNC shared many of the methods and goals associated with a more traditional concept of community organization, it also had important distinctive features. "Its claim to distinction is best supported in its recognition of a broad base of power in an industrial community which potentially provides a basis for democratic action, and also in its conception of a close tie-up between local and larger-scale action." Beyond that, however, the social-work committee found little to praise and much to be suspicious about— suspicions that read more like accusations. The committee wondered, for instance, if Joe Meegan could be considered a genuinely "indigenous" leader. "It must be noted that despite the theoretical devotion to the qualities of local leadership, in all discussions and written accounts of [the development of the Back of the Yards Council], the dynamic qualities of Mr. Alinsky and Mr. Meegan are stressed as central factors." Was "the principle of broad participation" being honestly implemented? the report questioned.

There were other unfriendly questions. Were the Council's current accomplishments of the same magnitude as its earlier ones, which had attracted a "strong nationwide publicity build-up"—deeply resented, of course, by the social-work professionals. Or what about the current in-volvement of the CIO? "The fact that the CIO and the Catholic Church were cooperating in a local community was responsible for much, if not most, of the publicity in popular write-ups at the beginning," the commit-tee contended, somewhat inaccurately. "If the labor group is now much less active, as some evidence suggests, the organization becomes predomi-nantly a grouping of Catholic churches with a community program."

Alinsky delivered a blistering reply to these implicit charges. He had met once with the committee before the preliminary report was written, but because it was so clearly interested in discrediting the BYNC and had gathered little evidence to bolster its contentions, he had been inclined to ignore the report until a friend in the Sociology Department at Northwest-ern, Professor William Byron, prevailed on him to put down his "criticisms in black and white." "I want to strongly reiterate that this statement is not forthcoming in response to the report (because it isn't deserving of the time involved), but because of your request and our personal friendship," Alinsky replied, and then went on for fourteen pages, attempting a point-by-point refutation.

Some allegations were easy to refute. "Despite this being a 'prelimi-nary report,' I cannot help having a large question mark in my mind regarding a study of an organization which has been unstudied," Alinsky wrote. "I don't know . . . of the Committee ever having had a single contact during the past year and a half with any of the officers or board members or heads of committees of the Back of the Yards Neighborhood Council." This was apparently accurate, except for possibly one former board member who spoke with the committee. Alinsky chose to focus on differences in style and purpose, and only indirectly touched on fundamental differences in philosophy.

> The last contacts within the community with a professional worker came at the time of the first Community Congress of the Council which occurred during a period of grave labor crisis. . . . At that time, a strike [at Armour] was imminent. . . . One professional social worker present at the Congress took the vociferous position that the Council should abstain from any involvement in this dispute [because] it was unprofessional and it meant staining the Council with partisanship and bias. The kind of "objectivity" professed by this social worker is not shared by the Council. . . . The Council admits openly and frankly that it is biased and that it is partisan. It is partisan and biased in favor of its people. After all, that is the reason it was conceived.

Alinsky was able to dismiss easily several of the other criticisms raised by the social workers, including their doubts about BYNC's recent programmatic accomplishments. The Council tended to claim credit for apparent successes when other agencies or factors had also played a role—for instance, in establishing a new infant-welfare station or in lowering infant-mortality and delinquency rates—but Alinsky could show that its contributions were important. When it came to questions about Meegan's work and his own, however, Alinsky's answers were less convincing.

Privately, Alinsky had long since indicated mixed feelings and frustrations with Meegan. And he had opted for co-executive secretaries in his other councils to avoid a repetition of Meegan's tendency to dominate the BYNC. Publicly, however, Alinsky sang a different tune. To doubts about whether new, diverse leadership would be encouraged, Alinsky's reply was vague and weak: ". . . the turn-over of officers and the development of the present leadership speaks for itself. Of the present slate of officers who are leaders of the Council, it is of interest that with two exceptions there has been a complete turn-over of leadership." As for why journalistic accounts of the Council's success focused heavily or nearly exclusively on Meegan and him, Alinsky replied lamely: "The emphasis on one or two personalities is generally regarded as making a story much more interesting than a completely impersonal account. Your criticism is more properly directed at the press than the Council."

In practice, day-to-day leadership of the Council came largely from Meegan and a few priests—the president of the Council, Father Ed Plawinski of St. John of God, one of the Polish parishes; the well-liked Ambrose

Ondrak from the Bohemian church, St. Michael's; and two or three others. Within this core group, Meegan was the main force.

As to whether Meegan was a "purely indigenous leader," Alınsky scoffed at any doubts.

> I may be somewhat naive [he wrote sarcastically], but I am unfamiliar with criteria or measurements of "purity" in indigenous leaders. . . . [As for definitions of purity], I think of the dairy industry where we have Grade A Milk, Grade B Milk, Pasteurized Milk, Homogenized Milk and various degrees of butter fat content. Using this field as an analogy, I admit that, while I can't say that Mr. Meegan is homogenized . . . , he is all milk, and unquestionably a native, indigenous leader of the community.

And yet, Meegan was hardly typical of the Back of the Yards: he was Irish in a heavily Polish and Lithuanian area; he was first-generation American in a community where immigrants still made up a majority of the adult population; he was a college graduate and former teacher in a community where the typical adult had, at best, a grade-school education.

Yet Meegan was virtually indispensable to the daily operation of the Council, just as Alinsky remained the indispensable strategist and spokesman who interpreted for mostly friendly journalists the Council's larger, national significance. Alinsky was ambivalent about his role: although he enjoyed the recognition, he didn't want to appear like a behind-the-scenes puppeteer who pulled all the strings. Indeed, during a quiescent period, Alinsky tried to expand the horizons, understanding, and leadership potential of the priests by organizing a book discussion group that met regularly. Yet whenever the Council faced a political conflict or crisis the leaders turned to him.

One such conflict that arose in 1944 involved the University of Chicago Settlement House, which was located in the Back of the Yards. The narrow issue was ostensibly which organization, the Settlement House or the BYNC, was better able to house a new infant-welfare station. The larger issue, however, was the competing philosophies of the social-work professionals on the one side and the BYNC on the other. In effect, the conflict continued the attack that the Chicago social-work establishment had launched in its "preliminary report" on the BYNC.

The University of Chicago Settlement House, one of the most prestigious settlements in the city, had been located in the Back of the Yards for more than fifty years. By the 1940s, however, the settlement-house movement had begun to lose its romantic appeal. In an earlier period, it had been an enlightened and adventurous calling for upper-class people to help the poor, often by moving into and working out of settlement houses located in lower-class immigrant and slum neighborhoods. To whatever extent the University of Chicago Settlement House, most of whose board members had traditionally come from the university community, had in bygone days been accepted in the Back of the Yards, by now it was clear that it was not the most popular local institution. In fact, it and its workers were deeply resented, if not hated, by, among others, the old pastor at St. John of God, Father Louis Grudzinski.

Grudzinski, perhaps the most intensely nationalistic of the Polish pastors, had been in direct competition with the University of Chicago Settlement House from as early as 1915, when he was the leading force behind a successful effort to raise money, buy land, and build the Guardian Angel Day Nursery and Home for Working Girls at the corner of Forty-sixth and Gross, a few doors away from the Settlement House. Guardian Angel was built specifically to counteract the Settlement House, for Grudzinski viewed the University of Chicago crowd as a corrupting influence, non-Polish, non-Catholic interlopers who were not to be trusted. Nearly three decades later, by the spring of 1944, nothing had happened to change Grudzinski's early evaluation.

The BYNC could not take for granted the support of the Polish priests. They could be rigid and difficult about many things, including the BYNC. Indeed, the pastor at St. Joseph's, Stanislaus Cholewinski, would have nothing to do with the BYNC and his parish did not support it until after he retired. A constant political priority was to ensure that the BYNC's base of support was firm, which, above all, meant the local parishes.

In the spring of 1944 the Infant Welfare Society's branch station in the Back of the Yards was forced to vacate its space at Davis Square Park. When Alinsky heard that the University of Chicago Settlement House had offered to house it in its building, he must have heard as well the bells and whistles of opportunity. Here was an incident that could be turned into an issue, an issue that could be used to line up the villains on one side and the good guys—the parishes and the BYNC—on the other.

The BYNC quickly notified the president of the Infant Welfare Society that if the Society moved into the Settlement House, all the priests in the community would take to the pulpit and tell their parishioners not to use it; the BYNC and the churches would set up their own infant-care facility. The Infant Welfare Society, which had the support of many in Chicago's Social Register, had run public-health programs in Chicago's parks for thirty-three years. Sensing trouble that she wanted to avoid, its president contacted Bishop Sheil. Sheil suggested that representatives of the Settlement House and the BYNC meet to discuss their differences.

The Back of the Yards delegation, led by Alinsky, went on the offensive immediately when the two sides met in August 1944, with Wilfred Reynolds of the Council of Social Agencies trying to act as a mediator. Alinsky growled that the people in the Back of the Yards did not like "do-gooders," outsiders who knew little about the neighborhood people. That salvo was only a warm-up. Before the meeting had ended, the BYNC delegation had charged that the Settlement House was anti-Catholic because it gave out birth-control information, helped local women in divorce proceedings, and spoke critically of the Church; anti-labor because it had denied its facilities to the CIO and had not supported an earlier Packinghouse Workers' strike; and anti-Semitic because it allowed the local Kiwanis, which barred Jews as members, to use its facilities. Throughout the dispute, Alinsky's primary interest was not the issue itself—where an infant-welfare station would be housed—but how the issue could be used to solidify community support for the BYNC and affirm its role as the community's voice.

While denying many of the charges made by the BYNC delegation, the Settlement House representatives admitted that its leadership, particularly its board of directors, did not reflect the composition of the Back of the Yards community. They promised to do better. Alinsky was unimpressed. He then gave them an ultimatum: either they could sell their building to the BYNC—for one dollar as a gesture of goodwill, he later suggested—or they could continue as before, in which case, he said threateningly, when the war ended the BYNC would construct its own facility and, he implied, drive them out of the neighborhood.

Before this first negotiating session ended, the Settlement House leadership made a counterproposal that to Alinsky and the BYNC was nothing short of preposterous: the Settlement House would withdraw its invitation to provide space for the Infant Welfare Society if the BYNC also dropped its offer to do the same. That proposal was, of course, dismissed out of hand. Not long after, the Settlement House leaders suggested quietly to the Infant Welfare Society that it might be better for all concerned if the Society disregarded their earlier invitation.

But Alinsky had expanded the issue well beyond the question of where a new infant-welfare station was to be housed. The larger question was now whether the Settlement House should be allowed to survive in the neighborhood, and, further, whether social-work professionals and like-minded Settlement House boards of directors ought to control institutions and programs in lower-class industrial communities. At one point, as negotiating sessions continued, the BYNC proposed that if the Settlement House would not sell its building to the BYNC for a dollar, the only acceptable alternative was to elect at least half of its board of directors from among the officers of the BYNC.

The effrontery of Alinsky and his cohorts must have been infuriating to the Settlement House leadership. They struck back, saying at one point that their own investigation had turned up many people who were critical of the BYNC:

> The procedures of the Council were said to be undemocratic in that it is controlled by a very few key persons who initiate important movements without conferring with their board of directors. There were charges of financial mismanagement. Many felt that the BYNC was not representative of the region, since a number of organizations, among them the American Legion, the Chamber of Commerce, and one of the large Catholic churches, had withdrawn, and other Catholic churches had never participated. Pressure, intimidation, propaganda, and open attack were declared to have been employed, the present campaign against the Settlement being only one example, and it had been frankly admitted by Mr. Alinsky that their ends justify the means taken.

These charges had little credibility, not only because they were made in the form of a self-serving counterattack but also because the Settlement House freely confessed that they had come "from certain people of the community [who are] admittedly prejudiced against the BYNC."

As weak as the anonymous sources were for the Settlement House's offensive, the sources that came to the defense of the BYNC were devastatingly potent. The most potent was Bishop Sheil, who at the beginning had been asked to provide his good offices to head off a dispute. Perhaps the Settlement House leaders had misgauged the closeness of the friendship between Sheil and Alinsky. Perhaps they had not considered the inevitability of Sheil's decision if he were forced to choose between the Catholic-based BYNC and the non-Catholic University of Chicago Settlement House. In any event, as the dispute dragged on, whatever sympathy Sheil might have had for the Settlement House leaders as individuals began to fade, and whatever political or social constraints he might initially have felt also began to diminish. The Settlement House leaders had been both inept and inconsistent, he thought, and then, having raised questions about the honesty, integrity, and legitimacy of the BYNC, they made an incredible about-face. Now they claimed that, "despite obvious and serious objections" to the methods of the BYNC, "an effort should be made to work with the BYNC for the good of the community as a whole." Whereupon, explaining "that the only way of determining whether the Council was an agency with which our resources might eventually be combined was to work with it from the inside," they applied to the BYNC for membership. With undisguised relish, Joe Meegan wrote in response: "It is the unanimous decision of the Board of Directors . . . that [the] agency known as the University of Chicago Settlement House is wholly unfit by character, purpose, or spirit to be part of the movement known as the Back of the Yards Neighborhood Council."

The flip-flops, arrogance, and hypocrisy of the Settlement House leaders were too much even for the fair-minded Bishop Sheil. In a letter to the BYNC, which the BYNC conveniently made public, the bishop minced no words:

> I withdraw my request for the Back of the Yards Council to explore all possibilities of approachment with the University of Chicago Settlement House board of directors. I want to congratulate the officers of the Council for their infinite patience in talking and trying to work out an understanding with those people. . . . The kindest thing that I can say for the Settlement House directors is that they exhibit an outstanding intransigence. The Board of Directors and the staff of the University of Chicago Settlement House do not have the remotest understanding, feeling, or real heart-felt sympathy with the problems, the desire, and the hopes of the people of the Back of the Yards. To continue negotiations with them would be a tragic waste of time.

If the bishop's public chastisement was not enough, a newspaper account by Agnes Meyer in the Washington *Post* made the entire Chicago social-work establishment flinch. Meyer, wife of the *Post*'s publisher, came to Chicago early in 1945, met Alinsky and Bishop Sheil, and was captivated by both. Not long after, she wrote:

> This fine building is almost idle because of a bitter feud between the settlement house workers and the neighborhood. The battle has become even more embittered now that the people have shown ample proof of being able to look after themselves. . . . The Chicago University Settlement trustees remain in an obstinate, righteous isolation, indifferent to the creative activity and the dynamic democracy swirling about their disintegrating institution. Seen through the eyes of the surrounding population, who are struggling for dignity, self-respect

and self-expression, the Chicago University Settlement makes social work look like the meaningless play-thing or the hypocritical subterfuge of a morally bankrupt civilization.

Alinsky's virtuoso performance had left the University of Chicago Settlement House bloodied and bruised. One might say that it never fully recovered from this battle, although a few years later its relationship with the BYNC improved. Alinsky had won this round. But because Alinsky represented a fundamental challenge, he and much of the social-work establishment would have other fights on other grounds.

The episode with the Settlement House reveals a part of Alinsky's extraordinary ability, indeed genius, to envision the dramatic potential in a seemingly ordinary event. His love of battle and keen tactical sense were also on display here, though in this instance the opposition was less than Herculean. How he might fare against a more formidable opponent was an interesting speculation. In Chicago, there was no better test than to do battle with the Kelly-Nash Democratic Party machine. For Saul Alinsky, Joe Meegan, and the BYNC, the big test began within the first days of the new year in 1944.

E D   K E L L Y was elected mayor of Chicago in 1935 and won reelection in 1939 and 1943. In the process, Kelly and the chairman of the Cook County Democratic Committee, Patrick A. Nash, a wealthy sewer contractor, teamed to build one of the most powerful, if not the most powerful, big-city political machines in the United States.

Soon after he was first elected in 1935, Kelly and the party machinery that had helped elect him began to earn their own well-deserved reputation for a rich assortment of corrupt practices—for padded payrolls, for payoffs in return for favorable tax assessments, for kickbacks in exchange for lucrative city contracts, for bribery within the police department. Kelly's personal priorities were sometimes revealed humorously if not quite intentionally. One such incident that Alinsky loved to recount to friends concerned an address the mayor gave to a graduating class entitled "The Real Values in Life." "Money cannot buy you success; money cannot buy you prestige; money cannot buy you happiness," Kelly proclaimed, but then unexpectedly departed from his text to ad-lib: "Confederate money, that is."

Of course, the Chicago machine, like other big-city political machines, also claimed a sunnier side. Among the virtues often cited by political scientists of the period were the care and attention they could provide to poor immigrants. In exchange for their votes, immigrants got not merely recognition at City Hall but also tangible rewards such as jobs, better garbage collection, parks, and street repairs. But the implicit and explicit bargains between immigrants and political machines were inevitably inequitable, and the Back of the Yards was a good case in point.

The Back of the Yards neighborhood spread over four of Chicago's fifty wards. The heart of the neighborhood, however, was in the 14th Ward, which had, albeit with some boundary changes and other numerical designations over the years, an unbroken history of Irish leadership and domination. Before the turn of the century, Tom Carey was not merely the alderman of the 29th Ward (as it was then numbered) but was called its "king"—and, of course, he behaved and was treated accordingly. By 1914, the emerging leader of Carey's old turf was Judge John J. Sullivan. In short order, Sullivan, a Superior Court judge by 1916, became boss of the 14th Ward because he was smarter and tougher and worked harder than any of the other politically ambitious ward politicians. The Judge, as he was called, picked the alderman and the ward committeeman, the latter a party official who usually made the most important political decisions, such as which precinct workers deserved to get on the city payroll. In the 14th Ward, however, the Judge made those decisions. Every Sunday morning all the precinct captains and others in the ward organization met at his home on Garfield Boulevard, the grandest street in the ward, with the largest and best houses. They filled him in, say, on what had happened on Tuesday night, which was Ward Night, when anybody who lived in the ward who wanted help with a political problem could go with his precinct captain to talk with the alderman and ward committeeman. One supplicant might want a job or maybe a building permit, another might be seeking to get a relative out of jail or out of the old country. Sometimes people in the 14th Ward would go straight to Judge Sullivan's house for advice about family or financial problems. It was said that there were people from the 14th Ward at Judge Sullivan's house every night of the week asking for his advice or for a favor. The Judge knew a lot about the 14th Ward.

Under Sullivan's reign, it was a gross understatement to say that the 14th Ward was a bastion of Democratic support. In the 1938 election, for instance, the Democrats won the 7th Precinct in the 14th Ward by a vote of 524 to 4, and the 8th Precinct by 470 to 2. The 25th Precinct in the 14th Ward went entirely for the Democrats, including the votes of the Republican election judges. With that kind of political base, and because Judge Sullivan was an astute slate-maker at election time, by the 1930s and 1940s he was one of the most powerful Democrats in Chicago, along with men like Pat Nash and Jake Arvey.

By the 1930s, the Democratic votes that Judge Sullivan and his hand-picked alderman and ward committeeman, James McDermott, were delivering from the 14th Ward were not Irish. The Irish, except for a few, had long since moved out of the Back of the Yards. Yet the Irish still dominated political life in the 14th Ward, which is to say that Irish leaders dominated a good part of life itself.

Every alderman of the 14th Ward from the early 1930s through the mid-1980s has been Irish. The South Side Irish politicians, a tight-knit clan, passed along political offices and politically connected jobs from one generation to another. The political family tree on the South Side, whose branches often crossed ward boundaries, revealed various combinations of inheritance: from father to son, from father-in-law to son-in-law, from uncle to nephew. Many of the lines of inheritance, especially for 14th Ward politicians, crossed at Visitation parish. In fact, every 14th Ward alderman, committeeman, and any other Irish politico of consequence was a parishioner at Visitation, located less than a mile south of the stockyards and on the edge of the Back of the Yards neighborhood.

The Irish domination of the 14th Ward was not maintained without tensions and conflicts. The other ethnic groups in the ward and throughout the Back of the Yards disliked, even hated the Irish—in part because of their commanding political power and corresponding attitude of superiority. And since the Slovaks, Bohemians, Poles, and others had been shut out of the Regular 14th Ward Democratic Organization, each ethnic group organized its own Democratic club—the Slovaks' club was organized around St. Michael's parish, and the Bohemians, Lithuanians, and Poles had their own clubs, too. While these clubs worked for the Democratic ticket at election time, they also functioned as a small power base from which to prod and push the Irish in the Regular 14th Ward Democratic Organization. Most of the time, it was clearly understood by everybody that the regulars could not be pushed and prodded very far. On rare occasions, however, perhaps on the order of once every two or three decades, somebody would make a gigantic miscalculation of the local power relationships, perhaps when his political judgment was warped by hatred of the Irish and by fantasies of political glory and riches. One such episode occurred in the Back of the Yards in 1942, in anticipation of the election the following year.

The Poles, as the largest ethnic group in the Back of the Yards, had the biggest political grievance, and received only a modest portion of the political rewards. At the Polish Regular Democratic Club of the 14th Ward, the leader was John Kluczynski, or Johnny Klu, as he was known, who had been a precinct captain as a young man and was elected to the state legislature in 1930. Johnny Klu had made his accommodations with the Irish leadership in the 14th Ward. His club, which included the best Polish precinct captains in the 14th Ward, worked with the regulars, got the vote out, and, in return, received a certain number of patronage jobs and other rewards. His own role was to get as much as he could from the Irish while keeping any restive Polish troops in line. He did a good job and went from state representative to state senator in 1940 and, later, to the United States Congress.

In spite of Johnny Klu's successes, not every Pole was happy with the status quo. When Jim McDermott announced that he was not going to run for reelection as alderman of the 14th Ward in 1943, some members of the Polish club thought they saw an opening to push for a Polish alderman. Joseph Palka, a top Polish precinct captain who also held a city job, announced his candidacy. A group of Poles, including the pastor of St. John of God, visited Judge Sullivan to ask for his support. When they declared to him their conviction that it was time to have a Polish alderman, the Judge replied, "Well, I don't see nothing wrong with it." Pressed to give Palka his support, Sullivan said: "I'll be with whoever the precinct captains nominate and I'll be with him heart and soul. If they nominate Palka, I'll be with him a hundred percent, financially and every other way." Whereupon, after a time, Sullivan appointed a committee of five trusted lieutenants who then recommended the man the Judge wanted for alderman of the 14th Ward, Clarence Wagner. Wagner was a precinct captain, a lawyer, and—more to the point—Irish on his mother's side and a member of Visitation parish.

The Poles were insulted and angered. Palka was more determined than ever to make the race. Judge Sullivan and Jim McDermott, who was to continue as ward committeeman, did not take political challenges lightly, however. Palka (whose own wife, interestingly, opposed his candidacy) found himself quickly removed from his city job. It was rumored that Sullivan and McDermott were also responsible for putting another Pole on the ballot, Thomas Tomaskiewicz, who might help split the Polish vote. In addition, Judge Sullivan made it clear to all the ward organization precinct captains, including the Polish ones, that anyone who failed to deliver the vote for Wagner would likewise lose his city job. So most of the precinct captains dutifully made their rounds to explain that Palka was not qualified, or that Wagner would have more clout downtown with the Kelly-Nash machine, or that too many people in the ward would lose their jobs if Wagner lost the election.

When the votes were counted on election day, Wagner received 11,794, Palka 3,696. All illusions about who was in control were dispelled. Both Palka and the Polish Regular Democratic Club quickly tried to make peace with Judge Sullivan and his ward organization. Palka said that it had all been a mistake, that the leaders of several Polish societies had forced him to make the race. Even after this act of contrition, it was a full year before Palka got another patronage job. The leaders of his club emphasized that in the future they would be "100 percent regular Democrats at all times" and requested a picture of Alderman Wagner to display in their meeting room.

To outsiders, the Polish revolt in the 14th Ward appeared to be over. To Democratic machine insiders, the satisfaction of crushing the revolt was tempered by the fact that an uprising in a machine stronghold had occurred in the first place, a serious embarrassment for leaders such as Judge Sullivan. And embarrassments could have corrosive effects on his heretofore unquestioned respect and power. The Judge did not want any more embarrassments, uprisings, or surprises. But whenever he left his house and drove north on Ashland Avenue, he could look over his shoulder and see another possible problem as he passed Davis Square Park.

Saul Alinsky and Joe Meegan kept the BYNC out of the fray over the aldermanic race in the 14th Ward. In one sense, the fight among the machine Democrats was not the Council's fight. The Council's agenda included delinquency-prevention programs, neighborhood cleanup projects, health-care and nutrition programs for children, support for the Packinghouse Workers Union. That was a full plate of activities, and an important part of the Council's image was that it was above partisan politics. Unlike selfish, crass politicians who often seemed most interested in perpetuating their own power, the Council was perceived as a unifying force that could harness the energy and latent goodwill of the residents themselves to solve the community's real problems. The Council might pressure government officials and agencies to provide better services, but it would not become a direct participant in party politics. So in one sense, it was understandable that, as a general principle, the Council would keep its distance from the Democratic machine, especially when the specific conflict was, at best, a mixed bag of motives, personalities, and grievances—not anybody's idea of a glorious political battle.

In another sense, however, the *idea* of challenging the 14th Ward machine was consistent with the Council's, and Alinsky's, philosophy. The Democratic machine in Chicago was a great contradiction to the raison d'être of the Council, which was summed up in its motto: "We the people will work out our own destiny." For the Democratic machine, the only political poison for which there was no known antidote was unbridled independence. In a variety of ways the machine could remind people of their dependence. Some of the more creative precinct captains would even invent problems that they would then solve to show how indispensable they were. They would arrange, for example, with a postmaster or postman to hold up the delivery of someone's relief check. When in desperation the person turned to his precinct captain for help, the precinct captain could say, "I'll fix it for you." As long as enough people felt that they depended on the machine—on its personifications in precinct captains, aldermen, ward committeemen, lawyers who knew which palms to grease—the machine could run smoothly, subject only to internal breakdowns caused by avarice, ego, or stupidity.

Then, slowly and subtly during the first two years, a little less subtly by 1942 and 1943, the BYNC became an alternative institution to which people could turn when they had problems. Still, the challenge to the machine was indirect. On a practical level, there was nothing in the offing to suggest that the Council would actually try to challenge the machine. For all the national press notices the Council had received, back in Chicago, in the glare of reality in the 14th Ward, the Back of the Yards Neighborhood Council was still merely a grape to the boot of Judge Sullivan—or so it must have seemed to the machine leaders when they decided to squash the Council.

In February 1943, Joe Meegan started to get none too subtle warnings from local machine leaders that the 14th Ward would be a lot better off if he went on a long trip. "What's your draft status?" ward committeeman McDermott asked Meegan when their paths crossed at a party one evening. Within days, the local draft board called Meegan in for a chat about his deferment. The harassment continued, with Meegan receiving ever more pointed warnings from local leaders that his job as director of Davis Square Park was in jeopardy. Perhaps they thought they had not acted swiftly enough to stop Palka and others from mounting a challenge and were not going to wait until it was too late again. They had been wary of the BYNC from the start, in part because of its skill at uniting diverse groups: adept as the machine was at playing on ethnic hatreds and rivalries, they did not want anybody or anything to disturb, for example, the local axiom that a Lithuanian would never vote for a Pole and vice versa. Perhaps even more threatening was that the BYNC had been rapidly expanding its nutrition program for local children, a most important organizing device, administered by Meegan, that placed the BYNC at the center of a network of local parishes, each of which sent children to Davis Square Park for free milk and lunch. This program was beginning to worry machine leaders for both obvious and, up to this point, not so obvious reasons. The time had finally come for verbal warnings to be translated into action.

On the morning of January 3, 1944, a front-page story in the Chicago

Sun reported that the Chicago Park District had denied the use of Davis Square Park to the Back of the Yards Neighborhood Council. In addition, the *Sun* reported, the head of the Park District had ordered the transfer of Joe Meegan from Davis Square, where he had continued to earn his living as park director while also functioning as unpaid executive secretary of the Council. Now, while the BYNC might be able to find other suitable facilities for its meetings and programs, it was less certain how well the BYNC could survive the transfer of Meegan to a full-time job away from the stockyards neighborhood.

It was no accident that, of all the Chicago daily newspapers, this story first appeared in the *Sun*. The *Sun*'s owner and publisher was Alinsky's benefactor Marshall Field, who had started the paper in 1941 as a liberal competitor to archconservative Colonel Robert McCormick and his Chicago *Tribune*. Nor was it an accident that the *Sun* ran the story when it did. Alinsky and Meegan had known, at least in general terms, about the Park District's intentions for some time. They had tried, to no avail, to head off Meegan's transfer through a variety of informal channels. Once those efforts failed, Alinsky needed time to develop a public strategy and to coordinate a public response. The Park District, an instrument of the Kelly-Nash machine, wanted to get Meegan out of Davis Square quietly, with a minimum of fuss. Alinsky's strategy was to set off as many sirens of protest as he could invent.

After many late-night meetings in the waning days of December with Meegan and the young priests in the Council, Alinsky was ready to take action, and the front-page story in the *Sun* was his first move. A large, four-column photograph above the story, with the caption "Children Pray for Continued Use of Fieldhouse," was a close-up of four children, with many others in the background, looking solemn, innocent, and hungry, hands folded in prayer, their small heads barely above the church pew. The cutline gave the names of the four children—a not unintentional ethnic mix of Polish and Bohemian names—and said that they were among "scores of children attending an all children's mass . . . yesterday to pray that the Back of the Yards Neighborhood Council be permitted the continued use of the Davis Square Park fieldhouse for their free lunch project."

Part of the story identified the Council as "the organization which won the fight last summer for the nation-wide penny milk and hot lunch programs for schoolchildren" when Meegan and Council president Father Edward Plawinski lobbied in Washington and in the state capitol in Springfield. Indeed, there had been a large letter-writing campaign by schoolchildren in the Back of the Yards to elected officials, and Meegan, on a trip to Washington, had enlisted the help of Illinois's senators, Representative

John McCormack of Massachusetts, and others in the effort to save the milk and hot lunch programs.

But most of the story in the *Sun* consisted of the statement read the previous day in the one Lutheran and seven Catholic churches in the Back of the Yards that belonged to the Council—a statement that, either in large part or in its entirety, was almost certainly drafted by Alinsky. In its powerful blend of populist, patriotic, and democratic appeals, it displayed the kind of wickedly effective rhetoric of agitation, reminiscent of John L. Lewis, that left no doubt as to who were the villains and who the heroes:

> Just as our children and brothers and fathers are fighting Fascism all over the world, so must we continue to fight it at home. Yes, my people, we have Fascists at home, too. We have persons in high places who tremble in fear at any prospect of popular rule by the people and democracy in action. . . . We have long heard that attempts would be made to torpedo the greatest example of democracy in the City of Chicago. . . . [T]he sabotage has begun. Joseph Meegan . . . has been ordered transferred from this community. . . . The Council offices have been ordered out of Davis Square Park. This means that hundreds of our children will lack proper nourishment. . . . The Park District and its head have completely disregarded the desires of the people of our neighborhood. . . . We are the people. Our cause is just, and the democratic spirit embodied in the Back of the Yards Neighborhood Council itself will long survive these saboteurs.

Thus did Alinsky succeed in turning a behind-the-scenes power play by the machine forces into a public controversy. Justin McCarthy, assigned to cover the controversy for the *Sun* (he later became press secretary for John L. Lewis), started to spend so much time at the BYNC offices in Davis Square Park, Meegan recalls, that it seemed as though he lived there. During a two-week span, a story by McCarthy ran on the front page of the *Sun* nearly every day, each one reporting a new development in the controversy.

The point man for the machine forces was Robert J. Dunham, Park District board chairman and a perfect target for Alinsky's ridicule. Now he had to explain why both the Council and Meegan were being evicted from Davis Square Park, a task that he performed with a conspicuous absence of skill. The BYNC's activities were interfering with other recreational programs in the neighborhood, Dunham said, and Meegan had to go, too, because "he became more interested in Council activity than with his park duties."

Dunham was a well-known society figure in Chicago, a financier with a Gold Coast address who had become vice president of Armour in 1909. In subsequent years, he became known as the "crown prince" of the Armour empire and was in line to succeed J. Ogden Armour. By 1920, however, Dunham had left his wife to become the frequent companion of Elizabeth Preston Drown, a married San Francisco socialite. The notoriety surrounding their romance was followed by Dunham's resignation from Armour. When he resigned, he reportedly took with him, as a form of severance pay, a large block of stock in a new company with patents on an oil-cracking process. The company, Universal Oil Products, became a big success, and in 1931 Dunham sold his stock for $8 million. Until 1934, Dunham had been known as a loyal Republican, but his friend the Democratic mayor asked him to be the head of the newly consolidated Park District. From then on, he was one of the powers within the Democratic machine.

It was not difficult to portray Dunham as an upper-class, blue-blooded fat cat insensitive or even hostile to the concerns and problems of working-people and the poor. It was a portrait that Alinsky was eager to paint and one that Dunham, in his arrogance, was willing to pose for. When Dunham tried to soften the harshness of his original directive by proposing a sixty-day extension of the use of Davis Square Park until the BYNC could find new facilities, Alinsky arranged to have one of the Council's priests quoted as saying: "Sixty-day reprieve? What does Dunham think we are, criminals? You don't give kids sixty-day reprieves on their feeding." When Dunham refused to back down, another Council leader proclaimed that the battle had become a "clear case of bankers versus babies."

Invective was not the only means of discrediting Dunham. Alinsky and the Council's leaders, and Justin McCarthy, researched the use of other Chicago parks to demonstrate that Meegan and the Council were being singled out for special attention. Dunham, for instance, had made the charge that the BYNC was the "only welfare agency in the city expecting such use of the park facilities." The BYNC countered that the private Infant Welfare Society was operating nearly forty centers in the parks. And McCarthy rebutted Dunham's contention that many neighborhood residents were unable to use Davis Square because of the Council's activities.

Alinsky's full-court press included letters from neighborhood children to Mayor Kelly's office, and even heartrending letters from servicemen—or press interviews with Catholic nuns, local businessmen, and prospective servicemen. "I am soon to be inducted in the Army," a man from the Back of the Yards told a *Sun* reporter. "I told Mr. Meegan I was leaving my children in his hands. Now he is gone, and so are the children's lunches.

Their mother works in the stockyards, but she will have to give up her job now to take care of the children at noon. We won't have our kids running the streets and eating pop and candy bars at the noon hour."

It took only four days after the front-page *Sun* article for Alinsky's retaliatory campaign to triumph. On January 7, a meeting with Mayor Kelly was arranged—probably by Bishop Sheil—for Alinsky and Father Plawinski. Kelly, it was said in Chicago, was interested not only in power but also in respectability, and it wasn't easy to predict when the latter might prevail over the former; neither was it inconceivable that the two might, at times, be compatible. Thus, Alinsky could have framed an argument to Kelly that appealed to both his pragmatic and his public-spirited interests—asking for support of the BYNC because under Dunham's attack the machine was antagonizing people in its own political base and appearing to bully children and clergy.

Whether or not Kelly fully accepted that argument, he soon announced that the Park District order would be rescinded. Then, in the presence of *Sun* reporter McCarthy, he phoned Dunham to tell him of his decision. The front-page headline in the *Sun* the next morning blared the sweet news: "Back of the Yards Council Wins Battle to Serve Free Lunches, Milk in Park."

Indeed, it seemed like a great victory for Alinsky. He wrote excitedly to Morris Ploscowe, his friend in New York: "The Back of the Yards Neighborhood Council has been front-page news for a week running and the end of the scrap was that the Kelly machine publicly backed down for the first time in its history. I am pleased as punch to report that it was the little Back of the Yards Council which forced him to do so." It also seemed like a great victory for the people in the neighborhood, who could see immediate results from their collective action. A homecoming celebration was quickly planned around the first lunch to be served when the program was resumed at Davis Square Park.

But what about Meegan? The "Meegan issue" was obscured in these press reports heralding the BYNC victory. After Alinsky and Plawinski's meeting with Mayor Kelly, Meegan announced in a formal statement that he had applied for a sixty-day leave of absence from his Park District job, during which he would continue to work with the BYNC. He went on to say a number of conciliatory things—that the fight had never been personal, that his "heart has always been with the constructive work of the Chicago Park District and with the Back of the Yards Neighborhood Council." Now that the Council's lunch and milk programs had been allowed to stay in Davis Square, the implication seemed to be that Meegan could, too. The leave of absence was intended as a face-saving device; after the whole controversy faded from public view, Meegan would resume his paid job at Davis Square. That was the scenario that evolved out of the meeting with Kelly.

From the start, it had never been clear how strongly Kelly himself felt about the move to oust Meegan and the Council. But clearly, others did, including Dunham, which was why Alinsky's big victory was short-lived. Only a week later, the Park District announced that Meegan's request for a leave of absence had been denied. Dunham, as chairman of the three-member civil service board that denied his request, also announced that if Meegan did not report to his new job at Ogden Park on the following Monday, he would be "removed from the payroll." When a reporter asked Kelly about assurances that he had given Alinsky and Plawinski regarding Meegan's leave of absence, the mayor replied with studied innocence that he had not imagined then he would have any trouble arranging it. Since the Park District was independent of the mayor only by statute and not in the way things really worked in Chicago, this answer was not taken seriously.

The day of reckoning had arrived. If Meegan took the new park job, his work with the BYNC would become a part-time, weekend affair. As far as Alinsky and the other BYNC leaders were concerned, this was unacceptable.

On the weekend of January 15, Alinsky and Joe and Helen Meegan got together. In spite of the tension between them and their differences in background and style, Joe and Saul were fond of each other, as were Helen and Saul's wife, Helene. The four of them occasionally dined together. Saul and Joe used to buy clothes together—at Finchley's on Jackson Boulevard, especially during winter sales, when both bought tweedy, collegiate coats. They had been through a lot and had enjoyed the fun and recognition of building the BYNC. But they knew that they had come to a crossroads. Now, on a dark, unusually rainy winter night, Alinsky told Meegan that he should quit working for the Park District, that the future of the BYNC depended on it: they had both put in too much to see the Council crippled or possibly go under, and there was no guarantee that Meegan would be free of future harassment from Dunham and the machine crowd. The most difficult issue was financial; could Meegan earn enough from the BYNC to support his family? The original summer festival, the Jungle Jamboree, had been expanded into a large fund-raising success, and there was also some revenue from the Community Fund and from local businessmen. Nonetheless, Meegan would be taking a risk. Helen Meegan thought it was a big risk, as she sat next to Alinsky in the front seat of his leaky Ford convertible. As the rain poured down, Helen Meegan started to cry. How is Joe going to support a wife and two children now? she asked Alinsky. "Don't worry, it'll be okay," Alinsky replied, perhaps with no more confidence about the outcome than she had.

With Meegan's resignation, Alinsky took on a more public role in the continuing controversy. Up to this point, he had stayed behind the scenes, out of public view, except when the BYNC had announced the formation of a strategy committee with Alinsky as chairman. (The composition of the six-man committee also served as a rejoinder to a statement Mayor Kelly made about not wanting to become involved in a "religious controversy"— implying that the dispute involved only a few Catholic parishes that wanted to have special, privileged use of a public park. The BYNC announced—and emphasized—that the committee was composed of a Lutheran minister, a representative of the CIO, a Jewish social worker [Alinsky], as well as three Catholic priests.)

Now Alinsky publicly leveled a sarcastic blast at Dunham. "The people of the stockyards aren't angry with Dunham," he started, warming up. "They could no more be angry with him than they could with one of our favorite childhood characters—Winnie the Pooh, who was 'just a bear with very little brain indeed.' " A few days later, when the BYNC announced that it was moving all of its activities, including its lunch and milk programs, out of Davis Square Park into temporary facilities at Holy Cross Church, the strategy committee released a scathing attack on both Dunham and Kelly. (By now, of course, the committee was synonymous with Alinsky.) The BYNC was moving out of Davis Square Park because it was a waste of time to continue to work with "Double Talk Dunham," it reported. As for the supposed agreements with Mayor Kelly that had collapsed:

> At no time was there the slightest insinuation that these agreements were conditional upon Dunham's approval or that Dunham was not completely obedient to the mayor. . . . Everybody knows that Kelly can make Dunham observe his wishes. This Edgar Bergen Kelly–Charlie McCarthy Dunham act has become an old story. . . . As for Dunham, he is now clearly understood by the people of Chicago. He is a bull-headed and bigoted dictator whose only claim to fame is his consummate stupidity.

As if that were not enough, Alinsky also sniped at "Dunham's snoopers and Gestapo agents" who had been hanging out at Davis Square trying to dig up information to discredit Meegan and the BYNC.

Alinsky was enraged because of the double-cross that he had been dealt by Kelly, but also because he had lost. He did not like to lose; nor did his pride allow for having his nose rubbed in the dirt. He was not willing to see the battle end without striking back, without getting in the last licks.

So his next ploy was to have the BYNC announce it was sending a letter of protest to President Roosevelt. While this may have sounded farfetched, it was a way to embarrass Kelly and keep the controversy going. In fact, news coverage of the letter appeared in still another front-page story in the *Sun*. "We, the people who are members of the Back of the Yards Neighborhood Council, . . . respectfully petition you, our President and commander in chief. . . . During the last few weeks the highly dictatorial and faithless conduct of two public officials of Chicago, namely, Robert J. Dunham . . . and Mayor Edward J. Kelly, has brought about a condition that we believe should be called to your attention." A BYNC spokesman was quoted as saying, "We thought that the mayor, who was once one of our own people and who was born and reared in the Archer Road district, would keep his word and force his political subordinate . . . to stop fighting our people."

The ploy of sending a letter to Roosevelt and of publicizing it may have looked transparent and contrived. But in the bare-knuckles world of Chicago politics, a personal attack on a political opponent was a provocation that demanded retaliation. In this instance, a special "citizens' committee," made up of civic and business figures friendly to the Kelly machine, announced it was going to investigate the activities of the Back of the Yards Neighborhood Council during the time it had been housed in facilities at Davis Square Park. That prompted one of the priests in the Back of the Yards to crack, with Alinsky-like sarcasm: "Expecting a fair investigation from the citizens' committee is like expecting Hitler to keep an open mind toward Czechoslovakia or Poland." But Dunham greeted the citizens' committee with undisguised enthusiasm. He "hoped the investigation would smoke out some vital facts concerning the activities of the Back of the Yards Neighborhood Council . . . which heretofore have been steadfastly concealed, . . . including astonishing disclosures on the role of Saul Alinsky and the astounding growth of the organizations he has sponsored."

These cryptic remarks were followed by stories in the Chicago *Tribune* that were intended to expose Alinsky as a mysterious and, therefore, sinister behind-the-scenes force, and to suggest by inference and innuendo that the BYNC was making money from its lunch and milk programs. The *Tribune* had remained virtually silent early in January, its virtual blackout of Alinsky's efforts to flush out Dunham and Kelly being its way of siding

with the machine. Now that the machine was launching a public counterattack, it was ready to provide generous coverage. The attack on Alinsky
was a good old-fashioned hatchet job, run under the headline "Reputed
Head Refuses to Discuss Finances." The story characterized Alinsky as the

> man behind the scenes in the yard council setup . . . [who] is listed
> in council records as its technical consultant and strategy committee
> chairman. Alinsky, a 35 year old promoter, within a brief time has set
> himself up in a Michigan av. suite of offices from which he reputedly
> directs . . . council maneuvers. . . . [He] has set up organizations
> similar to the council [in other cities] thru his executive directorship
> of the Industrial Areas Foundation, another little publicized but well
> subsidized product of his promoting ability. Alinsky has a University
> of Chicago education and calls himself a criminologist. When ques-
> tioned yesterday regarding finances of his organizations he refused
> information, parrying with, "What's the pitch, bud?"

No sooner had the *Tribune* article appeared than Alinsky and Justin
McCarthy worked on a response that ran two days later in the *Sun*. The
only part of the *Tribune* article that probably rankled Alinsky was the
suggestion that he and his work were not widely known. In rebuttal, part
of the *Sun* headline read: "Noted Sociologist Is 'Man Behind the Scenes';
Foundation Has Been Widely Praised," and the accompanying story discussed the laudatory press accounts of Alinsky's work and the prominent
members of Alinsky's board of directors.

Alinsky was thoroughly enjoying both the combat with the machine
and the attention he was receiving. He wrote to his friend Sidney Hyman,
who was away in the Army, to bring him up to date on what had been
happening. "Mr. Dunham decided that there was very little room in this
metropolis for a large and ever growing people's organization which was
not bound to any political machine. After a few preliminary skirmishes,
war was declared on both sides." He told Hyman about the *Tribune*'s
attack on him and the ensuing notoriety: "For the next few weeks, when
people would call me, the opening statement would be, 'What's the pitch,
bud?' "

The *Tribune* also tried to make a case that the BYNC was playing fast
and loose with thousands of dollars of state and federal aid for its milk and
lunch programs. Less than a year earlier, in the summer of 1943, the BYNC
had sponsored free milk and hot lunch programs for only seven neighborhood schools, it reported. Then, when a change in federal policy substituted cash subsidies for the free surplus foods that the Department of

Agriculture had been supplying—a temporary arrangement, as budget-cutting and anti-New Deal forces in Congress were bent on ending the aid programs—at this point "Saul Alinsky got busy. Organizing an impressive delegation, he led it to Washington not once but several times, for a campaign that finally resulted in the federal cash subsidies for low cost milk and hot lunch programs for school children being retained in the department of agriculture's 1943–44 budget. Fifty million dollars was appropriated, of which $2,040,000 was allocated to Illinois." In its zeal the *Tribune*'s account ludicrously exaggerated Alinsky's role: in actual fact, many others from around the country were pressing for federal aid, and among the BYNC delegation that went to lobby in Washington, Meegan and Plawinski did much of the important legwork.

The *Tribune* also reported that Alinsky "led his lobbyists to Springfield" and successfully pressured the state legislature to provide supplemental state aid. With federal and state subsidies disbursed on a per-pupil basis, a sizable cash kitty was now in place, and suddenly the BYNC started to recruit additional schools to participate in the milk and lunch programs, the *Tribune* reported. Within a matter of months, the number of schools had grown to forty-four, including many west and south of the Back of the Yards. The BYNC sponsorship had grown so large that its claim for federal and state reimbursement for one month, January 1943, was more than $9,000.

The *Tribune* report did not charge that the BYNC had stolen money or padded its claims for reimbursement with phantom schoolchildren, but merely tried to plant the idea. No evidence was ever produced to substantiate these innuendos, and it was not long before the tables were turned, when another Chicago paper, the *Daily News,* reported that the Democratic machine had been using the school milk program as a source of political kickbacks. This revelation also showed why it was not merely the political independence of the BYNC that had attracted the wrath of Democratic leaders. The BYNC's school program was cutting into an important subterranean source of funding for the machine. The BYNC had contracted directly with dairies for milk, usually paying three to three and a half cents per half-pint. With a federal subsidy of two cents per half-pint and a state subsidy of an additional penny, the BYNC was able to provide milk free to many of the parish schools; in some instances, children paid a penny every other day to make up the amount not covered by the subsidies—that is, when the cost from the dairy was three and a half cents instead of only three. Chicago's Board of Education, however, had slightly different contracts with dairies, which gave the dairies four cents for each half-pint, with the children paying an additional penny to supplement the three-cent federal-state subsidy. The so-called penny milk in Chicago was, in practice, a penny-per-half-pint subsidy for the machine, for the four cents that the Board of Education paid was an intentionally inflated price: there was a clear understanding among the dairies doing business with the city of Chicago, the *Daily News* reported, that a substantial portion of the inflated cost, which may have added up to as much as $250,000 a year, was to be "contributed" to the Kelly political machine—whose treasurer at the time was none other than Robert J. Dunham.

Although the *Daily News* exposé was well researched and almost certainly true, bringing formal charges and winning convictions regarding alleged political kickbacks was another matter entirely. Nonetheless, the news stories about milk-money kickbacks were revelations that Kelly and Dunham could do without. Dunham also made two public-relations mistakes. He ordered the eviction of the Infant Welfare Society offices from the public parks, and he publicly attacked Bishop Sheil's integrity. The ouster of the Infant Welfare Society was Dunham's clumsy, self-defeating attempt to show that he was being evenhanded in ridding the parks of private organizations. The reaction to Dunham's demonstration of "even-handedness" was one of incredulity and angry criticism. As for Dunham's other blunder, he announced that Bishop Sheil had broken his word that he would work privately to persuade the BYNC to leave Davis Square Park. "Normally, I would not dignify such patently absurd remarks by stooping to answer them," the well-loved bishop replied. "In this instance, however, my personal wishes must stand aside. As a bishop of the Roman Catholic Church it is my duty to reply to any and all aspersions upon my office, no matter what the source of the outrage." He went on to castigate Dunham and to defend the integrity of the BYNC and its leaders.

There was still the matter of the citizens' committee investigation. Dunham had raised expectations in his public statements that the investigation would turn up wrongdoing, and a field audit by state officials had now been promised. Whether an honest audit was possible or likely, however, was an open question. Moreover, the Civic Federation, another Chicago group allied with the Kelly machine, suddenly came forward with an unsolicited "report" that the BYNC should have been evicted from Davis Square Park and that Meegan had spent much time working on private (that is, BYNC) affairs while on the public payroll.

Alinsky needed to find allies for the BYNC; otherwise it would become politically isolated and increasingly vulnerable. In Lewis's fight with Roosevelt in 1940, Alinsky had seen from a front-row seat how an outcome is determined not merely by the two contestants themselves but by the relative strength of the alliances around each. What support did the

BYNC have? The Chicago *Sun*'s support, of course, had been extremely important, and Alinsky could continue to count on it. The *Sun,* however, was not the city's most important paper. And Bishop Sheil's support was by no means decisive: he could not deliver the archdiocese, for elements within the ethnic and geographic factions of the archdiocese had their own relationships and agendas with the Kelly machine. Where could Alinsky and the BYNC turn for additional support?

It was with a roll of the dice that Alinsky and the BYNC leaders decided to schedule a special Little People's Congress. Invitations were sent to hundreds of welfare, civic, labor, athletic, religious, nationality, and similar groups all over the city. First scheduled for March 13 and then postponed until March 27, it would be a large rally, a show of popular support for the embattled BYNC. The stated purpose was "to give the common man an opportunity to voice his opinion about the kind of tactics that Robert J. Dunham [has employed]. . . . From time to time dictators are spawned in a democracy. The common folks call them big shots," the BYNC statement read. "These arrogant 'big shots' contemptuously refer to the common people as the 'little people.' They forget that it always has been, and always will be, the 'little people' who keep the fires of democracy burning. . . . Under Fascism people are permitted only a single, unqualified loyalty to the totalitarian state," not unlike the humble obeisance demanded by the Chicago machine, the statement suggested.

It was by no means certain that Alinsky and Meegan could pull a rally off. In Chicago, there were not all that many important and respectable people who would be eager to travel to the Back of the Yards, stand up in the Holy Cross social center at Forty-fifth and South Wood streets, and say for all the city to hear: "Yes, Mayor Ed Kelly and his rich, fat sidekick the arrogant Robert J. Dunham are behaving like Fascists." Fortunately, perhaps, for Alinsky, the Little People's Congress never took place, because ten days before the scheduled event, a meeting was arranged between Dunham and the BYNC leaders at Bishop Sheil's office at the Catholic Youth Organization headquarters on East Congress Street.

Memories are hazy as to who made the first move to call a truce, but both sides were ready. Still, the meeting was by no means a perfunctory one. The wording of the truce was important, especially to Alinsky, not merely for the sake of his ego but for the credibility of the BYNC. He wanted words that would suggest, at a minimum, that the BYNC had held its own against Kelly and Dunham, even words that he could use to claim victory.

Reporters waited for three hours while the bishop mediated the negotiations. When the parties emerged, Dunham read a statement: "The controversy between the Park District and the Back of the Yards Neighborhood Council is deeply regrettable. The purposes of the Back of the Yards Neighborhood Council are laudable. We recognize that community organizations, formed by voluntary act of groups of people, perform a valuable function in the community. The Park District will welcome the public use by the Council and its members of Davis Square Park and field house and all other park property."

Within hours, the banner headline in the early edition of the Chicago *Sun* trumpeted a dramatic victory for Alinsky and the BYNC: "DUNHAM GIVES IN TO YARDS," and then: "Head of Parks Calls on Sheil," "Offers Full Use of Facilities to Neighborhood Council." In fact, however, this was only a partial victory, rather than the total triumph claimed by the *Sun.* For one thing, Dunham had earlier succeeded in forcing Meegan to quit his job rather than accept a transfer out of the neighborhood. Moreover, although Dunham announced that the BYNC could use Davis Square facilities, the BYNC made it clear in its own conciliatory statement that it was going to remain in its own new headquarters in a storefront at Forty-sixth and Ashland. Nonetheless, *Sun* reporter Justin McCarthy characterized Dunham's statement as "no less" than what both Bishop Sheil and the BYNC had come to expect, a public apology and retraction of Dunham's charges. "Thus, as in all previous battles," the article concluded in the exuberant, partisan style of Chicago journalism, "the 'little people' of the stockyards district, through their own organization, the Back of the Yards Neighborhood Council, have won again."

Saul Alinsky had every reason to be ecstatic—and he was, Joe and Helen Meegan remember. His contempt for Dunham was genuine, and therefore he enjoyed the public spectacle, which he had largely choreographed, of the blue blood Dunham, hat in hand, coming respectfully to Sheil's office to settle a dispute with the leaders of the Back of the Yards immigrants. He also enjoyed the little accident that befell Dunham when he was leaving Sheil's office after the statements had been read: he slipped and fell down a flight of stairs, breaking his glasses and injuring his knee. A small crowd gathered, and when a reporter asked how Dunham had fallen, Alinsky muttered loud enough for most to hear: "Maybe the bishop pushed him."

That night, Saul and Helene Alinsky and Joe and Helen Meegan went out to celebrate. Alinsky could have expected that McCarthy would write the kind of "victory" story he wanted, although the glorious 22-point headline was a surprise bonus. The headline and story in the early edition of the *Sun* made the celebration at the Piccadilly in Hyde Park especially joyous. It must have felt like a perfect night to Alinsky—until the four of them left the Piccadilly and crossed the street to pick up a *Trib* at the corner newsstand.

Alinsky flipped through several pages until he saw the headline. "USE PARKS AS DO OTHERS: DUNHAM TO YARDS GROUP." Anger quickly rose to fury as Alinsky read the *Trib*'s report, especially: "Later Mr. Dunham, saying that a misinterpretation had been placed upon his first statement in a story printed in a morning newspaper [a reference to the *Sun* story], made a second statement to the press." Dunham's second statement said in part: "Nothing that I have said can be interpreted as an apology by myself or the members of the park board for our action in this controversy. We are not retreating one step from the position we originally took—namely, that the Back of the Yards council was usurping rights in Davis Square park and must cease using the park as its headquarters for its private functions."

Alinsky's instinctive reaction was that Dunham's second statement was a double-cross. After all, both sides had agreed on the wording of the statement read at Bishop Sheil's—and it was simply too bad for Dunham that the *Sun* had run the kind of story it had. From Dunham's perspective, however, that his vaguely worded platitudes of goodwill should wind up as an admission of defeat on the front page of the *Sun* was something he was not going to let pass.

After Alinsky cooled down, he realized that there was no point in reopening the battle with Dunham. Instead, the BYNC replied eventually that both Dunham and the BYNC's strategy committee had "given their word of honor" after the statements at Bishop Sheil's office that they would make no further remarks about the controversy. Dunham had now broken his word, but the strategy committee would not; in fact, the committee was disbanded, and as far as the BYNC was concerned, the controversy was over.

THE BATTLE with Dunham and the Kelly machine was a milestone for the Back of the Yards Neighborhood Council. It had compelled the BYNC to become a real organization. Indeed, it could be argued that the organizing process that Alinsky had begun in the winter of 1939 was now finally completed five years later. The Kelly machine had forced the BYNC to stand on its own two legs—and to discover that it had two legs to stand on.

The mythology about Alinsky only grew. When Agnes Meyer wrote in the Washington *Post* that "the Council has already clashed with the powerful packing industries and the no less powerful Kelly-Nash machine and defeated both of them," she was writing another paean to Alinsky, as other journalists had before her. There was, of course, much to praise, and Alinsky had become adept at encouraging such praise, not only by projecting his considerable charm and intellectual substance but also by parlaying one good news story into another. The stories continued to spread that Saul Alinsky was a uniquely talented, even heroic figure and that his methods might change the fabric of American democracy.

These glowing accounts of Alinsky and his work in the Back of the Yards were, however, one-dimensional. For the outcomes of the morality plays that Alinsky had fashioned were far from conclusive. As Alinsky was learning firsthand, the perception of reality and reality itself were often indistinguishable, the line between fact and fiction faint and ragged. Yet Saul Alinsky was not about to discourage anybody from perceiving him as a fearless dragon slayer who never lost a battle. Indeed, his next project helped to encourage just such an image.

13

Reveille for Radicals!

James Bryant Conant, the brilliant forty-year-old chairman of Harvard's Chemistry Department, already well known for his studies on chlorophyll and hemoglobin, was elected president of Harvard in 1933. From this prestigious platform, Conant played an important role in the national debates on both the growing international crisis and domestic issues. By 1940 and early 1941, he had become an outspoken, controversial interventionist, among the first to call for all-out aid to England, and an early advocate for universal conscription. But Conant was especially concerned with America's domestic problems, for he saw fundamental inequities in its social and economic arrangements.

In an article in 1940 in *The Atlantic Monthly,* "Education for a Classless Society," Conant warned that a dangerous elitism had infected American democracy, that a basic principle of the Republic—that inheritance shall not determine the opportunity for education and advancement—had been eroded. "The privilege of higher education" was an insidiously influential phrase, he wrote. "It would be a hardy soul indeed who would be willing to say in public that there should be one type of education for the rich, another for the poor." Yet that is what had happened. It was a practice Conant wanted to challenge by argumentation, public exposure, and example. At Harvard, he pushed for scholarships that would open the door of opportunity to deserving students.

Conant's article on education and democracy attracted much attention, and so did another one three years later, in the spring of 1943. The provocative intent of this second piece was set forth in its title: "Wanted: American Radicals." Conant was concerned now with the direction that American society would take in the postwar period. He thought that a stratified, socially immobile American society could become a powder keg when millions of men returned to civilian life, and worried that the war had merely postponed the necessity of coming to grips with such "difficult questions as the relation of management and labor, and the control and ownership of the tools of production." Unless speedy progress could be made on these kinds of fundamental questions—questions of social and economic justice—then Conant foresaw the possibility of rancorous upheaval, even a civil war within a decade after the end of the war.

It was highly unlikely, Conant believed, that effective ideas and leadership would come from liberal or conservative intellectuals, both of whom had "nearly disappeared from view." Neither was he optimistic—indeed, he was troubled—about the country's finding the right course if the debate was merely a choice between two extreme alternatives. For Conant, these two extremes were being pushed by the "chief vocal groups now discussing the American future—whom I shall designate 'American' reactionaries and 'European' radicals." Conant's American reactionaries, most easily personified by American businessmen, "promise to restore the American system of free enterprise and with it American prosperity" if government will, after the war is over, "move out and leave us alone." Conant's European radicals, whose predecessors were "found on the lists of the Fabian Society" and whose approach was now to be seen in Russia, offered a vision of communal ownership and police supervision. It was "the lack of a third choice" that Conant aimed to correct. He wanted to stimulate "a new group of thinkers and speakers [to] arise: a group of modern radicals in the American tradition who will . . . contribute elements which are lacking in the present picture."

The new American radical could trace his lineage to "the men who abolished primogeniture at the founding of the Republic," he suggested, and "who with zest destroyed the Bank of the United States in the time of Andrew Jackson." He "will be a fanatic believer in equality," indeed this "is the kernel of his radical philosophy," Conant continued—by which he meant equality of opportunity, not equality of rewards. But to preserve this notion of equality, the size of the rewards—that is, of accumulated wealth—should be limited, for radicals would favor effective inheritance taxes and the confiscation (by constitutional methods) of all property once a generation, Conant wrote enthusiastically.

Conant emphasized that there was a strong pragmatic spirit in the radical tradition, too. "Being rooted in the American soil [the radical] will be endowed with a considerable amount of common sense and a certain willingness to apply to the changes which he effects the typical American question, 'Does it work?' " Like Jefferson, he "will compromise his objections to governmental action from time to time. He will be ready to invoke even the Federal government in the interests of maintaining real freedom among the great masses of the population but . . . never cease to hope that such remedies may be only passing sins."

Conant knew that much of the current leadership of both capital and labor would feel threatened by the new American radicals. To what extent radicals could reinvigorate and democratize American society, Conant was not sure, but he thought that their "individual contrariness" was much needed. The radical's spirit and love of battle reminded Conant of an old New England story about a man who was stopped by a friend on his way to the town meeting. "Don't you know, Ed," said the friend, "there ain't no use in going to that there meeting? Old Doc Barnes and his crowd control enough votes to carry everything they want and more, too. You can't make any headway agin 'em." "That's all right," Ed replied, "but I can worry 'em some."

"THE DESCRIPTION and the table of contents of *Reveille for Radicals* is just what I wanted," said the director of the University of Chicago Press to Saul Alinsky. A year after Conant's second article appeared, Alinsky had begun to write a book. It seems very likely that Conant's article gave him the idea for the title and framework of his book, if not the idea of writing one. (Although he never met Conant, Alinsky added his name to a list of friends and journalists to whom the press sent complimentary copies when the book came out.) Alinsky, however, never acknowledged Conant's influence. This was not surprising—he was not inclined to share the credit for a good idea. There were two predictable consequences to this tendency: for some people he seemed ungracious and ungrateful, while a good many more considered him the originator of good ideas. It was a trade-off that Alinsky never lost sleep over.

Alinsky had been interested in writing a book based on his experiences in the Back of the Yards long before Conant's article appeared. He had kept a journal for several years—a three-ring loose-leaf collection of reminiscences, observations, and anecdotes about his earlier prison work, about his community organizing experiences, and about human nature as it was revealed in the course of daily encounters. But if there was any one person who encouraged Alinsky to go beyond thinking about writing a book and actually doing it, that person was most likely Jacques

Maritain, whom Alinsky repaid by granting him the book's foreign rights.

This French Thomist philosopher was a man of international stature who had written and lectured both in Europe and in the United States. He had lectured for a time at the University of Chicago, where he and Alinsky may have been introduced by Professor John U. Nef, George Shuster, or perhaps by Bishop Sheil. Maritain was a man of exceptional compassion as well as great intellect. In the late 1930s, several years before he became French ambassador to the Vatican, he had suggested that as an appropriately dramatic display of mercy, the Pope ought to ride into Berlin on a mule and plead with Hitler on behalf of the Jews. Maritain was, perhaps, as much a democrat as he was a Catholic and a philosopher. He was deeply concerned with the connection between morality and politics. He had become excited about Alinsky's work, about the promise it offered as a possible democratic response to the despair that had swept across Europe. He saw the Back of the Yards as a microcosm, where for generations ethnic hatreds and rivalries had mocked Christian teaching, but where now there was a powerful hope for both a renewed spirituality and democratic citizenship. Alinsky had demonstrated, Maritain thought, that "starting with selfish interests, [people can] succeed in giving rise to the sense of solidarity and finally to an unselfish devotion to the common task. . . . It becomes obvious that in the very bosom of the humblest, most material needs of a community of men, an internal moral awakening is linked with the awakening to the elementary requirements of true political life."

Beginning with Alinsky's earliest discussions with the University of Chicago Press in the spring of 1944, it took him about a year to write *Reveille for Radicals*. Perhaps Alinsky's wife, Helene, read the work as it progressed, but not even his closest friends ever saw the manuscript. Walter Johnson, a good friend and history professor at the University of Chicago, remembers Alinsky being secretive about the progress of the book, partly because "he loved to be secretive about certain things"—it added a touch of mystery—and partly because "he wanted to write his own book and didn't want anybody to be a critic." As the people at the press also discovered, Alinsky was not an author in search of an editor.

Reveille for Radicals is a forceful, even powerful, and yet uneven book. Much of it was written as a polemic, and Alinsky was at his best when on the attack, depicting villains and villainous ideas with broad, true strokes. When he shifted to a fine pen for detail and analysis, however, his touch became less sure. The prose was stylistically inconsistent, an unpredictable mix of eloquence and rhetorical excess, and the varied tone produced a cacophony of compassion, contempt, optimism, and anger. Alinsky was bluntly honest but sometimes contradictory and confusing.

Actually, *Reveille for Radicals* was more nearly two separate books, rather than the two parts into which Alinsky divided it. And that was part of the problem. If Alinsky had confined himself to a straightforward account of how he had organized the Back of the Yards Neighborhood Council, and why such democratic experiments can make a difference in the lives of people, he would have had a good, solid book. But Saul Alinsky was after much more than a good, solid book. He wanted to write a historically significant book, one that Maritain would later call "epoch-making," one that flowed with the same blood and passion as Tom Paine's *Common Sense.* (The book's epigraph came from Paine: "Let them call me rebel and welcome, I feel no concern from it; but I should suffer the misery of devils, were I to make a whore of my soul.")

Part One of *Reveille for Radicals,* only seventy-four pages, sounds like Alinsky's response to Conant's call for a new generation of American radicals. What is a radical? Alinsky asks, and answers by quoting from Jefferson's letter to Henry Lee in 1824, that "men by their constitution are naturally divided into two parties: Those who fear and distrust the people, and wish to draw all powers from them into the hands of the higher classes . . . [and] [t]hose who identify themselves with the people, have confidence in them, cherish and consider them as the most honest and safe, although not the most wise depository of the public interests." Indeed, in tone and style, Alinsky's celebration of radicals here was reminiscent of Sandburg's epic "The People, Yes." American radicals were present at all the glorious battles for freedom and justice—and Alinsky ticks them off:

> They were with Patrick Henry in the Virginia Hall of Burgesses; they were with Sam Adams in Boston; they were with that peer of all American Radicals, Tom Paine, from the distribution of *Common Sense* through those dark days of the American Revolution. . . . They were in the shadows of the Underground Railroad, and they openly rode in the bright sunlight with John Brown to Harpers Ferry. . . . They were in the vanguard of the Populist Party leading the western rebellion against eastern conservativism. They built the American labor movement . . . and finally spearheaded the fateful drive that culminated in the Congress of Industrial Organizations.

Radicals were not to be confused with liberals, who did not have the passion, the unfettered commitment to the underdog and downtrodden. "Liberals like people with their head" was the kindest thing Alinsky could

say about them. "Radicals like people with both their head and their
heart." Or:

> Liberals give and take oral arguments; the Radicals give and take the
> hard, dirty, bitter way of life. Liberals frequently achieve high places
> of respectability ranging from the Supreme Court to Congress; the
> names of Radicals are rarely inscribed in marble but burn eternally
> in the hearts of man. . . . Liberals play the game of life with white and
> occasionally red chips; with the Radical it's only the blue chips, and
> all the chips are always down. . . . Since there are always at least two
> sides to every question and all justice on one side involves a certain
> degree of injustice to the other side, Liberals are hesitant to act. Their
> opinions are studded with "but on the other hand." Caught on the
> horns of this dilemma they are paralyzed into immobility. They
> become utterly incapable of action. They discuss and discuss and end
> in disgust.

The attack on liberals was a good example of the "hard-boiled" rhetoric that Christopher Lasch calls typical of radical discourse of the 1930s,
1940s, and 1950s, when the outcome of debates depended to a "considerable
degree on the success with which each side was able to depict the other
as sentimental, timid, effeminate and 'utopian.' " In Alinsky's case, little
effort was needed to cultivate this style, for it came easily as an extension
of his personality.

That liberals and radicals often shared goals was of little consequence
if liberals were incapable of inspiring action and unwilling to compromise
their self-imposed ethical standards, Alinsky suggested contemptuously:
"The Radical . . . will realize that in the initial stages of organization he
must deal with the qualities of ambition and self-interest as realities. Only
a fool would step into a community dominated by materialistic standards
and self-interest and begin to preach ideals."

In Alinsky's view, reason was to the liberal what power was to the
radical. He did not develop this argument in *Reveille for Radicals,* yet it
was central to Alinsky's notion of how a more just social order could be
achieved.

> [Liberals] fail to recognize that only through the achievement and
> constructive use of power can people better themselves. They talk
> glibly of a people lifting themselves by their own bootstraps but fail
> to realize that nothing can be lifted or moved except through power.
> The fear of popular use of power is reflected in what has become the

motto of Liberals, "We agree with your objectives but not with your tactics." . . . [Throughout American history] every issue involving power and its use has always carried in its wake the Liberal backwash of agreeing with the objective but disagreeing with the tactics.

The values and priorities of Alinsky's American radical were similar to Conant's. American radicals, Alinsky said, placed human rights above property rights, favored inheritance laws that would destroy the present caste system, and recognized that free, universal public education was a cornerstone of democracy. Alinsky's radical, like Conant's, was also ambivalent about the role of government, particularly federal, power. "The Radical . . . knows that ever since the Tories attacked the Continental Congress as an invasion of local rights, 'local rights' have been the star-spangled Trojan Horse of Tory reaction. It is one of the reasons that the American Radical frequently shifts his position on this issue."

Alinsky's political analysis and vision picks up where Conant's left off. Conant saw the implicit ideology of the American radical tradition as a third choice, interposed between a European-flavored Marxism and American laissez-faire reaction. While calling provocatively for new, radical leadership, he placed his American "radicals" in the middle. He envisioned a new clash of ideas, a new intellectual struggle, but he did not address the issue of whether new, radical political action would require a new political form. In *Reveille for Radicals,* however, Alinsky was ready to make a clarion call for a new political form, for what he called "People's Organizations," which would offer an alternative to "both monopolistic capitalism and organized labor."

Like Conant, Alinsky tried to position his radical alternative as a third choice between industry and—most originally—organized labor. Many "Radicals are convinced that the current of organized industry leads to perdition, and they have little doubt but the current of organized labor flows to the promised land," he wrote. "If the facts should indicate that both of these currents are actually running in the same direction, then our Radicals may truly find themselves in danger of foundering. Is the faith of the Radicals justified?" Alinsky's answer was an only slightly qualified "No."

As the bright promise of the CIO's glory years began to fade by the close of the 1930s, so, too, had Alinsky's expectation that the labor movement represented the cutting edge of a new, democratic force. The conservative AF of L, after having been nearly pushed off the political map by the upstart CIO in the mid-1930s, had made a strong comeback. Oh, Alinsky still identified with the progressive spirit of a few of the CIO unions, such as the Packinghouse Workers, Auto Workers, and Electrical Workers, but these were the exceptions. By 1945 in *Reveille for Radicals,* he was almost ready to conclude that, taken as a whole, the leadership of the labor movement—cautious, unimaginative, and interested most of all in its own preservation and prosperity—had taken it so far down the wrong track that nobody, including radicals, had the energy and strength to reverse the direction. Part One of *Reveille for Radicals* is replete with Alinsky's illustrations of the greed, selfishness, stupidity, and bigoted practices of organized labor. These were largely familiar criticisms (except for the attack on racial discrimination), but more familiarly delivered by conservative, anti-union propagandists, not by someone closely identified with the Packinghouse Workers, still viewed as a left-wing union.

Looking beyond the labor movement's old, fiery slogans, which he felt no longer had much to do with reality, Alinsky saw that "the organized labor movement *as it is constituted today* is as much of a concomitant of a capitalist economy as is capital. Organized labor is predicated upon the basic premise of collective bargaining between employers and employees. This premise can obtain only from an employer-employee type of society. If the labor movement is to maintain its own identity and security, it must of necessity protect that kind of society." Radicals, on the other hand, "want to advance from the jungle of laissez-faire capitalism to a world worthy of the name of human civilization. They hope for a future where the means of economic production will be owned by all of the people instead of just a comparative handful. They feel that this minority control of production facilities is injurious to the large masses of people not only because of economic monopolies but because the political power inherent in this form of centralized economy does not augur for an ever expanding democratic way of life."

What was Alinsky implying or suggesting? That a capitalist economy did not lead to economic and social justice, but that the labor movement— because of its "reactionary leadership"—was not going to fight for an economic alternative? And what was the preferred system, democratic socialism?

There were many doubts about the prospects for capitalism in the early 1940s. As Godfrey Hodgson reminds us: "As late as the war years, most American economists, led by Alvin Hansen, predicted that capitalism was entering a phase of chronic stagnation. Most other intellectuals took the economists at their word and assumed that the task was to replace capitalism with some more promising system." Indeed, Joseph Schumpeter, a conservative, unhappily and reluctantly concluded that socialism was inevitable.

But was Schumpeter's prophecy Alinsky's advocacy? Not quite, or not exactly—here Alinsky was uncharacteristically ambiguous. At one point in *Reveille for Radicals,* while he was willing to observe that "the position taken by organized labor is consistent with their role in a monopolistic capitalist economy," he took off in a different direction. Suddenly, he shifted away from an economic perspective, short-circuiting his discussion about laissez-faire capitalism and socialism, and leaving his own position unclear. Because the labor movement had lost its progressive spirit, he now suggested in safe, broad strokes, People's Organizations were needed to fill the void—and, if possible, to reinvigorate and reorient organized labor. People's Organizations would move beyond labor's narrow agenda of higher pay and shorter hours, beyond what Alinsky referred to as straight trade unionism, and develop instead a recognition that "the welfare of its constituents does not depend solely upon an improvement in economic earnings but upon a general improvement of all of the standards in the life of a worker."

Alinsky's lecture to labor seemed to parallel the lectures on social disorganization and delinquency of his former sociology professors at the University of Chicago. In criminology, the traditional anti-delinquency approaches had only limited success or flat-out failed because they did not address the many causes of social disorganization—of which delinquency was but one result. Similarly, Alinsky was arguing, the labor movement could not address the fundamental problems of American society if its focus was limited to winning higher wages. Not only did America's social problems transcend the economic sphere but, by focusing only on the economic well-being of its members, organized labor had made these problems worse. To harness its full potential as a democratic force, Alinsky called for

> a complete change in the philosophy of the labor movement so that instead of viewing itself as a separate section of the American people engaged in a separate craft in a particular industry, it will think of itself as an organization of *American citizens*—united to conquer all of those destructive forces which harass the workingman and his family. . . . [But] if the organized labor movement cannot stretch to the broad horizon of objectives, it must then help in the building of a broad general People's Organization whose very character would involve an over-all philosophy and attack. In its simplest sense it would be an extension of the principles and practices of organized collective bargaining beyond their present confines of the factory gate.

Thus did Alinsky attempt to construct a rationale for the multiplica-
tion of People's Organizations on the model of the Back of the Yards
Neighborhood Council. There were forces at work in American industrial cities that gravely threatened American democracy—and neither big
business, organized labor, nor the federal government was interested in
or capable of confronting them. In spite of his apparent sympathy for an
unspecified American brand of socialism, Alinsky positioned himself
above the familiar ideological battles. He blurred the importance of the
class struggle by lumping together organized labor and big business, and
by focusing on "participation" itself as a key concept. He also made it
clear that the power of the federal government was a two-edged sword
and, in general, should not be the first answer to complex questions
about how the intricate web of social, psychological, and political forces
in community life could be enriched. Alinsky seemed to be saying that
even if in theory there were a better set of economic arrangements, the
first order of business was to arouse a democratically minded citizenry in
working-class areas. At least initially, the *process* of becoming a participant was more important than the content of any particular program.
What was most important, Alinsky explained, was "the breaking down
of the feeling on the part of our people that they are social automatons
with no stake in the future, rather than human beings in possession of all
the responsibility, strength, and human dignity which constitute the heritage of free citizens of a democracy. This can be done only through the
democratic organization of our people for democracy. It is the job of
building People's Organizations."

How to build People's Organizations was the subject of the second and
larger part of *Reveille for Radicals.* This was an inspirational handbook of
sorts—Alinsky's dos and don'ts of how to achieve a People's Organization.
An organizer must have "faith in the people, [he] should have faith that
they will evolve a people's program. If it is not a program to [his] liking,
remember that it is to their liking." Or: ". . . the most difficult job confronting an organizer is the actual identification of the local leadership, [who]
with few exceptions . . . are completely unknown outside of the community." Or: ". . . many organizers inwardly feel superior toward the people
with whom they are working. An organizer who has this superior attitude
cannot, in spite of all his cleverness, . . . conceal his true attitude" and will
fail. Or: "Many organizers will speak of the difficulties of trying to overcome local traditions and local taboos in creating a people's movement.
One should be constantly on guard, however, against attacking local traditions. . . . This course of activity only leads to hostility, conflict, and the
creation of an impossible condition for a real People's Organization."

Alinsky larded these admonishments and axioms with anecdotes drawn from his own organizing experiences. But not only did a good number of the anecdotes seem contrived to make a larger point, but the use of pseudonyms instead of real people and places added to the sense that Alinsky had infused fact with fiction to make his truths bigger and more compelling. His name for the Back of the Yards, for example, was "Across the Tracks," and the People's Organization there did battle with "the Tycoon's Department Store" and their powerful and arrogant law firm, "Van Snoot, Van Snoot, Van Snoot and Snoot." It was true, of course, that academic sociologists sometimes used such a style—William Foote Whyte's *Street Corner Society* was one example. Moreover, the University of Chicago Press, which had published Whyte's book as well as *Reveille for Radicals,* was extremely concerned about possible libelous attacks on national leaders, organizations, and corporations. Because the press's editors thought that Alinsky's book was going to be controversial, they were exceptionally fussy about avoiding any possible libel problems. (For example, in an essentially harmless passage where Alinsky was critical of how car dealers sold automobiles to unsophisticated buyers, the editors changed "Buick" to "the Golden Glamour," "Pontiac" to "the Silver Star," and "Ford" to "the Poop.")

But there was another reason for Alinsky's reliance on pseudonyms. In his anecdotes and illustrations, Alinsky adopted the voices of both chronicler and political strategist of a new, progressive movement, quoting and interpreting "reports" from "organizers" in Muddy Flats, Oak Root, and Bagville—all pseudonyms for Kansas City, Kansas. There were also references to "an organizer's report from a western city" and "from a northern town." In truth, nearly all the anecdotal material came from Alinsky himself, and involved not the numerous cities implied in the text but only his projects in Chicago, Kansas City, South St. Paul, and, to a very limited extent, the Norwood section of Cleveland. Although Alinsky presented these anecdotes straight-faced, one is somehow reminded of the old comic vaudeville act in which a lone performer becomes an entire cast of characters with a little imagination, a multitude of costumes, and a backdrop of ever-changing scenery.

The simple truth was that lack of empirical evidence prompted Alinsky to write Part Two of *Reveille for Radicals* as he did. He did not have compelling proof to back up his assertion—and here was one of the few times in the book that he mentioned the Back of the Yards Neighborhood Council directly—that "the tremendous speed with which the organization developed confirmed the validity of the premises, procedures, and objectives of a People's Organization." Indeed, it was not quite the case.

After the rousing first-year success of the BYNC in 1940, the crucial test was whether Alinsky's experience there could be replicated elsewhere—that, after all, was the purpose of setting up the Industrial Areas Foundation. And while the results of Alinsky's efforts elsewhere by 1944 had been fair, perhaps even good, they were not spectacular. The war effort had most certainly limited the level of energy and activity in Alinsky's two other major projects, but he had also not succeeded in training or attracting full-time organizers for them or for Los Angeles. Yet Alinsky wanted to say in *Reveille for Radicals* that his success in the Back of the Yards

> had spread out—and [is] still spreading—so that today more than a quarter of a million Americans are involved in the building of similar People's Organizations. . . . They have shown by positive, concrete action in every field of human endeavor, from housing to food, from wages to health, from child welfare to civic administration, that an organized people can achieve limitless objectives through the democratic process. They are great by their accomplishments, and glory in the deadly hatred and fear in which they are held by native Fascists.

The hero of this glorious undertaking was the organizer ("radical organizer" was redundant), and the handbook portion of *Reveille for Radicals* was aimed at would-be hero-organizers. One could almost envision Alinsky's organizer flying high in a Superman cape, swooping into a forlorn industrial community, ready to fight for "truth, justice and the American Way!" Clearly, Alinsky saw the organizer—especially himself—in heroic terms, leading the "war against the social menaces of mankind." Notwithstanding Alinsky's sometimes mawkish prose, there was much in his concept of the organizer that *was,* indeed, heroic, for fundamentally the organizer's goal was to create a setting in which victimized people could experience and express their self-worth, power, and dignity.

Alinsky's effort to define the organizer's role was a major part of *Reveille for Radicals.* In previous writings, especially in the statement of purpose of the Industrial Areas Foundation, Alinsky had talked mainly of the purposes and structure of a People's Organization. Much of that was repeated in *Reveille for Radicals:* the centrality of native or indigenous leadership; the representative nature of the organization (really an organization of organizations); the gradual establishment of new norms of behavior, with an emphasis on collective action, cooperation, and unity. But now, for the first time, Alinsky tried also to give a coherent account of the role of the organizer.

In Alinsky's conception, the organizer was by necessity an outsider:

The organizer of a People's Organization will shortly discover one simple maxim: *In order to be part of all, you must be part of none.* In dealing with the innumerable rivalries, fears, jealousies, and suspicions within a community the organizer will discover that not only must his own moral standing and behavior be impeccable, but . . . he cannot enjoy the confidence even to a limited degree of all other groups as long as he is personally identified with one or two of the community agencies.

This neutrality had another effect. For both practical and ideological reasons, the effective organizer did not make value judgments about a community's values, traditions, and attitudes: an elitist, heavy-handed approach would not work and was not democratic. This had been an important part of Clifford Shaw's philosophy, though for all their respect for a community's values, Shaw and his workers were interested in changing some of those values—not by unilateral action, but by raising alternatives, by engaging community members in a kind of Socratic dialogue, and by working with them to implement those alternatives in an indigenous community organization. For his part, Alinsky insisted that "the objective of securing a people's program absolutely precludes the organizer's going beyond . . . broad general principles into a detailed blueprint for the future." The organizer might push for certain priorities—health care, housing, delinquency prevention, with the organizer prodding when things went off track and, if he was trusted, acting as a private counselor to the various leaders and subgroups—but the details and implementation should be the result of discussion, debate, and negotiation among the leaders of the People's Organization.

There were some community "values" and practices, of course, that Alinsky's organizer—as well as Alinsky himself—was not going to tolerate, practices that were "undemocratic." Racial discrimination was one. A shrewd organizer should not attack discriminatory attitudes and practices at the start, while he was still establishing his own credibility and new, trusting relationships. Nor would he act unilaterally or self-righteously. But he would look for an opening, a circumstance that he could use to force people at least to modify their prejudices because it was in their interests to do so.

Alinsky seemed to be saying that an organizer was not forcing an alien, unwanted value system on people, because, down deep, people were yearning for fraternity, mutual respect, and community. "Frequent demonstrations of brutality, selfishness, hate, greed, avarice, and disloyalty among masses of people . . . are the result of evil conditions. . . . Radicals are not repelled by moral malignancy and evil in people, but on the contrary regard with wonder the fact that the masses of people, subjected to the kind of society in which they have lived, should retain so much decency and dignity." If Alinsky would not go so far as to say that man's nature was unequivocally selfless and loving, he did believe that contemporary man—for him, particularly the urban immigrants and their children—had deep-seated, although submerged qualities and needs that were consistent with the requirements of building democratic, communal life. It was the organizer's noble task to create circumstances in which these submerged qualities could be expressed and trusting relationships would grow across boundaries of race, religion, and ethnicity.

If Alinsky's idealized organizer-radical did not *feel* superior to the people he was organizing, he was nevertheless above the human scramble, motivated by "his love for his fellow men." As the years unfolded, Alinsky's critics would have doubts about whether this was his primary motive. But in 1945, many were willing to accept a simplified, hopeful explanation without too many questions; after all, "love for his fellow men" was a more promising motive than the loathing for most of mankind that had plunged the world into a long war. In a rousing peroration filled with combative optimism, Alinsky wrote about "the job ahead. It is the job of building People's Organizations which are all inclusive of both the people and their many organizations. . . . It can be done only by those who believe in, have faith in, and are willing to make every sacrifice for the people. Those who see fearlessly and clearly; they will be your radicals. . . . Sound it now. Whether it be the hoarse voice, the bell, the written word or the trumpet, let it come. Sound it clear and unwavering. REVEILLE FOR RADICALS."

A MONTH AFTER its publication in January 1946, *Reveille for Radicals* made the *New York Times* best-seller list, right up there with such other nonfiction works as Arthur Schlesinger, Jr.'s *The Age of Jackson,* Bill Mauldin's *Up Front,* and, by the spring, William Allen White's autobiography. In Chicago, too, the book was soon at the top of the best-seller list, as it was in several other cities. This was a remarkable, almost unprecedented performance for a University of Chicago Press book. Except for Friedrich von Hayek's conservative manifesto the previous year, *The Road to Serfdom,* the press's books were typically aimed at a small audience of scholars. But a new editor at the University of Chicago Press was interested in reaching a broader audience and took a chance on Alinsky's idea for a book.

Two strong early reviews in the New York *Herald Tribune* and *The New York Times* no doubt helped the sale of the book. Calling Alinsky's organizing work "one of the most amazing movements of our time," J. Raymond Walsh said in the *Herald Tribune* that "his success is a tribute to his passion and his political sagacity. He seems a saint with the skills of a ward heeler." Walsh, like others, believed that Alinsky had an important answer to the question of "how can a little man participate, or even feel that he participates in the determination of his destiny" in a society that had grown "larger and more intricate, the sources of power more remote and obscure." Walsh was also impressed with the broad coalitions Alinsky had created: "Most important in the long run perhaps is his uniting of workers and the small business people, whose customary outlook disposes them to feel kinship with Big Capital, and in the pinch to side with it against the workers. Recalling the swing of Europe's lower middle class into the army of Fascist reaction, one senses the profound importance of this." A corollary was noted by a reviewer in *New Trends,* who saw "great importance" in "Alinsky's emphasis . . . insofar as it combats the growing acceptance of the leader principle, of greater centralization and government control, by the exponents of the fascist right and the Marxist left abetted by the liberals of the 'Nation' variety."

Time magazine said that Alinsky had "glimpsed a vision . . . which is no less than the revitalization of democracy [and which] explains why Chicago's Auxiliary Bishop Bernard J. Sheil calls *Reveille for Radicals* 'a life-saving handbook for the salvation of democracy.' " Indeed, in Chicago, Sheil's own exulting review of his friend's book ran on the front page of Marshall Field's Chicago *Sun.* The Chicago *Tribune,* surprisingly, selected two friendly reviewers, Jacques Maritain and a University of Chicago anthropology professor named Wilton Krogman. At least Krogman's review turned out to be friendly, possibly contrary to what the *Tribune,* perhaps anticipating a more skeptical, scholarly evaluation, had expected. "I was impressed by the author's stirring sincerity," Krogman wrote. "He has a surging hope that the people can and will work out their own social salvation." Maritain wrote that he saw in Alinsky's concept of People's Organizations "the manner in which one of our great problems—how real leaders can emerge from and be chosen by real people—is to be solved. . . . Saul Alinsky's book is specifically American," but Maritain nonetheless concluded: "I do appreciate and admire the constructive value and the universal import of the essential concepts it proposes, and the new possibilities it discovers for that 'orderly revolution' which Mrs. Agnes E. Meyer anticipated in describing the work started in Chicago's Packingtown."

Alinsky's growing friendship with Agnes Meyer, whom he had met toward the end of the war, was also very helpful. In 1943, Meyer had traveled around the country writing articles for the Washington *Post* on various aspects of the war effort. She was deeply affected by the poverty, bad housing, lack of health care and educational opportunities, and general suffering she witnessed. Meyer, an energetic, feisty, though also at times erratic woman, launched something of a crusade to arouse the conscience of the country, at first through the news articles she wrote and later through speeches and lobbying efforts in Washington.

Agnes Meyer came to Chicago to meet Alinsky early in 1945, at the suggestion of Alinsky's friend Sidney Hyman, who had become friendly with the Meyer family through one of the Meyer children, Kay, a classmate at the University of Chicago in the late 1930s. Hyman gave Alinsky and his work a big buildup, and the meeting with Meyer could not have gone better. She spent several days in the Back of the Yards and talked to various people active in the Council. She was deeply impressed by what she saw and heard. Afterward, Alinsky fired a letter off to Hyman:

> Mrs Meyer arrived on schedule, went through the Back of the Yards with a fine comb—and is now writing four or five articles on it—is utterly convinced that the Back of the Yards movement is *the* hope for the future . . . , and feels that Bishop Sheil is one of the great moral leaders for the country to look to in the future—and (I am trying to avoid the use of Hollywood adjectives) is completely enthused and sold on the approach. I must also say that the situation operated in the reverse in that we are also sold on her. I think that it was wonderful of you to have done what you did, Sidney, and the Bishop knows the full details of how the contact was made and has asked that I send you his love.

When Meyer returned to Washington, she wrote six long articles in the *Post* about Alinsky's Back of the Yards experiment; they were reprinted in the New York *Tribune* and the Chicago *Sun*. Meyer referred to Alinsky's work as "an orderly revolution," which served as the title of the series—as good a phrase as any, perhaps, to capture the spirit and scope of what Alinsky was doing. And if the word "orderly" seemed to contradict or at least dilute the power of the word "revolution," that did not seem to bother Alinsky very much—although "orderly revolution" was not a phrase that he went out of his way to use, since "orderly" made his work and approach sound much tamer and safer than what he was interested in projecting. And, in fact, Agnes Meyer's own account focused on the dramatic, exciting change that she believed had occurred in the Back of the Yards, where "this desolate area is now transformed, in spirit if not in appearance, by the most powerful upsurge of organized individualism yet to come into being in the U.S.A."

Alinsky had arranged a luncheon meeting for her at a neighborhood Bohemian restaurant to meet the BYNC leaders. "What a gathering!" Meyer wrote. "I felt as never before what it would mean in terms of human development if our country could really become democratic." Meyer, as the daughter of a Lutheran minister, was generally hostile toward the American Catholic hierarchy, but in the Back of the Yards she had a chance to praise the Church and its local leaders—and to demonstrate her open-mindedness. "In other places [in the country] I have seen the authoritarianism of the Catholic Church clash so sharply with democratic principles that the possibility of another conflict between Church and State has long oppressed me," she wrote. "These priests in the Back of the Yards have demonstrated the regenerative force of Catholicism when it has the faith to rely on spiritual rather than political power. Acting upon the Catholic belief that all human beings alike reflect the face of God, they are finding a path on which democracy and Catholicism can go forward harmoniously toward a mutual enrichment."

Meyer's enthusiasm went well beyond many of the earlier favorable stories, rivaling the New York *Herald Tribune*'s hyperbolic editorial in the fall of 1939, which had seen Alinsky as the possible savior of American democracy. Her heightened enthusiasm can be measured in the small exaggerations that crept into her story—for example, the characterization that "the Back of the Yards movement has in the five years of its existence leapt like wildfire to Kansas City, to South St. Paul, to Cleveland"; or that the "movement [now] represents well over a million people." Even Alinsky claimed only that 250,000 people lived in the areas where he had been organizing—and that the most active participants represented 5 to 7 percent of this total population. Meyer also overstated the popular interest in better race relations in the Back of the Yards, especially when she wrote that because of the Council's influence, "the churches constantly emphasize the fact that race prejudice in any form is un-Christian." But her tone, even more than her presentation of details, made her account special, a tone of near-euphoria over what she had discovered—and she fancied herself as someone who discovered important new ideas, movements, and people, who celebrated and promoted them. Since Saul Alinsky was interested in being celebrated and promoted, he and his new friend Ag Meyer were on the same wavelength from the beginning.

In Chicago, Meyer thought she had discovered not only a new idea for urban democracy but also the two men who made it possible, Bishop Sheil and Saul Alinsky. Actually, it was Sheil who made Agnes Meyer's heart beat fastest. She had not expected to meet a ranking Catholic who had Sheil's charm, dynamism, and physical attractiveness, and who shared many of her views about social conditions and, like her, was eager to speak out about them. "Powerful but not tall of stature, he is a robust saint with the integrity, compassion and joyousness of a person who has the courage to live as he thinks," Meyer wrote. "His spirituality presents no barriers to a non-Catholic, because it permeates his whole being. Like that of the great poets, it has been forged by the role of mediator between heaven and earth."

As for Alinsky, Mrs. Meyer described him as having walked into a hotbed of animosities five years earlier, "a young Jewish criminologist and Chicago University graduate, armed with an invincible weapon—a disinterested passion for democracy." She quoted Alinsky at length, especially his attack on the social-work profession and the contrast it provided with his approach: "They come to the people of the slums not to help them rebel and fight their way out of the muck. Most social work does not even reach the submerged masses. . . . In the rare instances where it reaches the slum dwellers it seeks to get them adjusted to the environment so they will live in hell and like it." Mrs. Meyer herself may not have been willing to go quite so far in condemning social work and other professional help: "[T]here is no doubt," she pointed out, "that the work of the Council would profit by more expert advice on its health, housing and welfare problems than its own membership can provide." On the other hand, she took the Council's side completely in blasting the arrogance of the University of Chicago Settlement House, and she understood the deep, psychological importance of its rallying cry, "We the people will work out our own destiny."

"The Orderly Revolution" was a great advertisement for Alinsky and his work. The editors at the University of Chicago Press were frustrated, however, that the articles appeared so far—nearly six months, it turned out—in advance of the book's publication. One editor told a colleague, "Although we cannot use this in promotion anywhere it is heartening to know that on the basis of Mrs. Meyer's articles . . . describing Alinsky's works, Harry S. Truman ordered 100 reprints of the articles . . . in booklet form." When the book did come out, Agnes Meyer arranged to have Alinsky appear at the Washington *Post*'s Book and Author Luncheon; and when he came to Washington for the event, he stayed at the Meyers' home on Crescent Place.

Saul Alinsky promoted *Reveille for Radicals* with great energy and determination. He saw to it that a long list of influential friends and acquaintances received advance copies. He pushed the idea of an autograph party in the large book section of the Marshall Field department store in Chicago's Loop, where he would be introduced by Bishop Sheil—an event that did not come off, however. He appeared at a number of other book signings, and on radio interview programs in Chicago, Washington, and New York, sometimes through the help of Agnes Meyer or through Happy and Valentine Macy in New York, two wealthy and well-connected friends whom Alinsky had met on a trip to New York in 1944. A friend of the Macys, Paul Hollister, then at CBS, wrote personal notes to his friends at several of New York's largest department stores and bookshops, urging them to promote *Reveille for Radicals*.

Alinsky initiated much of the book promotion himself because of his growing disenchantment with the University of Chicago Press. To Sidney Hyman, it was not surprising that Alinsky had chosen the press to bring out the book rather than a commercial New York publisher, since being published by the press was not only a mark of intellectual respectability but also identification with a great university and whatever social status that conveyed. (Hyman recalls: "I used to play tennis with Saul, and there were lots and lots of tennis courts around Hyde Park that were not filled, but Saul would rather play on the [university faculty's] Quadrangle Club court than anywhere else, even though it meant that we had to wait around for two hours [to get a court].") But if Alinsky had been attracted to the University of Chicago Press because of its prestige, the final editing process of *Reveille* was difficult, and relations between author and publisher were strained. The press's lawyer recommended six pages of changes, especially an elimination of "bloody passages" that "might by the wildest stretch of the imagination have any connotation in connection with the syndicalism law," as the director of the press explained to Alinsky. The lawyer recommended, for example, that the word *turmoil* be substituted for "*bloodshed* of the Civil War" and that *heartbreak* be used instead of "the *blood* of battle"—and that Alinsky's quotation from Tom Paine on the French Revolution—"To Arms! To Arms!"—be moved to another section of the book where it could not be misinterpreted as Alinsky's own advocacy of violent change. "Despite your obvious intention to effect an orderly and bloodless revolution," the press's director wrote to Alinsky, "there is danger, in view of the placing and nature of the passages [that the lawyer cited], of some readers considering the book as an incitement to be incendiary or promote a blood bath." Alinsky made many if not all of the recommended changes, although a dull, toned-down substitute title, *The Radical and the Job Ahead,* was discarded, and his exasperation did not peak until after the book had been published. When sales started to lag a bit in the second month, Alinsky believed it was because of the press's incompetence and stinginess. He told the director: "As to whether or not you choose to increase your advertising expenditure, and judging from your letter you apparently will not, that is entirely between you and the Press. I think that 'Reveille' has already made its mark of at least being one of your five all-time best sellers and is making a very good profit for the Press. I make it five all-time best sellers although outside of the Goodspeed Bible and the Hayek Handbook for the National Manufacturers Association I don't know of two other titles."

NOT ALL of the reviews of *Reveille for Radicals* were effusive valentines for its author. In Chicago, Alinsky's colleague in the Back of the Yards, Joe Meegan, was angry. Although he and Alinsky had usually been referred to as co-founders of the BYNC in various press accounts over the years, Alinsky never once mentioned Meegan in *Reveille*. Meegan felt that Alinsky's account made him seem as though he had been a mere puppet in Alinsky's grand theatrical production.

Since Alinsky was eager to distinguish himself from traditional liberals, and had done so by attacking their integrity and fortitude, it was not surprising that some liberal reviewers proved eager to retaliate. This is not to say that *Reveille* went without liberal praise; some liberal critics, moreover, chided Alinsky for exaggerating the differences between liberals and radicals. Nonetheless, it was true that most of the negative reviews came from liberals who had serious reservations about Alinsky's methods and concept.

One such person was a well-known Chicago cleric, the Unitarian Leslie T. Pennington. In a sermon, Pennington acknowledged that "Alinsky has laid hold of something so fundamental, so realistic, and so pertinent to the struggle for power in which democracy has become immersed, whether we like it or not, that we cannot afford to ignore either his diagnosis or his prescription." Yet he was troubled not merely by Alinsky's prescription of rough-and-tumble tactics but also by his celebration of the necessity for them. "He comes very close to the doctrine that the end justifies the means, that it is right to lie and apply ruthless social pressure for a good end," Pennington observed. "Who is going to determine the methods used and against whom they are to be used? If you once break away from principle, as he himself writes, there is no end to the evil in which you become involved," he said, sounding exactly like the liberal whom Alinsky scorned. Pennington also thought it was more than a coincidence that Alinsky "has worked extensively and has been most widely acclaimed by Roman Catholics whose influence in history, at least in one of their major Orders, has seemed to bear with it the doctrine that the end justifies the means." Among Protestant clergy and intellectuals, and among people hostile to the Catholic Church, this would not be the last time that Alinsky's association with the Church became a reason—sometimes a major reason—for suspecting his motives and methods.

Other largely negative reviews of Alinsky's book appeared in *The New Republic, The Nation,* and *Commentary.* Under the sarcastic headline "Awake to What?" the reviewer in *The New Republic* wrote that there was "no indication [in the book] of how many people's organizations there are, where they are located or the extent of their membership. Until we are given these facts, it will be fairly hard to assay the value and importance of this particular sort of social organization." Even without the "facts," the reviewer concluded that "rather than socialism, the 'people's movement' of Mr. Alinsky's radicals sounds more like a move in the direction of the corporate state—in form, and perhaps in spirit." He was suspicious of the bullying tactics of Alinsky's organizers and of the possibility that the various local groups in a community would be forced into obedience by the "People's Organization." "The book is important not because, as the publisher's blurb states, it is a 'blow-by-blow account of an orderly revolution already under way,' but because it expresses a point of view which runs the risk of developing *away* from the democracy that the author speaks of with such fervor."

The review in *The Nation* was similar, bemoaning the vagueness of Alinsky's program and ideology: "Chapter 11 completely puzzled me. Labor today has accepted the capitalist outlook, Mr. Alinsky begins, and he attacks William Green, Dubinsky, and Mr. Reuther in a fashion that made me believe he was about to talk about socialism. Then came a quotation from Laski and, after this, nothing except vague references and much about the necessity of going to the people." Although Alinsky was "a sincere democrat," in the "absence of a hard program his organization would be easily captured by demagogues, and worse. Doubtless he means to regenerate democracy . . . but in some parts of the world fascism has made use of exactly this sort of 'radical' talk."

In *Commentary,* Daniel Bell's main criticism was of a different kind. Bell acknowledged that an experiment such as Alinsky's "that attempts to give people a sense of participation and belonging becomes important as a weapon against the cynicism and despair on which a fascist movement feeds." Like other social critics, Bell saw as dangers of the industrial age both urban anonymity and the "increasing bureaucratization extending into all major organizations with which people are identified. As societies grow more complex, the distance between the loci of power, the places where decisions are made, and the grass roots and pavements becomes greater. With the centralization of decisions arises a related growth of dependence and helplessness on the part of the people." Although Alinsky was apparently interested in addressing such fundamental problems, Bell was disappointed—almost angry—that *Reveille* was mainly "shrill pamphleteering . . . [and] handbook material for organizers. . . . What obviously should have been the core of the book, a coherent picture of what the People's Organizations actually *are,* is just never developed."

Bell, though, wanted more from Alinsky than description; he wanted a serious, extended discussion of how democratic theory and practice might be reformulated in response to the new landscape of a mass urban society. He was skeptical, if not quite unconvinced, about Alinsky's concept of People's Organizations. While he understood the usefulness, even possible importance of the concept, he also wondered about limitations. How far could a People's Organization go, for instance, in developing a political program? At times in *Reveille,* Alinsky gave the impression that not only small businessmen but perhaps sizable corporations could eventually become a part of a People's Organization through their enlightened self-interest. Bell was skeptical. "Our radical Founding Fathers recognized the existence of class interests and sought a means of balancing them one against the other so that no single one could become dominant." He was also skeptical about the long-term staying power of a broad coalition of diverse interests. "In his initial experiment in Chicago, Alinsky was able to proceed only because of the support of the Catholic Church and, later, of the left-wing union in that area," Bell wrote. "The basic pulls of both of these power groups, however, are not rooted in the people's lives in the neighborhoods, but in some larger institutional commitments. If the two groups were to clash on some larger ideological or power issue, what would stop the People's Organizations from being rent apart?" Or, Bell might have also asked, if a People's Organization had to avoid divisive issues to maintain unity, to what extent was its program likely to be diluted?

"If I have been harsh with this book," Bell concluded, "it is because the activities of Alinsky's Councils raise explicitly the questions of the limits of individual activity in a technologically organized and power-massed society, and yet fail woefully to define them. One of our crucial jobs is to explore the range of activities through which people can genuinely share in the basic decisions that affect them and in molding a society responsive to their economic and emotional needs."

To be sure, *Reveille* addressed these legitimate questions only by implication or not at all. Down the road, Alinsky would be forced to provide more precise answers. In *Reveille,* however, he was not interested in talking about limits or in suggesting that some activities or issues were beyond the capacity of People's Organizations. The sky was the limit—that was very much part of Alinsky's exuberant, pugnacious call to action. In tone and hopefulness, it fit nicely into "the sense of wonderful possibilities," Eric Goldman's phrase to describe the near-manic optimism that swept much of the country after the Japanese surrender in August 1945. For millions of Americans, the sense of wonderful possibilities meant a better-paying job, a new house, and a chance to go to college under the GI bill. For Saul Alinsky, now the author of a best-selling book and of an idea whose time appeared to be coming, the future was obviously bright, too. And he knew how to make his star shine even brighter—in ways that were not merely self-serving but also helped to advance the cause of building democratic citizen organizations in industrial areas. Saul Alinsky set out to capitalize on the unexpected success of his book. How he went about it revealed his remarkable facility for nurturing friendships with important people and manipulating them to his advantage. Alinsky did not like surprises, or events he could not control. But out there over the horizon, beyond the bright future that lay immediately ahead, there was an unexpected event that nobody could have foreseen. How Alinsky reacted to that would reveal a part of him that even his closest friends had never known.

14

The Cruelest Summer

From late 1945 into the summer of 1947, Saul Alinsky was riding high. It was the busiest and most promising time of his life.

As wartime travel restrictions were lifted, he was increasingly on the road, often for a week or two at a time, paying more frequent visits to the community councils of Kansas City and South St. Paul, and starting a new council in another stockyards setting, this time in Omaha. He was working out a deal with Henry Holt & Co., in New York, to write another book, and was continuing to lecture to criminologists and social workers. And, increasingly, he was on the road to mine new sources of financial support for the Industrial Areas Foundation.

Marshall Field's money had gotten Alinsky and the IAF started in the winter of 1940. Over the next several years, Field and Bishop Sheil were regular contributors to the IAF, each giving up to $5,000 a year. By 1943, Adele Rosenwald Levy, a daughter of Sears, Roebuck founder Julius Rosenwald, joined the IAF's board, probably through the intervention of Leonard Rieser, and began to contribute $5,000 annually. Rieser, a Chicago attorney who was related to Helene Simon's family, had done the legal work on Julius Rosenwald's estate, and he was now doing the IAF's legal work, too. As for the other IAF board members, by 1944 Howland Shaw was the only one who could be counted on for sizable contributions. Only modest financial support was forthcoming from the others, such as Dutch Smith or Kathryn Lewis, who brought in small contributions from her father's United Mine Workers union.

With not much more than a $20,000 budget, Alinsky felt that he was constantly tottering at the financial edge. After paying the rent on his two-room office, his traveling expenses, and the salaries for himself and a secretary, there was little left over for additional organizers who could help create more People's Organizations or work more closely with the existing councils.

One spring evening in 1944, on a fund-raising trip to New York, Alinsky met Valentine and Harriet Macy at a dinner party. The three of them talked into the morning hours, with Alinsky telling them stories about his experiences with delinquents and gangsters and, now, with organizing in urban slums. It was more than a memorable night for the Macys; it was entertaining and inspiring. "Val and I have felt that next to having a shot in the arm, you were the best tonic we'd found in years," Happy Macy told Alinsky soon after. "Hearing your story gave us the feeling that all was not lost after all in this world of chaos—if we could [only] find a quick way of turning you into about 100 more of you, so's to spread your understanding and energy all around this country!"

The Macys were very wealthy, from a fortune already well established at the time of Val's grandfather, Josiah Macy, who had held an interest in an oil refinery with John D. Rockefeller. The family holdings now ranged from a chain of newspapers in Westchester County to a bottle-cap factory to coal mines in Alabama. Val and Happy Macy were in their mid-forties when Alinsky met them. Both had been divorced previously, but this time they had found a match filled with complementary attractions. Val—of medium height, trim, with dark brown hair and blue eyes—was reserved, quiet, even shy. Happy—short, plump, with dark eyes and curly hair—had earned her nickname from her warm, outgoing, and effervescent temperament. Neither Val nor Happy was much involved in partisan politics, although Val's father had run successfully as a Republican for office in Westchester County many years earlier (at one time, he had been a Democrat). Both Val's and Happy's interests were not unusual for their class: Val collected paintings, and Happy ran a little summer theater in East Hampton and served on the national board of the Girl Scouts.

The Macys were fascinated by Alinsky because he was different. Maybe their friends in the Hamptons could exchange stories and gossip about a Marshall Field, but Saul Alinsky could do that and more: he could tell inside stories about Frank Nitti, "Golf Bags" Hunt, and other Capone characters; he could tell them what really happened in Miami at the attempted assassination of Roosevelt; he could tell them about the time he arranged to have Bishop Sheil appear with John L. Lewis, and how the good bishop was shot at for his efforts; he could tell them about the offstage, private behavior within the Catholic hierarchy, always an intriguing subject for upper-class Protestants; he could tell them in colorful detail about the subculture of the urban underclass. Saul Alinsky was a great bridge to many mysterious, enchanting, even exotic cultural islands for those who felt marooned on the Upper East Side of New York.

The Macys thoroughly enjoyed their new friend. Happy Macy in particular was excited about the ideals of the Back of the Yards Neighborhood Council and the emphasis Alinsky placed on promoting understanding among ethnic and racial groups. That reminded her, she told Alinsky, of a woman whom she knew and admired who had been promoting better race relations in the Detroit area Girl Scouts, and how her efforts seemed to parallel what Alinsky was attempting to achieve. Happy even suggested that Alinsky might want to contact the woman to see if she would be interested in a place on his staff. Alinsky told Happy, "I quite agree with you that this particular woman who seems to be the spark plug . . . would be an excellent addition to our staff." Since, however, Alinsky had no interest in having a woman on his staff, he let Happy's suggestion sink quietly into oblivion.

Within months the Macys sent a check to the IAF for $2,500, followed by another contribution in the same amount a few months later. Less than a year after their first meeting, Happy accepted Alinsky's invitation to serve on the IAF board. She wanted to help Alinsky with fund-raising, and was full of optimism that many of her wealthy friends would share her enthusiasm for his work.

When Alinsky told Happy in 1945 that he was heading out to California both to investigate the possibility of starting a new community council and to raise funds, she suggested that he call her and Val's friends the J. Cheever Cowdins. Cheever Cowdin was chairman of the board of Universal Films. "They live in Bel Air on something called Tortuoso Way," Happy told Alinsky. "They are both grand people and I shall tell them all about you. They'll be out there in July after the Republican convention in Chicago." Dutifully, Alinsky checked in with Cowdin and was invited to the Cowdins' home on the Fourth of July. Prospecting for gold in the hills of Bel Air turned into a minor disaster for Alinsky, as he recounted to Happy:

> During that afternoon session at the Cowdins', they suggested going up to a party given by a Lady Mendel, and it was there that I promptly began to put my foot into it at every whip, stitch and turn. This Lady Mendel, who is a dumpy, little dame with fallen-down garters, and who seemingly spends her life passing out hors d'oeuvres and cocktails to loads of people, greeted us at the door. After getting into the house, I noticed lots of pillows around the joint with all kinds of different slogans on them, such as "If you fail, keep trying and you

are bound to succeed," signed by Neville Chamberlain. I was intrigued at such a statement coming from such a guy, and while staring at the pillow, I noticed Lady Mendel heading my way. Her approach was fascinating to me as the closest thing to it that I can think of is a barrel cantering down the floor. She said that she noticed that I was interested in the pillows, and before I could restrain myself, I asked her if she got them down at Atlantic City. I assumed that they were the kind of thing that you get with Kewpie dolls—you know, when you throw the three little balls into the right little slots. She became quite huffy and I later discovered that the pillows were a rather expensive proposition, being handmade, handwoven and whatever else runs into money.

It was often unclear, even among Alinsky's oldest Chicago friends, whether his bad manners, sarcasm, and pranks in these social situations were spontaneous, intentional, or a complex hybrid of the two. Although Alinsky was capable of self-censorship—of being on his "good behavior"— there were many occasions when he did not practice it. On such occasions, it sometimes seemed that he was being indulgent, that, for instance, the great pleasure and pure fun of—figuratively speaking—picking up a cream pie at a fancy dinner party and casually sticking it into the face of a phony, stuffed-shirt guest was too powerful to resist. Yet mere spontaneous indulgence did not always seem his motive either. Alinsky was often eager to tell others—as he told Happy Macy—about his "misadventures," even when the results, such as no financial support from the Lady Mendels of the world or embarrassment to the Macys, could have been costly to him. For Alinsky wanted others to see him as he did—as a man who was so contemptuous of elitism, pretentiousness, hypocrisy, and worse that he would go out of his way—even at great cost—to thumb his nose at them.

Happy Macy was not very successful in helping Alinsky to raise money, although she tried. She and a friend came up with an idea for a pamphlet that would explain the work of the Industrial Areas Foundation and would feature a collage of newspaper clippings extolling Alinsky's successes. She thought that if each IAF board member would send a personal note along with a pamphlet to ten or fifteen friends, new money would come rolling in. Happy sent letters to, among others, DeWitt Wallace of *Reader's Digest,* Averell Harriman's wife, Marie, Clare Boothe Luce, Cheever Cowdin, and John D. Rockefeller. The response was quite modest—after a long delay, Marie Harriman sent a check for $250, and another Macy acquaintance gave $500—and even those who contributed apparently did so out of politeness, for hardly anybody gave a second time.

When Eustice Seligman sent a check for only $100, Alinsky wrote Happy Macy, sarcastically, that he would send Seligman a copy of Agnes Meyer's stories on the Back of the Yards movement "so that he will know that his hundred bucks went into REVOLUTION." After Happy was again unsuccessful with a follow-up, Alinsky told her, "Don't be too discouraged about DeWitt Wallace, after all, remember that he did send me a free three-year subscription to *Reader's Digest.* With that accouterment in our bathroom, it makes home more like home. I am seriously considering sending Mr. Wallace a quarter for a cup of coffee and a doughnut. He really sounds as though he is hard up." And when Happy told Alinsky that Rockefeller had turned her down, Alinsky remarked in a more serious vein, "I was not too surprised by Mr. Rockefeller's reaction. Mr. [Howland] Shaw had discussed the matter with John D. III a couple of years ago and my own feeling . . . is that the program and operations of the [Industrial Areas] Foundation are much too (as they say in the Armed Forces) 'rugged' for their tastes. In all honesty, we certainly do not fall into the class of 'benevolent' or 'welfare' organizations."

Happy Macy was disappointed that she had not been more successful—and somewhat mystified. She speculated that her Eastern friends felt remote from Alinsky's Midwestern projects, although that did not seem to be a totally satisfying answer. "What really gripes me," Happy said to Alinsky, "is that the burden of fundraising still rests on your shoulders along with everything else, which just doesn't seem right." No one felt that burden more intensely than Alinsky and, therefore, since every dollar that Happy Macy contributed and raised was urgently needed, Alinsky showered her with attention and compliments, regularly sending her warm, chatty letters, telling her about trips he had taken or new developments in the Back of the Yards. When he had heard that she was not feeling well, he sent her a telegram: "Will be in New York tomorrow and will call you as soon as I get through speaking and will come over laden with aspirin, Freud, Papal encyclicals, a Jewish mezuzah, detective stories, dirty stories, candy, flowers and your obedient servant." On Happy's train trip West one summer to join Val for a vacation in Wyoming, she stopped off in Chicago to see Alinsky, who gave her a grand tour, including dinner one night at the Pump Room. On another occasion, during a typical after-dinner conversation with the Macys in their New York apartment that stretched to 2 a.m., Val started to talk proudly about photographs he had taken of a pastel watercolor portrait of Happy that hung above the fireplace. Alinsky made a point of asking Val to send him one of the photos, and after it arrived, he wrote to them that he was going to put it in the most honored position he knew of—on his office wall between pictures of "the Most Rev.

Bernard J. Sheil and the Hon. Jacques Maritain." He gently teased Happy that her picture "will be slightly out of place, particularly when one notes the suggestion of—shall I say the unadorned shoulders which sort of go off into nothing (how much did you wear anyway while this business was going on)?"

Alinsky's solicitousness toward the Macys may have had opportunistic roots, but as the relationship grew, so too did Alinsky's real feelings of friendship: nearly two years after they had met, Alinsky wrote to Val:

> As you know, I have some rather unorthodox standards and one of them is the valuing of friendships infinitely above any of the other things that most people regard as treasures—and in my heart there are few friendships equal to the feelings that I have for both Happy and yourself. See, I have gone sentimental and I am glad that there are nearly 1,000 miles separating us right now because if you read this letter in my presence, I would be blushing from my ears down and that would be disastrous to my reputation of being hard-boiled.

Friendship also meant that Alinsky could be more candid about his and Happy's money-raising ventures. After Alinsky met Marie Harriman at a party the Macys gave for him, weeks went by without Harriman sending a promised financial contribution. Alinsky complained to Happy: "You would think that after all of her cracks to me about 'these pissy-eyed Park Avenue bastards,' plus her articulated strong support for our work, she would be the first to contribute." And about another wealthy acquaintance of the Macys, Alinsky said bluntly to Happy, "I think you ought to write him and say, 'OK, Bud, you may be over-extended this year, but put us down for a definite contribution immediately after January 15th of 1946.'"

By the time *Reveille for Radicals* was published, the Macys and Alinsky had known each other for more than a year and had gotten to understand each other. It was fortunate, perhaps, for Alinsky that his friendship with the Macys had matured, for Val Macy—while politely generous in his praise for the book as a whole—was troubled by certain passages that he read in the unbound proofs of *Reveille* that Alinsky had mailed to him and Happy before publication. Specifically, Val was concerned about Chapter 2, where Alinsky discussed with great passion the evils of capitalism and the American labor movement. It was Alinsky's statements about the former that concerned Val Macy, the capitalist. "P. 33, last sentence," he wrote to Alinsky. The passage in *Reveille*, at once crystal clear and ambiguous, read:

Radicals want to advance from the jungle of laissez faire capitalism
to a world worthy of the name of human civilization. They hope for
a future where the means of production will be owned by all of the
people instead of just a comparative handful. They feel that this
minority control of production facilities is injurious to the large
masses of people not only because of economic monopolies but because the political power inherent in this form of centralized economy
does not augur for an ever expanding democratic way of life.

In his letter, Val asked Alinsky:

Does a Radical have to be against private ownership of means of
production? If so, should he favor state ownership (Socialism or Communism) or ownership by co-operatives? Is *ownership* the important
point rather than what is produced and how it is produced? If by
definition a Radical must be against private ownership of production
per se, you automatically rule out and often antagonize many who are
otherwise good Radicals. Few but small companies are operated by
the "owners," the stockholders, and this would be true to a large
extent no matter who the "owners" were. Do the People's Organizations oppose such private ownership?

Val Macy's letter brought a quick clarification from Alinsky. "On the
discussion of 'private ownership of means of production,'" he began,
"what I really was driving at was not kicking up Hell on what would be
the best kind of economic organization. . . . I did not mean there that I
am opposed to private ownership, but I believe that there are certain major
services that are basic to the American public which could stand considerable modification and possibly public ownership in the sense of the Postal
Service." And then, after giving what he must have thought was the
appropriate amount of reassurance, Alinsky added:

With reference to your [other] question on whether or not there is
"deliberate 'conspiracy' to hold down production" . . . there is no
question in my mind but that [for example] within the building trades
there is definite collusion in restraint of production both on the part
of capital and labor. You are quite right that from the point of view
of having the book sell the work, making statements of this kind is
like slapping the faces of some people, but knowing me as you do I
think you would have been awfully surprised if I hadn't swung a few
punches—and I know nobody would have been more surprised than
myself.

Val Macy and Saul Alinsky remained friends for many years, and it is doubtful that their brief exchange here had much effect on Alinsky's thinking about economic theory, which he was not very much interested in, and in any event the postwar boom quickly changed the political discussion of economics. Before the end of the war, economists and other intellectuals could talk seriously about the possible end of capitalism. Now, after the war, even those who were critical of capitalism seemed to accept it—as many intellectuals did in the 1920s—not as an ideal but as a fact. But Macy had pointed up Alinsky's vulnerability, and the exchange posed the question of how far Alinsky would go in the future to accommodate his views to financial pressures, which sails he might trim and, more insidiously, which sails he might never raise. He was not indifferent to such matters. At least for now, he was willing to make small gestures to ingratiate himself to a benefactor or, for example, to calm Macy's edginess. Six months later, he made a point of sending Macy a short note about the highly negative review of *Reveille* that appeared in *New Masses:* "If you want to have a picnic lay your hands on a back issue of the Communist *New Masses* . . . They have not only hit me with the kitchen sink but have followed up by pulling out the plumbing and throwing that my way too. You and Happy will have a tremendous chuckle out of it." And to his friend Agnes Meyer, Alinsky treated the *New Masses* review as a badge of honor: "They not only toss everything including the kitchen sink at me but there are some points that make you sit up and mumble to yourself, 'Well, I'll be God damned,' such as where they charge these people's organizations with being controlled by big business!! In case you did not know it I am 'a trickster,' 'a mixer of the oil of elusive idealism with the water of capitalist-bred cynicism,' a 'petty bourgeois reformist,' . . . and a lot of other things."

AGNES MEYER started by giving Alinsky's Industrial Areas Foundation $5,000 a year. The contributions of the Macys and Agnes Meyer in 1945 represented a nearly 50 percent increase in the IAF's budget. In the case of Agnes Meyer, Alinsky did not have to ask for financial support; she pressed the issue. For, as she wrote to an acquaintance, she thought that "Saul Alinsky has the most pronounced talent for genuinely democratic organization work of any person that I have encountered in this field."

Agnes Meyer was a gadfly, and Saul Alinsky came to know her during one of her more productive periods. She was a good, energetic writer with a strong social conscience. After the war, she continued to travel around the country, writing for the Washington *Post* on a variety of social problems, from race riots in Columbia, Tennessee, to the plight of coal miners. She also used all of her considerable social and political connections to lobby strenuously for federal aid for health, education, and welfare.

Agnes Meyer may not have been a perfect ally for Alinsky, but she was still a very useful one. She may have thought she was more sophisticated about social and political issues than she actually was, and this meant Alinsky had to deflect many of her suggestions and ideas. On the other hand, she and Alinsky agreed on many current issues and they could talk easily about events and gossip about many political characters. She also understood how important the press could be in promoting Alinsky's work and was, of course, in a good position to help.

Alinsky was an occasional guest at the Meyers' residence on Crescent Place in Washington. The house was baronial, atop a rise and set back from the road, with a driveway that was perhaps designed more for carriages than for limousines. Agnes and Eugene were wonderful hosts; they would go out of their way to make a guest comfortable, assisted by a full retinue of footmen and maids.

Saul Alinsky liked the idea of staying at the Meyers'. It was another indication that his work was important. He could casually mention to Happy Macy that before coming up to New York, "I'll be staying with Mr. and Mrs. Eugene Meyer for a few days in Washington." He could also bring back good stories to his friends in Hyde Park—about joining Agnes and Eugene, and Kay and Phil, their daughter and son-in-law, at the symphony, "if you can stand some music," Agnes would say. Or there might be a story to tell about some famous dinner guest that he met or some mischief that he had committed. On one occasion, a Hyde Park friend, Ralph Helstein, happened to be in Washington on business, and Alinsky brought him along to the Meyers' for dinner. Helstein, who had become president of the Packinghouse Workers Union in 1946, was a lawyer, a tough-minded man of strong opinions, but also a decorous man, even a bit prudish about personal matters. That night at the Meyers' he was embarrassed by his friend's behavior, as he had been in other social settings. "After dinner," he recalls, "we retired to the library, where we had after-dinner drinks in front of a beautiful fireplace. We sat and discussed issues of grave import to the world and society. I remember being shocked [at some of the things that Saul said]. He'd use incredible language and say the most outlandish kinds of things that even he didn't believe. I'd know, but they didn't." Alinsky's calculated crudity or vulgarity also embarrassed Helstein, like the story Alinsky told about his experience at a Hollywood cocktail party given in his honor shortly after *Reveille for*

Radicals was published. "A dame asked me, after I autographed her book, what I was doing that night, and I, looking her right in the eye, said, 'Lady, I only autograph with my fountain pen.' " Nonetheless, Helstein thinks that Alinsky's uninhibited, saucy style made a powerful impression in these otherwise predictably dignified social encounters. "Saul had a way with him—and I think it was one of the things that knocked people like this off balance, and either endeared him to them or they rejected him. But if it endeared them to him, he could get away with anything."

Many of Alinsky's get-togethers with Agnes Meyer centered on him and Bishop Sheil. Typically, Agnes Meyer would invite them both to spend a few days or a week with her during the summer or early in September at the Meyers' vacation retreat at Mount Kisco, New York, an even more splendiferous place than the Meyer residence in Washington. Before Alinsky's first trip to Mount Kisco, Mrs. Meyer jokingly prepared him for the spectacular setting and size of the estate by cracking that, unlike Marshall Field, she had no guilt feelings about being rich and living accordingly. Alinsky often interspersed a few days at Mount Kisco with a few days in Manhattan, visiting friends and checking out fund-raising possibilities. On one occasion, he told Agnes Meyer that he would be with Bishop Sheil in New York before they headed up to Mount Kisco and that if she wanted to leave a message for him, "you may address me as follows: His Eminence Saul D. Alinsky (the kosher Cardinal), c/o Bishop Bernard J. Sheil, Waldorf-Astoria." When Mrs. Meyer made an occasional trip to Chicago, she would stop for an afternoon visit or for dinner at the bishop's house on the North Side, where Alinsky would join them. Or the three might meet for a sentimental lunch at Mario's, the Italian restaurant below the Catholic Youth Organization office, where Mrs. Meyer had first been introduced to Sheil. Sometimes the setting for one of her forays into Chicago was more public, as when Alinsky reminded her that "you are expected at the [bishop's annual] corn beef and cabbage dinner . . . and we will sit at the same table because women do not sit at the speaker's table. It will be a rare experience and you will see some of these things I have told you about."

Agnes Meyer was determined to see Bishop Sheil anointed an archbishop and, eventually, a cardinal, and she lobbied for his promotion in both subtle and not so subtle ways. It was she and her husband, for instance, who helped to arrange for President Truman's appointment of Sheil to the commission studying the conditions of children in Europe and recommending American aid. But in spite of her wealth and influence, her self-directed campaign to elevate the bishop ranged somewhere between futile and ludicrous. For all of his popular following in Chicago's neighborhoods and among liberals—many of them non-Catholic—Sheil had only limited support within the Church hierarchy, where his style, liberalism, and independence were widely resented. Nonetheless, Mrs. Meyer plowed ahead and saw Alinsky as her co-conspirator and confidant in this adventure, a perception that Alinsky encouraged mainly by being a sympathetic ear for her frustrations and anger.

New York's Francis Cardinal Spellman, the most powerful American prelate, epitomized much of the worst of the Church, as far as both Meyer and Alinsky were concerned. Once, when Agnes Meyer told Alinsky that Spellman had given her a hard time on some matter of mutual interest, Alinsky's retort was: "You say that Spellman gave you the 'devil.' I sincerely hope you returned it to him since he might be lonesome without it." Another time, Alinsky told her he was thinking about writing a magazine article and one of the titles he was considering was "Sheil vs. Spellman: Democracy against Fascism." So much, however, did Mrs. Meyer want to advance the cause of her beloved Bishop Sheil that she finally arranged to have an audience with Spellman, who she thought was blocking Sheil's ascension, to plead her case. She was not a woman who groveled, but she came close to it in her unsatisfying talk with Spellman. After she related this episode to Alinsky, he told her: "I have . . . a brilliant vision on how to have a perfect vacation at Mount Kisco. If I had Mount Kisco and the bowling alley in the basement and your dough, I would get a good craftsman who could carve bowling pins in the form of certain bishops and archbishops that we both know—and could we have a picnic!!!"

Alinsky's own interest in the Catholic Church centered largely on its politics, both internal and in relation to other institutions and forces in American society. The rituals and dogma of religion were of far less interest, and indeed, among friends, he could be openly contemptuous about not only Catholic rituals but religious rituals generally. When he found himself at a mass, he would have nothing to do with any friendly suggestion that he kneel politely in prayer. When Mrs. Meyer heard a rumor that Bishop Sheil was on the verge of being made an archbishop, she chided Alinsky: "I can already see us at the ceremony, me being very embarrassed because you won't kneel. Really, Saul, it wouldn't hurt you a bit." Even at a Seder dinner with friends during Passover, Alinsky could be irreverently uncooperative. Fran Gitelson, who was Gentile but whose husband, Max, was Jewish, invited Helene and Saul and another couple to the first Seder dinner that she hosted. Of that memorable night, she recalls: "We tried to start the Seder service [with] Saul taking an active part. He knew Hebrew and could read from the Haggadah. It wasn't very long, however, before it got to be an absolute panic because he just hammed it up so . . . and at the same time sort of poked fun [at the whole thing]. [It] turned out to be a real fiasco in terms of anything serious, but it was a fun evening eventually," since no one in the group was offended.

On theological and related philosophical issues, Alinsky had a stronger interest but still not the kind of intense intellectual curiosity that might have led him to serious study. In his relationship with Jacques Maritain, for instance, one has the impression that it was Maritain who believed he had learned something important from Alinsky, but not the reverse. For Alinsky, Maritain mainly confirmed what he already believed—that democratic values and the ideals of social and economic justice ought to be central concerns of the Catholic Church. Alinsky was not oblivious to Maritain's analyses and argumentation, but simply not much interested in studying them closely. His conversations with Maritain were often about his own observations of the Church's rigidity. After the war, as anti-communist sentiments began to run strong in the United States, Alinsky told Maritain that his community councils continued to work with all groups, including communists, as long as the latter cooperated and did not interfere or try to take them over. "I am not so concerned with [the communists] as I am about the shortsighted position taken by a number of leading Catholic prelates who denounce Communism and do nothing else. . . . They do nothing but moan and wail about the fears of Communism and advance nothing constructive, no positive program, no willingness to share the problems of mankind and to cooperate in the fight for their solution." In a similar vein, Alinsky also told Maritain about his reaction to Roberto Rossellini's film *Open City,* about the fight of the Italian Resistance against the Nazi occupation. The protagonists were a Catholic priest and a communist, of whom the latter reminded Alinsky of his friend Herb March. "I don't mind telling you," Alinsky related to Maritain, "that I was deeply moved by the picture. The presentation of the human, really spiritual values, apparent in both the Communist and the Catholic priest through the Nazi ordeal, made a tremendous impression on me. I think that I was just as surprised to see the rich, spiritual beauty inside the heart of the Catholic priest as I was at that inside of the Communist (this may be a terrible thing to say, but I know that you will understand)."

Alinsky also had ongoing discussions about religious and political philosophy with another friend, Gretta Palmer, a journalist who met Alinsky when she wrote a story on the Back of the Yards Neighborhood Council for *Coronet.* Palmer, who was in the process of converting to

Catholicism, was increasingly preoccupied with religion and had begun to look at nearly all political and philosophical issues from a religious perspective. Because Alinsky otherwise liked her and also enjoyed a certain amount of philosophical jousting, he put up with this. On one occasion, when Alinsky referred to Jeffersonian ideals, Palmer replied:

> Will I be accused of a further tiresome attempt to proselytize if I point out that the sanctity of the individual is a conception (radical, indeed, as you say!) which is tenable only in a religious frame-work? If a man is a child of God and half-divine, then he is safe from persecution for his political views. . . . But as soon as you remove the religious support for the idea, it seems to me that you are almost forced to accept the Statist view: the idea that the good of the majority, living or to-be-born, is primary and that any individual who gets in the way must be sacrificed. That, of course, is the first step to Dachau.

To which Alinsky responded: "The question of course arises, what and whose religious framework? I think that, for example, Tom Jefferson and Tom Paine were deeply religious persons even though from an orthodox religious point of view, they might be considered as agnostics." Then, while essentially agreeing with the logic of Palmer's statement that the sanctity of the individual was possible only within a religious framework, Alinsky argued from another perspective:

> [Your] statement cannot stand completely by itself as for example, take the Nazis. I hate dictatorship, totalitarianism and Fascism with all of my heart and soul (and you know that). I would have been in favor of wholesale execution of the Nazis and, sister, I mean *wholesale.* Yet I suppose a Nazi is a child of God. But on this point of the conflict between the basic love for all individuals which is fundamental to organized religion, as over against the expression of hate which I have just given vent to, there seems to be [a] fundamental contradiction. This is one of the subjects that Maritain and I have had long conversations about. . . . As yet I have not found the answer. I hate injustice; I hate persecution; I hate people that for their own personal reasons degrade great parts of humanity; I hate them with a burning passion and yet they are individuals and I firmly believe, I completely believe in the concept of the dignity and sanctity of the individual. We shall go into this philosophical contradiction on our next breaking of bread and coffee (but believe me it won't be at a communion breakfast).

Even with Gretta Palmer, Alinsky found opportunities for light-hearted banter about religion. She once asked Alinsky how much she would have to spend to buy a pectoral cross for a prelate with whom she had become friendly. Alinsky told her it would cost hundreds of dollars, maybe more. Doubtful, Palmer asked another friend, who told her she could get one for as little as seventy-five dollars, an estimate she triumphantly relayed to Alinsky. He growled:

> Don't be silly about the $75 Pectoral Cross. You can believe in the Immaculate Conception; you can believe in the Divine Mysteries; you can believe in the Resurrection; you can believe in the Miracle of Christ feeding the people on a loaf of bread and some fish but believe me, Gretta, and take it from a hard-headed and yet religious guy like myself who has gone through the valley of the shadow of the commercial aspects of the church, there just ain't no 75 buck Pectoral Cross!!! I'll make a deal with you. You get me a six bit Pectoral Cross and I'll split the Red Sea for you—or if I am too busy to take a long trip, will you settle for Lake Michigan? Faith is faith, kid, but you better confine it to elements less tangible than a Pectoral Cross.

THE CATHOLIC PRIESTS who had worked closely with Saul Alinsky and Joe Meegan to build the Back of the Yards Neighborhood Council became critically important during the Packinghouse Workers' strike in January 1946. The call for a strike was a historic, dramatic, and potentially dangerous move by the still fledgling union, and its first major walkout. Chicago labor disputes were historically violent—memories were still fresh of the Memorial Day Massacre and even of the viciousness of the packers' union-busting activities earlier in the century. This time, the prominent support of the priests, and of the Back of the Yards Neighborhood Council, helped to produce a climate more favorable to the striking workers.

Alinsky created a visible role for himself as the strike date approached. With the approval of the union leaders, he chaired a citizens' committee to support the Packinghouse Workers' demands. The citizens' committee was neither innocuous nor peripheral, for the companies were hoping that public antagonism would break the union. In fact, Mrs. Meyer warned Alinsky that she thought the union was making a big mistake, that even though the workers were underpaid in comparison with other industries, a strike—coming on top of postwar strikes in other basic industries—

would trigger a hostile reaction, especially if the public could not buy meat. She suggested to Alinsky that he keep his distance from the national leadership of the strike and also think of a way to insulate the Back of the Yards movement from becoming a secondary target of the likely public and press hostility.

Alinsky had no such cautious approach in mind. He identified closely with the Packinghouse Workers and respected its best leaders such as Herb March. Moreover, it had always been one of his primary aims to rally the Catholic community to support the union, and he agreed, besides, with both the necessity of a strike and the timing of it. He called Walter Johnson, his history professor friend at the University of Chicago, and gave him his marching orders: "You're going to be chairman of the All-Chicago Committee for the Packinghouse Workers, and we're going to have a meeting and press conference at your house." As Alinsky began to round up other prominent Chicagoans, he wrote to Agnes Meyer that "I am going to have some fun with these Liberals . . . who are so bold and do so much grimacing but run like Hell when anything happens." He told her of a letter of invitation he was thinking of sending to the president of the University of Chicago, Robert Hutchins.

> I am asking you to become a member of the All-Chicago Committee for the Packinghouse Workers [it would begin]. I assume you will be glad to become a member because in your opening address before the Political Action Committee mass meeting at the Stevens Hotel . . . you stated, "Now is the time for every man to stand up and be counted." Despite the fact that I am a University of Chicago graduate, I have spent the last ten years . . . with working people of this country and thinking in their terms and having adopted their idioms and never having studied the Great Books, I am wondering if what you meant is what we all mean when we say, "There comes time in the life of every man when he either has to get off the pot or let go." Will you please inform me of your intentions?

Alinsky asked gleefully, "Do you agree with me that a picture of Hutchins trying to make up his mind on the pot would definitely be the picture of the year?"

While the All-Chicago Committee provided useful public relations and moral support, the priests and the BYNC provided much more. When the first picket lines went up in the Chicago stockyards at 12:01 a.m. on January 16, Alinsky and Meegan were there, bundled in heavy overcoats, together with two Catholic priests, who were officers in the BYNC, and a minister from the Lutheran church. (A photo of the picketers, with the clergy wearing "On Strike" signs draped from their necks, appeared the next day on the front page of the Chicago *Sun.*) Picket-line priests were not a common sight in Chicago. Their presence not only was a moral endorsement of the workers' cause but also conveyed a message to the companies and to the Chicago police. Only several weeks before, the police department's labor detail had raided CIO picket lines outside a struck gear plant, an action that was applauded and encouraged by the Chicago *Tribune,* which spoke about the menace of labor "mobs." Some leaders of the Packinghouse Workers Union thought the police action was intended to establish a precedent for action during their coming strike, but with priests manning and endorsing the picket line, the police were less likely to make a decisive partisan move—and, in fact, there were only minor incidents during the ten-day strike. Still, as symbolically important as the picketing priests were, other, tangible expressions of community support were at least as important. During the strike, the BYNC contributed $1,000 to a strike fund, helped with a mobile soup kitchen, supported efforts of the sisters at the Guardian Angel nursery who served thousands of meals to strikers, and worked with the union to persuade local merchants to extend credit to union families. The strike, which led to a wage increase, was a success, a glorious victory for workers in an industry that had been, with few exceptions, ruthlessly dominated by the bosses. In one postmortem in the *Nation,* it was observed that "the strikers in Chicago gained a degree of community support which in the old days would have been inconceivable." Notably, the absence of a violent police assault was "due [especially] to the extraordinary support mobilized for the workers by the so-called Back of the Yards Council. This curious institution is, in a way, the lengthened shadow of one Saul Alinsky. . . . [A]mong Chicago packinghouse workers there is complete agreement about the usefulness of the Yards Council."

The negotiations and strike were big news. Alinsky had made a point of slipping interesting, juicy tidbits of information about behind-the-scenes events to Agnes Meyer, the Macys, and other financial supporters. He knew that they would be interested and that they would appreciate having a good source at the center of action. Sometimes, to heighten the drama, Alinsky would suddenly write in the middle of a letter about a fast-breaking piece of news: "I just got a flash that Secretary of Agriculture Anderson has just fallen into the packers' trap," he told Agnes Meyer. With one potential supporter in New York, he took a different, more prudent tack:

... the union is completely dependent upon my personal efforts to try to avoid the downpour of public indignation—when the American people find . . . there is *no* meat to be had. I am personally in violent disagreement with the position taken on certain issues on both sides, but never having been cut out to be a philosopher and to enjoy the luxury of the grandstand seat and always believing, as I have, that in a fight neither side is completely right—that you have to pick one side and get into it—therefore I am where I am.

Although Alinsky seemed willing here to adjust his rhetoric to suit a conservative, he nevertheless had genuine doubts about the compromises the union made. When Alinsky heard that the Secretary of Agriculture was likely to recommend that the government raise the ceilings on meat prices (war price controls were still in effect) if the workers won their hourly wage increase, he told Agnes Meyer:

This really puts me over a barrel. You know and I know . . . that an increase in the cost-of-living—particularly in food—will wipe out whatever economic gains are made and as you will remember from the second chapter of my book, I raise hell with labor unions for doing this very thing, and yet there is not a union in the country that has its membership sufficiently educated to understand what ceilings are all about and the fact that a union member is also a consumer. In a sense it is a tribute to the narrow trade-union selfish power bloc philosophy which has developed in this country. [But yet] if the union's officials say that they refuse to accept a raise unless the ceilings are maintained their membership will drive them out of office.

The BYNC and Saul Alinsky gained additional prominence because of their support of the strike against the packers. The priests and nuns on the picket lines seemed to symbolize the new spirit of community flourishing in the old stockyards neighborhood. A scene like that would make the perfect climax to a movie, thought a young screenwriter by the name of Larry Bachmann. Bachmann had been sent in 1947 to Chicago by his boss, Pare Lorentz, an outstanding film critic who had also made two great documentary films during the Depression. Lorentz, who was married to one of Agnes and Eugene Meyer's daughters, Elizabeth, and had heard about Alinsky from his mother-in-law, was working on a series of films for the War Department to be shown in Japan and Germany as part of an effort to reorient and educate the people in democratic values and methods: one movie was intended to deal with tensions among antagonistic ethnic and racial groups—problems that Americans themselves, obviously, had not been wholly successful in solving. Mrs. Meyer told Lorentz that Saul Alinsky's work in the Back of the Yards was a dramatic, conspicuous success story in intergroup harmony. But Bachmann was doubtful about the feasibility of doing such a movie. "When I was given the assignment by Lorentz . . . I thought it absurd; there was no way quickly to do it, nor were there [good] examples. Then, when I read *Reveille for Radicals,* and talked to Lorentz, and then met Saul, I realized that this was the way to do the film and what a splendid film it would make."

Bachmann arrived in Chicago "in the bitter January of 1947 and spent a month with Saul. We became great friends." He was impressed with Alinsky's intelligence and sincerity.

> He also had a great sense of humor about himself—as though part of him was looking over his shoulder and kidding him, telling him he was doing a stupid thing or being pompous; [he] had an insight, a perspective into himself. He sort of chuckled and thought it amusing that he was so close to Bishop Sheil—what was a nice Jewish boy doing with a Catholic priest? Sure he was serious [about himself] but it was leavened by humor which although not modesty—Saul was never modest—still made him fun and warm. . . . Saul was endearing, and his ego didn't bother me, for I'd been raised in the hotbed of egos—Hollywood.

Sometimes Alinsky was an unintentional source of amusement to Bachmann, especially when Alinsky tried to appear more cosmopolitan or accomplished in certain social graces than he actually was. They were walking down the street one day when, Bachmann remembers, he abruptly pulled me into a cafeteria just under the elevated rails of the Loop.

> "I want to show you something great," he said. "You want coffee, don't you?" It was cold and I readily agreed. He insisted I have pumpkin pie. "But I don't want pumpkin pie," I protested. "You have to have it." Then, when we sat down, he revealed his discovery. He scooped the whipped cream from the top of the pie and put it on top of the coffee. "Delicious," he said. I agreed—but the Viennese had discovered this quite a few years before and called it *Kaffee mit Schlag.*

Bachmann finished his screenplay—the climax was the priests and nuns on the picket lines—but then, unexpectedly, the War Department for budgetary reasons canceled the remaining films Lorentz was working on. Bachmann was almost as disappointed as Alinsky. Alinsky asked Mrs. Meyer to intervene. She subsequently told Alinsky that Secretary of War Robert Patterson himself had informed her there was no chance of the project being continued, but he asked her to try again. She was puzzled by Alinsky's adamancy, for the movie on the BYNC, like all the other films in this project, was to be shown only overseas. But Alinsky had his own special audience in mind: he had envisioned screening a print of the movie at private fund-raising sessions. What would have been more powerful and persuasive with wealthy supporters than a movie the American government was using to educate Europe and Japan! He could even see himself being invited to Rome or to Paris or to Tokyo to lecture and to consult. But no sooner had this golden opportunity slipped through his fingers than another important media opportunity came unexpectedly his way when he received a phone call from Bob Shayon.

Robert Shayon had gone to work for CBS Radio in 1942, served overseas as a war correspondent, and worked with the most famous American broadcaster in Europe during the war, Edward R. Murrow. After the war, Murrow became vice president in charge of public affairs for CBS. One of his first decisions was to establish a documentary unit that would do shows about major social problems and issues. Shayon, who became one of Murrow's producers, remembers that Murrow and "a number of his colleagues, myself included, . . . having recalled that radio did an outstanding job of public service during the war years . . . had a vision that this same trend could be continued into the postwar years." Shayon's first assignment from Murrow, in the aftermath of the bombing of Hiroshima and Nagasaki, was to do an hour-long program on the promises and dangers of atomic energy. The radio show—broadcast from the Library of Congress and including an array of eminent people such as Albert Einstein, Supreme Court Justice William Douglas, and the poet Archibald Mac-Leish—was considered a huge success, Shayon recalls, and led quickly to his second assignment, a program on juvenile delinquency.

Although the war had helped to end the Depression and had brought a measure of prosperity to most Americans, it also produced many social dislocations—prolonged and often permanent family breakups as husbands went off to war; old roots torn up as families moved to unfamiliar cities where defense-plant jobs could be had; housing shortages; new racial tensions as blacks began to migrate to the North and West. In the midst of such rapid changes, there seemed to be a new, ominous wave of juvenile delinquency, so much so that it once again reached the lofty status of a "major national problem." Traveling extensively, Shayon spent months researching his assignment, visiting juvenile facilities, death-row cells, and other examples of a failed system. "It was a totally depressing experience," he recalls, "because you saw that youthful crime is an endemic phenomenon of our capitalist society. Every once in a while there is a flurry of concern, an investigation and a proposed program. But when that's over, nothing ever happens; there's no way out of it. Well, I had that feeling as I came to Chicago, which was my last stop."

One of the resource people to whom Shayon had been directed was Howland Shaw, Alinsky's friend and a member of his board. Shaw impressed Shayon as a strange anomaly—an aristocrat, an elitist in the State Department tradition, who nevertheless had a passionate interest in and commitment to Alinsky's work. Shaw told Shayon to see Alinsky in Chicago. After a phone call and a meeting in Alinsky's office, Shayon suddenly had a new perspective on his heretofore dismal inspection tour. He soon had the feeling that "I had done the swing around the country to meet Saul Alinsky. He impressed me as a gentle, arrogant individual, very fascinating, very much concerned with his own world, but a charming fellow." Alinsky gave him a tour of the Back of the Yards and introduced him to Council leaders. "I lit up like an electric tree because in his neighborhood council ideal I saw a vision of hope, of democracy solving its own problems."

Inspired, Shayon wrote a powerful script, and he searched for the best radio actors to read it. Joseph Cotten would do the narration. Shayon wanted Luther Adler to play Alinsky, but with deadlines fast approaching, Adler could not be found; he was somewhere in Florida. Shayon got a CBS affiliate in Florida to broadcast a message that he was looking for Adler. The actor heard it, called Shayon, and agreed to come to New York to do the role.

The uplifting message of "The Eagles Brood" was that America's delinquent-prone children could be saved and the epidemic of delinquency wiped out, not by individual "treatment," reform schools, or incarceration, but rather by cleaning up the "swamp" in which delinquency breeds— specifically, by the kind of "grass-roots democracy" that Saul Alinsky had planted in the Back of the Yards. Shayon's script, which followed the sequence of his own research findings as he had traveled around the country, reached a climax soon after Alinsky was introduced. Two-thirds of the way into the show, the radio program's narrator asked whether there was a way to get out of the morass of juvenile delinquency, which was a threat to the country's future. "In a slum in a stockyard neighborhood that had fed more juvenile delinquents to the prisons of our nation than any other, I met a man who answered my question. He was young, but there was gray around his temples. He'd been a welfare worker, a criminologist; he'd studied gangs, worked in prisons, written books. He was a man with a vision, the director of an organization helping to start neighborhood councils all over America. He spoke with drive and boundless enthusiasm."

Neither Alinsky nor the BYNC was mentioned by name in "The Eagles Brood," but Alinsky was ecstatic about a broadcast that was "as outstanding a public acknowledgment of our work and philosophy as we can ever expect to get." He told Happy Macy that "the reaction to the broadcast was quite terrific and we understand that CBS is being deluged with requests for identification of the 'young criminologist with graying temples—the man with the vision' so that they can get him into their communities."

WITH GREAT OPTIMISM, Saul Alinsky was off again to California to track down new fund-raising leads and to launch a long-delayed project on the West Coast. His optimism was understandable: during the past fifteen months he had been on a roll, with a best-selling book, acclaim for his role in the Packinghouse Workers' strike, and now the CBS radio program. If the spring and summer of 1939 in Chicago, when he met Bishop Sheil and John L. Lewis, had been a pivotal time of his life, then the spring of 1947 was an apogee. Although he was not yet forty, his star was shining brighter than ever.

The trip to California was reasonably successful. Near the end of his stay, Alinsky had to turn down an invitation from the film actor Melvyn Douglas to host a small fund-raising gathering because he was due back in Chicago for a party celebrating his fifteenth wedding anniversary. Alinsky was supposed to arrive in Chicago on Sunday, June 9, shortly after noon, in time for the party that night. At noon on Sunday, however, Alinsky's train was stranded on a siding in a flooded Iowa cornfield. He didn't arrive in Chicago until the next morning.

Fran Gitelson, who helped Helene to prepare the food for the party, recalls being angry at Alinsky for not showing up. She remembers thinking that, regardless of the weather and the train delay, Alinsky could have been there had he planned differently. "I had some negative feelings about Saul. I was fond of him; we had many good times together. [But] there was a side of him that was selfish, narcissistic, and really not terribly considerate about other people. I had the feeling that he used Helene a great deal in the sense of always depending on her to be [available] and to take up the slack." Fran and her husband, Max, who had worked with Alinsky at the

state prison in Joliet and was a close Hyde Park friend, were both psychiatrists. At one point, they speculated "about Saul perhaps needing to be analyzed to try to work out" the needs and feelings that were producing his most conspicuously self-absorbed behavior. "We finally decided that that probably was not the way to go with him because he might lose some of the drive he had to achieve—and he was doing such important [and] significant work, and it would have been a shame to have lost his capacities with that."

Fran Gitelson knew that Helene loved Saul deeply and that the two were compatible. Helene was a woman of such genuine warmth, friendliness, and pragmatic, commonsense intelligence that none of the Alinskys' Hyde Park friends ever saw her as playing the mouse to her husband's lion. She understood people, including her husband, and, as Fran Gitelson saw it, "she held her own, but she didn't try to outshine Saul." Helene was loyal and supportive; she considered Saul's work important, and a contrast to the conventional, materialistic world of Elkins Park which she had escaped when she married him.

With Saul doing a lot of traveling after the war, Helene spent much of her time raising Kathryn, who was now eight, and David, three. During the week, with David in tow, she might meet Fran Gitelson and her child at a park, midway between the Alinskys' apartment on Blackstone and the Gitelsons' apartment near Lake Michigan, in East Hyde Park. Once a week, Helene and a group of mothers with young children—Marian Despres, Dot Liveright, Bea Mayer, Mary Meltzer—would meet for what they called their sewing group, but these sessions were devoted mostly to gossip.

These women provided the impetus for a new amateur theatrical group that was started after the War. A play by Jean-Paul Sartre, *The Respectful Prostitute,* had recently been banned, and the women thought it would be fun to get a copy and perform it at one of their houses. Over the next twenty years, about fifteen Hyde Park couples met periodically at one another's homes to read and act out plays. It was good fun, but also done with some seriousness; there would be a rehearsal, costumes, and scenery. A memorable scene from one of the early productions featured Saul Alinsky. It was the Greek comedy *Lysistrata,* a play in which one character (Alinsky's) suddenly has an enormous erection. Leon Despres remembers that "Saul was wearing a white gown, and he had a big stick that he pushed through the gown. He just thought that part was wonderful." Despres also remembers that even in performing the plays, Alinsky could be difficult. "He wasn't very disciplined . . . and wouldn't accept direction very well."

Helene and Saul had a pleasant, comfortable niche in the social life

of Hyde Park. In addition to the drama group, there was a regular poker game, and there were small dinner parties on the weekends, with Helene and Saul going over to Tink and Walter Johnson's house, or to Rachel and Ralph Helstein's. Everybody liked Helene, and if people's opinions about Saul were often mixed, he could at least be counted on to be interesting and amusing.

Soon after Alinsky returned from his California trip, Helene and the children left for Beverly Shores in the Indiana Dunes, a popular summer vacation place on the other side of Lake Michigan, just below the Michigan-Indiana state line. The summer before, Helene and Saul had rented a cabin in the Smoky Mountains, near Gatlinburg, Tennessee, for August. It had been a favored spot—they had been there shortly after they were married, and again in 1939—but the vacation had a number of snafus as far as Alinsky was concerned. They hadn't been able to find babysitters, which meant that they had to stay close to their cabin and with their children, not Saul's idea of a great vacation. "It was impossible to get into a hotel dining room because two-and-a-half-year-old David would jump out of his high chair and wreak havoc over the dining room," Alinsky told a friend. Like the acerbic comedian W. C. Fields, he tended to think that young children should be neither seen nor heard. "The two restaurants that we did eat in," he wisecracked, "promptly posted signs over their shambles as we left, reading, 'Restricted, and particularly so to any future Alinskys.' " Still grimacing at the thought of the experience, he told a friend later from the safety of his Chicago office:

> All of the crawling insect life of the Smokies came out during the month of August, and after slugging lizards all over the living room and having their tails break into three and four pieces and go crawling around in different directions, plus myriads of spiders and an occasional black widow, I finally turned to Helene, at the end of three weeks, and said, "Now, you know that I have a terrific schedule ahead of me, so please give me a break and let's go back to Chicago so that I will have one week to recuperate from this vacation."

After the experience in the Smokies, Helene and Saul's plans for the summer of 1947 seemed like a good compromise: Saul took Helene and the kids to the cottage in the Dunes, where they were to stay from July 1 through early September. The beach was fun for Kathryn and David. There were many Hyde Parkers who vacationed in Beverly Shores whom Helene knew. And late in August some of the women from Helene's sewing group went out to see her and to enjoy the cool Lake Michigan breezes and

to swim a little. Meanwhile, Saul, restless and with a busy summer agenda, commuted to the cottage on weekends. During the week he was often traveling: he and Bishop Sheil spent the better part of a week at Mount Kisco with Agnes Meyer and her family; late in July he was in Kansas City and in early August in Butte, Montana, to look at the possibility of starting a community council there. Back in Chicago, there was an occasional out-of-town visitor, such as Val Macy, on his way West to vacation at a Wyoming ranch.

Dorothy Liveright was part of Helene's sewing group. She and her husband, Sandy, were Hyde Park friends of Helene and Saul. As the summer wound down, Dot and Sandy invited Saul to a casual, neighborly after-work dinner in Chicago on the first Tuesday in September. Labor Day had just passed, and Saul's weekday bachelor life was about to end: in a few more days, he would be picking up Helene and the kids and bringing them back to Hyde Park.

Dinner at the Liverights' was over, or maybe the three of them were still sitting at the table, drinking coffee and having an after-dinner ciga-rette—Dot Liveright cannot remember for sure. But she remembers the phone ringing. She remembers a voice asking if Saul Alinsky was there. Yes, he is. Do you want to speak with him? No, the caller wanted to speak with her husband first. So it was Sandy Liveright who was the first to hear what had happened, and it was Sandy Liveright who somehow had to walk into the next room and tell his friend Saul the unimaginably horrible, incredible news that there had been an accident, a terrible, tragic accident, and that Helene was dead.

It was the worst of nightmares, and nobody could believe it was real. Helene had drowned in Lake Michigan, the caller said. When Saul first heard Liveright say something about an accident and saw the expression on his face, he thought something had happened to one of his children. It was beyond his comprehension—it was really beyond everybody's compre-hension—that Helene could have drowned. Helene had always been mar-velously athletic and was an outstanding swimmer. As a girl she had been the captain of the water-sports team at the fancy summer camp in Maine she had gone to and had taught swimming and Red Cross lifesaving classes.

There were different versions of what happened in Lake Michigan off the Beverly Shores beach early that Tuesday evening. Probably the most accurate account is this: The Alinskys' daughter, Kathryn, and another girl were playing on a sandbar off the beach. A woman and her nine-year-old son were also on the sandbar. Suddenly, an undertow dragged the children into deep water. Helene, who was on the beach, rushed into the water and began to swim out to the children. A college boy who was also there, the brother of the nine-year-old, did not know how to swim but quickly paddled out in a rubber raft. He rescued his brother while his mother made it safely to shore. Then the college boy paddled out beyond the sandbar again to help Helene and the other children. When he got to her, Helene's head and body were underwater but, with her strong arms and shoulders, she was somehow holding Kathryn and the other girl above her head and above the surface of the water. The rescuer pulled the girls into the raft; they had been saved. He then dragged Helene in, too. She was already unconscious. On the beach, he applied artificial respiration until a pulmotor squad arrived. But it was too late.

The Liverights and Ralph Helstein drove Saul to Beverly Shores late that night, and the next day they all came back with the kids. Saul was devastated, weeping for the loss of Helene, blaming everybody, including himself, for what had happened. He was a man who needed and wanted to be in control, and now his life was out of control, turned upside down and inside out. He was desperate for help, for the kind of help that his psychiatrist friend Max Gitelson might be able to provide—as much for himself as for Kathryn and David. He tried calling Max, only to discover that the Gitelsons were in a remote area of the Sierras in California on a backpacking trip. But Alinsky's urgent message was somehow passed along, and as Fran and Max had just climbed on horseback to the top of Army Passage late in the afternoon, they were met by a forest ranger who told them the sad, shocking news. First thing the next morning, Max and Fran left on horseback, riding over Mount Whitney and back to civilization, where Max was transported to a plane and a flight to Chicago in time to attend the funeral.

There was no great psychiatric wisdom, of course, proportional to this cataclysmic tragedy. Rather, the simple human virtues of love and compassion, and a neighborly instinct to help with the daily demands of life, were most important and comforting to Saul Alinsky. The many expressions of support had already begun. The women in Helene's sewing group and others in the neighborhood started to make plans to help with the children. Ralph Helstein canceled his trip to Canada to help Saul with the funeral arrangements. And at the funeral, even the Italian kids from the West Side with whom Saul had worked fifteen years before—Felix, Stiff, Nick—came to express their friendship and sorrow. Saul Alinsky would need all of these expressions of affection and support, for the pain and loneliness had only begun.

·   ·   ·

IT WAS EARLY in the evening, a decade or so after that fateful telephone call at the Liverights'. The sun had nearly disappeared from the Chicago sky, and darkness was filling Saul Alinsky's office above South Michigan Avenue. His secretary, who was about to go home, opened the door to say good night. It was a small office, sparsely furnished, with a desk, a chair, and a bookshelf. There was also a black leather lounge chair, and in the last flicker of the day's light through the blinds covering the window, the secretary could see Saul in the chair. He had apparently dozed off. She gently asked him, "Saul, is everything all right?" He, startled in the darkness, called out, "Helene?"

15

Good Fortune, Bad Luck

Without his friends, there is no telling how Saul Alinsky would have survived the weeks and months after Helene's death. In total despair, he had told his stepsister in Los Angeles, Kay Mann, that he didn't want to go on with life. She told him that the children needed him. The children did provide him with an immediate reason for carrying on, but they were also a constant reminder to him of Helene, and of how much he had depended on her, especially in caring for them. It was not only a matter of her being at home when he was out on the road. It was also a matter of Alinsky not having a great interest in, or the patience to relate to, small children. For Alinsky, the saving grace of children, any children, was that someday they would become adults.

Helene and Saul's friends, especially Helene's women friends, knew this side of Saul even if they had not found it attractive. But in the aftermath of the sudden tragedy, they also saw a vulnerable side of Saul they had not witnessed before. "[He] was absolutely helpless in terms of knowing what to do, how to provide, how to manage alone," Fran Gitelson remembers. They all pitched in to help him: Miriam Elson went shopping with him to buy clothes for the children; Rachel Helstein and others helped with the meals.

It was not long before Alinsky found a housekeeper, a Swedish woman everybody came to know simply as Karen. She was a warm, competent person who took care of Kathryn and David and, to a degree, became a substitute mother. And during the fall and winter after Helene's death, Alinsky drew closer to his new friend, Ralph Helstein, whom he had met in January 1946. Helstein, who was also in his late thirties, was born in Duluth, Minnesota, the only son of an Orthodox Jewish family. They later moved to Minneapolis, where Helstein went to school, eventually receiving a law degree from the University of Minnesota. During the Depression, he worked for the National Recovery Administration in Washington and by 1942 was general counsel of the Packinghouse Workers Union in Chicago. As the union was moving closer to a strike in January 1946, Helstein recalls, Alinsky was furious over the maladroit public statements and general ineptitude of the union president, Lewis J. Clark. Helstein doesn't remember if he called Alinsky or vice versa, but they had their first meeting over the problem of Clark's leadership. They hit it off immediately, like the brothers whom neither of them had. "We stayed in the car until four in the morning talking about [the tactical statements that should be made] and about everything under the sun—women, politics," Helstein remembers. "It was the sort of thing you did in college, but at this point," he says, smiling, "I was thirty-six or thirty-seven years old." They both recognized on that first night that they shared many values and a similar political perspective. "We were both very sophisticated at this point and rather knowledgeable about how power operated," Helstein says. Not long after the strike in 1946, Helstein became president of the Packinghouse Workers, one of the few lawyers ever in the American labor movement to lead a union.

Within a few weeks of Helene's death, Alinsky was spending many evenings at the Helsteins' house, a few blocks away from his own apartment. Throughout the fall and then into the winter, Alinsky was either at the Helsteins' or with Dot and Sandy Liveright. Karen would serve dinner for him and the children, and then he would be off until midnight or later. He craved companionship. With the Liverights, he would tell the same stories over and over again, Dot and Sandy never letting on that they had heard them before. At the Helsteins, Ralph and Saul played a kid's game called Photo Electric Football, a board game of sorts that required one player to select a defense that would stop the opponent's offensive. The various defensive and offensive strategies were on large cards that Ralph and Saul would push into a slot and slide along the surface of the Photo Electric box. Then a light would shine from under the transparent cards, revealing whether or not the zigs and zags of the offensive play had eluded the defensive configuration. "We sat by the hour until one or two in the morning playing that game and loving it," Helstein remembers. Alinsky was never in a hurry to go home, because there was nothing to go home for. "One more cigarette," he would say several times before leaving, as each Pall Mall made the night a little shorter.

Nearly three months after Helene's death, Alinsky told Agnes Meyer that he was beginning to feel he was getting back a little of his fighting spirit:

The best example that I can give you is to quote one simple sentence from a speech I gave yesterday morning before the Illinois State Welfare Conference: "The meat packing industry has never been able to distinguish between a Hereford Steer and a Homo Sapiens." I am beginning my old anger at the meat packing industry and, well, I am just beginning to feel lots of things as I did before. [But] I haven't yet reached the point of doing any writing since that means sitting down alone with your thoughts.

But sentimental family occasions were especially difficult. With the first Christmas without Helene approaching, the otherwise happy memories of earlier celebrations only served to recall the terrible loss:

After two weeks of no tears one of my kids turned on the radio last night and the first Christmas carol came through, "Silent Night." Here after three months of always keeping myself under complete control in the presence of the kids . . . I suddenly cracked and wept for an hour. . . . The children took my outburst as they have everything else, with magnificent courage and real understanding. I felt somewhat ashamed of myself with an eight-year-old girl and a three-and-a-half-year-old boy each holding my hand and pressing it affectionately.

Alinsky's thoughts about Helene, and the sadness those thoughts evoked, were never far from his consciousness.

The acute, immobilizing mourning over Helene's death that afflicted him for many months slowly, gradually began to diminish, though for the rest of his life, on each June 9, his wedding anniversary, he would inevitably become withdrawn and morose. One incident supposedly helped to break the grief that had consumed him. He had been visiting Helene's grave regularly, he recounted many years later, despondent and mourning her loss, when one day he was interrupted by a cemetery worker who told him that he was mourning at the wrong grave. He suddenly recognized the futility, even the absurdity, of what he had been doing, and that helped him to focus on the future, to move forward with his life. Perhaps there was such an incident, but the passage of time and the stark reality that he had two children to support, plus a new, full-time housekeeper, helped, too, to refocus his attention and energy.

. . .

SAUL ALINSKY told his friends that because he needed the money he signed a contract with Putnam's to write a biography of John L. Lewis, which provided him with a $10,000 advance. By the spring of 1948, when he started to work on the Lewis book, the financial situation of the Industrial Areas Foundation was not good. A few months earlier, he had told Agnes Meyer, "As things stand now, I would say that we are roughly about $20,000 a year short (in other words, $40,000 for the next two year period). If we had that sum, I could operate without feeling any kind of concern or pressure." As it was, Alinsky had reason to be concerned. Bishop Sheil, through the Catholic Youth Organization, had apparently contributed $10,000 to the Foundation in 1947 or early 1948. No other single contribution had ever exceeded $5,000, the standard annual contribution from Alinsky's handful of ardent supporters. By the fall of 1948, however, Sheil was in a tight financial situation of his own—his financial house ranged regularly between chaos and a shambles—and he was forced to "redeem" his contribution to the Foundation. Val Macy arranged for a loan to carry the Foundation—which is to say, Alinsky—through the end of 1948. By 1949, however, Alinsky's financial fortunes had not improved. After Helene's death, Alinsky's board of directors had authorized a 50 percent increase in his salary, bringing it to $15,000 a year, and a new appropriation of $5,000 annually for a retirement fund. But in spite of the board's good intentions, none of the additional money was raised, and for the next several years, Alinsky deferred both his salary increase and the retirement-fund contribution. Happy Macy once again lamented that "something must be done to lift the Foundation out of the curse of being run like a charity organization, dependent on donations—it's undignified and unsatisfactory and there must be a better way."

In the meantime, Alinsky began to work on the Lewis book. Perhaps the advance, which was high for its time, and the prospect that a successful book would make even more money provided his immediate motives for doing the book, but it was also clear that Alinsky liked the idea of being a writer, if not the process of writing itself. He had enjoyed the acclaim, the attention, and the new forums that had resulted from *Reveille for Radicals.*

Lewis never let journalists or writers get too close to the inner workings of either his mind or his union business. There were some writers with whom he was more open than with others—for example, during the glory years of his CIO leadership, Louie Stark of *The New York Times* was one, and the young C. L. Sulzberger was another. (Sulzberger wrote a short biography of Lewis in 1938.) Of course, Lewis perceived advantages to himself in having a cordial relationship with a *Times* reporter and a member of the Sulzberger family. More typically, however, Lewis, who was a master of using the press and publicity to his advantage, kept reporters at arm's length; potential biographers were likely to be rebuffed totally. Thus, Lewis quickly rejected Alfred A. Knopf's proposal, including a substantial cash advance, that A. J. Liebling write his biography. And when Sidney James, assistant managing editor of *Life* magazine (and, coincidentally, a friend of Alinsky's), tried to flatter Lewis into cooperating on a biography in a series *Life* was doing on prominent world leaders such as Winston Churchill and Douglas MacArthur, Lewis was not interested.

Alinsky, of course, had nothing to do with Lewis's daily activities at the United Mine Workers. Lewis did not see Alinsky every day as he saw his union colleagues—men like Lee Pressman, Jett Lauck, or Phil Murray. Then again, even these colleagues were not close friends. Lewis did not have close personal relationships outside of his family.

There is no clear record of what, exactly, led to Alinsky's book about Lewis. How did the idea for the biography originate? Did Kathryn Lewis, John L.'s daughter and Alinsky's friend, first suggest the possibility? Did she do it out of sorrow for Alinsky's terrible tragedy, knowing her father would be sympathetic? A good friend of Kathryn's, Grace Kaplan, believes there was also a romantic motive on Kathryn's part, and that her father recognized it, and wanted to be helpful. Apart from that, many years later, Alinsky wrote of John L.'s own sensitive response some weeks after Helene's death. "I went to Washington and did what I had done every place else—walked alone. As I passed the White House the gate swung open and a big Cadillac came out. It braked to a sudden stop and out came Lewis. He had just left the President and suddenly saw his friend and knew of the ordeal. Without a word he put his arm through mine, and we walked for some hours in utter silence except for the frequent reassuring squeeze from the hand of that man."

Although friendship and sympathy probably had a lot to do with it, there were other factors, too. James Wechsler's *Labor Baron: A Portrait of John L. Lewis,* published in 1944, gave a highly unflattering account of John L. So, too, did Wellington Roe's *Juggernaut,* published in 1948, in which Lewis was discussed at length. In addition, many other critics were unforgiving of Lewis's behavior during the World War II coal strikes, especially in 1943 when he defied both the federal government and public opinion by leading 450,000 miners out on strike. By 1948, Lewis and his union "confronted opposition on all fronts," labor historians Melvyn Dubofsky and Warren Van Tine write. "Press and public opinion clearly aligned against them, with story after story portraying Lewis as a national ogre." Even if John L. Lewis did not profess great concern with this portrayal of him, his daughter, Kathryn, probably thought differently. "Katie had a sense of his role in history," says Len De Caux, who worked closely with Lewis when he headed the CIO and who also knew Kathryn. "She probably encouraged the old man [to help Alinsky write the book]. . . . [S]he wanted to have history tell good things about the old man and explain his role as much as possible."

Alinsky's sympathetic treatment does just that in *John L. Lewis: An Unauthorized Biography.* The phrase "unauthorized biography" is itself confusing, if not misleading, for it was literally true only in the narrowest sense. In a foreword, Alinsky wrote on the one hand, "I am most grateful to John L. Lewis for the unlimited time he placed at my disposal." On the other hand, he also said that he "made no commitments [to Lewis] of any kind. He knew that in this study the sharp edge of criticism would cut everywhere and everybody including himself—and it has." And after the publication of the Lewis biography, Alinsky told a doubtful Matthew Josephson, himself at work on a biography of Sidney Hillman, head of the Amalgamated Clothing Workers Union: "When I wrote the biography, I insisted that there be no strings attached and that Mr. Lewis would have no right nor would I permit him to look at any materials, conclusions, statements, or anything else. As a matter of fact, Mr. Lewis did not see a single word of the biography until it was published. I know that this sounds somewhat unlikely but you will have to accept my word that it is so."

The use of the phrase "unauthorized biography" gave both Lewis and Alinsky some small benefits. For Lewis, it was a matter of dignity: a great leader of his rank did not lower himself to promoting the story of his life. For Alinsky, the phrase connoted a measure of independence for him as the author and projected a degree of credibility into a book written by an admitted friend and associate. But Alinsky's contention in the foreword that his "sharp edge of criticism" fell equally on Lewis and others with whom Lewis worked or did battle is simply preposterous. Alinsky largely or totally ignored the seamier parts of Lewis's career, including the internal workings of his union; Alinsky's "criticism" of Lewis was, at its sharpest, done with a dull butter knife, applied lightly. Future labor historians were to be highly skeptical of the accuracy of Alinsky's treatment of several important episodes in Lewis's career.

Yet the book is not without virtues, providing as it does a glimpse into the always intriguing Lewisian mind. Lewis's verbatim accounts of the founding of the CIO, his break with President Roosevelt, his split with the CIO and his longtime associate Phil Murray, the coal strikes of 1943—all make for fascinating reading. Although the book was not a best-seller, it did receive a good deal of attention. It was excerpted in *Look* magazine, serialized in newspapers through the Des Moines *Register* syndicate, and reviewed widely.

One of the clear results of the book was that Saul Alinsky was now perceived publicly as an intimate of John L. Lewis. A photograph at the beginning of the book shows Alinsky sitting in a chair, pen and notebook in hand, while Lewis stands next to him, explaining his version of history. Footnotes cited the dates and places of interviews that Lewis gave to Alinsky in 1948 and 1949. The account of Alinsky and Bishop Sheil working together back in the fall of 1940, trying to head off the historic break between Lewis and Roosevelt, was included. And most suggestive of Alinsky's "intimate" relationship with Lewis was his account of a show-down meeting in October 1941 between Lewis and Murray. Murray had been Lewis's handpicked successor to head the CIO after Lewis stuck to his promise to resign if Roosevelt was reelected in 1940 over Lewis's opposition. Soon thereafter, however, Lewis became the target of virulent criticism by almost every CIO union, especially because of his continued isolationism. Even the communist-dominated unions, which had approved of this stance before Hitler invaded the Soviet Union in June 1941, were now attacking him. Lewis wanted Murray, as CIO president, to stop these attacks, and the confrontation between the two men became front-page news. Of that confrontation, Alinsky wrote:

> The author was in Atlantic City during those two days at Lewis's invitation, stopping at the President Hotel, where Lewis, Mrs. Lewis, and their daughter, Kathryn, were also staying. He was continuously present in conversation with the Lewis family immediately before and after Lewis's visits with Murray. There had been a brief meeting the previous afternoon, and on this day there were to be two meetings between them, one in the afternoon and the other in the late evening. Lewis was extremely upset that day and recounted his conference with Murray in great detail. The writer has no question of the unvarnished validity of Lewis's statements . . . of that day. Lewis was talking to his wife and daughter, and if ever there was a situation when one could be certain that Lewis was giving the bald facts, it was here. Immediately following these meetings with the Lewis family, the author, unknown to Lewis, retired to his room and made copious notes of what had been said, with the belief that it was important historical material.

After the last, fateful meeting with Murray, Lewis invited Alinsky to join the Lewis family in the nearly deserted hotel dining room. He began to rail against Murray, how Murray would not acknowledge that others in the CIO were maneuvering against Lewis, how Murray was totally unprepared, in Lewis's view, to provide tough, decisive leadership on a range of labor issues. Then, as Alinsky wrote,

> Lewis looked about the empty dining room. I realized with a shock that he was moved to the point of tears. The muscles of his face were working, and he seemed to be fighting to keep his emotions under control. Suddenly tears rolled down his cheeks. Lowering his head, he said, "This is the same hotel, this is the same dining room, and this is the same table where in 1935 a small group and myself walked out of the AF of L convention, which was a few steps away at the boardwalk, sat down here at this table, and organized the CIO." Then turning to me, Lewis continued, "Where you are sitting, Saul, David Dubinsky sat. And Mother, where you are sitting, sat Sidney Hillman, and [Charles P.] Howard sat where you are, Kathryn." Lewis then paused, clenched his fist, pushed against the edge of the table, and arising said, "Here I conceived and built the CIO, and it is here that I leave it!"

In the years to come, there was an association of Alinsky with Lewis in terms of their organizing ability and style—the aggressiveness; the gamesmanship; the deliberately provocative challenges and insults to opponents; first the promotion of conflict, then the negotiated resolution of it to win political advantage; the use of power. His Lewis biography—his obvious access to Lewis and his firsthand accounts of important episodes in Lewis's career—allowed Alinsky later to invoke Lewis as "my teacher." And in the 1940s, being a student of Lewis's in the field of organizing, tactics, and power conferred a status that might be akin, say, to a young cellist studying with Casals or a young artist with Picasso.

But one must nonetheless ask just how close the relationship was and whether much of Alinsky's learning was done by long-distance observation rather than through personal tutelage. Alinsky's "firsthand" accounts of Lewis's thought and motivations draw skeptical comments from later biographers of Lewis such as Dubofsky and Van Tine. "Nothing in the surviving Lewis papers," they write, "suggests that Alinsky and Lewis were close, met often, or engaged in long conversation." They doubt that Lewis "would have opened his soul to Saul Alinsky." And there is no trace of any correspondence between Lewis and Alinsky in either man's papers.

To Alinsky's friends, however, there was little doubt that Lewis and Alinsky were close. Ralph Helstein feels certain that Alinsky and Lewis had a close "personal relationship" in the 1940s and early 1950s. He remembers attending a lunch in Chicago that Alinsky arranged for Lewis and has the impression that Alinsky saw Lewis in New York and Washington. Helstein is not surprised that there is little documentation of their relationship, in large part because Lewis quite intentionally avoided leaving a paper trail about his activities whenever possible. One controlled the public record by *not* leaving a record: that was Lewis's mode of operation. Another friend of Alinsky's, Julius C. C. Edelstein, who then worked in Washington on the staff of Senator Herbert Lehman of New York, remembers that "every time [Saul] came to Washington, he would have lunch or dinner with Lewis. It was either [lunch or dinner] with me or with John L. Lewis; we divided up his social life." And others who knew Alinsky also recall similar social settings. Palmer Weber, for example, an organizer of the CIO's political action committee in the mid-1940s, remembered, "I met John L. Lewis with Saul in Washington in the Carlton Hotel in the dining room," a hangout for Lewis. "He was completely at ease with Saul." As for Alinsky's book, Weber thought the time had come when not only Kathryn Lewis but John L. himself—who was nearly seventy years old when Alinsky's biography was published—"wanted to have somebody do a book that would keep other people from reviling him. His main great period in life was over, and he knew it. [A friendly book] was preparatory against the time when some idiotic academic s.o.b. would turn him into a monster or vilify him. He wanted a portrait done [by] somebody he knew was fundamentally friendly to him, understood him, felt the same way he did about what had happened."

Saul Alinsky more than understood John L. Lewis; he identified with him. The rousing final lines of the biography suggest the attitude, spirit, style, and accomplishment that Alinsky admired—and perhaps found in himself. When the time comes for John L. Lewis to pass from the scene, Alinsky concluded,

> America will sigh with relief, and yet America will sorely miss him. We shall miss . . . his unbearable insolence to all authorities, the grimness of his unparalleled, stiff-necked determination, and his colorful epithets. We will miss cursing, ridiculing, fuming over him, and giving that grudging admiration for his doing what so many people would like to do: openly and successfully defy the political as well as the economic royalists. We shall realize that his defiance of every power was a note of reassurance for the security of the democratic idea, that his dissonance was part of our national music. . . . But until that time, today, as before, and to the end, Lewis will continue. . . .

The years of thunder in the earth will roar on as Lewis lives on, for he is, as he has bellowed at his miners, "something of a man."

So, in Alinsky's final analysis, it came down to a question of manhood. The measure of a man was his bravery, his fearlessness, his courage, his strength. Those qualities had been important to Sollie Alinsky, too, the young boy in the old neighborhood in Chicago. Ten-year-old Sollie, whose own father was such a weak, forlorn figure, would go into the pool hall on Twelfth Street, around the corner from the Alinskys' apartment, where the older, tougher neighborhood guys hung out. One of the older guys would tell the ten-year-old to raise his arm and flex his muscle and, feeling it, would say to Sollie, "No, you're not ready yet, kid, to fight the Polacks." This little ritual went on for several years, until one day, when Sollie was thirteen or fourteen, one of the guys in the pool hall felt his muscle and told him he was ready now, that he had made it. It was a day Saul Alinsky never forgot, the day he became a man.

The biography of John L. Lewis was written quickly, in about five months, according to Alinsky. He apparently had a research assistant. Sidney Lens, a Chicago writer and labor-union activist, remembers such a person calling on him for material and him handing over a thick stack of papers that contained information critical of Lewis, none of which Alinsky incorporated in the book. Carol Bernstein Ferry, who was a young copy editor at Putnam's, spent a frantic week or so with Alinsky near the end of the project, when the book needed last-minute editing and polishing to meet a deadline. To show his appreciation, Alinsky took her out to dinner at Le Chambord, one of the most expensive French restaurants in New York. Alinsky had been there before, with Lewis, and there was a "Lewis story" about it that Alinsky told to Carol Ferry, and to many others as well. Alinsky and Lewis, whose regal presence was frequently on display at the grand hotels and exquisite restaurants which in Lewis's mind were appropriate for a great leader, had been shown to a table when a young serviceman and his girl wandered into Le Chambord, apparently thinking it was an ordinary restaurant; after looking at the menu they decided they would split the least expensive item on it. Lewis and Alinsky noticed all this, which prompted a pseudo-serious discussion between them as to whether it was possible for two people at Le Chambord to run up a tab of over $100 (perhaps the equivalent of $400 or $500 today). They bet they could, and after a great intake of both food and drink, if they didn't quite make the goal, they got very close.

But the person who helped Alinsky in the writing of the Lewis book more than any other was Babette Stiefel. In fact, Ralph Helstein thinks it might never have been completed without her. Babs Stiefel was in her late twenties when she met Alinsky. Like Helene, she had been born in Philadelphia; also like Helene, she was attractive, broad-shouldered, and fair-skinned—and again like Helene, she was interested in ideas and social problems. She was the director of community relations of the Chicago Public Housing Authority (CPHA) while Alinsky was active in the Chicago Public Housing Association, a citizen support group of the CPHA. This was a period of increasingly bitter political battles in Chicago over the intertwined issues of public housing and racial integration, battles that foreshadowed the larger, uglier struggles over race and housing of the 1950s and 1960s. Babs Stiefel's and Saul Alinsky's paths crossed probably in 1948, and it was not long before Babs was helping Alinsky with the Lewis book. After a trip to Washington, where, for example, Alinsky would have access to the records of the United Mine Workers, he would return home and, according to Helstein, Babs "worked all kinds of hours [in the evening] going over the materials with him, [helping] him to put it together." When he would get discouraged or depressed, still suffering from the loss of Helene, Babs would encourage him. She even began to help him at the office with typing and other secretarial work. It was not long before the relationship began to develop into more than a friendship. Alinsky's friends approved, not only because he needed her support but because they liked Babs for many of the same reasons they had liked Helene.

DURING THE TRIP Alinsky made to California before his wife's death, he had an opportunity to check out a lead on a new organizer, a man by the name of Fred Ross. Alinsky had first heard about Ross at one of his poker parties in Hyde Park. One of the players, Louis Wirth, a professor in the University of Chicago Sociology Department, was complaining that a guy out in California who was working for the American Council on Race Relations, a Chicago-based operation, was causing problems: he had been hired to do surveys of several communities but, instead, was organizing people around the issues of racial discrimination. Wirth said that they were probably going to fire Ross. Alinsky was interested, asked for Ross's address, and wrote him to set up a meeting.

Fred Ross recalls their first meeting at a hotel restaurant in Los Angeles. He had heard a little about Alinsky, had read *Reveille for Radicals,* and, in anticipation of their meeting, was slightly in awe of this apparent tough guy from Chicago who used to pal around with the Capone gang. But no sooner did they shake hands and sit down than Alinsky—

whom Ross expected to be oozing toughness through every pore—ordered not a double bourbon but a root-beer float. Alinsky proceeded to inhale it in two quick, violent sucks on the straw.

Alinsky was impressed with Ross, as he had every reason to be. Soon after their meeting, he wrote to a friend: "I have hired a guy [in California] who I think is a natural for our work. It will really be the first time that I have had a capable associate who understands exactly what we are after. His name is Fred Ross and he was the head of the 'good' government transient camp that Steinbeck described in *The Grapes of Wrath*. His heart is completely in the right place." The last observation was right on the mark. Tall and slender, with a square jaw and brown eyes, the thirty-seven-year-old Ross had the look of a still youthful, still dedicated Eagle Scout.

Born in San Francisco in 1910, he was graduated from the University of Southern California in the depths of the Depression with a teaching degree. With no teaching jobs in sight, he became a case worker with the state relief administration. From there he took a job with the Farm Security Administration, one of the more radical of the New Deal agencies, not only servicing the rural poor but being an advocate for them. Ross was eventually put in charge of the camp at Arvin that Alinsky referred to as the real-life camp described in *The Grapes of Wrath*. When the war broke out, Ross's superiors made it clear to him that, as part of the overall war effort, certain accommodations had to be made with the growers. Since he was unlikely to look the other way while the growers took advantage of farm laborers, or *braceros,* this was, in effect, like being fired, and he went to work with the War Relocation Authority.

Fred Ross's life changed dramatically during an all-night session with two people in a small southern California town shortly after the war. He had started to work for the American Council on Race Relations as a consultant helping communities that were setting up interracial councils. One evening he found himself with two people who felt passionately about the plight of Mexican-Americans in southern California. One was Ruth Tuck, who had lived in a *barrio* for a year and had written a book, *Not with a Fist,* based on her experiences. The other was Ignacio Lopez, who published a Spanish-language newspaper. After that night, Ross decided he wasn't going to be a consultant anymore. Tuck and Lopez had convinced him, Ross remembers, that "the main thing that was needed throughout the whole Southwest was someone to start organizing the Mexican-Americans. They didn't have any organization—nothing. They were the only ones who didn't have their own organizations. The Japanese-Americans had theirs, the Chinese-Americans, the Filipinos, the Jews had plenty of organizations, the Negroes had the NAACP and other organizations, but the Mexican-Americans didn't have anything. Well, before I realized it, I was an organizer for them." When Ross told his superior, Larry Hewes, what he wanted to do, he received a friendly warning. "He was married to a Mexican woman, and he said, 'Well, Fred, you're going to break your heart—they're going to break your heart. I know, I'm married [to one].' He had had experience with Mexican people. And he knew how hard it was going to be."

When Alinsky and Ross met for the first time in early June 1947, Ross told him about his organizing experiences of the past year, the work that had gotten him into trouble with the American Council on Race Relations. In the citrus belt, east of Los Angeles, in Belltown and in the Casa Blanca *barrio*, for example, where Ross had realized that much of the discrimination experienced by Mexican-Americans derived from the fact that they were, in effect, noncitizens, he went to the voter registrar and found that in the precincts in Casa Blanca only 10 percent of the registrants had Spanish surnames. A door-to-door voter registration drive had encouraging results: in Casa Blanca, the new, larger Mexican-American vote defeated the incumbent City Council representative, an orange grower who had been unresponsive to the Chicanos' problems; in Belltown, a school-bond proposal that would have perpetuated segregated schools was suddenly in danger of being defeated because of the opposition of a sizable number of newly registered Chicanos—along with blacks and others who simply did not want to pay more taxes. The minority voters' new political leverage forced a revision of the school-bond proposal and cracked the segregated school system. Here, Ross began to learn valuable lessons. In Belltown, what motivated Mexican-Americans initially to register to vote was not the large issue of segregated schools but rather "a subsidiary grievance: the use of their school taxes for the benefit of an all-Anglo school, which, to them, was more painful and insulting than straight segregation." As an organizer, Ross began to see that he had to be patient and to accept what the people felt was important so that a process could unfold, a movement "from irritating doorstep issues," as he called them, "to those problems farther removed from them . . . , often from symptom to cause."

Ross thought that he was on to something important; inspired by the modest but, he thought, telling successes in the citrus belt, he wanted to build on those successes elsewhere in California. Alinsky, however, before meeting Ross, had thought about putting him either in Butte, Montana, where there was the possibility of a new project, or in Kansas City, Kansas, where the most recent man Alinsky had hired to help with the Armourdale Community Council had not worked out. After they talked for a while,

Ross made it clear to Alinsky that he wanted to continue to organize Mexican-Americans in California. Alinsky was apparently so impressed with Ross's dedication, energy, and sincerity, and so much in need of a dependable organizer who could help spread the work of the Industrial Areas Foundation, that he offered Ross a job to organize Mexican-Americans. Ross accepted, in part because he thought that he was about to be fired from his current job—but also because he liked what he knew of Alinsky's work. The two of them talked generally about starting in Los Angeles, perhaps in Boyle Heights, where, Alinsky told Ross, his father used to put him up when he came out for summer visits during his high school years.

There was one other point that Ross wanted to raise. He told Alinsky that the organizing approach with Mexican-Americans would have to be different from Alinsky's approach in Chicago. In the Back of the Yards, nearly everybody belonged to groups or organizations, or so it seemed—to a parish and, within a parish, to a sodality or Holy Name Society; to a union local; to an athletic club; to the neighborhood chamber of commerce; to the political ward organization. The BYNC was an organization of organizations. But the poor Mexican-American neighborhoods in California did not, for the most part, have anything like that: Chicanos had few formal, organized groups, few recognizable leaders who could speak for more than a small number of friends or relatives. While Mexican-Americans came out of a Catholic tradition, allegiance to the Church tended to be weak and church attendance spotty at best. An organizer in the *barrios* could not expect as much leadership from young priests as Alinsky had enjoyed in Chicago.

Ross went on the IAF payroll in August 1947, but before he and Alinsky could talk much about organizing approaches and strategies, Alinsky's wife died, and it was not until 1948 that Alinsky began to give more attention to Ross and the California project. For the next two years, he came from Chicago to see Ross about every three or four months, each time for a week or so. A top priority early in 1948 was fund-raising. He had hired Ross at $3,000 a year but told him that he was certain that he could get another $1,000 for Ross from the film star Melvyn Douglas and his wife, Helen Gahagan Douglas. The two men went to see the Douglases, who were interested in the project. Mrs. Douglas was a congresswoman at the time (two years later, in a savage campaign, she was to be defeated in a race for the U.S. Senate by a young lawyer, Richard Nixon). Ross had already met her years before when he was running the migratory labor camp. "She used to bring some of her rich friends from Beverly Hills up there to see the migrants, and then she'd hit them up for money . . . for powdered milk for the migrant kids [and for other necessities]. She wasn't a typical politician at all, and she was interested in this whole business of getting the Mexican-Americans into the mainstream." It was not long before the Douglases contributed the $1,000 that went for the rest of Ross's salary.

Ross marveled at the way Alinsky operated when he met with a group to raise money. Another time at the Douglases' house, Alinsky told stories about John L. Lewis and the Flint sit-down strike against General Motors.

> There was a break in negotiations, as I remember the story Saul told. Lewis took occasion to go over and sit next to Alfred Sloan, the head of GM. He starts giving him an explanation of something that has to do with the workers but, more to the point of Saul's story, Lewis gets Sloan to agree with him on one point. Once he gets his agreement on that one thing, that's all he needs, because that's like getting people to admit that they believe in Christ. If you can't get them to believe in Christ, well, then, forget it, because you're not going to get them to take the next step. What Lewis was doing was like getting somebody to believe. So then he carries on to the next step, and Sloan has to agree on that, too, if he already agrees on the first one. And then Lewis takes him to the third point, and Sloan has to agree on that, too. By the time they go back to the bargaining table, Lewis has the head of the whole company practically on his side. That was the last time anybody ever left Sloan alone at a bargaining session, was Saul's punch line. Well, that's the sort of stuff he was just regaling these people with up at Helen Gahagan Douglas's that afternoon. I always contended that Saul could tell a better story than he could write it. He gave it certain inflections and body language, and he was great with a deadpan delivery.

Alinsky was also a big hit with a small circle of Jewish businessmen in Los Angeles who supported liberal causes. Although he had failed to get enough support to start a project when he came to Los Angeles in 1943, he had made a few contacts, one of them apparently with Harry Braverman. When Alinsky returned to Los Angeles in 1948, Braverman suggested that he call one of his friends, Seniel Ostrow. Ostrow recalls Alinsky's phone call and the conversation: "I said I just don't have the time, I'm too busy. I was running a business then. He said, 'Well, you have to take time for lunch.' And I said I'll only grab a sandwich. He said, 'I'll come by and we'll have a sandwich together.' So all right, I agreed. He came out at twelve o'clock, and I never got back to the office. Six o'clock I came home.

He was just so imbued with what he was talking about and what he had to sell that I just decided to sit and listen." From that six-hour lunch, Ostrow became Alinsky's entrée to many others, such as Ike Greenberg and Harry Davidson. Ross remembers one of the first meetings with the men at the Beverly Hills Hotel. "Alinsky just charmed the pants right off of them. Before the meeting got started, he joked with them, used a few Jewish expressions or idioms. And then he started talking about the national situation." He wove into his analysis of domestic politics a colorful story about his friend John L. Lewis. Then he made a transition to his own work and to the CBS radio program that had praised it, "The Eagles Brood." The program was still available on a set of twelve phonograph records, and Ross remembers that Alinsky brought the records to the meeting "in an album of Haydn's quartets . . . and he'd play the records to start off the discussion." It was an impressive performance that conveyed a simple but strong message, Ross recalls: the message that "this guy Alinsky knows his business." Stressing a major theme in "The Eagles Brood," Alinsky emphasized the importance of stimulating participation, of getting people involved in the democratic process. "And, of course, he would play up the fact that there was hostility on the East Side [of Los Angeles] between the people in the Jewish and the Mexican communities. . . . [The businessmen] had a stake in that, too. And, of course, he knew that the Jewish community . . . was interested from a humanitarian point of view in doing something to help other people as well as from a self-interest point of view."

Alinsky's meetings produced donations and pledges from both the businessmen and the Jewish Community Fund of more than $10,000 over three years, the period, Alinsky told the contributors, it would take for an organization to become self-supporting. Meanwhile, there would be no shortage of issues and problems: in 1948 and 1949, many of the streets in the East Side *barrio* were unpaved; there were no streetlights; police brutality was widespread; the schools were inferior; good housing was in short supply.

Another priority soon became a focus of much of Fred Ross's energy, and that was the candidacy for the Los Angeles City Council of an attractive, articulate, young social worker, Edward R. Roybal. Of Spanish descent, Roybal was born in Albuquerque, New Mexico, and could trace his ancestral roots to the San Jose area in 1610. Before he went into the service in World War II, he had been active in public-health education, as the person in charge of the first mobile X-ray unit used to test people for tuberculosis. After the war, a group of Mexican-Americans persuaded Roybal, who had just turned thirty, to run for the East Side seat on the

City Council against an incumbent who was in his eighties and, as Roybal says, "was already senile and was a very heavy drinker." Roybal, attempting to become the first person with a Spanish surname to be elected to the City Council in the twentieth century, lost a close election in 1947. The next day, he remembers, "I received a telegram from Saul Alinsky. The telegram said, 'What are you going to do next?' That's all. He didn't say congratulations on a good race or anything else."

Roybal had met Alinsky in the early 1940s at a social-work convention in Texas, introduced to Alinsky by the convention's keynote speaker, Archbishop Lucy of San Antonio. Lucy, along with Bishop Sheil, was among the few Catholic bishops in the forefront of liberal and even radical movements. "One evening I was invited to go to the bishop's room," Roybal recalls, "and among the other people there was this man whom I had never met by the name of Saul Alinsky." Roybal had a vague memory of having read something about Alinsky, but thought he had not been favorably impressed by it, thinking of him as too much of a leftist. "We had been fighting communism and communists in Boyle Heights for many years. They did everything they possibly could to get us involved in the Communist Party. We fought them, and we were trigger-happy when it came to any communist. . . . I was young and foolish enough to ask [Bishop Lucy], 'What about this man? He's quite a leftist.' And the bishop smiled and said, 'Well, he is a leftist, but so am I.' "

Roybal's narrow election loss and Alinsky's fortuitous discovery of Fred Ross occurred almost simultaneously. Roybal and his campaign cadre decided soon after the election that they were going to make another run at a City Council seat in the 1949 election. In the meantime, they wanted to build an organization that would keep interest in Roybal's candidacy alive. The first name they picked for the organization was the Community Political Organization, but in Spanish the acronym CPO (pronounced "say-pay-oh") sounds very much like the idiom *se peó,* which means "he farted." CPO was quickly changed to CSO, for Community Service Organization.

In the next two years, voter registration became the hub of CSO activity, linking together many of the community's grievances. It was a major challenge, Roybal says, "to be able to register something in the neighborhood of seventeen thousand people in a community that hadn't had that kind of activity. This was the first time, and you had to sit down and convince these people."

Ross entered the scene as the CSO was born. At the beginning, Roybal says, "I didn't trust him. It was prejudice on my part." Small symbols sometimes shape first impressions, and for Roybal the cowboy boots Ross was wearing were an ominous sign. "I said to myself, 'What the hell is this guy doing with cowboy boots? He must be a Texan, and Texans don't like us.' " Ross was going to have to earn his acceptance by the community—it was not enough simply to be associated with Saul Alinsky, himself little known there.

In fact, Ross had spent weeks looking for "a hole into the community." He visited the Carioca, the Red Rooster, and other bars along East First Street. But he felt himself floundering until he met up with Roybal and his band of campaign workers at a meeting one night in a small room in the East Side YMCA. Ross liked what he saw of Roybal: he seemed soft-spoken and sincere, in contrast to the bluster and phoniness Ross had seen often enough in Mexican-American men among the small middle-class leadership on the East Side. There were real people at this YMCA meeting—workers from foundries and garment factories, short-order cooks and young students—and they were interested in more than a political campaign and electing someone. They were especially interested in rooting out the injustices. Slowly Ross began to work his way into the inner circle. After one meeting, he joined five or six at the Red Rooster, where they talked and drank East Side brew until two in the morning. Then Ross began to visit the homes of each of the fifteen or so people who continued to come to the weekly meetings—the numbers had dwindled as the election campaign receded into history. They talked—with Ross doing most of the listening—about their families, about their hopes and problems.

Finally, Ross was ready. He talked to Roybal. At the next weekly meeting, after Henry Nava reported on civil rights and Maria Duran on housing, it was Ross's turn:

> It was a terrific strain just sitting there, both feet on the brakes, waiting for my turn. It was difficult to keep my mind on the meeting. I wanted so badly to get on with it, to prove to them and to Saul and probably to myself that I could do something no one else had ever done—to organize the Mexican-Americans so they could move forward and catch up with the rest of the population and make a better life for themselves and their children. As I looked around at all the vacant chairs and heard the leaders blast the politicians who wouldn't move on the problems of the neighborhood, the old flood of urgency rushed through me. I wanted to hurry, hurry, hurry out into the streets and drag the people in and fill those chairs and that room until they were packed in, standing belly to buttocks, clear to and through the door.

The words "Fred Ross" suddenly yanked him back into the present, as Roybal was announcing that Ross had a plan to present and afterward the group would discuss it and vote on it. Ross stood and explained that he wanted to be a part of what the CSO was trying to do—to stop the police brutality, to stop the gerrymandered school boundaries, and all the rest. But they needed an organization that had the power to compel the changes they were talking about. Somebody asked Ross how he would go about creating such a force, and he told them:

> You'll be organizing me at least as much as I'm organizing you; and you'll also be doing just as much organizing of others as I will, and probably more. Whenever I'm out there corralling people into this organization, at least one of you is going to be right along with me. You want to know why? Well, first of all, this is *your* organization, not mine, and if it's going to continue that way, you've got to organize it. Otherwise someday it's liable to turn out to be mine.

But how were they going to get other people to join, somebody asked, especially since their own ranks had already been shrinking? Ross said, "How do we make something happen? You've tried. At the last meeting each of you said you'd bring two other people with you tonight. But after the meeting things got very busy and it completely slipped your mind until tonight—and then it was too late." Smiling, he added, "You know, some of the ones who made the loudest brags didn't come back themselves. By the way," he continued, as he began a Socratic dialogue such as Alinsky had often used in the Back of the Yards, "*why* do you suppose those folks didn't come back tonight?"

A woman named Maria replied, "I don't know. I think they weren't really interested in what we're trying to do. After the last meeting, I heard one of them griping because we don't spend enough time on politics."

"How long had he been coming to meetings?" Ross asked.

"Oh, two or three weeks," she replied.

"Ah, maybe we've got something. Do you think that fellow really knows what you're trying to do in the CSO?"

"Probably not," Maria said.

"Do you?" Ross asked.

"Sure I do." She rattled off a number of problems and grievances. "We know why we want to be together. We think about it a lot, and we're always talking about it."

"So you know all the reasons we don't discuss politics at these meetings?"

"Why, sure. We've been all over that dozens of times."

"But had this fellow been here when you were talking about these things?"

"No, I guess not," Maria said. "Say, maybe that's it! When we come to a meeting we bring along our memories of all the other meetings, we don't expect too much at any one time. If tonight doesn't go too well, we won't get mad and drop out. We'll just figure, oh, well, you can't win 'em all, and maybe next week it'll go better."

"And why don't the others take it that way?" Ross asked.

"Well, probably because all this is so new to them. Most of them have never been in organizations before. They haven't thought much about these things."

And so it went, as Ross illustrated what he meant by self-discovery and education. Thousands of people on the East Side would have to be educated—not only about what the CSO stood for but about why it was important for each and every person to understand how his hopes for a better future were wrapped up in the hopes of a better future for the East Side community. There could be no shortcuts, Ross warned. "If you do vote me in, it'll be like taking a vote to put yourselves to work, because I'm going to want some volunteers to start working with me tomorrow night." They would begin by going to one house a night. Ross and Maria would visit a friend of Maria's. The next night Ross would go with somebody else to the house of that person's friend or relative—and so on each night of the week. At each meeting, Ross would try not only to recruit the new contact to membership in the CSO (which cost two dollars a year) but to get him to arrange a follow-up meeting with a friend or relative. During the next two years, Ross and other CSO leaders held house meetings virtually every night. Group meetings evolved at which five or six or eight people would gather together. Roybal says that Ross was "tireless and he was not afraid to impose upon you. If something had to be done, his attitude was 'Well, let's do it.' And if somebody said, 'But it's already nine o'clock,' Ross would say, 'That's all right, we'll get up an hour later tomorrow.' " When he first came into Boyle Heights, Ross had been just a gringo with cowboy boots who spoke hardly any Spanish, but he eventually won the trust of nearly everybody.

Alinsky told Ross to send him monthly written reports—long-distance phone calls were taboo, since the Industrial Areas Foundation did not have enough money. Sometimes several months would go by before Ross heard anything back from Alinsky, and he would think, Oh hell, I bet that bastard isn't even reading them. But when the response came, it was likely to be simple, crystal clear, and on target.

> One of the first questions I ever asked him [Ross remembers] was after I had been organizing in Boyle Heights for about four months. We had been holding house meetings every night. I was already starting

to think where I wanted to go next. So I made a tentative calendar. You know: by such and such a date I'll be through with Boyle Heights, then I'll go to Lincoln Heights and spend so much time there, and then I want to go to Matavia and spend so much time there to set up a third CSO group. So I wrote to Saul that we had to expand, but, on the other hand, was I sort of rushing things? He wrote me right back. And I remember the exact words he used: "In work like ours, we very seldom have the luxury of being able to predict what we're going to do next week, let alone next month or next year." And he was absolutely right. I never got to start a couple more CSO groups that first year. I was just flooded with all kinds of things with this growing organization—because once people joined, they wanted to produce. They would say, "You told us about all the things that the CSO could help us do. We want them. Now." We had to set up committees on health, employment, civil rights, housing, education— wherever there was discrimination. I had no time.

Ross was not systematically or formally trained by Alinsky, but he understood Alinsky's orientation, and he could easily extrapolate from the specific situations they discussed together. One ongoing dilemma was the role of the organizer vis-à-vis the citizen leadership—when was the organizer justified in stepping out front and temporarily assuming the leadership himself? During an instructive episode early in his work with Alinsky, one that involved a protest over school policies, Alinsky asked him why he stayed outside the meeting room when a CSO leader and her delegation went in to confront the board of education. "Because I wanted her to get in the habit of standing up on her own and demanding her rights without my help." But Ross had slipped in later, and Alinsky asked him why.

Well, I tell [Saul] that was the first time in her life she had ever gone up before a public official of any kind, and she was very nervous. I wanted to be on hand to help her out in case she got stage fright and started to muff the thing.

And Saul is right on me: "And what difference would it have made if she had muffed it?"

"Well, it would have been a terrible blow to the organization."

"Certainly"—Saul nods his head—"and that's so obvious you'd think that anyone could see it, wouldn't you? But many people don't, particularly people who go overboard about being nondirective. They get so busy trying out their little theories, they forget they've got a flesh-and-blood organization to consider. We all have to remember that while it's the organizer's function constantly to push responsibilities on the people, he must always be ready to jump in and take over himself in case the people, for some reason or other, fail to follow through. Oh, of course, many times it's okay to let them drop the ball and fumble around for a while, so they'll learn. But very often you aren't allowed that luxury.

"And there's something else that's equally, if not more important, and that's the effect on the individual. How do you think this woman we're discussing would have felt if she had dropped the ball, and you hadn't been around to help her pick it up? The moment you see she's going to muff it, you take over and give her the backing she needs and—even more important—'on the spot' leadership training she has to have to meet the same or similar situations in the future. No real learning takes place unless it's tied into real experiences."

Such exchanges were meaty but sporadic, and Ross wished they were more frequent. He would anxiously await Alinsky's visits to Los Angeles because, as he describes his feelings then, "I was aching to tell him what I had been doing. But I had the hardest time getting him to listen." Alinsky *could* be a good listener, but he probably had mixed feelings about going to California after Helene's death, for there were always minor crises with the kids. In the summer of 1948, for instance, his son, David, contracted polio—as it turned out, a mild case from which he fully recovered. Still, it was frightening: in the late 1940s polio was a crippler and killer of children and young adults, and it spread fear and terror through families, neighborhoods, and even entire communities.

And while Alinsky's fund-raising conquests in California could be fun, not every contact resulted in conquest. He had a short fuse when it came to some of the film industry people he met. "I found it was impossible to raise money among the picture people for this kind of work unless I spent five or six weeks selling them on the idea," Alinsky wrote to Agnes Meyer:

They were not too interested because there was no social prestige attached to making a contribution to the work, and they seemed to be a little frightened of the ungentlemanly tactics employed by our organizations. One picture person after another uses the term "Oh, well, so and so wasn't *important.*" People out there are judged like chattels on the basis of their income or social position. I blew up with a producer after he had used that phrase and said, "I have never believed that there could be so many physically grown up people who are mentally adolescent, who are pathetically insecure, who are damnably maladjusted, and who are completely inhuman as yourself and those that are associated with you and your industry." I walked out without a contribution.

Alinsky also told Meyer about another incident:

> [An] important picture guy [with a] very cynical look on his face said, "Alinsky, you're talking about all these poor people and how you feel about them. You seem to be well dressed and as a matter of fact . . . I noticed the wristwatch you are wearing. If I'm not mistaken, that's an Audemar Piquet, which happens to be one of the most expensive watches made in the world." He then leaned back and literally leered. I glanced down at the face of my watch. . . . Then without a word I unstrapped the watch and handed it to him with the back side up and waited until he read the inscription, "To Saul Alinsky from Chicago's Packinghouse Workers," etc. etc. I then reached over, took the watch back, looked at his face, which was the color of a full-ripened cherry, turned around and walked out. I guess I don't have the tact for money raising.

Ross soon noticed that Alinsky had a little stratagem for protecting himself from people and situations that were dull and boring. When he made an appointment with somebody, he would warn them that he had a busy schedule crammed with meetings and that he probably couldn't spend much time with them. "But then, if something I was talking about happened to interest or fascinate him, for example, he'd 'cancel' out on some of those other things." Ross knew that usually there were no other appointments to cancel and that Alinsky would rather go back to his hotel or find a tennis game than be bored. Or he would escape to a beautiful walkway above Santa Monica Beach, where he could walk alone for miles.

As the 1949 election for the Los Angeles City Council drew near, the CSO was increasingly preoccupied with voter registration. Roybal recalls that more than 125 men and women attended classes to become deputy registrars. Their pitch was that there was a connection between fighting discrimination and winning a measure of political power on the City Council. Two-person teams—always a man and woman because such a combination was more presentable with the Mexican-Americans—combed the East Side. The formal position of the CSO, which was formed as a nonpartisan organization, was that the registration drive was also nonpartisan, that neither the CSO nor the deputy registrars were explicitly talking up Roybal's candidacy. Fred Ross tried to be careful, too, for he was on

Alinsky's payroll and could not jeopardize the Industrial Areas Foundation's tax-exempt status. It just so happened that of the approximately 17,000 new people that the CSO registered, approximately 15,000 had Spanish surnames, and the CSO received much of the credit when Edward Roybal was elected to the Los Angeles City Council in the summer of 1949, the first time in the century that a Spanish-speaking Hispanic had been elected to the City Council. It was a landmark, euphoric victory. Ironically, a situation then developed that graphically demonstrated the connection between Roybal's election and the CSO's larger political agenda. Roybal was sworn in on July 1, a Friday.

On the following Monday, I went to a housing development where they had a big sign that said "GI Housing." I went there, presented my check for $250 [as a deposit on a house]. [A salesman] said, "Well, I'm sorry, young man, it's not my fault, but I'm instructed that I cannot sell to you because you're a Mexican." Here I was a veteran. I met all the qualifications. I said nothing. I took out my card—I already had my City Council cards printed—I gave it to him, went back to my city car parked right in front of his office, and before I got the car started, he was there and he said, "I'm sorry, but I can sell to you because you're different." It had taken me thirty seconds to change from an undesirable to a desirable person. I said nothing. Had that happened to me before, I would have torn that house and man apart whether it was his fault or not.

I went back to the City Council—don't forget, this is my second day—and asked for unanimous consent to speak. I was awarded ten minutes. I told them the story. This got nationwide publicity—"GI Refused Housing in Los Angeles." By that time, the CSO had grown to 650 to 700 people attending meetings every Thursday. We had a picket line up by the afternoon of the following day. The head of the company called me. We went out and negotiated with him. We said, "The only thing we want is that you sell to any one regardless of race, color, or creed." He agreed to do it, and we withdrew the picket line.

WHILE FRED ROSS had been a great find, and the CSO was developing into something potentially significant, nearly two years after Helene's death Alinsky's personal life back in Chicago was still shaky; he was still struggling to move a half-step forward without soon falling a step backward. The summers seemed to be a little easier, with Kathryn away at

camp and David occasionally staying with friends, such as with Sara and
Al Kamin's family in suburban Skokie. Alinsky's happier days and weeks
usually involved time with friends like the Kamins. There were also tennis
games with Walter Johnson, and dinner with Dot and Sandy Liveright. He
passed along a lighthearted anecdote to Agnes Meyer:

> I went up to the North Shore this weekend to pick up David and met
> a very stuffy society dowager (who is completely devoid of any sense
> of humor). She was very brusque with me and afterwards I discovered
> what had happened. It seems that she has one of the most expensive
> modern homes in Chicago's swanky North Shore where everything is
> glass, chrome and what have you. My friends with whom David was
> visiting brought him over to this house . . . and this stuffy gal was
> holding forth on the beauty and originality of this extreme modern
> house when David suddenly burst out with "I think this is the most
> beautiful airport I have ever seen!" Do you think he is being brought
> up right?

But perhaps the best times, the most fun and distracting times, were
with his friend Ralph Helstein. By the spring after Helene's death, the two
of them were going regularly to Comiskey Park to see Chicago White Sox
baseball games. "We were really involved in those games," Helstein
remembers. They made bets during the games and argued constantly and
vehemently about strategies and about the prospects of young players—
twenty-five years later, Helstein still remembers one of their spirited arguments over an obscure journeyman outfielder named Luis Olomo. Neither
would easily give in or concede to the other, and they would argue stubbornly not only about baseball but about all the late-night, after-dinner
subjects of both practical and intellectual consequence—about politics,
philosophy, and the books they read. If they enjoyed anything more than
arguing with each other, it was to team up and turn their gamesmanship
and intellectual combativeness on others. Helstein remembers when the
two of them signed up for a series of evening classes given by Milton Mayer
and Mortimer Adler—star performers in the Great Books movement at the
University of Chicago. "Saul talked me into going," Helstein remembers.
"I thought it was a lot of nonsense. He said that he thought it was a lot
of nonsense, too, but that we ought to do it anyway." Actually, they were
both avid readers—Helstein was impressed that Alinsky had read Voltaire
more closely than he had—and they were curious about the Socratic
method that was used for teaching the Great Books. Alinsky wrote to a
friend: "I have exactly an hour and a half to do something which has to

be done—when I tell you what it is, you will howl like hell! I have to read fifteen chapters of Thucydides in an hour and a half! Yes, I am taking the Great Books Leadership Course just to see what the hell tricks they have in their seminar that I don't have in mine"—a reference to the periodic book-discussion group that Alinsky led for some of the priests in the Back of the Yards.

Helstein thoroughly enjoyed the intellectual pranks, the baseball games, and the many late-night hours with his friend, but both he and his wife, Rachel, were hoping that Alinsky would marry Babs Stiefel. It was now more than two years since Helene's death. They sensed that Alinsky did not feel he was ready, but nonetheless they thought it would be the best thing for both him and the children. Like most of Alinsky's friends, they genuinely liked and respected Babs. Ralph remembers that Babs encouraged Alinsky "to do things that were important for him to do and that would bring him great credit." At the same time, Babs was also committed to her own career at the Chicago Public Housing Authority. As director of community relations, it was her job to anticipate the social and political problems that were likely to develop in a neighborhood where the CPHA planned public housing. Ed Holmgren, one of her co-workers, has described her job as requiring "a keen understanding of the communities, their makeup, the various elements of the bureaucracy, and the aldermanic structure which was so important because each alderman had the site selection veto over new public housing projects." It was a challenging assignment that this warm, outgoing, and vivacious woman carried out intelligently and competently.

The summer of 1950 turned into a scorcher in Chicago. Saul and David Alinsky headed for a long fishing weekend on a cool Wisconsin lake. The Lewis biography was out, and Alinsky had a little time to relax. In the foreword he had apologized to his children for his nightly absences, and he dedicated the book to the memory of Helene; but he also paid tribute to Babs—for her "selfless help . . . in research, editing, scolding and cajoling." She had kept his nose to the grindstone when he would rather have been any place but hunched over a typewriter. And it was a matter not only of her help with the book but also of her help and kindness to his children, and her obvious love for him.

Friends like the Helsteins were becoming a bit annoyed with Alinsky because Babs had given so much of herself to him while he had given much less in return. But now, this summer, Alinsky began to talk of getting married. Maybe he would have some time to think about it while he and David were away.

The oppressive August heat probably did not make it any easier for

Ralph Helstein to think clearly, to begin to imagine which words, in what order and with what tone and expression, could possibly soften the catastrophic news he had to deliver to his friend Saul just after that long weekend. "Polio" was not a word that could easily be surrounded by comforting adjectives. Babs had gotten sick that weekend, and the diagnosis was bulbar poliomyelitis. She had been taken to Chicago Contagious Diseases Hospital, where she was now in an iron lung. Before the month was out, she was dead.

Saul Alinsky did not cry when Babs Stiefel died. He was too numb and too confused. How could this be happening to him again? It was hard to express how he felt because all the words had been used before. It all felt futile. If the passage of time was, in fact, a healer of wounded feelings and personal tragedy, then Alinsky might well wonder if there could ever be enough hours left in his days to relieve his pain and loneliness.

16

An Anti-Anti-Communist

For Saul Alinsky, the postwar period had started with springtime promise. But after the deaths of Helene and Babs—and for some time after—he did not live with the feeling that each day was bound to be brighter than the last.

The euphoric optimism and good feeling that had swept the country right after the war were also short-lived. It was, perhaps, Winston Churchill's Iron Curtain speech at Westminster College in Fulton, Missouri, that symbolized the beginning of the new era. In March 1946, with President Truman in attendance, Churchill reminded his American college audience that the world had not heeded his early warnings in the 1930s about Adolf Hitler's Germany. He hoped now that the Western democracies would not make the same mistake about a new threat to freedom and world peace, the Soviet Union. For, Churchill said, the danger signs were already there for all to see. "From Stettin in the Baltic to Trieste in the Adriatic, an iron curtain has descended across the Continent allowing 'police governments' to rule Eastern Europe."

In the fall of 1946, when the Republicans swept the congressional elections, at first it did not appear that foreign policy and the Soviet threat would be high on the agenda of the new Eightieth Congress. Rather, what seemed certain was that the conservative forces would turn back the clock on New Deal legislation and, in alliance with Southern Democrats, keep the clock just where it was on the matter of civil rights. However, when the British, economically pressed, told the United States that it could no longer provide aid to Greece to counter the communist threat there, the Truman administration was galvanized into action. The administration considered a massive, unprecedented peacetime foreign-aid program.

Would the country and the conservative Republican Congress back such a radical proposal of $400 million in economic and military aid for Greece and Turkey? President Truman received some advice from a friendly, influential Republican, Senator Arthur Vandenberg of Michigan. "Mr. President, if that's what you want, there's only one way to get it," Vandenberg said. "That is to make a personal appearance before Congress and scare hell out of the country." Truman did both; he spoke to a joint session of Congress, declaring in no uncertain terms that the communist actions in the eastern Mediterranean were a serious threat to American security. Swiftly, he won both congressional and public support. Within a month of his speech to Congress, a new term, "the Cold War," entered the national vocabulary, a term that provided an ominous echo to Truman's scary rhetoric.

That the new anti-communist foreign policy would have a domestic political effect was predictable; what was not readily predictable was its scope, duration, intensity, and ugliness. After all, even the zealous, demagogic reactionaries who had seen communists at the heart of all social and economic protests of the 1920s and 1930s—who had seen the New Deal itself as communistic—had been largely silenced during the war, when the Soviet Union was an ally. But the political climate had now changed. Alinsky told a friend in the spring of 1947, "It has reached the point out here that if you even say (with reference to the Truman Foreign Policy), 'Well, I'm not so sure'—then there is a long silence and people look very suspiciously at you. If we have reached the point where issues can no longer be discussed on the basis of logic and truth, where hysteria has wrapped us up to a point of utter irrationality and fear, then it is one hell of a situation."

Alinsky was not a major casualty in the anti-communist hysteria of the late 1940s and 1950s. That is not to say that he was untouched by the climate of fear, suspicion, and innuendo. In fact, rumors and Red-baiting by political enemies would follow Alinsky well into the 1960s. But he was never called, for example, before a congressional investigating committee or raked over the coals in the public press. His friend Walter Johnson thought that he escaped such treatment for a combination of reasons—that he had a network of influential (sometimes wealthy) friends in the Catholic Church, in the press, and in the public eye and that he would have been a highly combative witness before any congressional committee. Alinsky preferred to think it was his toughness and the ridicule he would have heaped on the congressional witch-hunters that made the difference. Herb March, the most prominent communist with the Packinghouse Workers in Chicago, says, "I would place a little more emphasis . . . on the Church influence. I think undoubtedly [government authorities] must have had him under close surveillance, and they must have concluded that they didn't have anything [on him]."

March was right about the surveillance—the FBI had reports on Alinsky's activities in the postwar period, especially concerning his work on behalf of the Packinghouse Workers during the strike in 1946. Its subterranean, mysterious surveillance could be played out in a variety of insidious ways, and insidious anti-communism touched Alinsky periodically. For instance, a State Department official gave Walter Johnson a questionnaire to answer dealing with national security and loyalty matters after he returned from a trip abroad on a Fulbright program assignment. Johnson was furious when he came upon a short series of questions about his relationship to Alinsky implying that Alinsky might be a security risk. One question read: "To what extent, if any, have you been aware of his alleged Pro-Communist sympathies and activities?" He thought Alinsky ought to "do something about this."

Alinsky was eager to tell Agnes Meyer about the State Department questionnaire and about Johnson's suggestion that he was one person who had the guts to strike back. It was the kind of appraisal from friends that Alinsky loved to hear and encouraged.

> I wouldn't mind doing something on this. It seems to me that in the face of the terrifically repressive and police state climate which this country has been degenerating into, . . . those Americans who have not been and are not Communists should stand up and slug back when this kind of stuff is tossed their way. I know that one of the big arguments against that is that you just put yourself open to a lot more smears. On that score, I don't give a damn as I am not running to be President of the United States or to be a Cardinal. The other big argument against trying to fight this kind of slimy character assassination is that it is like trying to fight shadows because these guys will never tell you exactly what the charges are so that you can stand up and disprove them or, at the very least, explain exactly what was happening so that the interpretations would be vastly different. By that I mean, suppose they say, "You are known to be seeing a Mr. Herbert March at regular intervals through the year of 1939 and also in 1943, 1944 and 1946." Well sure, I saw plenty of Communists as a regular part of my organizational work and also plenty of Fascists. And also plenty of other kinds of individuals but I was not converted to any creed or religion by associations.

Alinsky's close association with the Packinghouse Workers in Chicago might have been reason enough for him to be called before one of the congressional investigating committees. For a union like the Packinghouse Workers, with some communists in leadership roles and with a maverick president like Helstein, political attacks and investigations came not only from the likes of the House Un-American Activities Committee but also from within the labor movement, from the CIO leadership, which was now running scared and toward the right, purging from its ranks political undesirables, especially suspected communists. In spite of such attacks and pressures, Helstein says:

> I was able to retain the [broad] support of my membership [although we] didn't like a lot of the things that Russia did, and we said so, and had trouble with some of the communists in the union for saying so. But we [also said] it was essential that the civil liberties of everybody be protected, and that people who didn't agree have a right to say so without its affecting their status in the union. Well, sometimes that was easy, but usually it was very hard. We were in trouble with other unions, on the verge of being thrown out of the CIO, all the time. We were investigated more than any other union in the CIO by the CIO.

Helstein takes great pride in the philosophical underpinning of his freedom-of-speech policies, which he says Alinsky shared. "I was influenced by Oliver Wendell Holmes and Brandeis. It was important to me [to keep the doors open] just so long as argument was possible. The question was, how do you keep argument possible?" While unions around the country were adopting prohibitions to bar communists or fascists from holding union office, "our union never did," Helstein says. It was bad enough, he thought, that Congress, with the Taft-Hartley law of 1947, prohibited communists from holding union office—"the law was ridiculous," he says—but it was "stupid" for a union to pass its own internal prohibitions, too. "There were people in Hyde Park over the years that Saul and I both felt great respect for who used to go around Hyde Park calling us crypto-communists, [because we] wouldn't be part of this liberal anti-communist attitude. We weren't about to conform."

Alinsky was unflinching in his support of Helstein when his friend was being Red-baited. For example, when a news story ran in the Washington *Post* in the winter of 1947, less than a year after Helstein had become union president, that suggested that some thought he was a communist collaborator, Alinsky fired off protests, first to Agnes Meyer and then to her son-in-law, Philip Graham, the *Post*'s publisher. He suggested to both of them that the *Post* run a profile of Helstein that would, in effect, correct the record by showing him to be a man of great integrity who was committed to democratic ideals. Graham was at first amenable to Alinsky's proposal, but a few months later another issue arose somewhat inadvertently that triggered a sharp exchange between them. Graham sent Alinsky a clipping from the communist newspaper *The Daily Worker* of an article that praised the Packinghouse Workers for their willingness to cooperate with other groups on the political left. Alinsky wrote back:

> The write-up is a distortion. The Packinghouse Workers did go on record to begin to organize all Progressive forces so that the Progressives would have (a) A higher degree of organization for bargaining power within the Democratic Party and (b) If in the course of events, it becomes necessary to devote their efforts towards building a third political party, that they would then do so. Personally, I see nothing wrong with that. Last week, I addressed a Packinghouse Workers' meeting of all of their leaders, and my fellow speaker was Palmer Webber of [the CIO] PAC (with whom I was deeply impressed) and I could see no contradiction between the Packinghouse Workers line with that of PAC. . . . I stick by everything I [have] said about Ralph. . . . I am willing to bet anyone odds of 100 to 1 that if you were to sit down and talk and get to know Helstein, you would feel just as I do—that more labor leaders of his type would make the American future a lot brighter.

Alinsky was surprised and annoyed when he received Graham's reply. Setting aside the matter of Ralph Helstein, Graham said he was troubled by Alinsky's enthusiasm for organizing all the progressive forces. "At first blush, no one could object, but where we get into trouble is—what the hell do you mean by 'all Progressive forces'?" Graham feared that such a strategy played into the hands of "the Party boys." "I simply can't believe that it's 'progressive' to agree with every act, black or white, committed by the Soviet Union. Nor can I believe that we can pretend this problem [of communist influence or control] doesn't exist in such things as the current drive—'Unite the Progressives.' "

Alinsky's immediate, lengthy response was a mixture of defense and offense. "For Christ's sake, Phil, you're writing to a guy who has been a 'war monger,' who fought them in trying to get Lewis to support Roosevelt for a third term, who came out in full support of the Lilienthal plan for control of atomic energy, etc. etc. etc.," he began, stringing together a list of issues where his disagreement with the official communist position was of little consequence. But the heart of his response was a forceful rejoinder: "I *don't agree* that it's 'Progressive' to agree with every act, black or white, committed by the Soviet Union but neither do I think that it makes as much sense to disagree with every damn thing that the Communists profusely favor. The way things are going we would certainly find ourselves in a hell of a situation if the Communists came out in favor of sexual relations and ham and eggs for breakfast, and don't think that I am being facetious!" As to what to do about domestic communists, Alinsky sounded less driven by philosophical principles than Ralph Helstein recalls. Asserting that the issue of whether communists should be barred from unions and other organizations was moot, he argued that the question was essentially "whether there can be developed an American Progressive Movement in which the Communists are forced to follow along or get out on the basis of the issues—a movement so healthy, so filled with the vitality of real American Radicalism, that the Communists will wear their teeth down to their jaws trying to bore from within. I know that the latter can be done."

In the final analysis, Alinsky told Graham, "certain Fascist mentalities" posed a far greater threat to the country than "the damn nuisance of Communism." Unlike many liberals and others, he did not believe that communists generally were endowed with extraordinary persuasive capabilities or that people en masse would follow communist exhortations like sheep. Moreover, from his personal experience, there were communists and communists. While Alinsky was not oblivious to many party members' tunnel-vision determination, he also knew that in the Back of the Yards, Herb March and others had understood his approach and its value to the Packinghouse Workers and that March had never been a problem, only a help.

As discouraging as things had become for progressive-minded people in 1947, the next year was even worse. The Packinghouse Workers Union found itself in a bitter strike, Alinsky again playing an active role as he had two years earlier—organizing another citizens' committee to support the union's position, consulting closely with Helstein, asking Agnes Meyer to arrange for favorable editorial support in the Washington *Post,* and helping to write some of the union's broadsides. This time, however, the union lost the strike, and it was marred by violence (three men were killed). In debt and demoralized, the union and its leaders were vulnerable to many outside pressures, including those from the fiercely anti-communist leadership of the CIO. One of the post-strike casualties was Herb March.

March resigned as district director shortly after the losing strike, at the point when the AF of L Meatcutters Union moved in to challenge the Packinghouse Workers at a number of plants. Prior to the strike, he had refused to sign the Taft-Hartley noncommunist affidavit. He still refused to sign after the strike, but his party affiliation had become more of a problem, so he resigned his union leadership position because, he said, "I felt it was necessary for the union to be in compliance in order to be able to meet the challenge of these elections [with the Meatcutters]." March was given a job on the union staff, but that did not satisfy the national CIO leaders, who began to pressure Helstein and his colleagues to fire March outright. Finally, March recalls, Helstein and another leader, Tony Stevens, called him in and asked him to resign. It was a sad, painful experience, all of them feeling like victims. March, however, felt he was the prime victim, and now, as he saw it, he was not about to let Helstein and the others get off the moral hook. "Gentlemen," he remembers telling them, "this one is going to be on you, not me. I'm not going to resign. You can fire me. I'm not concerned so much about what it's going to do to me; it's what it does to *you,* because, if you're firing me, you're firing me for only one reason." When they fired him, March knew that "it hurt the guys to do it."

Alinsky did not like what was happening to March. March recalls: "I met Alinsky at union headquarters. . . . He made a point of telling me, 'Herb, I think that was a serious mistake Ralph and a few other people made. I had a bitter argument with them. I just wanted you to know that.' " March appreciated Alinsky's sentiments. Although they did not always agree on issues and priorities, he believed that Alinsky was fundamentally an honest man, and it was nice to know how he felt.

Alinsky reached out to help others who had gotten caught in the web of anti-communism. One was Larry Adler, the harmonica virtuoso (he preferred the term "mouth organ" to "harmonica"). Adler was not only a brilliant musician and international star but a great raconteur. By the mid-1940s, he and the tap dancer Paul Draper were famous for their duo concerts. By 1949, however, Adler, who was sympathetic to liberal-left causes, had been blacklisted and was losing bookings. When his and Draper's libel suit against a Connecticut woman who called them pro-communist ended in a hung jury—even though Adler swore in a preliminary affidavit that he was not a communist—his career in the United States was at a dead end. Alinsky met Adler during this period and introduced him to friends in Chicago and arranged for Adler to stay with the Macys in New York. "I would appreciate it if you can have him over for dinner and listen to his story," Alinsky wrote the Macys. "Larry wants only one thing and that is advice. . . . He was in for the weekend and I saw a good deal of him . . . and was actually heartsick about his situation."

In Monteagle, Tennessee, another remarkable person, Myles Horton, was frequently in trouble during the McCarthy days. Horton, who had met Alinsky in Chicago through a mutual friend, Walter Johnson, founded the

Highlander Folk School, which became a mecca for progressive union activists, civil rights workers, and others who came not only to learn leadership and organizing techniques but also to discuss and think through new ideas and strategies for social change. It was a radical operation, especially in the segregated, anti-union South, and Alinsky admired it. Highlander and Horton, besieged by political and legal attacks from conservative forces, were often in serious financial trouble. Alinsky was among the many who helped to bail the school out of one economic emergency after another. One day, Walter Johnson remembers, he and Alinsky were playing tennis at one of their regular morning sessions at the University of Chicago's Quadrangle Club, when Johnson received an urgent phone call. A voice on the phone said that Myles Horton needed bail money. As Johnson was confirming the details, Alinsky suddenly took over. "Give me the fucking phone," he demanded, and then quickly called Helstein at the Packinghouse Workers' office and arranged to have $500 wired to Monteagle. He also helped to set up Chicago-area fund-raising events for Highlander and was instrumental in getting for Highlander a grant of more than $40,000 from the little-known, newly established Emil Schwarzhaupt Foundation. Not only was Schwarzhaupt a godsend for Myles Horton; it would also become a financial angel for Saul Alinsky.

Alinsky's willingness to help a friend in trouble and his interest in being a writer came together when another friend—like Larry Adler—found his name listed in the book *Red Channels,* an anti-communist tome that listed alleged "Reds" and "pinkos" in the entertainment and broadcasting industries. Robert Shayon, who met Alinsky in 1947 when he wrote and produced the CBS radio documentary that praised Alinsky's work on juvenile delinquency, was about to take a new job in Europe when charges surfaced about his alleged communist connections. "My name found its way [into *Red Channels*] because I had signed a couple of petitions, made a couple of speeches," Shayon says. "I had no connection with the Communist Party. I never was a member or a fellow traveler. But I had been president of the radio and television directors' guild. I had some recognition in the field." (Shayon adds that friends who were generally on the opposite side of the political fence from him, shocked that he had been named, later arranged a luncheon meeting for him with the publisher of *Red Channels* and a few of his cohorts. "He just quite candidly said, 'It was a mistake, you should have never been listed.'") Nonetheless, "I couldn't get any work," Shayon says. Then Alinsky called. With Shayon's life at a low point, "and Saul being very sensitive, we would talk a lot about writing something together, and we decided to write a play about the labor movement. We signed a contract," and over a period of time in 1951, they wrote the play. In Chicago, they would work late into the night, with Alinsky often insisting at one or two in the morning that they go off to a neighborhood restaurant, where he loved to order chicken livers and eggs. When Alinsky came to Westport, Connecticut, to stay with the Shayons for a couple of days, "he drove my wife crazy. She loved him, but Saul would get up at noon, and then he would make crazy demands of what he wanted for breakfast." With the Shayons' two small children and Mrs. Shayon's mother also in the house, Alinsky's pleasures and nocturnal habits added to the household havoc. "He would work late into the night, thoroughly on his own schedule," Shayon says. "But he loved the family and they loved him."

They had a wonderful time writing the play, Shayon remembers. He discovered the extent to which Alinsky viewed the world in dramatic terms, and was fascinated with the various masks and roles Alinsky created for himself. As it was, Shayon surmised that the process of writing the play gave Alinsky "some of the most enjoyable moments of his life." It was a drama about labor leaders and the conflict between the exercise of power and their commitment to other values and ideals. "I would essentially guide the construction of the play, and depended on Saul for the racy dialogue because he lived with these people," Shayon says, referring to the characters drawn from the labor movement—mostly, in Alinsky's view, a bumptious assortment of dim-witted endomorphs, greedy schemers, and well-meaning mediocrities whose natural habitat was a macho land of bourbon, beef, and broads. "Saul did all the characterizing. He would lie back on the bed or walk up and down" giving character sketches and creating dialogue, including an incident—which Alinsky claimed he had witnessed in a hotel room during a union convention—when an insurgent started to argue with a union leader and suddenly found himself being picked up by one of the union's strong-arm guys and dangled out of a hotel window, twenty stories above the street.

Two characters in the play stand out from the rest. One is based on John L. Lewis. "Saul would invent the dialogue for the Man, which is what we called Lewis," Shayon says. He would walk up and down mimicking Lewis's grand oratorical style, as well as the way in which he made play-things of his intellectually inferior subordinates. In a land of mental pygmies, the John L. Lewis character towers over everyone except for Socrates McGuinness, the title character, who is, of course, based on Saul Alinsky. In a surprise twist, the Lewis character, president of a CIO-like confederation of unions, sells out his confederation membership when the President of the United States, with whom he has had a long-running feud, offers to make him his vice-presidential running mate, a position he has long coveted. Into the moral gulch rides McGuinness. He is outraged by a sense of personal betrayal and by the betrayal of the workers, who have now lost their chance to gain a historic pension program. Logically if not artfully, McGuinness symbolically slays the monster that the Lewis character has become—and that McGuinness believes he created—by cleverly rallying the other confederation leaders to rise up in opposition.

Shayon and Alinsky—especially Alinsky—at first thought that they might have written a big hit, and they retained an agent. Alinsky eagerly sought out his friends to get their reactions. "I can remember Saul sitting me down in a hotel room and reading [the play to me]," recalls Sidney Hyman. "He thought that it was great. I thought it was a morality play. I am Vice, I am Virtue, I am Doubt, I am Certainty. And I told him so, and he got very distressed. 'What you've done,' I said to Saul, 'is to write a morality play. It'd be fine for a church pageant, but you'd have to change a few things.' That didn't break our friendship, but he didn't like it."

Alinsky also took *Socrates McGuinness* to his friends in Hyde Park who still met to perform plays at one another's houses. It was probably the only time *Socrates McGuinness* was performed. Slowly the verdict began to sink in that it just wasn't a very good play.

AS THEY were writing their play, Shayon remembers having many late-night conversations with Alinsky about the anti-communist hysteria, McCarthyism, and the role of the Catholic Church in all of this. Liberal Catholic leaders such as Sheil and a very few other bishops, and editors at *Commonweal* and *America,* opposed McCarthy's methods, but they were a distinct minority and, in the heyday of McCarthyism in 1953 and early 1954, their voices were often drowned out in the applause of popular approval of McCarthy. The Irish-Catholic McCarthy's support was especially strong among American Catholics. Although Gallup polls by the winter of 1954 showed substantial support for McCarthy and his anti-communist crusade among Protestants, too, the figures were even higher among Catholics. In January, after his round of attacks on Pentagon generals for "coddling communists" in the military, nearly 60 percent of all Catholics approved of what McCarthy was doing and, apparently, what he had come to stand for. Politically, not only were American Catholics a key component of McCarthy's support but their attitudes also posed dangers for the Democratic Party in deciding how to oppose McCarthy, since the Catholic vote was an important part of the party's base.

The strong rank-and-file approval for McCarthy among Catholics was amplified if not molded by much of the Church's hierarchy. From Spellman on the East Coast to Archbishop McIntyre of Los Angeles, anticommunism became a rallying cry. In fact, Alinsky had a confrontation of his own with McIntyre, who had previously served as an assistant to Spellman in New York and was one of "Spelly's boys," one of many former aides to Spellman who later headed a diocese elsewhere in the country. "I had almost an hour and a half 'audience' with Archbishop McIntyre," Alinsky told Agnes Meyer after a trip to the West Coast in March 1951. "I'm sure that you remember him from your expeditions to the New York Chancellery when he was Cardinal Spellman's right hand man. My audience bogged down when the Archbishop at one point said to me, 'And what precisely is your position on Communism?' I replied, 'I'm agin it completely, just as I am completely opposed to any kind of totalitarianism, regardless, Archbishop, of what symbol it uses.' There was about a ten minute, very, very icy silence."

Alinsky's little gossip about his meeting with McIntyre was something that Meyer would have enjoyed, for she admired Sheil not only because of his values and courage but also because he was, in her view, such a wonderful contrast to other leaders of the Catholic Church, such as McIntyre and Spellman, whom she detested. Because of her liberalism generally, and her writings and speeches in opposition to McCarthyism and its supporters in particular, she herself was a favorite target of right-wing writers in the Catholic press and elsewhere. One such attack on her in the fall of 1953 prompted Alinsky to tell her:

> I suppose that you know that after our little fascist friend from New York [Spellman] gave that statement endorsing McCarthyism in Europe last week . . . the *Herald American* here in Chicago (a Hearst paper) ran a lead editorial supporting him and denouncing as Exhibit A none other than Agnes E. Meyer. You are the only one named. I assume that your cell will be close to ours [his and Sheil's] and we ought to have a lot of fun while they round up the American patriots. I must tell you that when I talked to the Bishop yesterday he was so God-damned mad at the *Herald American* and at the idea of anyone "picking on Agnes" that I thought he was going to blow up the damn paper.

By the spring of 1954, the saga of the junior senator from Wisconsin was about to reach a climax. During the last weeks leading to the fall of McCarthy, one of the events of some significance involved Bishop Sheil and, in a supporting role, Alinsky.

Long before the spring of 1954, Spellman had, for all practical purposes, endorsed McCarthy. Still, it made a difference—it made newspaper
headlines throughout the country—when Spellman stepped forward to
appear with the senator on April 4 in New York. At a communion breakfast of a Holy Name Society chapter of New York policemen, most of
whom were Irish Catholics, McCarthy blasted away at "bleeding hearts"
who did not understand or care that "we are at war" with communists.
With his police audience cheering him on, McCarthy also vilified fellow-
traveling "college professors" who are "ten times as dangerous" as a traitor
in an atomic plant, because they have "captive audience[s]." McCarthy
finished to thunderous applause. Spellman's presence on the speaker's
platform, his handshake and appearance with McCarthy, were widely
interpreted as a personal endorsement.

Sheil and Alinsky shared much the same views on the issue of communism, as they did on labor, race relations, and many other social and
political issues. This made Sheil highly unusual if not unique among American Catholic bishops. In private, he was apparently willing to chastise a
fellow bishop for being obsessed with the dangers of the Red menace. As
early as 1945, he had written a tough, critical reply to a letter that he had
received from the bishop of Fort Wayne, Indiana, which dwelled on the
danger of communism in the labor movement. With barely controlled
contempt, Sheil replied:

> Your Excellency, I am somewhat perturbed over what I can only
> consider your over-emphasis of the Communist danger. . . . Numeri-
> cally, Communists are not strong. Some of them do occupy positions
> of influence in labor unions; but we should be on our guard lest we
> exaggerate their strength even here. . . . I have always believed that
> Communism is no danger in a society where justice and charity
> prevail. Communism, I believe, is no threat in a decent and human
> economic structure. . . . [W]e Americans, and especially we American
> Catholics, should work indefatigably [to bring about economic jus-
> tice] in accordance with the magnificent teachings of our Popes. . . .
> We Catholics possess the most far-reaching and radical (in the best
> sense of the word) plan for social reconstruction; we *must*, we are
> bound to, put it into effect.

From the perspective of the vast majority of other bishops, Sheil's
views on communism, and his willingness to express them, stood out like
a sore thumb. Now, it was no doubt especially painful for him to see the
Catholic Church leadership increasingly perceived as at one with

McCarthyism. Perhaps the final straw for Sheil was Spellman's personal appearance with McCarthy, which prompted the liberal New York *Post* to write that the senator had used the occasion "to strengthen the impression that he is the beleaguered spokesman of Catholicism in America." Only five days later in Chicago, Sheil spoke out with a hard-hitting condemnation of McCarthy. Given the timing of his speech, it was seen as not merely a response but a counterattack to both McCarthy and Spellman from a leader of the Church's liberal wing. Some of Alinsky's friends thought he might have written Sheil's speech—and it is at least possible that he contributed to it. But a draft was prepared by one of the editors of *Commonweal,* John Cogley, who remembered getting a telephone call in which Bishop Sheil said to him, "I've had it with this guy McCarty," mispronouncing the senator's name in the classic Irish Chicago way. He wanted Cogley to write a speech for him against "McCarty" that would be "tough."

What is known is that Alinsky did advance work for Sheil, and this may possibly have included the selection of an appropriate national forum: an educational conference of the United Automobile Workers, a large gathering of 2,500 delegates at the monumental Civic Opera House.

"An invocational address was scheduled by Chicago's Auxiliary Catholic Bishop, Bernard J. Sheil," Alinsky wrote in a magazine article he composed later. "Here and there sleepy-eyed delegates yawned as they settled into their seats for the opening. Everyone, including the UAW's officials, expected some words on the morality of the living age; that is not what they got." Perhaps few if any among the UAW leadership knew what was coming, but Alinsky had apparently made certain that the press did. The press section, he reported, was overflowing with motion-picture cameras, photographers, and reporters. And the speech, Alinsky wrote, "sent newspaper editors ripping open their front pages for new headlines that were to make Bishop Sheil's name the most celebrated among the clerics of the nation."

Indeed, Sheil went vigorously after McCarthy and, by clear implication, after the good cardinal of New York as well. While insisting that on political matters "a Catholic's statement—even a bishop's—bears no more authority than whatever he can bring to it as a citizen and public figure," Sheil nonetheless roundly criticized McCarthy and his Catholic cheerleaders. "The Church does take a position on lies, calumny, the absence of charity, and calculated deceit," he said, and all of these were demonstrated by the junior senator from Wisconsin. "They are morally evil and to call them good or to act as if they were permissible under certain circumstances is itself a monstrous perversion of morality."

How the thin-skinned, autocratic Cardinal Spellman felt about being
called party to a perversion of morality can only be imagined. But for all
those who opposed McCarthy, Sheil's speech became an instant rallying
point. In addition to the newspaper headlines and a variety of favorable
editorials, there was a heavy mail response. "Altogether the Bishop has
received 21,763 letters and telegrams," Alinsky wrote in his article, "The
Bishop and the Senator," in *The Progressive*. Alinsky (identified by the
magazine's editors as a "sociologist and author, [and] an intimate associate
of Bishop Sheil") reported that all but several hundred of the responses to
Sheil's speech had been supportive, often enthusiastically so. "I can't tell
you how much I enjoyed the privilege of reading that speech," former
President Harry Truman was quoted as having written. "[Y]ou represent
the Catholic hierarchy in this country in the best way that I know."
Truman's was one of more than a score of letters from a variety of people—
senators, congressmen, labor leaders, Catholic, Protestant, and Jewish
clergy—that Alinsky quoted, and indeed the show of support for Sheil's
position was Alinsky's major purpose.

Alinsky told a friend in New York, "For the last two weeks I have
been literally living with the Bishop. I had to handle the public relations
and the press and a number of other things—a good number of other things
on what has happened." While Alinsky had helped to fan the embers of
Sheil's red-hot oratory, it may have been one of McCarthy's Republican
colleagues, Senator Ralph Flanders of Vermont, who used Sheil's words
to best effect. Flanders, alone among Senate Republicans, kept prodding
his colleagues to censure McCarthy. On June 1, 1954, Flanders took to the
Senate floor to attack his colleague's recklessness and, in a significant
passage, quoted "a high and respected member of the Catholic Church"
to buttress his claim that McCarthyism had to be stopped. Before the year
was out, McCarthy was censured by the Senate, and his career was over.
But sadly, in Chicago, the career of Bishop Sheil was—for all practical
purposes—over, too.

Within days of Sheil's speech, Alinsky told a friend, Miriam Jackson, that "the battle [inside the Church] as a result of this was the bitter-
est, dirtiest fight I have ever been in, and believe me, Toots, I have been
in some pretty bitter and dirty ones in my lifetime." Just five months
later, the Bishop "resigned" as director general of the Catholic Youth
Organization, the largest of his enterprises and the one that had provided
him with much of his public identity and fame. The speculation in Chicago and elsewhere was widespread that Sheil's resignation was forced by
powerful pro-McCarthy elements within the Church. Sheil did little to
dispel such impressions. But the sanitized explanation that dribbled out

was that Sheil was a bad administrator who had allowed the CYO to fall deeply into debt.

It was true that Sheil was a terrible manager of his myriad projects—which also included a radio station, dog kennels, and other disparate ventures. He was almost legendary in the Chicago Archdiocese for the staggering array of bills and debts he could accumulate. Agnes Meyer came to know that side of Sheil before many outsiders did. Long before the McCarthy episode, in August 1948, she had told Alinsky:

> I realize how vulnerable he is to attack from the hierarchy because he is so impractical and impetuous about his social program. If they ever caught him over-extended in his financial responsibilities, they would certainly close in on him and punish him somehow—and it is that thought that really makes me tremble with fear for him. . . . I'd die of rage and pity and sheer hatred if the Spellman crowd ever got anything on him.

It was not only the Spellman crowd that did not share Meyer's adoration for the bishop. For all the popularity that he enjoyed among Chicago's Catholic parishioners, his relations with his fellow priests were often cool and distant. Sheil was not a priest's priest. He was not one of the boys. In a sense, he was a loner who had built his own power base and who, some thought, needed the public spotlight to keep his ego warm and glowing. Even within the relatively liberal hierarchy of the Chicago Archdiocese, Sheil was hardly a favorite. Cardinal Stritch was no Spellman, either in political beliefs or in administrative style. Yet even Agnes Meyer knew that Stritch's aides, if not the cardinal himself, were antagonists of Sheil. In the fall of 1946, when she was especially active in promoting Sheil for an archbishopric, she had had an audience in New York with Spellman, who cited a long list of particulars against Sheil, one pertaining to an alleged act of insubordination—he had supposedly taken a trip to Rome without asking Cardinal Stritch for permission. Meyer later told Spellman that she had checked and that Sheil had, in fact, talked with the cardinal beforehand. A false rumor had been planted, she told Spellman, "that is typical of the cold hostility of Cardinal Stritch's entourage [toward Bishop Sheil]."

So there were many reasons and motives within the Church to get Sheil. These included, of course, Sheil's controversial stance on many social and political issues, leadership on which Alinsky had cited approvingly in the *Progressive* article, reminding readers of Sheil's long record of fighting demagogues such as the fascist radio priest, Father Coughlin; of embracing John L. Lewis and the cause of the CIO during their most radical phase; of fighting anti-Semitism within the Church. Little did Alinsky realize that he had written Sheil's epitaph.

The bishop had been skating on thin ice for a long time, but taking on the junior senator from Wisconsin finally sank him. There was little Mrs. Meyer could do to help him within the Church. Frustrated and angry, she exploded at Alinsky. He was not doing enough to save Sheil, she charged, and he was selling the bishop down the river during his time of greatest need.

It was true that Alinsky had begun to develop a personal relationship with Cardinal Stritch, one that had been helped along by Monsignor Edward Burke in the chancellery office. But Alinsky's budding relationship with Burke and then Stritch had preceded the anti-McCarthy speech. Indeed, before Sheil delivered the speech, Cardinal Stritch began to sound out Alinsky about the possibility of doing a study of South Side neighborhoods. It was something in which Alinsky had great interest; the racial and other changes and problems on the South Side were symbolic of what was rapidly altering nearly every major city in the North. Until Sheil's anti-McCarthy speech, Alinsky had been able to keep his relationships with Sheil and with Burke and Stritch on separate tracks. But now that was no longer possible, apparently because Sheil was making demands on Alinsky—it was either me or them, Sheil felt. Helstein, who served with Sheil on the Industrial Areas Foundation board then, feels strongly that it was not Alinsky's intention or preference to abandon Sheil. It was characteristic of Alinsky to reach out to friends—Myles Horton, Bob Shayon, and Larry Adler—who were in trouble and being battered by powerful forces. "Saul had a very deep sense of loyalty and commitment to friends of long years' standing. . . . [If they] were losing some of their power or influence or that sort of thing, I don't think it would have been a major consideration."

It was a hurt, angry Saul Alinsky who fired back an answer to Agnes Meyer when she accused him of betraying Sheil. His discussions with Stritch and his acceptance of the offer to conduct a study of the South Side occurred *before* Sheil's sudden resignation, he explained, and the bishop knew about it and voiced no objections. "[T]hroughout, including the only meeting to date on August 19th with the Cardinal, neither I nor any member of my Executive Committee nor any member of my Board of Trustees had any idea whatsoever that within the next two weeks Bishop Sheil was to resign as Director of the Catholic Youth Organization, or that in the slightest sense his position was to change within the time following."

Then, proclaiming his willingness to "remain [the Bishop's] friend," Alinsky let loose with a parting shot: "Knowing completely the utter lack of justification and responsibility of your charge, either by the logic of the facts or, more important, the actual intrinsic character of my actions in this specific instance, I cannot react with anger, rancor, bitterness or anything else except shock that such a baseless idea should even have entered your mind and that an old friend was not accorded the hearing you would have given to a stranger."

These were the last words that Alinsky and Mrs. Meyer exchanged. Close friends for a decade, their relationship had nonetheless pivoted around Bishop Sheil. With the pivot gone, their friendship was over. While he made an effort to save it, it was no more than he might have done with any less rich or well-connected person. All of his relationships were, essentially, on his terms. Sometimes, as with his wife, Helene, that made him seem selfish or self-centered. In other instances, as in the parting of the ways with Agnes Meyer, one could see the integrity of it. The writer Milton Mayer, who knew Alinsky well then and had a hard time liking him because of his aggressive personality, thought that Alinsky was a radical, in part, because "he was not afraid to break with the establishment, with one level or another of the establishment"—and that included breaking with symbols of the establishment, even enlightened and liberal symbols like Mrs. Meyer.

There was no rapprochement with Bishop Sheil either. He sent a letter of resignation from the board of the IAF to Marshall Field. At the IAF's annual board meeting in New York six weeks after Sheil had resigned from the CYO, the trustees unanimously declined to accept his resignation and telegraphed him accordingly, but to no avail. Although Sheil stayed at his North Side parish in Chicago for another decade before moving into full retirement in Arizona, he and Alinsky never again spoke to each other.

17

Pennies from Heaven

Early in 1952, Saul Alinsky surprised all of his friends in Chicago when he suddenly announced that he was going to marry a woman whom he had met in New York. It had been a quick, nearly whirlwind courtship, nothing at all like his unfathomable reluctance and procrastination with Babs Stiefel. Not only did Alinsky surprise his friends with his announcement, he surprised them even more when he told them about Jean Graham, an attractive, slim brunette in her thirties with a debutante background, divorced from an executive of Bethlehem Steel. "Her antecedents are not those with which I would have predicted marriage," Alinsky told Milton Mayer. "To wit: Scotch Presbyterian, Vassar graduate, Park Avenue and all of the other stuff which I have always cordially detested—and still do." Alinsky delighted in the semi-shock of his friends and of the horror he claimed he had elicited in his prospective mother-in-law. "Jean's mother," he told Mayer, "hates three things in life above everything else. One, the Catholic Church. Two, Jews. And three, John L. Lewis, and she has charged Jean with having scoured the entire nation to find the one person who would embody all three of these horrible tie-ups. The old dame is quite a character. She wears a DAR dog license around her neck as though she were in the finals of a top dog show and just above it is a thin strip of black velvet which gives a mournful dirge-like cast to the medallion as well as the neck, and above it is a puss which makes the dame in Grant Wood's *American Gothic* look like a happy-go-lucky babe." Fortunately, Alinsky added, Jean's mother and the rest of the family ("they being little chips off the old block") were ensconced in Montclair, New Jersey, safely removed from the new house in Hyde Park where Jean, Saul, and his two children were to live.

When Jean Graham introduced her mother to Alinsky, she was careful to invite her mother into New York, where Jean was living in an apartment on Park Avenue, rather than have Alinsky trek to the inhospitable setting of Montclair to face the entire family. Jean remembers that Alinsky charmed her mother, an effort in discretion and judicious cultural compromise that Alinsky conveniently left out of his tales to friends back home. As far as Jean's impending marriage was concerned, it probably would not have mattered whether her mother approved, because Jean Graham had been swept off her feet. "I remember when he asked me to marry him, twenty-four or forty-eight hours after we first met," Jean recalls. "And I said, 'I thought you would never ask.'" They had been introduced by Jean's roommate, Terry Robinson, a woman whom Jean met in Reno, Nevada, where they had both gone to get divorces. They became friends and roommates, sharing Robinson's Fifth Avenue apartment most of the year and Jean's place in Canada on Lake Ontario the rest of the time.

Jean immediately found Alinsky exciting and appealingly different. Alinsky told Milton Mayer that Jean "has rebelled against [her family's upper-class elitism and prejudices] from the time she can remember and has always been regarded as the pink sheep of the family. I think, for the first time in her life, she has finally found what she is looking for and it has been perfectly wonderful." It was an assessment Jean agreed with, at least in spirit and principle. But she was not involved in social or political causes; in fact, she had virtually no interest in or awareness of them, although she made a valiant effort after she met Saul to educate herself about his world. Still, Jean's first love was the world of museums, art, and architecture, a world in which Alinsky had no interest and felt no need to cultivate an interest.

A few of Alinsky's Hyde Park friends gossiped that Alinsky might have seen Jean as something of a trophy—that he, the son of Jewish immigrants, author of *Reveille for Radicals,* and friend of John L. Lewis, had successfully crossed enemy lines to bag one of *their* attractive women. And as he suggested to Milton Mayer and others, he savored the delicious irony of his marriage to Jean. But there was also the matter of timing. Alinsky was simply ready—in the spring of 1952, five years after Helene's drowning—to get remarried. He also wanted to have a full-time mother for Kathryn and David, which Jean, who had no children from her first marriage, was looking forward to being. Soon after their marriage, Alinsky reported enthusiastically that Jean "and the kids . . . have latched on to each other so that within four weeks of the marriage I found myself in a peculiar situation. After having wiped the noses, the rear ends and other parts of these two kids for the past five years I was suddenly relegated to the position of a father which was a combination of a sort of necessary evil, a nice guy to have around at certain times and above all economically desirable. I can't say that I have resented this in any way. On the contrary, it has come as a great relief."

Alinsky found a new home in Hyde Park for his new family, a handsome, three-story brick house at 4919 South Woodlawn. Before Jean moved in, he asked Helen Meegan to take a look at it and she, startled by its size, asked Saul only half jokingly who was going to wash the windows. After Saul and Jean moved in, Alinsky invited Milton Mayer and his family, who were then living in Carmel, California, to stop over for a visit on their next trip to town. "Believe me, we have ample room," Saul reported to Milton Mayer:

> Outside of our facilities, there are three guest rooms and since the domicile also includes seven bathrooms there will be plenty of places to go wee-wee. You may or may not know the house. It was the Kunstadter House, and they spent a pot of dough on the thing and we got it through a funny deal for about $28,000, which included all of the carpeting and a million built-in things. The place is so filled with built-in stuff that David's room, for example, has not only a built-in desk and built-in cabinet work all around as well as his own bathroom and carpeting, it was so furnished that the only thing we could use from our apartment was his bed. . . . We practically had no expenses in furnishing the house.

Jean won quick acceptance in the neighborhood. "She was friendly and open and took part in the community," Len Despres recalls. "I don't think everybody who comes into this community can do that. She was just very nice and we liked her." Six months after they were married, Alinsky told the Macys in New York, "At home all goes quietly and routinely. Jeannie is Cub-Scouting, mothering, cooking, cocktail partying and walking the dogs." The dogs, two black Labradors that had been Jean's when they married, were a constant source of annoyance to him. "The dogs," he told the Macys, ". . . well, they eat, shed and shit. Tang, the older one, has been prospering to such an effect in the Alinsky household and on the Alinsky budget that I am planning to enter her in the Madison Square Garden Dog Show next year as a new breed—a cross between a dachshund and a Labrador. I am really not exaggerating. When she walks her belly literally scrapes along the ground." The next year, in the summer of 1954, when the Alinskys took a trip out West to Aspen, Colorado, Saul recounted to Miriam Jackson, we found [ourselves] up on top of the mountains in a spot where they raise the only Husky dogs in the country. What do you think happened? You're right! We now own a Husky pup, which is four and a half months old and looks like it is going to be the size of a horse. We know that it will be much larger than a St. Bernard, and we also know that the neighbors are already terrified of its oriental slanted eyes. We also know that the neighbors are getting very jittery because of the long wolf howl that goes up each morning. We are calling the dog the Fifth Amendment.

Actually, the dog's name was Pangnanya—Pang for short—and Alinsky was quick and a little boastful in explaining that the word "in Eskimo talk means 'tough.' "

THE MARRIAGE to Jean was a fresh start. Finding a woman whom he loved and making his family whole once again was, in a sense, a triumph over his personal tragedies. It was also a triumph amidst a variety of professional failures and disappointments, although Alinsky did not readily admit to himself or to friends—and certainly not to strangers—when he failed. Except for Helene's death, Alinsky almost always appeared undaunted by everything, ready for the next battle and the next success. It was an attractive quality that conveyed strength and contagious optimism. Nonetheless, the early 1950s were, to an objective eye, a disappointing time for Alinsky on several fronts.

Alinsky's career as a writer stalled. In the spring of 1951, he had lunch in the Pump Room in Chicago with Alfred Knopf to discuss a new, more scholarly effort, a book on social disorganization. Alinsky had accepted a teaching position for the summer session in 1951 at Catholic University in Washington, D.C., and he told one of Knopf's editors that the preparation for the course he would be teaching there on social disorganization would give him a good start toward organizing and writing the book. Alinsky worked on the book in fits and starts, but it never progressed very far, perhaps because his enthusiasm for it was never high. Three years later, when Knopf asked him if he might be interested in writing a biography of Bishop Sheil—the query coming only months after Alinsky's break with the bishop—Alinsky replied, "I am not your man on that one." He also told Knopf that he was already busy "working on three different books at once. Each is entirely different and depending upon my mood and time of the day I pick the one to work on at that time. It's a damn good thing that

I don't depend upon my writing for my living," he acknowledged, hinting that the discipline of writing did not come easy to him.

During this period, a writer whom Alinsky admired and sought out was the longshoreman-philosopher Eric Hoffer, whose book on social movements, *The True Believer,* was an Alinsky favorite. After Alinsky finally made contact with Hoffer in San Francisco—for years he lived a spartan existence in a small apartment that had no telephone—the two of them saw each other occasionally. Alinsky may have been surprised to discover that Hoffer had a similar but even more extensive practice of collecting and filing aphorisms and other quotations from a wide assortment of philosophers, historians, revolutionaries, poets, and prophets. In Alinsky's case, after reading into the early morning hours in his study, he would appear at his office the next day with passages in books and magazines underlined, ready for his secretary to type on 3 × 5 pieces of paper and file.

One of the books Alinsky was working on—perhaps the only one to which he actually gave a considerable amount of his time and energy—was a biography of Monsignor John O'Grady. Alinsky and O'Grady, at that time director of the National Conference of Catholic Charities in Washington, had met in the early 1940s and almost immediately felt a strong affinity for each other. O'Grady had emigrated to the United States from County Clare, Ireland, fresh out of the seminary, in July 1909, the year that Alinsky was born, a coincidence that each of them bantered about as somehow symbolic of their cosmic brotherhood. O'Grady was a lovable, good-hearted, witty character whose brogue had grown richer and thicker the longer he lived in the United States—and which became especially pronounced late at night amidst good conversation and an increasing number of glasses of good Jack Daniel's.

John O'Grady was known in Washington as the Catholic Church's lobbyist on a wide range of progressive causes—on minimum-wage and other labor legislation, on public housing, on the plight of migrant workers, on anti-discrimination initiatives. He was an avid supporter of every progressive impulse of the New Deal. By the early 1950s, he was taking a lead role in fighting the reactionary McCarran bill that restricted immigration from Third World and other "undesirable" countries. So he and Alinsky shared not only a friendship but also the same broad concerns on matters of social justice. (There was also another connection: as a young priest, not long after he had landed in Omaha, Nebraska, O'Grady finagled his way to the University of Chicago, where he did graduate work with, among others, one of Alinsky's old professors in the Sociology Department, Ernest Burgess.) In Washington, O'Grady saw the Catholic Charities job as a good base from which to advocate legislation dearest to his heart—causes he felt ought to be at the heart of the American Catholic Church.

(As the firstborn in his family and always intellectually curious, O'Grady had never wanted to be a man of the cloth but was forced into the priesthood by his mother, he told many of his friends. Palmer Weber, a young congressional aide when he first met O'Grady, who worked with him successfully on legislation to extend the minimum wage to migrant workers in California, once asked him how he could stand the corruption in the Church. O'Grady replied: "Palmer, I had been a priest for eight years and I was thirty years old before I realized the Church was corrupt. It really put me in agony. I thought, What am I going to do? Shall I leave the priesthood, shall I go out and become a doctor or a lawyer? What shall I do?" After thinking hard about it, he came to realize that every institution in society was corrupt. So he said to himself, "If I stay in the Church, at least here I'll have the word of God. I'll have the example of Jesus Christ. I'd have Jesus Christ on my side here but in the other institutions I wouldn't. So I decided to fight it out on this line. I'll never make it to bishop, but I might become a monsignor." Six or seven years later, he did.)

Howland Shaw, who served on the board of directors of Catholic Charities as well as that of the IAF, and Lowell Mellett, a friend of Monsignor O'Grady at the *Evening Star,* wanted Alinsky to write O'Grady's biography. They wanted to honor him with a biography that would trumpet his many important but often behind-the-scenes accomplishments—and, perhaps, through the story of his life present a view of a humanitarian Catholicism that many non-Catholic Americans remained unaware of.

Alinsky and O'Grady spent many long sessions together, often with a tape recorder running, engaging in a kind of Socratic dialogue, which was the form Alinsky considered using to organize the book. Taking the role of both friend and social critic, Alinsky would press and prod O'Grady toward the "truth." In addition to covering O'Grady's many glorious legislative battles, Alinsky wanted to establish that O'Grady—perhaps because of Alinsky's own influence—had a new, postwar, post–New Deal view of the role of government. In his outline of the biography, he wrote: "He is beginning to see that the New Deal was important, it was good, it was what he fought for, yet it carried an opposite side to the shield, in terms of a gravitation of power and the establishment of enormous bureaucracies which were evil. He is beginning to rebel against superimposed plans and the specialist up on top and [instead] turning to grass roots organization and decentralization. The contradiction of this change of attitude as over against the character of his own authoritarian institution" was of great fascination to Alinsky. He envisioned a climax to his dialogue with O'Grady where he would "point out contradictions and inconsistencies and raise questions and points" on Catholic censorship of motion pictures and books, the rigidity of the Church hierarchy, the domination of the Irish within the Church, and, broadly speaking, the hierarchy's willingness to exercise political power to further a narrow "Catholic agenda." In short, he wanted O'Grady to come to grips with the anti-democratic image that the Catholic Church held for many non-Catholic Americans.

By the time Alinsky had completed a draft of the biography, it was apparent that there were major problems. O'Grady was reluctant to speak out critically on the regressive personalities and positions that typified a significant part of the Church. Also, O'Grady's career, although speckled with colorful, dramatic episodes, was largely composed of good but un-dramatic work as an important cog in somebody else's machine. Shaw suggested to Alinsky that the perspectives he had employed be put aside in favor of an account of O'Grady as an inspiration for parish priests, church activists, and social workers. He even suggested that Alinsky consider O'Grady's contributions to the theology of Catholic social case work—a suggestion that might well have produced a thud in Alinsky's mind, the telltale sound that the bottom of a dry well had been reached. Finally, without rancor, they all agreed—Alinsky, O'Grady, Shaw, and Mellett—that it would probably be best if the biography was put on the shelf indefinitely.

Alinsky's writing was not the only activity that was not producing satisfying results in the early 1950s. His community organizing work, with two important exceptions, had lost its momentum, if not stalled. The Back of the Yards Neighborhood Council, of which Alinsky was still technical consultant, was going strong under Joe Meegan's energetic leadership. The Community Service Organization in California was back on track, after a temporary derailment, and expanding beyond the confines of Los Angeles because of the work of the quietly inspirational, indefatigable Fred Ross. But a problem arose when there was no money to pay Ross in 1950. Alinsky did not come out to raise money in Los Angeles that year, which was around the time of the sudden death of Babs Stiefel. Ross tried to do it himself but wasn't very good at it, partly because organizing—not money—is what interested him. "With Saul, I started with peanuts, and I never got much further along than peanuts. I think I got up to around maybe $6,000 eventually [by the end of the 1950s]. But even then that [was not very much]. But I was above all that. I was the saintly type. Money was dirty stuff." But Ross's indifference toward money and fund-raising affected the stability of the CSO. He rarely pushed CSO leaders hard enough to make the organization self-supporting and, consequently, it became shaky when outside funding dried up. Ross recalls:

> They accepted me as their organizer, but they knew that the freight was going to be paid by somebody else. And they talked about how difficult it was to raise money among the Mexican-Americans because [in the past] so-called established leaders had raised money among them and then had gone south with the money. Or they would say that it was a bad time to try to get them . . . and on and on. So I swallowed all of this. Well, hell, they had started out at $2.00 a year in dues, and I finally got it up to $3.50. But what's that?

In 1950, Ross held on as long as he could, with him and his family living off the savings they had accumulated from war bonds. Finally, nearly broke, he took another job with the California Federation for Civic Unity. More than a year went by and then one day Ross ran into Monsignor O'Grady, who wanted to know how the CSO in Los Angeles was doing. Not too well, it's practically folded, Ross told him. "Oh my God, we can't let that happen," O'Grady said, and the next thing Ross knew, Alinsky's interest in the West Coast had been reawakened.

As for the other organizing projects, Alinsky tended not to talk about them anymore. On rare occasions, he was willing to admit that not all of his projects had been unequivocal successes, although he always rationalized the failures with a mixture of truth and fiction, plausibility and revisionism. In a letter in November 1952 to a New York–based organization that monitored the activities of foundations, Alinsky wrote that all of his organizing work during the IAF's first twelve years had been "experimental demonstrations." The "various handicaps, such as drastic lack of personnel and insufficient field visits, were regarded and used as tests for various procedures, with negative results being considered as significant as those of positive character. We knew from the Chicago experience and also that in Los Angeles how basically important adequate personnel is to insure a positive result." The question about staff was clearly important, even critical, and Alinsky, in the privacy of his own mind, was probably unsure if a single answer fit all situations. What was supposed to happen after the first two or three years, when the original organizer and/or fund-raiser left the community council on its own? Interestingly, back in 1946, Alinsky had made a point of telling Happy Macy that "at the next Board meeting there will be an ironing out of policy, whereby [the IAF's] affiliation with most of these councils will be formally severed. This will be in keeping with our own policy. After all, we are not a holding company of People's Organizations." He took this position at the very time when things were not going well for the community council in Kansas City and probably not so well for the one in South St. Paul either. Was it now entirely up to "the people" to regenerate their community organizations because that was what democracy was all about? Or had Alinsky invented another convenient rationale so that he would not have to deal with such problems? With money always scarce, with his problem of recruiting organizers, and with his low threshold of boredom, Alinsky had enough reasons to say—and to want to believe—that these community councils were now on their own. And yet he continued to ride the circuit, and now it was abundantly clear in Los Angeles with the CSO that the IAF's support of Fred Ross was essential if the Mexican-American effort were to survive, let alone flourish.

Alinsky developed a plan late in 1950 for a new, ambitious national drive to organize "between twelve and sixteen million people"—he referred to it as a three-year program: "First, it takes that length of time (on the average) to establish these organizations to the point where they are self-financed, independent and have a developed native leadership. Secondly, it is almost impossible to secure competent personnel without guaranteeing three years' tenure. Third, this kind of a program would be subjected to a severe disadvantage if there were constant interruptions because of financial crisis." How serious was Alinsky about such a national program? As serious as he could be without having any of the money to implement it. Two years earlier, he had talked with Palmer Weber and J. Raymond Walsh in New York about his idea, and also to Carey McWilliams. Alinsky tried to interest his old friend Sidney Hyman, too. He told Hyman that a new opportunity was on the horizon.

> We are trying to raise about a million-dollar budget to carry us over a three-year plan of organization through the country. We are taking the position that all of our present projects . . . are pilot projects and that we have now finished our period of experimentation and are ready to really go ahead. I have been acquiring what I think is really the best staff in the country and the guys that are coming in are really terrific. I don't know whether or not you ever heard of Palmer Webber. He used to be in charge of CIO-PAC for the South. Palmer is coming in on administering Southern organization. Yes, we plan to go into the South, into Atlanta, Birmingham, New Orleans and other places. Carey McWilliams is going to work with us and supervise the Southwest. J. Raymond Walsh is coming with us, and I could name others.

Alinsky was right about one point: this group of men was extraordinary, each of exceptional intellect, compassion, and commitment to democratic ideals. What a team they might have made! Alinsky, however, had no money to pay them. So he played a familiar chicken-and-egg game, implying to people like Hyman that big money was highly probable, while greatly stretching the truth when telling potential big-money sources that people such as Hyman, McWilliams, Walsh, and Weber were "on board." In truth, Alinsky had neither chickens nor eggs.

One of his early leads led him to the Avalon Foundation, where he put in an application for $75,000, and he quickly turned to Happy and Valentine Macy for help. "As you know," he told Happy, the head of the Foundation "is buying a house in Westchester County, and he wants to meet the newspaper and radio tycoons of Westchester County. So here is the pitch. Call the guy some time next week and . . . set him up for a dinner date at your house on either November 7th or Thursday the 8th. . . . If he is tied up and can't make it during those days then work on Thursday the 15th or Friday the 16th. BUT GET HIM. With Val to serve as the ultra smooth host and with you slinking around in that extra low cut dress and with me playing gangster at the door—we ought to get him." In spite of such blandishments, little was accomplished with the Avalon Foundation.

In approaching the Ford Foundation, Alinsky enlisted the help of Jacques Maritain, since Maritain was a good friend of Robert Hutchins, late of the University of Chicago and now at the Foundation. Alinsky asked Maritain to write a letter focusing on themes popular with Hutchins and the Foundation: "You should say that you saw a good deal of me during your trip here and that you discussed civil rights and peace and the potentiality of our new program in that direction." Maritain's letter to Hutchins, while not following Alinsky's precise instructions, was, nevertheless, a glowing endorsement. "I am writing this on a personal basis," Maritain began, "because I have known Saul Alinsky for about ten years and because I admire and love him as a great soul, a man of profound moral purity and burning energy, whose work I consider the only really new and really important democratic initiative taken in the social field today." In spite of Maritain's good words, Ford Foundation support was not forthcoming.

Later, when Hutchins had gone to California with the Fund for the Republic, a spin-off of the Ford Foundation, Alinsky was after him again, this time through Milton Mayer, and he came up with still another slant that he thought might work: "Our major objective and the character of our whole program is targeted primarily for the breaking through of this climate of repression against civil rights," he told Mayer, trying to suggest that such concerns, in keeping with Hutchins's interest in civil rights and civil liberties, were not merely by-products of community organizing work. Mayer's intervention was to no avail, however; Hutchins was simply not enthusiastic about—or was uncomfortable with—Alinsky's deliberately abrasive, often belligerent style. With no infusion of new, big money, the best Alinsky could offer to Palmer Weber and Ray Walsh was a salary of $12,000 a year, and they would have to raise the money themselves. It was an offer that neither was in a position to accept.

There was also no money to put into an IAF retirement fund for Alinsky, although the $5,000 yearly contribution that the IAF board approved after Helene's death was carried on the books as a liability owed to Alinsky. After Helene's death, the board also had approved a $5,000 increase in Alinsky's salary to $15,000 a year, but for four years he did not draw the increase because there was no money. By the beginning of 1952, the IAF's budget—a little less than $30,000 a year—was virtually unchanged from what it had been in the mid-1940s; the annual contributions from the same seven people—Marshall Field, Happy and Val Macy, Howland Shaw, Adele Levy, and (before their split with Alinsky in 1954) Agnes Meyer and Bishop Sheil—made up most of the total.

But just as Alinsky seemed to have struck out in the early 1950s in finding new financial support and in attracting talented men to work with him, there began to emerge slowly a new set of relationships and resources that would significantly improve his fortunes.

THE FIRST important change came by way of a friend of his, a Chicago lawyer named Leonard Rieser, whom he had met through his first wife. Rieser, more than a generation older than Alinsky, came from a Philadelphia family related to Helene Alinsky's. After studying at Harvard Law School, he joined the Chicago law firm of Sonnenschein, Berkson, Lautman, Levinson and Morse. This was not long after the establishment of the first federal income tax, and Rieser soon became a highly regarded, pioneering tax attorney. Among the firm's clients was Sears, Roebuck founder Julius Rosenwald. Through another partner in the firm who handled much of Rosenwald's legal work, Rieser eventually became involved in Rosenwald's affairs, too, especially in Rosenwald's estate and the establishment of the Rosenwald Fund, well known for its support of Negro colleges such as Fisk in Nashville, Tennessee.

In the 1940s, Rieser, a short, slightly stocky, fast-talking, energetic man, handled the modest amount of legal work generated by the Industrial

Areas Foundation, and he and Alinsky grew closer after the tragedy of Helene's death. By 1950, Rieser was an IAF board member. Coincidentally, within months, one of the clients of Rieser's law firm, Emil Schwarzhaupt, died. Schwarzhaupt, a German-Jewish immigrant bachelor, had made a small fortune in the liquor business. Anticipating Prohibition, he had cleverly stockpiled huge quantities of whiskey before 1919, some of which he and a few partners sold for medicinal purposes during the 1920s, but when Prohibition was repealed, they pooled their inventory with a number of other concerns and formed the National Distillers Corporation. Later, Schwarzhaupt acquired the Bernheim Distilling Company from the Bernheim family and in 1937 made a big financial killing when he sold out to Schenley.

"Emil, being the kind of man that he was who made an awful lot of money, he always felt that he came to this country with nothing, that this was the greatest country in the world . . . and that, therefore, he owed this country something," recalls Adolph Hirsch, whose uncle was a partner of Schwarzhaupt's. "He was never married, so he figured that he wanted to leave a good deal of money to do something for this country or for the people of this country." Schwarzhaupt wanted to do something to help immigrants become functioning American citizens, but he was vague about how, exactly, he wanted it done. "We were together one evening," Hirsch remembers, "we had a couple of drinks, and I said to him, 'Emil, you know, you keep talking about what you want done but suppose you died tomorrow . . . what do you really expect us to do?' And he said, 'You goddamn fool, don't you think if I knew I would write it out?' "

Thus, after Emil Schwarzhaupt's death and his bequest of $2.3 million to the Emil Schwarzhaupt Foundation, its trustees—a small group of his friends, relatives, and business associates—had no specific criteria for deciding what citizenship programs should receive Emil's money. They brought in experts to advise them and finally held a meeting at a New York hotel, where a number of potential grantees were invited to make presentations. Saul Alinsky was there at the urging of Leonard Rieser. (Rieser was not a trustee, but his law partner, Hugo Sonnenschein, who had been Schwarzhaupt's lawyer, was.) Because of Rieser's work with the Rosenwald Fund and his interest in foundations and progressive causes, his opinion was given great weight by many of the trustees. In fact, the Schwarzhaupt Foundation had been set up along the lines of the Rosenwald Fund, including the rather unusual provision that the Foundation would give all its money away and go out of business within twenty-five years.

Alinsky's presentation at the meeting in the New York hotel—with an emphasis on his work in that famous immigrant slum, the Back of the Yards—was good but not memorable. And, ironically, it was Rieser's law partner, the conservative Hugo Sonnenschein, who wanted no part of him. "Sonnenschein was of the old school," Hirsch says. "He was giving us more trouble with Alinsky or Alinsky's philosophy than any other trustee. . . . He believed that in the old days people came over here, they went to school and that's the way they became Americanized." But Rieser pushed Alinsky's cause, and the other trustees were open to different, innovative approaches.

Before they made a decision on Alinsky, the trustees agreed that Hirsch should go to Chicago to examine firsthand the Back of the Yards Neighborhood Council. Alinsky, leaving nothing to chance, was Hirsch's tour guide. By the end of a week, Hirsch was dazzled. It was exactly what his late good friend Emil had envisioned without being quite able to articulate it: "They were doing the things that Emil wanted them to do." What he saw "made me feel all the more certain that Alinsky's methods were on the right track. . . . He had gotten the people involved to help themselves."

When he returned to New York, Hirsch brought with him photographs and dramatic stories to capture what he had seen, along with an ecstatic recommendation that the Schwarzhaupt trustees support Alinsky's work. Thus it was that the Schwarzhaupt Foundation's largest grant in 1953 went to Saul Alinsky's IAF—a three-year grant of $150,000.

The Schwarzhaupt money, intended for Alinsky's work in California, came in the nick of time. At first hearing, it sounded like a magnificent sum, but it did not dramatically alter Alinsky's level of operation—for several reasons. First, the high hopes that Alinsky had had for financial help from the Fund for the Republic were not materializing—and never did. Second, his split with Bishop Sheil and Agnes Meyer in 1954 cost him at least $10,000 a year in contributions from the two of them. More money was needed for Fred Ross's work in California, including additional funds for a new, young organizer, Cesar Chavez, whom Ross discovered in San Jose. Then there was also the matter of Alinsky's back salary and the deficit in his annuity account. Therefore, the new Schwarzhaupt money, while giving Alinsky a little breathing room and a relative measure of financial stability, largely covered work already in progress.

IN THE VERY PROCESS of establishing new ties to powerful Church leaders after the regretful end of his relationship with Bishop Sheil, Alinsky stumbled upon a young man who had the potential to become what

Alinsky had found to be so elusive: a crack organizer with whom he could work as a brother, or perhaps as a father, sharing and rejoicing in the adventure, the jousting, the fun, the power, and the nobility of fighting for a just cause.

It all started, more or less, with a phone call. Saul Alinsky called one Father John J. Egan, at the suggestion of Jacques Maritain. Jack Egan was in his early thirties, a small-boned man of medium height, whose family had moved to Chicago from New York when he was six. He grew up on the North Side; he was "North Side Irish," as they say in Chicago. "We didn't have the tribalism that they had on the West Side," Egan says by way of contrasting a distinguishing influence of his formative years. "I think that we had a better ecumenical spirit." After his seminary days at St. Mary's, as a young priest Egan gravitated to the Catholic left in Chicago. Although he was not an intellectual, his heart and sentiments were with the bright men and women, many of them college students, of the Young Christian Workers and the Young Christian Students movements, which he served as chaplain. (Egan's formal base was as director of marriage programs for the archdiocese, a program that was a symbol of progressivism in the most populous archdiocese in the country.)

What had prompted Alinsky's phone call to Egan was a letter from Jacques Maritain telling Alinsky that a good friend of his was coming to Chicago, a Father Voillaume, who would be staying with Father Egan. Voillaume was the founder of the Little Brothers and the Little Sisters of Jesus, who worked with the poor in missions all over the world—from the slums of Rome to the pygmies in Africa. Why don't you come to the United States, Egan had asked Voillaume, where we have a lot of poor people, too? He had tried, Voillaume told Egan, but had been refused permission. By whom? Egan asked. By Cardinal Spellman, Voillaume replied. Egan, who had the considerable, and useful, political instincts of a good Chicago Irish ward committeeman, did not miss a beat. "Everybody gets off a boat and asks Cardinal Spellman for something," he replied creatively. He told Voillaume to come to the Midwest, to Chicago, where he would find that Cardinal Stritch was kind and understanding. By the winter of 1954, Voillaume was on his way, and when Alinsky phoned Jack Egan to talk about what they would do with Voillaume, Egan invited him to his office for lunch.

Egan had kosher salami sandwiches for the two of them, which Alinsky found amusing. (When they discussed taking Voillaume out to lunch and Alinsky suggested one of his favorite haunts, the Grill at the Palmer House, Egan tactfully remarked that Voillaume might feel out of place there, an understatement of about the same magnitude as the sinfully large steaks that were a Palmer House specialty. Alinsky was impressed by this and other signs of Egan's sensitivity. "Maritain told me many years later," Egan recalls, "that Saul had written him and said that he had found a priest in Chicago who was sensitive to the needs of poor people.") In two hours, they covered a waterfront of subjects—the Catholic Church, community organization, their backgrounds. When Egan asked him how he happened to get into the kind of work he was doing, Alinsky summed it up by saying, "Oh, Jack, I hate to see people get pushed around." Egan was deeply moved. "That meant a great deal to me," he says of Alinsky's simple answer. Egan was also moved when Alinsky, recounting how Helene had died and how much he had loved her, broke down and started to cry. "He was so warm and so human." Egan was intrigued both by Alinsky's style and by the work he was doing.

At about the same time, Egan was also pointed in Alinsky's direction by the ubiquitous Monsignor O'Grady. A group of young people with whom Egan was working were trying to organize Puerto Ricans (a few had begun to settle in Woodlawn, a neighborhood just south of the University of Chicago and Hyde Park). They were poor, they didn't know English, and they were being abused, Egan told O'Grady, and these young people wanted to help them. O'Grady said that it sounded important and that Egan's friends ought to meet with Saul Alinsky and get his advice.

The "young people" to whom Egan referred were a remarkable group. They were mostly Catholics, but a conspicuous exception was Lou Silverman, conspicuous because he was a six-foot-seven, 218-pound Jew from New York who had come to Chicago to attend the university. After the war, there were many veterans on campus, and because of these older, politically aware students, colleges all over America were especially interesting and "yeasty." Silverman moved into one of the large courtyard apartment buildings in Woodlawn, across the Midway from the university, where he joined about a dozen other students, all men. They were a varied bunch with few common ties; sharing the apartment was a matter of convenience. Silverman remembers that there "wasn't a Roman Catholic among them," mainly Protestants and agnostics. In this and other respects, Silverman's apartment was in sharp contrast to an apartment that mirrored his across the back courtyard.

There were eight or ten women, older than us, some grad students, some undergrads, who were all part of the Young Christian Students. A couple went to the University of Chicago, some went to De Paul or whatever. One entrance over, but still on the same level, were the men of the Young Christian Students. The Young Christian Students, the men and the women, were much more purposeful than us, not a hodgepodge that shifted and changed like the group in my apartment. They had come together to live a communal life, not with a capital "C," but to live together and work together and to help each other. . . . Some of the men in our group joined them in an eating co-op. Nothing fancy, nothing very organized. Everyone kicked in a certain amount of money and people ate in different shifts. In those days, women still did the cooking, some of the men did the shopping, and I was appointed treasurer.

The more that Silverman got to know the Young Christian Students, the more fascinated he became. "They were bright and all Catholics, and this was new to me. I had had a certain impression of Catholics being rigid, and these people weren't like that at all. They were liberal. Some were highly anticlerical. . . . They were concerned about democracy in the Church. They had a feeling that the Church had lost its way as the protector of the poor." Some were Marxists; some wanted to emulate the worker-priests who were transforming much of clerical life in France. Silverman thought of them as left liberals, but "they weren't faddists. They came from a strong theoretical base. They were theologically trained. It was not an emotional thing. [Theirs] was a concept of what Christ had in mind."

Silverman valued his enhanced intellectual understanding of Catholicism, and he also enjoyed the company of his new, stimulating friends. One of these was Ann Byrne. One day, Silverman recalls, "she started bringing home a long-haired, very shaggy, handsome guy, a charming guy, an artist-intellectual whose main work was writing a novel." The young man began to hang around with the group, but "the difference with him was that he wasn't paying anything to the co-op. Not only that, he wouldn't take his turn washing dishes as I did and everyone else did. And that was a fellow named Nicholas von Hoffman." Eventually the co-op decided to throw von Hoffman out because he refused to do any of the communal work. "But I took up a very Jewish tradition. I told them that you have to put up with him; he is a real talent. It's only right to put up with him; it's charitable. So we allowed Nick to continue to come, and Nick and I became friends, not because of that but because we liked each other."

During the next several years, Silverman and von Hoffman both moved back across the Midway into their own apartments in Hyde Park. Von Hoffman married Ann Byrne; Silverman got into politics, challenging Democratic machine candidates in a few aldermanic campaigns. He was learning along the way about precinct work, door-to-door canvassing, and tactics. "In those days, I used to ruminate in Hyde Park at a bookstore, Clark & Clark. One day I found this book there called *Reveille for Radicals*. I paid a nickel for it. I don't think I understood what all of Alinsky's theories were, but as a book on campaign tactics I just soaked it up." "The guy's a genius," Silverman thought, himself a young man of considerable nerve, audacity, and cleverness. He discovered that "you could invent your own tactics. The book was my own reveille just for getting someone elected. When I began to canvass [Hyde Park], I began to look for nodules of community political leadership," which was like Alinsky's emphasis on finding the indigenous leaders in any community and then building an organization around them.

Silverman, who also started a public relations business, began to experience some electoral successes as a political activist. At the same time, Nick von Hoffman and some of the Young Christian Students were working in Woodlawn with the Puerto Ricans and their myriad problems. By 1953, they had approached Father Egan for some help, especially for some financial aid from the archdiocese. They formed the Woodlawn Latin American Committee, and Egan, acting as their advocate with the chancery office, eventually raised a small amount of money. Nonetheless, in spite of their good intentions and energy, von Hoffman and his friends were not making great headway, and soon Silverman the public relations man was drawn into the noble effort. As he recalls, von Hoffman spun out a grandiose prognostication: what was happening in New York, where tens of thousands of Puerto Ricans had immigrated to escape horrendous poverty only to find themselves trapped in unspeakable slum conditions, was obviously soon going to be repeated in Chicago. The Puerto Ricans' plight in New York, according to von Hoffman's analysis, was due to their lack of an identity. Therefore, even though Chicago's Puerto Rican population was still minuscule, it was a matter of the utmost urgency that they, Nick and Lou, create an identity and culture for the Puerto Ricans. And with equal parts of insolence, ignorance, and imagination, they hatched a campaign. Silverman was hired as press agent for what was eventually called the Cardinal's Committee for the Spanish Speaking. He had the services of twenty seminarians at his disposal. But before things really got off the ground, Silverman wisecracked to von Hoffman, "Nick, I've been to the library and to the Britannica—*what* Puerto Rican culture? There is no Puerto Rican culture." And Silverman remembers von Hoffman answering, "You're the public relations man, invent one." In short order, a series of new "cultural" events hit Chicago, a city where public displays of ethnic solidarity—St. Patrick's Day parades and Polish festivals—and political recognition are related. "We had the Puerto Rican presidential candidates and famous people coming in. . . . And then we invented stuff. We invented a national tree and a national flower," Silverman remembers, "and all sorts of customs. We would tell Lester Hunt, who was working with Nick and who spoke Spanish, what we wanted and he came up with the name for it in Spanish. We made the lamb the national animal of Puerto Rico. It was all a ball. We picked things that in those days the media just lapped up. We would dream up things for television and for newspaper photographs . . . including presenting the lamb to the mayor," who, by then, was Richard J. Daley.

> It was a real lamb, a live lamb. Great p.r. Six little girls in their communion dresses and the lamb. I called up the mayor's press aide, Colonel Riley. Want to present a lamb to the mayor, I told him. National animal of Puerto Rico. He said, "Sure, Lou, sounds great, good picture opportunity. We'll do it in the mayor's office." We walked in with the lamb, and Riley screamed, "I thought you meant a lamb that you put on your table. You're not going to bring that animal in on this carpet." I started to say, "But, Colonel," but at this point the guy who was the breeder of the lamb—we had rented it—started hollering, "Do you think I'm crazy? I plugged him up." The colonel could care less if the lamb was corked or not. He hollered, "Get out of here." There was all of this hubbub and cameras were whirling and the headline on the front page of the *Tribune* became, SCRAM LAMB SAYS MAYOR'S MAN. But Daley stuck his head out of his office and invited us in. What did he care if the lamb pissed on the carpet.

These, then, were the kinds of stories that Saul Alinsky heard when he first met Nicholas von Hoffman. The meeting, which O'Grady had suggested to Egan on an earlier trip to Chicago, finally took place when O'Grady came to town on a return visit some months later. The four of them—Alinsky, Egan, von Hoffman, and O'Grady—met in the dining room of the Blackstone Hotel on Michigan Avenue, where O'Grady always stayed when he came to Chicago because the man who ran the hotel was an old friend who put him up without charge. Alinsky asked von Hoffman what he was doing, and von Hoffman went on at length, prideful and enthusiastic, explaining why and how he had been organizing Puerto Ricans in Woodlawn. Alinsky finally interrupted. "You're full of shit," he said. "You're going about it the wrong way." Von Hoffman became angry and laid into Alinsky. "Well, you're over the hill, you're a has-been, and you've sold out." Egan recalls, "There was shouting and yelling, waiters thought there was going to be a fistfight." Alinsky argued that any serious, effective strategy had to include the other Puerto Rican enclaves on the North Side of Chicago, and he chastised von Hoffman and his friends for their irresponsibility. They were having a good time, he said, doing something they thought they should be doing, but they were doing it all wrong. A lot of people were putting their faith in them, giving the project their time, but it had little chance for success. Egan, watching the verbal slug-fest, thought Alinsky was intentionally goading von Hoffman, exaggerating the ineptitude and incompetence, testing him, since he was so obviously something special—handsome, extraordinarily bright, and charismatic. He was not surprised, therefore, that within a month Alinsky offered von Hoffman a job. Of course, Alinsky had additional incentives for doing that. For von Hoffman and his young friends were not the only ones interested in the Puerto Ricans' problems in Chicago; Cardinal Stritch himself was also taking an interest. Von Hoffman and the others had run up $10,000 worth of bills with the Woodlawn Latin American Committee, which, as Egan says, "was a lot of money in those days." Egan went to see Monsignor Edward Burke in the chancery office, and Burke, with Egan in tow, went to Stritch's house. "Jack, tell the cardinal all about it," Burke said. Eventually the cardinal agreed to put up some money and, perhaps, to look more closely at Alinsky's suggestion of expanding the work beyond the small Puerto Rican enclave in Woodlawn. Not long after, Egan introduced Alinsky to Burke and, in short order, Burke introduced Alinsky to the cardinal. These new connections were being established just as Alinsky's old friend Bishop Sheil was on his way into oblivion. Maybe Lou Silverman had considered von Hoffman's interest in Chicago's Puerto Ricans a nutty idea, but it was turning into a fortuitous opportunity for Saul Alinsky.

As for von Hoffman, Alinsky said to him, "I'll give you a job, a hundred bucks a week, provided one thing."

"What's that?" von Hoffman asked.

"Provided you go out and get a haircut and buy yourself a decent suit."

18

The Big Eight Ball

"They were the most interesting months of my life," Nicholas von Hoffman says about his start with Saul Alinsky. Von Hoffman's entry into Alinsky's life coincided with a marked upturn in the volume of Alinsky's work—partly a matter of coincidence, since a developing set of social forces made Alinsky's analysis and methods newly relevant—and von Hoffman himself was an important part of Alinsky's renaissance. He quickly developed under Alinsky's tutelage and influence in the manner of a highly talented, precocious rookie who had, as they say in baseball, all the tools.

At first von Hoffman thought Alinsky regarded him as a mere throw-in in a two-for-one sale, "that he was just sort of stuck with me." And when, still shaggy and without a decent suit, he first walked into Alinsky's office, the assignment he was given did nothing to dispel his worries about Alinsky's enthusiasm for him. Alinsky said, "Look, you go out to the near West Side, and I want you to write me a report every week. You figure out how the near West Side is put together. I don't want to see you. You can send in your expense account. We'll send you your check. Don't call, don't do anything except send that weekly report. And when, and if, I ever want to see you again, I'll tell you."

Dutifully, young Nick von Hoffman, blond and bohemian, went off to the largely Italian near West Side. "I just talked to everybody and every week I would write these things," von Hoffman says. "This went on for I don't know how long—weeks and weeks and weeks. Finally, the telephone rings one morning, and it's Dorothy." Alinsky's secretary told him that Mr. Alinsky would like to see him the next morning at eleven o'clock. "So I go in to see him, scared shitless, and he's got this real puzzled expression on his face."

"I've been reading this stuff you've been sending me every week," Alinsky said. "I think you may have smartened up."

"Well, what does that mean?" von Hoffman asked.

"That means I want you to go back out to the West Side and keep doing what you are doing. Don't call me, I'll call you."

That is what von Hoffman did.

> I learned more during those weeks than I ever learned in my life. I really think I did. It was day after day of going out and finding out about other people and other things, taking it home, putting it down, thinking about it, trying to make sense out of it. Day after day after day, making the connections and trying to understand people's motives and activities. I cannot think of anything I have ever gone through that was more valuable.

One of the people von Hoffman discovered during the early weeks of his adventure on the West Side was Nick Taccio, who, twenty years earlier, had been one of the kids Alinsky befriended in that same neighborhood when he was working in Clifford Shaw's juvenile-delinquency program.

> I was getting absolutely nowhere, because I had no leverage—why the hell should they tell me anything? And I was at a meeting and, afterward, Nick Taccio came over to me. He said, "You work for Saul?" I said yes, and he slipped me a match cover with a phone number on it. He said, "Call me." So I called him, and we arranged to meet in some coffee place. "If you're working for Saul, you gotta be all right," he said. "Tell me anything you want to know." I think it really jarred Saul when he realized I had come across the trail of Nick Taccio.

Von Hoffman's ingenuity, insights, and intellectual sophistication impressed Alinsky. So, too, did his exceptional writing talents. His handwritten weekly reports, some of which were retyped by Alinsky's secretary, were composed in a fluid, vivid style that Alinsky no doubt admired and perhaps even envied. Von Hoffman, who had rejected college as too dull and confining and had pursued his own intellectual interests—he had, for instance, learned French on his own—passed Alinsky's assignment on the West Side with flying colors. "I may have been the only person he did this with. He told me later that he did it out of craft, but I am sure he did it because he didn't have anything else for me to do."

While von Hoffman was out on the West Side, Alinsky was putting the finishing touches on his new relationship with Samuel Cardinal Stritch. After Alinsky's dinner meeting at the Blackstone Hotel with Monsignor O'Grady, Jack Egan, and von Hoffman, he met with Stritch at the cardinal's residence on August 19, 1954. They agreed to proceed with a feasibility study to determine whether a community organizing project with the Puerto Ricans in Woodlawn was doable. Stritch agreed to contribute $4,000 to the Industrial Areas Foundation; this was the first time it received financial support from the archdiocese (it was, in effect, money for von Hoffman's salary), and Alinsky pledged that the IAF would match the grant. That same day, the IAF executive committee approved the study and Stritch's financial support of it on a motion made by Bishop Sheil. It was the bishop's last official act with the IAF. Within a few months, Cardinal Stritch had presided over Sheil's resignation as head of the Catholic Youth Organization and Sheil had resigned from the IAF board and ended his friendship with Alinsky.

Soon Alinsky contacted the cardinal with a revised proposal. It made much more sense, he said, to expand the study of Puerto Ricans to other areas on the North Side where Puerto Ricans lived in greater numbers than in Woodlawn. Moreover, it would be a study not only of Puerto Ricans but also of the surrounding communities. That was, of course, the central point: that the problems affecting Puerto Ricans were part of a larger picture. If the Puerto Rican population in Chicago, as in New York, was growing so rapidly, it would strongly affect the surrounding neighborhoods and communities—their housing, schools, and, of course, Catholic parishes. The archdiocese had many interests in the outcome of a possible large-scale immigration of Puerto Ricans to Chicago, some essentially humanitarian, others of a more practical nature. Although the "Puerto Rican question" was not at this point its major concern, it went along with other population shifts that had begun to change the face of the city, notably an influx of blacks from the South. Stritch agreed to Alinsky's revised proposal. And soon Lester Hunt was given a job at Catholic Charities, where he began to set up a Latin American Program. Hunt, who thinks he was perhaps the first non-Catholic to work at Catholic Charities, later joined his friend von Hoffman on Alinsky's staff. In the meantime, having received a green light from the cardinal, Alinsky dispatched von Hoffman to the near North Side to do a survey.

Von Hoffman's survey was of the same near North Side community that had been the subject of an earlier, landmark study in sociology, *The Slum and the Gold Coast*. The book, a best-seller in Chicago when it was published in 1929, was written by Harvey Zorbaugh, a graduate student in the University of Chicago's Sociology Department several years before

Alinsky started there; Zorbaugh's methodology was based on the same kind of detailed work that Alinsky came to in his own graduate assignments. Now, in 1954–55, Alinsky was giving von Hoffman a similar assignment. Within the boundaries of the near North Side—from the fashionable shops and nightclubs north of the Loop and stretching from the luxurious high-rise apartment buildings overlooking Lake Michigan to the transient hotels and public-housing projects in the west—von Hoffman once again set out to discover virtually everything he could. He pored over federal census data. He combed through reports by local planning commissions, comparing their often contradictory projections of population shifts. He compiled lists of all the institutions in the area. He collected statistics from each school and church, from which he derived the exact number of Puerto Ricans that attended each institution. All this information went to Alinsky in weekly typed reports. If Alinsky was especially interested in, say, an analysis of existing housing stock, he would ask von Hoffman for an expanded, additional study.

But only part of von Hoffman's work had to do with the collection and analysis of this quantifiable material. Much of his time was spent on a canvass of the area, interviewing hundreds of people, ranging across the entire spectrum of community life and up and down both the formal and informal leadership ladders. There were precinct captains, transplanted hillbillies, the president of a local civic association, priests and ministers, bank executives, housing-project tenants, the owner of a rooming house, realtors, and the biggest bookie (who did business at the corner of Grand and State, under the Waiters Union headquarters). After almost every interview, von Hoffman would write up a report for Alinsky. With each report, he could see and feel a new piece of yarn being woven into the fabric that was this community—the modest hopes and avaricious ambitions; selflessness and prejudice; signs of community spirit and competing power centers. Von Hoffman absorbed all this and speculated about it, in anticipation of the day when they would be ready to start building a community organization.

After nearly a year, von Hoffman may have known more about the near North Side than anybody else in Chicago. He was Alinsky's eyes and ears. And by the end of 1955, Alinsky informed Cardinal Stritch that he was ready to build a community organization on the near North Side and asked the archdiocese to fund a three-year project for just under $150,000. Jack Egan recalls that Stritch was impressed with the work von Hoffman and Alinsky had done. But the cardinal was not yet ready to make such a commitment—not in that part of Chicago. It was not only a matter of money. There was also the sticky matter of politics. There would inevitably be suspicions in Chicago about the archdiocese's motives in "hiring"

Alinsky: was it doing so only in hopes of preserving the ethnic parishes on the near North Side from an expanding population of poor Puerto Rican families? In his recommendation to Stritch, Alinsky himself argued: "It should be emphasized that one of the issues involved in community organization [on the near North Side] is the development of certain population controls in terms of housing and occupancy standards and the enforcement of the latter. It is important to bear in mind that it would be a serious mistake to permit a community to become all Puerto Rican, just as it would be to permit it to become all Negro. This kind of segregated pattern is mutually detrimental to those who are being segregated as well as to the general population." Alinsky had a long track record as a staunch integrationist, which included his chairmanship of a citizens' group, the Chicago Public Housing Association, in 1950. One of the hottest political battles in Chicago at that time was over the site selections of public housing, which, for the most part, meant whether integrated public housing was going to be built in white neighborhoods. Alinsky and the CPHA favored it; the ward politicians and their white constituents did not. But in spite of Alinsky's own impeccable credentials as an integrationist, Stritch was bound to envision the dangers of archdiocesan sponsorship of Alinsky's recommendation. Tensions and conflicts between Catholics and non-Catholics in Chicago, as elsewhere in urban America, were real and often ugly. If given half a chance, many in Chicago would assume the worst about the Church's motives.

In the case of the near North Side, Alinsky envisioned a community organization that would promote the integration of Puerto Ricans into the life of the community, including its Catholic parishes. He thought that Stritch and others in the hierarchy were sympathetic to this enlightened and realistic strategy. Stritch, however, was not ready to fund an outside agency to handle what eager critics would portray as "a Catholic problem." Moreover, the Puerto Rican population on the near North Side, while growing, was still small, about 4,000. In other parts of Chicago, population shifts and neighborhood dislocations were already more advanced and more troublesome.

Nearly a year went by before the cardinal decided he wanted Saul Alinsky to take a look at some of the problems on Chicago's South Side. In the meantime, Alinsky devoted his energy to another project.

FOR A LONG TIME, Alinsky had wanted to make a big splash in New York City. He had many friends and acquaintances there, including his most steadfast financial supporters, Marshall and Ruth Field, Happy and Val Macy, and Adele Levy. He was eager to show off his talents in their backyard. A big, showy success in New York would not be bad for future fund-raising either. And, not least important, Alinsky's attraction to New York was also heightened by his Second City complex. True, he extolled the virtues of Chicago to his Eastern friends, especially his city's tough, he-man image and the corresponding myth of "if you can make it in Chicago, then you can make it anywhere." But Nick von Hoffman, who had grown up in New York, spotted the familiar, Broadway-inspired stars in Alinsky's eyes. When Alinsky spent an increasing amount of time angling for a project in New York, von Hoffman says, "I used to tell him, 'Listen, you're just another rube. I've seen you guys ever since I was in diapers come running in here with your tongue hanging out to your belt buckle.' " But like a moth to a flame, Alinsky was irresistibly attracted to the city's bright lights. As he maneuvered to get money and sponsorship in New York, not only did he overlook a series of political danger signals but he was blinded to them.

Alinsky had been daydreaming about a New York project since the mid-1940s, but it was not until the early 1950s that a glimmer of opportunity appeared on the horizon. It started casually, almost accidentally one night when Alinsky was visiting with Julius Edelstein in New York. Edelstein, administrative assistant to Senator Herbert Lehman, had known Alinsky only slightly prior to the Democratic National Convention in 1952. But during the convention in Chicago their friendship blossomed, thanks to their mutual friend Monsignor O'Grady. O'Grady had worked closely with Edelstein and Lehman in Washington on immigration legislation, and had often told Edelstein about Alinsky. "O'Grady thought I would want to meet him because he was Jewish," Edelstein says. Edelstein and Alinsky immediately became good friends, seeing a lot of each other both in New York and in Washington, where O'Grady frequently joined them for dinner.

Edelstein liked the idea of Alinsky's coming into New York to organize. Late one night in New York, he thought of a person who might be able to help him. Dr. Leona Baumgartner remembers the phone call she received from Edelstein as she and her husband, Nat, were getting ready to go to bed. "I want to bring a guy down to meet you," Edelstein said. Within minutes, Alinsky and Edelstein were at the door of the Baumgartners' converted coachhouse in Greenwich Village, and with Alinsky in great storytelling form, the two of them did not leave until 4 a.m. "We spent most of [that night] listening to Saul tell us about the Back of the Yards and how that got started, how [he had] played church groups [off against] each other," Leona remembers. "We were all fascinated by it."

Alinsky went out of his way to let her know that he approved "very much of the attitude I had to public service." Baumgartner, whose career after medical school had been in public health, had recently been made New York City's Deputy Health Commissioner. "I wanted to see that people [had the necessities like] bathrooms, running water, [and] I wanted to be very practical about what was going on. . . . We were not communists. You know what I mean by that—left wing—but we were pragmatists. Saul convinced me that he agreed entirely with me." As she discovered later when she saw Alinsky operate in other settings, he was masterful at leaving such an impression with many different kinds of people. "This is one of the charming things I used to watch him do at meetings. Saul would [make it a point] to agree with someone or, if he didn't agree, he would come around to something else."

Alinsky and the Baumgartners became fast friends. And when Leona left her city job to become executive director of the New York Foundation, she was in a position to help her new friend. Baumgartner was at first dismayed by the unprofessional, clubby way the New York Foundation dispensed its considerable largesse. "The board was largely Jewish. We met in Arthur Sulzberger's office. I had quite a time because the Foundation had been run in what I thought was an amoral way. Each board member came in for about two meetings a year with a little list of the favorite things he wanted to do. . . . No set of criteria. . . . For an hour and a half they'd give [each other] tips on the stock market." Baumgartner insisted on internal reforms—a published annual report, an agenda for meetings, and explicit criteria for making grants. She put everyone's pet social-welfare projects on a separate Christmas list, which, she says, "gave us time to talk about creative ideas. That's what gave us time to talk about Saul."

A large migration of poor, unschooled, and unskilled Puerto Ricans had poured into New York after the war to escape the devastating poverty of their island homeland. Their numbers—nearly 500,000 by the early 1950s and growing—placed great demands on New York's health and welfare agencies, and were also changing the character of several neighborhoods within the city. Adequate housing, already in short supply in New York before the Puerto Rican "invasion," was almost nonexistent for the newest arrivals. It was not uncommon for several large Puerto Rican families to live in shifts in the same modest-sized, roach-infested, run-down apartment. Even in New York, with its history of immigrant slums, the plight of many Puerto Ricans was especially grim.

Many New Yorkers—perhaps the majority—were hostile to the Puerto Ricans, who were viewed as dirty, lazy, Spanish-speaking parasites.

But another, more constructive view prevailed among some of New York's leaders—a view, based in some cases on enlightened self-interest, in others on simple humanitarianism, that something needed to be done to ease the Puerto Ricans' problems and, in turn, the city's neighborhoods and institutions. A major difficulty was the Puerto Ricans' almost total lack of integration into mainland American life: even in the densely populated Puerto Rican neighborhoods, the usual dynamic of immigrant groups was not in evidence. Puerto Ricans were not forming or joining religious, fraternal, or political groups whose leaders, in turn, might speak for them and for their housing, jobs, medical care, education, and other social needs.

Alinsky's theories and concepts seemed relevant to the situation in New York. Leona Baumgartner and Julius Edelstein thought so. Still, Alinsky's set of assumptions and values about urban life were very different from those promoted by powerful figures and forces in New York in the 1950s. This was the era of Robert Moses, the city's master builder and power broker, who by mid-decade had proven so adept at removing people and neighborhoods to make room for urban expressways that envious planners and engineers from other cities came to learn his wondrous methods. It was Moses who put New York City at the forefront of urban renewal, which, on a much smaller scale, had already dislocated thousands of poor people in Chicago. By 1957, the total expenditure of public monies on urban-renewal programs in New York was $267 million, compared with $133 million for all other cities combined. New York's social-welfare professionals, similar in outlook and style to their Chicago counterparts with whom Alinsky locked horns, were another significant political force—indeed, a "welfare industry" was growing so rapidly that by the close of the 1950s a four-hundred-page book was needed to list all of the public and private agencies servicing the needy. Nonetheless, at the New York Foundation, where Senator Lehman served on the board of directors, Baumgartner and Edelstein went to bat on Alinsky's behalf. Senator Lehman sent a letter to David Heyman, the Foundation's president, suggesting that Alinsky's work in Chicago, about which he heard good things, might now be put to good use in New York with Foundation assistance. Leona Baumgartner obtained positive appraisals of Alinsky's work from several people in Chicago, and then wrote to the board:

> In view of the tremendous strides that Puerto Rico itself made in its "Operation Bootstrap" in getting the lower economic groups to help themselves in addition to the tremendous strides made by the government and business there to have Puerto Rico help itself, it has frequently been suggested that a similar self-help movement might be the

answer here. In view of all this, I have given some study to various self-help movements in this country. The Back of the Yards movement in Chicago has been apparently a notable success. I was therefore delighted when Dr. [sic] Alinsky got to New York.

The term "self-help" was one Alinsky never used—he found it too tame and apolitical. And her memo also put a favorable spin on Alinsky's biography: "Alinsky himself is a person trained in archeology who found himself out of work during the depression and went in to do a series of studies in the field of criminology. He finally got tired apparently of study and seeing little happen, despite the fact that he was a high public official in the State of Illinois and was handsomely financed by the Rockefeller Foundation. He gave it all up . . . to try to help people help themselves." The embellishments—Alinsky of course was never out of work in the Depression, he was never a high public official in Illinois, and it was Clifford Shaw, not Alinsky, who had been funded by the Rockefeller Foundation—are not very significant. Nonetheless, it is another instance of Alinsky's desire to create or suggest a persona a little bigger, a little more dramatic, a little more successful than was actually the case. And, of course, it is fascinating to see how often people were willing and inclined to embellish his embellishments.

By December 1953, Baumgartner and Edelstein's collaboration yielded an $8,000 grant from the New York Foundation to Alinsky for a study to determine whether his methods could be implemented in New York, but the Foundation was not yet ready to underwrite a big, costly community organizing campaign directed by an unfamiliar figure from Chicago. Alinsky told them he would spend about a month (September 1954) in Puerto Rico, learning about the culture and the prospects of continued emigration to New York, followed by two months in New York, with a report and recommendations to follow.

It was another six months after his tour of Puerto Rico and inspection of New York before Alinsky finally submitted his report. In the meantime, he lost an important ally when Leona Baumgartner resigned from the New York Foundation to become New York's Health Commissioner, but gained a new friend. Alinsky's new contact at the Foundation was a consultant, Dean Paul McGhee of New York University. Mrs. Baumgartner introduced Alinsky to the McGhees one evening in New York, and soon they were on a Paul-and-Saul basis. But when Alinsky submitted his report and recommendations, he was shocked to receive a highly critical reaction from his new friend. "You completely screwed my weekend," he wrote to McGhee. "I know from trying to phone you over the weekend, including today, that while I have been sweating out about a fourteen-page memorandum (which you should be receiving in the next mail delivery) all this time you were sunning yourself around Martha's Vineyard." It was not only a matter of substantive criticisms; Alinsky was offended by McGhee's formality and what he saw as a breach of friendship. "Why in the hell did you wait three weeks . . . ? Are you a slow reader? Was there a telephone strike on? . . . Did the report have a wax seal of sacred finality on it? Don't you think that our relationship is such that you can discuss things with me?" In truth, McGhee had been embarrassed for Alinsky after reading the report, which, he felt, was filled with generalities and showed little evidence that Alinsky had spent time in Puerto Rico or New York working on the issues. "We can never sell this," he finally told Alinsky. And he did his best, because he genuinely liked Alinsky, to break the news in a way that would make Alinsky understand what had gone wrong:

> You assume that everyone knows what you and the IAF have done in Chicago, the Imperial Valley and parts West and South, that they probably have read your *Reveille for Radicals,* know your philosophy (and Tocqueville's) and your methods, and are prepared to come to a meeting at which I will say, "Saul and the IAF have agreed to come and work in two neighborhoods for three years, and all they need is three million dollars and so how will we split the tab?" Now the fact is that I'd be willing to gamble on your fresh (and I mean FRESH) approach and be happy to have you come in here and go to work. But about all I could contribute personally would be about $7.50 and you need more than that. . . . I don't know what is going to be the end of all of this but somehow you have got to give us a package we can try to sell.

Alinsky wrote a long, rambling defense, arguing that his methodology did not lend itself to a detailed plan with prepackaged programs and flow charts specifying when goals would be met. "I know this sounds very strange to you, but the fact remains that this kind of operation does not proceed on an orderly blueprint chart." The challenge facing an organizer, he stressed, was to "exploit (not in the evil connotation of the word) every opportunity for citizen participation which presents itself (and if they don't, you make them) for the purpose of community organization." The timing and nature of such "opportunities" were rarely if ever predictable, and neither to a large extent were the staff needs of an organization until issues emerged, Alinsky told McGhee. "Suppose I tell you right now that I can't even guarantee that the [staff] breakdowns and functions would remain as they are listed in the proposed budget. I am not saying that we would exceed the budget, but I am saying that I might very well find out within two months of operations that salaries allotted for three or four full-time staff members may be better expended on eight or ten part-time staff people who would be residents in the community. . . . Does that surprise you?"

Part of what Alinsky loved about being an organizer was that it meant applying one's imagination, intuition, experience, and judgment to a kaleidoscope of events, personalities, and motives. His attitude was reflected in Bix Beiderbecke's line: "One of the things I like about jazz, kid, is I don't know what's going to happen next." Still, he was also interested in minimizing surprises—that was part of the purpose of discovering early who were likely allies and enemies or which issues might be embraced or avoided or, finally, whether a community was ripe for a strong organization based on democratic values and directed by local leaders. There is no question that Alinsky's survey in New York was far short of the meticulous work that von Hoffman was doing for him on the near North Side of Chicago. Two months was far too little time for such a study or survey, he acknowledged. The more important issue, however, which he tried to disregard by glorifying the inherent unpredictability and spontaneity of the organizing process, was whether a more rigorous, systematic survey was needed. Alinsky was not interested in dealing with that issue. Out of habit, laziness, shortsightedness, and hubris, Alinsky assumed that if he got the money now, he would figure it all out later.

Alinsky assured McGhee that he had "no pride of authorship" in the report and would gladly incorporate whatever suggestions McGhee thought necessary to sell the project. By the fall of 1955, with the help of McGhee, Alinsky submitted a revised, expanded version. In simple yet eloquent terms, he sketched out the IAF philosophy and commitment.

Alinsky proposed that either of two New York neighborhoods be the site of a community organizing project—in the South Bronx or in Chelsea, on Manhattan's Lower West Side. His three-year budget for Chelsea was $289,927; for the South Bronx, a much larger area, $547,767.

Alinsky told at least one friend that he purposely submitted a large budget in hopes that he would be turned down, since a big New York project would consume too much of his time. That was nonsense, merely another defensive gesture. Even before he had submitted the revised proposal, he had probably picked up enough gossip and vibrations to know it was in trouble. The opposition was especially strong among parts of the professional social-work and settlement-house leadership in New York. It was not only a matter of their resenting an outsider from Chicago going after a big chunk of New York foundation money, although that was certainly part of it. It was also Alinsky himself—his arrogance and his reputation, dating to his days with Clifford Shaw, for being antagonistic toward social work.

One of Alinsky's most outspoken opponents was Helen Harris, the influential executive director of United Neighborhood Houses of New York. Along with nearly twenty other social-work and civic leaders— including Trude Lash, Madeline Low, Stanley Isaacs, Don Kingsley, Sara McCaulley—she met with Paul McGhee in December 1955 to discuss Alinsky's proposal. With few exceptions, the comments were negative. On the other hand, Alinsky still had the support of Senator Lehman via Edelstein, and he had enlisted Monsignor O'Grady's help, suggesting, for example, that O'Grady should soften up James McCarthy of the New York City Youth Board, who, "as you may remember my telling you, is part of the Helen Harris bloc which is so uncompromisingly opposed to the Industrial Areas Foundation coming into New York." There was also help from Leona Baumgartner, who now, as the city's Health Commissioner, was even fiercer in support of Alinsky. "[S]omething must be done to help stem the increasing trend to dump responsibility on government and private philanthropy to do some of the things that people should be doing for themselves," she told Paul McGhee. "As I see it, even from the narrow point of view of improving health conditions in the city, the residents of local areas must be awakened to carrying some responsibility for them-selves. Any approach that gives hope of stimulating such actions should be vigorously tried out." And Arthur Sulzberger had also weighed in with a measure of interest and support. He had read Alinsky's proposal and was impressed with his fundamental positions. He had also asked one of his associates at *The New York Times,* William Ogden, who followed city affairs, for his appraisal. Ogden was favorably impressed, too. He told Sulzberger that while he had heard Alinsky could be difficult, he had to be credited with considerable accomplishments, and it would be worth a try to bring him to New York. He recommended the smaller area of Chelsea, where there was already an excellent organization to work with, the Hudson Guild, one of the most respected settlement houses in New York, run by an able man named Dan Carpenter. Sulzberger endorsed Ogden's suggestions.

In fact, Carpenter had been shopping around for foundation support for one of his programs, and he and Alinsky had already met. As early as March 1955, Alinsky had begun searching for new allies and different wedges into New York, and he apparently suggested to Carpenter that he, Carpenter, should approach the New York Foundation and the Schwarzhaupt Foundation for support for small citizenship projects that might be combined with Alinsky's own proposal. In addition, at about the same time, Alinsky wrote a letter on Carpenter's behalf to Alinsky's friend Dutch Smith, who served on the Field Foundation's board. "The Hudson Guild is now the recipient of a grant from the Field Foundation," he wrote, "and is coming up for renewal of this grant. . . . Dan Carpenter is one of the most level-headed, conscientious, capable persons that I have met in the field. His ideas are similar to ours and in all my contacts with him he has shown an open mind and an intense desire to extend himself in every possible way that would be beneficial to the community in which he works." Alinsky made certain that Carpenter received a blind carbon copy of this effusive praise.

Thus had Alinsky positioned himself for the compromise decision that was finally made in the spring of 1956. The New York Foundation let it be known that they would contribute a sizable grant to the Hudson Guild provided that Alinsky would act as a consultant and that the community organizing project in Chelsea would employ Alinsky's philosophy and methods. But Alinsky was not pleased. "The proposal you outline," he told Carpenter, "is a completely different animal, philosophically, structurally and in terms of objectives, from the project [I] recommended." He was especially disturbed by Carpenter's emphasis on avoiding controversy; by the fact that the Hudson Guild controlled the funds, which implied a lack of trust in Chelsea's people; by having only a half-time director, a job that Carpenter intended to fill while also directing the Hudson Guild; and by what he thought was an unrealistic appraisal of the power relationships and realities in Chelsea. Still, he was conciliatory, and so was Carpenter. When the New York Foundation finally agreed to provide a grant of $120,000 for three years, Alinsky was able to deliver the additional needed funds, nearly $60,000, from his friends at the Schwarzhaupt Foundation. A small portion of the grants went to the IAF for Alinsky's services—$100 a day for forty-five days per year of consulting in New York. (The three-year commitment was later amended to two years, with the third year of funding contingent on progress made.)

Privately, Alinsky was not completely sanguine about the most important part of the compromise deal—his own role as consultant. He talked with some of his IAF board members about the "positives and negatives," a typical mode of analysis for Alinsky. He ruminated that this was the first time that he and the IAF would have responsibility without control. Yet he also saw that it was perhaps the most practical way to spread the philosophy and methods of the IAF. A lack of money and his own wavering interest in recruiting a larger, permanent staff had put limitations on new projects. If Chelsea worked out, then maybe the same format could "at least partially carry out the ideas of the IAF [elsewhere]," Alinsky theorized. "Certainly a partial projection of some of the ideas and concepts of the Industrial Areas Foundation into community organization is better than none at all."

Not all of the elements in the Chelsea situation could be broken neatly into positives and negatives. Alinsky was especially conflicted about the Hudson Guild and Dan Carpenter. When he met with the IAF board for its annual meeting in New York, he speculated about the possible difficulties of working closely with

> any organization which is oriented philosophically as well as pragmatically by the standards of professional social work . . . , of working [for] rather than with people. We know from experience that we can go into a community and be effective where the power center lies either in a social group, a religious group, an economic interest group, or most lay non-professional organizations—but we do not know, and our experience to this date has not been particularly encouraging on this point, whether we can do this with a social work agency.

Alinsky thought there was a reasonable chance of educating Carpenter—and if he could do that, then he might be able to sway a portion of the world of social work beyond Chelsea to his way of thinking, too. "If Saul got a reputation of reliability," Lester Hunt says, "then he could begin to make speeches to social-work groups and they'd say, 'Ah, that's what we should be doing, we shouldn't be going out with Band-Aids,' or whatever it was that we called them in those days. He was anxious to influence social work." It was not merely an academic interest either. Social workers had resources—agencies, staff, credibility, and budgets—that Alinsky could use. So he had a self-inflicted incentive to believe—or at least to hope—that "in the case of the Hudson Guild, the kind of leadership which we have encountered impresses us at this point as being more emancipated from the professional philosophy and more sympathetic to [our] basic concept than most social workers. . . . Carpenter has been reassuring on this issue."

Alinsky, however, was not reassured by what happened next. In the summer of 1956, without mentioning a word to Alinsky, Carpenter hired an assistant director—the top staff job after his own—who would in effect be the organizer of the new project. Alinsky thought there had been an understanding that he would be intimately involved in selecting and training staff (at one point, he had even argued for a veto power over staff hiring). So, it was bad enough when Alinsky heard that Carpenter had hired somebody, but Alinsky nearly went through the roof when he heard that Carpenter had hired a woman.

Alinsky's attitude toward women (which changed somewhat by the end of his life) was typical of the male world of Chicago politics and especially of the CIO subculture. "The female of our species was inevitably referred to [by Saul] as broads," Nick von Hoffman says with only some exaggeration. "They were good to lay but not to hire." Alinsky fashioned a polite public rationale for his bias, but it was not entirely persuasive. "We have a general policy against hiring any women on our staff because of the working conditions," he explained to a friend. "There [are] many occasions when following a community or organizational meeting . . . I sit down with my staff people in hotel rooms, or park alongside a road, and discuss the events of that evening and the plans for the next week or so—and this would be very difficult to do with a woman." Since Alinsky relished thumbing his nose at decorum and propriety, his sudden obeisance to them was not convincing. It was closer to the truth to say that Alinsky had a very compartmentalized view of the roles of men and women. Organizing, power, politics, and toughness were all related to manhood—and vice versa. And women organizers could be a threat to manhood. If a man in the community were to make a pass at a woman organizer and she turned him down, Alinsky hypothesized earnestly, he would be inclined to interpret her rebuff as an attack on his manhood and would, therefore, reject her as an organizer. In Chelsea, was a woman organizer really going to be effective and credible with Catholic priests or longshoremen on the waterfront? These were not unrealistic concerns in the 1950s, but his sweeping generalizations about women blinded him to the possibility that talented women could be good organizers.

With each bit of information Alinsky learned about Marjorie Buckholz, the woman whom Carpenter had hired, the angrier he became. She was also a social worker! And she was not only a social worker but—"Nick, you're not going to believe this"—she worked for the goddamn Camp Fire Girls in Cleveland! "When Saul walked down the street and felt a drop of rain," von Hoffman says of one of Alinsky's many idiosyncrasies, "he was convinced it was God pissing on him." He must have felt a similar sensation when he heard about the hiring of Marjorie Buckholz.

Since it was both too late and too early to back out of the Chelsea project, Alinsky sought the advice of a trusted friend, Gordon Clapp, who had recently joined the IAF board. Clapp, who had grown up in a small northern Wisconsin town, was an unassuming, quietly brilliant man who had been David Lilienthal's number two man at the Tennessee Valley

Authority in the 1940s and had succeeded Lilienthal there. He was now working with Lilienthal again on international economic development projects. Clapp had done graduate work at the University of Chicago in the early 1930s, and Alinsky may have met him there or at the TVA in the late 1940s, when he took several priests from the Back of the Yards on a tour of the TVA's citizen-participation programs. Gordon Clapp's bland, even seemingly dull manner belied a deep-seated, passionate commitment to democratic values and ideals, many of which he identified in Saul Alinsky's principles and philosophy. There was no need for Alinsky to contrive stories to impress Clapp or to perform great intellectual exercises. He was not only Alinsky's friend but a perfect sounding board and counsel.

Clapp tried to help Alinsky sort through the politics and psychology of Alinsky's relationship with Dan Carpenter and the Hudson Guild. They concluded that a key to success was to convince Carpenter that Alinsky was not a rival but a collaborator, even a promoter of Dan Carpenter's interests and career. A few days later, Alinsky wrote to Leonard Rieser in Chicago:

> I feel much more optimistic now because for the first time I can see a course of action. There are two major points to be clarified. . . . One is that the word "consultant" is erroneous for the kind of relationship which I am supposed to be having with the project. It becomes a stumbling block. . . . In actual fact, my function and relationship here is more in the capacity of what the Russians would describe as a "commissar" (perish the word and destroy this letter). Gordon feels that if the title were changed to "advisor" that might clear up some of Mr. Carpenter's difficulties in this area. Secondly, Mr. Carpenter has to understand in a statement given not only in Technicolor but wired for sound that the exclusive objective of the Industrial Areas Foundation is to see whether we can work out this arrangement of teaching others to do it with all of the credit going to those who are doing it.

While Carpenter had pulled a fast one on Alinsky by hiring Marjorie Buckholz, he had not been completely candid with her either, for he told her nothing of Alinsky's involvement until she herself brought it up. "A friend wrote to me and said that Alinsky was involved in this project, and I probably should know about him," Buckholz says. "So I said to Carpenter, 'Well, what's Alinsky's involvement?' I knew of Alinsky's hostility towards social work. [Years before] I had read [Reveille for Radicals] and I admired it. [Then] I heard him as a speaker and I didn't admire it." "He got up and said—here's a thousand social workers at a meeting, and at the same time the Packinghouse Workers Union is meeting in Chicago—and he said: 'You could bomb this social workers' meeting and nobody would know the difference, but if it were the packinghouse workers, that would make a big difference.' " Carpenter downplayed Alinsky's involvement in the Chelsea project almost to the point of nonexistence. "I received the proposal for the grant from Carpenter, which I read," Buckholz says. "I later learned when I got [to New York] that the front page had been removed, which said [that the program was supposed] to test Alinsky's method of organizing in New York. . . . When I asked about Alinsky's role, they said, well, they had to write him in in order to get the grant, and he was to come into New York five days a month, and we would listen to what he had to say but that's all we had to do about it."

Because New York was also enticing to her and because she was ready to leave Cleveland, Buckholz, who was in her thirties, accepted Carpenter's offer without inspecting Chelsea—a decision she later regretted—and without, of course, having met Alinsky. "If I had realized what role he was going to have in the thing, I would have insisted on meeting with him," she says. "If I had met with him, I'm sure I never would have taken the job because, I know, his tactics would have been to be as mean as hell, which he was good at." Alinsky often subjected prospective organizers to a vigorous verbal hazing, as he had done to von Hoffman. As it was, Buckholz was on the receiving end of Alinsky's sarcasm—and hostility—as soon as she started her new job. When he first met with her and Carpenter in New York, she says, he treated her virtually as a nonperson. "Oh, well, she can take the PTA's, the women's part," was a typical gibe.

Despite an unpromising beginning, a better relationship between Buckholz and Alinsky began to develop when they found themselves on the same side of an internal debate. After the foundation money had been committed and the project was ready to start, an administrative committee was created. Four of the nine members were on the Hudson Guild board; only four actually lived in Chelsea. Buckholz recalls that Carpenter thought there should be a so-called Chelsea Citizens Participation Council, "which would be the community people, and that their action program [would have] to be approved by the administrative committee." But Buckholz—sensing that she was surprising everybody—took a strong position that a community could not be organized on that basis. Alinsky, of course, was on the same side of the fence. Buckholz remembers him driving his point home by saying, "If the people in Chelsea want to spend the money tying balloons on telephone poles, that's up to them."

The Christmas season slowed the hiring of additional staff, and it was well into 1957 before the organizing process began to come alive. About 60,000 people then lived in Chelsea—roughly, the part of New York that stretches from Sixth Avenue to the Hudson River and from Fourteenth to Thirty-fourth streets. The population was diverse, ranging from very poor to upper-middle-class, the poorest being the Puerto Ricans in the southern part of the area. Irish Catholics had predominated in Chelsea, but many of them had been moving to the suburbs in recent years, and they were being replaced by Jews, some blacks, Greeks, and a variety of others. Buckholz and three junior organizers divided Chelsea into three sections; within each, they met with leaders of virtually every organization— churches and groups within churches; social agencies; unions; nationality, fraternal, and political clubs; business associations, block clubs, and PTAs. What are the problems? they would ask, and the answers gave them an agenda for a community organization: a housing shortage, pockets of juvenile delinquency, a lack of parking facilities on the waterfront. In each of the three sections, the organizers then brought the various leaders together. Steering committees from each planned a Chelsea-wide meeting for June, which was attended by representatives from more than fifty organizations. With guidance from Buckholz, who reported regularly to Alinsky, the leaders voted to draft both a program and bylaws for a community council to be officially created at a convention in the fall.

Throughout the summer, Buckholz and the other organizers were on the prowl for effective leaders, especially one to be the first elected president of the new community council. It did not take a genius to figure out that this person should be a Catholic—not only because half or more of Chelsea was Catholic but also because the Hudson Guild and its leadership, which was non-Catholic and heavy on Ethical Culturalists (of whom Dan Carpenter was one), was viewed with suspicion and even hostility by many of the local Catholics. "They came into a very Catholic community to do good, and there was conflict from that day forth," was Buckholz's belated discovery of the history of the Hudson Guild in Chelsea. The contemporary conflicts manifested themselves in different ways. Just before she arrived on the scene, Buckholz heard, the Guild had been passing out birth-control literature, and the hostility and rivalry reached into other, diverse areas. If the Guild organized a Boy Scout troop, then a Catholic parish would organize its own Boy Scout troop. As far as Buckholz was concerned, she had not yet found the right man—the right Catholic—with the talent, experience, and personality for building new bridges of understanding in Chelsea. "There was a meat cutter who was active," Buckholz recalls, "who wasn't a leader, really, but he was the best we had. And I suggested him. Well, Carpenter said no, he would rather have Dunn than one of Dunn's puppets."

Father Robert Dunn was an assistant pastor at St. Columba's. A native New Yorker, he had come to the parish in 1944, and he had learned not to trust the Hudson Guild crowd. So when Dunn first heard about a new community project emanating out of the Guild, he was suspicious. He did not want "to get into anything that was worthless," nor did he want "to compromise my own position as a Catholic priest." But somebody at Catholic Charities, where Alinsky had a few contacts, suggested that he might want to take a look, and then Dunn met Alinsky. The two of them liked each other, and Alinsky invited Dunn to Chicago to see the Back of the Yards Neighborhood Council. In Chicago, Alinsky made certain that Dunn was given royal treatment, including a meeting with Cardinal Stritch and dinner with Monsignor Ed Burke and Jack Egan, a duet who sang the praises of Alinsky and the accomplishments of the BYNC. Alinsky also sent him on a grand tour of the Back of the Yards, where he was impressed by everything he saw and heard—by the modest but well-kept houses ("everything was so clean," he says); by the credit union that the BYNC had started; by the unmistakable community spirit. Dunn, who had been roosting for thirteen years on his modest perch at St. Columba's, left Chicago impressed by Alinsky's lofty Catholic connections and excited by what he had seen in the Back of the Yards.

Bob Dunn was elected the first president of the Chelsea Community Council (CCC) in November 1957. By his own admission, he was a rookie when it came to such basic organizational skills as running a meeting, soothing interpersonal conflicts, and building coalitions among diverse individuals and subgroups. When Alinsky came to New York for his monthly visits, he spent a lot of time coaching and teaching Dunn, sometimes over dinner at Cavanaugh's on Twenty-third Street, often at the rectory at St. Columba's until the early-morning hours. He would force Dunn to reexamine a troublesome situation—what went wrong, why, how he could have handled it better. An actual crisis or problem presented the best possibilities for learning, Alinsky believed. Principles, concepts, and theories were distant abstractions unless they could be related to one's real and immediate problems and solutions. Buckholz also worked with Dunn, challenging him to consider new responses to problems and to sharpen his understanding of how he could use his position as both a priest at St. Columba's and the president of the Council to advantage. For instance, it had never occurred to Dunn, Buckholz recalls, that he could use his relationship with a state senator, a member of his parish, to get an appointment with the mayor or to gain access elsewhere. Slowly, gradually, Bob Dunn began to gain both confidence and leadership skills.

There were a goodly number of other examples of people in Chelsea gaining new citizenship and leadership skills through the CCC. For some, there were small but important triumphs in being able to speak effectively at a big public meeting. For others, there was a new, more sophisticated understanding of the art of politics. The organizers made certain that the Catholic groups who backed Dunn for president also understood that they had to back non-Catholics for the other offices so that Dunn might have a cooperative, broad base of support. Buckholz helped leaders of some of the smaller groups in the CCC, who feared being overshadowed, to understand that from time to time it might be useful for them to form a bloc to improve their bargaining position.

Alinsky was especially aware of the link between participation and influence, and thought that the structure and bylaws of a democratic community organization had to express that link. Early on in the Chelsea project, he spelled out his thinking for Carpenter, who he thought placed too much importance on winning the endorsement of titular heads of Chelsea's mainstream organizations:

> We must never lose sight of the actual lodestar of this entire program, to wit, to involve as many of the citizens of the Chelsea community as possible in citizen participation activities. Through experience, we have learned that if there is a policy adopted of equal representation from all organizations regardless of their size, sooner or later large organizations resent it (and do so legitimately). Their position is just, and the issue has been met logically . . . with a controlled proportionate representation in the [annual] Community Congress and equal representation on the board of directors.

Programmatically, the CCC eventually achieved several victories. After it pressured the Board of Estimate to overrule the City Planning Commission, the city agreed to build 1,300 low- and middle-income housing units in Chelsea. There was also a fairly successful rent strike organized by the CCC to force landlords to maintain services. The CCC could claim credit for cajoling the city to set up three health-care stations in Chelsea one day each month. But these modest victories were few, dwarfed in both importance and number by the problems that would not go away.

One such problem involved the goal of financial self-sufficiency for the CCC. The idea that a successful community organization would discover ways to support itself within three years was a nice one: skillful organizers, committed to democratic values, would arouse ordinary citizens, help them create their own independent organization to improve community life, and then fade into the sunset; it all hung together—the temporary role of the organizer, faith in the competency of ordinary people. But in practice it was a goal that his other community organizations had found difficult to achieve, except in the Back of the Yards.

Alinsky, an optimist who was selling a concept that he believed in, chose to emphasize what had succeeded in the Back of the Yards, not what had failed elsewhere. Bob Dunn had witnessed the BYNC's fund-raising success when Alinsky brought him to Chicago in the summer of 1957—the BYNC's annual Free Fair, which was by now a Chicago institution. It had grown to enormous size from the first Jungle Jamboree that Alinsky and Meegan put on in the early 1940s. Every night for most of July, thousands of people from all over Chicago streamed to Forty-seventh and Damen streets for the carnival rides, games of chance, and the nightly raffles. Not only turkeys and televisions were raffled; there were luxury vacation trips and automobiles, too. The raffle was a big deal and so was the size of the profits the BYNC reaped. The Free Fair, like other highlights of Dunn's Chicago tour, had impressed him. So, a year after the CCC began, he was eager to try out Alinsky's suggestion for a similar fund-raiser in Chelsea.

As the CCC's version of the Free Fair drew near, however, disaster loomed ominously. Little was going according to plan with the raffle and bazaar. The raffle, which was supposed to provide the bedrock of success, looked instead like a big loser. Raffle tickets were not getting sold. Alinsky was especially angry at one of the leaders of the Longshoremen's Union whom he had tapped to organize the raffle and sell tickets. The man did little work and he sold not one of the hundreds of tickets he had promised to sell. Removing his consultant's hat, Alinsky jumped into the act, bailing furiously to keep the fund-raiser from sinking into the red. His most tangible contribution was to get the BYNC in Chicago to buy a thousand dollars' worth of raffle tickets. Even with such charity, a week before the fund-raiser Alinsky calculated that the deficit, attributable mainly to the costs of the prizes for the raffle, might run as high as $6,000 or $7,000. That potential loss would be cut significantly, Alinsky wishfully told a friend, if the BYNC won a major prize—either the Cadillac or the trip for two to Europe—which, of course, it would return to the CCC. As it turned out, although the BYNC did not win a major prize, neither was the fund-raiser a losing embarrassment. In fact, a small profit was turned, thanks in part to money from the bazaar and from profits from a roulette wheel—which the Dan Carpenter crowd found appalling—set up in the basement of one of the Catholic churches. Nonetheless, the modest profits—ranging from $1,300 the first year to a high of about $12,000—were far short of what was needed for financial independence.

Success in organizing Puerto Ricans in Chelsea was not much better than with fund-raising. Indeed, one of the oddities of the CCC was that

Puerto Ricans in Chelsea did not become its central focus. Twenty-five years later, Dunn has gone so far as to say that "the Chelsea Community Council was not formed for the sake of the Puerto Ricans by any means. It was for the people of the whole community, who were not doing anything to work out their destiny." Still, approximately 20,000 Puerto Ricans lived in Chelsea, nearly a third of its population. Marjorie Buckholz soon learned, however, that not many other Chelseans wanted the Puerto Ricans around. Although the Guild had a program that attracted a few Puerto Ricans, especially children, Buckholz sensed that Dan Carpenter and other middle-class residents who lived in Chelsea's attractive brownstones wished that the lower-class Puerto Ricans would somehow disappear. This attitude existed all over Chelsea. Buckholz remembers an incident at St. Columba's that involved Dunn's boss, Father Kane. Kane, who was not in good health, had let his assistant priests carry out the parish's daily activities. Apparently, he had not realized that CCC organizers had been bringing Puerto Ricans to St. Columba's for meetings. "Well, [we] had a group [of Puerto Ricans] at St. Columba's, and one night good old Kane was feeling good enough to come around, and he saw them, and he went over and chased them out. And he said he didn't want those little men in his church."

Kane's attitude was not unusual. But in the higher reaches of the Archdiocese of New York a few people had responded differently to the Puerto Rican situation. One was the chancellor, Bishop John Maguire, who persuaded Cardinal Spellman that the Church should help Puerto Ricans for practical reasons; otherwise they would remain a drain on Church resources and would disrupt financially stable Catholic parishes. Others apparently got Spellman's attention by suggesting that if the Roman Catholic Church did not get the Puerto Ricans, the communists would. Such arguments helped to provide an opening for another man who eventually won Spellman's support on behalf of Puerto Ricans, Ivan Illich, an idiosyncratic young priest who had already launched a variety of community projects to help Puerto Ricans. Variously regarded as brilliant and something of a screwball, Illich had studied in Rome and was close to Jacques Maritain. When Illich came to the United States in the early 1950s, Maritain told him there were three people whom he must see: Dorothy Day, the radical Catholic activist; Gregory Zilboorg, a Catholic convert and prominent New York psychiatrist, who had counseled Marshall Field III; and Saul Alinsky. Illich met Alinsky in New York and was impressed and influenced by his theories of community organization.

When the Chelsea project began, Alinsky paid a courtesy call on Cardinal Spellman, the man whom he and Agnes Meyer loved to hate. He recognized that the Puerto Rican situation gave him an opportunity to establish a beachhead in the Archdiocese of New York. On the one hand, the Church had to find ways to recruit Puerto Ricans, nominal Catholics who did not readily gravitate to parish membership. On the other hand, at the parish level Father Kane's attitude at St. Columba's was fairly typical. Alinsky's creative approach was to fashion a strategy that fused the Church's seemingly mutually exclusive interests. In Chelsea, for example, that meant bringing Puerto Ricans into parish life and thereby into the CCC; then, the CCC, with Puerto Ricans actively involved, would demand that the city both enforce building-code violations to stop overcrowding and build new low-cost housing; the housing initiatives would relieve the pressure on established parish neighborhoods, thereby stemming neighborhood deterioration and the flight of Irish parishioners to the suburbs. In theory, almost everybody was a winner, perhaps getting three-quarters of a loaf if not a whole one. It was an ambitious scheme, to say the least, similar to the plan Alinsky had sketched for Cardinal Stritch in Chicago, where the Puerto Rican population, however, was much, much smaller.

Unfortunately, the Puerto Rican aspect of the Chelsea project was in trouble from the beginning. It was not only a matter of overcoming hostility or indifference to Puerto Ricans, although that was a basic problem. There was also a problem of finding the right organizer. During the first year, a talented young man who had been recruited to the CCC organizing staff because of his experience in working effectively with Puerto Ricans, died when a plane on which he was a passenger crashed into Jamaica Bay. At another point, Buckholz hired a young woman who, she says, "was probably sort of upper-class Puerto Rican. . . . She wasn't experienced, I'll agree to that, [but] she looked like the best I could find at the time. Saul came in and threw a fit."

On several occasions early in the project, Alinsky sent Lester Hunt into Chelsea to help out, the first time for three weeks beginning on Washington's Birthday in 1957. (Hunt and von Hoffman's work with Puerto Ricans in Chicago was known to Ivan Illich, and he organized the first San Juan Day in New York because, Hunt remembers, "he thought that was a great idea.") Trying to figure out how to get a handle on how things could be done, Hunt soon found that all the handles were short and slippery. He had a few leads, names and telephone numbers from Puerto Rican friends in Chicago. He also checked the local unions, especially the International Ladies Garment Workers Union, which had some Puerto Rican members. "But the control of the ILGWU was not in the hands of any Puerto Ricans and there wasn't any way to get them represented through that." The city-wide Puerto Rican organizations were too political and, in any event, few Puerto Ricans in Chelsea were involved in them. The churches were not much more fertile hunting grounds. "There was a Pentecostal church with quite a few members from Chelsea, and I had contact with them. [And] I used Joe Fitzpatrick a great deal, a sociologist at Fordham who knew more about New York Puerto Ricans than anybody in the world. [But] what I came up with just wasn't much to work with."

Since the organizers could find no existing Puerto Rican organizations to bring into the CCC, Hunt suggested that new ones be created. Mike Coffey, whom Buckholz and Hunt had hired, began to organize the Knights of Santiago, a kind of men's support group similar to others that Hunt and von Hoffman had organized in Woodlawn in Chicago a few years before. It operated out of St. Columba's, where, from the outset, Father Kane was a stumbling block. Hunt reported to Alinsky:

> [Mike Coffey] will have to do some education of Father Kane. . . . These priests are used to having their best Catholics in their [own church] organizations and even when they get watered down to some of the "not so good Catholics," as a Holy Name Society sometimes does, they are still used to having their members show up to Mass every Sunday and make use of some of the other sacraments besides baptism on occasions. Of course, this is not true of Puerto Ricans. If 5 to 10 percent of Mike's men go to Mass at all he will be lucky, and Father Kane will not easily, at first, understand this is a Catholic organization. . . . Furthermore, these priests are not used to having their parish organizations spend much time on social and civic activities.

Even with Father Dunn, who was sympathetic, Alinsky and Lester Hunt were not subtle in appealing to his own pastoral interests.

> The advantage to the church in all of this is, of course [Hunt told him], that as soon as some Knights begin to go to church . . . the others will shortly follow along, as will their families and many of their friends. . . . Once you've got them inside willingly, you can work on them as far as religion is concerned. The equally important advantage will be that the Knights will soon learn that they are incapable of solving a lot of their problems by themselves because they don't have the power to do it, but allied with the Catholic Church as a Catholic organization they can get a lot done. Furthermore, your interest in them and in the things which they feel are important will create a bond of loyalty to the Church which is hard to do by just teaching catechism or reminding them of their religious duties.

With Coffey's help, the Knights of Santiago gained members by helping families in their negotiations with the city over enforcement of housing-code violations, by helping others gain eligibility for public housing or social security benefits. But the going was slow and the overall impact modest.

Under the best of circumstances, organizing Puerto Ricans in Chelsea would have been very difficult. There appears to have been an implicit decision that a more determined effort would have to wait until more progress was made elsewhere in Chelsea. But meanwhile much of the time, energy, and attention of the CCC staff and leadership was siphoned off into two major internal conflicts, and the Puerto Rican piece of the project never had a chance to succeed.

One of the conflicts was over Dan Carpenter. After twenty-five years at the Guild, probably the most visible institution in Chelsea, Carpenter would have been the leading contender in any local contest for a "Mr. Chelsea." He, more than anyone, was Chelsea's spokesman, and it was a role he was not inclined to give up, especially to somebody like Bob Dunn, who had rarely been involved in community-wide endeavors. Alinsky had badly misjudged Carpenter, deluding himself into thinking that Carpenter could be satisfied and won over if he got the credit for a "successful" organization in which he was merely a behind-the-scenes player. Rather, Carpenter strongly resisted relinquishing control and leadership. It was not only that Carpenter insisted on simultaneously being head of the Hudson Guild and head of the new community organi-zation—and that he only reluctantly gave up the second position under pressure from the foundations—and not only that he initially saw noth-ing contradictory about having an administrative committee, many of whose members did not live in Chelsea, control the purse strings. There was disagreement and confusion about other issues, too. Buckholz remembers that Carpenter and Alinsky differed on how the organizing should proceed. Alinsky felt strongly that Carpenter should not continue to act as the community spokesman; Carpenter did not see it that way. Nor did he seem to understand that Alinsky's approach involved more than merely "signing up" titular leaders of Chelsea's various organiza-tions. Alinsky wanted organizers to identify natural, nontitular leaders within local groups and organizations, and he wanted to organize on the basis of issues and self-interest so that participation was not merely sym-bolic—a ritual of "good citizenship"—but tied to matters of real value and importance. He wanted his organizers to agitate and mobilize hereto-fore quiescent people into active, protesting citizens who, if necessary, would publicly confront city officials and make demands. The approach was both foreign and repugnant to Carpenter, a veteran insider with access to city agencies and City Hall whose settlement-house style stressed consensus and avoidance of conflict.

But there was apparently no conflict on the night of June 20, 1956, at a meeting of the Hudson Guild board when, according to the minutes, the board approved in principle plans for an ILGWU-sponsored cooperative housing project in Chelsea. At the same meeting, Dan Carpenter also reported that the foundation grants had been received for the new, Alinsky-style community organization project. It would not be surprising if neither Dan Carpenter nor anybody else at the Hudson Guild on that fateful night imagined any connection between the two.

The proposed ILGWU housing project was a mammoth series of high-rise apartment buildings spread over six blocks just south of Penn Station. Buckholz had heard that the staff on the City Planning Commission opposed it because it was out of sync with the architectural nature of the nearby neighborhoods, where brownstones and low, four-story houses predominated. But from the beginning, Penn Station South had powerful support—from the ILGWU to Robert Moses and other political and civic leaders. In the community, Dan Carpenter thought that the housing project was a beginning for a new Chelsea, where moderate-cost housing would replace the old housing stock, much of it deteriorating. But the new cooperatives would also replace old, lower-income residents who were largely Catholics. In all, about 10,000 of them were going to be driven out of the neighborhood, casualties of "progress" and of a "consensus" on a revitalized new Chelsea. Indeed, in Chelsea there *was* a consensus. The Hudson Guild, the Sloane YMCA, the General Theological Seminary, the French Hospital, and the Episcopal churches—all institutions with limited local membership—favored Penn Station South.

But as the organizing process of the CCC unfolded, opposition slowly began to form. It was not an issue the organizers pushed; in fact, Buckholz says, "I don't think even as an organizer that I realized how far down the road [Penn Station South] was. . . . The CCC didn't take action on it until into the second year." Why not? Because in every respect the fledgling, stumbling community organization was a mismatch for Penn Station South, with its great size and powerful sponsorship and backing. So the organizers did not think of making a major effort to stop Penn Station South. But eventually, the relentlessly growing, swirling conflict over the leadership of the CCC between Carpenter and Dunn became a powerful force of its own, a vortex of conflict that swept up virtually everything in Chelsea, including the heretofore nonissue of Penn Station South. When the question of whether to support or oppose the housing project finally came before the CCC board of directors for a vote, more was at stake than a vote on Penn Station South. The vote was about the conflict between Catholics and non-Catholics, between lower-class and middle-class interests, and between two men, their leadership and integrity. Alinsky was foursquare on Dunn's side—not because he thought it was possible to stop Penn Station South or that to try to stop it was a good tactical move, but because of the rightness of Dunn's position. After all, the poorer, weaker people of Chelsea were being pushed out in the name of progress. Maybe it was true, as Buckholz had heard, that the archdiocese was not protesting Penn Station South because it had bigger fish to fry in another real estate deal elsewhere in town. If Father Dunn did not speak out for the interests of the four Catholic parishes in Chelsea and for other lower-class, soon-to-be ex-Chelseans, who would? By a vote of 29–27 the Dunn forces prevailed in tabling a motion to support Penn Station South, but with virtually everybody's chips in the center of the table, the game was almost certainly over. Soon Dan Carpenter and the Hudson Guild and their allies withdrew from the CCC amid much anger and acrimony. As the last, painful passages were being written in Chelsea, Alinsky told Carl Tjerandsen of the Schwarzhaupt Foundation, "I do not in any form or fashion like the smell of what is happening and having the fight develop on religious lines. It is an ironic commentary that the big job was to break out the Catholic Church from their parochial cocoons only to get them into a situation with a person like Carpenter."

"How Chelsea Was Torn Apart" was the title of a magazine article that soon appeared which pointed a large finger of blame at Saul Alinsky and his methods for the debacle in Chelsea. From Alinsky's perspective, of course, the main problem was that he and his "methods" never had much of a chance to get going. But his biggest failure was not to realize before he undertook the project that Chelsea was the wrong place at the wrong time. Joseph Fitzpatrick at Fordham, the expert on Puerto Ricans, had been disappointed that Alinsky had gone into Chelsea rather than into the South Bronx. Marjorie Buckholz, whose organizing abilities were considerably better than Alinsky had expected, was frustrated by the deep divisions and lack of overlapping membership in Chelsea's social, civic, and religious groups. She found it virtually impossible to find common issues that could bridge the gulfs. Alinsky's plan or approach was to have the organizer identify issues that would stimulate participation. Those issues became "the program." The trick was for an organizer to be creative enough to spot possible issues that others might glide over and to imagine how they could be used to attract participation. In Alinsky's eyes, Buckholz, while diligent and devoted to democratic methods and goals, was not very creative or inspiring—two qualities he valued highly—or comfortable

with an open-ended, ambiguous situation. Although she and Alinsky exchanged dictabelts through the mail every week, it was not a satisfactory
substitute for either extensive face-to-face meetings or more frequent firsthand inspections of Chelsea by Alinsky. When the project first began, Don
Kingsley, one of the few people in New York's social-welfare world who
was sympathetic to Alinsky's coming into New York, told Paul McGhee
that he was concerned that five days a month might not be enough time.
"There is as much art as there is science in the approach he makes,"
Kingsley told Paul McGhee, "and the institutionalization of art is difficult." As it turned out, Buckholz felt shortchanged, because Alinsky often
did not give a full five days to Chelsea when he came to New York,
spending time instead with his other New York contacts and old friends.
Yet Alinsky stubbornly refused to court a new circle of contacts—he was
snooty about New York intellectuals—that might have given him social
and political prestige and support to neutralize Dan Carpenter's advantages as the New York insider. "Saul didn't have the troops in Chelsea,"
von Hoffman thought, and challenged him to explain how he could possibly succeed there. "I was really saying, 'What are you going to fight with?
You got no army, . . . no base, absolutely no power base.' You know, New
York is not Chicago."

too did the first black migration to Chicago and other Northern cities. But during and after World War II, a new wave began—and did not stop. There were many reasons, among them the decline of labor-intensive agriculture in the South and expectations of postwar economic prosperity in the North. During the war, labor shortages provided blacks with a chance to get better-paying jobs, especially in the North and West; their success attracted still more blacks to the North after the war was over. In addition, many blacks had new expectations about racial equality. Blacks who served in the armed forces came home with a new attitude and determination to escape from the old humiliations of a segregated society. A yearly average of 160,000 blacks came North in the 1940s; the rate was only slightly less in the 1950s and 1960s—about 147,000 a year. Of course, nobody could predict with certainty the ultimate scope and duration of this great, historic migration. No national crystal ball was available to show what the great cities of the North would look like two decades later, to show the scenes of racial violence and political upheavals. One thing was quite apparent by the 1950s, however, and that was that the question of race, in terms both of morality and of politics, could no longer be completely ignored. As long as segregation in its most complete and odious form had been restricted to one section of the country where the vast majority of blacks lived, it had been possible for the rest of the country to go about its business with considerable detachment. Even in the North, a long-practiced "strategy" was to ignore the black population generally, let alone the injustices of segregation and discrimination. In Chicago, even until the early 1960s, a daily reading of the newspapers gave little indication that there were black residents in the city, although by 1960 the total black population had mushroomed to 813,000, the second largest of any city in the country. A veteran Chicago newspaper reporter, Jerome Watson, recalls working the night shift one Saturday for the City News Bureau. When a report came in of a shooting, Watson's editor gave a typical response: "Colored? Cheap it out," meaning that if it was about blacks, then it was worth only a sentence or two since the story would be buried or ignored.

In Chicago on the South Side, in the 1920s, 1930s, and through much of the 1940s, a neat, slender rectangle not much more than a dozen blocks wide, which started a little south of the downtown Loop and extended south for about forty blocks, contained the majority of the city's blacks. By the mid-1950s, that rectangle suddenly lengthened and fattened by nearly 40 percent. Moreover, as the city's black population increased, the white population of Chicago declined. Cause and effect was not the only explanation of this demographic phenomenon, but it was a major, troubling one. It was troubling to those, like Saul Alinsky, who believed in the

19

Race

Alinsky may have been adrift in Chelsea, but at the same time he was firming up his power base within the Catholic archdiocese back in Chicago. His services were in demand, but by now it was not Puerto Ricans but blacks that concerned the archdiocese—and for good reason.

The migration of blacks from the Southern states to Chicago, Detroit, Cleveland, Philadelphia, and other big cities in the North had started during and immediately after World War I. The prospect of better jobs was a powerful allure but not the only one. In 1917, a black migrant from Texas, according to Godfrey Hodgson's account, wrote that he was off to "Chicago or Philadelphia. But I don't care where so long as I go where a man is a man." Had he fetched up in Chicago, he might well have landed a job in one of the meat-packing plants. He would have probably found a place to live in the South Side ghetto east of Wentworth Avenue, about a mile away from the killing floors at Armour or Swift. It was not a long walk—over the dividing line into the white neighborhood—except at certain times such as during the race riot of 1919 or any day after the sun went down. Rather than walk, most black workers took the streetcar or the elevated train.

For twenty years, until World War II, most blacks in Chicago lived in this South Side ghetto. During this period the black population in Chicago, as in other cities in the North, remained relatively small and constant, between 5 and 10 percent of the total. This relative stability was one reason that there was no great push for new, better housing in white neighborhoods; another reason was economic; a third was discrimination—restrictive covenants made it nearly impossible for blacks to buy houses outside the ghetto.

Soon after World War I, when the wartime labor shortages ended, so value of an integrated society. It was troubling to those who feared that the loss of the white middle class would result in a city too poor to provide improved housing, health care, education, and other services for needy people. It was also troubling—and threatening—to many in the city who liked things the way they had been: many businessmen, ward politicians, their white, homeowning constituents, and others who had various "investments" in the old Chicago that was all too suddenly changing before their eyes.

IN 1957, Saul Alinsky's Industrial Areas Foundation received a three-year grant from the Archdiocese of Chicago for $118,800. This not insignificant sum was a measure of both the archdiocese's concern with the rapid changes that were occurring in Chicago and the respect and trust that Cardinal Stritch and other archdiocesan leaders had in Saul Alinsky.

The money, except for 10 percent that went to the IAF for administrative expenses, was allocated for a study, Alinsky told his board of directors, "of changing communities resulting from population shifts. Issues such as the consequences of its impact upon local institutions, power rearrangements, areas of vacuum of community life, . . . will be analyzed in terms of the philosophy and experience of the Industrial Areas Foundation to the end of attempting to develop the most feasible plans for community organization under these circumstances." As part of this extensive study, a number of priests were to receive training in community analysis and organization. "Today one of the outstanding priests of the diocese," Alinsky reported to his board, "has been almost completely released from his clerical duties and is now being trained by the Industrial Areas Foundation." That priest was Jack Egan.

Indeed, since they first met over salami sandwiches less than three years before, Egan and Alinsky had been friends. Not only that, but Egan was a good bridge for Alinsky to others in the archdiocese, including the well-placed Monsignor Edward Burke, chancellor of the archdiocese and a very powerful man, being the archdiocese's chief executive officer. (His frequent rival in the archdiocesan office was Monsignor George Casey, vicar general. Nobody knew exactly how Burke and Casey's duties were divided. "At times," Egan recalls, "you didn't know which one to go to. Casey was generally the man on financial matters, and Burke on appointments. Cardinal Stritch knew that there was a certain rivalry between them; he didn't do anything to stop it.") Casey and Burke had been two of Cardinal Mundelein's boys. Mundelein, a large man himself, would suffer no small priests, and Burke, who was in the vicinity of six feet three inches and two hundred fifty pounds, was at once well endowed and well qualified for a position of influence and power. Although there was nothing subtle about Burke, he was not easy to pigeonhole—and not merely because of his size. On the one hand, in both politics and religion, he was traditional and conservative. On the other hand, he was impulsive, intelligent, pragmatic, and loyal to friends. If you were a priest, even a liberal priest, and Ed Burke liked you, he would go to bat for you with the cardinal. In fact, he was the liberals' man in the archdiocesan office downtown.

In just a few years, Alinsky had discovered a valuable new double-play combination: Egan to Burke to Stritch. His relationships with these men were not those of mere convenience or opportunism. Not only did they share many similar values; they also developed a genuine fondness for each other. In the case of Stritch, Alinsky's friendship was formal, his personal contact limited to purposeful discussions. To Burke, Alinsky quickly became a close friend and trusted, brotherly adviser. It was commonplace for Burke to phone Alinsky several times a week to ask for advice on even the most sensitive personnel and political matters. When he phoned, after the customary chitchat with Alinsky's secretary, Dorothy Levin, Burke would ask, "Is God in today?" It was a playful tribute that Alinsky did not discourage.

Alinsky enjoyed kidding and teasing Burke, even about the most sensitive of subjects. Nick von Hoffman recalls one such memorable occasion. "Somebody had made a movie about Martin Luther. Burke decided that it was shameful that such a movie should play in Chicago, which, after all, was a Catholic city. But the movie was scheduled to be shown on WGN, the Chicago *Tribune*'s station. Burke called up Green, Kirkland and Ellis, the law firm that represented both the *Tribune* and the Archdiocese of Chicago—imagine the clout they had!—and told them, 'You tell your other clients that that movie is not to be aired.' Well, that was enough. The law firm apparently passed the word and said that the chancery office is very unhappy about playing Martin Luther on the air. So the ACLU and all of the liberals were up in arms, and I was taking an enormous amount of abuse from all of these people about this Catholic stuff. So I finally told Saul, 'You got to do something about this nonsense.' He says, 'What do you expect me to do?' I said, 'I expect you to talk to Burke and get this thing reversed and put the movie back on the air.' He says, 'You're crazy.' I said, 'I'm not crazy, you can do it.' So he invited Burke out to Barney's, at Halsted and Randolph, where we ate a lot. All the big aldermen and monsignors ate there; you herniated your eyes looking at the steaks—I mean, this was beef-eater territory. It was the kind of place Saul loved.

Bourbòn, steaks, macho land! And so we went over there, and after drinks, and at what Saul thought was the propitious moment, he said, 'Ed, I want to talk with you about this fucking Martin Luther thing.' "

"Saul, I don't want to hear anything about it," Burke said. "My mind's made up. You're a great guy, I love you, but you're not a Catholic and don't understand it and, furthermore, you're Jewish, so it isn't even your fight. It's strictly between us and the goddamn Protestants."

"Now wait a minute, Ed," Alinsky began.

"No 'wait a minute,' " Burke said, but then relented. "All right, I'll wait a minute, but the answer is no."

"Listen, I've got a way to solve your problem," Alinsky said, "including the objections of the ACLU and all of that. It's very simple; you've got nothing to worry about."

"Well, what is it?" Burke asked.

"Let them put the movie on—"

"No," Burke interrupted.

"Now wait a minute, let me finish," Alinsky pleaded innocently. "Let them put the movie on the air with one proviso, Ed."

"Well, what's that, Saul?"

"The one proviso," Alinsky deadpanned, "is that they show it backwards so that Martin Luther will end up a Catholic."

Whereupon the table exploded in laughter, with Burke staring at Alinsky. "You son of a bitch, Saul." But it was not long before Burke relented. "I'll let them show the damn movie," he told Alinsky grudgingly.

Alinsky enjoyed telling stories about Burke, especially to his non-Catholic friends, who he knew would appreciate a glimpse into the culture of powerful monsignors. A visit with Burke at the Loretto Hospital, where he was being treated for an embolism, produced an anecdote that Alinsky passed on to his friend Leonard Rieser:

> I stopped in the day before yesterday and was treated to a brand-new experience as to what constitutes the new hospital routine. I should say the hospital routine in a Catholic hospital when the Catholic chancellor of the archdiocese is a patient. His room is lined wall to wall with presents and every single present is in the form of a bottle! A quick glance indicated proportions of 70 percent scotch, 20 percent brandy, and 10 percent bourbon. A portable bar has been set up in his room! The guy who owns Barney's Market Place sends over baskets of steaks and other goodies twice a day. The moment I showed up, Burke promptly pressed the button for "room service," and a demure sister showed up and was greeted with the order "Let's have some setups, Sister." In about two minutes flat she returned with the glasses

and ice. I understand this has been going on from the moment he entered the hospital, and I told him that I felt that it was only a matter of time before those nurses would have to take out membership in the Bartenders Union!

But Jack Egan's life became even more intertwined with Alinsky's. And the more Egan saw of Alinsky, the more fascinated he became with both the man and his ideas about social change, power, democracy, and human nature. On the personal side, he came to see that although Alinsky could be self-centered—"Saul never wanted to be inconvenienced; I would never ask him to pick me up at the airport, but he wouldn't mind asking me to pick him up"—he could also be compassionate and concerned about other people's feelings, especially when those people were vulnerable.

Egan jumped at the chance to work with Alinsky when Cardinal Stritch gave the IAF the grant to study population shifts. The first part of that study had to do with relocation procedures and other effects on the people uprooted from their homes to make room for the Dan Ryan Expressway on the South Side. Egan considered the displacement of hundreds of families a serious moral concern. "That was the beginning of my two years with Saul," Egan remembers. "I was still doing the job with the marriage program . . . but I was also working two-thirds time with Saul." Egan and Lester Hunt spent long days over several months visiting practically every home and institution between Thirty-fifth and Fifty-fourth streets and from State Street to Cottage Grove Avenue—the Grand Boulevard section of Chicago, in the heart of the old South Side ghetto. Their survey was like the one von Hoffman had done on the near North Side. Egan remembers that it was hard work, but when the report was presented to the cardinal, Stritch was once again impressed. He rewarded Egan by appointing him to the Cardinal's Conservation Committee, the archdiocese's forum for addressing problems of urban blight and decay. While Egan had already proved to be a useful ally, the connection with him now yielded its first tangible benefit for Alinsky.

By 1957, "Saul and I were developing a very close personal relationship," Egan says. It was a relationship that often included Nick von Hoffman and Lester Hunt, a social cluster that Egan found stimulating, exciting, and fun. Periodically, in the evening after dinner and after Alinsky walked Pang, he would invite Egan to join von Hoffman and Hunt at his place for a quasi staff meeting and bull session. "We would talk about the events of the day, what was happening to each of us," Egan says. "I was the foil of a lot of their fun. They were so damn smart. They loved to kid me. They would kid me about the Roman Catholic Church . . . and about women and celibacy. Saul would say, 'I'll buy the celibacy but don't try to put that chastity on us.' They would kid me about all the rules and the nutty priests and bishops. Saul loved to do that. They would expect me to defend every single priest and sister. Then there would be some serious conversation about a book, about music, or a play. It was a joy to be with them. Jean would have gone to bed when, near midnight, Saul would say, 'Get the hell out of here.' "

Egan felt privileged to be the fourth man at these gatherings, to be a part of what he felt was "the very precious relationship between Saul, Nick, and Lester." Von Hoffman and Hunt had quickly become Alinsky's protégés. Although half his age, they were both precocious, well read, irreverent, and witty. They were the kind of young men whose great admiration and respect for Alinsky had no chance of becoming idolatrous. (When, for instance, Alinsky suggested that they read and discuss the philosophical implications in *Alice in Wonderland*—he enjoyed discovering allegedly important insights from unlikely sources—von Hoffman and Hunt showed up at the appointed lunch hour at the Palmer House Grill with information they had dug up on Lewis Carroll's sex life. Alinsky was not amused.) It had not been long, however, before the three of them had formed a mutual admiration society. Their feelings were never uttered directly. To the contrary, barbs and sarcasm were the preferred style, compliments were nonexistent, and von Hoffman and Alinsky in particular loved to argue with each other over virtually everything from Plato to the Chicago White Sox.

They had great fun together, the three of them. Von Hoffman and Hunt were fascinated with Alinsky's style, idiosyncrasies, and audacious sense of humor. Alinsky had a small collection of tastes that he had picked up from John L. Lewis and other, lesser CIO barons, von Hoffman observed. "He loved Jay Sulka's," a haberdashery in the Loop, von Hoffman remembers. "It was terrible—true AFL-CIO taste right out of their executive committee. We would always stop and look in the window at Jay Sulka's. And Saul smoked Dunhills but never took them out of his pocket and put them on the table if he possibly could because he thought someone might filch one." Then there was Alinsky's mischievousness. "He loved to throw confusion everywhere," von Hoffman says with delight. "And since he was a fairly combative person by nature, he produced a never-ending furor. Of course, it was just wonderful. One of the things he liked to do was to go into a restaurant where the menu was: 'Number 1, small sirloin with baked potato and sour cream, and chef salad; Number 2, lamb chop with french fries,' and so forth. Then he would say to us, 'Watch me disorient her.' And he would order: 'I want the potato from Number 1, and

the chops from Number 2 . . .' and before long there would be massive
confusion. And he'd sit there with his little boyish face as happy as he could
be while everybody is ready to shoot him. He loved it. He was quite
convinced that he was illustrating important points in human psychology,
and I kept telling him, 'All you're doing is causing trouble!' "

One person who could sometimes top Alinsky when it came to causing
trouble in public places, although usually unintentionally, was the peripa-
tetic Monsignor John O'Grady. O'Grady's appearance in Chicago inevitably produced a small warehouse of stories. O'Grady was a good source of
intelligence for Alinsky. He had the confidence of certain influential people
through his work at the National Conference of Catholic Charities, he
knew all the rivalries in the Church, all the key players and bishops, and,
as von Hoffman says, "he could sort out the promising bishops from the
clunkers." In turn, while O'Grady was a man of compassion and commitment, he did not possess Alinsky's political instincts, so he would listen to
his friend's advice. O'Grady would describe a situation to Alinsky, von
Hoffman remembers, and Alinsky would say, "No, you can't do that, John,
it won't work. You can't approach so-and-so that way, John, you have to
approach him this way."

On one occasion, because it was Friday, Alinsky, von Hoffman, and
Hunt rented a room in the Palmer House so O'Grady could have a steak
in private. O'Grady hid behind the door of the bathroom as room service
rolled in the never-on-Friday treat. On another memorable occasion, von
Hoffman says,

> O'Grady was forced to have a great piece of Lake Michigan whitefish,
> grilled, and when it came, O'Grady starts eating it but gets a bone
> stuck between his dentures and his gum. I don't know what the hell
> we were talking about but the next thing I know is that his hand has
> gone into his mouth trying to get the bone out. He can't get it out.
> Finally, even Saul stops eating; he's watching in silence as O'Grady
> is fishing around. The bottom of his dentures comes out and goes on
> the table. There was a great groaning sound. Uggggrrr. All the people
> around us are hysterical, and Saul finally says, "For Christ's sake,
> John, go in the men's room."

The lunches and dinners with people such as O'Grady and Burke
were, in effect, part of the education that von Hoffman and Hunt received
in the attitudes, agendas, and style of players in both Church and Chicago
politics. Working for Alinsky was exciting for two young men like von
Hoffman and Hunt. Von Hoffman says:

For a while, I was kind of an unofficial go-between between the cardinal and [Mayor] Daley through Saul's auspices. One thing I did for a while, on the race relations problems, is that I would go around and get information. Then, every so often, I would get a call from Burke saying, "The cardinal would like to see you tomorrow." And I'd go up there, sometimes to the cardinal's residence on North State Parkway, sometimes to the chancery office. I'd hear the click of the pectoral cross—a heavy diamond number—against the cassock buttons and the rustle of red moiré, and there he'd be. We'd sit down, and he would put his hand on his forehead, lean forward, and say, "Now, sonny, tell me what is happening." He always called me sonny.

T. GEORGE HARRIS, a journalist who was based in Chicago for *Time* magazine in the mid-1950s, became preoccupied with the new dynamics of American cities because, as he says, "of Alinsky's effect on me." Soon after he came to Chicago, he began to organize small lunches with various movers and shakers. He recalls inviting Alinsky to join him at one of these lunches, along with the banker Gaylord Freeman and the industrialist—and founder of the Aspen Institute—Walter Paepcke. Harris was intrigued with Alinsky's sense of the transformation of the city. "I was desperately trying to understand what the hell was happening in cities," Harris says. When Henry Luce, the head of Time Inc., came to Chicago, Harris remembers that "I locked him up in a car and hauled him around the city, saying, 'Look, there are things happening here that I don't understand, but they're fundamental. It's not [merely] a matter of city planning; the whole damn city is being transformed, but I can't quite figure out how to write about it." Luce went back to Holly White at *Fortune* and told him about his visit; he agreed that Harris was onto something, and that, perhaps, it was time for a major series of articles on the American city.

The result was a five-part series published in *Fortune* in late 1957 and early 1958, "The Exploding Metropolis." It was, Harris thinks, the era's first major journalistic piece of urbanology. Though Alinsky was never mentioned by name in the series, Harris insists that a significant perspective in it was influenced by him. "I think that Saul broke up our somewhat architectural view of the city. I think that one of the nice things that he did was to help us think of the city much more in terms of muscle and minds and people, more so than in terms of buildings and streets." In fact, the series was at its pungent best when it addressed the problem of the flight of the middle class to the suburbs, and how government policy, politicians,

the real estate industry, and city planners had abetted the flight: by generous funding of highway and expressway construction, which made the
suburbs so accessible, while providing little money for housing and urban
renewal; by failing to deal creatively with expanding and worsening slum
conditions; by failing to appeal to the middle class (the "vast barracks-like
superblocks are not designed for people who *like* cities, but for people who
have no other choice").

Alinsky would not have disagreed with these and similar observations
in the *Fortune* series, but his frame of reference was different. It was related
to Chicago and, especially, to his experience in the Back of the Yards.
Alinsky argued his case early in 1959 in a paper that he presented at Notre
Dame University for a symposium, "Roman Catholicism and the American Way of Life"—an appropriate forum for what Alinsky had to say,
since the Church and many of its parishes and parishioners were at the
center of the racial changes occurring in Northern cities. To put it more
graphically, many Catholic parishes stood in the way of expanding black
ghettos.

Alinsky framed his analysis by contrasting the sociology of the old
urban immigrant experience with that of the new urban immigrants, the
Southern blacks. The old urban immigrants, such as those who arrived in
Chicago in the early part of the twentieth century, formed "large national
and religious communities which were literally European cultural islands
transported and grafted onto the body of the American cities," Alinsky
explained. One's entire life, including one's job at the nearby steel mill or
meat-packing plant, could be lived within the confines of one's own community. These communities, Alinsky argued, remained "stable" for longer
than they otherwise might have because of various factors—the end of
unrestricted immigration in 1924, the Great Depression, and an acute
housing shortage during World War II. And at the center of these stable
communities stood the Catholic immigrant church—"a central anchor of
security to these immigrants," Alinsky said. "[The Church] was the one
familiar part of their life and experience which was the same here as it had
been in their native home. . . . [It] was not only the spiritual fountainhead
for the new immigrant, but the place where he went for advice and guidance in all other areas of his life, ranging from his social problems to his
political activities."

Quickly, within the space of only a decade from the end of the war,
the familiar sociology changed. In the case of the old immigrants, the
process of Americanization, which would have led them into the mainstream of American society earlier had not the Great Depression and
World War II intruded, was now being played out, aided by the new

postwar prosperity. "Out of the situation of today is coming a new kind of people, a people who are being exposed to and accepting new areas of interest; new allegiances; new places to look for with reference to counsel and guidance in different areas; a trend toward looking for advice from specialists in specialized fields, and the acceptance of multiple memberships, so that no longer does any one institution, whether it be organized labor or organized capital or organized religion, carry the power, the influence, or the authority over more than its one particular area of interest and activities." While these changes in world view and aspirations were perhaps most dramatic among the Slavic immigrants, Alinsky maintained that they also applied to other people and communities as well—which in Chicago included largely Roman Catholic communities such as the working-class Irish communities on the South Side. "No longer," he argued, "can the Roman Catholic Church, or any church, or any other institution, go it alone."

In the late 1950s, it was said in Chicago that each week another block changed from white to black, and many of those blocks were on the edges of largely Catholic neighborhoods. The whites—often white Catholics—frequently considered this nothing less than an enemy invasion, and often enough responded with ugly violence. For Alinsky, however, it was essential to reject both the racial segregation that kept blacks out and the other kind of segregation that resulted if whites abandoned their neighborhoods because of their fears and prejudices. Much of Alinsky's argument rested on the value he placed on racial integration as an end in itself. And his strategy was to secure racial integration by using racial quotas—quotas that would allow for a limited number of blacks to move into white neighborhoods.

The use of quotas for "liberal" goals was not a unique idea, although the term in the 1950s usually carried the opprobrium of discrimination. Elite universities, for example, had quotas to restrict the number of Jewish students they admitted. Alinsky referred to quotas as that "ugly word, . . . an anathema to any believer in the democratic way of life, and yet every attempt in school and community integration falls back upon the use of some kind of control." In fact, leaders of the public housing movement in Chicago had been surreptitiously employing quotas to further racial integration for some years, and Alinsky himself spoke favorably about the use of quotas to further racial integration in the late 1940s.

Now, Alinsky argued that the Catholic hierarchy should support—even embrace—the use of racial quotas as an interim, good-faith device. "The churches," Alinsky said, by which he meant here Protestant ones as well as Catholic, "are made up of people, with all of their weaknesses, fears, prejudices, and the general irrationality of much of human behavior. Those in positions of responsibility [in the churches] owe and bear responsibility to their people and their organization, as well as to the [urban] newcomer." Clearly, however, there were a number of important "ifs." Putting aside for a moment the question of the morality of his proposal, the scheme of racial quotas had a chance to be effective only if the white homeowners could be sold on the concept, if blacks saw it as a useful step toward progress, and if it was possible to implement.

As for the white homeowners, Alinsky claimed that he had already done a little informal test marketing, asking some on Chicago's South Side if they would accept the quota scheme—if they were guaranteed that blacks would not exceed 5 percent of the neighborhood population. According to Alinsky, they all thought that was a deal they could live with because their greatest fear was not of blacks per se but of the inevitable transformation of a white neighborhood after the first black moved in.

As for the blacks' reaction to his idea, Alinsky said that he expected sympathy, even agreement in private that "this is the only way under present conditions that a beginning can be made towards the development of a natural integrated community which would not have any kinds of controls operating except the usual ones of economics and personal preference." There would be no disagreement, Alinsky suggested, with his definition that—under present conditions—a community remains integrated only between the time when the first black moves in and the last white moves out. Privately, there would be little disagreement about the desirability of preventing resegregation when the ghetto spilled over into white neighborhoods. "Many Negro leaders, even more anxious than certain whites to have integrated communities, know that there is no control over their own people's movements wherever housing opens." Nonetheless, Alinsky said that black leaders would publicly criticize his idea—and some did—"because of the principle involved." Such public criticism, Alinsky implied, would be mostly ritualistic and not by itself a serious obstacle.

Far more serious and uncertain for Alinsky was the question of whether racial quotas were workable, not merely in a small, government-controlled public housing project, or in a small neighborhood dominated by a single powerful institution, but in a much larger community—in a chunk of Chicago, for example, where racial violence had already flared. Had Alinsky been forced to bet on success or failure, he would have put his chips on failure. He was doubtful—perhaps just short of highly doubtful—that something like this could be pulled off.

20

Church's Last Stand

Alinsky's call for racial quotas was an act of desperation to fit an increasingly desperate situation. He saw no viable alternatives, at least in the short run, and was playing for time. If the scheme could be sold in the white community on the Southwest Side, and if it could work, at least for a while, then maybe something else might happen in the meantime—some other partial solution might arise. Alinsky did not know precisely what form the other solutions might take, but he did have one possibility in mind: he thought it might be possible to organize a black community contiguous to or at least close by a white one, so that the leaders of the two could negotiate agreements on such issues as housing sales and rentals. Each organization would have accumulated enough power, he theorized, to be able to control real estate and mortgage lending practices, which had so much to do with the stability—or lack of it—in transitional communities.

In fact, in 1958, when Jack Egan and Lester Hunt surveyed the Grand Boulevard community where blacks lived, Alinsky might have given fleeting consideration to the possibility of organizing there. Hunt and von Hoffman were especially eager to organize a black community, for although the first, dramatic events to crack segregation in the South had only just begun to unfold, they were convinced that race would eventually become a dominating force in all the major cities of the North. Alinsky, von Hoffman recalls, thought that ultimately "the crucial history of race relations would be written in the Northern cities." By successfully organizing a large black section in Chicago like Grand Boulevard, Alinsky and his protégés could be on the cutting edge of historic social change.

For Alinsky, there might have been another, more personal reason for starting a community organizing project in Grand Boulevard: the neighborhood nearly bordered the Back of the Yards on the east, and by then the Back of the Yards—which was virtually synonymous with the Back of the Yards Neighborhood Council—was gaining a reputation for segregationist policies and actions. While the black population on the South Side had begun to expand around the boundaries of the Back of the Yards, not one black family had been permitted to move into the old stockyards community. (Nationally, there was little awareness of this aspect of Alinsky's creation. For example, in 1959, when Jane Jacobs praised the Back of the Yards Neighborhood Council for its housing revitalization program in her influential book *The Death and Life of Great American Cities,* she was unaware of the community's position on race.) And the segregationist attitudes and practices of the Back of the Yards community were not significantly different from those in many other white neighborhoods. But because the Back of the Yards that he organized was supposed to be different, Alinsky was embarrassed. After all, he had taken pride in the fact that during the early years of the BYNC it had a committee on race relations which actively worked to stop the harassment of blacks in community retail stores, restaurants, and bars. Moreover, the Council's vigorous support of the Packinghouse Workers Union, with its large black membership in Chicago, represented an implicit show of support for the idea of racial unity. But the Council's race relations committee was apparently Alinsky's idea and in a sense had been grafted onto the Council's main body. In reality, the Council's focus on black-white relations was never as prominent as the picture Alinsky eagerly sold to journalists, especially out-of-town journalists.

One who clearly understood what Alinsky had accomplished in the Back of the Yards was Elizabeth Wood, the head of the Chicago Housing Authority from the 1930s to the early 1950s. A legendary, charismatic figure, she and a devoted band of assistants were largely responsible for the early successes of public housing, including integrated public housing—as limited as those successes were—in Chicago, until she was unceremoniously canned by Mayor Martin Kennelly in 1954. Now in her eighties, Wood says that the Back of the Yards Neighborhood Council was never a "model of anything that we think to call peaceful integration. . . . It wasn't integration. It was a job of negotiating peaceful relationships, not on a theoretical basis, not moralizing, but just simply practical." She admired Alinsky then—and still does—for bringing a measure of civility, for keeping things "peaceful," among alien groups, including blacks and whites. "I think that was the major contribution Saul made," she says.

Whatever progress Alinsky achieved on race in the Back of the Yards was tied closely to the necessity for black-white unity among the packinghouse workers in their struggle for recognition and survival. After the war, however, the meat-packing industry in Chicago began to decline rapidly, and by the 1950s many fewer Back of the Yards residents—which is to say, whites—were employed in the packinghouses. At least within the neighborhood, black-white issues within the union were of lesser concern.

So it was not accurate to say, as many liberals and other critics in Chicago were saying in the late 1950s, that the Back of the Yards had *become* segregationist. It had always been a neighborhood where only whites lived; it had been one of the unquestioned "givens" of the racial life of Chicago. But now, because integrated housing had become a live issue, and because Alinsky had won acclaim for organizing the Council on the basis of "democratic values," he was embarrassed, especially since he needed the BYNC as a model to show that his concepts of community organization had succeeded. Much of his public identity—which is to say, his credibility—continued to be linked to the Council.

Thus, when Alinsky phoned Joe Meegan and asked if they could talk over dinner, he was concerned not only with what was happening in Chicago—not only with his idea about racial quotas and the new project that he was getting into in the white Southwest Side community—but also with his inevitable identification with the tarnished image of the Council.

Ironically, while the Back of the Yards was becoming actively anti-black, it was also winning acclaim from the Chicago newspapers and from progressive urban-policy writers like Jane Jacobs for its ambitious and successful housing program. With the postwar population shrinkage in the Back of the Yards—in which the decline of the meat-packing industry, the emergence of new job opportunities elsewhere, and new suburban housing were all factors—blight was afflicting the neighborhood's old, inexpensive housing stock. Joe Meegan and the Council mobilized the community, including the local banks and savings and loan associations, to stem the tide. Billboards went up asking "Why Move Away?" and listing the attractions of churches, schools, playgrounds, and convenient shopping. In the Council offices, one room contained floor-to-ceiling bookcases filled with binders in which every building and vacant lot in the Back of the Yards was listed—a complete listing of each property owner, together with mortgage information, a history of building-code violations, and other data—which made rehabilitation and building programs much more efficient. Up-to-the-minute property surveillance also gave the Council a measure of control for other purposes—for example, being able to arrange housing sales and rentals before they were advertised on the open market. Within five years, 4,000 houses had been rehabilitated. To heighten community awareness and support, the Council held contests for outstanding exteriors, interiors, and landscaping among the refurbished dwellings. In addition, more than 150 new houses were built on vacant lots, following an intricate process of matching up lots with families who had the means to build a house. And by the late 1950s, the Back of the Yards was clearly on an upswing. This housing program was carried out without a cent of government money—a point that gained the attention of, among others, editorial writers and representatives of other working-class communities. Every remodeled and newly built house was financed through local institutions. The working-class people of the Back of the Yards were exceedingly thrifty—in and near the community of fewer than 100,000 souls were twenty savings and loans institutions, nearly 10 percent of the total in all of Cook County. By 1958, the Chicago *Sun-Times* celebrated the BYNC achievements by proclaiming that "the home conservation and modernization program of the Back of the Yards Neighborhood Council . . . has hung up a record unsurpassed in the city or suburbs."

Exactly what Alinsky said to Meegan when he phoned to arrange the dinner is not clear. Nobody who was at the dinner remembers precisely when it occurred, although it was probably in late 1958, for it was the kind of uncomfortable, unpleasant evening that one tries to forget but of course cannot. At the appointed hour, Alinsky arrived at the Meegans' house for dinner accompanied by Monsignor Egan, the latter in his priestly garb. Meegan had invited his priest, too, the relatively new pastor at St. Basil's. He also had invited his friend Patrick O'Malley and O'Malley's wife. O'Malley, who was well connected in the upper echelons of Democratic politics in Chicago and who would later become president of Canteen Corp., was also an adviser of sorts to Meegan. After dinner, they adjourned downstairs to the Meegans' oak-paneled recreation room. (The Meegans' handsome, big house on the corner of Fifty-fourth and Damen, just within the southern boundary of the Back of the Yards Neighborhood Council, had more in common with the even larger, gracious homes on Garfield Boulevard, a block south, than it did with the small, shingle-sided houses to the north, in the heart of the Back of the Yards. Garfield Boulevard, or Fifty-fifth Street as it was also called, was one of Chicago's Mason-Dixon lines, with an all-white segregationist district on the north side. The expanding black population, shut out of the Back of the Yards, had started to arrive in Englewood—south of Fifty-fifth Street—by migrating from the East.)

Now, in Joe and Helen Meegan's pleasant home, Alinsky started to talk about the next batch of new houses that Meegan and the Council were planning. Alinsky suggested that the time was right for Joe to sell a few of those houses to blacks, and that Joe was also the man who could sell the community on the idea. He explained his notion that people in the Back of the Yards feared that if one black moved in, then the neighborhood would inevitably "go colored." The Back of the Yards would be different, Alinsky said, because Meegan could assure the community that he and the Council could control the number of black move-ins.

"Saul's plan for the evening," Jack Egan recalls, was that "we would sit down and talk rationally with Joe about the possibility of moving a few black families in. I remember Saul saying that the black families would be on the same economic and cultural level as the people in the Back of the Yards, so that they would really become friends." Egan, playing the role of the good priest, chimed in with a moral appeal. "I backed Saul up. I said, 'And what a wonderful thing this would be for the city, and how the Back of the Yards, which has had a racist reputation, would be looked upon by the rest of the community' " for its enlightened leadership.

At first, Egan says, "I didn't know how big a hole we were digging for ourselves." Neither Pat O'Malley nor the Meegans' priest had much to say; they mainly listened. But then Egan began to notice that the more he and Alinsky pressed on, the redder Joe Meegan's neck became. Then the shouting started, shouting and yelling. Things went downhill very rapidly. Helen Meegan was especially angry with Saul. Livid, she angrily reminded Alinsky that it had taken years, nearly two decades, just to get the various nationality groups in the community to stop hating one another and to live together in peace and with a measure of cooperation. She challenged Saul Alinsky at point-blank range: if you think that you have such a great idea, Saul, she said, then you come down here, you live here, and you bring in the Negroes. When she finished speaking, the night's get-together had effectively ended.

"I was naïve, and Saul was dumb," Egan says, suggesting that they should have known that, from the Meegans' perspective, he and Alinsky were asking for the impossible. Egan's previously friendly acquaintance-ship with the Meegans was a casualty of that stormy evening. "The relationship after that night between the Meegans and me could never be the same. That night was just too violent."

As for Alinsky, although he never talked to Egan again about the disaster at the Meegans', his friendship with them survived. One bad night could not wipe out all that they had shared over twenty years, or the fondness he and the Meegans felt for each other. Alinsky was usually very loyal to his friends, and his continuing friendship with Joe Meegan had much to do with loyalty.

Perhaps, too, Alinsky knew in his heart that the risk he had asked Joe Meegan to assume was unrealistic, doomed from the outset. Years later, when a friend of Alinsky's, the Chicago journalist Mike Royko, heard about Alinsky's proposal at the Meegans' house, he was surprised. "I mean, Jesus, Saul was really asking for a lot. And I can understand the Meegans' position. Those neighborhoods out there [on the South and Southwest Sides] were mean." When Royko himself was growing up on the Northwest Side in the 1940s, he didn't think much about race because it wasn't an immediate problem. But on the South Side things were different, and he never forgot a chilling, revealing episode that occurred when he was eighteen: He had gone to a friend's sister's wedding in Bridgeport, a working-class Irish neighborhood north of the stockyards. He hung out in Bridgeport because he and his buddies could drink beer there, no questions asked. The wedding was in a hall in the back of a tavern—there were cold cuts and beer, a bleak place for a wedding, Royko thought. Then he remembers a flurry of excitement.

> Guys started getting up, getting their coats and leaving, saying, "Let's go." And my friend's older brother came over and told us what was going on: we were all expected to join in. There had been some crime against a white person committed by a black—I don't recall what it was. They were all getting in their cars and getting guns and railroad flares, and they were driving to the nearest black neighborhood, and they were going to shoot up houses and throw flares through windows, things like that. These were not people who fucked around. I was stunned by this. And you had that all over the white South Side. You're not dealing with a bunch of pantywaists from the suburbs. These are hard people. . . . If Saul were here today, I'd say, "Saul, what were you thinking of?" I mean, Jesus, Meegan would have been committing suicide. That would have been the end of Joe Meegan. He might as well have just taken his bundle and moved out to the burbs. He would have been done.

None of this was unfamiliar to Alinsky. He knew about Studs Lonigan's South Side and, because he did, he had been very reluctant to undertake a community organizing project there. "Saul didn't want to do it," Jack Egan recalls. "But gradually we pushed and shoved for it." Beginning in 1957, Egan worked on Alinsky, telling him about the problems priests were having on the Southwest Side. He reported to Alinsky, for example, about a lunch meeting he had with a young priest, John Greeley, the acting pastor of St. Margaret of Scotland, at Ninety-ninth and Throop. "Father Greeley requested my advice regarding community organization in that general area because he wanted to maintain the high living standards in that neighborhood and knew that many of the homes were getting older and that very soon there would be the need for conservation. He also wanted, since he still has time, to make very sure that anybody who desired would be able to move into that neighborhood and would be welcomed. He knew because of the geographical location . . . that Negro people would be gradually moving in greater numbers into that immediate neighborhood. Father Greeley wants to so prepare his people that any family moving into the parish will be warmly accepted no matter who they may be." But, Egan also reported, Father Greeley did "not want to happen to St. Margaret's parish what had happened to so many more when black people moved into the neighborhood and so many, if not all, of the white people would move away." There was no getting around it: if you were a Catholic pastor on the Southwest Side of Chicago, you were concerned about saving your parish from the possibility—even the probability—of a mass exodus of your white parishioners.

Alinsky's reluctance was not confined to white neighborhoods; it extended to black communities as well. The Grand Boulevard area that Hunt and von Hoffman had canvassed was black and Baptist; except for the packinghouse workers there, Alinsky had few ready-made contacts and little prospect for money to pay for an organizing staff and campaign. Von Hoffman had tried to interest Alinsky in the Englewood community, which bordered the Back of the Yards on the south and, unlike the Grand Boulevard area, contained some Catholic parishes that might provide both a source of money and an avenue of communication. Alinsky had also been approached by a Catholic priest in Woodlawn, which by now was largely black, but he was hesitant about all these possibilities. Part of his reluctance had to do with money: there was no firm commitment to fund a project in a black community. Moreover, he apparently also had doubts not only about using white organizers in a black community but also about whether von Hoffman and Hunt had enough experience to be the day-to-day organizers. Since his days in the Back of the Yards, Alinsky's own role in his other projects was largely that of the commanding general who plots strategy and tactics. But it would be von Hoffman, for instance, who would actually be on the streets in a Chicago ghetto, who would have to make the myriad personal contacts, who would have to size up and evaluate the capabilities of potential leaders, who would have to inspire trust and induce people to take risks, who would have to function as Alinsky's eyes and ears when it came to deciding when an issue ought to be cut or avoided. Alinsky's reluctance was not only keyed to the question of whether von Hoffman or someone else had enough experience and maturity to do the job; he also did not know if a black ghetto *could* be organized into his vision of a strong community organization. It had been one thing, eighteen years earlier, to organize in an almost exclusively Catholic community, with the support of Bishop Sheil and the young priests. It would be quite different—it would be virtually another world—to organize in, say, Woodlawn.

So, partly by default, partly because a modest amount of Catholic money became available, and partly because Alinsky wanted to tackle the problem of race in Chicago, he finally agreed late in 1958 to begin a community organizing project on the white Southwest Side. But it was also partly that Chicago's Southwest Side was symptomatic of a national urban problem. As Lester Hunt recalls, there was "a question of how many projects Saul really wanted to do. The Industrial Areas Foundation provided a place for him to operate to influence the country, which I think he thought was more important than developing [a lot of] other organizations. . . . One of the reasons he published *Reveille for Radicals* was to change people's minds. I think he saw that as a very important function, and he didn't want to get bogged down in a whole lot of projects where his time was taken up with one neighborhood organization or another." This, of course, was a different vision or ambition from what Alinsky had professed earlier, when he had talked of organizing People's Organizations throughout the country. This vision faded when he failed to persuade potential funders to underwrite it, and failed as well to persuade talented friends to join him. But his interest in promoting his ideas through speeches and writings had not changed. If anything, that had become more appealing to him. Hunt remembers:

> Saul was always talking about how we had to change people's minds by rhetoric, by publishing things of some kind. And Nick, of course, was very interested in that because Nick wanted to be a writer. I didn't want to sit around and watch Saul write books. I wanted to go out and save the poor or whatever. And so I wasn't very enthusiastic about that. But I don't think that we ever thought, any of us, that the things Saul was doing would ever become important to the country simply by being organized [one] after the other. Saul certainly didn't. . . . Saul used to say, "We never organize a similar neighborhood twice. We organized the Back of the Yards, and then that can be imitated by all the working-class Polish neighborhoods in the world. So we don't do that again." . . . He saw [each] organization as being important for its publicity effect.

. . .

THE AREA on the Southwest Side of Chicago where Alinsky agreed finally to build a community organization contained nearly ten Catholic parishes, including two of the largest in Chicago. The pastor of one of those large parishes, Monsignor John McMahon, was concerned not only with the future of St. Sabina's but also with the fear, mean-spiritedness, and violence that were growing on the Southwest Side. It was he as much as anyone who wanted to find an alternative between a strategy of "keeping the colored out" and seeing the entire area turn all-black. McMahon, a tall, slender, quiet-spoken man, had once before experienced the traumatic dynamics of a racially changing community, while serving as pastor of an inner-city parish. It had been a painful experience for this genteel and gracious man to be engulfed and overwhelmed by an outpouring of racial hatred. Now, at St. Sabina's, with its 3,500 families—14-15,000 parishioners in all—and its convent, rectory, and school, McMahon was deeply concerned that history was going to repeat itself. No blacks lived within the parish boundaries yet, but by the late 1950s they were headed in Mc-Mahon's direction.

Several years earlier, in 1955, he had taken steps to maintain the attractiveness of the neighborhood within the parish boundaries. This heavily Irish-Catholic, largely residential neighborhood had been settled in the 1920s and '30s. As in a good portion of the older, closer-in Southwest Side, there were three-story walk-ups and a sprinkling of larger apartment buildings, but the blocks around St. Sabina's consisted mostly of single-family homes. Although generally the houses and commercial buildings were well kept and in good repair, there were pockets of blight in the neighborhood. McMahon interpreted such blight—on the basis of his previous inner-city experience—as a danger sign. He got a conservation program underway that included exhortations to parishioners to maintain the community's appearance. "Many people who are older than they were a few years ago are neglecting their property," a church newsletter warned. "The rest of us, younger and able, should be willing to give them a hand. Watch out for signs of blight. Report all illegal conversions [when, for example, a three-flat house was divided into four or five units]; attend conservation meetings. Work for the common good."

But McMahon knew that more was needed on the Southwest Side than a parish conservation program. He had talked to Egan about a large-scale community organizing strategy, and he had also talked with Monsignor Vincent Cooke at Catholic Charities about money; he was also prepared to contribute money from the parish treasury. Soon he was sounding out other pastors on the Southwest Side and trying to persuade Alinsky to take on the project. While these discussions were coming to fruition in the spring of 1958, Cardinal Stritch, on a visit to the Vatican, became ill and died; Alinsky's project did not officially begin until some months later, when the new Archbishop of Chicago, Albert Meyer, was appointed.

Stritch's nearly twenty-year reign had perpetuated the progressive image of the Archdiocese of Chicago, an image symbolized earlier by Cardinal Mundelein, a visible, strong supporter in the 1930s of Roosevelt and the New Deal. But for many liberals in Chicago, including some Catholics and many non-Catholics, "progressive" did not accurately describe the entire archdiocese. At the parish level, with a few exceptions, there was little that was progressive when it came to attitudes about race, and the most violent opposition to racial integration was typically in heavily Catholic neighborhoods. The fact that many such neighborhoods were physically close to the expanding black ghettos only heightened the political dilemmas for Church leaders. Alinsky had a great deal of respect for Stritch, especially for his concerns about race relations and the potential for violence. But Alinsky also appreciated the difficult position Stritch was in when it came to race—that he was often caught between the liberals, both Protestant liberals and those on the Catholic Interracial Council who often sounded holier-than-thou, and the fearful working-class Catholics on the South Side who resented the liberals' self-righteousness. "The blue-collar masses of Chicago, that was Stritch's main constituency," von Hoffman says, implying that when it came to race, the influence of religion took a back seat to the power of social and economic class. "He had a real problem, a problem that has taken many American liberals until now to recognize. But he understood it very well then and, of course, I think Saul and I understood it, too, but you simply could not explain it to some of these liberal nudniks."

Stritch's replacement, Meyer, who had earlier been Bishop of Milwaukee, was, in his own way, genuinely interested in trying to ameliorate the racial tensions in Chicago—and, of course, to find a way to preserve racially endangered parishes. Egan and Burke, who introduced Alinsky to him, talked to him about Alinsky's project. "Cardinal Meyer was very much in favor of it," Egan recalls. "He, Saul, Nick, and I went out to meet with the pastors [on the Southwest Side] and talk to them about it. [The cardinal] told them what it would cost and asked each pastor to contribute and said that they had permission to do so. Saul was very eloquent that day when he met all the pastors. These men didn't really know Cardinal Meyer yet. He was a scripture scholar. He was a humble, open man with a great social conscience but not the kind of man you'd find on a picket line." "He allowed us to do it" is the way Egan characterizes the overall message that Meyer delivered to the pastors on the Southwest Side. As another indication of his own progressive inclinations, Meyer appointed

Egan to a full-time position as executive director of the Cardinal's Conservation Committee.

At the beginning, there were mixed motives and understandings about the purpose of the project among the Catholic pastors on the Southwest Side. While Egan, for example, thinks that the motives of both Stritch and Meyer were quite honorable, he also says that a number of the priests "were only worried about blacks moving into the area." There was also more than a little ambiguity about Alinsky himself. Alinsky had not talked to these pastors about racial quotas. He had not brought up the ideas and themes he had discussed in his speech at Notre Dame. Rather, he talked more generally about the problem of racial violence, saying that if it continued it would destroy the community and that a broadly based community organization was needed to deal with racial change. They probably had only a dim awareness or understanding of who Alinsky was. His primary identity was with the Back of the Yards Neighborhood Council, and in Chicago in those days the Council was identified with keeping blacks out of the neighborhood.

The organizing process began in earnest in January 1959. Time was an important factor because the violence in transitional neighborhoods was worsening. In the neighborhoods nearest to the expanding ghetto, many whites had already left. Von Hoffman recalls that in sections of some neighborhoods the vacancy rate was as high as 30 percent. Alinsky and von Hoffman had only one clear goal: to set up a community congress as soon as possible. A congress would mean recognition and legitimacy; delegates from church groups, social and fraternal clubs, neighborhood associations, and local businesses would ratify a constitution, elect leaders, and adopt a program. In form, it would mirror the Back of the Yards Neighborhood Council and the Citizens Federation in Lackawanna, New York, where von Hoffman had been dispatched by Alinsky in 1956 to set up a community organization.

Funded in part by the Schwarzhaupt Foundation, the Lackawanna project was the result of Monsignor O'Grady's efforts to spread Alinsky's concepts—especially citizen participation and democratic processes—into more working-class Catholic communities. O'Grady had initially wanted Alinsky to organize a community in St. Louis, which Schwarzhaupt agreed to fund. But the leadership in St. Louis turned out to be too reactionary for O'Grady's tastes and he thought he had found a better situation in South Buffalo. When that fell apart, O'Grady, Alinsky, and the Schwarzhaupt money landed in Lackawanna, a town of 30,000 adjacent to Buffalo and dominated by Bethlehem Steel. It is more accurate to say, however, that Alinsky rarely landed in Lackawanna. The place held little interest for him, and he went along with the project only because of his friendship with

O'Grady. But it did provide some firsthand organizing experience for von Hoffman, who was there for six months, and for Ed Chambers, whom von Hoffman hired. Chambers worked there for two years and helped to organize the first community congress of the Lackawanna Citizens Federation. Lackawanna was a good learning experience for Chambers, but after two years he had had enough and joined Alinsky and von Hoffman in Chicago to help launch the project on the Southwest Side.

Chambers, who had grown up in a small Iowa town, had hitchhiked to Harlem after being bounced out of a Catholic seminary in 1954. "I lived for about two years in a settlement house in Harlem called Friendship House," he recalls, "working in this kooky commune, male and female, black and white all together. Our pay was six dollars a month. You could buy toothpaste, a couple of quarts of beer, that was it," says Chambers, an earthy, gangly, six-foot-four, small-town boy who never pretended to be an intellectual and whose heart as much as his head had taken him to Harlem. "One day, I went over to Harlem Hospital to give blood, and this black guy says, 'I don't know what you are doing, but you'd better start eating some beefsteak because your blood ain't no good, we can't take it.' " He periodically visited Dorothy Day, the inspirational radical Catholic whose newspaper *The Catholic Worker* took up the causes of labor, social justice, and world peace. When he was on the verge of being drafted into the Army, "she kind of tutored me," he says. He had had a deferment from the military while in the seminary: "In those days they were sending Roman Catholics to three years in jail because [we were] not recognized as conscientious objectors." A month before his case was to be decided, however, Chambers turned twenty-six, was no longer eligible for the draft, and no longer had to agonize over a possible jail sentence. It was about then that von Hoffman, who heard about Chambers's work with tenant organizations in Harlem from a professor at the University of Chicago, got in touch with him. "I had been using *Reveille for Radicals* in Harlem," Chambers says. "I said to myself, Jesus Christ, this guy I'd like to know." So when von Hoffman called, Chambers was more than interested. On a trip to Chicago, he met with Alinsky, O'Grady, and von Hoffman, and agreed to go to Lackawanna to organize, although he was somewhat worried—in spite of his familiarity with Alinsky's book—because he did not know how to organize a community from start to finish in line with Alinsky's methods. Not to worry, he was told by von Hoffman, who assured him that they would work closely with him and that he would receive intensive training. Little did Chambers know how eager von Hoffman was to get out of Lackawanna and how indifferent Alinsky was to the entire project:

I flew out of Midway Airport in Chicago, the first time I'd ever flown, and landed in Buffalo. Nick was going to meet me at the airport. No Nick. I called the hotel where he was staying. No answer in his room. I had him paged at the bar in the hotel dining room. "Oh, Ed, glad you're here. Grab a cab and come on over." Nick wasn't even living in Lackawanna; he was staying at the Lenox Hotel in Buffalo and going to the racetrack in the afternoon with a bartender friend. The next morning we went down to Lackawanna in a cab—Nick didn't have a car. I got a room in the Lackawanna Hotel. It was really a rooming house. It had no room phones—you had to go down to the main hall to use a phone—no air conditioning, no nothing. On the third day, Nick flew out of town. He said that he would be gone for a couple days. And I said, "Hey, you made me a promise to give me two months of intensive training." Nick says, "I'll be back." I did not see him for about six weeks. He gave me thirty-two Polish names . . . and I started to scratch around.

Chambers's training was mainly on-the-job and through the discussions he had with von Hoffman about the weekly reports he sent in. When it came time to set up the first community congress, Chambers got some long-distance help from von Hoffman and also relied on passages in *Reveille for Radicals*. On the day of the congress, Alinsky, Egan, and O'Grady came to town. "To my knowledge, Saul was in Lackawanna for one day," Chambers says. "Of course, he stayed up at the Statler Hilton in Buffalo."

Chambers came to Chicago in January 1959 as one of Alinsky's organizers for the Southwest Side project. "I moved into a basement apartment at Sixty-seventh and Peoria where I shared a closet with the lady who lived in the other basement apartment. I was paid $4,200, which was astronomical," Chambers says facetiously. "And I had to fight to get it, too." Von Hoffman's first assignment for Chambers immediately after he arrived in Chicago, where he had visited briefly only once before, was to get a handle on the Protestant churches on the Southwest Side. ("I was given the Protestant churches," he says, "because I was a young ex-seminarian and Alinsky was worried I would start talking theology to the priests, which, of course, they wouldn't understand.")

Nick said, "Find out where the Protestant parishes are. Saul wants to know what's out there." So within two days I gave him a rundown of every Protestant church—names, location. We had those dictabelt machines we talked into and I sent my report down. And so, within

two days, Alinsky sees this total rundown of all these fuckin' Protestant churches. This guy must be good, Alinsky must have thought.
Well, what I had done was, I got a map, went to the yellow pages,
and did a little driving around. I checked to see if the pastor's name
would be on that thing in front of the church. I just did a quickie
windshield survey, threw all that shit in a report. So I got off to a good
start.

　　Chambers was one of three organizers who began working in a rectangular area approximately fifty blocks long and thirty blocks wide—
bounded on the north by Sixty-seventh Street, on the south by the city
limits, and stretching from State Street on the east to Western Avenue.
Most of the organizing work was to be concentrated in a narrower rectangle centered on Eighty-seventh and Racine, but it was still a lot of territory
and people—about 200,000—to cover. Joseph Vilimas, who knew von
Hoffman and was hired by him, was in his early thirties, had grown up on
the South Side, and had been active in a community organization in the
Chatham-Avalon neighborhood, just east of Alinsky's project. Chatham
was a prime example of a changing neighborhood that seemed to symbolize
many of the problems, fears, and, for some, opportunities associated with
the changing racial scene in Chicago.
　　Among those who saw opportunity in the blacks' great need for
housing were real estate speculators. The mainline real estate industry in
Chicago had a long history of establishing and maintaining practices that
kept housing in white areas of Chicago out of reach of the black population.
As far back as the 1920s, for example, the Chicago Real Estate Board and
the Chicago Title and Trust Company cooperated with neighborhood
"improvement associations" to enforce restrictive covenants. Now, however, a number of aggressively entrepreneurial realtors were eager to sell
houses to blacks in certain white neighborhoods. Their tactics were simple:
scare white homeowners who lived in or near a transitional neighborhood
into selling cheap and then turn around and sell at a handsome profit to
black buyers. This was a feasible plan: white homeowners feared that if
blacks moved in, the value of their houses would plummet and they would
have difficulty selling them even at reduced prices. On the one hand,
mortgages from conventional sources dried up in such situations; on the
other hand, a real estate speculator, with the promise of a cash deal, could
buy from panicky white sellers at well below fair market prices and then
sell at inflated prices. A "panic peddler" or "blockbuster" could buy a
house from a white homeowner for, say, $10,000 and turn around and sell
it to a black for $19,000. The black, shut out of the mortgage market, would

buy on contract from the speculator with a small down payment and exorbitant monthly interest charges—at three or four times the going rate—and if he missed a payment, he lost everything. The speculator then merely started the process over again by finding another black buyer. By the time the house had been recycled through a number of buyers, as was often the case, he could often afford to walk away from the property, into which he had put little or no money, with a substantial profit. For an especially ambitious speculator who had a score or more of such houses, the profits could be considerable.

When von Hoffman hired Vilimas, he was taking on a volunteer neighborhood activist who had firsthand experience with the dynamics of a racially changing neighborhood. Vilimas thinks that what piqued von Hoffman's and Alinsky's interest in him was a successful organizing campaign that he helped to run to shut down the bars and dives along Seventy-ninth Street between State Street and Cottage Grove. "We essentially took on the mob in a referendum," Vilimas recalls of the strategy based on a Chicago law that permits voters to vote their precinct dry.

Vilimas, Chambers, and von Hoffman started to work behind the shaky "Berlin Wall," the racial dividing line that ran along Sixty-seventh Street, the northern boundary of Alinsky's new project. Although there was a division of labor among the three organizers, there was little else that was orderly or predictable about their task. For example, while Alinsky's men could depend on Monsignor McMahon at St. Sabina's from the beginning, the support of Monsignor Patrick J. Molloy at St. Leo's was another matter entirely.

P. J. Molloy headed one of the largest parishes in Chicago, which meant that it was one of the largest in the United States. The size of the physical plant at Seventy-eighth and Emerald awed von Hoffman and Chambers. "They had two churches in that parish that operated every Sunday," von Hoffman says, "one in the official church and another in the parish high school. Starting at five-thirty or six in the morning on Sundays, they had a mass about every three-quarters of an hour in both buildings. They were all filled. You're talking about a very big operation, about five thousand families." In addition to the church and high school, there was also a grammar school and a rectory.

P. J. Molloy's style was Chicago crude. He was unpolished and bigoted, shrewd and politically well connected—he was a good friend of Mayor Daley and South Side ward politicians—and according to various stories and rumors, had had connections with the mob. In *The Bootleggers,* for example, Kenneth Allsop's account of the Capone era in Chicago, Allsop tells the story of how the family of the famous florist-gangster Dion

O'Banion sought a proper Catholic burial for their loved one after a burly gentleman in a fedora and overcoat had walked into O'Banion's Wabash Avenue shop with two short, stocky companions and pumped six slugs into his upper body. Cardinal Mundelein would not permit O'Banion's burial in consecrated ground, nor would any bishop or monsignor officiate at a graveside service—which left the spiritual duty and civic honor to young Patrick J. Molloy. Apparently this was not the last time that Molloy crossed paths with Chicago mobsters. When he was in his mid-thirties, he either fled to South America to escape the wrath of disgruntled mobsters or was banished there by Mundelein for consorting with them, according to differing but similar tales.

The now older Molloy was no less shifty and colorful, a source of fascination and amusement to von Hoffman in particular. Von Hoffman started to visit Molloy frequently and developed a relationship with him. It was not a dull assignment. Somewhere in his checkered past, Molloy had acquired a reputation as a great wheelman. His skill had not atrophied, as von Hoffman discovered on a visit to the rectory one day during the baseball season:

> When it got to be twelve or twelve-thirty in the Molloy head, he would suddenly hear the plunk of horsehide on ash, and he would say, "Let's go to the ballpark." We'd go downstairs and get in the world's most powerful Buick. Molloy never accepted that they had made Wabash Avenue a one-way street going south. He was not prepared to deal with that. So it was one-way south except for the world's most powerful Buick. It was lump-in-your-throat time, and I will tell you that that was the world's most hair-raising automobile ride as we went north to Thirty-fifth Street, where he made a screeching left. There was this police sergeant on duty in front of Comiskey Park. Molloy would drive the world's most powerful Buick up on the sidewalk right in front of the main ticket booth behind home plate, get out of the car, flip the keys to the sergeant, and we'd roar into Molloy's box. Daley was often there, John McGuane, a county commissioner, and all those wonderful people.

One did not have to be sanctimonious to be repulsed by Molloy's character deficiencies, including his blatant bigotry. (There had been news accounts in the not too distant past of his angrily shooing away a black who had strayed into St. Leo's to attend a church service.) Nevertheless, because Molloy was an influential figure who ran one of Chicago's biggest parishes, Alinsky's organizers could not dismiss or ignore him. He had to be dealt with—and so, too, did the attitudes that he reflected in his working-class Irish parish.

According to the definitions of Alinsky's organizers, the ultraconservatives, those who were violently opposed to blacks moving into the Southwest Side, were not as numerous as the moderates, who, while frightened by the changes swirling about them and hopeful that the invasion in their area could be stopped, were not inclined toward violent opposition. Many of these people, who liked their neighborhood, would not necessarily move out merely because one or two blacks had moved in. Then there were a small number of liberals scattered around who were pro-integration—a few journalists from the downtown newspapers, for example, some labor-union activists, and a number of young families who had been active in the Young Christian Workers and now were part of the Christian Family movement. The ultraconservatives were especially important, however, because they tended to set the dominant tone. Some of them were literally violent, ready to stop a black move-in by any means. Others encouraged or supported violent opposition.

There was no easy way for Alinsky's men to deal with these conservatives. In the early stages, Chambers had an unexpected, scary confrontation with some of them near the north end of the organizing area, where much of the violence was occurring. A man whom Chambers had identified as a conservative ringleader agreed to a one-on-one meeting. "Ten o'clock tonight at my house," he said. They sat in his kitchen, a bottle of Jim Beam on the table, the man shooting down a number of jiggers as his friends began arriving—much to Chambers's surprise. Seven or eight guys, each coming in through the back door, surrounded Chambers, and the talk quickly became angry. He began to suspect a setup. "You're a commie," one said, a slightly lesser offense than being a nigger-lover, although Chambers was soon called that, too. "And Alinsky's a nigger-lover," somebody added. Chambers's best defensive weapon was to remind everybody that he was working with people like Monsignor Molloy—and that they were trying to "stabilize the neighborhood," the ambiguous code words that he and the other organizers used in the beginning, almost never the words "integration" and "segregation." And then Chambers went on the offensive: "You guys are kinda dumb. I've been talking to some of the ladies in the neighborhood and—I know you guys don't do this—but some of the porches are getting blown off people's homes, like it happened the other night. I talked to a couple of those ladies the next morning, and you know what they said? They said, 'Chambers, I'm not going to raise my kid on a battlefield. What if they put the dynamite under the wrong porch? It's dark, and what if they make a mistake? I'm moving.' This kind of activity induces white flight even though you think it's preventive." Chambers invited them to keep tabs on what he was doing in the neighborhood—and finally, by 1 a.m., they let him go, unconvinced but unprovoked. "I don't think they *planned* to hurt me," Chambers says, "but that night was tough."

For the first three or four months, little headway was made. But, perhaps equally important, Alinsky's men at least had not riled the conservatives into active opposition. And on the plus side, they had started to recruit supporters. McMahon gave von Hoffman and Vilimas entrée to a number of lay leaders of parish clubs at St. Sabina's. The organizers would get the names of thirty or thirty-five people and would start to call on them. "Monsignor McMahon suggested I talk with you," they would begin, and then they would start to get to know these people. The going was much slower at other Catholic parishes, including Molloy's, and Christ the King and St. Barnabas in Beverly, the upper-middle-class neighborhood farthest from the expanding black ghetto, where many Chicago executives, professionals, and powers in the Democratic Party lived. Part of the problem at Christ the King was that the pastor wanted to distance himself from the potentially controversial project. So he directed an assistant, the young Andrew Greeley, to be his contact with the Alinsky organizers.

Cardinal Meyer's support had been essential, of course, but the tough old Irish priests on the South Side did not move until they were ready to move. Alinsky understood this, and warned von Hoffman that men like Molloy could not be bullied by the archdiocesan office downtown. Von Hoffman recalls that, in the early going, Ed Burke, who often spoke for Cardinal Meyer, "said to me, 'You can say that you are talking for me whenever you think it is necessary out in any of these parishes.' Which is just enormous formal power. But afterward, Saul says, 'But don't ever do it!' "

One of Chambers's early Protestant contacts was the Reverend Bob Christ at Seventh Presbyterian. Christ, who had come to this small church after graduating from McCormick Seminary in Chicago in 1954, was immediately appreciated by Chambers and von Hoffman as someone special, intellectually gifted and politically adroit. He had been in the service at the end of World War II and then did graduate work in philosophy for two years at Princeton, where he was influenced by Alinsky's good friend Jacques Maritain, who was then at Princeton's Institute for Advanced Study. "The reason I moved from graduate school and philosophy was because of Maritain," says Christ, who did not discover Alinsky's relationship with the Thomist philosopher until the project on the Southwest Side was further along.

Obviously I did not become a Catholic, but Maritain showed me that there was a respectability to Christian theology. . . . He was a gentle, loving, open, sympathetic person who showed great depth and strength. At the time, I know, I would have said I was being impressed with his rational, well-worked-out neo-Thomistic theology, less than with who he was as a person. But in retrospect I think I would reverse that. The man showed me that a Christian could use his mind to explain the world and where the world was going, and that in Christ there was an answer. This was 1949 to 1951. The Cold War was pretty much at its peak. We were aware of the nuclear holocaust happening and our dream that we had at the end of World War II—that now the millennium had come—was pretty well shattered. And Maritain, showing that there was an answer within the Christian faith to these dilemmas, . . . turned me toward theology.

From his self-described boyhood as "Presbyterian in the backwoods of Pennsylvania," Christ landed the urban assignment at Seventh Presbyterian after going through the urban studies program at McCormick. When he arrived in 1954, race was not yet seen as a problem in his primarily blue-collar congregation set in the middle of a Catholic neighborhood. But things began to change faster than anybody, including Christ, had expected. By 1958, his congregation was both "apprehensive and head-in-the-sand" regarding the changing population. "They were no more enlightened than what Pat Molloy or John McMahon had to deal with. I would say almost identical," Christ observes, suggesting that social and economic class was, again, more potent than religious affiliation.

Christ had many conversations with Chambers and von Hoffman and, eventually, with Alinsky. There was an early meeting of minds. Christ did not see himself as a conventional liberal. "In all my life in the church, I had never belonged to a social action committee." But he seems to have associated his own proclivity toward independent thought and action with a similar proclivity in Alinsky's men. And there was another attraction:

This sounds like *True Confessions,* [but] Nick, Ed, and Saul in their own way offered people like me and some others who were hungry to make our mark in the world a way to do it. We sure as heck couldn't do it in a two-bit church in Englewood or Chatham, where things were sort of going down the tubes. And we were, I think, authentically concerned about some of the wrongs, but the way we were going at them was so trivial that we knew that it was only a finger in the dike. Alinsky offered an opening, an opportunity to make it in an area of concern. It was more than selfish ambition, more than trying to get to be a church executive and that sort of thing. What Saul had to offer was a device, a methodology and a vision that something could be done.

Christ was not put off by the heavy Catholic involvement, as some Protestant clergy were. On the other hand, he does not deny that "I pretty much had the standard middle 1950s Protestant point of view that, you know, Catholics fought Martin Luther, they played bingo, they had confession, and they weren't intellectually respectable." In fact, in the early stages there was a great amount of suspicion in some Protestant circles in Chicago about Alinsky and the Southwest Side project. When word started to spread that the seed money for the project had come from Catholic sources, some Protestant clergy wondered whether the project was primarily an anti-integrationist ploy, and in the case of one churchman, suspicion turned almost immediately into hostility. Walter Kloetzli, in charge of urban programs for the Lutheran Church, did not approve of Saul Alinsky and his methods. He did not approve of church involvement in power politics. He also had little doubt that Alinsky was doing the bidding of the Archdiocese of Chicago and was trying to organize an essentially segregationist community group whose highest priority was to preserve the large, important Catholic parishes. Kloetzli was ready to lead a campaign to discredit Alinsky and his methods.

In spite of such rumblings, Bob Christ continued to be impressed with what von Hoffman and Chambers were saying, and he soon began to meet with Catholic clergy. He also began to spend a great amount of time and energy educating his own parishioners. It was quickly obvious to Christ that he was much more amenable to the kind of community organization that Alinsky's men had sketched than his parishioners would be. "I think that if I did a couple of things right, it probably was my beginning to work with the congregation and with its leadership relatively early to move them along on this. Some of the other clergy did not do that. . . . I had enough political sense to realize that if I was going to do anything in this, then I had to have a strong political base and that involved informing, explaining, trying to bring along the leadership."

Christ's persuasive approach with his congregation was both subtle and purposeful. He wanted to help his lay leaders discover for themselves that a new community organization on the Southwest Side was "an answer" that the congregation should embrace. He seldom dealt with the

Saul Alinsky, thirteen years old, 1922.
(Courtesy of Kathryn Wilson)

Saul's mother, Sarah.
(Courtesy of Kathryn Wilson)

The first meeting of the trustees of the Industrial Areas Foundation, at the Waldorf Astoria Hotel in New York, August 24, 1940. *Left to right:* G. Howland Shaw, chief of foreign service personnel at the U.S. State Department; Kathryn Lewis, daughter of CIO president John L. Lewis; Marshall Field III; Bernard J. Sheil, auxiliary bishop of Chicago; Saul Alinsky.   (UPI/Bettmann Newsphotos)

Fr. Edward Plawinski, first president of the Back of the Yards Neighborhood Council; Joseph Meegan, executive secretary of the BYNC; and Alinsky. Early 1940s. (Courtesy of Joseph Meegan)

A landmark moment in Chicago labor-union history, when clergy—who were also leaders of the Back of the Yards Neighborhood Council—joined the Packinghouse Workers' picket line at the Chicago Union Stockyards, January 17, 1946. *Left to right:* Herman Brauer, pastor of St. Martini's Evangelical Lutheran Church; Miss Ellseabelle Goss of the YMCA; Alinsky; Joseph Meegan; Ambrose Ondrak, assistant pastor of St. Michael's Church. (UPI/Bettmann Newsphotos)

Alinsky and unidentified man on a Wisconsin fishing trip, probably in the late 1940s. (Courtesy of Irene McInnis)

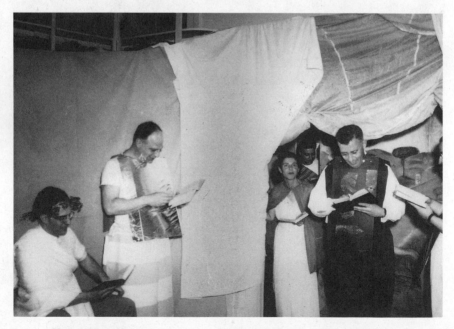

Hyde Park play-reading group presenting *The Road to Rome*, 1947. *Left to right:* Leon Despres; Richard Meyer; Marie Meyer; Alinsky. (Courtesy of Marian Despres)

Saul's daughter, Kathryn, 6, and her mother, Helene.
(Courtesy of Kathryn Wilson)

Saul with Kathryn and David, 2.   (Courtesy of Kathryn Wilson)

Meegan and Alinsky outside the BYNC office, 1949.
(Courtesy of Joseph Meegan)

Meegan and Alinsky, and Bishop Sheil, ca. 1949.
(Courtesy of Joseph Meegan)

Alinsky interviewing John L. Lewis, 1948.
(Courtesy of Chase Washington)

Leaders of the Community Service Organization (CSO) in Los Angeles, 1954. *First row, beginning second from left:* Edward Roybal; Fred Ross; Alinsky.   (Courtesy of Fred Ross)

In 1955, Cesar Chavez (first row, fifth from right) was completing his second year on Alinsky's IAF payroll, working with Fred Ross (first row, fourth from left) to organize CSO chapters throughout California. A decade later, he set out on his own to organize farm workers, successfully employing a national boycott of California grapes to force growers to the bargaining table. Saul Alinsky is at far left in the second row.   (Courtesy of Fred Ross)

The boss with his protégé Nicholas von Hoffman in Alinsky's office, late 1950s.
(Courtesy of Nicholas von Hoffman)

A portrait of Alinsky by the Chicago artist
Annette Cremin Byrne, 1961.
(Courtesy of the artist)

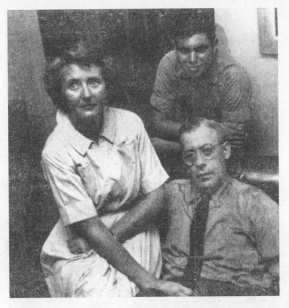

Alinsky with his second wife, Jean, and his son,
David, 15, 1959.   *(The Southtown Economist)*

Alinsky (second row, fourth from left) at an audience in 1958 with Pope Pius XII.
(Courtesy of Irene McInnis)

Alinsky in Woodlawn, the Chicago South Side community where he won national attention for establishing the Temporary Woodlawn Organization (TWO) in the early 1960s.   (AP/Wide World Photos)

Alinsky in a pensive pose in his office, 1964.
(AP/Wide World Photos)

TWO's leader, the Reverend Arthur Brazier (leaning forward), preparing to speak at a civil rights rally in Chicago's Soldier Field in 1966. Seated to Brazier's right is Dr. Martin Luther King, Jr.; the rally was part of Dr. King's Chicago Freedom campaign, his first major effort to confront racial discrimination in a Northern city through the nonviolent tactics he had pioneered in the South.   (Courtesy of Arthur Brazier)

Brazier addressing a Monday night meeting of TWO's steering committee in 1969. Seated to Brazier's right is the newly elected Congressman for the Second District, Abner Mikva. (Courtesy of Arthur Brazier)

In Princeton, New Jersey, 1966. *Left to right:* Msgr. John J. Egan; the Thomist philosopher Jacques Maritain; Alinsky; and Irene McInnis, whom he married in 1970.   (Courtesy of John J. Egan)

Alinsky speaking at an April 1967 demonstration in Flemington, New Jersey, to protest Eastman Kodak's refusal to honor a minority job hiring agreement. Kodak's annual stockholders' meeting was in progress nearby. The man directly behind Alinsky is Minister Franklin D. R. Florence, president of FIGHT, the group Alinsky had played a key role in organizing in Rochester, New York, Kodak's headquarters.
(Courtesy of the Industrial Areas Foundation)

FIGHT supporters listening to Alinsky in Flemington.   (AP/Wide World Photos)

Alinsky at a FIGHT meeting in Rochester, shortly before the protest demonstration at Kodak's annual meeting.   (AP/Wide World Photos)

Alinsky and the militant civil rights leader Stokely Carmichael share a platform at a meeting in Detroit in January 1967, when Carmichael acknowledged FIGHT as a prime example of Black Power, the controversial phrase he helped to popularize. (UPI/Bettmann Newsphotos)

Alinsky receiving a briefing from Ed Chambers, his organizer in Rochester, in 1966. Upon Alinsky's death six years later, Chambers succeeded him as IAF executive director.   (NYT Pictures)

Alinsky and Gordon Sherman, president of Midas Muffler International, in Chicago, sometime in the late 1960s. Sherman's foundation helped Alinsky launch his training institute for organizers. (Courtesy of Mrs. Gordon Sherman)

Lecturing, early 1970s.
(UPI/Bettmann Newsphotos)

Alinsky commissioned this portrait photograph
by Yousuf Karsh in the late 1960s.
(Courtesy of Irene McInnis)

In his office, February 1969.   (Declan Haun)

Near his home in Carmel, California, in December 1968.   (Declan Haun)

issue in his Sunday sermons, but rather talked to people in one-to-one encounters or small groups. To doubters, of whom there were many, Christ's gentle but firm challenge—"probably something I consciously or unconsciously picked up from Ed and Nick and Saul"—was the question of whether anybody had a better answer. Except for the most stubborn or incorrigibly racist, it was difficult to come up with a better—or at least a more convincing—response. It took a year or more before he felt that he had a fairly good base within the congregation—a group of people who at least had come to think that a new approach was worth a try. After a time, he was able to lead many of his parishioners to take unfamiliar but important interim steps, to say to them, for example, "Let's take a chance and go to the parish house of that Catholic church and talk to some Catholics who want to do something about the community's problems." Such small ecumenical acts between Protestants and Catholics were rare at that time in Chicago, radical departures from the status quo.

By the spring of 1959, Alinsky's men were ready to call a meeting to announce the formation of the Provisional Organization for the Southwest Community (POSC). Until then, they kept a low profile. Chambers says that they intentionally did not have an office for the first several months to avoid calling attention to themselves. He also remembers when Molloy, who had not yet made a cash contribution, donated office space. "We ended up in a place Molloy gave us on Seventy-ninth Street, church property he had bought to put in a parking lot. He let us use a commercial storefront, but we had to have windows all the way through it. He says, 'You put glass in so that people who walk by on the street can see in and see that there is no hanky-panky going on.' "

Molloy was one of about "300 community leaders from 80 organizations," as the Chicago *Daily News* reported, who showed up at the Park Manor VFW hall to launch the POSC on May 25. Molloy and John McMahon were there, along with several other Catholic pastors. Steve McMahon, pastor of St. Theresa, Little Flower, was not, however. Neither was Monsignor Patrick Gleeson, the pastor of Christ the King in affluent Beverly, on the southern edge of the project. As for the Protestants, Bob Christ was joined by more than a dozen of his colleagues. Chambers had done a magnificent job with the Protestant churches. And, as with the Back of the Yards Neighborhood Council, there were also representatives from civic and fraternal organizations and businesses, too. In fact, the man who was elected president of the POSC at the first meeting in the VFW hall was a well-known South Side banker and former real estate man, Donald O'Toole.

O'Toole, whose first contact with Saul Alinsky in the early 1940s had been unpleasant, saw himself as a tough-minded businessman who was also concerned about social problems. He had followed in his father's footsteps when he went into the real estate business on the South Side after graduating from the University of Notre Dame in 1931. As a youngster, he was as fascinated with the nuances and lore of real estate as other boys were with baseball. "I had worked in [my father's business] every summer since I was in the sixth grade as an office boy," O'Toole says. "My father used to take me to lunch at an inner club of the real estate board he belonged to. I would listen in fascination to these fellows," old-timers who would talk of their experiences rebuilding Chicago after the great fire of 1871. So O'Toole appreciated that real estate was more than a way to make a living; it was also a way to understand the social and political history of a great city. Later, during the Depression years when O'Toole often had nothing to do, he spent a lot of time at the library reading real estate histories of the city. "I learned a great deal about the cycles of the real estate business and the development of Chicago and the influences that caused deterioration." Soon he had firsthand experience with some of the causes of neighborhood deterioration. "I moved back into the house where I was raised in Woodlawn just east of the University of Chicago in 1937. We spent three very uncomfortable years there and finally moved out. It was bad when we moved in; we didn't realize how the neighborhood had deteriorated. What had happened was that for the World's Fair of 1893 a lot of bad buildings had been put up throughout Woodlawn, badly laid out and badly constructed. Unfortunately, they were terribly durable buildings." Although he knew that the deterioration of a neighborhood was always due to a complex set of linked factors, O'Toole had a clear vision of what he thought was the essential sequence: When a stock of older dwellings falls into disrepair, "an area becomes undesirable. When an area becomes undesirable, undesirables move in."

In O'Toole's view, this process of deterioration was well along in Woodlawn by the late 1930s. The "undesirables" were poorer whites, not blacks, who had been unable to move east of Cottage Grove Avenue into Woodlawn, thanks in part to the joint efforts of local property owners and the University of Chicago. (O'Toole was an officer of the Woodlawn Property Owners League. "Being vice president, my job was membership, getting people to join. I had nothing to do with getting restrictive covenants signed, and I would have nothing to do with it. I didn't like it," he says.)

After three years of working very hard on the problems in Woodlawn, he felt he had reached an end. "I hated the injustice of it, but mostly I hated the ignorance," by which O'Toole meant the unrecognized futility of saving Woodlawn through the efforts of the property owners association and the university. "It couldn't be done," he thought. On a rainy Sunday afternoon, he wrote a letter to the university telling them just that. "You and I are engaged in the stupidest venture we ever got into," he remembers writing. "The economic pressure on the blacks to get in here is far greater than the economic pressure of the whites to stay," anticipating that poor Negroes recently arrived from the South would inevitably push into the area.

O'Toole's next instructive experience with neighborhood deterioration, housing, and the companion factors of class and race occurred in the early years of World War II, when he and some investors attempted to build housing for black defense workers on the South Side, a row-house project on an eighty-acre parcel, farmland bought from the Pullman Company on Princeton Avenue between Ninetieth and Ninety-fourth streets. For O'Toole, however, Princeton Park turned into a series of nightmares. He and his associates argued with the sewer and water departments over standards that, O'Toole believed, were intentionally set higher than they were for white developments. Then he ran into problems with mortgage financing. A financially desperate O'Toole found doors being slammed shut because he was developing housing for blacks. The ugliest episode involved a protest by some whites who lived in the nearby Roseland neighborhood. A mob descended on his office after he was vilified in a local newspaper. Even his own relatives grew hostile, and a cordon of police was called out to ward off protesters when construction finally began.

Soon, as an honor of sorts for the trouble he had had, O'Toole was invited to serve on the board of the Metropolitan Housing Council, a collection of civic leaders, academics, and progressive businessmen in Chicago who supported programs to improve housing. Coincidentally, Alinsky also joined the board at about the same time, and he and O'Toole quickly tangled over a proposal made by Elizabeth Wood to build a large housing project just to the south of Roseland. "I came out of that with a healthy respect for Alinsky's ability and a wholesome fear of the man," O'Toole remembers. "He meant no harm to me, but I was a roadblock . . . and mowing me down was unfortunate but necessary to the gaining of his ends."

More than fifteen years later, O'Toole took Alinsky, Nick von Hoffman, and Ed Chambers to lunch at the Chicago Athletic Club. O'Toole was ambivalent about assuming a leadership role in the Southwest Side project. On the one hand, he had both an interest in the well-being of the community and attachments to the Catholic parishes there. He was running the Standard Bank at Seventy-ninth and Ashland, which he had organized in 1947, and from the beginning the bank did well. "We drew a lot of our support from the pastors of Catholic churches," he says. "They used to say it became a matter of confessing if you weren't banking at Standard. We supplied personnel for their carnivals, we did a lot of things." On the other hand, O'Toole could see that the old arrangements were in jeopardy, and he had a special appreciation of the magnitude of the Church's jeopardized real estate investment. But he had not forgotten his bitter experiences in Woodlawn and with Princeton Park. He did not want to experience again the hatred and turmoil that the issues of race and community control generated.

Finally, however, O'Toole agreed not only to get involved but to become president of the Provisional Organization. "Either this works or I'll never touch anything like this again," he remembers saying. He was intrigued with the concept of priests and ministers in key roles helping a community to pull together and to initiate a politically effective program. And he was even comfortable with Alinsky's notion that, if everything went according to plan, the Southwest Side would peacefully accept a limited number of black residents. For him, social class, not race, was the critical factor. So when Alinsky talked about blacks of a similar class moving into the neighborhoods, he was, in effect, articulating a theory that O'Toole understood and agreed with.

In spite of O'Toole's growing enthusiasm for the project, Alinsky was very guarded at the luncheon meeting with him. He had agreed to the meeting reluctantly, and only after O'Toole demanded it. Before O'Toole went out on a limb, he wanted to talk with the boss. Perhaps Alinsky was no more guarded at the luncheon than his organizers had been in the community, especially when the subject of race came up. It was a topic to be downplayed or deflected, as Chambers had tried to do in his tense late-night kitchen debate. Suddenly, however, the rug was pulled out from under their attempts at deflection, subtlety, and subterfuge. And the one who pulled the rug was none other than Saul Alinsky.

The occasion was a hearing in Chicago on housing discrimination by the President's Commission on Civil Rights. Alinsky had less than forty-eight hours to get his testimony written, and the small IAF office was thrown into a tizzy. Although his statement would be similar to the speech he gave at Notre Dame several months before, he told von Hoffman to prepare a revised draft.

Alinsky's testimony focused on his call for racial quotas in neighborhood housing, and it hit the front pages of the Chicago newspapers, not only because his proposed solution to the city's most menacing problem was controversial but also because of an accompanying bombshell, the virtual endorsement of Alinsky's plan in a statement submitted to the commission by none other than the Archbishop of Chicago. (Archbishop Meyer's statement was presented on his behalf by Jack Egan.) If it dovetailed nicely with Alinsky's, there was a good reason: Nick von Hoffman had written not only his boss's testimony but also the archbishop's. While deploring racial discrimination that affected all blacks, a key passage of Meyer's statement stressed that an emerging black middle class, like its predecessors of European extraction, "ought to have the choice of leaving the ethnic community if they so wish . . . [and] it is not rash on our part to suggest that the time has come for practical measures to that end. . . . We must have community organization to ensure that Negroes do gain access to our communities, but not to the degree that we merely extend the boundaries of the racial ghetto."

Alinsky reveled in the commotion that he had started. He wrote to Gordon Clapp, his friend in New York, who had recently joined the IAF board:

> This whole town is suffering from severe, chronic color constipation, and I was out to administer a sizeable mental laxative. You should have been here to have seen the urban bowels move as they have! . . . The city was horrified when I stated a few simple truisms such as "No white neighborhood wants Negroes," and other obvious facts of that kind. The ensuing situation has made a Gilbert and Sullivan comedy look like a Greek tragedy. The Catholic Interracial Council now believes that I am "immoral," but they don't want to discuss the Archbishop's position. All of the do-gooders who have always ostensibly been against segregation are shocked by this, and are off in the metaphysics of means and ends. . . . I am bemused by the fact that all those who talk about integration, such as the kind of re-districting of schools now being contemplated in New York City, or any other kind of "integrated situations," talk about *percentages, ratios, proportions, balanced population,* and every other kind of synonym for quota, and then throw up their hands so high in righteous indignation when somebody comes out and says it openly. . . . The problem simply could not continue to be swept under the carpet because the stuff under the carpet was already six feet high!

Alinsky claimed that "the Negro community as a whole has responded with 'Amen!' . . . [while] the white bigots in this town have gone into a frenzy where the name of Alinsky today is infinitely more unpopular than the Supreme Court. All in all it's been, and is, a gay show."

Things were not so gay, however, on the Southwest Side. Personal attacks and rumors about Alinsky started to fly around the neighborhood bars. But as they were reported back to him by von Hoffman, he was inevitably ready with a quip. When he heard that some were saying that he was illegitimate, he smiled and said, "Sometimes I have wondered." They are saying that you raped a thirteen-year-old girl, he was told. "If I only had the vitality!" he cracked. "I assume that by next week it will be thirteen-year-old Negro girls, and that by the week after that we will be opening the doors to the Protocols of Zion and I will be drinking their blood, eating their flesh, etc.; and after all, who knows, as inflation grows and the cost of living keeps rising, why anything is possible." However crude, clumsy, and absurd each attack was, cumulatively they seemed to lay the foundation for one of the most menacing slanders: that Alinsky was a communist. On the Southwest Side, communists were as dangerous and unwelcome as lepers. The Red-baiting of Alinsky on the Southwest Side sprang from the wacky logic that American racists have used in the United States through much of the twentieth century. In this instance, the bogus syllogism was: integration is supported by communists, Alinsky is for integration, therefore Alinsky is a communist. That Alinsky was working with the Catholic Church, or that he had had a long, close, and public relationship with Bishop Sheil, did little to offset the slander. And, of course, Alinsky's comrades—von Hoffman, Chambers, and Vilimas—were tarred with the same brush.

Not long after Alinsky's testimony, some of the most rabid anti-integrationists called for a community meeting to discuss the new threat to the Southwest Side. At the scheduled hour, the VFW at Eighty-seventh and Brainerd was packed. Von Hoffman had arranged for Monsignor McMahon to speak on behalf of the POSC organizing effort, and he and the other organizers decided they would go to the meeting to observe. Chambers recalls:

> They start the meeting right on time, everybody is in place, and these other guys are crowding in from the bar, so we're not right up against the back wall. There are these guys who had gotten between us and the back wall. Somebody announced, "We're going to start tonight's meeting with the singing of 'The Star-Spangled Banner' and the Pledge of Allegiance." I mumbled through "The Star-Spangled Banner," and then as we were starting the Pledge of Allegiance, all of a sudden I feel—I don't know what the hell it is—like a finger or a gun: "Say it, you commies, say it," right in my ear, and another guy on Nick says, "Say it, you commies." I say to Nick, "Nick, you haven't got your hand over your heart."

They had barely survived the Pledge of Allegiance when the first order of business was an announcement summoning von Hoffman, Chambers, and Vilimas to the front of the hall, where they were told that they were being expelled from the meeting. They were immediately grabbed by a number of men and unceremoniously hustled toward an exit at the rear of the big hall.

Had Alinsky known just how powerful a charge his and the archbishop's testimony would become, he might have found a different forum or approach. By the end of May, nearly three weeks after his appearance before the President's Commission, he wrote again to Gordon Clapp: "Today at a luncheon with a number of priests I finally got across the idea of accepting the quota proposal (obviously not through any moral argument) but through the analogy of vaccination and this scored to a telling degree—the idea of being inoculated with a certain quota of Negroes for white immunity. Gad, the things you have to think of in this work!"

But in fact, the dust refused to settle. Throughout the summer of 1959, Alinsky's organizers continued to run into the tireless efforts of the hardcore anti-integrationists and self-styled anti-communists. One such ragtag operation, We, the People, fired off a steady barrage of scurrilous attacks. The Committee to Preserve the Southwest Community also employed sleazy, Red-baiting tactics. The racial-quota plan, the committee wrote in one typical broadside, "is the plan of Saul Alinsky, radical sociologist who was the front man in Chicago for Herb March, National Committeeman of the Communist Party U.S.A., according to Joseph Poskonka, Communist agent for the FBI, who testified before the House Un-American Activities Committee in Chicago (May, 1959) and whose testimony is published by that Committee under the title 'Communist Infiltration in the Chicago Area.' " The lies and distortions sounded like plausible truths to enough people on the Southwest Side so that Alinsky's organizers regularly encountered hostile questions and attacks at community meetings. At the height of the Red-baiting in the summer of 1959, Joe Vilimas recalls, "people that I went to high school with and that I knew in the neighborhood, I mean, really some friends, told me never to come to their homes again. And then they pulled out of the organization. Even my mother got the pamphlets. She wondered what the hell I was doing with my life—did I understand the implications . . . of being called a communist? . . . And there was a very tense period when parishioners of the various churches were coming to their pastors and telling them they better get out or I'm going to get out of the church."

Since Alinsky's identification with the community organizing project had become an albatross, by the middle of August he and the Industrial

Areas Foundation officially severed ties with the POSC. Behind the scenes, however, nothing changed: Chambers and Vilimas still reported to von Hoffman, who became discreet about being seen in certain neighborhoods on the Southwest Side, and he in turn reported to Alinsky. It was a cosmetic, tactical maneuver that apparently had little effect by itself, except that it did temporarily seem to tranquilize some of the nervous stomachs among the POSC leaders.

Ironically, for all of the problems that were triggered by Alinsky's testimony, there was also an important—albeit serendipitous—benefit. It started the night at the VFW hall when von Hoffman, Chambers, and Vilimas were told to leave the meeting. As they were being pushed toward the rear exit, Chambers heard somebody call the name of a man whom he had been trying unsuccessfully to meet with for weeks.

"You're not Jim Norris, are you?" Chambers asked. James R. Norris, a man in his fifties, was a grade school dropout who had left his native Kentucky as a teenager and eventually migrated to Chicago in the 1920s; he was president of the East Gresham Community Association, one of the many homeowners groups that dotted the Southwest Side. He was an ironworker, hard-drinking and strong.

"Yeah, what's it to you?" Chambers recalls Norris answering.

"Are you part of this kind of crap? Did you see what just happened to us?"

"Serves you right, coming around here trying to have a nigger on every block," Norris replied.

"Buy you a drink," Chambers said.

"No."

"What's the matter, you afraid of me?"

"Nah, I'm not afraid of any commie nigger-lovers."

"Why don't you sit down and talk to me? I've been trying to reach you."

"Yeah, my wife said you called all the time."

"Well, if you're not afraid to talk, can we schedule something for tomorrow? When's a good time? You name the place."

And that is how Ed Chambers finally met one of the most important neighborhood leaders among the conservatives on the Southwest Side. "He was the head of a powerful civic association, and he was raising havoc with us," Chambers says. "Every place we'd go, he would come behind or he'd been there before, saying, 'Watch out for these Alinsky communist organizers.'" Chambers also believed that Norris was playing a pivotal role among lending institutions and the police and fire departments to keep blacks out of the Southwest Side. Alinsky's men knew that some of the banks would buy houses to prevent blacks from buying them and keep the houses off the market until white buyers could be found. Chambers heard that Norris was one of the key bird dogs who spotted houses that were for sale and possibly in danger of being sold to blacks.

If blacks slipped into certain blocks and neighborhoods despite the banks' efforts, there were often second-line attempts at harassment and violence to drive them out. Sometimes a black family would be burned out, the fire department slow to answer the call for help or maliciously zealous. As Chambers says, "To whom do you complain? To the parish priest? He'd say, 'It serves you right.' Where are you going to go? To the police? Norris had the police department, the fire department, and the banks all wired."

Chambers's first meeting with Norris led to many others during the summer, and on a personal level the two of them hit it off. Norris was willing to discuss, to argue, to listen; Chambers did a lot of listening, too. Slowly, he began to persuade Norris that the biggest immediate threat to the Southwest Side was posed not by blacks but by the real estate companies and agents—the blockbusters—who were systematically scaring white homeowners into selling cheap and moving out. (Of course, Chambers's argument was helped by the fact that several of the most active blockbusters were blacks.) Eliminate the blockbusters and the violence, reduce the fear of a massive black invasion, Chambers argued, and the Southwest Side could be stabilized.

The anti-blockbusting work became the centerpiece of the Provisional Organization's emerging program in the summer of 1959. The organizers had been feeling their way—listening to people and looking for opportunities. Von Hoffman says, "We already knew we were facing an avalanche of blacks and, of course, having walked those neighborhoods and having talked to all of those blue-collar white people, we knew we had to come up with something that would appear remotely plausible, that would not sweep their communities away. You cannot merely say, 'Have faith, believe in interracial justice.' You've got to give them something concrete." The organizers tried to make the blockbuster into public enemy number one. The newspapers loved the rhetoric of anti-blockbusting and the POSC's attacks on "panic peddlers," and their coverage added a measure of credibility to the POSC's work. Privately, however, as far as von Hoffman was concerned, real estate speculators were only a small symptom of a much larger, perhaps overwhelming set of basic problems. But there was no point in saying so. "We were improvising," von Hoffman says. "The one hope we had was to be able to tell them *something;* we had to give them some kind of hope."

By the end of the summer, Chambers had established a measure of trust with Jim Norris. Alinsky's men now had an important new avenue of communication to many of the conservatives, especially those active in the homeowners associations. Not to all of them, to be sure. In Norris's parish, for example, the outspoken and combative Jane Crawford remained hostile, typical of the hard-core "antis" who would never be won over. Still, Norris's growing participation was significant, and Chambers had effectively opened up new organizing opportunities. Norris was now his special project, as Molloy was for von Hoffman.

Von Hoffman had ample reason for self-congratulation when word started to spread through the Southwest Side in mid-August that Pat Molloy had made a $5,000 contribution to the POSC. Molloy's out-front, public endorsement, which is how this was interpreted, stunned many community leaders—not least, perhaps, the most virulent of the antis and McCarthyites, such as police captain William Hennessey and Jane Crawford's crowd in Brainerd. The wild charges that Alinsky was tied to communists were systematically exposed and ridiculed in the *Southtown Economist,* a local newspaper run by Bruce Sagan. Soon after Molloy's contribution, von Hoffman reported to Alinsky:

> Even the people in Brainerd have begun to soft-pedal the communist thing and are restricting their charges against us to mere integrationism. The Captain [Hennessey] seems to be forgetting the communist issue or at least soft-pedaling it for the time being. He has a new line, which is that the whole operation is being directed by 719 N. Wabash [the archdiocesan office], and he said to several people that Donald O'Toole is the handpicked man of Archbishop Meyer. The Captain must feel awfully funny going around knocking the Catholic Church. Of course he does it rather gently and always adds that naturally you can't beat them.

Even Alinsky was mystified by Hennessey's cockeyed logic and manic swings of rhetoric. From his working vacation in California, where he, Jean, and David (daughter Kathryn was now living on her own) had moved into a new vacation house they had bought in Carmel Highlands, Alinsky responded to von Hoffman on a dictabelt:

> The enormous contradiction of a sudden switch from a communist plot to a Catholic archdiocese-engineered project is . . . about as irrational as the original charges were, but sooner or later there is going to be some catching up . . . I mention this because the contradictions are so glaring. It is also interesting and a lesson for you to learn

that the moment you begin to mobilize any kind of power and it begins to show itself . . . , the opposition begins to disintegrate and run for the dark corner. This is something to keep in mind as you go into different situations and run into the same kind of opposition. When I have used remarks such as Pekinese snuffing at the leavings of a Husky or little jackals in the night, I have not been kidding. They are that kind, and while they may have nauseated you, yet the moment you raise a club or even turn around with anything at all behind you, they scatter before the wind or even the slightest breeze. That's the reason I was not perturbed by all this stuff that was going on.

It was not only the hard-core conservatives who had been affected by Molloy's apparent embrace of the POSC. Von Hoffman reported to Alinsky that Harry Fisher at the Mutual National Bank was amazed, speculating that Molloy must have been coerced by superiors downtown—until O'Toole told him that no such orders had ever been issued and that if Fisher were a Catholic he would understand that what he was suggesting was not the way things worked in the archdiocese. Molloy, one of Fisher's largest depositors, even promised von Hoffman he would get Fisher to make a contribution, too, a possibility confirmed by one of the bank's board members, who told von Hoffman he thought the bank would come in for one or two thousand dollars. But von Hoffman was studiously contemptuous, suggesting that if that's all the bank could come up with, they should keep their money. It was the kind of cocky, poker-playing attitude that Alinsky appreciated, although von Hoffman later had second thoughts, telling his boss that "perhaps I shouldn't have said this, but I find that what is paying off is a kind of bandwagon psychology atmosphere here. Merely by giving the impression of complete confidence in the future we evidently are able to attract more and more people."

Molloy's growing support of the community organizing effort expressed less a transformation of his views on race, brotherhood, and Christian charity than a growing appreciation of new political realities. One of these was that his old political connections—his friendship with the mayor, for example—were not enough to solve the problems of St. Leo's parish. The variable of race had turned heretofore simple problems into untouchable ones. In the "old days," perhaps only a few years earlier, after Dick Daley was first elected mayor in 1955, it might have been different. Then, when racial problems had not yet reached the borders of St. Leo's, Pat Molloy could have told his old pal about an eyesore of an apartment building in the neighborhood, and the city's building inspectors would soon be on their way. Now it was all different. As von Hoffman told Alinsky:

The situation regarding that building on Seventy-seventh Street in St. Leo's parish, the one that has the Negro family in it, drags on. There are now two vacancies and the fear in the immediate neighborhood is that more Negroes will be moved in. If that happens a number of other people in the immediate vicinity will put their houses up for sale and we may have one of these Chinese firecracker things going. . . . [Molloy] talked to Daley once about this building, particularly about getting it torn down. It's a complete dump and it ought to be torn down. Daley put him off . . . [and] Molloy told me later that he didn't think Daley was going to act too quickly on the matter.

Indeed, Daley's inclination to ignore his old friend once race became part of the discussion was not unique. Donald O'Toole remembers sitting in his office one day at the Standard Bank when somebody said, "The mayor is here." Daley had popped in to shake some hands while in the neighborhood. O'Toole, whose daughter had gone to school with Daley's daughter, walked out on the bank floor, where the two of them greeted each other. "You got a couple of minutes?" O'Toole asked, and Daley said sure. They went over to a corner of the bank floor, just outside the tellers' cages, where O'Toole told Daley with considerable gusto about the new community organization on the Southwest Side. O'Toole himself had become excited about the progress that the organization was making, especially on the racial issue. "I suppose our faces were this far apart," O'Toole says. "And I was explaining, 'Dick, I don't think that you really understand what this organization is doing. The way it is put together is a fascinating thing.' I was very enthusiastic about it, very worked up over it. And we continued to be just that far apart. And when I reached the end of my pearl of an oration, he said, 'Don, when did your dear old dad die? God rest his soul.' "

Daley and his political henchmen preferred to look the other way when it came to issues associated with race, but occasionally they ventured forth to initiate "solutions" to "problems" of a burgeoning black population on the South Side—and then one might think inaction and avoidance might have been a more enlightened strategy. Shortly before the community organizing project on the Southwest Side started, for example, near the end of Cardinal Stritch's tenure, von Hoffman met with Daley to report on some of the conditions affecting Catholic parishes. The mayor had an idea: Meet with my man John McGuane, who's also a friend of Monsignor Molloy's; he'll come up with something that will satisfy the city and His Eminence. McGuane, a Chicago Park District commissioner, commanded von Hoffman to meet him for lunch in the Walnut Room of the Bismarck

Hotel, where Chicago pols and their conspirators sketched deals on napkins and tablecloths. Von Hoffman recalls:

> It should have been set to music. McGuane's basic lunch consists of five martinis and an ice cream sundae. You get rich enough, you just do what you want, even to yourself. So we're into this thing, and he says to this guy from the Chicago Real Estate Board, "Put the map on the table, put the map on the table." McGuane's got his knife and he's pounding the map of the South Side, and says, "Look, I don't care where the line is. You draw it. You guys decide where the line is. You go to Dawson [the powerful Negro congressman who controlled five wards in the South Side ghetto] and to all your other friends. But once the line is drawn, you stay on your side." I'm saying to myself, this is an American primitive. I was talking to Saul, who asked afterward, "How did it go?" "Have you heard of a communication problem?" I said. "Well, what is less than a communication problem?"

Now, toward the end of the summer of 1959, Molloy had begun to realize there was new handwriting on the wall. Strong crosscurrents were cutting into personal relationships. Molloy's own friendship with John McGuane was but one example. When Molloy mentioned to von Hoffman that McGuane had been bad-mouthing him, von Hoffman replied that it was not only a matter of personal dislike. McGuane also had a different agenda on the Southwest Side, von Hoffman said. "I explained [to Molloy] that what I meant was that my orders and my sole concern was to help the various parishes. At that point Molloy interrupted and said, 'Yeah, and you mean that McGuane is mainly interested in real estate,' and I said, 'Yes, that's right, Monsignor.' " Much to the delight of both Alinsky and von Hoffman, Molloy—perhaps more than most of his peers on the Southwest Side—saw the wisdom and necessity of developing a powerful organization.

Because Daley continued to stonewall Molloy, von Hoffman told the monsignor that the only recourse concerning the dilapidated apartment building in the parish was to move all of the people out and throw up a picket line around it to prevent anybody else from moving in. The picket line would have to have blacks on it, von Hoffman explained. Molloy accepted this plan at first, but Alinsky wanted to brainstorm about better ways to use the situation to advantage. If the owner of the building were pressured into making expensive repairs, he speculated, the building might no longer be profitable and Molloy could then buy it cheap—and the renovation could be turned into a symbolic community project. Molloy's renovated six-flat would include a black tenant, evidence of the monsignor's commitment to the quota scheme. Alinsky told von Hoffman that Molloy was both sufficiently influential and pragmatic to pull this off, although "nobody recognizes more than I do that this business of using a little pot of money to buy up places and then knock them off is an impossible economic job and in the long run just gets nowhere except wasting a lot of money down the drain." Still, Alinsky thought maybe this particular situation could be used to get the community interested in alternatives to violence and white flight.

Molloy, however, while apparently interested and sympathetic to such an approach, was not ready to move so fast and so far. He had even become tentative about the suggestion of a picket line. Uppermost in his mind was the kind of publicity such a tactic would receive, which might backfire against the Daley administration. He wanted to talk again to his friend the mayor before he did anything, for he was torn between his loyalty to Daley and the interests of his parish and the archdiocese. It was a new, puzzling dilemma that Molloy and others on the Southwest Side, where the Daley administration won some of its biggest pluralities, didn't know how to solve.

21

Tears of Joy

While the situation with the apartment building in Molloy's parish dragged on, the attention of Alinsky's organizers turned to plans for the founding convention. In May, committees were created to develop a program and to make plans for a permanent organization and constitution, and it was important to recruit the right people to head up the committees. Bob Christ, for example, was picked to chair the important program committee. The organizers, mainly Chambers and Vilimas, each worked closely with several committees, not only helping to shape their agendas but also being on the lookout for trouble, especially for proposals that raised the divisive race issues.

From the perspective of Alinsky's men, the conservatives and liberals were both potential sources of trouble. It was not uncommon for a conservative to ask whether "this organization is going to be for the niggers." Chambers's response, firm but not self-righteous, was to say, "We don't talk that way." "I started saying, 'You can't raise that kind of word in a public arena, you'll lose the monsignors, you'll lose the support of the Catholic Church in trying to stabilize things.' Gradually they learned how to get out their feelings [about race] in a public forum." As for the liberals, whose vociferous participation belied their small number, many were determined to push for explicit, pro-integration policies, which was also a problem. The organizers warned them they would lose the moderates if they pushed too hard and too soon. Chambers would sometimes explode at them, partly for effect and partly because they genuinely angered him. They "kept bringing up their goddamn motions on race all the time." "You sons of bitches keep bringing this up," Chambers remembers hollering at them, "and you'll kill this organization." If Chambers heard or suspected that a liberal was going to propose a pro-integration resolution at, say, a meeting of the education committee, he would alert conservatives to get their troops out. It was a tricky role that the organizers played in the months leading to the founding convention. Chambers says, "Privately I would tell both sides, 'Now, you know I've got to work with both people, so if you're telling me what you're planning to do, I'll have to share it with the other side . . .' Both sides got the idea that while I was neutral, I would give tips. It was a constant balancing act." It was also an honest con job.

The date for the convention was set for October 24. Von Hoffman reported to Alinsky:

> That's a Saturday. The reason for the choice of Saturday is that our Dutch people are intensively Sabbatarian and feel that it would be ungodly to have a convention on Sunday. The organization committee was snagged over this point for three weeks. They took no less than three votes, and Saturday finally prevailed. The Catholics' reasoning was that it would be wrong of the convention to go ahead and do something that would violate the religious principles of one of the federated groups. . . . The Dutch people are mighty pleased and, in a certain way, so are the Protestants, who are becoming ever more impressed by the fact that they are not the victims of any sort of Catholic steamrolling.

During this critical period, von Hoffman reported to Alinsky almost daily, both to keep him up to date and to get his reaction and advice. When, for example, the pastor at St. Margaret of Scotland seemed to be getting nervous about the direction of the POSC and threatened to complain to Archbishop Meyer, von Hoffman anxiously suggested that Alinsky ought to get to Meyer first. Alinsky did not disagree, but he wanted to approach Meyer carefully and thought that there was enough time to do so. Meyer was still a relative newcomer to Chicago, and Alinsky wanted his Catholic friends to run interference for him on this problem and, moreover, his main interest was to parlay the immediate relatively small problem into larger future opportunities. He was very precise about a sequence of meetings: first he wanted Burke and McMahon to talk to the archbishop, and then to have another discussion involving Burke, Egan, and himself. (Even though Egan wasn't involved in the immediate controversy, Alinsky wanted him there to boost his visibility and prominence in the eyes of the new archbishop.) Alinsky was confident that he could use the second meeting as a springboard to advance the general relationship of the IAF and the archdiocese.

He also had specific advice for von Hoffman about the ongoing problems with Captain Hennessey and other Southwest Side opponents. "I think it is infinitely more effective rather than batting those kinds of worms over the head to say to somebody, like in the case of Hennessey, that [Bob] Hartigan [an influential Democrat who lived on the Southwest Side] is the guy who's really doing this and that Hennessey is just his cat's-paw." That way, Alinsky theorized, Hartigan had an interest in reining in the good captain. Alinsky's advice was much the same when he heard from von Hoffman that Morgan Murphy, a young executive at Commonwealth Edison and a Democratic Party regular on the Southwest Side, had chastised Donald O'Toole for associating with Alinsky because, Murphy allegedly said, Alinsky had recently been thrown out of a meeting because he was a communist. Maybe, Alinsky suggested, some effort ought to be made to make Murphy's superiors at Commonwealth Edison feel responsible for Murphy's "wild, irresponsible charge. While it is true that there isn't much point in wasting time with this stuff, it is also true that when some of these characters reach so far out of the ballpark, as is now the case with them, their jugulars ought to be nicely sliced."

Not all the politicians on the Southwest Side were sniping at Alinsky and his project. Reactions varied from one alderman or ward committeeman to another, and even from one precinct captain to another. In the 18th Ward, the alderman, Jim Murray, had been friendly from the beginning. As the convention approached, Murray, whose father was a leader in the Electricians Union, even offered to arrange for free or cut-rate electrical work for the installation of the public-address system. Despite his friendliness, Murray's political antennae had twitched when, earlier in the summer, he heard the POSC's president, Donald O'Toole, brag in a speech to a local group that the POSC was going to become a powerful organization. When Murray asked von Hoffman if that meant the organization was going to get involved in politics, von Hoffman assured him that it wasn't, that it was only natural, however, to expect a few exuberant leaders like O'Toole to flex their muscles.

More difficult to mollify was the committeeman in the 19th Ward, John Duffy. Alinsky speculated that Duffy may have been the "real fountainhead . . . way back of the scenes" who was responsible for the troublemaking of Hennessey and some others. He warned von Hoffman not to expect cooperation from him. "I'm not at all surprised that Duffy is having his troubles with Daley," he said. "Duffy's had his troubles with everybody who's been in. He was quite in the doghouse under Kelly and as a matter of fact he is probably closer to Kennelly [the previous mayor, and one of the Democrats whom Daley defeated in the primary election in 1955].

Duffy is one guy who I'm sure doesn't have any love for me because I had two sharp tussles with him and in one of them I made him back down and both of them, as I remember, were on the race issue involving discrimination or racial policies in public housing projects."

Opposition to the PSOC by the City Hall crowd was limited to occasional sniping, since the support of such influential monsignors as Molloy and McMahon dampened it. When the PSOC's street signs announcing the place and time of the convention were cut down in the middle of the night, for example, a few phone calls to Daley's office the next day by one of the Catholic pastors abruptly ended the political sabotage.

A stifling string of ninety-degree days that extended into September did not slow the organizational bandwagon. A different kind of heat was being felt by Harry Fisher at the Mutual National Bank, who was increasingly uncomfortable and conspicuous in his neutrality and was about to join the PSOC front ranks. Elsewhere, the reluctant pastor at St. Margaret's, Alinsky was told, had apparently reconsidered taking his complaints to the archbishop and instead was going to commit himself to at least a $1,000 contribution. Fisher was a big catch, but even the addition of much smaller fish, such as several men's social clubs, counted. "The name of one of these groups is the Boneheads," von Hoffman reported of one of the clubs. "They are basically composed of guys who went to school and through the war together and grew up in the neighborhood and still live there. These guys are going to be the sergeants at arms at the convention. There's another group called the Selohssa Club, or 'assholes' spelled backwards, who, I hear, will be affiliating before long. So with the boneheads and the assholes, I really don't see how we can lose."

The sense that the incipient organization was on a roll boosted the energy and enthusiasm of many of the POSC's committee members. Not only were more churches and other groups joining up but the PSOC was receiving a great deal of press attention. The *Southtown Economist* was providing extensive coverage and conferring new status on the POSC leaders. Bruce Sagan, the friendly editor, saw to it that many of the POSC's press releases were published verbatim. And the downtown Chicago newspapers also took note: shortly before the convention the *Daily News* ran its long series of articles on blockbusting on the South Side.

The POSC's committees were working hard. The publicity committee was busy responding to the many controversies and rumors in the community. The program committee was rushing to formulate a set of policies to be voted on. The finance committee was showing new spunk and self-reliance, which von Hoffman traced to the official departure from the project of Alinsky and the IAF. The organizers' salaries, office rent, and other expenses were no longer paid out of a special IAF bank account, and with all funds going into the POSC's own account, the finance committee members seemed to exhibit a greater sense of responsibility and commitment. With the guidance of Alinsky's men, the finance committee developed a fund-raising plan: they targeted twenty local companies and institutions, sent out letters of introduction to each, and followed up with personal visits by committee members.

As the convention drew near, the work of the credentials committee became especially important and sensitive. Eight weeks ahead, the credentials committee sent out invitations to churches, businesses, and neighborhood associations on the Southwest Side. The letterhead on the invitation was loaded with names of people who represented organizations in the area. All of the invitations were sent by registered mail, return receipt requested—a gimmick the credentials committee used to make sure that no "anti" group could claim it had not been invited. A noteworthy exception was the group in the Brainerd neighborhood, which seemed only interested in demolishing the project. The related question of geographical boundaries was quietly and intentionally sidestepped by Alinsky's organizers. Exactly which streets on the Southwest Side marked the beginning and end of the POSC's territory was left approximate and ambiguous, so as to dampen possible controversies and confrontations on two fronts: it discouraged intractably hostile whites from screaming that they had been gerrymandered out, and on the other side, the absence of a boundary line that explicitly excluded black neighborhoods absolved the POSC from charges of racism.

But it was one thing for Alinsky's men to finesse the boundary lines during the first nine months of the Provisional Organization and quite another to unveil formally an all-white organization. Yet just days before the convention it appeared that all the delegates would be white because they were coming as representatives of white groups. Although blacks lived here and there within the effective boundaries of the POSC, there were no black institutions within those boundaries.

In May, the reaction to Alinsky's speech calling for racial quotas had merely confirmed the obvious—that it was virtually impossible to talk about even limited integration on the Southwest Side without inciting heated opposition. So Alinsky's men had backed off through the summer and into October. At some late point, however (none of Alinsky's men seems to remember when), the moment of truth arrived: Alinsky realized they must be sure to have black delegates at the convention. Not only would an all-white founding convention look bad and be open to criticism, not only would the archbishop be embarrassed by its being an all-white, heavily Catholic community organization, but Alinsky did not want to be associated with an organization that appeared to be segregationist, and he knew that if the organization started without black representation, this situation would inevitably and quickly become divisive, ugly, and, perhaps, fatal. What he had told Gordon Clapp in May, what then sounded a little like a rationalization to justify his speech on racial quotas, now seemed prophetic: if the necessary ingredients were not placed in the cake during its making, the result would be a white cake.

The convention, which von Hoffman's preliminary estimate said would attract 500 delegates, was only a week away when Alinsky's men arranged for the credentials committee to receive an application for membership from a black Methodist church located on the northeastern edge of the POSC's conveniently imprecise boundary. The sympathetic chairman of the credentials committee, a lay liberal named Richard Bukacek called an emergency meeting of the committee for October 23, on the eve of the convention. The organizers guessed that a full vote on admitting the black church would be close, perhaps by a margin of only one or two in favor of admission, a narrow victory that would be a loss. There would inevitably be angry, bitter feelings, and if the conservatives were voted down, many—maybe most—of them would walk out, turning the founding convention into a funereal disaster.

Earlier in the week Alinsky gave the go-ahead to von Hoffman and Chambers to enlist the help of the one man who might be able to pull off their eleventh-hour gamble, Monsignor Molloy. His public endorsement of the POSC, while a shock to many antis in the community, had not diminished Molloy's standing with the people, both Protestants and Catholics among them. There was no indication that his old views on blacks and integration had changed much: he was still known for such pronouncements as "There will be no burr heads in this parish as long as I'm pastor." So Ed Chambers made the pilgrimage to St. Leo's, hoping to get Molloy's cooperation, a signal from him that the admission of the black church was something that had to be done. However, after a long talk, Molloy made no promises.

A number of stomachs had butterflies the following night when members of the credentials committee sat down to make their fateful decision. Before the meeting, the organizers had learned that virtually nobody wanted to initiate action. A number of members were shaky; a panicky pastor from a Methodist church arranged for an open telephone line to his bishop during the meeting. Even Monsignor McMahon, whose initiative and money were largely responsible for bringing Alinsky into the picture, was nervous. "Why can't we have the convention first and quietly admit the Negro church afterward?" he had asked. McMahon was now on the spot, too. The organizers told him before the meeting—in effect, ordered him—to make the motion if Molloy did not do so. Chambers told McMahon, "If this vote does not go the right way tonight, you might go on having the convention without us." It was not a mere bluff. Alinsky and his men were now prepared to pull out of the project if blacks were excluded.

The first positive sign of the evening for Alinsky's men was the appearance of Molloy: he arrived on time and sober, neither of which could have been taken for granted. All the key pastors were in the room, both Catholic and Protestant. The organizers had instructed Bukacek to let the discussion run for about a half hour and then look to Molloy. After some discussion, suddenly Molloy spoke up. He said that he had questions about this Methodist church that wanted to join.

First, about the pastor, Molloy asked, "Is he a jackleg preacher?"

"No," Bukacek answered. "He is an ordained minister of the Methodist Church."

All eyes were riveted on Molloy as the monsignor asked his next question. "Is this, uh, this, uh, parish or whatever they call it, they got a building, or is it a storefront thing?"

"Monsignor, they have a building," Bukacek replied. "It is an old, established Methodist church that used to be white. Now it is about a ninety percent Negro congregation. It's a standard building, and it's maintained very well."

"And is the church in our area?"

"Yes, Monsignor."

There was a short pause. Then Molloy said, "Well, if they haven't got a jackleg preacher, and if they've got a building, and you say they fall within the boundaries of this organization, I move we admit them."

That was it; the crisis was over, and nobody felt more triumphant than Alinsky's organizers—a euphoric mix of victory and power.

THE FOUNDING convention the next day might have been an anticlimax for the organizers except that the growing enthusiasm in the community and the amount of time and energy that went into planning the convention kept their adrenaline flowing. They had been working on the convention virtually around the clock for days. The auditorium doors at Calumet High School opened at one o'clock sharp that Saturday afternoon. It took nearly two hours for delegates to register and have their credentials checked. The turnout exceeded von Hoffman's earlier optimistic projections. Shortly after three o'clock, more than 1,000 delegates packed the floor; half again as many observed the proceedings from the balcony. The scene looked like a high-spirited political convention. Red, white, and blue bunting was fastened to the side walls and hung from the balcony. Placards on long wooden poles with the printed names of the various delegations dotted the convention floor. Down front was the Westchester Highland Civic Association; off to the other side was Faith United Church of Christ; farther back, the Ridge Council of the Knights of Columbus. It was a wonderful sight for the organizers, who were always playing a numbers game, as they scanned 104 delegations.

The program opened with a color guard and the Pledge of Allegiance. Five or ten minutes after the proceedings had begun, with virtually everybody in place, the delegation from the black Methodist church arrived. Their appearance came as a big surprise to most of the people there. As they walked down an aisle to their seats, the entire auditorium fell ominously silent. The spectacle is etched in Ed Chambers's memory; it was the tensest situation he had ever been in, and the few minutes it took the delegation to get to their seats seemed like an eternity. If something were to happen . . . If there were an incident . . .

But the tension, like a puff of smoke, quickly disappeared, absorbed into the day's busy agenda. The voice of the chairman of the day's proceedings boomed over the public-address system, instructing delegates on the next order of business. The organizers, once again, could breathe easily.

The convention turned into something of a marathon session, lasting until past midnight. Much of the work was ritualistic, but there were still decisions to be made—a constitution to ratify, officers to elect, and a program to adopt. The tenor was mostly one of discussion and debate rather than of hot controversy, though at one point a resolution was offered from the floor that all staff members and elected leaders of the community organization be required to sign a noncommunist loyalty oath and Bob Christ gave an impassioned rebuttal; the resolution was rejected by a voice vote.

The organizers had taken several measures to avoid divisiveness at the convention: they had encouraged the leaders of the Provisional Organization to exclude the group from Brainerd; they had worked closely with the committee chairmen; and they had recruited a slate of candidates, the officers-to-be of the permanent organization, who would symbolize unity. The two bankers, Donald O'Toole and Harry Fisher, candidates for president and treasurer, not only signified that the new organization was a serious venture but, as a Catholic and Protestant respectively, provided religious balance. So, too, did the men slated for vice-presidential slots: the

Catholic monsignors, McMahon and Molloy; the Protestant pastors Bob Christ and Royald Caldwell; Jim Reed, an assistant pastor at Trinity Methodist Church, who was a last-minute substitution for the lone woman candidate, who declined to run after she became pregnant; several lay leaders who represented churches where the organizers had failed to recruit the pastors, such as in Beverly at Christ the King; and representatives of neighborhood improvement associations.

With a lineup of officers that bespoke unity so strongly, no rancorous opposition was going to resonate in the high school auditorium. All ten resolutions presented by the program committee were adopted by the convention: proposals for the development of a new home-loan program to attract young families to buy older houses in the area; the continuation of an anti-blockbusting campaign; a series of measures to improve the local schools; hiring planners to investigate strategies to redevelop and rehabilitate residential and commercial areas. Nowhere was the issue of race mentioned. Interestingly, the extensive press coverage in Chicago of the founding convention also virtually ignored the topic of race.

I T W A S "one of the thrills of my life," Jack Egan says about standing in the back of the auditorium of Calumet High School and casting his eyes over what he knew was an extraordinarily unlikely collection of people: Pat Molloy, the blacks from the Methodist church, the Irish and Protestant working-class homeowners, the Protestant pastors—all of them at least willing to think about ways to enlarge the small piece of common ground that they now shared, however tentatively. The romantic Egan was nearly moved to tears of joy by this living, breathing testament to democracy. He felt great pride that his friendship with Alinsky had helped to make it possible. For the quite unromantic Donald O'Toole, the founding convention had been no less exhilarating. It had made him feel as he imagined some of the Founding Fathers must have felt when they came together in Philadelphia to fashion a great, new experiment in democracy. O'Toole was not only happy with the results thus far; he was also fascinated with the process—the way relationships were being forged and a shared responsibility for the community was emerging.

Individuals, swept up by the new group dynamics, found their lives spinning in new directions. A case in point was Jim Norris. Soon after the convention, Ed Chambers persuaded von Hoffman and Alinsky to let him offer Norris a full-time job on the staff of the Organization for the Southwest Community (OSC). At the time, Norris was unemployed. He was overweight, and the ironwork was getting tough for him. He had expected that Harry Fisher would give him a community-relations job, Chambers heard, but that did not happen. There was some risk in offering Norris a job at the OSC, Chambers knew: if Norris became disenchanted and reverted to his old ways about race and housing, there would be trouble. But Chambers knew that Norris's thinking on those issues had begun to change, and he also knew that Norris was a pretty good organizer himself and had the trust of many of the conservatives. "Hiring him was the signal to the conservatives that we were for real, that we were willing to have on the staff not only good bleeding-heart types but also a community man like Norris."

Just several months earlier, nobody would have guessed that Jim Norris's hard-line opposition to integration would waver, let alone turn completely around. But not long after the convention he accepted the concept of limited integration, essentially Alinsky's idea of a 5 percent solution. Then he also began to undergo a psychological transformation. He no longer thought of blacks as the enemy. Rather, he began to believe that they, like the white homeowners on the Southwest Side, who wanted to stay in their neighborhoods, were also victims. And if you had victims, you had to have victimizers. From Norris's new perspective of the world on the Southwest Side, the most immediate, tangible enemies were the blockbusters and panic peddlers and their fellow travelers. It was a subculture Norris knew well. He knew which cop or fireman—or teacher, mailman, or truck driver—who lived near a racially changing block or neighborhood was in cahoots with which real estate agents. He knew which cop, for example, was receiving a commission or a finder's fee for tipping off a real estate broker that a certain white homeowner wanted to sell fast. He often knew who was most likely to be spreading rumors about violence and—as Chambers surmised before he had met Norris—who might be responsible for carrying it out.

Norris quickly became an enormous asset to the OSC. When the OSC distributed 25,000 copies of the *Daily News* series exposing the practices of blockbusters, Norris followed up by meeting with neighborhood groups to explain what they could do to stop inflammatory rumors and in other ways stabilize their areas. But Norris's activities went beyond education. He became famous in the OSC for his middle-of-the-night raids to appropriate "Sold by" signs that some real estate agents planted illegally in front of houses to scare homeowners into thinking that their neighbors were selling out before an influx of blacks arrived. Norris, big and strong, would cruise the streets after midnight, stopping here and there to yank the signs out of the ground, throw them in his car, and bring them to the OSC office for display in the morning. His lone raids evolved into communal actions. Scores of "Sold by" signs were confiscated, and after notifying the press the OSC staged a large bonfire of the signs to protest both the realtors' practices and the city of Chicago's complicity in not enforcing the ordinance that prohibited such signs. Norris also helped to organize the picketing of downtown real estate offices after discussions with realtors proved fruitless.

By the end of his first year on the OSC staff, Norris was spending much of his time on problems of substandard housing, illegal conversions, and other forms of neighborhood deterioration, especially in Molloy and McMahon's parish neighborhoods. It was part of the service that, in effect, the OSC provided in exchange for the monsignors' support and part of Alinsky's strategy to organize and stabilize neighborhoods a mile or so "behind the line" of the advancing black ghetto. The volume—the number of houses and commercial buildings that were problems—quickly became more than Norris could handle effectively. Chambers began to insist that Norris should go downtown to confront the city's building inspectors only if a delegation of local people cared enough to go with him. "Norris got the idea. If you want to hire me to do it, he'd say, you're not serious." It was the same reasoning and approach that Alinsky had used in the early days in the Back of the Yards to prod people to take the initiative. Alinsky called it the Iron Rule: don't do for people what they can do for themselves.

Another man whose life took a dramatic turn on the Southwest Side— who felt that his life had been "saved"—was the young Methodist minister Jim Reed.

"My introduction [to Alinsky's project] came on a spring day in 1959 when Bob Christ, whom I knew slightly, called me and said that something new was happening and that he wanted to talk to me about it and to bring someone along, who turned out to be Ed Chambers. You know how the South Side was then. I mean, the race thing was like grit, it was in everything. You could never wash it out of your food. It just impregnated everything." Reed's early experiences at the Washington Heights Methodist Church, when he was fresh out of seminary school in 1952, attested to this. The Washington Heights neighborhood was adjacent to Beverly on the west and Morgan Park on the south. East Morgan Park was an isolated, old black community east of the Highland railroad tracks, where blacks who worked as domestics and servants in Morgan Park and Beverly lived. A Beverly–Morgan Park Human Relations Council was an effort to foster interracial understanding, but it was not politically effective and it was still dangerous for the Council's blacks and whites to meet in a white neighborhood, even in a church. There was also a spreading sense of hopelessness about community survival in the midst of racial transition. So when Ed Chambers came around, Jim Reed was primed to hear his message. "Ed was a low-key kind of guy, really, but there was an evangelical kind of an overtone as I recall. He was immediately convincing."

Although Reed's congregation joined the community organizing project, in the summer of 1959 he accepted an offer from Amos Thornberg, pastor of the big Trinity Methodist Church in neighboring Beverly, to join him as an associate. It was not Reed's ideal career move because he had had a romantic vision of serving in an inner-city church, but he also felt it was time to move on. At Trinity, Reed's involvement in the Provisional Organization continued while Thornberg was on summer vacation, although Reed was not formally representing the church. But this was a distinction that others did not always make. When Thornberg returned, he suggested that the two of them explain Reed's involvement to the church's board of trustees. One of the trustees said very quietly, "Isn't that the organization that Saul Alinsky is involved with?" Reed said it was. And the trustee replied, "Well, he's a communist." Some of the trustees, Reed discovered, were executives in the meat-packing industry; they remembered Alinsky's involvement in the union organizing of the 1940s and matter-of-factly believed he was a communist. The trustees, of course, were not at all interested in belonging to an Alinsky-inspired organization that would promote integration in Beverly.

But that was not quite the end of it. While the board of trustees vetoed any church affiliation with the POSC, they gave Reed permission to continue his participation, representing the Beverly–Morgan Park Human Relations Council. But when newspaper stories announced the OSC's new leaders, Jim Reed was identified as a pastor at Trinity. "Trinity really went up in smoke on that," Reed recalls. "And it was at that point that the man who was the chair of the staff-parish relations committee, a vice president of Continental Bank, came to the parsonage to talk to my wife, Jane, and me and told us that if we would leave town and go to Florida until next June when my appointment was up, they would send my salary down there."

Reed held his ground and, consequently, was called to appear at an official church hearing. On his way into the church, Thornberg pulled him into his office. Emotional, with tears flowing down his face, he pleaded with Reed not to press the OSC issue with the trustees, saying that to do so would be highly embarrassing. Apparently, at his former church in California, one of Thornberg's parishioners was Branch Rickey, and Thornberg took some credit for getting Jackie Robinson into baseball because he talked to Rickey about it. But now his liberal reputation was going to go down the drain because he was going to have to side with the trustees. Stunned by Thornberg's outburst, Reed told the trustees he would resign from the OSC. "And as soon as I said it, I knew it was wrong."

Soon Alinsky and von Hoffman saw an opportunity to help Reed do what was right and, in the process, to steer the OSC in the right direction. They fantasized a delightfully diabolical chess move: since one of the OSC's vice presidents was under attack because he somehow threatened Beverly with racial integration, all of the neighborhood groups in the OSC were going to have to come to his aid, even though they didn't like integration either. Yes, Jim Reed may be wild-eyed and liberal, but he's one of ours and no Methodist bishop is going to tell us whom we can have in our community organization, Alinsky's organizers would explain. Unfortunately, however, Alinsky's and von Hoffman's scheme was overtaken by events. The trustees offered Reed one last chance, promising a transfer to a comfortable suburban parish if he dropped the whole thing. He refused and furthermore informed them in a letter that he had changed his mind and would not resign from the OSC. Having done the principled thing, he thought he'd be able to stick it out at Trinity, but after he told von Hoffman about his letter, Nick told him, "You're dead now."

Shortly thereafter, Reed received a special delivery registered letter informing him that he had been assigned to another parish in Chicago, Wesley Church. He had never heard of it and didn't know where it was. "Nick went up with me to look at it. We drove into the neighborhood and I couldn't believe it, it was what I'd always wanted. Even Nick was excited about it. Sometimes it's a good thing to let your enemies punish you. They never awakened to the fact that what I really wanted was an inner-city church."

WITHIN THE space of little more than a year, Saul Alinsky and his organizers had ushered in—had provoked—a new era in Catholic-Protestant relations in Chicago. It was seemingly only a by-product of the community organizing project, but it was significant and important, an early indication, years before Vatican II, that even in Chicago ecumenism was possible.

Jim Reed, who remained in Chicago, says now, "I would say that that was the first time that I had a sense of Protestant and Catholic clergy actually sitting down together and talking about issues." Within the larger Protestant community in Chicago, these new alliances were viewed with suspicion and distrust. Bob Christ remembers being warned that his increasingly frequent contacts with Catholic clergy could cause him trouble. One presbytery official told him, Christ says, " 'You better start documenting everything you do because you can be defrocked on this.' It sounds dumb, doesn't it, that in this age that someone can be deprived of his ordination because he was working with Catholics." Anti-Catholicism was alive and well in Chicago at the time, but it was only one reason that some Protestant critics did not like Saul Alinsky's project, with its heavy Catholic presence and funding. They also disliked Alinsky's philosophy and style, which they thought were inimical to Christian teachings. On the Southwest Side, Alinsky's organizers spoke in terms of Jeffersonian democracy, the American Way, and people working together for the common good. But elsewhere, Alinsky had talked in different terms, arguing that social change could take place only through conflict, by appeals to self-interest, and by the exercise of power. A few Protestant churchmen, in Chicago and elsewhere, alarmed by the inroads Alinsky was making among their brethren, began to attack him and his assumptions and methods. It was an attack that Alinsky could not ignore, partly because it raised legitimate issues about the role of the church vis-à-vis social change in the United States and partly because the attack was threatening Alinsky's plan for bringing the civil rights movement to Chicago.

22

Civil Rights in Chicago

It is indisputable that Saul Alinsky brought the first large-scale modern civil rights effort to Chicago, the most segregated city in the North.

Not long after the bus boycott in Montgomery, Alabama, in 1955, Alinsky began to think seriously, albeit ambivalently, about a strategy for attacking residential segregation in Chicago. The incubation period, which eventually yielded a new project on the South Side in 1961, was not quick or easy. Indeed, it was a frustrating and sometimes even a painful process, and Alinsky saw several old friendships founder on the rocks of controversy.

Even in his family life, this was a period of new torment and distress, sadly reminiscent of the old bad luck that had befallen him, first as a boy when his father left for California and later with the sudden deaths of Helene and Babs Stiefel. Alinsky himself had experienced some nagging health problems, especially a thyroid condition that had first flared after Helene's death and left him with slightly bulging eyes. But far more serious and troubling was the sudden appearance of a mysterious illness in Jean only a few years after they were married.

In 1956, the family planned to spend most of a second summer on the West Coast, in and around Carmel, where the summer before they had had such a delightful time. Their second visit was cut short, however, when Jean became very ill, and the family flew back to Chicago. At first, Jean's illness, which caused her great pain, was diagnosed as facial neuralgia. For a time, the pain was so bad she could not touch her face and was forced to take much of her food through a straw. The symptoms finally abated, only to reappear. Then there were other symptoms and other diagnoses, which included hysteria and depression.

Alinsky sought the advice of Friedy Hiesler, a friend who was a psychiatrist. Hiesler believed it possible that Jean was suffering from a combination of emotional and physical problems, and recommended to Saul that she see a neurologist. After another round of consultations and examinations, there was at last a diagnosis: multiple sclerosis. At first, Jean was not told, partly because of other, emotional problems and partly because of the possibility that the early physical manifestations of the illness might subside. Saul wrote to Ruth Field, Marshall's wife:

> There seems to be no doubt in the mind of the neurologist . . . but all these diagnoses are based on clinical findings which can only be corroborated by time. . . . [T]he doctors took the position (and after listening to their arguments I concurred) that at this point nothing should be said to her except that she has "an inflammation of the cerebellum." . . . On the optimistic side, it is to be hoped that the present process will abate and that it may be years before there would be any recurrence, if ever. On that point once it does abate, too, there would be a substantial recovery of the functioning of her left arm. The arm is not in any sense paralyzed. She can move it, as well as the fingers, but it is as though it were "asleep." The next few weeks should pretty much indicate what the course will be.

Saul was horrified at the possibility that the news of her true condition might somehow trickle back to Jean before the time was right for him to tell her. He had emphasized to Ruth Field how important it was for her not to tell anybody else. But Jean now began to suspect the nature of her illness herself. On another family trip out West, while Saul was in a filling station making a telephone call, Jean read a story about multiple sclerosis in a newspaper that was lying on the car seat. When he returned, she told him that what she had read seemed like the illness that she had, and soon the whole truth was out.

A very difficult time followed. The Alinskys sold their handsome three-story house on Woodlawn Avenue when it became too difficult for Jean to navigate the stairs, and moved into an apartment in Hyde Park. Jean's illness continued to be a tangle of physical and emotional problems. Kathryn, Saul and Helene's adopted daughter, now a teenager, continued to have her own problems, too. When Alinsky told his friend and IAF board member Leonard Rieser that he needed a salary increase, he added with grim humor, "Correctly speaking, it isn't me who needs it, but two psychoanalysts. I'm convinced that any drug addict who goes around talking about 'having a monkey on his back' has got a very light load compared to carrying two analysts on one's back."

Alinsky did his best to reconcile the demands of his work and travel with Jean's growing dependency on him, but it was not easy. At first, there was always the hope of an extended remission or even a reversal for the better. But both Jean's condition and Saul's ability to cope with the consequences slowly deteriorated.

Still, at this juncture in his life, Alinsky was usually able to juggle things so that he was not away from home too often. He spent most of his time in Chicago, except for the four or five days a month in New York on the Chelsea project, a trip to the West Coast every two or three months or so to see Fred Ross, and occasional out-of-town speaking engagements. In Chicago, the surface rhythms of a typical day were similar to what they had been when Alinsky first opened the office door of the Industrial Areas Foundation in February 1940. After most commuters had already arrived in the Loop, he rolled in from Hyde Park at ten or ten-thirty, after a late night of reading or writing in his study at home, to the same two-room office on the seventh floor at 8 South Michigan Avenue. His secretary would have all the correspondence opened and arranged on his desk. There was dictation to give and phone calls to make.

But now there were also important differences. For the first time, Alinsky had a full-time staff. In another office at 8 South Michigan were his protégés Nick von Hoffman and Lester Hunt. They were the IAF's "Research Department," as Alinsky called it. For the better part of two years, beginning in 1957, Jack Egan was a nearly full-time intern. And, of course, Egan's presence symbolized another difference: Alinsky's acceptance by the archdiocese as a trusted and valuable resource.

IN AT LEAST one respect, Martin Farrell was an unusual parish priest in Chicago. Soon after being ordained in 1938, he had volunteered to serve in a primarily black parish on Chicago's West Side. It was not an assignment that was forced on young white priests coming out of St. Mary's of the Lake, and the volunteers were few. As Farrell recalls: "The Catholic apostolate to the Negroes was more or less left up to Orders and Missionary Orders . . . but a couple of us in seminary [wondered], why shouldn't ordinary parish priests do this work? . . . Back then, there was no concept that when a neighborhood goes black—even though traditionally Negroes are not Catholic—one should go out and get them into the Church." From those early days, Doc Farrell served more or less continuously in the Negro Leagues, as some within the archdiocese used to call such parishes.

By the late 1950s, Farrell had landed as pastor of Holy Cross parish in Woodlawn, the community just south of Hyde Park. Woodlawn was in

the midst of a tidal wave of change. At the start of the 1950s, Woodlawn
was about 60 percent white; ten years later, it would be more than 95
percent black. The community problems that predated the population
shift—overcrowded housing, illegal conversions, delinquency and crime—
were getting worse. In February 1958, Farrell wrote to Alinsky, whom he
had never met:

> After long and tedious work with people and organizations in Wood-
> lawn . . . it is quite evident to me that all and any effort for neighbor-
> hood betterment must come from the people without any outside help.
> I call upon you to consider probably the most interesting neighbor-
> hood ever in your career. . . . Woodlawn itself is the most disorganized
> community in the United States. There is no leadership. On the other
> hand, I have found many ordinary people in the community waiting
> for somebody to lead them to effective democratic organization ac-
> cording to American and Alinsky principles.

It did not take Farrell long to arrange an audience with Alinsky, and
he was impressed with Alinsky's gentleness and sincerity, quickly ap-
preciating the contrast with "his reputation of being a big, tough organizer." Farrell, a ramrod six-footer with piercing blue eyes, could be tough
himself when an opportunity presented itself. "Mr. Alinsky, you just think
you're a great organizer," Farrell remembers saying to him, "but you're
not a great organizer until you organize blacks."

In fact, only three months before he met with Farrell, Alinsky had
sent Cardinal Stritch a private memorandum proposing that he organize
the Grand Boulevard area, where Lester Hunt and Jack Egan had been
conducting a door-to-door survey. Part of the problem with moving ahead
was lack of money, the same hurdle that had to be surmounted if anything
were to be done in Woodlawn. But Farrell, tenacious as well as tough-
minded, refused to be discouraged. He asked for a specific budget, which
Alinsky and von Hoffman worked up—nearly $150,000 for three years in
Woodlawn. "I foolishly said, 'Okay, I'll get you the $150,000,' " Farrell
remembers saying. "I didn't know what I was doing."

Farrell started to shop around the archdiocese for allies and support.
But Cardinal Stritch died in the spring of 1958, and more months passed
before his successor, Archbishop Meyer of Milwaukee, was installed. In
the meantime, several of the Catholic pastors on the predominantly white
Southwest Side, who were able to tap their parish treasuries, had persuaded
Alinsky—with Jack Egan's help—to start the project that became the
Organization for the Southwest Community. Not until well into 1959 did
the Woodlawn project become more than Farrell's fantasy.

The first sign of real progress was a commitment of $50,000 that Farrell wangled from his friend who ran Catholic Charities in Chicago, Monsignor Vincent Cooke. Cooke was a good man to be friends with; he shepherded an annual budget that approached $20 million. As long as Cooke didn't lean back in his chair after hearing your plea for money and say, "That sounds like a bucket of steam to me," you had a good chance of getting his help. But as was a common practice of his, a string was attached to the money: it was contingent on Farrell's (or Alinsky's) coming up with the balance of the budget, another $100,000.

The prospect of funding was not the only thing that was moving Alinsky toward organizing his first black community. Not only were Nick von Hoffman and Lester Hunt lobbying him to move in that direction, but so was his closest friend, Ralph Helstein, who, as president of the Packinghouse Workers, was developing a friendly, supportive relationship with Dr. Martin Luther King, Jr. (Among Alinsky's friends there were only two or three others—Gordon Clapp and Leonard Rieser, perhaps—whose opinions and respect meant as much to him as Helstein's.) Helstein wanted Alinsky to speak out against the Back of the Yards Neighborhood Council for its anti-integrationism. "We got into a terrible argument one night," Helstein recalls. "I told him he ought to publicly repudiate the Council. Well, he wasn't going to do it. They've gone through too much together, he said. I said, yes, don't repudiate [the past], repudiate this particular behavior. Well, he wouldn't do it, and I'm not so sure that you could separate it." Helstein was right: you couldn't; Alinsky's interest in a black community was related to his interest in offsetting, modifying, or combating—he wasn't quite sure which—the BYNC's growing racist reputation.

But the most important reason for attempting to organize on the Southwest Side was to test Alinsky's idea—his experiment—of a quota system to break the pattern of residential segregation. The negative, panicky reaction of the whites, however—it was as if somebody had pulled the pin of a grenade in a crowded room—had forced Alinsky's organizers to heave the quota proposal completely out of sight. From that experience, Alinsky projected a similar dismal fate in other hypothetical situations. He told von Hoffman: "A white community, once it reaches the point where it believes it has the strength to accept and control a quota, will very probably assume that it has the strength to have no quota or to operate on a straight 'keep them out' basis." Again, he could see elements of such transformations and rationalizations in the history of the BYNC. "There may be ways of avoiding this turnabout, such as keeping the issue out in front [of a community] continually and conspicuously so that they cannot make this fatal turn in the road," Alinsky said, but "we were not able to do this in the Southwest Side project, and I question whether that experience is unique."

Thus, what was needed in Chicago—and as a model for other Northern cities—was a powerful black community organization that could "bargain collectively" with other organized groups and agencies, private and public. Alinsky told von Hoffman, "There is no substitute for organized power. . . . We know all of the opposition which would come, including many of the Negro leaders and agencies who actually depend upon segregation for their very existence. We also know that there is no Negro organization in the field equipped or able to do the kind of job that has to be done." Then, speaking into his Dictaphone with a sense of mission and history, Alinsky gave von Hoffman marching orders:

> I want a memorandum prepared which will be used in a number of ways—as a basis for application to the Field Foundation and to the Schwarzhaupt Foundation; as a statement of the issue; as a statement of purposes and procedures; as a statement of the situation as it prevails in the city generally; as a detailed statement of the Woodlawn community. . . . I want a discussion of the importance of this issue of residential segregation. I want a discussion of what this kind of [community] organization means as far as the whole field of urban renewal. . . . We are fed up with the moving out of low-income and, almost without exception, Negro groups and dumping them into other slums, building houses for the middle-income groups, and all of this in the name of urban renewal. . . . I want you to devote full time to this. I want these materials prepared. I want to be able to cut them up, throw them back at you with specific instructions on write, rewrite and rewrite. I will put them into final form. . . . I want you to start right now, today.

Within several months, Alinsky and von Hoffman had produced a foundation grant proposal for a community organizing project in Woodlawn. Von Hoffman says, "I kept saying to Saul: no Woodlawn, it's a disaster, it's the wrong place, it's got the University of Chicago, it's just going to be a pain from start to finish. But, you know, that's where the money was; it had to be Woodlawn."

Von Hoffman's prescience had more than theoretical roots, for he had had an extraordinary muckraking and rabble-rousing adventure which involved the University of Chicago in the spring of 1958. While there had been some wonderfully comic aspects to it, it had also raised important and divisive issues that would likely be raised again in Woodlawn.

Von Hoffman's escapade began when Alinsky departed for his first trip abroad, to Milan, to consult with Archbishop Montini—a trip arranged by Jacques Maritain, who thought that Alinsky could give Montini some organizational ideas for stopping the Italian Communist Party from making further inroads among Catholic workers. As he left Chicago, von Hoffman recalls Alinsky telling him, " 'Now stay out of trouble. Just don't do anything. Go on an extended snooze.' Because he knew that I had inherited his mischievous qualities. He made a marvelous boss. When there was nothing to do, he did not expect you to pretend to be doing something. Go out to the ballpark, go away. Only come around when there is work to be done."

Gliding down the well-greased political pike in Chicago, but due to make a pivotal stop at a City Council hearing, was a plan for the largest, costliest urban-renewal project ever in the United States. The mastermind of the Hyde Park–Kenwood urban-renewal plan was Julian Levi, the son of a rabbi and a shrewd, aggressive lawyer. Levi had a long association with both Hyde Park and the University of Chicago—he had grown up in the neighborhood and attended the university's undergraduate and law schools in the late 1920s and early in the Depression. Although the university went through hard economic times during the Depression, not until the 1940s did the surrounding community of Hyde Park begin to experience problems of its own. Until then, Hyde Park had been one of Chicago's more prestigious communities, a mix of generally solid, even handsome single-family houses and small- to medium-sized apartment buildings. But some of the new residents attracted to Chicago for war-related jobs and the university's Manhattan Project landed in Hyde Park. After the war, problems multiplied with alarming speed as the Hyde Park population increased. As in other Chicago neighborhoods, whites began to leave as blacks arrived. In Hyde Park–Kenwood, from 1950 to 1956, 19,989 whites left while 23,162 nonwhites moved in; the nonwhite percentage increased from 6.1 percent to 36.7, and the total population rose from 71,689 to nearly 75,000. Meanwhile, the downward spiral of conditions in the community seemed to be moving at a geometric rate. Crime had become such a menacing problem in parts of the neighborhood that university officials said they were having difficulty attracting and keeping first-rate faculty, although perhaps these claims were exaggerated. Amidst talk that the university might move out of both Hyde Park and Chicago if conditions did not improve, Levi became the executive director of the newly created South East Chicago Commission. Although its title connoted the authority of a governmental agency, the Commission was a private entity, essentially an arm of the University of Chicago and supported mainly with university funds.

Levi's style at the Commission soon became famous or infamous in

Hyde Park, depending on one's point of view. As arrogant as he was clever, Levi was determined to make the world of Hyde Park safe for the University of Chicago. He had the money, staff, and political connections through the university to make life miserable for owners of apartment buildings who had made illegal conversions or for the proprietors of run-down taverns and other disreputable, unsavory eyesores in middle-class Hyde Park. He was not bashful about picking up the phone and screaming threats and epithets at such targets, calling in the police and building inspectors, trying to engineer the cancellation of an uncooperative real estate owner's insurance or financing, or pressuring a liquor distributor to stop selling to a troublesome tavern owner. While this knee-to-the-groin approach apparently caused some wincing among the large, genteel professional class in Hyde Park, the cause was sufficiently noble—the salvation of their property values and neighborhood, not to mention a great university—that few complained loudly. Such was apparently the case, for example, when Levi sprang into action after being tipped by liberal activists from the Hyde Park–Kenwood Community Conference that a real estate speculator had bought a six-family apartment building and promptly moved in nine Negro families. According to one reliable account, "the day after the nine families moved in, Julian Levi visited the speculator, threatened him with legal action for violating the housing code, and confronted him with evidence of overcrowding; at the same time a generous offer to buy was made by the University real estate office. The speculator sold the apartment dwelling to the University on the next day, and one day later the nine Negro families were moved out by the University's real estate managers."

As energetic and expensive as were Levi's piecemeal assaults on the causes of neighborhood deterioration, they were small potatoes compared with a massive urban-renewal project that he and his talented planner, Jack Meltzer, began to work on. Hyde Parkers prided themselves on being concerned, active citizens, and many individuals and neighborhood organizations got involved. Nonetheless, the planning process was dominated, if not completely controlled, by Levi and his staff. "The Final Plan" was unveiled to the rest of Chicago early in 1958. Nearly five years in the making, the numbers—of acres, dollars, buildings to be demolished and people displaced—were unprecedented. In one grand plan, Levi was going to get rid of most, if not all, of the "rotten apples" that were turning Hyde Park and adjacent Kenwood into a slum. As announced, the plan covered 900 acres and would cost $130 million, which included federal and local government funding as well as private investment. This bold plan immediately captured the support of Chicago's establishment. One downtown newspaper hailed it as "a redevelopment miracle," and the *Tribune*, reflecting the clout and social class represented by the university and the professionals in Hyde Park, put aside its usual rhetoric of anti-federal spending and called it "a great program."

The cheerleading for Levi's plan often focused on the fact that 80 percent of the buildings in Hyde Park–Kenwood were to be maintained or rehabilitated, while "only" 20 percent were to be demolished. This was a different kind of urban renewal, observers noted approvingly, from the then more typical approach of total demolition and clearance which, for example, had occurred in another South Side area a few years earlier to make way for the huge Lake Meadows housing development. In that instance, 100 acres had been cleared and poor black families uprooted to make way for new, middle-income housing, an early episode in what was becoming a disappointingly familiar story.

In Julian Levi's sophisticated plan for Hyde Park, removal of blacks was not, of course, a stated goal. He also attempted to downplay a prime goal of the university, which was to lay claim to land for expansion of the campus. Rather, the goal was spoken of in lofty, public-spirited terms. The *Sun-Times,* for example, grandly elevated the Hyde Park–Kenwood proposal into "a national test," to see whether "the older, partly blighted parts of a city can be made livable and urbanely attractive." Removing the "blighted parts" of Hyde Park, the key to Levi's plan, was its most expensive goal. Essentially, by using the powers of eminent domain, 20 percent of the buildings in Hyde Park were to be demolished—buildings that were judged substandard and too costly to renovate. Many small businesses would be forced out—and not only dives. The truly big numbers, however, involved residential units and the people who inhabited them. It was population density—"overcrowding" was the middle-class description— that Levi's plan intended to do away with. In all, nearly 20,000 people in Hyde Park–Kenwood would be forced to move, a high percentage of them low-income blacks and whites. Although many of the cleared sites would be rebuilt, virtually all of the new housing was for decidedly middle- to upper-middle-income people.

The more Nick von Hoffman read about the details of the Hyde Park–Kenwood plan, the angrier he became. From his perspective, government money was going to be spent in a way that would make life worse for thousands of poor people. There was no provision for even a modest number of scattered public housing units, as some in Hyde Park had proposed; relocation procedures, abysmally inadequate in earlier urban-renewal projects in Chicago, were sketchy at best; and it seemed that many more structures were to be torn down than were necessary. Von Hoffman also resented the implicit arrogance of the proposal. Here was the country's largest urban-renewal project, conceived and written by private, self-interested parties, which would monopolize the city of Chicago's bond money. Other Chicago neighborhoods worse off than Hyde Park, but without a University of Chicago, a Julian Levi, or the political power at their disposal, would be cut off from funds and starved into further deterioration. "Jesus Christ, look at this. Do you see this, Lou?" Jack Egan remembers von Hoffman exclaiming to his friend Lou Silverman as the three men discovered another outrage among the details of the Hyde Park–Kenwood plan. "Their anger began to mount," Egan says, and Nick or Lou said, "Boy, we ought to kick the hell out of them. We ought to do something about this."

Their talk did not turn into action, however, until Alinsky had taken off for his six-week tour of Milan and other European stops and they had gone to see Cardinal Stritch. They told him about their analysis of Hyde Park–Kenwood. The cardinal, Egan recalls, said, "I want you to oppose this plan. It is designed only to preserve one institution. There are other social considerations to consider, so oppose it." With that, the public campaign began.

The first newspaper criticism of Levi's plan appeared in the archdiocesan newspaper, *The New World.* Ghostwritten by von Hoffman, as were the others that followed quickly, this new drumbeat of opposition caught Levi, Mayor Daley, and other leaders in the city off guard. For it was rare, virtually unprecedented behavior: the archdiocese did not assume public partisan positions on issues that were only indirectly or tangentially related to the Church.

Von Hoffman's trenchant prose and Silverman's cultivation of the press quickly turned both the Hyde Park–Kenwood plan and Jack Egan into controversial subjects on the front pages of the regular downtown dailies. With all this going on, Egan was set to testify—to represent, in effect, the views of the cardinal—at a City Council hearing on the urban-renewal plan. Von Hoffman drafted his testimony. "Nick had a very hard time working with me, and so did Saul," Egan says, "because I am sort of a gray person. Nick said, 'Unless you go for the jugular and unless they believe you're going to destroy the plan, they won't change it.' Politically, I know that's right, but I couldn't get myself to do that; I thought it was dishonest." In truth, Egan believed that there was an urgent need for some kind of sweeping urban-renewal program in Hyde Park and that, without it, the future of the university and the community was endangered. So he slipped a qualification into the last part of his testimony—that although he was demanding certain changes in the plan, on the whole he supported a renewal effort. "I presented [the watered-down statement] to Monsignor

Burke," Egan says, "and he truly, literally threw me out of the office. He was so mad. 'You SOB, get the hell out of here,' he said. 'We put all this money and time and effort into this [and this is all you're going to say?]' " Egan made a hurried check with friends at *The New World* and received the same kind of angry reaction. In the meantime, however, Silverman was already delivering advance copies of Egan's testimony to the downtown newspapers for their next editions. In a panic, Egan located Silverman, who had already made several deliveries. "I said, 'Lou, I don't care what you do, we got to get it back, Monsignor Burke is totally against it.' " Silverman's mad dash to retrieve the statement was barely successful, and the next day Jack Egan's testimony flat out *opposing* the Hyde Park–Kenwood plan was front-page news.

It was around this time that Alinsky returned to Chicago, and he heard about the uproar almost as soon as he stepped off the plane. Alinsky summoned von Hoffman, Egan, and Silverman to lunch at the Palmer House Grill. Silverman remembers Alinsky's opener—"What the fuck are you doing, you assholes?"—and watched as von Hoffman and Egan seemed to evaporate. Alinsky's ire was directed mainly at von Hoffman, who, he knew without giving it a second thought, was responsible for instigating and directing the whole fuss. "While he was away, his little mice had blown up the city," von Hoffman says. "It wasn't that he disagreed with our position. It was 'What are you guys doing? You can't possibly win. You're crazy. Yeah, yeah, you just had nothing to do; I told you to go fishing, but you just can't stay away from playing games.' Saul used to have a wonderful thing he would say about political stuff. People would come up with a stratagem of one sort or another and he'd say, 'Okay, now let's suppose you do it, and A works out the way you think, and B works out the way you think, and C works out the way you think, and D works out the way you think, and it all works out the way you think that it's going to work out—which, incidentally, it won't. But we'll say that it will. Then what have you got?' And in this case with Hyde Park, not much." Alinsky was angry about Hoffman's thoughtlessness, even recklessness, in leading the archdiocese, especially Egan, Burke, and Stritch, down a lonely, dead-end road. Who were Egan's allies, or even potential allies, in this eleventh-hour, quixotic misadventure? Alinsky asked, the answer painfully evident in the question. There had been nothing on the horizon, for example, to suggest that leaders of other religious denominations in Chicago would join Egan's late-blooming crusade. Levi had already taken steps to co-opt many of them.

Egan was not only isolated from other clergy. Earlier in the planning process, the liberal leadership of the Hyde Park–Kenwood Community

Conference, a large network of block clubs formed in 1949 to combat crime and blight while preserving the neighborhood's interracial mix, had raised many of the same issues that Egan was now raising. But after protracted negotiations, and in spite of divisions among their membership, the Conference gave its support to the final plan. Ironically, Egan's eleventh-hour criticism had a perverse effect on the Conference vis-à-vis Levi. Suspicious of the archdiocese's motives and fearful that the entire plan might begin to unravel, the Conference closed ranks *behind* Levi.

Then there was Mayor Daley. Serving his first term and not yet entrenched, Daley saw a big, successful urban-renewal project in Hyde Park as a feather in his cap. Only belatedly, after Egan's opposition became public and pronounced, did Egan learn that the mayor was angry with him for rocking the boat. "[We] totally miscalculated the reaction of the mayor," Silverman says. Now it became clear that Daley thought the Church, and Egan especially, had intruded into an area where it did not belong. Daley was fond of saying that Chicago was a city of neighborhoods, and he believed that cutting a deal with the recognized leaders and institutions in each neighborhood was his job. "Most important," Silverman says, "Daley, who was *really* Catholic, counted the cardinal in his power base. And now someone had co-opted all of that."

It is possible that Daley contacted Alinsky upon his return from Europe to ask him to talk to Egan and Burke. But one call that Alinsky certainly did receive was from his friend Hermon Dunlop Smith. Dutch Smith was not only on Alinsky's board but also on the board of trustees of the University of Chicago. Alinsky apparently told Smith that he thought Egan and the other archdiocesan leaders had made a mistake in opposing the plan but that, at this stage, there was not much that could be done except to let them play out their hand.

In fact, as the public debate continued through the summer and Egan remained at center stage, he also remained a largely solo figure. With Stritch's death in Rome and with his replacement not yet named, the authority of Egan's statements was diminished, and it was evident that other Catholic clergy and influential lay leaders were not joining him. Even when the NAACP, although hardly a potent force in the city's politics, came out with a critique similar to Egan's, it avoided outright support of his efforts, not wishing to be too closely identified with the archdiocese and its many anti-integrationist parishes. In Hyde Park, many but not all liberals—the alderman, Leon Despres, was a conspicuous exception—were willing to accept the trade-offs in the renewal plan as the price of stopping white flight and maintaining Hyde Park as an integrated community. "I never felt more lonely in my life," Jack Egan remembers. His opposition had delayed the City Council's final approval for several months, and "because of our protest the relocation policies and programs in the city [showed] . . . more care, more attention, and more compassion," but the Hyde Park–Kenwood urban-renewal plan was nonetheless approved in the fall of 1958.

NEAR THE CLIMAX of this long process, two ex–Hyde Parkers, the young satirists Mike Nichols and Elaine May, returned to their old stomping grounds for a benefit performance sponsored by the Independent Voters of Illinois at the Piccadilly Theater in Hyde Park. Now with a national following, Nichols and May were only a few years removed from their more humble show-business origins at a bar on Lake Park Avenue. "We're glad to be back where Hyde Park used to be," was Nichols's opening dig. He said he heard there was a new slogan in the community: "White and black together, shoulder to shoulder, against the lower classes." The laughter seemed a little strained, for Nichols's arrow was on target, landing at about the same place as the arrows Jack Egan had been shooting.

But Egan's painful lesson was that being a straight shooter was not enough. "I learned a hell of a lot," Egan says, suggesting that, in spite of nearly three years of informal tutelage by Alinsky, there was no substitute for the experience of being on the firing line. Above all, Egan learned, "you don't go into a battle unless you have your troops."

Not long after the Chicago City Council's approval of the Hyde Park–Kenwood renewal plan, the University of Chicago and Julian Levi were at it again. This time the land in their sights was across the Midway, the wide expanse of grass that, not unlike a moat, separated Hyde Park from Woodlawn—or, more to the point, separated the University of Chicago from the predominantly lower-class black area that Woodlawn had become. The Midway lay between Fifty-ninth Street, the southern boundary of the university's campus, and Sixtieth Street, where Woodlawn began. Beginning in the 1930s, the university had employed various stratagems, including an alliance with the Woodlawn Property Owners Association, to control the housing market and population in that neighborhood—to prevent, in effect, the spread of Woodlawn's problems across the Midway onto the campus and its surrounding Hyde Park neighborhood. Now it seemed to university officials that the Midway was shrinking as both a physical and a psychological barrier. In fact, the university's students and faculty had learned to avoid the Midway after dark, for muggings and robberies had become commonplace there.

During the early phase of urban-renewal planning, university ad-
ministrators had advocated a less than subtle solution to their "Woodlawn
problem": widening Sixty-first Street into an expressway that would cut off
Woodlawn from Hyde Park. At least some people assumed that the scheme
had been concocted by the unabashed Julian Levi. Although it was eventually dropped, it was well known that the university was buying up land in
Woodlawn, especially in a long, skinny stretch a mile long and a block
wide, running east to west from Stony Island to Cottage Grove avenues
between Sixtieth and Sixty-first streets along the length of the campus, just
where university officials had once fantasized an expressway. University
officials did not, of course, talk about their interest in pushing the ghetto
farther from their doors, but, rather, about the need for expansion; eventually they referred to the mile-long strip in Woodlawn as the new South
Campus project.

Nick von Hoffman, of course, knew about the University of Chicago's
interests in Woodlawn. He also knew from firsthand experience that, in a
political fight, the university could throw very heavy leather. So it was not
surprising he thought organizing in Woodlawn was a bad idea and tried
to persuade his boss accordingly.

No doubt Julian Levi had heard through the grapevine in Hyde Park
that Alinsky was thinking about organizing in Woodlawn. Bad feelings and
conflicting interests between Levi and Alinsky went back before the von
Hoffman fracas—as far back as the early 1950s, when Alinsky had received
a small grant from the Field Foundation for a project in the West Kenwood
area to stop white flight and stabilize a racially changing neighborhood. As
project supervisor, Alinsky worked primarily with the Howell Settlement
House, run by Presbyterians, and several Catholic parishes. Levi was
already at work with his own plans for Kenwood and, apparently, saw
Alinsky as a troublesome interloper.

The two men had no reason to have changed their opinions of each
other in the intervening years. But several other things had changed—for
one thing, Alinsky's power relationships with men on the university's
board of trustees. By 1959, he was no longer close to Agnes Meyer's
son-in-law, Philip Graham; Marshall Field, his friend and benefactor who
provided the seed money that started the IAF, had died in 1956; Dutch
Smith, still a friend and also still on both the university and IAF boards,
was also on the board of the Field Foundation in New York, which meant
that he was about to be caught in the middle.

Alinsky and von Hoffman drafted a proposal for a Field Foundation
grant to supplement the $50,000 that Catholic Charities in Chicago had
committed for a Woodlawn project. Significant funding from a non-Catho-

lic source was crucial even if Farrell were able to come up with, say, an additional $100,000 from other Catholic sources. In theory, the proposal seemed like a natural, for the Field Foundation was committed to breaking down racial barriers and promoting intergroup understanding. Moreover, the application to the Field Foundation was being made collectively by the IAF, Farrell's Roman Catholic Holy Cross parish, and the First Presbyterian Church in Woodlawn, whose co-pastors, a black and a white, were Farrell's allies. But the Field Foundation did not eagerly embrace the proposal when it was received in February 1960. As noted in a staff memo, Smith requested that the Field board take no action—"to permit further exploration of the subject with the University of Chicago."

Levi's and the university's specific interest was the mile-long strip in Woodlawn, but they were also generally concerned about the effect of Woodlawn's problems and people on the university. From his base at the South East Chicago Commission, Levi tried various approaches to smooth the way for the university in Woodlawn; he needed at least some cooperation from groups and institutions there—which is why he included some Woodlawn residents on the Commission's advisory board, among them Doc Farrell and the new co-pastors at First Presbyterian, Charles Leber and Ulysses Blakeley.

Alinsky was surprised at the first, quick sign that funding from the Field Foundation was less than a sure thing. But Smith, the man in the middle, wanted to see if there was a mutually satisfying solution, a way the university's interests could be assured *and* Alinsky's project funded. Alinsky was willing to talk about it, and a meeting between Alinsky and university officials was arranged. Alinsky and von Hoffman approached this as a bargaining session and began to plot their strategy. (The two of them worked together so closely during this period that it is difficult to say which ideas originated with Alinsky and which with von Hoffman.)

Von Hoffman's opinion was that the Woodlawn operation would not be jeopardized by conceding the strip of land, which he thought was of limited importance compared with the larger issues facing blacks in Woodlawn. They decided that Alinsky's "offer" to the university would be his side's neutrality when the university went to the city government with its plan for the strip of land; in return, the university should promise neutrality on his community organizing project in the rest of Woodlawn. Alinsky would emphasize that Levi's opposition to him at the Field Foundation was not decisive, since Alinsky could easily come up with sufficient funding elsewhere (meaning the archdiocese). And if Levi did not agree to this kind of trade-off, there would be a good chance that the university's land grab in Woodlawn would be attacked, and attacked vigorously.

Von Hoffman thought that Levi was susceptible to attack because of problems with the university's renewal program in Hyde Park and urged Alinsky to show, if necessary, how those problems could be related to Woodlawn. "In the event of a brawl in Woodlawn," von Hoffman said to Alinsky, "he has no assurances the battle would not be carried back into Hyde Park, where he is vulnerable on two counts. . . . The prices being paid for properties are suspiciously high, very likely high enough to cause a little scandal if they got out. . . . He is also vulnerable because his renovation program is a flop. What is more, Negroes are now moving into many Hyde Park buildings *NOT* scheduled to come down. Therefore, he should be told that we know that he must come back and ask for another Hyde Park clearance program. Without neutrality from our side, he cannot get it!"

Since Alinsky was not intimately familiar with Woodlawn, von Hoffman briefed him on the details that might come up at the meeting:

> The street pattern must remain absolutely as it is. This is important. The people from the slums use the Midway as a park, in the summer particularly. If the streets leading to the Midway are cut off, the people will not be able to get to it. Please do not concede this point. . . . If you can get it, I would try for an agreement that no public facilities like firehouses, police stations, boys clubs, etc., should be located on the Woodlawn slice. With clearance programs of this sort, it is easier to get the land sometimes than to dispose of it (buyers are not usually interested in small parcels next to slum sections). So promoters like Levi are tempted to fill up empty spaces by getting the city or some other government body to take the excess land off his hands. The trouble is that most of these facilities are badly needed in the *heart* of the slum districts. They should not be sucked out of them.

The rebuff that Alinsky received at his meeting with university officials was a dreary anticlimax. There is no way to know precisely what happened; it is not even clear who was at the meeting—not Levi, Smith, or von Hoffman—and none of them remembers the details of what Alinsky might have said. The university's logic in rejecting Alinsky's deal, however, is not difficult to discern. They could not entirely trust Alinsky; even Smith admitted he could be very difficult to deal with; and it was incredible that he should claim to speak for forces whose "neutrality" could help the university. The only ace that Alinsky had or was likely to have in hand was his relationship with the leadership of the archdiocese, but that could be trumped. The other cards that Alinsky brought to the meeting were laughably low, and his threat to go ahead, even if he did not get Field

Foundation money, and build a community organization in Woodlawn was preposterous.

About a month later, the university made its definitive response to Alinsky's proposed deal. On July 18, 1960, Julian Levi appeared before the Chicago Land Clearance Commission to request a land survey of the mile-long strip of land in Woodlawn, the requisite first step leading to the university's new South Campus project. He did not come downtown quietly or alone, but with public-relations men, maps, and charts, and the press had been alerted. In effect, it was a news conference to announce the university's plans, and the CLCC chairman, Phil Doyle, was an unwitting and unhappy participant. "We wired the room up on Doyle," Levi says. "He was on TV and couldn't make a move. This meeting had to be forced because Doyle didn't want it. He worked against everything I wanted." (Doyle and Levi had crossed swords before on other urban-renewal projects and Levi knew that Phil Doyle would be in no hurry to advance his cause. Levi had successfully lobbied in Congress for legislation that gave the city of Chicago financial incentives to approve the university's expansion plans. Specifically, through Section 112 of the Housing Act amendments of 1959, this meant that the university's spending for South Campus would generate $21 million in federal urban-renewal credits that could be used anywhere in Chicago. Doyle disliked this on principle because it pressured the city to support a project for reasons other than its intrinsic merits.) At the CLCC, one could almost hear the sound of bureaucratic feet dragging.

But Levi's high-profile announcement of the university's plan to cross the Midway reinvigorated Doc Farrell and his clerical core group in Woodlawn. As far as Farrell was concerned, any pretense that the university was interested in a broad, cooperative effort to revitalize Woodlawn was shattered. Farrell was ready to move, but it was not clear whether his Protestant colleagues would move with him. More than a year earlier, before Levi unveiled the South Campus plan, Alinsky had met with leaders of the archdiocese, the Illinois Synod of the Lutheran Church, and the Presbytery of Chicago, and the Protestants knew about Farrell's commitment of $50,000 for a Woodlawn project. But a number of them had doubts not only about Farrell but about Alinsky. The meeting did not go well, with Lutheran leader Walter Kloetzli being the most antagonistic toward Alinsky. Kloetzli was not alone, however, as Protestants elsewhere began lining up to attack Alinsky and his methods. Some of the sharpest criticism appeared in the liberal Protestant magazine *Christian Century*. An article entitled "How Chelsea Was Torn Apart" had been preceded by an attack on Alinsky headed "Machiavelli in Modern Dress." "Can anyone be a follower of the gentle Christ and at the same time play the game of power politics?" is how Wayne A. R. Leys put it. "We get the impression [from *Reveille for Radicals*] that nothing can be accomplished without power, [and] it is claimed or inferred that power can be used for good ends, even though it is built up by deception, [and] by fabricated disputes." In Leys's view, such "power maneuvers" were incompatible with—if not the antithesis of—Christian doctrine.

Since Alinsky wanted the support of Protestant churches, he could not shrug off such attacks, and he was thinking about writing a new book that would address these ethical issues. "Whenever the word power is mentioned," he wrote in a paper he delivered at a conference in Chicago in 1957, "sooner or later somebody will quote the classical statement of Lord Acton . . . 'Power *tends* to corrupt, and absolute power corrupts absolutely.' Lord Acton never said, nor intended to say, that power itself was corrupt, because he knew that power in itself is absolutely amoral. . . . The corruption of the concept of power is not in power, but rather in ourselves. . . . [And] the morality of the use of power is not in the power instrument but in the user."

But the morality of Alinsky's argument rested principally on the assumption that the goal of social or economic justice was not possible, or not as likely, without attaining and exercising power. "Prevailing arrangements or power patterns can only be altered by power," Alinsky maintained. Essentially, power flowed from two sources: money and people—organized people, that is, who through their numbers could effect political change. This was an insight that was understood by an idealistic young man in California, Douglas Still, who was now on his way to Chicago to assume a key position with the Protestant Church Federation.

AFTER WORLD WAR II, Doug Still had graduated from college, married, and, along with his wife, Hannah, who was interested in social work, decided that he wanted to work with churches that provided social services to the poor. In 1951, he joined a project sponsored by the National Council of Churches to educate the children of migrant workers. But dissatisfied with his lack of influence within the church structure as a nonordained employee, he went to New York and enrolled at the Union Theological Seminary as preparation for entering the ministry. He also took courses in social work and community organization at Columbia. After working again with migrants in California one summer, Still returned to Union with an idea of establishing rural slum ministries: each would consist of a small church, someone to teach Christian education, and another person as a community organizer. The community organizing that Still had in mind was not the kind he had learned about at Columbia, which was mostly oriented toward coordinating the work of existing social-service organizations. But during his summer in California, Still had heard about Saul Alinsky from Dean Collins, associate director of the Migrant Ministry program. Collins, excited by Still's idea of rural slum ministries, used Alinsky's connections to secure a three-year grant from the Schwarzhaupt Foundation, and beginning in the fall of 1956, young Protestant clergy in the Migrant Ministry began to be trained in community organizing techniques by Fred Ross, Cesar Chavez, and Alinsky.

Still, the first trainee and the director of the program, worked as a participant observer with Ross and Chavez, all living in a motel in East Los Angeles, where they worked with the local Community Service Organization. At the end of his six-week experience, Still met with Ross, Chavez, Alinsky, and William Koch of the NCC to discuss his experience. Alinsky, of course, was the center of the discussion, and Still recalls that "Saul was full of anecdotes of his experiences. His basic question was, Who is calling the shots [in a community] and how do they call them? His discussion helped us all to grow into an understanding of what the real world was about."

Alinsky often transformed these wrap-up sessions, repeated at the end of each trainee's fieldwork assignment, into intense debates. He had little patience with people whom he found naïve: "Most of us were raised nice middle-class boys," says Chris Hartmire, also a graduate of Union Theological Seminary, who eventually succeeded Still as the director of the program, "and [in our experience] everybody likes everybody else, nobody gets too mad at anybody—and the people in the Migrant Ministry were probably like that." Alinsky was more than willing to disabuse them of any expectation that Christian love would dissolve the differences between migrants and the growers. Alinsky was teaching them tough-mindedness as much as teaching technique. "It was just getting accustomed to the fact that there was an enemy out there and that the enemy was willing to use all kinds of methods to attack you personally," Hartmire explains, "to attack your organization, to try and take your financing away, all the things that the growers did."

Alinsky was also determined to smash illusions the ministers had about their own motives. Doug Still says, "He felt very strongly that if you are a do-gooder, you're never going to make it, and don't kid yourself that you are committed to helping others, because you are primarily interested in helping yourself. You had better get to the root of your own motives because you are not going to save yourself by helping somebody else." At first Still was shocked by these attitudes, but he was also "titillated by the appropriateness of them, the truth of them." Alinsky's "chiding of me was done in my interest. I always trusted his integrity." Others did not, however. On more than one occasion, Alinsky's chiding turned into something darker. Still remembers that there was "one guy on our staff whom Saul couldn't stand, whom he treated viciously . . . a young, black fellow from the Church of God in Anderson, Indiana, [and who] believed that he was called to do good, to love the Lord and spread the gospel. Saul pulled all his defenses from under him and exposed him, and he couldn't take it. He just collapsed under it." In another instance, Alinsky hounded one of the trainees so much that everybody—there were other trainees present—was devastated by the onslaught. "It was beating a dead horse too long," Still says. "It was the only experience [with Saul] that I felt was senseless."

More frequently, however, Alinsky's humor, wit, and playful irreverence enlivened his meetings with clergy. He would tell the clergy that the Bible ought to be read as an organizer's training manual and that much could be learned from Moses and Paul, two terrific organizers (Alinsky admitted his bias for Moses). Then, with tongue partially in cheek, he would spin out an analysis of, say, an exchange between Moses and God when the Jews had begun to worship the Golden Calf. Moses, like any good organizer, never relied only on facts or ethics to persuade. "Moses did not try to communicate with God in terms of mercy or justice when God was angry and wanted to destroy the Jews," Alinsky explained, noting that

a great organizer, like Moses, never loses his cool as a lesser man might have done when God said, "Go, get thee down: *thy* people, whom *thou* hast brought out of the land of Egypt, hath sinned." If Moses had dropped his cool, one would have expected him to reply, "Where do you get off with all that stuff about *my* people whom *I* brought out of the land of Egypt? . . . Who started that bush burning, and who told me to get over to Egypt, and who told me to get those people out of slavery, and who pulled all the power plays, and all the plagues, and who split the Red Sea?" But Moses kept his cool, and he knew that the most important center of his attack would have to be on God's prime value that God wanted to be No. 1. All through the Old Testament one bumps into "There shall be no other Gods before me," "Thou shalt not worship false gods." At this point, trying to figure out Moses's motivations, one would wonder whether it was because he was loyal to his own people, or felt sorry for them, or whether he just didn't want the job of breeding a whole new people, because after all he was pushing 120 and that's asking for a lot. At any rate, he began to negotiate, saying, "Look, God, you're God. Whatever you want to do you can do. But you promised them not only to take them out of slavery but that they would practically inherit the earth. Yeah, I know, you're going to tell me that they broke their end of it so all bets are off. But it isn't that easy. The news of this deal has leaked out all over the joint. The Egyptians, Philistines, Canaanites, *everybody* knows about it. But go ahead and knock them off. What do you care if people are going to say, 'There goes God; you can't make a deal with him. His word isn't even worth the stone it's written on.' But after all, you're God and I suppose you can handle it." . . . *"And the Lord was appeased from doing the evil which he had spoken against his people."*

As much fun as all this was, many of the clergy found it difficult to accept Alinsky's theory that nobody operates outside of his self-interest, and many of them were troubled by his ideas about the use of conflict. If you are going to arouse people who are demoralized and apathetic— whether in a meat-packing plant or a community—you have to "agitate to the point of conflict," he would say bluntly, "fan resentments" and "rub raw the resentments."

The trinity of conflict, organization, and power that Alinsky taught was profoundly disturbing to those who were committed to the old assumptions of the Social Gospel. Alinsky, of course, rarely missed an opportunity to disturb or shock. In late-night discussions with the young ministers, he would take a long drag on his cigarette and say, "Somebody once asked me whether I believe in reconciliation. Sure I do," his deep, confident voice delivering the proper mix of cockiness, sarcasm, and certitude, the cigarette smoke coming out slowly with the punch line: "When our side gets the power and the other side gets reconciled to it, then we'll have reconciliation." Still and a few of the others could appreciate both Alinsky's dramatic flair and the truth of his generalizations, while also taking into account that, in practice, Alinsky understood that motives were often mixed and complicated. Still quickly came to admire Alinsky because he thought that "Saul was one of the biggest idealists there ever was. He hated exploitation and felt obliged to facilitate an equalizing of opportunity." He was captivated by the humanity of Alinsky's social philosophy and its spiritual implications. "Saul felt strongly that you don't patronize people but instead have them experience their own authority and practice their own power. The assertion of personal value is the core of his whole philosophy."

Doug Still arrived in Chicago at the Church Federation just as Alinsky needed another ally among Chicago Protestants and when new, friendly relationships and lines of communication were developing between Egan's circle of Catholic activists and their Protestant counterparts. Indeed, among the Protestants, several who had earlier been somewhat reserved about Alinsky's work in Chicago were about to become his important foot soldiers. One of those was David Ramage.

Ramage had recently been appointed as head of the urban-church department of the Presbytery in Chicago. Previously, he had been pastor of a church in the Englewood section of Chicago and had worked in a delinquency-prevention program, the Hard to Reach Youth project. Ramage says that it was his experience in that project that "really convinced me to move more in the direction of community organizing . . . because I became increasingly convinced that it was the problems of the neighborhood that were [critical] for these kids and not that they were deviants in terms of their own personal makeup." Yet for all of his sympathy for a community-based approach to social problems, Ramage was "very, very, very cautious" when he first heard about Alinsky's plans in late 1958 and early 1959. By 1960, Ramage says, "I had to make the decision ultimately whether to give Presbyterian support [for the Woodlawn project]." Ramage could already feel the heat of controversy from several directions—from anti-Alinsky Protestants in Chicago, led by the Lutheran Walter Kloetzli; from the fallout in New York from the Chelsea project; from the hostility to Alinsky in *Christian Century;* and from Protestant antagonists on the West Coast who were aroused by Alinsky's infiltration of the Migrant Ministry program. Not totally convinced about Alinsky's motives, Ramage decided to have a "showdown" with him, hoping to discover a rationale that would legitimize church support of Alinsky's work in Woodlawn.

At eight o'clock one evening, Ramage, who hardly knew Alinsky, arrived at the latter's Hyde Park apartment, only a short distance from his own. Immediately, Alinsky assumed a neighborly conviviality and, as had happened so often before, by two-thirty in the morning, when Ramage was allowed to leave, Alinsky had made a new friend and supporter. He wowed young Dave Ramage—"my eyes just went like that"—as he colored in the multi-layered political map of Chicago in vivid, vibrant detail. More to the point, Alinsky "shared" his ideas about what could be done to integrate Chicago's neighborhoods and how the Woodlawn project would be the centerpiece of a grand strategy.

What Ramage heard that night was essentially an update of plans hatched several years earlier. Alinsky had been edging toward the possibility of creating a community organization in the black Grand Boulevard area. Because Grand Boulevard was adjacent to the Back of the Yards and, in theory, shared similar problems, he hoped that leaders from the two community organizations could negotiate agreements on urban-renewal, school, and housing issues—including agreements about limited numbers of blacks moving from overcrowded parts of Grand Boulevard into certain parts of the Back of the Yards. In his grant application to the Field Foundation, Alinsky stressed that the eventual integration of Chicago was a key goal of the Woodlawn project, although he carefully avoided any suggestion of even informal residential quotas:

> No more than an insignificant number of whites can be lured into joining interracial groups for principle's sake. There must be more immediate incentives to meet and cooperate with Negroes. The incentives do exist, but the Negro organizations to cooperate with do not. We lack one of the two essential elements or parties necessary for community collective bargaining. If even one substantial and powerful Negro organization were in existence now on the city's South Side, interracial cooperation could become a reality. Then, once men and women of both races are working together and getting to know each other as persons, we can only hope that people will judge each other as individuals, not as faceless members of groups.

To be sure, Alinsky told the Field Foundation—and Dave Ramage—that another key goal in Woodlawn would be to create "a regenerative force" to improve conditions in Woodlawn. But Alinsky's emphasis was clearly on his grand strategy in which a black community organization would help lead the way toward the integration of Chicago.

Personally, Alinsky was deeply committed to integration. But his emphasis on a long-range grand strategy to achieve it was also important in garnering support for community organization per se. "All of a sudden," Ramage remembers, Alinsky's strategy was seen as "not just this tough labor-union-type approach to community, but began to be minimally acceptable because it was in the context of a positive, pro-integration strategy that was serving 'good moral [purposes].'" Ramage became convinced; he was inspired and ready to deliver Presbyterian support for the Woodlawn project. "If Woodlawn had been just sort of a working-class, labor, Roman Catholic community organization, the Protestant Church would never have embraced it, but the moral crusade that was beginning to emerge of the civil rights movement enabled Alinsky to be perceived as one of the white horses to ride in on."

Nonetheless, Ramage had to marshal the argumentation to combat Protestant opposition. Although Reinhold Niebuhr and others were beginning to have an impact, by and large urban Protestant churches were still operating on the assumptions of the old Social Gospel, with the institutional church as a mechanism for dispensing social welfare services. The traditionalists recoiled at the thought of the church getting caught up in political struggles with, say, City Hall and having pastors and lay leaders talk openly—and approvingly—of self-interest and the exercise of power. But as Bob Christ, Ramage, and others had come to believe, the old Protestant assumptions and approaches were like a "finger in the dike," not only in Chicago but in most large Northern cities now being swept by racial change. Indeed, "the civil rights movement" and "urban issues"—discrimination, bad housing and schools, lack of employment opportunities, police brutality—were frequently viewed as one and the same. And related to all of this was an incipient urban quality-of-life movement: as middle-class whites fled the old cities, and as suburban lawns and nuclear families became smug symbols of success, an articulate minority of liberals, intellectuals, and clergy overtly hostile to suburbanization championed the cause of city life and spoke on behalf of the new urban immigrants. At least for churchmen like Ramage, there was now a golden opportunity—indeed a moral responsibility—for the white Protestant churches to move to center stage in urban America, where the Catholic Church had held sway. An important avenue into that urban scene, he argued within Protestant councils, was provided by Alinsky's concepts and practices.

For Ramage, a new chapter in his life started that night at Alinsky's apartment, along with new ideas for steering the Presbyterian Church toward a commitment to urban social action. "I became a major factor in strategizing and developing the framework and policy for the United Presbyterian Church, starting in Chicago and ultimately beyond, to embrace Alinsky's style of community organization as a basic, legitimate, and non-paternalistic mission of theology for the urban church. It all started that night."

It took most of 1960 before Ramage, Still, Chuck Leber, and Buck Blakeley in Chicago and their co-conspirators in New York could shake loose some Presbyterian money. In Chicago, it was fortunate that Ramage, Leber, and other Presbyterian allies were experienced with the decision-making process because there was strong opposition by other Presbyterians. A vice president of U.S. Steel, a leading lay Presbyterian in Chicago, opposed Alinsky's project and so too did a businessman who was also "one of the big wheels in the social-welfare field," Leber remembers.

> He was a Presbyterian who served on one of the big welfare boards [in Chicago]. And when we finally brought all of this to a vote in our

own denominational meeting, he was there. Thank God I can't remember his name [because] he was poison and very nasty. He stood up in the middle of the meeting, slammed his fist, and said, "If this proposal goes through this committee to our Presbytery, not only will I resign from this committee, but I will stand on the floor of the Presbytery and oppose it and tell them why I resigned from this committee, and resign from the Presbytery." And then the chairman stood up, and he was about six feet six, the associate pastor of a very swanky church. He stood up and hit the table and said, "This committee will not be threatened by you or anybody else." And the businessman sat down, and the chairman sat down, and the vote went through. I think we had three votes against us out of about eighteen people who were there.

The Protestant imprimatur was especially important to Alinsky at this point because his pursuit of the Field Foundation was being derailed. Alinsky had been banking on the Field Foundation as a source of non-Catholic sponsorship and funds, but Julian Levi had his supporters on the Field Foundation staff. "From other foundations we have learned that Mr. Alinsky's prestige has lessened as a result of the Chelsea experiment," the staff reported. Then, while briefly noting that one foundation regarded Alinsky's work as generally significant, it said that none of six other foundations, "each of which has knowledge of the work of Mr. Alinsky and the Industrial Areas Foundation, or has supported it in the past, . . . indicated support for Mr. Alinsky's work in the future." It was the kind of devastating staff report that could kill a grant application, and when Dutch Smith saw it, his surprise and suspicion quickly turned into anger.

At first he demanded a detailed explanation, suspecting that the staff had been unfair. (In fact, the Schwarzhaupt Foundation was the only foundation that had ever examined Alinsky's work closely, and it, of course, continued to be supportive.) But Smith's ardor cooled when Field's executive vice president suggested he first talk to the University of Chicago's president, Larry Kimpton, and Julian Levi, implying that their negative reaction to Alinsky's proposal might "satisfy" Smith. Alinsky, who had exploded in anger when he heard about the staff report, did not wait for Smith's help; he went immediately to see Ruth Field, or at least he tried.

Marshall's widow, who was proud of the Foundation's record of support for the downtrodden, had liked Alinsky and respected his achievements, especially his pioneering work in the Back of the Yards. But she had no appetite for close-range, interpersonal warfare, which is what

Alinsky was proposing to drag her into. He phoned, outlined the problem, and set up an appointment at her Fifth Avenue apartment in New York to discuss it further. In the meantime, he sent her a very long "Dear Ruthie" letter detailing the hatchet job the Field staff had done on him. It was no longer merely a foundation grant that was at stake, he told her. "I do not relish having to write you, an old friend, and to tell you that I have evidence . . . that employees of a granting foundation did indeed use an application to begin a reckless attack on the name, character and reputation of an applicant." Looking forward to her help, he closed by saying, "Until we meet at the summit, 4:30 p.m., Monday, your place." But before they could meet, Ruth Field had second thoughts. "I must *beg* you to realize the awkward situation that you and Dutch have created, and do your best to remedy it . . . use tact!" And then, with the icy graciousness of the upper class, Ruth Field terminated an old friendship in two politely coded sentences: "I have become even more firmly convinced of the unwisdom of a talk between you and me. So will you stop in on Monday at 5:30 for a drink and a personal visit instead of 4:30 for a serious talk?"

THE TEMPORARY Woodlawn Organization (TWO) was born on January 5, 1961. The Presbyterians came through with $22,000, and the Schwarzhaupt Foundation, which according to its plan was on the verge of spending itself out of existence, had enough left to make a grant of $69,000. Over a decade, more than $700,000 of Schwarzhaupt money went into Alinsky's projects. It is hard to imagine how Alinsky would have fared without this support, or without the good luck of having the Archdiocese of Chicago headed by men of uncommon social concern who shared many of his values—first Cardinal Stritch and then Cardinal Meyer. By coincidence, Alinsky had been in Rome in the spring of 1958 when Stritch, who had been called to the Vatican, became ill and died; he was apparently the last non-Church official allowed to see Stritch before his death—an episode that was repeatedly described among Alinsky's Catholic friends in Chicago. It must have been difficult for Alinsky to imagine how, from his point of view, Stritch's replacement could possibly measure up. But Meyer did. One of his first acts was to make Jack Egan the full-time head of the Cardinal's Conservation Committee, an appointment that took on added meaning because it came on the heels of Egan's ill-fated opposition to the Hyde Park–Kenwood urban-renewal program. Now, little more than a year later, Meyer invited Alinsky to his office to finalize the archdiocese's financial support for the Woodlawn project. With a handshake, the cardinal committed himself to $50,000 a year for three years. "Your Eminence," Alinsky told him, "I hope you realize that when we develop this organization, there are going to be a lot of conflicts and controversies." To which Meyer replied, "Mr. Alinsky, it's all right. You know, you and I don't share the same faith, but for Christians there shouldn't be anything more controversial than a Man on the cross."

23

Woodlawn

Although the formal beginning of the Woodlawn project was in January 1961, the real action had started the previous July, with Julian Levi's announcement of the university's plans for expansion into Woodlawn.

Von Hoffman reported to his boss that he had heard that Mayor Daley, reelected the year before to a second term, might be inclined to support the university's newest land grab. Farrell, who had also heard rumors of this kind, told Alinsky that he wanted to meet with Daley and make certain that the mayor understood how displeased he was with the university's unilateral decision. Alinsky tentatively approved of this, but he wanted to be certain that a meeting with Daley was handled properly.

> I'll tell you what I had in mind [he told von Hoffman]. I had no objections to Farrell going in with a group and making a number of points as far as Daley was concerned. One, as far as they could see, this dough is [really] all being funneled into Hyde Park. You know the proportion of funds that have [already] . . . gone into Hyde Park as over against what has been spent in the city as a whole. . . . [Two], he should point out what happens when there is this kind of demolition [as would occur in the South Campus area] and that people are being pushed off into other slum areas and further compounding an already evil situation. . . . [Three], he should point out that the kind . . . of housing being provided in Hyde Park is not meeting the acute need of lower-income people. For the diocese and the Presbyterian Church—and I emphasized that Farrell should stay away from an all-Catholic presentation—their concern was primarily with people and secondly with buildings and universities.

It was important, Alinsky felt, to avoid reminding the mayor of the fiasco over the Hyde Park–Kenwood urban-renewal plan. He wanted Farrell to tell Daley about his, Farrell's, own commitment to Woodlawn, how unhappy the Catholic Church was, how unhappy the Presbyterians were, and that

> if Daley thought that he was just getting in good with the [university] trustees, some other elite of Hyde Park, and certain banks and newspapers, [then Farrell's delegation should make it clear] that there was a hell of a big tide . . . that might start running publicly and conspicuously the other way at any time. It's one thing for a trustee who lives out in Libertyville or someplace like that to make decisions with reference to the disposition of masses of people in the city of Chicago, masses with whom he has nothing to do socially, economically or in any other way, as over against the mayor of the city of Chicago.

Alinsky gave careful attention to the subtleties and nuances that he wished Daley to hear. He wanted the message to be firm but not threatening, although if it came down to a choice of erring on the side of going easy or of going hard, it was better, he thought, to tilt toward hard—to say explicitly that a number of Chicago institutions, both in and outside of Woodlawn, would not remain silent if the university moved ahead, and that their relative silence up to this point should not be mistaken for disinterest or weakness.

Alinsky wanted Daley to view Farrell's delegation as a red flag, or at least a yellow one. This was only August, and he needed time—to get money, a staff, an organization in Woodlawn. Von Hoffman had been worried that if Farrell was too aggressive, Daley would resent being "bulldozed." But Alinsky sized up the situation differently. The last thing Daley wanted, he thought, was trouble, and the first and foremost impression Alinsky wanted Farrell to convey was that there would be trouble if the university's plans were allowed to roll merrily along. Alinsky also wanted to appeal to Daley's vanity, to another facet of the mayor's self-interest. Alinsky told Farrell, "I think it ought to be emphasized to Mr. Daley that if he'd rather go down in history as the university's friend, why that's his business, but I don't know people who have gone very far in political [history] as being the university's friend."

Only three months before, Alinsky had been willing to concede the strip of land to the university if Levi and his colleagues would agree to stay out of the way of his project. Now, however, he jumped easily to the other side of the argument, urging Farrell to emphasize to the mayor that if the university's plan was readily approved, there would be much pain and suffering among the newly dispossessed poor people.

The university's announcement of its plans also gave Farrell's Protestant allies in Woodlawn—Leber and Blakeley—a reason to reactivate the local Ministerial Association. It was not long before Association members were approached with an "offer" of money for a new community organization in Woodlawn that the clergy would direct, a $50,000 annual budget to be provided jointly by the Ford Foundation and the University of Chicago, Leber was told. Leber and his friends suspected that the intermediary who presented the offer was doing so on behalf of Julian Levi, who wanted to establish a front group to pave the way for the university's expansion. Alinsky countered by having a front group created for him. First, Leber and Blakeley invited Farrell to join their group, changing the name to the Woodlawn Pastors' Alliance; then, with the patina of interfaith credibility, Leber, Blakeley, and Farrell, over the reservations of their white colleagues, exercised the prerogative of leadership and retained von Hoffman as a "consultant." The Industrial Areas Foundation now had a passport of legitimacy, however flimsy, to operate in Woodlawn.

The first public protest that would stamp the style of the Temporary Woodlawn Organization occurred before there was a formal organization, and it occurred on very short notice. Leon Despres, alderman of the 5th Ward, which included both Hyde Park and Woodlawn, phoned von Hoffman with a friendly tip: A notice had just gone out that Julian Levi was going to appear the following day before the Chicago Plan Commission. He wanted an ordinance approved that would allow the city to qualify for nearly $1 million in urban-renewal funds when the university built on a vacant lot it already owned in the South Campus area. But Alinsky envisioned this downtown public hearing as a perfect place both to create and to dramatize a larger "issue" about the university's encroachment into others' territory.

By the next morning, December 15, von Hoffman had rounded up a delegation of about fifty people—Leber, Blakeley, and Farrell, along with their black parishioners and friends, together with the leaders of several small community groups in Woodlawn. Leber remembers von Hoffman's phone call: "Nick told all of us there was going to be this big hearing. We didn't have the faintest notion of what he was talking about. And he said, 'You have to get as many people [as you can] downtown at ten o'clock tomorrow. We want to flood the place, everyone is going to be in all the hallways and everything. Bring everybody you can in your car and get down there.' Well, we had maybe fifty people, that's about it. But everybody thought we had five hundred." (When the Plan Commission chairman, Claire Roddewig, was asked how many people from Woodlawn were at the meeting, he said, "Hundreds, you might as well say a thousand." "Nick's big point," Leber says, "was that every time a black face shows up downtown in any of these kinds of places, people see seven or ten black people. Only one black face, but that's what they see. So if you have thirty or forty black people, they see three thousand black people.")

The headline in the *Sun-Times* the next day was "Uproar Stalls U of C Plan OK," and indeed, the Commission chairman postponed a decision until further study had been done. Back in the neighborhood south of the Midway, where Woodlawnites were never mistaken for the New York Yankees, it was not difficult to feel that even one small victory was a big deal. Alinsky, by pressing ahead with an early, hurried protest, had redefined and transformed a simple real estate transaction into a moral issue— and in so doing had painted Levi and the university with the tar of sinister motivations.

Weeks before this first public protest, Alinsky and von Hoffman knew it was time to recruit at least one black organizer who could work with von Hoffman. Von Hoffman had been making the rounds in Woodlawn sporadically for nearly two years, meeting a few black clergymen, gathering impressions and information, comparing his empirical findings with published reports and census data. Much of this found its way into occasional memos to Alinsky and then into Alinsky's nearly identical grant proposals. But it had been one thing for von Hoffman to cruise around Woodlawn by himself informally and quite another to direct a highly visible organizing campaign. It would be both unseemly and impractical not to have a staff right from the beginning that included blacks. In fact, Leber remembers that both his cohorts and Alinsky were initially deeply concerned about the racial question. "The big issue was could he, should he, as a white person, as a person of Jewish background, and his identity as a person, you know, with all of these other things, even consider working in a black community? How could any of this fit? After all, we were all white, too. My partner, Buck Blakeley, was black, but he was not in on the initial discussions although I kept him posted."

At almost precisely the right moment, as luck would have it, Jack Egan told von Hoffman that he knew somebody who would be perfect to hire as an assistant. Von Hoffman was immediately skeptical. "I love Egan, but I remember saying to myself, 'Oh God, it's another Catholic turkey.' I could almost hear the clink of rosaries. But I told Egan, 'All right, send him down.' " And one day, to von Hoffman's great surprise and delight, in walked "Mr. Charm, I mean Mr. Lovable, I mean he had all the moves, he was marvelous!" Bob Squires was handsome, glib, street-wise, fresh out of the Army, and now working at Marrillac House on the West Side. "No one who had ever spent any time around Bob Squires did not come to adore him," von Hoffman says. Squires, who was doing some organizing in public housing projects on the West Side, met von Hoffman in Hyde Park and, a week later, was taken downtown to meet Alinsky. It was not a typical job interview. "I didn't know who in the hell Saul Alinsky was," Squires says. And the first thing Alinsky said was: "I don't know who you are, I've never had a black organizer before, and I would never hire you if I didn't need a black organizer." Not to be outdone, Squires shot back: "Well, we've got something in common. I've never heard of you either." Alinsky asked him about his work on the West Side and then told him what he was looking for, or what he thought he was looking for. And then he told Squires: "Now, look, I'll tell you what. Do me a favor, don't fuck any women in Woodlawn. You do like women?" Right, Squires said. "If you have to fuck somebody," Alinsky advised, "go over to Hyde Park. The reason I'm telling you this is that if you start screwing and the word gets out, and it's good, then you won't have any time to organize."

Squires's introduction to the possibilities of organizing in Woodlawn came at about the time he was hired, around the Christmas holidays of 1960. "We got rolling just purely by accident," he says of an incident that had portentous significance for him. "There was a fire on Sixty-third and Maryland, at the Royal Arms apartment building right down the street from the old Persian Hotel. And it was cold. Because Doc Farrell's church was right down the street, I was there along with Doc, Nick, and Chuck Leber. That was the first time that [I] saw what Woodlawn people were made of. There was a drunk lady sitting in the Royal Arms. We were moving people out of the apartment building and putting them into the hotel. But one lady forgot and had left her baby in the back seat of a car. It was cold like a mother out there. And about ten minutes later she said, 'Oh my God, my baby.' And she ran out and got the kid, and the kid was damn near turning blue. And there was this drunken lady, sitting in a drunken stupor in the Royal Arms, and we were talking about [whether] there'd be time for the doctor to come and save the baby. She got up, and she performed first aid to save the kid's life. The woman was an ex-nurse. She was just a drunkard, but she saved that kid's life. . . . There [was] a lot of hardness in the community," Squires says, but the incident also showed him that there might be more humaneness and caring on the streets of Woodlawn than even he might have thought.

Von Hoffman's instant affection for Squires grew into respect and friendship. "One of the things about him was that he had a great deal of tact as well as energy," von Hoffman says. "He could reach a wide spectrum of Protestants. You could also ask him to go see any number of people to smooth ruffled feathers. He had a diplomatic ability. Also he had something else. He had a wonderful humbleness. He was quite willing to let some of us louts really tell him what to do. And he had a sense of humor. He would make endless jokes about the salmon faces, his favorite expression."

There were several small community groups in Woodlawn, such as the United Woodlawn Conference, which had attempted to tackle Woodlawn's growing problems in recent years but with limited effectiveness. None of these groups was a potent force or likely to become one. Still, they had a measure of legitimacy—reputations, members, leaders, and letterheads. According to Alinsky's usual approach, such groups might have been expected to become part of the new, larger community organization. But the Conference leaders were not inclined to that kind of cooperative effort. In addition, there was a recent history of bad feelings between Farrell and the Conference's leaders. Also Farrell thought several Conference members were, as von Hoffman told Alinsky, "obnoxious communists. I told him that their strength was so weak that he could simply ignore them, but emotionally this was too much for Farrell to do."

Alinsky's own attitude toward communists had changed over the years. In the late 1930s, before the Soviet-German nonaggression pact, Alinsky had been enthusiastic about a United Front strategy, and in the Back of the Yards he had worked amicably enough with the occasional communist. After the war, during the purges of left-wing unions and in the McCarthy period, he was disgusted by the professional Red baiters, spoke out against them frequently, and extended his sympathy and, occasionally, a helping hand to witch-hunt victims whom he knew. Still, he had little patience and sympathy for the relatively few communists he continued to encounter. To be sure, he didn't give more than a scintilla of psychic energy to them, and to the extent he thought about them at all, he held to a very strong stereotype: they were quarrelsome, rigid, dour, humorless. In any event, he thought that to be a communist in the United States was pointless at best and perverse and destructive at worst. In short, communists were trouble that his community organizations could do without. Within an organization, they were apt to be trouble because they were obsessed with pushing ideologically pure issues and otherwise manipulating the agenda for their own narrow interests. They were also trouble, especially if they occupied visible leadership roles, because they made the organization vulnerable to outside attack. In short, he did not like them, did not need them, and, as a general matter, wanted them quietly moved out of his community organizations. (Fred Ross and Cesar Chavez followed such a course with the CSO in Los Angeles. Alinsky's two organizers coached the CSO leaders on what to expect, how to respond to likely arguments, what parliamentary moves to make, and, above all, the importance of making sure that their supporters were at a pivotal meeting for the decisive vote. Doug Still recalls being impressed that Ross and Chavez were able to defeat a few communist insurgents democratically.)

Now, in Woodlawn in January 1961, Alinsky decided that the underbrush had to be cleared so that a single, strong community organization could be planted. The underbrush included the United Woodlawn Conference, of course, and a half dozen or so communists. After von Hoffman consulted with Alinsky—he would almost never make a move of any importance without doing so—he selected a time and place for a meeting: the evening of January 16 at St. Clara's Church. Although he invited the Conference and other Woodlawn groups, he was intentionally vague about the purpose of the meeting. But Alinsky's Woodlawn supporters knew what was expected since they were carefully rehearsed by von Hoffman as to who would make the motion creating the Temporary Woodlawn Organization (TWO, pronounced T-W-O), who would nominate the prearranged slate of officers, and so forth. All of this was to happen in rapid-fire order, with von Hoffman and Squires merely observing from the sidelines, having made certain they had enough votes to defeat any challenge. Taking no chances, von Hoffman, with a Chicago-like burst of inspiration, instructed Squires to recruit several of his bulkier friends from the billiard room in the Hayes Hotel, a local hangout, who might provide a certain nonverbal persuasiveness at the meeting—just in case there were any obstreperous dissenters. "Saul had no objections to vigorous democratic action," von Hoffman says of his boss's implicit approval.

One of the leaders of the United Woodlawn Conference, Ann Prosten, remembers that no sooner had the meeting begun than somebody was on his feet calling for a point of order, saying that the meeting ought to be chaired by someone who was not already a leader of one of the existing local groups. A motion was made to nominate the Reverend Robert McGee as temporary chairman. It was quickly seconded and passed by voice vote. Belatedly, Mrs. Prosten realized her side had been sandbagged. "We were outnumbered. The minute that person was put in, [their side] proposed a series of rules by which the discussion would be conducted: only by recognition of the chair, and if he didn't want to recognize you, that was it, you couldn't talk. And posted around the room were some heavyset fellows. . . . We were told immediately, 'These are the sergeants at arms, I want you to meet them.'" And in fact, several of the heavyset fellows were carrying billiard cues.

With an organizational name, temporary officers, and one issue that had already created a stir in Woodlawn, von Hoffman and Squires fanned out into the community to build an organization.

Indeed, "organizing" hardly seemed adequate to describe what von Hoffman and Lester Hunt thought Alinsky was all about, and what they were all about. They could walk with a swagger around Chicago, as they did, because they were not only organizers but also magicians, capable of making something out of nothing. Their attitude was easy to resent, as von Hoffman knew. But he reveled in being part of Alinsky's little fraternity of organizer-magicians.

> It is a very strange thing. You go somewhere, and you know nobody. You drive up in a car, and you know nobody, and you've got to organize it into something that it's never been before. You know, you're not a Democrat or Republican. You don't have much going for you. You don't have prestige, you don't have muscle, you've got no money to give away. All you have are your wits. You've just got your wits, charm, and whatever you can put together. So you had better form a very accurate picture of what's going on, and you had better not bring in too many a priori maps [because] if you do, you're just not going to get anywhere.

In Woodlawn, the area west of Cottage Grove Avenue was largely a middle- and working-class neighborhood in good condition, although showing signs of age. Von Hoffman emphasized to Alinsky that this section of Woodlawn had a history of healthy community life, and blacks had been living there for more than twenty-five years. The area was honeycombed with block clubs, and many of Farrell's parishioners lived in this area. Von Hoffman projected that if a few Protestant churches could also be brought into the organization, along with new block clubs, then "I believe we would be in fairly good shape [in that area]."

But the other part of Woodlawn, east of Cottage Grove to Stony Island, was a horse of a different color. He told Alinsky: "Moving across Cottage Grove Avenue . . . is like going into another planet. East Woodlawn is a classic example of a disorganized big-city slum. Anyone who claims to have anything remotely resembling a representative organization in East Woodlawn is either a liar or a fool. I have absolutely no faith in any of the organizational maneuvers which have been pulled in the past, and that includes my own. None of them will work, no matter how much energy and vigor is put into them."

After strategizing with Alinsky, von Hoffman started by dividing up the territory, which held about 90,000 people, into workable sections. Squires had the largest section, a stretch of East Woodlawn thirteen blocks long, from Cottage Grove to Stony Island, and five blocks deep, from Sixty-third Street south to Oakwoods Cemetery. Every day for months, Squires walked the streets—"our office was the street"—sometimes going door to door, sometimes hitting the commercial establishments and hot spots on Sixty-third Street. "Sixty-third Street from Stony Island to Cottage Grove, I knew every son of a bitch in that area. I knew every bookie, every whore, every policy runner, every cop, every bartender, waitress, store owner, restaurant owner." And at the end of almost every day, Squires dictated a report—whom he had met, his impressions of them, where they fit in the community, what they were concerned about—onto one of Alinsky's dictabelts. At night, he often compared notes with von Hoffman, first over in Hyde Park, where, Squires says, "Nick would be listening to Joan Baez or some broad singing about trials and tribulations, until I got Nick over there on Sixty-third and Cottage Grove, at McKee's or the Cotton Club, right in the middle of that smoke-filled, pot-smelling jazz room. And we'd be talking about the Woodlawn community, and he could feel it and hear it."

There was no office for many months. When von Hoffman or Squires needed a phone or a desk, they went to Farrell's or Leber's church. For a time, Squires and von Hoffman were the only two, but a number of others came and went. Much to their surprise, an earnest young man who became one of their best organizers was a white theology student from the University of Chicago, Richard Harmon. "Harmon just kind of turned up," von Hoffman says, "working his butt off. Squires and I watched him for a long time, and we determined that he would fit in the 'siditty' area, which was what we called West Woodlawn." ("Siditty," one of Squires's favorite expressions, was black slang for "hoity-toity.") West Woodlawn had some black professionals, homeowners, and many club ladies who liked Harmon, von Hoffman says, "because he was so pretty, had good manners, never used bad words, and was very patient." A young black theology student, Jeff Williams, worked with black churches.

Each organizer had his own style, but the most stylized of all was von Hoffman, who was very purposeful about the image he projected:

> I dressed very expensively, and I was impeccable. I would wear a
> bowler; I want you to know that I looked like a super pimp. I looked
> like I had it made, and that commanded respect. . . . Dealing with and
> trying to organize people who have this vast history of defeat, of being
> bopped on the head—they don't need to look at some raggedy-assed

[white] person who looks like he couldn't make it with his own people, you know. Even in talking about my own motivations, I would play down the idealism. People are going to ask you, "What's in it for you?" The thing to do is to say, "Well, if it works, I'm going to get rich and famous and powerful." That they relate to and trust. This is something Saul said many, many times.

Alinsky appreciated von Hoffman's theatrical embellishments in Woodlawn, though it was not the persona he would have felt comfortable with.

As the organizers made their rounds, they listened to what people told them about problems in the neighborhood, looked for leaders who might be able to head up a block club or committee, and agitated. The threat of dispossession by the university's urban-renewal plan was a powerful issue. "They're going to wipe you out," Squires would tell Woodlawn homeowners, sometimes adding that the university's secret plan was to push residents all the way back to the cemetery at Sixty-seventh Street. But there were other problems and gripes, too—for example, complaints that a number of local merchants were cheating customers, using short weights, overcharging them, adding on hidden interest charges. Alinsky and von Hoffman thought these issues could be used both to mobilize residents and to demonstrate that, once mobilized, people could make a difference and turn things around. On a Monday night in April, the organizers turned out six hundred Woodlawnites to parade down Sixty-third Street: this was the beginning of the Square Deal campaign, in which TWO organized squads of shoppers to investigate suspected merchants, scales were set up to spot short weights, and a boycott was organized against one merchant until he agreed to negotiate with a TWO committee.

Through the spring, the organizing process progressed better than Alinsky and von Hoffman could have expected. New block clubs were organized, a few black churches got more involved, fraternal groups were joining up. Then, suddenly and unexpectedly, an event occurred that changed the direction in which Alinsky's project was headed.

It started late in May 1961 with a long-distance, collect phone call to von Hoffman from a young man named Terry who had been in the Catholic Worker movement and a TWO volunteer but left Chicago to join a small interracial group, sponsored by the Congress of Racial Equality, that was going to ride a bus through the South to protest segregation in bus terminals. (Only months before, in December 1960, the Supreme Court had outlawed segregation in interstate transportation, including bus and train terminals, but the decision was being widely ignored in much of the South.) The Freedom Riders, as they became known, traveled through several

Southern states without major incident until they arrived in Anniston, Alabama, where a mob burned one bus and beat up the passengers in another. When more Freedom Riders arrived in Montgomery, they were greeted with even worse violence—an ax-and-chain-wielding crowd circled the bus terminal and attacked the Freedom Riders as they got off their Greyhound bus. Attorney General Robert F. Kennedy shortly dispatched five hundred federal marshals to Montgomery to protect both them and Martin Luther King, Jr., who came to lend his support. By the time the Freedom Ride ended in Mississippi, it had become one of the most dramatic episodes yet of the civil rights movement, the courage and determination of the Riders inspiring blacks and sympathetic whites throughout the United States.

Terry, who was calling von Hoffman from a New Orleans hospital where he was recovering from a beating he had received, said he and a few other Riders wanted to make their first public appearance in Woodlawn. Could Nick set up the meeting? Von Hoffman said he'd let him know, and told the TWO executive committee about the idea. Personally, he was not enthusiastic. Wearing his organizer's hat, he envisioned a failure, recalling not one civil rights rally or protest in recent Chicago history that had attracted much of a crowd. (Some years earlier, black leaders had called a civil rights protest rally in Washington Park after a black man had been lynched in Poplarville, Mississippi. When von Hoffman showed up, he recalled, he was the only one there.) Now, he could easily imagine an embarrassing, poorly attended meeting that gossipmongers in Woodlawn and, worse still, across the Midway at the University of Chicago would point to as a sign of TWO's weakness and incompetence.

But the TWO executive committee, which included many cautious black property owners, wanted to go ahead, and arrangements were made to hold a meeting in the big gymnasium at St. Cyril's Church, a parish that was now empty because all the whites had moved out. On a Friday night, two hours before the program was to start, the gym was empty and von Hoffman was nervous—his initial fears seemed about to be confirmed. An hour later, an elderly couple arrived, and then, to von Hoffman's total amazement, so many more people turned up that there was no room left in the gym, in the foyer, or on the stairs. Hundreds of people were out in the street, where loudspeakers were quickly set up. Woodlawn had turned out en masse for the Freedom Riders. Toward the end of the program, one of them said, "We have a song we sing, it's called 'We Shall Overcome.' How many of you know it?" Only a few hands went up. "We shall teach it to you," one of the Freedom Riders said, and they did.

At evening's end, von Hoffman was in an unfamiliar state of shock and euphoria. He went out with friends for a drink and tried to fathom how his expectations could have been so wrong. When he got home at three in the morning, he did not hesitate to pick up the special phone in his apartment that only Alinsky called on—to call the boss at his house in Carmel. "This better be good," was the boss's opening growl, to which von Hoffman replied, "It is good; mix yourself a drink, I got to talk to you for a while." Blow by blow, von Hoffman described what had happened, and when he finished, he said, "I think that we should toss out everything we are doing organizationally and work on the premise that this is the moment of the whirlwind, that we are no longer organizing but guiding a social movement." There was only a brief pause at the other end, and then Alinsky said, "You're right. Get on it tomorrow."

Only many years later did von Hoffman fully appreciate Alinsky's reaction. It pinpointed Alinsky's brilliance as a political tactician: he was able to shed even his most favored organizational concepts and assumptions when confronted with a new, unexpected reality. For all his stubbornness that would infuriate Ralph Helstein; for all his self-centeredness that would rankle Jack Egan; for all his even more extreme forms of self-absorption that his psychiatric friends diagnosed as rampant narcissism, Alinsky could also be flexible, open, and mindful that others might sometimes know better.

For some weeks, there continued to be a surface similarity to the organizing efforts in Woodlawn. But von Hoffman was no longer looking only or primarily for "specific, immediate, and realizable" issues, Alinsky's axiom for organizing. Now Alinsky had spotted an opportunity to capitalize on—and test—the growing identification of Woodlawn residents with the civil rights movement in the South.

As a consequence of a partisan feud in the Illinois state legislature over charges of vote fraud in Cook County, the voter registration lists were wiped clean and every eligible voter in Chicago had to register again before he could vote in the next election. "The moment that Saul heard about it," von Hoffman remembers, "he said, 'Get on this.' " Inspired by the large, emotional turnout to see the Freedom Riders at St. Cyril's, Alinsky and von Hoffman invented their own version of the Freedom Ride. TWO would organize a large bus caravan from Woodlawn to City Hall to register voters. Of course, success depended entirely on getting a huge turnout of black voters.

Most of the organizing for the bus caravan was crammed into several weeks, and much of the energy went into fund-raising. "TWO never put up any money for [this] because you knew that you'd never fill a bus unless the people who are going to ride in the bus pay for it," von Hoffman says.

"So we had these endless fund-raisers for the buses. One apartment house after another. We had chicken dinners, barbecues, we even had hookers running fund-raisers." As the Saturday of the big event drew near, Alinsky and von Hoffman did not want anything left to chance. "We wanted a list of every name, of every person who was going to be on every bus. And their address," von Hoffman remembers. With only several days to go before the buses were to roll, von Hoffman's hopes and fears gyrated wildly. He had upped the number of buses that he ordered to twenty, then to thirty, and finally to more than forty. The lists of people were looking good, but the complexity of the operation scared him. On the morning of the event, hundreds of people were scheduled for wake-up phone calls and buses had to make pickups at specific places and times, though many drivers did not know the area. "In many instances, we were working with people who had never been in any organization larger than a crap game," he says.

With the final preparations in place, the first near-disaster struck when the Chicago Transit Authority, under the control of City Hall, called to cancel all the buses it had agreed to rent to TWO. A mad scramble ensued, with von Hoffman scrounging buses from suburban transit systems and from the archdiocese.

The second near-disaster, just hours before the first wake-up calls on Saturday morning, shook von Hoffman up even more. Bob Squires, the ace organizer who was responsible for filling up more buses than anybody else, was assaulted and stabbed as he left McKee's Lounge after a night of listening to some jam and jazz. He staggered home and phoned von Hoffman, who raced him to a doctor, a member of Chuck Leber's church. Miraculously, by 6 a.m. Squires was ready when Lester Hunt swung by in his Volkswagen to drive him around Woodlawn, where he rousted would-be bus riders out of apartment buildings and houses. Von Hoffman, however, emotionally spent, vomiting, was bracing for the worst. "There's no way that this can be a success," he remembers saying to himself as the sun started to rise on a cool August morning.

But a few hours later, when he came over to the Midway, the morning's rendezvous point, his eyes fixed on "the most satisfying scene I have ever seen in my life. As far as the eye could see, buses, all jammed with black persons. Every bus was draped with a banner saying 'Better Housing' or 'Jobs' or 'Vote' and, of course, with the emblem of TWO." The caravan headed toward City Hall with forty-six buses and more than 2,500 black passengers.

The first stop the bus caravan made on its way to City Hall had been planned so that Chicago *Daily News* reporter Georgie Anne Geyer, who was in the lead bus, could phone in a story to meet an early deadline. (That

Geyer was the first reporter to cover the emerging TWO story was not happenstance: She had grown up on the Southwest Side and was still living there when Alinsky started the OSC project in 1959 and got to know both him and his organizers. She sensed immediately that TWO was an important, historic undertaking. What little newspaper coverage there was of the black community tended to be in the *Daily News,* though even that wasn't much. Geyer, however, was resourceful and persuasive, and she had a few sympathetic editors who wanted to give more attention to the black community.) The second stop was not planned. The caravan was escorted by black motorcycle cops and behind them were a convertible filled with several of TWO's black leaders, von Hoffman, and Jack Egan and a bus carrying a generous number of nuns. In tight situations in Chicago, you couldn't be too Catholic, was Alinsky's commonsense philosophy. Suddenly and unexpectedly, the black cops were confronted by a posse of white cops, a scene reminiscent of something out of *Bad Day at Black Rock.* Egan sprang from the car in full priestly attire, smoothing things over and averting still another possible disaster. But as the TWO contingent came within sight of City Hall, they saw more police who seemed eager to do battle on this otherwise quiet late-summer Saturday. In fact, City Hall was ringed by policemen, and Jack Egan had heard a rumor that many more heavily armed reinforcements were at the ready in the basement of City Hall. As the buses were parked and the riders started to get out, von Hoffman spotted Marshall Korshak, the usually unflappable, hard-bitten Democratic committeeman of the 5th Ward. Von Hoffman hollered to him: "Hey, what are you going to do, Marshall, machine-gun the nuns? These people are all your voters." "It's a mistake, it's a mistake," Korshak chanted, a kind of political prayer, it seemed, in the circumstances. "Yes, it is a mistake," von Hoffman said, "and you better do something about it. They haven't come here to burn the place down, which they should do. Maybe next time they will, but this time they want to register to vote—even the nuns."

The parked buses surrounded City Hall, too. Inside, it took most of the day for Election Commissioner Sidney Holtzman and forty-five extra clerks to register everybody. It was the largest single voter-registration event ever at City Hall. If one understands that Chicago's religion is politics, then one can also appreciate why the capacity to deliver votes in unprecedented numbers might attract as much of the city's attention as other supernatural acts—such as, say, the capacity to walk on water.

To be sure, one successful event, even of this startling magnitude, did not turn Chicago upside down. The vastness of the city always muffled political noise. Nonetheless, this was an event that none of the downtown media could ignore. It was not something that Levi and the University of Chicago could ignore. Nor could the mayor. In 1960, Richard J. Daley's efforts had helped to elect John F. Kennedy as President. Kennedy won Illinois by only 8,858 votes. Woodlawn's plurality for Kennedy was about 17,000. No, the mayor could not ignore a forty-six-bus caravan of 2,500 Woodlawn voters. And neither could Marshall Korshak. Alinsky's successful gamble caused political lights to flash like lights in a pinball machine. And like a crafty pinball player with a sense of timing and a little luck, he had started to run up a score by ricocheting the steel ball from one target to another.

The success of the bus caravan scored points with Korshak. Woodlawn sat astride three wards, the 5th, the 6th, and a little of the 20th. Alinsky's organizers did not have to worry about crossing swords with the powerful South Side black congressman William Dawson, because very little of Dawson's political territory touched Woodlawn. (Dawson controlled wards to the north and west of Woodlawn.) The 6th Ward was run by Robert H. Miller, the alderman and ward committeeman. Soon TWO would have de facto control of his ward but, as von Hoffman says, "Miller had so little clout himself that to control Miller was to control nothing." Korshak, on the other hand, had a lot of clout and Woodlawn contained a lot of his precincts. Those precincts were important to him because of the problems he had on the other side of the Midway in Hyde Park, where he could not count on the intellectuals, independents, and reformers. If he lost control of his Woodlawn precincts, he was in trouble. Although Alinsky had not initiated the voter-registration extravaganza with Korshak in mind, a nice bonus was that TWO suddenly had some leverage with him—Alinsky and von Hoffman calculated that TWO could claim as much as 30 percent of the 5th Ward, which translated into about 50 percent in leverage. So as long as TWO's demands were not excessive, it could call on Korshak for help and, in fact, it got him to cough up a number of patronage jobs. Someone like Korshak could also be useful in running interference for TWO in the courts when, for example, slum landlords pressed charges to stop TWO-organized rent strikes. All TWO wanted was to have friendly judges assigned to these cases—which well-connected committeemen could arrange—who would grant TWO's lawyers postponements. If the postponements continued more or less indefinitely, TWO's organizers had a good chance to win their rent strikes.

Emboldened by the success of TWO's "vote-in" at City Hall, Alinsky wanted to attack another civil rights issue: the unequal, segregated school system. In Woodlawn, there was great concern and anger about the deterioration in the quality of education. Woodlawn's schools were so overcrowded that the school day had to be split into double shifts, while schools in some white neighborhoods had empty classrooms. These inequalities and related problems were obvious, but the school board, and the Superintendent of Education, Benjamin Willis, refused to release statistics or to make surveys that would document precisely their scope and effect. Alinsky wanted TWO to challenge and expose Willis's Orwellian claim that there was no evidence of intentional segregation.

It was not that other groups in Chicago had not raised the issues of overcrowding and segregated schools before. But none did so with the forcefulness and imagination that TWO brought to the issue. In October 1961, a TWO delegation of more than three hundred appeared at a downtown school board hearing. Half went into the hearing room, led by the Reverend Arthur Brazier; the other half marched outside in front of the building. According to one account, after an hour, when only two of more than sixty scheduled speakers had testified, Brazier tried to get the floor. "We have been here for several hours and our people are working people and I feel that they should have a chance to testify," Brazier said. When the school board president refused to recognize him, Brazier and the TWO delegation walked out, joining the other pickets outside. They chastised Willis and the school board for "double shifts in black communities and double talk public relations." A week later, another TWO delegation was back, demanding Willis's resignation. And two weeks after that, TWO held its own public hearing at the Southmoor Hotel in Woodlawn. More than seven hundred people jammed into the hearing to listen to parents, students, and community leaders testify about inadequate facilities, lack of books, and the demoralizing effects of double shifts. Alinsky, who rarely appeared in Woodlawn or at TWO's public events, spoke on this occasion. But the dramatic highlight of the evening was a behind-the-scenes account and criticism of school policies by three teachers. To protect them from reprisals by superiors and for dramatic effect, the TWO organizers hid their identity by draping sheets over them. (As things turned out, only two of the three were teachers. When the third teacher failed to show up, Bob Squires, who somehow believed that three was significantly better than two, quickly recruited a sixteen-year-old girl whom he knew; instructing her not to say a word, he threw a sheet over her, put her on the stage with the two teachers, and kept his fingers crossed that her sheet wouldn't fall off.)

Alinsky felt strongly about the school-segregation issue but, more to the point of organizing TWO, it was also an organizer's dream, with both Willis and the school board as ready villains. TWO kept pressing the issue well into 1962 with a continuing barrage of highly visible, theatrical protests. Dressed in black capes to symbolize "the mourning of Negro parents for the plight of their children," "death watchers" appeared at regular school board meetings. "Truth Squad" mothers from Woodlawn descended upon elementary schools in white neighborhoods unannounced to document with cameras what Willis would not—that there were empty classrooms. Willis's remedy for the overcrowding in black neighborhoods like Woodlawn was to provide them with mobile classrooms, which TWO immediately renamed "Willis Wagons." "No one liked to sit around and think up these things to do more than Saul," von Hoffman says. And no one had more fun thinking up ways to ridicule and harass the deserving targets.

Indeed, Willis's plan to install mobile classrooms in Woodlawn elicited what was perhaps TWO's most impressive protest, the most convincing evidence to date as to how well organized and disciplined it had become. Alinsky and von Hoffman brainstormed about a school boycott to symbolize the outrage of Woodlawn's parents. But a picket line in front of a school to discourage attendance—the conventional tactic—might have the picketers facing arrest and jail. Instead, Alinsky decided to do the seemingly impossible: declare a one-day boycott and have an area of Woodlawn so tightly organized that virtually no students would show up at the local school. The TWO organizers targeted the large Carnegie elementary school and, with the help of volunteers, assigned one person to be in charge of six or eight apartment units—to educate parents about the issues, to erect TWO "school boycott" signs in every apartment window, and, on Friday morning, May 18, 1962, to make certain that students stayed home.

The result was a stunning success that surpassed even Alinsky's expectations: about 1,200 out of 1,350 Carnegie students stayed away. The Chicago press gave the boycott front-page coverage, and the ecstatic von Hoffman was eager to move ahead with a whole series of school boycotts. Alinsky, however, vetoed the idea. Von Hoffman was furious, and one night the two of them stayed up until dawn arguing about it. Alinsky's position was simple: He thought everybody would go to jail if the boycotts continued, whether or not there was a picket line; school and city officials would simply not let TWO get away with it. Already four TWO Truth Squad mothers had been arrested for trespassing. Nonetheless, von Hoffman insisted that they had to take the chance. Finally Alinsky laid down the law, saying he was the boss and that there would be no more school boycotts in Woodlawn, and von Hoffman relented—although it was the closest he had ever come to quitting.

A new tactic which TWO used to pressure slum landlords was quintessentially Alinsky. In addition to rent strikes, TWO began to picket the (often white) landlords who refused to repair heating systems or broken water pipes, but instead of picketing in front of the slum building in Woodlawn, a TWO delegation—black people, mostly, with only a few white clergy sprinkled in—traveled to the landlord's white neighborhood to picket his house and pass out flyers to his neighbors. "Do you know that one of your neighbors is a slum landlord?" the picket signs and flyers asked. "He is Julius Mark, 2409 East Seventy-third Street. He leases and won't fix a slum at 6434 South Kimbark, where the tenants are so mad they've called a rent strike." Like all the other demonstrations, the residential picketing was carefully planned. Von Hoffman called the police in advance to tell them that there would be peaceful picketing. The media were notified. Specially trained TWO volunteers became a team of regulars who went on these assignments. Later, in recounting the psychology of the tactic to reporters, Alinsky remarked, deadpan: "For this assignment, we practically used a color chart in Woodlawn to recruit pickets. We wanted to use only the darkest Negroes." Once again, Alinsky and his organizers used white fear and loathing of blacks to best advantage. For every positive there is a negative, and vice versa: this was one of Alinsky's fundamental operating principles. If blacks suffered discrimination because of their skin color, then, he said, there must be a way to "flip the coin" to their advantage.

From all accounts, the residential picketing by blacks from TWO usually produced results. Not only was the landlord embarrassed but his neighbors were furious if not hysterical. TWO also capitalized in other ways on white phobia about blacks intruding into their space. It forced banks, for example, to reveal the names of slum landlords who had tried to conceal their ownership by using corporate fronts. Leber recalls:

> Saul said that there was a very simple way to do that. You just line up people to open new accounts in the bank, and you . . . fill up the bank lobby, and do it peacefully. Train your people carefully. . . . And you do that for two or three days, and tie up their business, and of course you scare the hell out of every white person coming to that bank when they see all these black people in there. We only had to do it once to one bank, and every other bank knew what would happen if it didn't cooperate. And they had been warned. First the clergy would go in, with our collars on, for an appointment with the bank president. A very important part was when they would say, "Thank you, gentlemen, but we're sorry, we can't help you." We'd say, "Thank you, Mr. President. Just remember we've been here and we asked nicely." That's it, and we'd leave. No sassiness, no threats. And

then a group of our citizens would come and say, "The clergy were here and you wouldn't help them. What about us? We're homeowners in the area. Will you help us?" "Well, it's against bank policy." We'd have it all documented, how many times we went into these places. . . . When we had a chance to go out to the churches and youth groups and everywhere else to tell them what was happening, we'd go through this whole process for them. We'd say, "We used the regular methods for being open, thoughtful, decent, kind, all of the Boy Scout virtues, and everybody told us to go to hell." So we'd say, "All right, we have to use another way of communicating." And that's how we did the bank thing. That's how we found out where those slum land-lords—slumlords, we called them—lived.

Because of this process, black pickets went into white communities not feeling self-conscious about a publicity stunt, but with dignity, righteous-ness, and purpose in fighting for a just cause.

Slum landlords, school integration, and dishonest local merchants were issues that galvanized citizen participation in TWO during its first year (and it is worth noting that in the first year the "T" in TWO still stood for "temporary"). Many Woodlawnites became involved in TWO because they had a self-interest, to use Alinsky's language, in, say, the quality of schools or rental housing, but TWO also had a strong civil rights appeal, more so than any other large-scale effort in Chicago, and the battle with the University of Chicago defined its role, too. If TWO had a slogan or theme during its first year it was self-determination. The motto that the Back of the Yards Neighborhood Council had adopted in 1939 was: "We the people will work out our own destiny." No issue that TWO raised in its first year more clearly delineated what it meant by self-determination than "the war over urban renewal," as the newspapers began to call the struggle between TWO and the university.

THE PUBLIC ARGUMENT between the university and TWO turned nasty quickly, beginning at the hearing in December 1960 at the Chicago Plan Commission. From then on, TWO harassed Julian Levi and the university at every turn. For example, Doc Farrell and Chuck Leber, whom Levi had placed on the advisory board of his South East Chicago Commission (SECC) several years earlier, asked the Commission to en-dorse a resolution at its monthly meeting in January 1961 that said, in part: "The principle of community self-determination applies to Woodlawn as it does to all other communities. . . . The South East Chicago Commission pledges itself to find a means of open, public, and equal negotiation to settle the differences outstanding between it and the people of Woodlawn." It was obvious to Levi and others that "self-determination" meant TWO's determination of what was best for Woodlawn, and that the city of Chicago should approve no urban-renewal plan for Woodlawn unless TWO approved. Not surprisingly, the SECC called for "citizen participation" instead, which of course TWO rejected. Arthur Brazier, on behalf of TWO, said: "King George was willing to give the American colonies 'participation' but George Washington wanted 'self-determination.' . . . We may have our little differences of opinion between ourselves, but we are all firmly united against any attempt at foreign domination."

In fact, collective bargaining between union and management was a more fitting analogy, for Alinsky wanted TWO to be the bargaining agent for Woodlawn vis-à-vis the university. And TWO's bargaining position was that any plan for Woodlawn must be comprehensive—that is, the South Campus urban renewal must be a part of a larger scheme. This formulation appealed to several constituencies: for example, local businessmen located along Sixty-third Street, almost all of them white, knew, sometimes from bitter firsthand experience, that urban renewal could wipe them out. As Alinsky's organizers quickly discovered, similar fears existed, or were not difficult to excite, among homeowners and renters. And institutions in Woodlawn felt threatened, too. First Presbyterian, where Chuck Leber was co-pastor, was the oldest church in Chicago, although it had not always been at its present location. "It had moved seven times," Leber says, "and [now] the church decided they were not going to move again."

Finally, the brilliance of Alinsky's formulation was also that it sought to use the university's political power to benefit TWO. There was no reason to believe that TWO by itself could induce the city to implement a good urban-renewal program for Woodlawn, but with the university's help TWO might get at least some of what it wanted. (TWO soon hired its own planner and proposed its own urban-renewal plan, which focused on both rehabilitation of existing housing and construction of new low-cost units.) And to get that help, Alinsky's strategy was to create a bargaining situation.

But Levi would not sit down and meet with the TWO leaders. In the parlance of labor union–management disputes, Levi refused to recognize TWO as the bargaining agent for Woodlawn. He wrapped this refusal in respectable-sounding pronouncements and platitudes about the use of proper procedures to decide matters of public policy. "TWO has taken the position that this whole South Campus thing should be settled with us by

negotiation," he said. "Well, we're discussing here a public program involving public power and public money. There's only one way in which you
decide the content and the approval or disapproval of a program of this
kind. We have the people elected to decide it and to decide it with all of
the safeguards that arise under law." The statement was hypocritical, for
Levi had negotiated arrangements with private interests during the Hyde
Park–Kenwood urban-renewal process and dominated it from start to
finish. Still, implicit in Levi's rationalization was the important question
of how the decision-making process should be structured. Another voice
in American public affairs was not bashful about pointing out the dangers
of having groups like TWO influence such processes. James Q. Wilson of
Harvard University wrote: "Upper- and upper-middle-class people are
more likely to think in terms of general plans, the neighborhood or community as a whole, and long-term benefits (even when they might involve
immediate costs to themselves); lower- and lower-middle-class people are
more likely to see such matters in terms of specific threats and short-term
costs." The lower classes, he said, "are likely to have what one might call
a 'private regarding' rather than a 'public regarding' political ethos." Increasingly, according to Wilson, professional planners faced a dilemma: on
the one hand, from their lofty perch high above the multitudes, planners
had clear, broad visions of the larger public good; on the other hand, the
"lower classes," who did not share the planners' view of "progress," were
prone to participate in urban-renewal decision-making, fighting "progress"
at every turn. Although Wilson noted that federal urban-renewal policy
required citizen participation, he was not optimistic about the prospects if
participation was defined so that the lower classes—and he mentioned
Alinsky's TWO project specifically—were encouraged to become participants.

Levi's counter-strategy of refusing to recognize TWO as *the* spokesman for Woodlawn made less and less sense. As early as January 1961,
when the Chicago Plan Commission reconvened, the Commission made
two announcements that TWO claimed as victories: most important, at
least symbolically, it recommended to the Land Clearance Commission
that the urban-renewal eligibility survey be expanded to include more than
South Campus; second, it announced it would develop an overall plan for
Woodlawn. Even at this early date, Alinsky and von Hoffman could see
their position vis-à-vis the university improving. They sensed that if Levi
could not push his plan through quickly, he was likely to become, for their
purposes, an invitingly slow-moving target. To be sure, he still had the
power of the university's political connections. But the South Campus
project was not small or simple enough to manipulate easily. "You're

talking about federal forms from the floor to the ceiling," von Hoffman says. "Required reports for this, required reports for that, feasibility studies, disfeasibility studies, financial woowahs—this was just an open gearbox asking for sand to be thrown in it. You can't say, 'Look, tell Jones to get his ass out there and take care of it.' Crude power melts against this. You don't even know who to fire."

Since Levi did not suffer stubborn bureaucrats gladly, he must have been increasingly frustrated and angry, and almost certainly not the only one at the university who felt that way. After all, the university was a great institution, and great institutions—and their great leaders—ought not to be treated as ordinary players on the dusty floor of the political arena. Levi, in fact, told the writer Charles Silberman, who interviewed him during this conflict, "The university was the only first-rate thing in this city."

Normally, Alinsky's joy over shaking up the status quo in Chicago would have been total, but in this instance a pie chart might have shown a narrow slice of gray to indicate his more complicated feelings about the "war" with the University of Chicago. Alinsky was proud that he had graduated from the University of Chicago, though he never said so. His closest friends surmised, as Sidney Hyman did, that graduating from the university was his badge of honor, a shiny, proud achievement, a rite of passage from his dreary, not very respectable family background. There was something of a psychological tug that Alinsky felt as he directed TWO's assault against his alma mater. He also began to experience a measure of disapproval from some of his friends in Hyde Park, some of whom taught at the university, or had also graduated from it, and others who simply took pride in living in the shadows of the renowned institution. It was not that these friends were apologists for the university, but rather that many of them felt that somehow the conflict was getting out of hand. Some may have wondered whether Alinsky was being rougher on the university and its leadership than was necessary. (Even total strangers evidently considered Alinsky a rough customer if not something of a barbarian. One night he was walking Pang in the neighborhood when another man's unleashed dog started to come toward them. The dog attacked Pang, a gentle but powerful animal, and by the time the dog's owner appeared on the scene, his dog was lying on the pavement bleeding, mortally wounded. He demanded to know who Pang's owner was and when he heard the name, he exploded: "Saul Alinsky? It figures you'd have this kind of a dog.") Then, one day in the spring of 1961, there was a phone call from Dutch Smith. Smith, the president of the huge insurance company Marsh & McClennan, and a member of both the University of Chicago's board of trustees and Alinsky's Industrial Areas Foundation board, called to tell Alinsky that he was resigning from the IAF board. He did not go into great detail with Alinsky, but years later he recalled that he was upset because "Saul was making things very difficult for the university. He was calling them names, more or less. [He was] very unrestrained."

Smith had known Alinsky for more than twenty years, though he had never been completely comfortable with him. He used to take Alinsky to lunch at the informal, literary Cliff Dwellers Club on Michigan Avenue, but never to either the Attic Club or the Chicago Club, two prime meeting grounds for the city's Waspy corporate executives. "I don't think . . . Saul made a very good first impression. . . . His looks were against him to begin with [and] I was a little concerned about Saul's behavior. . . . His language wasn't very refined. I didn't know what he might do." It was essentially because of this unpredictability that Alinsky never received financial support from Smith's counterparts in the mainline foundations, such as the Ford Foundation. He could not be trusted to abide by the unspoken, traditional rules of genteel political argument and action. In Chicago, Smith did not know how much further Alinsky might go—what stunt he might pull next—to embarrass and to make trouble for the university.

For his part, Alinsky was saddened and disappointed by Smith's resignation. "Twenty-three years is a long time," Alinsky wrote regretfully to Smith. And he was especially angry about an article that had appeared recently in the university's student newspaper that tried to label TWO as a segregationist hate group funded by the Catholic Church and controlled by the archdiocese's unscrupulous agent, Saul Alinsky's Industrial Areas Foundation. The story had the byline of a student reporter, but he had no doubt it had been generated by university officials.

"To a substantial degree," he wrote to Smith, "many of these activities by the university representatives have been incomprehensible to me in the light of what our program and purpose actually is." Although Alinsky was clearly disappointed, maybe even hurt, by Smith's resignation, he made it clear that he valued their friendship. When it came to old friends and to keeping valuable contacts, Alinsky was characteristically slow to burn bridges.

Months later, in the fall of 1961, Smith phoned again, this time to arrange a meeting between Alinsky and the University of Chicago's new president, George Beadle. Smith hoped that the two of them might find a way out of the conflict.

Over lunch, Alinsky tried to persuade Beadle, who had only recently arrived in Chicago, that the picture he had of the genesis of the Woodlawn project was inaccurate, that it had not been his intention to make the university a target or scapegoat. But when Beadle asked questions about the Back of the Yards Neighborhood Council, Alinsky's conciliatory tone turned defensive and then hostile, for the implication was that Beadle, like other university officials, saw TWO as a Catholic plot—that because Alinsky had done such a good job for the Church in the old stockyards community, the Church was hoping he could do a good job again, this time by blocking a plan in Woodlawn that otherwise might result in the relocation of blacks in white Southwest Side parishes. Alinsky counterattacked and later wrote to Beadle: "Permit me to suggest that in any debate, the record of the Back of the Yards Council in the field of race relations, including its own present unfortunate orientation, could more than hold its own in comparison with any other community in the city, including Hyde Park." While telling Beadle that he thought TWO's interests in improving Woodlawn were in the university's best interests, too, Alinsky also warned that TWO would not stand passively by while the urban-renewal process unfolded.

Perhaps Alinsky sounded more menacing and uncompromising than he had realized. When he bumped into Ralph Helstein immediately after his lunch with Beadle, he told his friend he was very pleased—that he had laid it on the line, even suggesting something to the effect that since there were a lot of tough guys in Woodlawn, don't be surprised if you're looking down the barrel of a gun someday. Helstein feared that Alinsky had taken the wrong approach with the mild-mannered president, and Beadle himself confirmed his strong misgivings about Alinsky in a brief report to Dutch Smith.

"I'm convinced that nothing short of agreeing 100 percent with Saul could cure me of my sins. And if I did agree 100 percent, I'm convinced Saul would use that to enhance his position of power and privilege. I'm sorry I've come to this conclusion, but I really see no other way. . . . I just cannot believe he is honest and straightforward." The irony was that Alinsky had been very honest with Beadle, at least about TWO and Woodlawn. But he had also been harsh, threatening, and insolent. To Alinsky, it was all part of the game he relished, but in his zest he sometimes assumed incorrectly that the people on the other side basically understood the process as he did. Or, similarly, he sometimes assumed that people like Levi and Beadle were strong and secure enough so that he could say or do anything to them and they wouldn't be hurt or resentful.

Alinsky seemed genuinely surprised when Beadle told him that he was not interested in a second meeting. In a pointed reply, he said he wanted Beadle to understand that

> the issues [are] exclusively [between] the Woodlawn community, its TWO, and your institution, and NOT the Industrial Areas Foundation. The Industrial Areas Foundation's presence in the Woodlawn

community is . . . to provide technical services for the development of citizen participation and education in the best of American traditions so that they may democratically and effectively cope with those problems which beset them and their community. *Their policies, programs and decisions are completely their own.* . . . In the future, any discussions should be between the University of Chicago and TWO.

With that, Alinsky ended his communication with Beadle and, for the most part, any future relationship with the university as well. (Several years later, Alinsky agreed to donate his personal papers to the University of Illinois in Chicago rather than to his alma mater.)

There was a certain symmetry to this ending. Alinsky, the son of Russian Jewish immigrants, an outsider from the wrong side of the tracks during his undergraduate days, was still an outsider, this time from the wrong side of the Midway. It was a role, an identity, that had come early and naturally.

Through the remainder of the fall and into the winter of 1962, the urban-renewal issue was in a holding pattern. TWO—the Temporary Woodlawn Organization—was still aggressively pursuing the problems of overcrowding in the schools and poorly maintained slum apartment buildings when Alinsky decided the time had come for a founding convention of a permanent organization. Alinsky and the TWO leadership discussed the possibility of inviting prominent speakers to address the convention. They ended up with two men who reinforced TWO's dual identity. Through Alinsky's church contacts, they invited the Reverend Ralph Abernathy, a leader of the civil rights movement and associate of Dr. Martin Luther King, Jr., to give a keynote address; and for the welcoming speech, Alinsky arranged for the one man who would signify to the rest of political Chicago that TWO was to be taken seriously—Mayor Richard J. Daley.

The organizers usually had to scramble to produce a large turnout for a demonstration or public event, and filling the ballroom of the Southmoor Hotel with more than 1,200 delegates and onlookers was no exception. TWO's most dependable members came from among the homeowners in West Woodlawn, but some of the most enthusiastic participants came from the poorer area of East Woodlawn, where Bob Squires had organized a number of new block clubs.

The other prime source of participants in TWO was the churches. But a year earlier, five Protestant pastors—colleagues of Leber, Blakeley, and Farrell in the Woodlawn Pastors' Alliance—had withdrawn from the Alliance because they objected to TWO's—and Alinsky's—tactics and philosophy of power. One of them, the Lutheran C. K. Proefrock, also charged that TWO "make[s] use of antagonisms within the neighborhood—some dreamed, some real. If they don't have them, they create them." Alinsky was also concerned with a highly critical editorial in *Christian Century*, which used the resignations as a point of departure for an attack on him and TWO. "How can [Protestant ministers who support Alinsky's approach in Woodlawn] command respect for Christian moral standards when they advocate and practice the ruthlessness of the class war, magnifying hostilities and exacerbating differences?" the editorial asked, and also referred to the contentions that Catholic funding for the Woodlawn project was motivated by a desire to preserve racial segregation.

When the editorial appeared, Alinsky had not yet won Presbyterian support for Woodlawn and, beyond that, the continuing criticism of him in *Christian Century* was not helping his courtship of Protestant clergy. Alinsky's supporters wrote angry letters of protest to the magazine. Finally, one of his Protestant friends arranged to have him meet the editor of *Christian Century*, Harold Fey, in New York. Alinsky told an ally at the National Council of Churches, Meryl Ruoss, director of urban-church programs, that he and Fey talked for four hours over lunch. "I was calm, cordial, concerned about not putting him into a corner from which he would have to fight his way out," Alinsky reported, no doubt trying to reassure Ruoss that he had been on his best behavior. "I tried to reach an agreement with him towards the end when I said, 'Well, I believe we are in agreement on common goals,' and Fey replied with 'It's possible.' " In fact, the hot criticism in *Christian Century* cooled noticeably as TWO began to receive favorable attention among civil rights activists.

In Woodlawn, as the founding convention drew near, three churchmen deserved a large measure of credit for TWO's success. Doc Farrell was of course determined to make the project a success, and while he had a following and could encourage many in the community to participate in TWO, he also prodded von Hoffman to spend more energy on the organizational details. If delegates were absent from a meeting, he'd tell von Hoffman the next day in a quickly typed note: "Should be visited, heat put on, show necessity of TWO. Too many joined something they do not understand." Or a Farrell phone call would bring a string of blunt "suggestions": "Eliminate some meetings of the Block Club Council. Eliminate housing complaints from the agenda of TWO right away. Tell the people the truth—that we are not strong enough [yet] to do anything. Two to three block club people besides Crawford should be placed on the executive committee right away." Crazy Doc, as von Hoffman affectionately calls him, could be crotchety, but his good intentions, often perceptive insights, and full-speed-ahead style could be an effective combination.

If Alinsky's organizers had wanted to assemble, piece by piece, the perfect pastor who, because of his intellect, temperament, and savvy, could always be counted on in a pinch, they could not have done better than Chuck Leber. Leber had arrived at First Presbyterian in Woodlawn in 1957 with a fortuitously appropriate background. After World War II, he had been an intern at Dodge Community House in Detroit:

> When I first arrived, my supervisor said, "I want you to do two things. I want you to walk in this neighborhood and get to know it for the next week. I want you to put in eight hours a day on your feet, walking this neighborhood. When you come back each day . . . tell me some of the things you've seen and then make notes on what you've seen." And he was very tough on me. But the second thing, he just threw this book in my lap and said, "Now I want you to read this." It was *Reveille for Radicals,* which had just come out. So I was introduced to Saul early in life.

By the time Leber arrived in Chicago, he did not require much persuasion by Farrell to think an Alinsky project for Woodlawn made sense. "I was already committed to this kind of ministry, so it was just a natural."

It seemed ironic that Leber, a white, was more active in TWO's formative period than his black co-pastor, Buck Blakeley. But both wanted to establish role models for the congregation, which was 85 percent white, that would not reinforce old stereotypes. So Blakeley assumed most of the traditional pastoral duties while Leber became the community activist. "For the sake of a new ministry like this, it was my job to be sort of a more radical type and his to be more conservative," Leber says.

Leber, who gave a great deal of his time to TWO, was especially valuable to Alinsky's organizers because he understood that his role was mainly behind the scenes and that a key to a successful community organization in Woodlawn lay in developing new black leadership. So, for example, at community meetings Leber spoke only when necessary; the organizers could depend on him—either at a signal from them or on his own initiative—to interject a timely, tension-reducing comment when tempers flared.

The third churchman who was vitally important was Arthur Brazier, the black pastor at the Pentecostal Apostolic Church of God. To understand his importance, one has to recall that Alinsky was extremely critical of black civil rights organizations and leadership in Chicago: the Urban League was dependent on white sources for funding and did not have a large membership; the Chicago Chapter of the NAACP had essentially been taken over by Congressman Dawson—"by the simple expedient,"

Alinsky told an acquaintance, "of having his precinct captains bring in enough new members to win the annual election." The single most powerful black force in town was the Dawson machine. Alinsky and von Hoffman estimated that its "harvest of patronage" was in excess of four thousand jobs. Yet stories circulated in Chicago that Dawson felt shortchanged—that for all of the votes he delivered he did not get as much from Daley as he deserved. But the conventional political wisdom in Chicago, which Alinsky shared, was that the success of the Dawson machine was tied so closely to the success of the larger, Daley-led Democratic machine that a political upheaval by Dawson would endanger his control of patronage. Thus, on the explosive issues of discrimination in housing, the schools, and access to quasi-public facilities such as the downtown department stores, the Dawson machine was largely silent.

Several years earlier, Alinsky's assumptions about the Dawson operation were confirmed to him at close range when Lester Hunt and Jack Egan surveyed the Grand Boulevard area, part of Dawson's turf. Hunt recalls long, friendly discussions with one of Dawson's top lieutenants.

> He just told me everything. He knew more about Grand Boulevard, the 2nd Ward, than anybody in the world. He was a Catholic, and he probably [talked] because we had Catholic credentials. So we learned a lot of things. . . . He would tell me how they'd walk into the Olivet Baptist Church and throw two hundred dollars on the table every Monday morning. And the Baptist ministers would all put it in their pockets. . . . [And] he talked about the garbagemen who didn't do any work and got their salaries. It was his opinion that the way you control the area was through the use of patronage and money, which the machine provided.

Not only was Arthur Brazier not a Baptist but his congregation was small and obscure. He was a perfect example of Alinsky's theory that the best potential natural leaders in a community were often unknown beyond their immediate circle of followers. The way Alinsky talked about it, the theory took on a romantic appeal, akin to the legend of Hollywood in which a sharp producer spots a raw talent sitting on a drugstore stool, waiting to be discovered. Although his congregation was in Woodlawn, Brazier lived elsewhere on the South Side. (His residence outside Woodlawn was later cited by some of Alinsky's critics as evidence that he was not an indigenous leader. Never a purist, Alinsky thought that anybody who pastored a small church at Sixty-third and Kimbark was indigenous enough.) For many months, Brazier was reluctant to get involved in the

Temporary Woodlawn Organization; his conservative church members did not participate in civil rights and politics. "I received severe criticism from [other] Pentecostal ministers," Brazier says, as his involvement in TWO grew. As it was, he held back during the first year; his assistant pastor became TWO's president, while Brazier was listed as "official spokesman."

Brazier was wooed by Nick von Hoffman, who became excited about his leadership abilities the first time he heard Brazier preach. After months of meetings between them and von Hoffman's reassurances to the strait-laced, cautious Brazier that heading his church and heading TWO were compatible activities, von Hoffman decided the time had come for Brazier to meet Alinsky, who would nail down a commitment. At the appointed hour, the three of them met in the Palmer House Hotel's fancy Empire Room, a supper club of some distinction but where on this night, von Hoffman realized only after they were all seated, the featured entertainment was the bawdy, blue "Last of the Red Hot Mommas," Sophie Tucker, whose costume consisted of little more than sequined cowboy chaps and a pair of six shooters. Alinsky leaned over to von Hoffman and whispered, "You dumb jerk, you're supposed to check these things out." But Brazier was not offended, and the evening ended just as von Hoffman and Alinsky had hoped, with Brazier on board and committed.

By the time of TWO's founding convention, the face of TWO that the rest of Chicago saw was often Arthur Brazier's. When television coverage showed a TWO demonstration in front of the school board offices, the cameras zoomed in on Brazier. When TWO held a news conference to rebut the University of Chicago's latest maneuver over South Campus, the newspaper photographers focused on Brazier. And when the Chicago *Daily News* ran a promo for its six-part series on TWO in the spring of 1962, one of the advertisements featured a large close-up of a stern Reverend Brazier, his black clerical garb visible to the chest, with a bold one-word cutline three columns wide: POWER. It was not the sort of image of blacks to which white Chicago was yet accustomed—this was nearly four years before white America would be jolted by Stokely Carmichael's angry call for "Black Power."

But Arthur Brazier's face was not primarily an angry face. To be sure, he often articulated the anger and resentment of blacks in Woodlawn, and as a good preacher he was capable of oratory that aroused the emotions. But Brazier's face and manner communicated more than anger. A man of medium build and complexion, Brazier was rarely seen with a smile in public. And while there was even a hint of austerity about him, most of all he projected a no-nonsense determination.

In the embryonic stages of TWO, Brazier was a willing student, willing to take direction. He was disciplined, dependable, and intelligent. "I had never met with city officials," Brazier recalls, and it took a while "to get the knack of what was going on. We began to learn the jargon, we began to understand the levels of power. We began to understand how the city worked." During this period, Brazier met with Alinsky frequently, and he appreciated Alinsky's role as someone who stayed in "the background and acted as a confidant, who [gave] advice as to how we were going to proceed. He never made any demands, [never intimated that] 'you got to do this or we're going to take your money.' "

In retrospect, it is easy to understand why von Hoffman, and later Alinsky, wanted to cast Brazier in the role of TWO's leader. In every way, he projected the style and aspirations of TWO. He was not only a credible figure in Woodlawn but also a man who could not be dismissed easily by white Chicago. He mixed his militant rhetoric, often directed at Willis and the segregated school system, with other, softer phrases and images that suited the Chicago tradition of ethnic politics. "If our hopes are realized," Brazier told a Chicago reporter, "TWO will be the first big solid Negro community organization in Chicago and in the United States. We'd like to prove that Negro communities can organize themselves effectively, not only for their personal well-being but for the betterment of the entire city." That was the kind of language Mayor Daley could relate to—that, and the message delivered by TWO's forty-six buses filled with 2,500 voters.

Finally, on a chilly Friday night late in March, the Grand Ballroom of the Southmoor was heating up quickly as the first of an overflow crowd of 1,200 began to arrive. The anticipated size of the turnout and the appearance of Abernathy and Daley assured press coverage. Alinsky, acutely sensitive to the importance of the press, knew that what was unfolding in Woodlawn had national significance—or at least he wanted to encourage such thinking. By now he was friends or at least acquaintances with journalists and media executives in New York, like Jane Jacobs at *Architectural Forum,* Charles Silberman at *Fortune,* and Arthur Morse at CBS, whom he was now encouraging to cover TWO's founding convention. But it was really a Chicago event and on this memorable night Alinsky's organizers— and probably Alinsky, too—were preoccupied with parochial political interests which centered on Mayor Daley's appearance. Alinsky and von Hoffman worked up a two-page memo for the mayor suggesting themes and language the mayor could use in his welcoming speech. They wanted Daley to talk about how TWO's goal of "self-determination gives individual people self-respect"; how TWO "is putting Woodlawn in the race for the honor of being the outstanding neighborhood in Chicago"; how people in Woodlawn should "depend on [themselves], not government . . . [because] the city cannot do everything." As for the South Campus urban-renewal issue, Alinsky wanted the mayor to stress that "the city is not committed to any [specific urban-renewal plan for Woodlawn]. . . . We now invite you . . . to discuss . . . proposals and present your own [plan]. The final plan will be the best plan that can be made. It will be a democratic plan. The city does not intend and will never force the people of Woodlawn to accept a plan they do not want. The mayor of the city has always believed in working with people openly, frankly, in trust, and with faith in the final judgment of the people." But it did not really matter whether Daley followed the script precisely. The mayor's appearance itself sent a message to both the University of Chicago and the urban-renewal bureaucrats in the city government that TWO was to be treated as a legitimate player in the decision-making process.

The fledgling organization went all out to treat the mayor in an appropriately regal style. As the mayor's squat frame emerged from his car in front of the Southmoor on Stony Island Avenue, Doc Farrell's little flower girls and altar boys were there to greet him and escort him inside. Perhaps it reminded the mayor—briefly, to be sure—of his own beloved South Side neighborhood of Bridgeport. Of course, everybody in Bridgeport was white and—like the people in the nearby Back of the Yards—they meant to keep it that way. If Daley was at all uncomfortable when he entered the Grand Ballroom, filled to the rafters with black faces, he never showed it. "The son of a bitch was as smooth as silk," Bob Squires remembers, as Daley made his way through an enthusiastic crowd, television lights and cameras adding to the excitement. The mayor was introduced, received an ovation, and took to the podium. Just as the audience went silent, ready for the mayor's first words, a shot rang out. But it was only a piece of equipment from one of the TV cameras slamming to the floor. Daley's round Irish face turned beet-red, but he wouldn't flinch. "It's so wonderful to be here," he began, and nobody in the audience would have disagreed. The night had been a fantastic success.

AFTER DALEY LEFT and after Abnernathy spoke and after a constitution was adopted, it was time to celebrate. Nobody felt like celebrating more than Nick von Hoffman. It had been not only an incredible evening but an incredible sixteen months. As the party in the hotel was in full swing, von Hoffman spotted the most beautiful woman he had ever seen, a gorgeous black woman who had already attracted the attention of von Hoffman's buddy, Ed Chambers. As von Hoffman moved in, Chambers moved on. Soon, von Hoffman and his new companion were heading for more intimate surroundings.

"You cannot believe how dumb you can be," von Hoffman says in retrospect. "We ride around, da da ta da, and we go back to the hotel. Stupid me. Up in the room. Bang, bang. House dick. Shakedown. You're running around with nothing on. I knew she was a hooker. She had said, 'You know, I'm giving you my body for free.' Of course, because these guys were going to get [the money] out of me. They wanted five hundred bucks or something like that." It was now two or three in the morning and von Hoffman had no money on him. Facing a physical if not a spiritual crisis, he called his favorite clergyman, Chuck Leber.

"Chuck, I'm in trouble. I lost a lot of money in a crap game," he lied, saving the two of them a modest measure of added embarrassment. Leber, who did not have much cash on hand either, called Doc Farrell. "Fortunately, Father Farrell had some money in his safe," Leber says. "And we called my partner, Buck Blakeley. He had a hundred or so. We called the police chaplain, who was one of the wildest characters in the world—the only Protestant police chaplain they'd ever had in the city of Chicago. We set him up in the job. He was a roustabout-type guy, uncouth as hell. We got hold of him—he was about six feet, two hundred fifty pounds. My partner was a pretty big guy—he'd played football. Farrell's a good-sized guy. I'm a good-sized guy. We all had our clerical collars on. Three-thirty in the morning, we arrive at the damn hotel. Nick told us later, 'My God, it looked like the Marines had landed.' We gave him the money. . . . Within two minutes he was back, hugging all of us. And we all went out for coffee across the street. That was one of the wildest nights of our lives."

"I never told that story to Saul," von Hoffman says. "He'd never understand it." Alinsky would have been more disappointed than angry, von Hoffman knew. It would have been the reaction of a father to his smartest and most promising son, the son in whom the father saw both himself and talents and possibilities he did not quite possess. Von Hoffman had given Alinsky a chance to be the kind of father that Alinsky himself had never had, a father whom the son could respect and love, a father who could leave a legacy the son would carry on. And in the eight years they had worked together, Nick had come to respect and love Saul like a father. He respected and loved him for his intellectuality, steadfastness, and commitment to social justice—qualities, von Hoffman believed, that he possessed in lesser degrees:

> I got by for a lot of years being a singer of songs, a charmer. . . . I
> wanted to write stories, you know. This part of me was socially

irresponsible. . . . We shared a lot. . . . He had mischief in his soul. He loved to pull the feathers off the turkey, and we shared that. But he misjudged me, too. I was the Broadway Kid. . . . I was Dionysus, he was Apollo. The problem was that Apollo can't recognize Dionysus if he has a certain view of him. I could recognize it, but I couldn't say it. I did obliquely. I always said to him, I'll only work for you for ten years, then I'm going to do my number . . . [and] it's not political. . . . He had a moral dedication that I don't have and never did have. That does not mean that I could not be swept up in it from time to time, and somebody like Saul would inspire me.

We both hated the slums. I think that's very important. We both did. If he had not hated the slums, he could never have done what he had done. You have to have that kind of bond to all those god-damned garbage cans to want to get rid of them. But he worried about things I never worried about. . . . What I regret in our relationship was that in those kinds of discussions when he would really get serious, I often remained silent. Well, I was the junior and all of that, but I think I let him believe that we were more alike than we were. He wanted to believe that, he always wanted to believe that.

Von Hoffman had no desire to stay around to see "Alinsky & Son" stenciled on the frosted-glass office door of the Industrial Areas Foundation. When Alinsky, ignoring his hints, told him that he wanted him to start attending the IAF's board meetings, he felt especially claustrophobic. Also, he was very, very tired. He had worked nearly every day, seven days a week, for two years. There was one stretch of about fifteen months when he had worked literally every day in Woodlawn. And they weren't ordinary days, for von Hoffman was in constant motion. He might be at a staff meeting in TWO's office; or talking with others at the restaurant down the street; or at Leber's or Farrell's church; or meeting with Bob Squires late in the evening; or later, maybe around midnight, meeting with Ed Chambers. In between, he was still supervising the OSC project, on which Chambers reported to him regularly. When he wasn't meeting with somebody, he was on the phone, but even then he was in motion, rocking back and forth, his intensity increasing as a pivotal event drew near.

It was not only the sheer volume of tasks that could be enervating but also the precariousness and fragility of it all. Von Hoffman was like the circus performer who tends frantically to a number of dishes spinning on sticks; one mistake and the act is forever diminished if not over. Alinsky himself had to encourage him not to try to do everything himself but to develop leaders to keep things going. But this was easier said than done. Even when von Hoffman wanted to delegate work, there were often barriers. "This was an era," he says, "that when you went to meetings and there would be twenty or thirty black people in the room and you'd be the only white person, and somebody would make a very sensible suggestion, then every eye would look at you to see whether *you* thought it was." There was a constant tension between breaking down such doubts and building people's confidence and competence, on the one hand, and the sense that, organizationally, there was little room for miscue or defeat.

Even when a tactic or protest was well executed, von Hoffman discovered, strategically the options were limited. TWO's first campaign against dishonest business practices was a case in point. TWO used the grievances and issues to attract new participants—new members—and, in the process, to show that it was a force to be reckoned with in Woodlawn. But the Square Deal campaign was short-lived, intentionally terminated by Alinsky and von Hoffman after it had served its main purpose, for to carry on the campaign brought disadvantages greater than the benefits. On larger issues such as urban renewal, TWO would want the political—and financial—support of the local businessmen. Indeed, it was not until several years later that TWO moved to close down the bars and dives along Sixty-third Street—Baby Skid Row—one of the most notorious stretches of crime in the city. In the meantime, many of these "businessmen" also supported TWO financially.

On an even bigger issue, rental housing and slum landlords, von Hoffman also felt himself and TWO standing on a slippery, narrow slope. The reverse picketing was a terrific ploy that gained TWO attention and forced some apartment owners to negotiate. But the rent strikes, which may have been the first of the era, also showed von Hoffman the limited potential of the housing issue. About one of the early strikes, von Hoffman remembers:

> We got everybody organized; we were real good at this. So there is then the crucial meeting when the horrible landlord turns up with his lawyer: "I'm the attorney, and here is the deed of conveyance, and you tell us who to fill it out to and the building is yours." Everybody else in the room is cheering, and I'm thinking, Oh, this is *not* a good sign; these guys know something I haven't figured out. I learned! Not that many weeks later I said, "Saul, there aren't any more slumlords, there are just people stuck with turkeys." So we knew early, but we didn't know what to do about it.

By the fall of 1962, Nick von Hoffman was rapidly winding down; indeed, he was on the point of collapse. It used to be that when he left

Leber's house at two in the morning after an especially grueling day, he'd say, "Chuck, I've got to be up by ten," and Leber would say, "Okay, I'll be around your house by nine." But now he had completely run out of gas and was barely able to hold staff meetings from his bed. Alinsky realized he would have to bring in a replacement, even if only temporarily. Then Nick started to talk about wanting to write. He wanted to write stories and novels, and he wouldn't have thought seriously about journalism except that Alinsky encouraged it as a more practical alternative. Perhaps Alinsky thought, too, that it was a way to keep Nick in town, for he landed a job with the Chicago *Daily News*. But when the day finally came for von Hoffman to leave, saying goodbye was not easy. "It was terrible," he remembers. "We hugged each other and wept. It was that hard. Big, salt-laden tears."

Black and White

"In many ways the most impressive experiment affecting the Negro anywhere in the U.S. is going on now in Chicago's Woodlawn area," Charles Silberman wrote in March 1962, in an article, "The City and the Negro," which appeared in *Fortune* magazine. Alinsky cranked out reprints of Silberman's enthusiastic appraisal, sending them to friends and journalists.

But by the fall of 1962, the backstage realities at TWO contrasted sharply with such glowing journalistic accounts as Silberman's and Georgie Anne Geyer's long series in the Chicago *Daily News*. TWO was in disarray. A major part of the problem was the near-collapse of Nick von Hoffman. It was as though an indispensable director had been removed from a Hollywood movie production; there was still plenty of talent around, but without the talented director, there was more chaos than creativity. In theory, von Hoffman's withdrawal should not have been so debilitating. According to Alinsky's theory, TWO's citizen-leaders might have been expected to rise to the occasion. But the formal organizing process was less than two years old and even Alinsky, an optimist about the unrealized potential of neighborhood leaders, believed that two years was not long enough to develop the more sophisticated skills and new interpersonal relationships necessary for holding together a large community organization. Second, TWO as an organization was less developed than it might have been because both von Hoffman and Alinsky had decided to hitch its wagon to the star of the civil rights movement. When Ed Chambers finally replaced von Hoffman at TWO at the end of 1962, what he took over was more a ragged mass movement than a well-structured, disciplined organization. Although Alinsky probably did not fully appreciate Chambers's abilities at the time, he was an excellent choice to follow up on what von Hoffman had begun.

Chambers had been working in Alinsky's Southwest Side project, the OSC, for four years, the last three as the staff director, during which he had learned how to organize. The OSC under Chambers's guidance could claim a significant amount of credit for specific achievements. It had, for instance, helped greatly to reduce racial violence throughout a five-mile, snakelike corridor of the Southwest Side, ultimately its primary territory, where in the OSC's first two years a fairly broad cross section of residents accepted—with varying degrees of reluctance—the organizers' pragmatic argument that violence to prevent blacks from moving in was both ineffective and self-defeating. It became one of the OSC's chief themes, amplified and given credibility by OSC leaders who were not previously known for being sympathetic to black move-ins (such as Monsignor P. J. Molloy, at St. Leo's, and the neighborhood civic association leader James Norris). Partly because of OSC influence in the community and even at City Hall, the police became a more positive force in dealing with racial violence.

The OSC founding convention in the fall of 1959, which had brought tears of joy to Jack Egan's eyes, raised the possibility that united, constructive action might be possible on the Southwest Side. Alinsky's organizers hoped that reducing violence would help to stabilize the area, and stabilization, of course, was virtually synonymous with keeping whites from fleeing, also the objective of the OSC's home-loan program implemented through the neighborhood banks. It started out as a mechanism to keep young white families from leaving their old neighborhoods for the suburbs, specifically to keep young white families in St. Leo's and St. Sabina's parishes. The OSC persuaded several local banks, including those run by OSC officers Donald O'Toole and Harry Fisher, to provide home mortgages with below-market down payments of 10 percent rather than the standard 20 or 30 percent. The OSC served as a screening agent: a church would give the OSC the name of a prospective home buyer who was a good financial risk, and the OSC would then match up the buyer with one of the participating banks. Chambers remembers that it was difficult to persuade the banks to join the program, although he had the support of McMahon and Molloy, whose parishes were also among the banks' large depositors. Once a week, somebody from the OSC met with bank representatives to divide up mortgage applications—Mutual would take two, Standard would take three, and so on. In the first nine months of the program in 1960, eighty-three such loans, totaling $1.2 million, were made. Chambers says it was a very successful program; there were hardly any mortgage defaults, and he believes strongly that the combination of the home-loan program and the anti-violence efforts slowed white flight in the early 1960s.

Not everybody, of course, was comfortable with a home-loan program that, at least at its inception, was available only to whites. On the surface, it appeared to be a first cousin to the earlier ad hoc arrangements whereby local banks bought houses in white neighborhoods and held them off the market until white purchasers could be found. When faculty and students associated with the divinity school at the University of Chicago and the Chicago Church Federation published a sympathetic study in 1966 of the development of the OSC, they omitted any mention of the initial exclusivity of the program.

But the OSC was simultaneously bringing more blacks into the organization, at first from predominantly black organizations on the edges of the OSC's intentionally ill-defined boundary. Eventually, a young Protestant divinity student from the University of Chicago named Barry Menuez, hired to integrate the all-Catholic staff and ease any suspicions among Protestants in the community about Catholic domination, became responsible for working with black groups. (Alinsky was sensitive to accusations by the Lutheran Walter Kloetzli and by Harold Fey in *Christian Century* that he had been retained to protect Catholic interests; having at least one Protestant on the OSC staff seemed like a small but necessary gesture.)

Menuez was twenty-seven, midway through the divinity school after having worked at the Harris Bank, but needing money now to support his wife and two children. After he was introduced to von Hoffman and Chambers and offered a job by Alinsky's men, he asked two of his professors, Gibson Winter and Alfred Pitcher, for advice. "Alinsky's a wild man," they said, "but it might be an interesting assignment; Menuez could work for six months and write a paper about his experiences. So he took the job, knowing little about Alinsky, not much more about community organizing, and feeling a little frightened. A genteel Episcopalian, slender and of medium height, Menuez remembers "the first day of work when I went straight from the campus to the OSC office on Seventy-ninth Street. I was wearing a beret when I walked through the door. And the first thing Ed Chambers said was 'Get that fucking thing off your head and don't ever show up with that on again or you're through.' "

Menuez was assigned to the Monday-night seminars that were led by either Alinsky, von Hoffman, or, occasionally, Egan in the archdiocese's lovely old brownstone on the near North Side. But most of his training was on-the-job. Methodically, Menuez called on reluctant pastors; some of these courtships stretched into a year or more. Before his arrival, Chambers had done an effective job—with the help of Bob Christ, pastor at Seventh Presbyterian—of bringing some Presbyterian and Methodist churches into the OSC. But not much had been done with other Protestant churches, especially those farther out and not quite so close to the expanding black ghetto. Menuez soon discovered that his most persuasive presentation to reluctant Protestant pastors was to make them focus on the reality that institutional survival—the survival of their church—would be possible only if a way could be found to manage the inevitable social change that confronted them.

Menuez began to organize a support group of Protestant ministers who, with some exceptions, felt shaky and vulnerable on the racially changing, Catholic Southwest Side. Unlike the Catholic priests, they were dependent on the goodwill of their dwindling congregations for their jobs. Most of them didn't have much hope, Menuez discovered, and were worried that if they didn't make it here, they would have to get another church somewhere else. The support group was a way to boost their morale and improve communication, and it gave Menuez an opportunity to work with them both collectively and one to one. "I was like a doctor making house calls," he says, recalling the nearly endless rounds of appointments in parish offices or over lunch. For Alinsky's men, a church's pastor was usually the starting point, although the ultimate goal was to bring the lay leaders into the OSC's committee work and have the full congregation represented at the annual community convention. "These pastors were very protective of their people," Menuez says. "They were hard to get past until they trusted me." Even then, each relationship was different. It took Menuez nearly two years before the largest Lutheran congregation in the area joined the OSC. His contacts with the church's pastor were very formal. Menuez recalls, "He would say, 'What do you want?' I would say that I want some people to come to a meeting of the OSC's education committee. He would send them. He acted just like a monsignor. I never went to a meeting in the church. Never spoke to the church. He did it all, had total control over his people." At a smaller Lutheran church, Menuez and the pastor drank beer together one afternoon every week while the pastor's wife was at the hairdresser. Finally,

> I had a chance to do him a favor. His church was in a saturated Catholic neighborhood and every time he had a funeral, there would be a car, probably belonging to a Catholic, parked in front of his church, and the limousine and the hearse couldn't park there. And he said one day, "If you could get a 'No Parking' sign for my church I'd appreciate it." So Jim Norris went to work on it; I don't know for sure, but Norris may have stolen a "No Parking" sign. The sign went up and this guy was so happy. He could have his funerals and people could park in front of the church. And that opened the door for me.

Increasingly, Menuez worked with black churches and neighborhood groups. One of his proudest accomplishments was in East Morgan Park, an old black enclave near Beverly, where the black working class—former domestics and laborers who served Beverly and Morgan Park—lived. East Morgan Park, with about 12,000 people, was like a little country town in the midst of the Southwest Side. Basic municipal services, such as paved streets and regular garbage collections, were conspicuous by their absence. Through his Episcopalian connections, Menuez called on Ed Smith, the black minister of an Episcopalian church there, who in turn introduced Menuez to other local leaders. Menuez organized a steering committee and then, after many months, the East Morgan Park Civic Association, which became the umbrella organization for virtually all the churches and other principal institutions in the area. He began to take some of the black leaders to OSC committee meetings to show them that the OSC represented something very new and positive, unlike the degrading experience of being treated as second-class by the whites in Beverly.

At the OSC's second congress in the fall of 1960, at which the turn-out was even larger than at the founding convention, one of the vice presidents elected was a black. But a small problem developed when it became clear that there were more candidates for the vice-presidential slots than there were slots. As the elections committee was tabulating the votes, Ed Chambers saw that the result for the last vice-presidential slot was going to be less than ideal. Except for Jim Norris, president of the East Gresham Community Association, no conservative neighborhood leader was winning; Chambers realized that a liberal from the Unitarian church in Beverly looked like a narrow winner of the last slot. "[This guy] was going to be the third flaming liberal, and we would have been isolated with one archconservative," Chambers says. He was working with the three-man committee counting ballots when Chambers decided that one of the men, a realtor named Bob Dwyer, was his ace-in-the-hole. He pulled Dwyer off to the side and whispered, "Bob, Jesus, this guy's got to win," pointing to the name of the conservative. "Gotta put down five more marks," which Dwyer obediently did. Chambers says, "I stole the election. Dwyer and I were the only ones who knew it. We had a balanced slate."

It was also at this congress that the OSC moved toward an explicit position on race and discrimination. A community relations committee was formed, in part "to communicate with city and state legislative bodies the desire of [the OSC] to destroy racial and religious restrictive practices in housing opportunities." If the organizers could have avoided such an explicit pronouncement for another year or so, they might have done so, but it was impossible, for at virtually every monthly meeting someone would raise *the* question: is the OSC pro-integration or anti-integration?

A few months later, the community relations committee drafted a letter to Chicago's elected officials which ignited a heated controversy within the OSC. The letter said that the OSC supported "open occupancy" legislation. Those were fighting words in many, if not most, white communities in the North in the 1960s—whether affluent suburbs or working-class neighborhoods. Nationally, moreover, strong economic interests were opposed to anti-discrimination reforms in housing. For example, a year later, in July 1962, the National Association of Home Builders sent to President Kennedy the results of a survey of home builders which showed that they predicted a sharp drop in residential construction if Kennedy signed an executive order outlawing discrimination in federally assisted housing. In fact, Kennedy had avoided signing such an order in spite of his criticism during the 1960 campaign that President Eisenhower could have done so "with the stroke of a pen." On Chicago's Southwest Side, many of the "conservatives" in the OSC were adamantly opposed to open-occupancy laws and to the ultimate implications, as they saw them, for their neighborhoods. Yet open-occupancy laws, had they been implemented and enforced throughout Chicago, could have taken pressure off the neighborhoods on the edge of the ghetto, and supporting them was a logical, rather than simply a "liberal," position for the OSC to take. That was not, however, the interpretation by many of the OSC's conservatives. With many of them aroused, the monthly meeting in March 1961 of the OSC Council—elected officers and one delegate from each constituent organization—deadlocked on a vote to approve or disapprove the community relations committee letter. When the OSC president broke the tie in favor of the committee, representatives of two civic associations walked out in protest, and by the next congress in the fall, two distinct "parties" had formed within the OSC to contest for control of the organization.

The conservatives, calling themselves the Median Forum, pressed a number of issues at the third OSC congress. Chambers, still working to keep them in the OSC, helped them organize for the convention. And they were well organized—with floor leaders, walkie-talkies, and their own resolutions up for consideration. While they scored a few victories—they elected some vice presidents—they lost the most critical votes, including those for the top officers and executive committee, but nonetheless they did not pull out of the organization.

Several months later, however, a new crisis arose and, ironically, it was triggered by Alinsky and von Hoffman's tactics in protesting the overcrowded, segregated schools in Woodlawn. The Truth Squad mothers who, with cameras in hand, would invade elementary schools in white neighborhoods to document their charges of empty classrooms did so at an elementary school in Beverly, whose well-to-do residents were especially hostile toward the OSC. It is surprising that Alinsky and von Hoffman gave little or no thought to the effect that TWO's black mothers might have on the OSC when they entered the school accompanied by newspaper reporters and photographers. Perhaps they were surprised by the magnitude of the city-wide uproar, which included front-page newspaper stories and the arrest of the TWO mothers for trespassing (one of the few times that TWO demonstrators were arrested). As a general rule, Alinsky avoided such eventualities, presuming as he did that people did not flock to a new community organization in order to be arrested and jailed.

The Truth Squad invasion enraged leaders of the Median Forum, who rallied their forces and packed a meeting of the OSC's education committee in February 1962. A resolution condemning the Truth Squad's tactics went to the OSC Council for a vote. More than three hundred people turned out, although the voting was restricted to official delegates of the OSC's member organizations. The key vote was on the liberals' substitute resolution calling for an investigation of the issues the Truth Squad dramatized. When they prevailed, 53–38, many in the Median Forum left the OSC for good. In fact, over several years many of the most rabid anti-integrationist white people had been moving out of the area, and while the OSC rightfully claimed credit for a reduction in racially related violence, Alinsky's organizers also admitted that another factor was that the most violence-prone whites tended to be the first to leave when blacks moved in.

Losing the conservatives was, by itself, not fatal to the OSC. But the controversy and vote symbolized a turning point, the beginning of the end of Alinsky's long-shot gamble to establish—and maintain—residential integration on Chicago's Southwest Side. For the conservatives were merely among the first to abandon the community, to jump to the "safety" of outlying sections of the city or the suburbs, in the face of what von Hoffman calls the "great Mississippi flood" of blacks pouring into Chicago. To be sure, the flood did not overwhelm the OSC's portion of the Southwest Side in one or two gigantic waves. In December 1963, Alinsky proudly reported at an IAF board meeting that the OSC "has become widely recognized as a long step towards the achievement of an integrated community." His own estimate was that blacks comprised a little less than 10 percent of the approximately 200,000 people who lived within the OSC's boundaries. That figure may have been accurate, but the block-by-block change from white to black was continuing, although at a somewhat slower pace and with less violence. By the end of the 1960s, most of the area was predominantly black.

Racism in the form of simple prejudice—a white not wanting to live next door to a black—was certainly a factor behind white flight on the Southwest Side, but it was not the only factor and not always the most important one. Prejudice came in varying degrees and was modified by other considerations. For example, in defending his quota proposal, Alinsky clearly exaggerated the eagerness of whites to accept one or two blacks on their block if they could be assured that no others would follow, yet his hypothesis was not so farfetched as it might have sounded. For example, in St. Leo's, P. J. Molloy's working-class parish, Chambers found many families who valued their neighborhood associations and church commitment and who wanted to stay put. Chambers remembers that they did not put their homes up for sale until their immediate area was nearly half black, at which point economic considerations became salient. In spite of the OSC's effectiveness in combating blockbusters, it was an economic fact of life in Chicago that the last white family to sell its house in a racially changing neighborhood was risking serious financial loss, not a trivial consideration when one's house represented virtually all one's net worth.

The dynamics of the housing market had a profound, perhaps decisive impact on Alinsky's OSC project in another way, too. Just as affordable housing was difficult to find for the growing black population, it was relatively easy for whites to pull up stakes and move to the suburbs. As Kenneth Jackson has observed in *The Crabgrass Frontier*, it was not the "free market" or merely the allure of open spaces that encouraged the exodus of whites from older urban neighborhoods. A variety of government policies made new suburban housing cheap and accessible—a cookie jar of federal subsidies for such things as FHA and VA mortgage insurance; new, expanded tax breaks for homeowners; and a multibillion-dollar highway system that made commuting easier. Conversely, federal policies not only failed to provide much support for the modernization of aging urban transit and sewer systems but sometimes hastened the decline of older neighborhoods. For example, the practice by financial institutions of "redlining" certain neighborhoods—refusing to provide mortgage loans there—was reinforced, if not originated by the federal Home Owners Loan Corporation. The HOLC, in an effort to systematize lending practices, assigned codes to various neighborhoods—the "best" neighborhoods were designated "green," the worst "red." The "best" neighborhoods were homogeneous, which meant "American business and professional men." If a neighborhood had an "infiltration of Jews," it could not be considered "the best." Black neighborhoods were invariably "red." As Jackson explains, the HOLC "accepted as a given the proposition that the natural tendency of any area was to decline—in part because of the increasing age and obsolescence of the physical structure and in part because of the filtering down of the housing stock to families of ever lower income. Thus physical deterioration was both a cause and an effect of population change, and HOLC officials made no attempt to sort them out."

The OSC's home-loan program was, in part, meant to offset the effects of redlining. But it was too little and too late; too many whites had already fled the Southwest Side by the late 1950s, before the OSC was fully mobilized. Von Hoffman says that "a great deal of the spread of black ghettos had to do with the fact that whites had already moved out. Even now I don't think that is really appreciated, but those of us who worked there knew this very well. There were huge vacancy rates in some sections, 30 percent vacancy rates, and you couldn't rent these places to whites."

There are several important ifs that might have made a difference on the Southwest Side: if both local and federal government—and civic leadership—had pressed harder for real open occupancy throughout Chicago; if the housing market had been tighter for whites as well as blacks; if there had been a residency requirement for city employees (one was instituted years later)—then Alinsky's organizers might have won over a large, important subgroup of whites for whom fleeing to the suburbs was no longer an option. If the OSC had had a bigger budget and larger staff, it could have been a more potent force. When Joe Vilimas left the staff and von Hoffman moved over to Woodlawn, the core of the OSC's staff was Chambers, Menuez, and Norris. True, Alinsky's idea was to have a small staff organize and energize large numbers of people—to transform "people" into "citizens." But even so, the OSC's territory was too large and filled with too many problems for such a small staff. James Norris, as competent and tough as he was, often felt overwhelmed by the sheer volume of building-code violations, illegal conversions, blockbusting crises, and violent racial flare-ups that had to be tended to. Menuez had to steal time from other urgent priorities—beefing up support in weak white sections and servicing the dues-paying church congregations—in order to organize new black groups. Why wasn't the staff larger, the budget bigger? Why, in short, was there not greater support of the OSC?

For two men, the banker Donald O'Toole and Nick von Hoffman, who had differing views on many other issues, the answer was ultimately traceable to the quality of the leadership in the Archdiocese of Chicago. If the Catholic leadership had been more courageous, O'Toole maintains, it could have made an important difference. O'Toole, like the newspaper publisher Bruce Sagan, recognized that the archdiocese had taken a risk— "a terrible risk," Sagan believes—in embracing Alinsky's plan of limited racial integration as a price for stabilization. But then, O'Toole says, "the Church simply turned chickenshit, to put it in the most brutal terms, the whole gang." He feels bitter about his OSC experience. In spite of grave doubts initially about the feasibility of "saving" the Southwest Side, O'Toole reluctantly agreed to play a leadership role largely because the clergy—especially in the form of Monsignor McMahon's seed money and Cardinal Meyer's endorsement—seemed willing to exercise leadership, too. But this never turned out to be wide or deep or effective enough, he believes. Bob Christ's deep commitment and effectiveness was an exception to the rule that both Catholic and Protestant ministries were lukewarm on the issues; even the best-intentioned Catholics fell short of what was needed. "The trouble with John McMahon," O'Toole cites as an illustration, "is he was more of a saint than a doer. He found more of his answer in prayer than he did in actually getting up and fighting." And the kind of fighting O'Toole wanted to see was about principles. He wanted the cardinal, for example, to force the Southwest Side priests to speak out forcefully on the immorality of racial discrimination. If a movie came to town that they didn't like, full-throated condemnation "was thundered from all the pulpits. Why couldn't racial discrimination receive the same treatment?" Indeed, why couldn't the cardinal simply lay down the law? To be sure, it is arguable, as O'Toole knew, that Cardinal Meyer could not successfully bring additional pressure to bear. O'Toole knew, for example, that many Southwest Side pastors rebelled when the chancery office ordered them to turn over all the cash they collected; instead, they came to his bank to open special accounts under their control. When it came to important matters such as money or race relations, the Southwest Side priests did not march readily to even the cardinal's drumbeat.

Perhaps more courageous and enlightened leadership would not have made much of a difference in altering the strongly held racial views of the working-class Irish and other ethnic groups. Even in the 1980s, there remain white sections on the South Side, like Mayor Daley's Bridgeport, where the few attempts over the years by blacks to move in have been repelled by violence or the threat of violence. Nonetheless, Alinsky's men thought competent leaders could make a difference and were frustrated—and in von Hoffman's case, angry—that the Catholic clergy were so deficient. "With certain notable exceptions, the pastors on the Southwest Side are practically a caricature, a cartoon, of the sins of omission and commission of the Irish Roman Catholic clergy," von Hoffman reported to Alinsky in the spring of 1963, shortly after he had left the IAF staff. (Alinsky still sought him out for advice, in this case after Jack Egan had complained that the OSC was not organizing vigorously enough in some Catholic parishes.) Von Hoffman attributed the OSC's limitations to the weaknesses and lack of interest of the Catholic priests, identifying two as having severe drinking problems and others as being absent much of the time or simply not involved in parish life. "Somebody is finally going to have to speak bluntly about these appointments," von Hoffman wrote. "I think it has been little more than miraculous that the OSC has been able to [win as much financial support] as it has out of these parishes. Aside from divine intervention, it has required on everybody's part the most humiliating and disgusting kind of belly-creeping." He went so far as to suggest that without a better group of Catholic priests, the OSC would not survive. Even four years into the project, the archdiocese's leaders, he believed, did not fully comprehend the inextricable connection between the pastors, race, and the success of the OSC.

> With the type of Irish Catholic you have in many of those parishes, and with the sort of issue exercised in the community, to speak of going in and subrogating the pastor and organizing the people despite him is pure pipe-dreaming. The people, in nine cases out of ten, are staunchly behind their anti-Negro pastors with all their anti-Negro selves. What I am suggesting is that the time has come—indeed, it is long past—when the chancery office and the rest of them up there better stop tearing their hair and fiddling around with [neighborhood conservation programs] and start worrying about the big issue, which is race.

Real, sustained pressure from the top never materialized. Such pressure was needed not only in working-class parishes but in Beverly, too. Resistance to integration in Beverly was, in some respects, even more uncompromising. From the beginning of the OSC project, Alinsky and his organizers believed the key to stopping the spread of the black ghetto was to open up housing opportunities for blacks far *behind* the areas of transition, especially in places like Beverly and in suburbs just to the south of Beverly. But in Beverly, with its two large Catholic parishes, a prestigious Methodist congregation, and other Protestant churches, hostility to the OSC and the entreaties of Alinsky's organizers was commonplace. Indeed, Donald O'Toole's bitterness grew out of the kind of treatment he received as an OSC leader from friends and even relatives who lived in Beverly and who belonged to one or the other of the Catholic parishes there. It was the kind of nasty, mean-spirited treatment that O'Toole felt the clergy condoned. At Christ the King, for example, Monsignor Patrick J. Gleeson generally kept a certain distance from the OSC. O'Toole remembers being verbally "torn to pieces" one Sunday morning when he came to speak on behalf of the OSC to a packed room in the basement of the parish school.

The opposition was led by one of his own cousins. The leadership and attitudes at St. Barnabas, located toward the south end of Beverly, where many of the city's wealthiest, most influential Irish lived, were as bad or worse. For O'Toole, the ugliness of racism there, and the complicity of the Church, was epitomized by a man he knew well, a daily communicant at St. Barnabas, a wealthy businessman and friend of Mayor Daley, who "could go on entertaining violent anti-Negro feelings and never heard word one from the pulpit at St. Barnabas. This was the sort of thing that just sapped the strength of the whole thing."

(It is a bittersweet irony that two decades later, long after the rest of the OSC's territory changed from white to black, Beverly has become something of a model for managed integration. To be sure, its large, handsome houses are populated by middle- and upper-middle-class professionals, but any kind of stable integrated neighborhood in Chicago—or in most large Northern cities, for that matter—is still a phenomenon. In Beverly, residential integration has been "guided" by the Beverly Area Planning Association, which plays a role not unlike the one Alinsky envisioned for the OSC in the 1960s.)

In the late 1960s, the OSC became predominantly black, and it concerned itself primarily with school issues and other problems related to the quality of municipal services. It was not only financial institutions and the real-estate industry that wrote off whole chunks of Chicago as they became black; so too did Chicago's white political leadership, if they could get away with it. Thus, the OSC not only tried to pressure the board of education to open up less crowded schools in white neighborhoods west of Ashland Avenue but also negotiated an informal arrangement with the board on the appointment of school principals within its territory. The OSC also battled successfully to overturn the city's plan to build a regional library in a more "desirable" white Chicago neighborhood. In the larger scheme of things, the library, which now stands at the corner of Ninety-fifth and Halsted, is only a small symbol of success, even among those who know how it came to be built at its present site. Still, the small victories added up, and although the OSC failed to achieve its main goal of integration, it can take credit for moderating the full ravages of despair and decline that swept through many other Chicago neighborhoods on the heels of racial transition. A modest achievement, perhaps, but not one that should be taken for granted when one ponders the physical—and spiritual—conditions of similar neighborhoods in urban America.

The ultimate failure of the OSC occurred long after Alinsky's close identification with it had ended. Thus, it was not widely perceived as *his* failure. Moreover, even in the early 1960s, when the OSC was still a promising venture, Alinsky's major effort in Woodlawn eclipsed public awareness of his role—and interest—in the OSC. Also, in 1962 Alinsky had reluctantly undertaken another community organizing project on Chicago's Northwest Side. It was exactly the kind of place that no longer held much organizing appeal for him: a declining, Old World, heavily Polish-Catholic working class community reminiscent of the Back of the Yards. But Jack Egan once again pushed and prodded and, most important, raised the money—about $54,000 for the first year—which came mainly from the local parish treasuries. Alinsky's man on the Northwest Side was Thomas Gaudette, who left his job at the Admiral Corporation to begin a new career (he had gotten a taste for organizing when his own South Side community was invaded by blockbusters and he led a counter-assault). Gaudette was something of a natural: after an abbreviated four-month training period, and with only a modest amount of supervision by Alinsky, he did a wonderful job of forging the Northwest Community Organization (NCO), which continues to this day.

Had the OSC been Alinsky's only or primary Chicago project, he might have pushed the Church harder for more financial and political support. But by the end of the decade, the OSC project had more or less disappeared from Alinsky's résumé, a noble but lost cause that he rarely talked about, a cause little known or remembered beyond Chicago's borders. But he had reaped an enduring dividend: he had forged new, important links with bright young Protestant clergy who, in turn, spread a favorable message about Alinsky's concepts to their colleagues in other cities—or who themselves began to occupy key roles as denominational executives in Chicago and New York.

WHEN ED CHAMBERS moved over to TWO as von Hoffman's replacement, he was not Alinsky's first choice. Just before von Hoffman left for good, Alinsky talked with Fred Ross about coming from California to help von Hoffman. "The job out here is essentially that of consolidation," he wrote to Ross. "Nick has done a grand and extraordinary job of organization but consolidation is not his forte. I might also bluntly state that neither is it one of your great talents but it is my hope that the pooling of the different talents which both of you possess [will work out]." Then, only semi-jokingly, Alinsky added that the consolidation process was too much for any one individual except, "egotistically speaking, [possibly] your boss—after all, I not only consolidate them, but I have done such a good job that they stay on and on long after they should have died," the latter a bitter reference to the Back of the Yards Neighborhood Council. Alinsky, like all generals, never considered getting into the trenches himself, even though the future of TWO was precarious. So when Ross stayed put in California, Chambers was Alinsky's new man in Woodlawn by default.

Morale was so bad among TWO leaders at that point that Art Brazier, among others, was on the verge of quitting. Chambers asked Brazier to give him sixty days to shape things up, starting with a housecleaning of TWO's staff. One of his first moves was to decide what to do about von Hoffman's right-hand man, Bob Squires. Chambers knew that Squires was charming, bright, and capable of bringing out three hundred people on a street corner virtually any time of the day or night. "But when he gets them there, he doesn't know what to do with them," Chambers says. Von Hoffman liked Squires and had depended on him, and was willing to overlook his short-comings, which included a certain lack of discipline, but Chambers put a premium on discipline, especially since he believed that what TWO needed most was a disciplined staff. "I'm sick and tired of the stumble-bumble black organizers we've got; we're going to run this right," Chambers said when he took over. The staff consisted of "about four street blacks and Nick," he recalls. "I had to establish that Nick was out of the picture and I was boss, that I was a direct line from Alinsky." With Alinsky's approval, Chambers set out to create a fierce new image for himself and he quickly set Squires up for a kill. "Oh, it was calculated," he says. "And if I hadn't had a Squires I would have invented one. He had a bunch of silly cartoons pasted all around the office, and so at the first staff meeting I said, 'I don't know who put all this silly stuff up around here, but I want all that down by the end of the day.' " But at the next staff meeting, the cartoons were still on the wall. Chambers remembers his exchange with Squires:

"Didn't I say yesterday that all that shit should come down?"

"Well, yes, but you're new here, you're not . . ."

"That's the problem, you don't understand where the power is. You're fired. You're out."

"You can't do that."

"We'll see."

Chambers, with Alinsky's backing, easily weathered the protests of Squires's allies and, in true Alinsky style, felt he had established the right persona: "Here is a tough son of a bitch down from central casting sent by Saul Alinsky to clean up this mess; the motherfucker goes and fires the most popular guy right off the bat. He must be tough; he's six feet four, and he's Irish, and he hasn't got all that nice Nick bullshit." Chambers also moved quickly to hire a replacement, Squire Lance, a black reporter for one of Bruce Sagan's newspapers. But not all of the reforms were imple-mented quite so quickly:

I remember about a month after I was there we had a fund-raiser. It was a quarter party, starting on a Friday night. Everything costs a quarter—quarter for a drink, for a dance with a girl, for a piece of chicken—and you split the money with the ADC mothers fifty-fifty: they kept half to support themselves for the next week and, ostensibly, TWO got the other half.

At the Monday-morning staff meeting there was no staff. They had just kept spending the money as they took it in and bought more food. The goddamned thing had gone on all Saturday and all Sunday and it took me until Monday morning to close it down. Of course, everybody was laying everybody, you know, it was a hell of a good party.

Eventually, Chambers hired other new staff, many of whom were women.

Chambers was mystified to discover that TWO had run up debts that had gone unreported. As with Alinsky's other projects, a special IAF bank account had been established for Woodlawn. The money from the Archdiocese of Chicago, the Schwarzhaupt Foundation, and the Presbyterians went into the account and all disbursements for staff, rent, and other approved expenses were made from Alinsky's office. That's why Chambers was mystified to see unpaid bills for odds and ends totaling about $8,000. One of Alinsky's prime tenets, of course, was that a successful community organization ultimately had to be self-supporting; financial independence and organizational discipline went hand in hand. And during the previous summer, von Hoffman had tried to institute a fund-raising system. "Now is the time for TWO to stand on its own feet, pay its own bills, pay for its own staff, and be free of the dangers arising from having to depend on outside groups," he told them. He proposed a "Dollar for Equality" campaign, a door-to-door canvass conducted by TWO volunteers and organized by political precincts so that contributors could easily be tracked by the names on poll sheets. Churches would also be asked to help by setting aside one Sunday a month when each member would be asked to bring a Dollar for Equality. But the fund-raising plan had not progressed very far, and Chambers now made fund-raising a priority. By the end of December 1963, TWO had $14,500 of its own money in the bank, most of it coming from mandatory dues from each participating group and organization. Unlike Fred Ross and Cesar Chavez in California, who had great difficulty raising dues to a level that would make the CSO chapters stable and truly self-sustaining, Chambers was both persistent and uncompromising. Clearly, Alinsky was not uninterested in these kinds of money matters; nor did he usually allow his organizers great freedom to make these decisions on their own. (Chambers, for instance, had a big fight with his boss when it came to hiring Lance for a $6,000-a-year salary, which Alinsky thought was highly excessive.) As a rule, he was adamant about an organization becoming self-supporting. Still, he took a pragmatic, flexible approach in this as in other aspects of organizing. If Ross and Chavez in California, and von Hoffman in Woodlawn, were doing good work generally, he was willing to live with their deviations from the ideal.

Internally, TWO made rapid progress with its new staff during 1963. To the outside world—meaning especially the white Chicago media—it was perceived not only as a community organization but also as the most important new civil rights group in town. TWO's Arthur Brazier not only was leading large TWO protest delegations but was also the spokesman for the Coordinating Council of Civil Rights Organizations. And the demonstrations in Chicago in the spring of 1963 were played out against a backdrop of dramatic civil rights events in the South—sit-ins in Birmingham to protest segregated eating facilities; Martin Luther King's arrest and subsequent "Letter from a Birmingham Jail"; Bull Connor's use of police dogs and fire hoses on peaceful protesters; Governor George Wallace "standing in the schoolhouse door" to stop the integration of the University of Alabama; the assassination of civil rights leader Medgar Evers in front of his home in Jackson, Mississippi. Seeing TWO's protests as a counterpart to the conflicts in the South, the Chicago press, led by the *Daily News,* began to attach historic importance to them.

On July 10, when Daley met with an eighteen-member TWO delegation led by Brazier, the *Daily News* called it "one of the first negotiated sessions on civil rights in Chicago." Apparently, Daley requested the meeting to head off a large demonstration at City Hall that TWO planned for the next day. He tried to be conciliatory by pledging to help end job discrimination in Chicago and integrate the Washburne Trade School, which was dominated by the white craft unions. But he was less forthcoming about using mayoral power to force the school board to change its overall policies on race, insisting as he did throughout his tenure that he would not "interfere" with the board's decision-making even though he appointed all of the board's members.

But it was another issue that TWO was now especially concerned with—the long-simmering, unresolved dispute over the University of Chicago's South Campus expansion and urban renewal in Woodlawn. The TWO demonstration the next day was Alinsky's idea, designed both to pressure Daley and to vent the frustration that was growing within Woodlawn. TWO's initially successful, dramatic move in stopping the university's South Campus plan had now turned into a dull, unsatisfying stalemate. The city had come up with a preliminary, more comprehensive urban-renewal proposal for Woodlawn, but TWO rejected it, more because of the process than the substance: the city's proposal had not been developed in consultation with TWO. Then TWO hired its own planner, who was recommended to Alinsky by Jane Jacobs. He worked closely with TWO's leaders, helping them to understand the city's proposal and to develop their own plan, which emphasized the role of citizen participation and favored rehabilitation and conservation over massive land clearance. Although TWO's plan had merit, it was ignored. Basically, TWO couldn't overcome the law of politics that it is easier to stop somebody else's plan than to initiate and implement one's own. Also significant was that Mayor Daley had lost a bond issue in 1962, further drying up funds for urban renewal. Thus the Section 112 federal urban-renewal credits that the university received for its expansion programs in Hyde Park and South Campus were of renewed importance to TWO, which envisioned that some of that money would be used for new low-income housing and limited land clearance. But since the university had been blindsided by the upstart TWO two years earlier, it was not inclined to initiate a second offensive.

By now, in mid-1963, the South Campus issue was more than two years old. Many in TWO, frustrated and angry about the lack of progress, and increasingly confident about TWO's capacity to organize large-scale protests, began talking seriously about a massive sit-down demonstration on Lake Shore Drive during rush hour. Alinsky thought this would be a disaster, a scatter-shot attack that would give Daley and others a convenient excuse to discredit TWO for being irresponsible, for disrupting the lives of thousands of Chicagoans who had nothing to do with the South Campus issue. Chambers told Alinsky that they needed movement on the issue, so an alternative had to be invented. That's when Alinsky came up with the idea of a large demonstration at City Hall targeted at the mayor. TWO had visited this kind of effrontery on others, but unleashing black platoons on the mayor of Chicago was of another order. For Daley, it was not the breach of decorum that was nettling but rather the "evidence" that all was not well in Chicago—a reality the mayor was adept at airbrushing off the front page of the city's consciousness. So on July 10, he tried his best to dissuade Brazier from going through with the demonstration. He told Brazier he would call university officials immediately to arrange a meeting to discuss South Campus, and by late in the afternoon Daley announced that a meeting had been scheduled in his office between university officials and TWO on July 12. Instead of sending TWO's demonstrators downtown, the mayor said to Brazier, he would come to a meeting in Woodlawn the next night to explain his good intentions. To which Brazier responded coolly: "I'm afraid they'd rather hear it here."

The next day, July 11, ten busloads from Woodlawn—about six hundred people—descended on City Hall. The mayor's aides and the police were briefed in advance by TWO organizers about what to expect—how many buses, the route they would take downtown, how long the demonstrators planned to be at City Hall. Alinsky didn't want to surprise anybody; he wanted to make a statement, get media coverage, and pressure Daley into working out a settlement. Although South Campus was the major concern of the day, it was not the only issue promoted by the TWO delegation. Outside City Hall, some TWO pickets held signs that read: "Give Us Jobs," "Daley Equals Delay," and "Okay, So We're Not Irish." (The latter was not quite accurate since Doc Farrell was a conspicuous member of the TWO delegation; having at least one Irish priest with you at City Hall was de rigueur as far as Alinsky was concerned.) About two hundred TWO supporters conducted a brief sit-in outside the mayor's office while Brazier and other TWO supporters met with Daley. All the demonstrators were instructed to keep the protest nonviolent. "Our enemies want an incident," the instructions read. "We must not give our enemies a weapon." The demonstrators were also instructed by Chambers and the other organizers to remain silent when Daley spoke, to cheer only Brazier. "Silence is a terrific weapon," the organizers told the TWO troops. In a two-page statement that TWO distributed to the press, a key demand was for a "flat, unqualified commitment" from Daley in writing that the renewal plan for Woodlawn would be settled in his office with TWO and University of Chicago representatives.

But Daley was not yet ready to make binding commitments, and at one meeting after the City Hall demonstration, Brazier's growing confidence as leader of "the militant Woodlawn Organization," as the press frequently termed it, unexpectedly deserted him. At the appointed hour, Brazier and his troops arrived at City Hall. (The night before in Woodlawn, Brazier had led a big rally, and Chambers thought that he was ready to take Daley on, to pin him down on specific provisions of a Daley-endorsed settlement.) In the meeting room on the fifth floor outside the mayor's office, with about two hundred TWO supporters present, Brazier froze. After a few pleasantries, Daley went into a stock speech about working together and doing what's best for this fine city—while Brazier sat meekly and listened. Chambers, stranded in the back of the room, was mortified at what was happening. A few hours later, Alinsky was on the phone to Brazier. "Everybody in town is saying the mayor pissed all over you," he intoned flatly, somehow making the words sting even more. Alinsky's criticism had its effect, though, for at a follow-up meeting with Daley—perhaps arranged by Alinsky—Brazier appeared as fired up as Joe

Louis had been in his rematch with Max Schmeling. Hardly had Daley entered the room when Brazier leaped to his feet, threw his arm out in Daley's direction, his open fist coming within inches of the mayor's suddenly red face, and began to declaim on behalf of Woodlawn's right to self-determination. Except for Brazier's oratorical ambush, the room was deadly silent. The mayor was clearly shocked. Chambers was shocked. He noticed that the mayor's guards had started going for their guns. "It was stunning," Chambers recalls of Brazier's performance. "It seemed to shock Daley that a black man could speak that way to the mayor of Chicago, in a raised voice [and in a manner that] momentarily seemed to threaten his life."

Not long after, an agreement was hammered out ending the dispute. The demonstration at City Hall proved to be a pivotal scene in the public drama Alinsky had created, the beginning of the final act, when Alinsky arranged to have the mayor play one of his favorite roles—that of a successful mediator. Alinsky apparently went to see Daley and told him the "solution" he had in mind for South Campus, including the role Daley could play. He probably told Daley that TWO was ready to settle the issue but that neither he nor Brazier could go directly to the university because the university didn't trust them and wouldn't want to be perceived as caving in to TWO's demands. But if the mayor assured the university that he thought he could work out a deal, and if the mayor agreed that TWO would have a voice in the urban-renewal decisions in Woodlawn, then Daley could take credit for solving the South Campus problem.

The seven-point agreement that followed was extraordinary—almost certainly the first time that a black community in Chicago had, through sheer political power, won a major role in shaping an important urban-renewal program. Mayor Daley agreed that the administrator of the program had to be acceptable to TWO. The agreement also provided that the design of the final plan should "give Woodlawn residents continued access to the Midway recreation area. In other words, no Great Wall of China." But the most important concession was that "the majority of the people to be appointed to the groups or committees relating to planning and renewal in Woodlawn will be people from Woodlawn." And, in fact, in October, Mayor Daley appointed TWO supporters to a majority of the thirteen-member Woodlawn Citizens Committee, including a TWO leader, the Reverend Ulysses Blakeley, as chairman. (Flexing its muscles almost immediately, the seven-member TWO majority rejected the city's proposed urban-renewal ordinance and then approved a somewhat revised plan that changed the boundaries of the targeted area, the land to be cleared, and the location of new low-income housing.) The agreement between Daley and TWO also addressed another important point—the issue of relocation, which had been the subject of heated controversy in urban-renewal projects not only in Chicago but in other cities. The agreement specified that "the demolition for South Campus should be delayed until . . . new units of low-cost . . . housing have been built so that the people can be relocated directly out of the old housing on South Campus into the new." Finally, it seemed, poor people were being accorded a measure of dignity and consideration, an unusual if not unprecedented development in urban-renewal policy—if, of course, all went according to plan.

All in all, the TWO–South Campus episode—both the final agreement and the events leading up to it—epitomized Alinsky's philosophy, values, methods, and style. Two years earlier, a city official had said about Woodlawn: "There is nobody to speak for the community. A community does not exist in Woodlawn." So the agreement itself represented a proud moment for TWO's leaders, the mayor's testimonial that TWO had arrived. At the same time, TWO continued its attack on slumlords, and stepped up efforts to deal with unemployment (estimated at more than 30 percent in Woodlawn), by trying to secure a contract from the U.S. Labor Department for a job retraining and placement program and negotiating with several businesses for new jobs.

TWO's earlier "negotiations" with Marshall Field's yielded not only jobs but a story about an Alinsky tactic that became a classic among his admirers. For many decades, when one thought of Chicago's State Street— "that great street"—one invariably thought of Field's grand flagship department store. It was a place for browsing if not buying, a major attraction for generations of Chicagoans for whom shopping on State Street was a Saturday ritual—if, that is, you were white. Generally, blacks did not come downtown to shop on State Street; they were not welcome. Nor did stores like Field's hire many blacks, and rarely if ever did they employ them as salesclerks or in other visible positions. So when TWO's leaders first approached Field's about hiring Woodlawn residents, the response was predictably icy. What happened next was a variation of TWO's tactic of sending blacks from Woodlawn to picket white slumlords in their own neighborhoods. Alinsky claimed that he planted a "rumor" designed to reach Field's executives (actually, they were informed rather straightforwardly) that unless Field's agreed to hire unemployed Woodlawnites, a substantial group of them, perhaps several busfuls, would come to Field's on an upcoming Saturday for an all-day shopping spree. The image of several hundred blacks fanning out through the store, trying on fine silks or testing floor displays in the magnificent toy department, apparently gave Field's top managers the shakes. Suddenly, they were willing to discuss new job possibilities with TWO—and by the end of 1963, Field's had hired a number of blacks for entry-level positions.

(In 1982, Alinsky's tactic was recalled by the journalist Mike Royko in a newspaper column prompted by the civil rights leader Jesse Jackson's threat to have blacks boycott a city-sponsored summer festival, Chicago-Fest, because minority businesses were allegedly being discriminated against. Jackson's approach was all wrong, Royko explained, only somewhat facetiously, maintaining that racial attitudes had changed little since the early 1960s and that many white Chicagoans would welcome the prospect of a blackless festival. Indeed, if blacks stayed away, Royko predicted the major effect would be a sharp increase in white attendance. On the other hand, if Jackson really wanted to make a credible threat and get Mayor Jane Byrne's attention, he should borrow a page from Saul Alinsky's book and urge all blacks in Chicago to *go* to the festival.)

WHEN CHARLES SILBERMAN wrote an article for *Fortune* in the spring of 1962 on race and poverty in American cities, it attracted considerable attention. "It seems hard to realize in retrospect, but it was the first time that anybody had said that the problem of the city was the problem of race," he has said, and it was true that most American periodicals skirted the problem. Even *Fortune*'s own ground-breaking series several years earlier, "The Exploding Metropolis," emphasized other urban issues, and when Silberman himself began research for his article, he first thought the problem of the city was poverty; then he thought it was associated with migration; and only finally did he come to see that the essence of it was race. His powerful argument was timely, and elicited a strong response— Henry Luce himself told *Fortune*'s managing editor he thought it was the most important piece that had ever appeared in *Fortune*—so Silberman expanded it into a book. Two years later, the publication of *Crisis in Black and White* was even more timely.

One of Silberman's main, controversial points was that black frustration and rage were so deep and widespread that large-scale violence in Northern cities was an imminent possibility. This was not a widely held view among whites, including Northern white liberals, and in *The Nation* of June 29, 1964, a reviewer wrote: "In the world of created non-news which surrounds race relations, Silberman is probably stuck with the idle chatter about violence that takes up a number of his pages." Only nineteen days later, riots broke out in Harlem, the first of the era, presaging anguish and disorder in scores of cities for the next five years.

Silberman's book quickly became a best-seller. It was not only his perspicacity about violence that attracted an audience. He convincingly traced the effects of 250 years of slavery followed by a hundred years of oppression and discrimination on the daily lives of ghetto residents—their low self-esteem, the breakdown of family life, their lack of hope. Although much of this material was familiar, Silberman's lucidly argued contention that the day of reckoning for America was drawing near—he thought it surprising that blacks had been as docile as they had for so long—cast a new light on the historical interpretations and gave urgency to his discussion of remedies. Silberman warned—as others would later—that "unless the Negro position improves very quickly, Negroes of whatever class may come to regard their separation from American life as permanent, and so consider themselves outside the constraints and allegiances of American society." Both practical considerations and the moral self-image of the nation were at stake, he wrote, but a prerequisite to specific remedies was an understanding of the truth of race relations "that neither white nor Negro Americans have been willing to face, even to admit."

One such truth was that racism was deep and pervasive not only in the South but throughout the country—a condition white liberals were slow to recognize and in many cases unable or unwilling to recognize. Indeed, white liberals in the North were no longer so unequivocal about racial equality in housing and schools as they had been when the issue seemed confined to the South. "The tragedy of race relations in the United States is that there is no American Dilemma," Silberman wrote, suggesting that Gunnar Myrdal's conclusion twenty years earlier—that "the American Negro problem is a problem in the heart of America"—was fundamentally wrong. To the contrary, Silberman argued, "white Americans are not torn and tortured by the conflict between their devotion to the American creed and their actual behavior. They are upset by the current state of race relations, to be sure. But what troubles them is not that justice is being denied but that their peace is being shattered and their business interrupted."

In large part, however, *Crisis in Black and White* was addressed to Northern whites who might be persuaded that the hour was late and a crisis at hand, that it was "up to [them] to lead the way [because] the guilt and the responsibility are theirs. To insist that Negroes must change before whites abandon their discriminatory practices is to deny the very essence of the Judaeo-Christian tradition." But Silberman did not place the entire leadership burden on whites. The "Negro problem" was not just a white man's problem, as Myrdal thought. "If whites were to stop all discriminatory practices tomorrow, this alone would not solve 'the Negro problem,' "

Silberman went on. "A major part of the 'Negro problem' lies in what these three hundred and fifty years have done to the Negro's personality: the self-hatred, the sense of impotence and inferiority that destroys aspiration and keeps the Negro locked in a prison we have all made."

For more than three hundred pages, Silberman tied the legacy of oppression to the need for fundamental reforms in areas such as employment opportunities and education—reforms that whites could help bring about as their contribution to breaking down the prison walls. But *how* such reforms were initiated and implemented were at least as important as their substance, Silberman argued. And in his climactic last chapter, he presented a case study of Alinsky's work in Woodlawn as the prime example of how poor blacks themselves could break the psychological shackles that inevitably limited their progress.

The more Silberman had seen of Alinsky's work in Woodlawn, the more impressed he became. Two years earlier, when he was researching his *Fortune* piece, he had come upon Alinsky and TWO somewhat accidentally, via either Jane Jacobs or Jack Egan. Although TWO had created a stir in Chicago by late 1961, it had received little press attention elsewhere except in several church publications, where an often contentious debate swirled around the issue of church support of Alinsky's controversial methods. At that point, Silberman had little more than a vague notion about the importance of poor blacks "taking more control of their lives. I don't know how I put it or if I was even able to formulate it that way. I simply had this percolating in the back of my mind. As Saul began to talk, what he was saying rang all sorts of bells and helped lots of things come together in my mind." After talking with Alinsky, he visited Woodlawn, interviewed Nick von Hoffman as well as many TWO activists, and then drafted his article. The *Time* bureau chief in Chicago, Murray Gart, saw the draft and called to tell him that University of Chicago officials had seen it, too, and wanted to save Silberman the embarrassment of publishing a number of misconceptions—in fact, they had compiled a dossier which they would be happy to share with Silberman so that he could get the facts straight. "I got the dossier, it came by packet the next day," Silberman remembers. "And the main items were some income-tax returns of the Industrial Areas Foundation and a copy of the famous University of Chicago undergraduate article 'Church Supports Hate Group.' " Silberman told Gart he was puzzled: the only point about the tax return was that it showed the Chicago Catholic archdiocese had contributed money to the IAF. The university's "logic" seemed all too apparent; Silberman was appalled by what he felt was "a kind of vulgar anti-Catholicism." He had observed the sociology of race long enough to know that Catholics were as likely to be on the right side of the issue as anybody else, he believed, and he also knew that the Archdiocese of Chicago's leaders were different from, say, New York's. "People like Egan and Archbishop Meyer were good guys. If the university made some case or argument that the archdiocese was doing something wrong, it would have been different. But simply the fact that the archdiocese supplied the money was evidence of Saul's corruption."

As Silberman nailed down his facts, he became even more convinced that Alinsky's work in Woodlawn was of major significance. But the last chapter of *Crisis in Black and White* was no mere description of TWO's individual successes with dishonest merchants, slumlords, or the University of Chicago. "The Revolt Against 'Welfare Colonialism' " was a scathing attack on traditional American social work and the welfare system as well as a discussion of Alinsky's approach as an important alternative. Silberman's scorn for the welfare–social worker–settlement house approach was reminiscent of Clifford Shaw's criticisms in the 1930s; a growing number of critics, most conspicuously those reformers who were shaping the Johnson administration's federal War on Poverty, were similarly scornful. Like many of them, Silberman thought that a huge self-serving welfare industry only contributed to the dependency of poor blacks in ways large and small, blatant and insidious. It was an industry populated by social workers who placed far too much emphasis on symptoms rather than causes, who were preoccupied with case work and the study and treatment of individual maladjustment. "The goal . . . has been to teach maladjusted individuals how to adapt themselves to society as it is, rather than to change those aspects of society that make the individuals what they are," he wrote. Moreover, the inherent tensions between social workers and their "clients"—the tensions between superiors and inferiors—were exacerbated by social workers' tendencies toward a patronizing, holier-than-thou approach—"the white man's burden" was the way Silberman summarized the approach and attitude. Alinsky used similar but even harsher language and images. "They represent welfare colonialism to the nth degree. And by welfare colonialism what we mean is that if you consider our low-income communities as underprivileged nations, they come in [and set up] their agencies as colonial outposts, treating us as though we were in the Congo." Woodlawnites, Alinsky said sarcastically, were on the verge of greeting the next wave of missionaries "by having about 150 of our people in loincloths meet them to take them to our medicine man, and then hold out trays of beads for trade."

Silberman was convinced that black resentment of the welfare–social work apparatus—the ever-present symbol of white control and black subjugation and impotence—was so deep that "any paternalistic program imposed from above will be resisted and resented as 'welfare colonialism.' " He acknowledged that the Woodlawns of the country needed help—resources in the form of compensatory education, job retraining, advice on child-rearing, and preventive medicine. But *how* these resources were delivered and implemented, at whose direction and initiative, was critically important. To Silberman, "TWO's greatest contribution, therefore, is its most subtle: it gives Woodlawn residents the sense of dignity that makes it possible for them to accept help."

Silberman raised two cautionary flags about replicating Alinsky's success in Woodlawn. He was uncertain where additional support—seed money and sponsorship—could be found to launch more TWOs. Although the federal anti-poverty program was still in its infancy, he thought it was unlikely if not impossible that government, "however liberal, is going to stimulate creation of a power organization that is sure to make its life uncomfortable." Similarly, large foundations shied away from controversy and were too committed to paternalism and tied in with the welfare establishment. A case in point was one of the Ford Foundation's major efforts of the era, the "gray area" project (a euphemism that had prompted Alinsky to remark that in the genteel atmosphere where big-time foundation executives think great thoughts, "slums" no longer existed). In New Haven, Connecticut, one of the project's five cities, the Foundation announced that "a community-wide consensus" had been reached to attack a spectrum of urban ills, a consensus reflected in the board of directors composed of the United Fund, the board of education, Yale University, the New Haven Foundation, and so forth. As Silberman noted derisively: "Everybody, in short, except the people being planned for."

If money and sponsorship were not insurmountable hurdles, then Alinsky himself might be. "There is only one Alinsky," Silberman said, in much the same way one might talk about a Picasso or a Horowitz. It remained to be demonstrated that others could successfully use Alinsky's concepts and tactics. But even though Silberman urged that a great many approaches were needed—"it would be naïve to suggest that there is only one way—Alinsky's way"—he clearly had been persuaded. Alinsky's Woodlawn project was, he said, "the most important and the most impressive experiment affecting Negroes anywhere in the United States."

25

Smugtown and Stardom

"When that book came out, my stock split two for one," Alinsky told friends some months after *Crisis in Black and White* was published. It was a curious choice of metaphor coming from a man who cultivated the image of a radical. But he was also a man who might follow up on a stock-market tip, who at one point regularly visited the newsstand in the lobby of his Michigan Avenue office building late in the afternoon to check out the "final markets" in the *Daily News*'s "red streak" edition. But he was by no means a big-time player, for by the early 1960s his $20,000 IAF salary—soon to rise to $25,000—provided for a reasonably comfortable lifestyle but not a lot of money to play the market. His chief investment was in his and Jean's house in California. Jean may have had some stockholdings when she married Saul, and part of his interest in the market may have been related to that. But he did not have many stocks, nor did he have much luck. (Once, Alinsky's friend Seniel Ostrow, an IAF board member, gave Alinsky a small amount of stock in a book-publishing company—Pocket Books—that Ostrow's son-in-law was involved in. The stock had a great ascent before plunging nearly to sea level. In the meantime, Ostrow forgot the gift—until one day Alinsky, who had held on to the stock through both its rise and its fall, phoned Ostrow, furious that his friend hadn't tipped him off before the roller coaster changed direction.)

Taking a risk in the stock market appealed to Alinsky's sporting side as well as to his interest in making a little money. He was not indifferent to money; he couldn't afford to be. While not quite penurious, he was careful about spending money, always on the lookout for somebody to pick up a tab; it was one of the small bonuses of having lunch with Ralph Helstein, say, who had a union expense account. But making big money or accumulating wealth was not a primary interest—recognition, influence, and power were much more important. Indeed, about the worst thing that could happen to Saul Alinsky was to be ignored, which he rarely let happen. Even riding down the crowded elevator at lunchtime from his seventh-floor office was an opportunity to attract attention and have a little fun. He would ask his secretary, Dorothy Levin, to take dictation as they rode down together. And with everybody listening, he would start on a letter, invariably to somebody well-known and important like His Eminence Cardinal Meyer. To his secretary, these elevator escapades ranged from comical to embarrassing, but no more so than when she was required to bring Alinsky his mail at curbside on Michigan Avenue—meeting him around the corner on a mere side street would not do—whereupon his car blocked traffic while he opened the mail and dictated instructions.

The recognition he received from Silberman's book was of an entirely different order, of course, and marked his rebirth as a national figure. Not since the publication of *Reveille for Radicals* nearly twenty years earlier had Alinsky's name and concepts reached such a broad audience. In fact, the immediate impact of Silberman's book on Alinsky was greater than *Reveille*'s had been. For one thing, high praise for Alinsky was coming from an apparently objective source. After the book came out, Alinsky suggested to friends and journalists that Silberman's glowing account was all the more remarkable because, as a *Fortune* editor who represented establishment interests, Silberman had originally been unfriendly. (Nearly the opposite was true, actually.) In any event, the lavish praise in the book was not confined to calling TWO the most important experiment in the country affecting blacks. He also wrote that "Alinsky is that rarity in American life: a superlative organizer, strategist, and tactician who is also a philosopher (or a superlative philosopher who is also an organizer, strategist and tactician)." Or in another passage: "The essential difference between Alinsky and his enemies is that Alinsky really believes in democracy: he really believes that the helpless, the poor, the badly educated can solve their own problems if given the chance and the means."

The other reason for the book's enormous impact on Alinsky's fortunes was its timing. *Reveille for Radicals,* first published at the end of the war, also seemed to come out at just the right time. But the focus of national attention then shifted from grave concern about the viability of democratic institutions to other, seemingly more urgent, tangible matters like the economy and the Cold War. *Reveille* had made a big splash, but the ripples developed slowly over a period of many years. With *Crisis in Black and White,* Silberman anticipated a deterioration in race relations and the strong possibility of racial violence in the Northern states. And now, in the summer of 1964, Harlem erupted in violence and only weeks later so did the black ghettos in Rochester, New York, and Philadelphia. The following summer, the Watts section of Los Angeles experienced violent unrest—and for most of the rest of the decade, riots in black ghettos throughout the country gave new meaning to the phrase "the long hot summer."

Beginning in the winter and continuing into early summer 1964, a small study group at the Third Presbyterian Church in Rochester, led by an assistant pastor, Paul Long, met regularly to discuss public issues and to read, among other things, *Crisis in Black and White*. Third Presbyterian was one of the largest, most prestigious churches in town, its congregants well represented among the luminaries of Rochester. One of the people in Long's study group was John McCrory, a thirty-nine-year-old partner in the city's largest law firm, Nixon, Hargraves, Devon and Doyle, and widely regarded as the brightest young trial lawyer in Rochester. He was deeply affected by the readings and then by the city's upheaval. "Everybody in that group was to a very large extent radicalized by the experience," McCrory says, recalling that the readings and discussions had a big impact even before the riot. By his own definition, he was—and remained—a conservative, voting for Barry Goldwater for President later that year, although not with great enthusiasm. But McCrory was also a Quaker, and he felt a personal obligation to embrace "rational change," and the civil rights movement in the South had sensitized him to many of the issues addressed in *Crisis in Black and White*. But the chapter on Alinsky— followed by more reading about Alinsky's ideas—provided him, McCrory says, "for the first time with an appreciation of the concept of power." Suddenly, he began to understand that political power was not necessarily an evil to be associated with corrupt big-city bosses, but essential to blacks if they were going to move into the American mainstream.

Still, McCrory was as shocked as nearly every other white Rochesterian when the riot began in the predominantly black Joseph Avenue area on July 24. It had been a pleasant Friday night. By ten o'clock the temperature had dipped to a comfortable seventy-six, and a street dance sponsored by the Northeast Mothers' Improvement Association was in progress. Soon, however, the police were on the scene responding to a call from an organizer of the dance complaining about a man who had become disruptive. There were perhaps several hundred people in the street when a police K-9 unit arrived. There had been other incidents involving the police and the K-9 unit—in the black community, it was a commonly held belief that white police harassed blacks for the sport of it, especially on weekends, and that the police deliberately used the dogs to taunt blacks. On the night of

July 24, as the K-9 unit made its way into the crowd, blacks who had been in the street retreated but then regrouped between Joseph Avenue and Kelly Street. And then many started throwing rocks at the police, and then through store windows. As one policeman recalled later: "Things were getting out of hand. . . . We didn't have a lot of policemen at that time. . . . You've got to remember this was only the second major riot in the country. We were ill prepared." Quickly overwhelmed by the growing violence, the police now retreated and, for a time, were removed entirely from the area by their superiors. Even after they regrouped and were joined by state troopers, the violence continued. Eventually Governor Nelson Rockefeller ordered the National Guard into the city. Three days later the violence finally ended but only after four people were killed, hundreds injured, and nearly a thousand arrested. Scores of stores in the black ghetto, many of them white-owned, had been damaged and looted. The Joseph Avenue area looked like a war zone.

To be sure, the way the riot started—an incident involving white police in a black neighborhood—was to be repeated in many other cities during the next several years. And as in other Northern cities, Rochester's black neighborhoods had expanded dramatically in the previous decade, along with the familiar problems of bad housing, inadequate schools, and high unemployment. But these conditions alone didn't produce riots; it was, rather, a combination of factors, including the new tone created by the civil rights movement, which had not only inspired a new assertiveness among many blacks but raised expectations of better living conditions which were going largely unfulfilled. Many black Americans, especially young ghetto blacks, were running out of patience. Progress seemed to come at a snail's pace and then only after the specter of violence. At the March on Washington in the summer of 1963, 300,000 people had chanted, "Freedom Now! Jobs Now!" It took another year before Congress finally passed legislation to outlaw discrimination in employment and to establish the Equal Employment Opportunity Commission—and only after Martin Luther King, Jr., and other civil rights leaders continued to warn of widespread violence if these laws were not enacted. Nonetheless, the riot in Harlem began sixteen days after President Johnson signed into law the landmark civil rights legislation on July 2, and six days after that came Rochester.

Rochester's civic pride was deeply wounded. The city's civic leaders were shocked by what happened because, in their eyes, Rochester was different from other cities. It was certainly not like cities in the South; after all, Rochester had been a stop on the Underground Railroad for runaway slaves and the place where Frederick Douglass published his abolitionist newspaper. Rochester was a city whose history was not dominated by corrupt machine politics or by warring ethnic factions struggling for the spoils of patronage, or a place where the typical wage earner had scratched out a living in a smelly rendering plant or dirty steel mill. Rochester's history and style were different. This was a prosperous, genteel city of generally well-educated people who worked at highly skilled jobs at Eastman Kodak or Bausch & Lomb or, more recently, Xerox. In many ways, Eastman Kodak set the tone in Rochester. Kodak's massive Rochester work force—nearly 40,000 people—had never been unionized. Kodak, it was said, took care of its own, for it paid well and provided job security. It also gave handsome support to an array of civic institutions—the Eastman School of Music, the highly regarded symphony, the University of Rochester, hospitals, and other charities. Charitable giving was a hallmark of Rochester, and civic leaders took great pride in their city's reputation for having one of the nation's highest levels of per capita contributions to the Community Chest. Charity, civility, and voluntarism—these constituted a cornerstone of the philosophy that shaped the life of Rochester, both its public and its private institutions.

Unlike most cities of the time, Rochester continued to rely on private giving rather than government funding for many social programs. The old tradition of noblesse oblige had remained in force even as new, bigger social problems emerged, many related to the rapid increase in the number of poor blacks, especially immigrants from the South. At the turn of the century, blacks made up only 1 percent of the city's population. Even by the end of World War II, there were only about 6,000 blacks in Rochester, but between 1950 and 1960, the black population tripled from 7,600 to 23,600, and by 1964, it was approximately 32,000. The black population increased faster in Rochester than in any other city in New York State, largely because of the allure of good jobs there. But the rapid population increase had outpaced the number of unskilled jobs available. In some black neighborhoods, unemployment ran at more than 25 percent, and the average nonwhite income in the city was less than that in Buffalo, Syracuse, or other upstate cities. There was some evidence of a link between black migration and unemployment in the arrests made during the riot: more than 90 percent of those arrested—most of whom were black—were either unskilled laborers or unemployed, and 660 of the 720 blacks arrested had been born outside of New York State.

By 1960, the black population had increased to 7 percent of Rochester's 318,000 total, and by 1965 it was about 10 percent. In addition to unemployment, there was a serious housing shortage. At its worst, the overcrowding in black neighborhoods was reminiscent of Chicago's South

Side. "Houses that were built for one family, maybe two families, were beginning to hold as many as twenty-four or twenty-eight families," says Connie Mitchell, at the time a Monroe County supervisor in the black 3rd Ward. While doing voter registration on Greig Street she came upon a house that had forty-three mailboxes. In spite of such conditions, there was only one public housing project in the black community.

The white leaders were not unaware of the new problems in the black community, but they were apparently not fully aware of their magnitude. Blacks, confined mainly to the 3rd and 7th wards, had no representation on the City Council, which was elected at large. If the black community was not literally invisible, the traditional rhythms of the city muted its presence and problems. One community leader remembers organizing informal Saturday-morning meetings between white corporate executives and civic leaders and representatives of the black community who told about the housing shortages, unemployment, and lack of opportunity. He recalls that later "most of [the whites] would call me and say, 'Well, I agree with you. It's a growing problem. But we've still got to raise money for the university. We've got a hospital drive. And I think you're exaggerating the problem.' " The white leaders not only minimized "the problem" but resented the accusations that they were insensitive and unresponsive. After all, some of them—along with liberal church leaders—had helped to push through a police advisory board in response to black protests of police misconduct. And the board of education was beginning to address the issue of racial imbalance in the schools. Perhaps nobody articulated—and symbolized—the old establishment attitude better than Paul Miller, president of the Rochester-based Gannett Company and publisher of the morning and afternoon papers, the *Democrat & Chronicle* and the *Times-Union.* "I have been reading every word about the city's racial problems," he wrote in a column in 1963, "and I believe I have been reading about a Rochester that doesn't exist. I mean the Rochester pictured by those who seem to feel—and I have no reason to doubt their sincerity—that it is not alert and responsive to human needs in all areas. There is no such Rochester as some of these critics paint."

When the riot hit, Jack McCrory was out of town. He hurried back, not knowing exactly how he could help, but, he remembers, "I didn't want to be like a conservative old fart who sat around on the side saying this is a terrible thing." To him and others, it soon became clear that the existing institutions and the attitudes they reflected were ill suited to deal with the new dynamics of race. A poignant emergency meeting was called by Mrs. Harper Sibley, chairman of the biracial Commission on Religion and Race, at her mansion on East Avenue during the height of the riot.

Mrs. Sibley, a symbol of the old, monied, Episcopalian upper-class Rochester, alternately scolded the black clergy present—what are *you* people
doing to control *your* people? she asked—and pleaded with them to let
whites help, perhaps by temporarily housing blacks endangered by the
violence. She may have been well intentioned, but some black clergy
started to walk out.

Soon after the riot, McCrory found himself plotting strategy with a
small group of church leaders, and later he became chairman of the
Rochester Board of Urban Ministry, whose executive director was a young
clergyman named Herbert White. Six years out of the seminary, White had
left a small inner-city church in Buffalo at the urging of church friends
working with the Rochester Area Council of Churches, who were starting
an urban ministry. "I was very reluctant," White remembers. "That was
a big step in those days, to leave the church and go into a staff job. Also
my salary doubled, so I had all kinds of guilt feelings." White arrived in
Rochester in January 1964, a little more than six months before the riot,
and began to build relationships among both white and black clergy. Not
long after the riot, he began thinking about getting in touch with Saul
Alinsky. "I knew about Alinsky and the Industrial Areas Foundation, not
personally but as a Presbyterian because of all the hullabaloo about Woodlawn and the involvement there of the Presbyterian Church, and also the
articles in *Christian Century.*" Meanwhile, the Board of Urban Ministry
and representatives at the National Council of Churches arranged to have
several of Martin Luther King's top aides, including Andrew Young and
James Bevel, come to town. About this time King and his strategists were
beginning to think of expanding the work of the Southern Christian Leadership Conference to Northern cities. Their invitation to Rochester suggested, in part, the assessment of many in the city that Rochester's own
civil rights organizations were ineffective, a factor that may have helped
to precipitate the riot. But the SCLC men did not stay very long; after a
flurry of meetings with black clergy and white liberals, they left town
abruptly before any concrete program or agenda could be fashioned. (Besides their obligations elsewhere, their departure may have been influenced
by the atmosphere in Rochester's ghetto, where, according to one report,
an SCLCer's street corner sermon on nonviolence elicited a shout of "What
is all this Jesus crap?") With SCLC out of the picture, White started talking
to black clergy about Alinsky, who was virtually unknown to them. After
they read *Crisis in Black and White* and were favorably impressed, White
went to the Board of Urban Ministry, made up largely of representatives
of the mainline Protestant denominations, and received their approval to
contact Alinsky.

In November 1964, a delegation of five whites and three blacks—including Herb White and Paul Long, Dick Hughes and Marvin Chandler of the Rochester Area Council of Churches, Connie Mitchell, and Cannon St. Julian Simpkins—met with Alinsky for three hours in his Chicago office. Alinsky made no promises, except to say he would consider their invitation to organize in Rochester; he had similar offers from other cities. But White and the others sensed he was intrigued with Rochester, especially because of the riot and the national attention it had received. Alinsky told them how much it would cost—$100,000 for two years—and went out of his way to tell them that life would never be the same for them and the city if he *did* come, a warning that came across as both a promise and a boast. Before they left, Alinsky, who had never been to Rochester but who had listened intently to accounts of the city's stuffiness and smugness, said, "There's a tactic I've always wanted to try, and Rochester would be the perfect place." As earnest as Saul Alinsky could be when he was about to spin a story like this one, he continued: "You buy blacks three or four hundred tickets to the Rochester symphony. But before the performance, they'll all get together for dinner, except this won't be an ordinary dinner, it'll be a big baked-bean dinner. Then they'll go to the symphony and fart it out of existence. How would that go over in Rochester? Wouldn't people love that?"

When White and the others returned to Rochester, word spread about their meeting with Alinsky—and about the baked-bean-dinner story as well. Alinsky, who had been largely unknown to Rochester's corporate and civic leadership, soon became a familiar name and, with notable exceptions, the city's leaders were furious that he had been approached. The president of the University of Rochester, Allen Wallis, who used to teach economics at the University of Chicago, called his friend Julian Levi to get a rundown on Alinsky. And the Chicago banker Gaylord Freeman remembers getting similar calls from Rochester's corporate leaders. The Lutheran Walter Kloetzli, on a personal crusade to warn others about Alinsky's unscrupulousness, traveled from Chicago to collar anybody who might listen. The Gannett newspapers sent a reporter to Chicago to see what he could dig up. It was not only that Alinsky's style and philosophy were so alien to the Rochester establishment; more disturbing—even alarming—was the prospect of having Alinsky in town on the heels of the riot, "fanning the flames of discontent." To a *Times-Union* reporter interviewing Alinsky in Chicago, who told him the Rochester police had been taking riot training but might be "jumpy" about the possibility of violence, Alinsky retorted: "Somebody had better unjump them, then. I believe in nonviolence, but I'm not Mahatma Gandhi. I believe in self-defense." In the view of many Rochester people, Alinsky seemed like the antithesis of what was needed to avoid another riot.

For nearly five months, through the winter of 1965, the debate over Alinsky raged, with the white clergy—the core of the pro-Alinsky forces—leading the way against powerful opposition. As the newspapers began to editorialize against Alinsky and other anti-Alinsky civic leaders stepped up their opposition, questions and fears about him within local church congregations had to be addressed. Herb White, Dick Hughes, Jack McCrory, and others were on the hustings three or four nights a week for three months during the winter of 1965, rebutting the criticism and mobilizing support.

In January 1965, Alinsky made his first appearance in Rochester, meeting separately with white and black clergy. Afterward, he spoke to the press, avoiding specifics while stressing that he would not come to Rochester unless a broad cross section of the black community invited him. "We are not," he explained, "a foreign mission social agency that just goes in regardless." He also charged that "faucets are being turned off all over town" to sabotage the efforts to bring him in. It became known, for example, that the Community Chest was prepared to cut the funding of pro-Alinsky groups. (One well-publicized episode occurred in February. Radio station WHAM informed the Council of Churches that it might "reluctantly be forced" to start charging the Council $275 for its Sunday-morning church service broadcasts if Alinsky came to Rochester under the Council's sponsorship. The station's president said, "I would not like to feel that WHAM is contributing in any way to the support of Alinsky." Then a full-page advertisement in the *Times-Union* commented that Rochester could "do without hiring an overpriced Chicago 'organizer' who is noted for 'rubbing raw the sores of discontent' and staging class and race incidents that cause trouble and solve nothing.")

But if some faucets were being turned off, others were being turned on. Rochester had never had an Urban League chapter; and even in February 1965 the latest attempt to fund one seemed doomed when the Urban League's national director, Whitney Young, Jr., told city leaders he was throwing in the towel. "This is your problem," he said during a visit to the City Club. "I'm not coming here to plead anymore." But by March, a group of Rochester's corporate executives, newly inspired, pledged the money. While there were public denials that the money was raised in hopes of heading off Alinsky, privately everybody involved knew better—and Alinsky and his friends began referring to the new office as "the Saul Alinsky chapter of the Urban League."

Such countermoves, however, came too late. By February, many of the Protestant denominations had voted financial support to Alinsky through both their local and national bodies, led by the Presbyterians, who pledged $14,000 annually. (Alinsky's friends Dave Ramage, George Todd, and Bryant George were now on the national Presbyterian staff in New York.) The Lutherans were a conspicuous holdout among the Protestants—Kloetzli apparently had an impact—and the Catholic diocese remained neutral, although the Catholic Interracial Council gave its endorsement. In the black community, petitions supporting an invitation to Alinsky were circulated through the Negro Ministers Association, among sororities and fraternities, and on street corners and in pool halls. In a letter to Alinsky on February 5, White wrote: "It is very exciting to watch the underdogs of Rochester rally around this effort. Even if by some stretch of the imagination we still possessed some small glimmer of a euphoric desire to create consensus in the white community about this thing, we could not now break faith with our Negro clergy and the Negro community."

In March, with virtually all of the funding assured, Alinsky told the Rochester clergy he would accept their invitation. It was something of an eleventh-hour decision, for Alinsky had more or less agreed to a similar offer from Kansas City, Missouri. Clergy in Buffalo and the San Francisco–Oakland area had also mounted serious efforts to recruit him, and at one point it looked as though the Kansas City group would be the first to raise the necessary funds. In fact, Ed Chambers, whom Alinsky was pulling out of Woodlawn to be the organizer of the new project, had just gone to Kansas City to look for a place to live when Alinsky phoned.

"We're going into Rochester," Alinsky said.

"But, Saul, I've just rented an apartment here."

"Forget it; the money's come through in Rochester, and we're starting there as soon as we can."

It was an exciting, chaotic time. For the first time in Alinsky's career, groups were coming to him with prospects of underwriting organizing campaigns. But a prospect of financial support was not quite the same thing as money in the bank. And because the clergy who were leading these efforts were sailing in uncharted waters, there was always the possibility they would capsize in a storm of opposition.

Journalists like Silberman, who thought Alinsky's ideas and methods were important, rarely focused much attention on the critical role of the day-to-day organizer in Alinsky's projects—such as Fred Ross or Nick von Hoffman—and Alinsky himself usually glossed over them, a tendency that rankled Ross in particular. To both journalists and the clergy who wanted an "Alinsky" project for their city, it was all too easy to think of these men as mere extensions of Alinsky and to minimize their importance. In truth, Alinsky's success or failure in a community had always depended heavily on the experience of a well-versed organizer or on the capacity of a young one to learn. Now, however, except for Chambers, Alinsky didn't have an experienced organizer who had worked in a black ghetto. Barry Menuez, in Chicago, who had succeeded Chambers as the OSC's staff director on the Southwest Side, was ready to move on after four years at the OSC, and with help from Alinsky's Presbyterian connections, he had landed a job with a new, church-backed community organizing project in West Philadelphia. But the project collapsed before Menuez got started. When Alinsky heard that Menuez was going to receive three months' separation pay for his troubles, he said to him, "Well, that's wonderful. Now I've got a free staff assistant for three months."

"I was like an advance man in Rochester," Menuez says. "I literally carried his big satchel. I think Saul liked [the image] of having an aide-decamp. And I loved it. I didn't feel at all demeaned. It was exciting. We'd go into Rochester and the press corps would be at the airport, and the TV cameras, and he'd say these outrageous things. He was having a ball. And then he'd farm me out. He couldn't go to all the meetings, so, for example, I would meet with the Episcopal Clergy Association at Mrs. Sibley's house . . . and would interpret for them the theology of power."

As Menuez's three-month internship came to a close, Alinsky's day of reckoning with the Kansas City delegation drew near. Just as he was on the verge of telling them that Menuez would be their organizer, Menuez was unexpectedly asked by the national staff of the Episcopal Church in New York to develop an urban program with an Alinsky-style perspective. Alinsky liked the idea of having a well-placed disciple in the national office of a major Protestant denomination. "I tell you what," he said. "I think you should go to New York. I'm going to tell the Kansas City people that if they'll wait six months, I'll send them an organizer. It'll be beneficial to all parties if you go to New York because, with you there, they'll be getting a little national leverage." Then Alinsky leaned forward and said, "But I want your word of honor that if they don't agree to the delay you'll get on a plane Saturday morning and go to Kansas City." Menuez agreed, and when the Kansas City people also agreed to wait for six months, he was off to New York and a new career.

By the end of March, Alinsky and the Rochester clergy—white and black—were ready to announce the start of an Alinsky-directed project. A meeting was arranged in Syracuse, less than a two-hour drive east, where Alinsky was a consultant to a new anti-poverty pilot program. Although by this time Alinsky had had several meetings with the black clergy there, a few details had to be taken care of before an announcement was made to the Rochester press, which had also made the pilgrimage to Syracuse. Nobody in Rochester, for example, had met the man whom Alinsky said would be their organizer, Ed Chambers. After a long phone conversation with Chambers, White had reported to the black clergy that he sounded like a tough, experienced organizer and—making a plausible but faulty assumption—that he was black. White was horrified when, shortly before the black clergy arrived in Syracuse, he met Chambers. "Holy shit, I thought Chambers was black," he blurted out to Alinsky.

Alinsky began his meeting with the black clergy by telling them that the first order of business was for them to pick a temporary spokesman and leader, and that he would leave the room until they made their choice. After a long discussion—at first nobody volunteered—and with Alinsky growing impatient, Franklin Florence finally emerged as the choice. Then Alinsky told them to name the new organization. Alinsky chided them for their tame choices, saying they ought to come up with something that would play on the whites' fears. "What the hell are they most afraid of?" he asked. "And why the hell are we doing this anyway?" Somebody else said something about how the new organization should come out fighting, and one of the clergymen recalled St. Paul's words: "Fight the good fight of faith, lay hold on eternal light." "Then call it FIGHT," Alinsky said. Everybody seemed to like that, although the group had trouble finding the words for the acronym—they got as far as Freedom, Integration, Honor, Today but couldn't come up with a word beginning with "G." (The next day, Alinsky phoned Chambers with the answer. "It came to me at about 34,000 feet last night on the flight to New York. The 'G' stands for God; now God is in FIGHT.") With the name thus decided on, an aura of good feeling and accomplishment filled the room, at which point Alinsky called in Chambers, emphasizing in his introduction that he was giving them his best man. If anybody there was thinking of making an issue of Chambers's skin color, they probably decided this was neither the time nor the place.

Alinsky and the white leaders of the Rochester Area Council of Churches—with the black clergy bearing witness—signed the two-year contract in a ceremony that made clear that Rochester's white clergy would have no control over the $100,000, which went into a special IAF account in Chicago. Except for the Council's right to ask for a yearly audit, all future decisions were between Alinsky and the FIGHT leaders. When asked why he accepted the invitation to organize in Rochester, Alinsky indulged in delicious invective. "Because Rochester probably more than any Northern city reeks of antiquated paternalism. It is like a Southern plantation transported to the North. Negro conditions in Rochester are an insult to the whole idea of the American way of life. I have seen in Rochester people who are sick to death of being treated like chattel, who find themselves regarded as a necessary evil." Praising the clergy who "are willing to stand up and be counted," and calling on "intelligent white people in Rochester" to support his new project, Alinsky nonetheless made it clear that Rochester's white power structure was the enemy and he referred to Negro conditions in the city as a "little Congo."

While there was no shortage of establishment leaders to serve as Alinsky's foils, Paul Miller was among the most conspicuous by virtue of his newspapers' editorials and his own weekly column. As Alinsky had anticipated, even FIGHT's name raised the hackles of people like Miller. "If the organization you financed is to be continued," Miller told the white clergy after the organizing process was underway, "why not see that it gets a name somewhat less offensive to the total community? How about WORK or LOVE or DEED? Then see that it joins hands with many other organizations, working more quietly and more usefully." Alinsky gleefully observed that critics like Miller were playing right into his hands.

Alinsky's glibness notwithstanding, he tried not to pass up an opening, however small, to charm or co-opt an antagonist. It wasn't only a matter of ego; with poor, powerless blacks as his clients, whether in Rochester or Chicago, he understood that any tactical benefits of locking horns with a bigger, stronger foe were, at best, short-term. Thus, at nearly the same time as he was castigating Rochester's leadership for its plantation mentality, he was angling for a private meeting in New York City with none other than Paul Miller. Alinsky's friend and IAF board member Happy Macy was to be the go-between; her husband, Val, whose family owned a chain of Westchester County newspapers, was an old friend of Miller's. Their schedules, however, did not permit a meeting.

Alinsky was in more typical form at a private luncheon at the University Club in Rochester several days after FIGHT was launched, an affair arranged by Edward Harris, a prominent attorney in town, who spotted Alinsky aboard a flight to Syracuse, introduced himself, and suggested that it might be useful to all concerned if Alinsky and a small cross section of movers and shakers got together. About a dozen men showed up, including Sol Linowitz, former president of Xerox, a trustee of the University of Rochester, and then a law partner of Harris's. (Indeed, Alinsky told Linowitz, who was widely respected while at Xerox for his keen intellect and involvement in social issues, that he accepted the luncheon invitation only because he heard Linowitz would be there.) But soon after the group heard Alinsky's opening comments about his philosophy and racial conditions in Rochester, the three-hour affair turned nasty. Linowitz recalls that Alinsky's uncompromising criticism, punctuated with a liberal sprinkling of vulgarity, shook people up. "In Rochester, people didn't say the words that he said at that luncheon," Linowitz says. "It was a very strong, provocative and—for Rochester—if not unprecedented, a highly unusual encounter." If the luncheon group was unnerved by Alinsky, he was hardly soothed by their attitudes. "I had the feeling," Linowitz says, "of a man indignant at the apparent obtuseness of the group to the problem in the city. . . . He did not like it that the blacks were blamed for the way they had acted."

At one point, a longtime Rochesterian, Marion Folsom, who had served in the Eisenhower administration as Secretary of Health, Education, and Welfare, and was then Eastman Kodak's treasurer, said angrily: "Mr. Alinsky, what you have just said is a demagogic statement." To which Alinsky snarled: "Look, in spite of your age, you retract that, [because] I don't take that shit from anybody."

"Well, you have misstated the facts," Folsom said. "We have a Negro Ph.D. on our staff and he is called in on these questions and he represents the Negro community." At that point, Alinsky later told a friend, Linowitz put his head down and whispered: "You're going to have to be understanding, Saul. You have to be very patient with us."

Paul Miller wasn't at the luncheon, but his executive editor, Vincent Jones, was, and the next day he wrote his boss a memo that not only captured Alinsky's performance but also was insightful and prophetic:

> Alinsky is smart and mean. He is deliberately insulting and provocative. He flaunts his erudition and such unconventional experiences as time spent in jail. In the course of the afternoon he cited such sociological authorities as Machiavelli, Locke, Orwell, the Federalist Papers, Franklin Delano Roosevelt, Sir Winston Churchill, and, of course, Saul Alinsky. [He] ridiculed an editorial comment that we had no "resentment" against Negroes . . . and said we were "irresponsible" because we had hinted, editorially, that he might cause more riots here. . . . We're in for a rough time. I am one of those who believe that Rochester has failed miserably to organize a program to cope with this problem. I don't mean just the city administration but the real leadership. We resent his coming because it signals our failure. We are hurt because the Negroes don't concede that there is any good will in Rochester. This man thrives on opposition. He is going to tell these people that they have been shabbily treated, even abused, [and] stir them up to demand things.

The real organizing of FIGHT began at six-thirty the morning after the Syracuse meeting when Chambers met with Franklin Florence. Florence, the thirty-one-year-old pastor of the Church of Christ, was a relative newcomer to the city—he had arrived in 1959—and little known outside the black community. Pugnacious and volatile, sharp-tongued and given to theatrics, the stocky Florence was virtually the opposite of TWO's cautious, dignified leader, the Reverend Arthur Brazier. Their vastly different personalities symbolized how much the scene in Northern ghettos— and in the civil rights movement, for that matter—had changed in only four or five years, how much rougher and angrier the scene had become. "Minister Florence," as he preferred to be addressed, showed up wearing his uniform of bib overalls and a surly expression, the former a product of his civil rights trip to Selma, Alabama, where Martin Luther King, Jr., and his aides marched in similar clothes, the latter suggestive of his friendship with the Black Muslim leader Malcolm X. In fact, Malcolm had been a house guest of Florence's not long before his assassination in February 1965. Shortly before his death, Malcolm wrote that he wanted "an all-black organization whose ultimate objective was to help create a society in which there could exist an honest white-black brotherhood," and Florence was interested in this notion of a tactical and transitional "black power." He had asked Malcolm to start an organization in Rochester, but he was committed elsewhere. Florence was impressed when Malcolm said that he knew of Alinsky's work in Chicago, that Alinsky knew more about organizing than anybody in the country, and was further impressed when he heard Alinsky speak at the Mount Olivet Baptist Church where Alinsky first met with Rochester's black clergy. Recalling that meeting, Florence says, "Saul was at his best, laying the law down, talking right. His sincerity and honesty came through. A lot of clergy there didn't agree with power politics, but they were impressed with Saul's commitment to the dispossessed. And I was impressed with the independence of the process he was talking about."

Both Alinsky and Chambers had liked the little they had seen of Florence before he emerged as FIGHT's temporary spokesman. They liked his aggressiveness and were aware, of course, of his recent civil rights involvement. In addition to his Selma trip, in 1963 he participated in a sit-in at Rochester police headquarters to protest a celebrated case of alleged police brutality, and he had also been among the few clergy to speak out on behalf of the local Black Muslims when the police raided their headquarters. Florence's outspokenness and activism, which set him apart from Rochester's other black clergy, made him a natural choice as FIGHT's spokesman.

Still, Florence's general dislike and suspicion of whites had not softened, and he began to test Chambers at their meeting. "How do I know if I can trust you?" he demanded.

"I don't know if you can," Chambers shot back, fully aware that the question was really about race. "You gotta find that out, don't you? You better watch me—not only what I say but what I do."

It was an invitation that Florence took literally, for Chambers found himself being tailed during his first month in Rochester. "Florence was watching whether I was consorting with whites," Chambers says, "so I told Saul that the Rochester Area Council of Churches had to be off base for me." Florence himself went to tell Herb White that it would be best for both of them if they did not see much of each other. White was at first disappointed, even hurt. After all, he had invested much of himself in organizing the white churches and raising the money for Alinsky. But, White says, "I knew he was right. So I kind of ended the discussion by joking: 'Well, we'll see each other someday in heaven.' "

Staying as far away from white Rochester as he could, Chambers moved into a motel on the edge of the 3rd Ward and began one-on-one interviews, seeing more than a hundred people in the first ten days. In arranging a meeting, his credential was sometimes "Minister Florence told me to call," at other times "I'm Saul Alinsky's representative in Rochester and I'd like a chance to talk with you." Chambers kept notes of his impressions of people, the names of other people mentioned, and the community problems he heard about. Most of all, though, he was interested in personal histories and relationships. ("I'd ask: 'How long have you been pastor of that church?' 'How long have you been a deacon there? Do you like that work? Tell me about your pastor.' I'm getting a fix on everybody. I'm getting connections. I'm getting dos and don'ts. 'Anybody else you think I should talk to?' See who they list. They say, 'You should talk to so-and-so, but don't say I sent you.' ") But after only a few weeks, Alinsky and Chambers decided they couldn't follow the slower course they had used in organizing TWO. For one thing, expectations in Rochester were too great; the whole city seemed to be bracing for a grand opening act commensurate with the commotion Alinsky's name provoked. (When the *Democrat & Chronicle* conducted a poll in May, four out of five Rochesterians reported reading or hearing about Alinsky.) Fear of getting blamed for a second riot was another, even more urgent issue. With the summer less than three months off, Alinsky and Chambers decided the only way to give FIGHT a measure of legitimacy and some capacity to impose discipline—"controlled anger" was a phrase Alinsky used—was by quickly turning it into something resembling a real organization.

"Our genius," Chambers says, "was to hold a convention early. As soon as we decided on this, I had something for everybody to do—committees to write a constitution and program, delegates and alternates to be selected from the churches and other groups. By the time we finished, we had a movement convention that looked like an organization." Indeed, on June 11, after only about sixty days, nearly 2,000 people—including 1,200 delegates representing more than seventy-five community groups—jammed into the Rochester Institute of Technology gymnasium to elect officers (Florence became FIGHT's president) and adopt a constitution and program. A long list of resolutions was approved under the banner of black self-determination, including demands for black representation on city policy-making boards; "collective bargaining rights . . . with Negro leaders the people elect, not the hired 'yes' men or the 'rubber stamp Toms' chosen by downtown people"; "direct negotiation" on black job placement with Eastman Kodak, Xerox, and other corporations; an end to labor-union discrimination; revision of the local anti-poverty board to include true representatives of the poor. Coming less than a year after the riot, the dramatic effect of this large, aroused yet orderly crowd was unmistakable. "The white media were astounded," Chambers says. "They'd never seen blacks like that; their only experience with large groups of blacks was in a riot."

By the early summer, Alinsky's high-wire act in Rochester—"he has taken on a serious and dangerous situation," James Ridgeway reported in *The New Republic*—attracted national press attention. "Saul Alinsky in Smugtown," written shortly after FIGHT's convention, was Ridgeway's second Alinsky-in-Rochester story in six months. In *The Reporter,* Jules Witcover's article, "Rochester Braces for Another July," suggested that Alinsky was facing tough odds in a palpably tense city, and referred to him as "already the most controversial figure in the war on poverty."

While Alinsky enjoyed the notoriety that such articles brought him, the most extraordinary of all was a two-part interview, "The Professional Radical: Conversations with Saul Alinsky," that ran in *Harper's* in June and July. (Indeed, the interviews attracted such widespread, enduring interest that Harper & Row published a paperback version of both the original and a follow-up in 1970.) *Harper's* Marion Sanders, who conducted the interviews, envisioned them as something of a sequel to Silberman's book, which had focused on Alinsky's methods and success in Chicago, rather than on his life story. Thus, to most Americans who knew little or nothing of Alinsky prior to Silberman's book, the *Harper's* interviews became a prime biographical source. Much of what Alinsky said in them was reasonably accurate and by itself made for fascinating reading—his teenage adventures in California after his parents' divorce; graduate school and the Capone gang; prison work and his friendships with powerful people like Marshall Field and John L. Lewis. On the other hand, however, he piled on a sufficient number of embellishments and dramatic fabrications to sculpt an even bigger and better Saul Alinsky, one reminiscent of his other fictional creation, Socrates McGuinness. The embellishments included his suggestion that he grew up in, and pulled himself out of, one of Chicago's worst slums. His studied nonchalance about his University of Chicago career—"I graduated, cum laude I guess, in 1930"—somewhat obscured the truth that he had been on academic probation for his first two years. But his recollections about being arrested and jailed were perhaps his most elaborate fiction. Asserting that in ancient times wise men of action periodically went off into the wilderness to reflect on their experiences, Alinsky spun out a wonderful yarn:

> Well, my wilderness turned out to be a jail in a Middle Western city where I was organizing people living in a miserable slum. There was this police captain who was very anti-labor who figured my mere presence would contaminate his town. So whenever I walked down the main drag a squad car would pull up and I'd be invited in. They never booked me—just tossed me in the clink for safekeeping. I got used to it. I'd say to the jailer, "Will you please phone my hotel and tell them to expect a late arrival." I had a very good deal in that jail—I didn't suffer at all. I had a private cell; they treated me very nicely. Now there's no place that is better designed for reflective thinking and writing than a jail. . . . The only way you can escape is mentally. So you're attracted to writing. It becomes a compulsion. I wrote *Reveille for Radicals* in that jail. Sometimes the jailers would tell me to get out when I was in the middle of a chapter. I'd tell them, "I don't want to go now; I've got a couple of hours' more work to do." This really confused them. But after a while they got used to it.

Almost certainly, nothing like this ever happened. Rather, Alinsky had produced a tall story by spreading a generous amount of fertilizer on a seedling of truth. In the Bottoms of Kansas City, Kansas, where Alinsky organized the Armourdale Community Council in the early 1940s, there had been a police captain active in the Council. Neither his attitude toward organized labor, however, nor his later whereabouts is known; nearly everybody who lived in the Bottoms left the area for good after the great flood of 1950. And because Alinsky claimed in the *Harper's* articles that he was never booked—a comment he usually omitted when telling this story on other occasions in the 1960s—there is, conveniently, no record of time spent in jail. Nonetheless, Alinsky's telltale silence twenty years earlier, when the jailings supposedly happened, leaves little doubt that the

story is fiction; while he was writing *Reveille for Radicals,* he never mentioned such an experience to friends, nor did he ever refer to time spent
in jail when he was publicizing the book, which he did with great relish.

What prompted Alinsky to invest himself with a jail experience?
Nearly every prominent civil rights leader—a description the press also
began to use for Alinsky by now—had become prominent, in part, by
risking arrest and going to jail to protest discriminatory laws and policies.
The era's most dramatic episode involved Martin Luther King, Jr., and the
subsequent publication of his eloquent "Letter from a Birmingham Jail"
in 1963. Alinsky referred to it—along with King's earlier arrest during the
Montgomery bus strike—in *Harper's* and also in notes he was preparing
for a speaking engagement before law school professors in 1964: "Imprisonment not only results in the development of [more effective] revolutionaries
who have a complete strategy worked out as a result of their temporary
withdrawal, but another consequence is the creation of martyrs—Gandhi's
hunger strike, the emergence of Martin Luther King because of his being
put in jail." Alinsky suggested that repeated, prolonged "jailings [not only]
become badges of honor but they also become credentials and a license for
leadership." As a white man in a civil rights movement increasingly inhospitable to white participation, Alinsky may have felt a bit more comfortable with an added credential. Still, it was ironic that he was talking up
the value of martyrdom when it had never been a part of his style, either
when mapping out an organizing strategy or in his personal life, where his
idea of self-sacrifice was staying at the St. Moritz if his favorite room at
the Grosvenor was booked.

In the second part of the *Harper's* interview, Alinsky provided an
entertaining yet trenchant discourse on the tactics of social change, explaining, for example, that the status quo was an organizer's indispensable,
albeit unwitting ally. "You need [the opposition] for a very important
organizing tactic which I call mass jujitsu," Alinsky explained. Recalling
recent episodes in the civil rights struggle, he said:

> A Bull Connor with his police dogs and fire hoses down in Birming-
> ham did more to advance civil rights than the civil rights fighters
> themselves. The same thing goes with the march from Selma to Mont-
> gomery. Imagine what would have happened if instead of stopping the
> marchers that first day with clubs and tear gas, chief state trooper
> Lingo had courteously offered to provide protection and let them
> proceed. By night the TV cameras would have gone back to New
> York and there would have been no national crises to bring religious
> leaders, liberals, and civil rights fighters from the North into Selma.

I've always thought that just as King got the Nobel Prize there should be an IgNobel prize for people like . . . Alabama Governor Wallace and Governor Barnett of Mississippi.

The Saul Alinsky who emerged from the *Harper's* interviews was a swashbuckling Renaissance man of independent thought and action, fearless, engagingly blunt, passionate but without sentimentality. "I do not in any way glorify the poor," he boasted, distinguishing himself from "a lot of liberals" and many "civil rights crusaders." Although he was willing to give liberals their due—"I don't want to minimize their function. . . . I think the agitation of the white liberals through the years prepared the climate for the reformation which you have to have before you can have a [civil rights] revolution"—the skewer was always at the ready. "The trouble with my liberal friends is that their moral indignation and sense of commitment vary inversely with their distance from the scene of conflict." Or: "I have an enormous problem communicating with the academic liberals—particularly the social scientists. I'm not talking about the sociologists who have creative, seminal minds like David Riesman or Robert Ezra Park. I'm talking about the ones who are just sort of electronic accessories to computers. They suffer from verbal diarrhea and mental constipation—I don't know any other way to describe it politely."

Alinsky was less flippant but still sharply critical of both the tactical and strategic shortcomings of the civil rights movement. "The Achilles' Heel of the movement is the fact that it has not developed into a stable, disciplined, mass-based power organization. This needs to be said loud and clear. Many of the significant victories that have been won were not the result of a mass power strategy. They were caused by the impact of world political pressures, the incredibly stupid blunders of the status quo in the South and elsewhere and the supporting climate created particularly by the churches. Without the ministers, priests, rabbis and nuns, I wonder who would have been in the Selma march." Although he acknowledged that in the South, Martin Luther King's reliance on passive resistance was "the only possible tactic," he warned that "in the North you need a more sophisticated approach. . . . The segregated practices in the South are a kind of public butchery. It's visible. There's bleeding all over the place. Up here we use a stiletto, it's internal bleeding, it's not visible, but it's just as deadly."

Indeed, before King attempted his first Northern campaign in Chicago in the summer of 1966, Alinsky's friend Ralph Helstein, one of a small circle of labor leaders who met periodically with King, tried to interest Alinsky in joining forces with him. Helstein thought Alinsky could con-

tribute strategic thinking and organizing know-how. But Alinsky rebuffed
Helstein repeatedly. Helstein says, "His way of dealing with many things
[that he didn't want to be pushed into] was to just slough it off with sheer
sarcasm and ridicule. He spoke very slightingly of King." To be sure,
Alinsky could not have much patience with King's Southern-preacher
style, but Helstein suspected the real problem was "Saul's ego; it was very
important for him to be the key figure in a given situation. I don't say this
critically. I'm stating it as my understanding of his personal behavior and
drives. And by 1965 King was already a person of international stature."
King and Alinsky never got together, although Helstein never gave up on
the idea.

(Apart from Helstein's role as a would-be matchmaker, there was a
short-lived, low-level experiment in 1964 involving two young SCLC aides
who came to the Woodlawn project for training. Through church inter-
mediaries friendly to both Alinsky and the SCLC, the two came to Woodlawn. Ed Chambers remembers supervising the one he thought had the best
organizing potential. Each day for several days Chambers had him ringing
doorbells on Greenwood Avenue between Sixtieth and Sixty-third streets,
trying to identify potential leaders for new block clubs. "The first three or
four days it went pretty well," Chambers recalls. "But then the next
morning he didn't show up. About one in the afternoon I got a collect call.
The operator says it's from so-and-so in Atlanta. And I said, 'But he's on
Greenwood Avenue.' I could hear him on the phone saying, 'No, I'm in
Atlanta.' And I said, 'What the fuck are you doing in Atlanta? You're
supposed to be on the 6200 block on Greenwood.' He said, 'The Lord
called me.' I said, 'The Lord called you? Wait until I tell Alinsky this.'
Well, he came back, but after another week the Lord called him again. So
I told Saul, 'We can't compete with the Lord.' ")

By the summer of 1965, Alinsky was spending much of his time giving
speeches and playing the role of social critic, as the growing turmoil in the
cities made his ideas and methods even more relevant. Few whites of
Alinsky's stature who had access to "respectable" forums were so blunt
and provocative. In early August, thirty-five people died in a six-day riot
in Watts, the black ghetto in Los Angeles, confirming the worst fears of
many that the previous summer's riots in Harlem, Rochester, and Philadelphia had been harbingers, not aberrations. Two, three, sometimes four days
a week Alinsky was on the lecture circuit, speaking to religious organizations, social-work conventions, college students—he rarely turned down an
invitation—explaining that a riot was to a poor black ghetto as a suicide
was to someone overwhelmed by despair. "A riot can happen wherever a
mass of people feel utterly trapped, where they have no hope, no future.

So they explode almost in a death agony." Placing the ultimate responsibility for the riots on white racism, Alinsky was bitingly critical of white political and civic leaders who claimed to be surprised by the violence. "I don't know why the question is today 'Why did Watts riot?' . . . When you are living in that kind of misery and when you see your children denied any kind of hope for the future, and when you're caged by color just as though you were animals . . . it seems to me the big question is 'How come it took 'em so long before the thing blew?' "

Alinsky was also angry at the racism implicit in the methods used to contain the Watts riot and the complicity of the press in not reporting it.

> When [the riot started] the area was cordoned off. What happened inside the area was of no concern [to authorities]; the important thing was to keep it from spreading out. It was just as though some of the animals in the zoo had broken loose. . . . The important thing was not to let them come out into the white community. There were thousands of Negroes that were not involved who could have been raped, burglarized, or shot without a cop anywhere near. Can you imagine a riot taking place in a white community and the police simply cordoning off the community to prevent the riot from spreading?

Typically, Alinsky wove such controversial, topical observations into what was a standard speech. He continued to position himself in the mainstream of American political tradition, his rhetoric larded with popular, familiar references and images. He was, for example, still approvingly paraphrasing Tocqueville's assertion that American democracy would wither and die without the active participation of ordinary citizens in the daily affairs of their community—that "citizen participation" was a critical measure of democratic vitality. In Alinsky's view, of course, real citizen participation meant getting organized and getting power, but even here, his characterization of the methods and processes suggested Puritan values. Organizing, for example, was "hard, tedious work," and poor blacks cannot "get opportunity or freedom or equality or dignity as a gift or an act of charity. They only get these things in the act of taking them through their own efforts."

In his speeches Alinsky was much more explicit about the importance of power than he had been twenty years earlier in *Reveille for Radicals,* having sharpened his analysis and arguments when he worked with Protestant clergy who were skeptical about his social-change philosophy. Then, one of his important rhetorical challenges was to cleanse the concept of power of its stigma of immorality as in Lord Acton's aphorism, "Power tends to corrupt, absolute power corrupts absolutely." Power is amoral, Alinsky argued, fundamentally nothing more than "the ability to act." "The corruption of the concept of power is not in power, but rather in ourselves." Indeed, the exercise of political power was as American as apple pie, he was telling audiences, for pluralism—which he tended to equate with American democracy—was ultimately about power relationships and struggles among competing groups and factions. Perhaps the most insidious threat to the American democratic system, Alinsky was now arguing, was the powerlessness of blacks. Recalling Madison's writing in *The Federalist Papers* on the issue of power, Alinsky provided a contemporary translation. "[Our revolutionary leaders] knew that no significant sector of the American population could ever be permitted to be politically and economically disenfranchised or it would become a malignancy within the body politic and would provide the platform for closed-society demagogues who could derail our political progress toward freedom." In the America of the 1960s, Alinsky's argument went, the powerlessness of blacks was not merely their problem but a threat to the stability of American democracy. Having sketched a scene in which nothing less was required than a radical—or at least fairly radical—change in power relationships to preserve democracy, Alinsky made it clear that, in his view, *the* key actor in this scene—indeed, the savior-hero—was "The Organizer." "There is no higher calling in a free and open society," he pontificated.

As a social critic, Alinsky was at his best in his early scathing and prescient criticism of the federal government's War on Poverty, which by late 1964 he contemptuously tarred as "a prize piece of political pornography." The focus of his wrath was the War on Poverty's centerpiece, the federally financed Community Action Program. Ironically, both Alinsky and CAP's prime authors and planners, like Lloyd Ohlin, who as a sociology student at the University of Chicago had been several years behind Alinsky, shared the same intellectual heritage that shaped the basic orientation and provisions of this grandiose scheme. Moreover, despite its foggy bureaucratese, CAP's dictum of "maximum feasible participation" of the poor in poverty-program decision-making suggested Alinsky-like intentions. In fact, the man who may have invented the phrase, Richard Boone, was influenced in part by Alinsky's work. But Alinsky's influence was from afar; CAP's planners never sought him out for advice, and at a crucial fork in the road Alinsky and CAP's authors traveled in different directions. In Alinsky's view, the CAP planners had read their map with rose-colored glasses, failing to see "the differences between the world as it is and the world as we would like it to be." It was one of Alinsky's favorite axioms, simplistic and hardly profound—unless, of course, one pondered its full implications. Although the historian Allen J. Matusow later called the men who shaped CAP "closet radicals," in fact the War on Poverty was, as Godfrey Hodgson has accurately characterized it, "the archetypal liberal program . . . inspired by a characteristic blend of benevolence, optimism, innocence and chauvinism." And for precisely this reason the radical Saul Alinsky predicted that the war was doomed to defeat.

The forerunner to CAP had been an anti-delinquency program initiated by Attorney General–designate Robert Kennedy shortly after his brother was elected President in 1960. At the time it probably seemed like a safe, popular cause for the new administration to undertake—delinquency being one of the few social problems of widespread concern in the somnambulistic post-McCarthy years. Kennedy recruited his good friend David Hackett to get things off the ground, and by the fall of 1961 three essential elements were in place—a newly created institutional base within the Justice Department, the President's Committee on Juvenile Delinquency, with Hackett as executive director; a three-year, $30 million budget for grants to fund local anti-delinquency projects; and the intellectual leadership of Lloyd Ohlin, who left his post at Columbia University's School of Social Work to become director of the Office of Juvenile Delinquency, the federal agency that would actually dispense funds.

In typical Kennedyesque fashion, Hackett scoured the country looking for the best ideas and people to attack the delinquency problem, finding Ohlin, whose credentials not only included his University of Chicago training but also his leadership role in a new, ambitious anti-delinquency program, Mobilization for Youth, on New York's Lower East Side. The project was only in the planning stage when Hackett discovered Ohlin, but it had already attracted establishment interest and, shortly, $14 million in funding from government sources as well as the Ford Foundation. Echoes of the philosophy of Clifford Shaw's Chicago Area Project—Alinsky's old training ground—were easily recognizable in the Mobilization's prospectus.

(Three years later, however, in early 1964, by which time Mobilization for Youth was underway, Charles Silberman was rightly dubious about its potential effectiveness. Even on paper, it had looked like a fantastic hybrid, only partly constructed from Shaw's belief in the latent capacities of slum dwellers to solve their own problems. Silberman thought it was particularly naïve to expect that any unit of government—"no matter how liberal"— would tolerate for very long political pressure and opposition from community groups even if funded in large measure by government. Ohlin and his Mobilization collaborators were aware of this inherent contradiction, but it didn't stop them from pushing on.)

Essentially, Mobilization for Youth became the model for Ohlin and

Hackett's major programmatic effort in the spring of 1962. Planning grants were awarded in sixteen cities (sixty-five communities had applied) where mayors, social-service professionals, and other civic leaders were deemed most receptive to the idea of fundamental social change. Yet even in these relatively enlightened jurisdictions, few of the major actors apparently grasped the full implications of Ohlin's theories. One was that delinquency in slum communities was directly related to lack of opportunity, and lack of opportunity in turn was directly related to the failure of youth-serving institutions—schools with middle-class orientations that weren't really committed to teaching poor children; vocational agencies that trained kids for jobs that didn't exist; welfare departments whose practices undermined family stability; police departments that were overtly hostile. The purpose of the planning grant was to encourage—indeed to bribe—a city's leaders, especially in the youth-serving institutions, to develop a strategy for *comprehensive institutional change*—nothing less than a highly coordinated redistribution of resources. "Here at last," Matusow writes, "in the guise of fighting delinquency, was a Kennedy program with reformist, even radical implications."

While the President's Committee on Juvenile Delinquency was laying its plans, the Kennedy administration began to discover poverty as a major political issue. Articles and books, including Michael Harrington's influential *The Other America*, that documented the extent of poverty within the larger, affluent society impressed Kennedy officials. But the biggest influence on the administration—and on national politics generally—was the dramatic spread of the civil rights movement to Northern cities, where issues of racial discrimination became intermingled with poverty issues such as unemployment and inadequate housing. By the summer of 1963, the President's Council of Economic Advisers began studying "the poverty problem," and by October a special poverty task force was formed as the White House grew impatient for ideas and concepts that could be turned into a legislative proposal a few months hence when the 88th Congress convened for its second session. Task force members, however, found the going slow and frustrating. Not only would their plans have to be fashioned within narrow budget constraints but their intragovernment investigation revealed a surprising lack of understanding about poverty and, as a rule, few who offered creative solutions. In this policy desert, the conspicuous exceptions turned out to be Hackett and his associates at the President's Committee, who suddenly seemed to represent an oasis of knowledge and vision. As the pressure increased to produce laws attacking the poverty problem, especially in the politically tense atmosphere following President Kennedy's assassination in November, they quickly became key players.

What soon occurred was the conversion of an anti-delinquency program into an anti-poverty program. While the goals of the President's Committee were ostensibly about delinquency, they were fundamentally about poverty, about removing barriers to opportunity within poverty-stricken communities. Hackett's long memos to poverty task force staffers spelled out the enticing logic of the anti-delinquency–anti-poverty connection. And demonstration projects were already in place or nearly so—indeed, within a matter of only several weeks, the poverty task force proposed five urban and five rural demonstration projects, based largely on the concepts of the President's Committee on Juvenile Delinquency. Walter Heller, chairman of the Council of Economic Advisers, who submitted the final proposal for presidential consideration, called it the Community Action Program. But when it was discussed with President Johnson at his Texas ranch during Christmas week in 1963, the President was very unhappy with the puniness of it all; a scattering of demonstration projects did not add up to a Texas-style poverty program. Then, as Matusow reports, came the fateful decision: "In the end, Johnson would accept the program only if it was drastically amended. Any locality that wanted one could have its own community action program, could have it now, and could use it to mount instant programs—with the federal government picking up most of the bill. In one stroke Johnson escalated community action from an experimental program to precede the War on Poverty into the very war itself."

When it came time to draft the anti-poverty legislation, Richard Boone, another product of the University of Chicago's Sociology Department, was instrumental in assuring a pivotal role for "the poor." In Chicago after World War II, Boone had worked with Ohlin and Joe Lohman (a Clifford Shaw disciple and contemporary of Saul Alinsky's) on several projects; later, his friendship with Ohlin brought him to Washington from the Ford Foundation when Ohlin became a consultant to the President's Committee. At first, Boone's work was confined largely to another of Robert Kennedy's interests, the development of a domestic peace corps or national service program. He recalls: "Two interesting things happened to me. One was that I began to conceptualize the world in four parts—urban, rural, Indian, and migrant—which became ultimately the organizational focus of [the poverty program]. And secondly, I began to make contact with people who said, 'My God, you have an enormous opportunity. Why don't you listen to what the people need rather than what the professionals say they want?' And that became the basis for 'maximum feasible participation of the poor.'"

Boone did not need much convincing on this point. From his Chicago experience, both at the university and in the field working with street gangs in the manner of Clifford Shaw, he had developed a great suspicion of social-work professionals whose first priority too often seemed to be the protection of their professional interests. Later, at the Ford Foundation, Boone became interested in Alinsky's work—he had not yet met him but knew about him from his Chicago days—and was intrigued that enthusiasm for Alinsky triggered an angry, emotional reaction from the social-work people. "I had lunch with several very key people in the social-work profession. I told them I thought social work was amiss because it was not picking up on . . . Alinsky. They just went up in smoke—would not admit he had anything to contribute whatsoever to their field."

In early 1964, Boone pushed hard for explicit phrases in the anti-poverty law giving the poor a formal role to play in the Johnson administration's proposals. Since the President's Committee had discovered that there was no support for institutional reform among the professionals who ran the institutions, it was looking for a mechanism to mobilize a constituency among the poor themselves. Leonard Cottrell was an influential voice here as chairman of the delinquency program's Demonstration Review Panel—and, not incidentally, was still another link to the University of Chicago's Sociology Department (he had been a contemporary of Robert Ezra Park and Ernest Burgess). In February 1964, Boone made all his points on behalf of the poor at a meeting called by Sargent Shriver, the new "poverty czar" appointed by President Johnson. At one point Shriver's deputy, Adam Yarmolinsky, said to him, "You have used that phrase, 'maximum feasible participation of the poor,' four or five times now." "Yes, I know," Boone replied. "How many more times do I have to use it before it becomes part of the program?"

When Congress funded the Economic Opportunity Act in October 1964, Boone became director of CAP's Program Policy and Planning Division. CAP received $300 million, less than half of the total appropriation for the new Office of Economic Opportunity, where the Job Corps and Vista were other major programs. But CAP soon became the most controversial when the OEO Washington office began rejecting plans submitted by the mayors of Philadelphia, Cleveland, and Los Angeles. To be sure, most of the plans included *most* of what was apparently required by the poverty-program law—namely, the establishment of a new organization or the designation of an existing one as a Community Action Agency both to provide a range of new services to the poor and to coordinate all federal, state, and local services. Largely missing, however, from the first proposals were the Siamese twins of institutional change and participation of the poor in CAA decision-making. OEO reformers like Boone and his colleagues

Sanford Kravitz and Fred O'Reilly Hayes were convinced that the former could not be achieved without the latter. Within their frame of reference, a single line in the Economic Opportunity Act was both clear and critically important: a CAA must be "developed, conducted, and administered with the maximum feasible participation of residents of the areas and members of the groups served." To the rest of the world, however, including Congress, President Johnson and his top advisers, and the mayors, *no* importance had been attached to "maximum feasible participation" when the act was signed into law. Indeed, like the proverbial fine print in a legal document, the phrase was virtually ignored. Only in retrospect did the "oversight" seem so incredible, leading to a "maximum feasible misunderstanding," as Daniel Patrick Moynihan would later call it.

When mayors around the country began to understand, however imprecisely, what the OEO reformers were after, their anger and opposition kicked into high gear. The issue, of course, was power. Who was going to control the millions of federal dollars that would pour into communities throughout the country, especially into the big cities? In city after city, where poor black ghettos were increasingly restive and antagonistic toward City Hall, mayors were hardly sanguine about having to share decision-making. Equally disturbing, the federal requirement of maximum feasible participation was an affront which could undermine the authority of local officials, lending credence to minority accusations that white-dominated City Halls and social-service bureaucracies were largely impervious to minority concerns. Thus CAP was also controversial because it further exposed a raw nerve of truth.

In spite of their good intentions, Boone and his OEO colleagues found it difficult to translate their theories into practice, the broad strokes of policy into specific, workable plans. In practice, what did *maximum* feasible participation mean? How many poor had to be included to satisfy OEO? Even when OEO eventually announced that one-third of those appointed to the administration and planning of the local programs had to be "the poor," other issues remained. Who would select "the poor"? And whose poor were the "right" poor—the poor who happened to be friendly to City Hall, or the poor who were hostile toward the established power brokers, or some of each? OEO's Program Guide and, later, its Community Action Workbook rarely provided definitive answers to such questions. "It was our hope initially," Boone says, "that primarily through the churches, which were very active at the time at least in some cities, larger groups of people could be represented. We did not foresee how few and far between those organizations really were." To fill the gap, OEO tried to stimulate community organizing activities under CAP auspices, but not enough resources or energy went into the endeavor; anyway, a more vigorous effort might well have faced establishment opposition.

In fact, such opposition materialized early in Syracuse, New York, the site of the first CAP-sponsored demonstration project—which, oddly enough, became known as a test of the community organizing concepts of one of CAP's earliest, sharpest critics, none other than Saul Alinsky. OEO legislation provided that up to 15 percent of the CAP budget could be used on research and demonstration projects and that the projects need not have the approval of local government. A social-work professor at the University of Syracuse, Warren Haggstrom, impressed Kravitz and other OEO officials with his ideas about community organization, and by December 1964 he received word that his application for a CAP demonstration project had been approved. The federal money—a total of $314,000—started flowing on January 1, 1965.

Haggstrom was no typical academic. Through the 1950s, he had worked at various part-time jobs organizing with labor, farmers, and poor people. In the late 1950s, he read *Reveille for Radicals* and was favorably impressed; he first met Alinsky in 1963, when he raised the possibility of hiring Alinsky as a consultant with his Syracuse University Community Action Training Center. By the next year, when the OEO money was virtually assured, Alinsky accepted Haggstrom's offer to spend four days a month in Syracuse, leading seminars and giving advice to the new demonstration project. "I talked with Saul about where he wanted to get his money from," Haggstrom remembers. "He said he didn't want it from OEO, so we talked about alternatives and one was the university. It was about $10,000 for a year."

Haggstrom, no stranger to getting fired in the wake of organizing projects, knew that his OEO-funded project would inevitably be controversial, and he tried to warn university officials what they were getting into. "The president of Syracuse smiled and almost physically patted me on the head. . . . You couldn't convince anybody at that point in history that anything would happen."

Within months, though, the organizing drive, not to mention Alinsky's reputation, "ignited emotions ranging from indignation to near-hysteria among downtown community leaders," according to a national news story. Although Alinsky spent most of his time out of public view conducting seminars for student organizers, nearly everybody in Syracuse equated the project as a whole with him. Alinsky's longtime West Coast aide, Fred Ross, moved to Syracuse to direct the fieldwork; as he and Cesar Chavez had done so effectively in California throughout the 1950s, Ross used house meetings in Syracuse as the building blocks. Dividing Syracuse's low-income neighborhoods into six areas, he sent teams of two—usually one black and one white student—door to door in each, looking for leaders and issues. The men and women contacted were invited to group meetings, and after a number of them, an area-wide "action committee" was formed. The same process was repeated in each of the six areas until all the action committees were ready to form a single large organization.

Ross and his student organizers rallied people around issues—inadequate garbage disposal, excessive rents and gas bills, unjustified evictions—that often drew heated opposition from public officials. The Republican mayor of Syracuse, who was up for reelection in 1966, was angry that the program's early phase included a voter-registration drive—"Register for Power," the flyers read—that was allegedly adding Democratic voters to the rolls. "These people," Mayor William F. Walsh complained, "go into a housing project and talk about setting up a 'democratic' organization—small 'd'—but it sounds just the same as Democratic—big 'D'—[and] in a close election it could be decisive." At one point, a commissioner of the Syracuse Housing Authority wrote to President Johnson protesting the federal grant that was financing "activities which . . . will ultimately cause serious trouble in our community if allowed to continue." He was especially upset with student organizers "who are claiming that all kinds of benefits will accrue to the tenants of our housing projects if they will join these action committees. One of the promised benefits is the 'improvement of conditions' in . . . the Pioneer Homes. Conditions in the Pioneer Homes are as good as the tenants will permit them to be."

From afar, the opposition's vehemence might have seemed disproportionate to the potential threat—after all, there were only 12,000 blacks in Syracuse, about 6 percent of the population. But local officials deeply resented the challenge to their power and control—and especially resented the OEO grant that made it possible. In fact, there were now two, competing OEO-funded projects in town, Haggstrom's and a City Hall-sponsored Crusade for Opportunity. The Crusade, like other OEO-funded agencies around the country, was limited to mobilizing established welfare and civic agencies to combat poverty on a case-by-case basis, and the "representatives of the poor" were more or less handpicked by Crusade officials. Not only was there no militant social-action component but the Crusade's executive director spoke darkly of civic strife if OEO continued to support the rival Alinsky-style project.

Although OEO officially remained neutral on Alinsky, there was speculation in a national news story in the spring that if "Alinsky makes his mark in Syracuse, other anti-poverty community groups will want his help, and the conflict over federal financing of assaults by the poor on their own city halls will mushroom." Alinsky himself, however, was never excited about the possibility of shaping OEO's program, believing the Community Action Program was ill conceived and unrealistic. "Under present circumstances a poverty program based on a moral dynamism is not going to carry the thrust which comes from a threat," Alinsky wrote in the *Journal of Social Issues,* contrasting the motives that led to the current program with those that spawned the first U.S. foreign aid effort two decades earlier. "The only reason we embarked upon the worldwide anti-poverty program or the foreign aid program was that after World War II we were threatened by the Russians in the world political arena. We, like the Russians, were desperately trying to get all the other countries allied on our side and so the foreign aid program came into being. But its genesis did not spring from any moral principle but from a threatening political urgency." The good intentions of a corps of OEO planners, even with the support of a President who felt the historic allure of ending poverty, were no substitute for organized political power by the poor themselves. In its absence, Alinsky maintained, the War on Poverty had already degenerated into a "prize piece of political pornography," spreading cynicism rather than opportunity. It was not only that City Halls were effectively screening out the "uncooperative" poor, or that mayors were all too willing to co-opt local opponents by dispensing well-paying jobs. In Alinsky's view, the behavior of "the welfare industry," a pejorative he frequently employed, was equally reprehensible. "The anti-poverty program may well be recorded as history's greatest relief program for the benefit of the welfare industry," he said, asserting that in most cities a myriad of both public and private social agencies, knowing how to play the federal grantsmanship game, were feeding ravenously at the new trough.

> Graft wears many faces and one of the most sickening is the dedicated one. The use of poverty funds to absorb staff salaries and operating costs by changing titles of programs and putting a new poverty label here and there is an old device. . . . [But now] the war on poverty has [also] become big business. We now have poverty planning professional outfits which draw up poverty proposals and provide technical advice . . . for substantial fees. . . . A number of these firms have gone public and they represent the best growth stocks on the market. Poverty is a blue chip investment.

Alinsky followed his critical blast with a few obligatory suggestions for corrective action. The top priority, he argued, was to recognize that power was the central issue.

> Poverty means not only lacking money but also lacking power. An economically stable Negro in Mississippi is poor. When . . . poverty and lack of power bar you from equal protection, equal equity in the courts, and equal participation in the economic and social life of your society, then you are poor. . . . Therefore an anti-poverty program must recognize that its program has to do something about not only economic poverty but also political poverty.

What, in practice, did he recommend that Washington now do? "Specially trained federal representatives," he suggested, "who are in sympathy with the spirit of independence, have a faith in the democratic credo, [are] in opposition to the welfare colonialism of the welfare industry or that of the City Halls, should be sent into local communities" to identify community organizations, like TWO in Chicago, with whom programs could be developed jointly within a framework of mutual respect. Since, however, the TWOs of the world were in short supply, Alinsky proposed that in most instances federal agents would have to seek out individuals who are "defined by a substantial part of the community as leaders. That [the agents] will encourage the gathering together of community sources of power through block meetings and mass meetings whereby temporary representatives can be elected to help develop a poverty program such as they believe would meet their needs. That in the ferreting out of leaders and of power centers these federal agents would not be looking through the eyes of City Hall."

Alinsky's proposal was like the drive underway in Syracuse—bypassing City Hall, using an "agent" to mobilize local leaders, and so forth. That the Syracuse project was in deep political trouble from the start, however, was the best proof that Alinsky's "recommendations" were no more politically feasible than the CAP program he criticized. If anything, Alinsky added to the political pressures that quickly formed against the Syracuse project by his highly visible and voluble criticism of the poverty program.

Indeed, his alliterative broadside about the War on Poverty as a "prize piece of political pornography" riled the suave, usually self-assured Sargent Shriver, who spluttered: "That man—that man—that man called me a pornographer!" Ultimately, however, the abrupt demise of the Syracuse project was only partly the result of Alinsky's controversial presence and methods. In short order, the potentially radical part of OEO's Community Action Program was washed away by a tidal wave of political opposition. By the summer of 1965, less than a year after the poverty program started, Richard Boone departed OEO, and not far behind were other champions of maximum feasible participation of the poor. In Syracuse, Haggstrom's one-year OEO grant was not renewed, and he was later fired by the university. When a *New York Times* reporter asked Alinsky if he was disappointed that the project had come to an end, he cracked: "Have you ever been to Syracuse?"

BY THE SPRING of 1966, the four days a month that Alinsky no longer spent in Syracuse were easily absorbed by an array of other activities. In a fairly typical two-week stretch in March, Alinsky's schedule included speaking engagements at the University of Nevada in Reno; in Newton, Massachusetts, to a public schools conference; in Minneapolis for the Minnesota Welfare Association Conference; at the University of Wisconsin in Milwaukee to the Union Forum Committee; and in Washington, D.C., to consult with an ad hoc committee on community organization. In addition to lectures, his time was consumed by training seminars for clergy which usually took place on the West Coast near San Francisco; the book he was struggling to finish; supervising FIGHT in Rochester and, to a lesser extent, TWO in Chicago; negotiating the start-up of two new organizing projects in Kansas City, Missouri, and Buffalo. Although both projects eventually got underway, Alinsky's impending arrival in those two cities, where once again clergy were both the initiators and fund-raisers, was largely a replay of the bitter controversy that greeted him in Rochester.

Despite frequently frenetic weeks crisscrossing the country, Alinsky's closest friends, such as Rachel and Ralph Helstein, sensed that he was often lonely. Although Saul was interested, concerned, and helpful when his children needed him, David was in the Army, and Kathryn was married and no longer living in Chicago. He missed his intense relationship with Nick von Hoffman, who was making his mark as a journalist, first with the Chicago *Daily News* and then the Washington *Post,* writing dramatic accounts of the civil rights movement in the South. They continued to see each other, but only when their busy schedules allowed. The sudden death of Gordon Clapp, a man Alinsky greatly admired and sought out for advice, had also been a blow. And then there was his deteriorating relationship with his wife, Jean. Her decade-long affliction with multiple sclerosis had taken a great toll. MS can be an exceptionally cruel, exasperating disease, destroying one's physical capacities and impairing cognitive functions in unpredictable fits and starts. In Jean's case, a series of remissions and plateaus were only temporary, and her condition continued to decline. She had left Chicago and was living permanently with a full-time housekeeper, Dorothy Johnson, in the Alinskys' house in Carmel, where the California climate was more agreeable. While Saul continued to work out of his Chicago office and kept a downtown apartment, he was quick to accept speaking engagements on the West Coast as well as arrange two-week training seminars so that he could spend time with Jean. He also managed to be with her during a portion of the summer. Nonetheless, it was hardly an ideal arrangement. Indeed, the marriage itself had been less than a perfect match, complicated enormously by the onset of Jean's illness so soon after they were married. Saul's friends and acquaintances were split into two camps over whether he was doing the right thing by staying in Chicago or by traveling as much as he did since there were long stretches when he was not in Chicago either. Saul's old Hyde Park friends, who had seen him suffer through the deaths of his first wife, Helene, and Babs Stiefel, tended to sympathize with him. They thought his work was important and that in Woodlawn he had achieved a breakthrough with national implications. Around Carmel, however, where friends and neighbors witnessed Jean's condition at closer range, the judgment of Saul tended to be critical, even harsh. Some accused him of virtually abandoning her during a time of great need, selfishly expecting that friends and neighbors would assume the burden of looking after her in his absence.

Alinsky himself was hardly satisfied with the compromises he had been forced to make. A new, related dilemma began to emerge when he met Irene McInnis in April 1966, after a speech Alinsky gave at Boston's Copley Plaza Hotel. McInnis, who had just turned twenty-eight and was teaching philosophy at Boston College, had accompanied a friend to hear Alinsky. Afterward, they joined a circle of questioners around him. Before Irene could ask her question, Alinsky pointed to her and said, "I'll answer your question after I'm through with the others. Wait over there." Startled at being singled out for special attention, Irene and her friend were soon joined by Alinsky, who suggested they talk over coffee. Alinsky, never bashful, especially enjoyed engaging in playfully amorous behavior with women. His approach was not unlike a friend's description of Groucho Marx's modus operandi: "[He enjoys] accosting strangers—especially if the strangers happen to be girls. If they are girls, they don't usually remain strangers long." How often Alinsky's merely flirtatious overtures evolved into late-night trysts was a topic of speculation among his friends. He certainly talked a good game, coming back to Chicago after a string of out-of-town speaking engagements and, over dinner at the Helsteins', for example, suggesting—although not specifying—that the tour had included both physical and intellectual pleasures. Friends generally interpreted his accounts as at least plausible, if not probable—after all, he was a celebrity who posed as an uninhibited free spirit, courageously and successfully battling the establishment and fighting for the underdog at a time when his college-age audiences were robustly anti-establishment. Physically, the older Alinsky (he was fifty-seven when he met Irene) had grown more attractive, his gray-white hair softening his features.

Alinsky's relationship with Irene McInnis very quickly became more than a casual romance. Warm, intellectual, and interested in social and political issues, Irene reminded several of Alinsky's friends of Helene. Within six months, the situation was serious enough so that Alinsky needed reassurance that he was doing the right thing. He felt very guilty about Jean, despite bragging publicly—as he had done in the *Harper's* interviews—that unlike so many of his liberal friends, he was totally unencumbered by guilt. In October he requested a meeting with his old friend Jacques Maritain, who was at Princeton, and brought with him not only Irene but also Jack Egan, who flew out from Chicago. It was a remarkable gathering. Here was Sarah Alinsky's son from Chicago's old Jewish West Side with his Boston Irish-Catholic girlfriend and a support group consisting of one of the leading Catholic scholars of the century and Chicago's most prominent monsignor. Alinsky had come to Maritain for absolution, although he did not say so to either Irene, who was thrilled at meeting Maritain, or Egan, though Egan understood why Alinsky wanted him there. "He wanted a strong arm to lean on if anything went wrong because he didn't know how Maritain would react. I was sort of a crutch, a friend he could count on." When they all arrived in Princeton, Alinsky spoke to Maritain alone while Egan stayed with Irene. Later the four had an easy, lighthearted conversation over lunch and then the three visitors said goodbye and headed for Newark Airport. Although Alinsky said nothing about his private meeting with the eminent Thomist scholar, the implication was clear: Maritain had given Saul his blessing.

Meanwhile Alinsky's project in Rochester was also about to take a dramatic, unexpected turn. Since the first FIGHT convention in June 1965, the organizing had gone reasonably well. Two summers passed without the recurrence of a riot. FIGHT couldn't claim full credit for the relative peace, but neither could Alinsky's critics, such as Paul Miller, claim they had been right when they suggested that his methods would provoke violence. (FIGHT in fact devoted a lot of energy to riot prevention: when rumors circulated about an incident involving the police or a clash between rival gangs, Florence and other FIGHT leaders—never Ed Chambers—patrolled the streets and cooled hot tempers.)

It wasn't only the absence of another riot that made Rochester seem surprisingly peaceful. In January 1966, Alinsky had returned to public view in Rochester to warn everyone against assuming that FIGHT was faltering merely because the turmoil had subsided. "Everything is proceeding according to schedule," Alinsky told an overflow audience of one thousand at the Corn Hill Methodist Church. "Remember this: when you're building an organization, it's not very dramatic," an allusion to one of his postulates that organizing and playwriting shared the challenge of maintaining audience interest in Act Two, when the characters and plot had to be developed—"the tough, tedious work"—before the climax and resolution of the final act. Alinsky also chastised city leaders who remained intransigent and insensitive. "The people who stand for the status quo in Rochester believe that if there's no riot, nothing significant is happening. This is the zoo-keeper mentality that prevails in social agencies. And it has a predictable effect. It makes people on the bottom think like animals in a zoo. They begin to believe that the only way to get more attention is to cause trouble." Implicit was a veiled threat that in effect placed responsibility for future disorders with Rochester's civic leadership. Such subtle and not so subtle references were ever present in FIGHT's rhetoric. "I'm always glad to visit Rochester," Alinsky said, "because it makes so many of the right people so miserable."

Both Gannett newspapers were giving FIGHT extensive coverage and, despite Paul Miller's editorial opposition, the daily reporting was generally evenhanded. And there was much to report during FIGHT's first eighteen months; the organization raised issues—jobs, representation in the poverty program, inequities in the school system, housing and urban renewal—that appealed to a cross section of the black community and, at the same time, challenged white domination of some of the city's major institutions. In part, FIGHT made an impact in Rochester because of the sheer number of issues it raised. Even more important, though, was the way FIGHT contested the issues—with a disciplined militancy that the white community had never associated with Rochester's blacks.

Urban renewal in the 3rd Ward, where about a third of the black population lived, was FIGHT's biggest issue, similar in many respects to TWO's urban-renewal battle in Chicago. With a final round of public hearings on an urban-renewal program approaching, Chambers, with Alinsky's approval, mapped out a strategy that included a round of private meetings at which FIGHT leaders lobbied City Council members and the urban-renewal administrator, who, Chambers told his boss, "is not too bad a guy if the politicians will leave him alone." But the biggest push was to organize a huge turnout for the last, important public hearing, a place to demonstrate that there was a united front in the 3rd Ward for an alternative plan. In fact, Alinsky and Chambers used the urban-renewal issue, as they had in Woodlawn with TWO, as a tool to build FIGHT. Chambers told Alinsky, "We now have sixty-five different organizations from the 3rd

Ward, including all the churches, the block clubs, poolrooms, neighborhood associations, etc. We have the signed statements that FIGHT will represent them in any negotiations for 3rd Ward urban renewal."

Although there was a spring rainstorm the night of the climactic hearing, it did little to dampen FIGHT's enthusiasm. More than 2,000 FIGHT supporters turned out; the *Times-Union* reported 1,000. A long line of FIGHT speakers—Chambers says there were more than eighty; the *Times-Union* reported fifty—paraded to the microphone, keeping the meeting going until midnight. "Only one [black] testified against us," Chambers recalls. "Everybody else got up, identified themselves as, say, from the Clarissa Street block club and a member of FIGHT." Minister Florence was the star attraction. In a twenty-five-minute oration—which nobody dared curtail although the five-minute limit on speeches was generally observed—he charged that black Rochesterians had too often been "the victim of hypocrisy and empty promises" and warned that "politicians for the rich folk are not going to be allowed to gobble up all the rich land [in the 3rd Ward] and build exclusive apartments."

When the final plan was voted on, FIGHT claimed victory, taking credit for a number of improvements or modifications in it, including the construction of new housing on vacant land before demolition of existing housing started, the establishment of a nonprofit public housing corporation, and an increase from two to 250 units of low-rise, scattered-site public housing. City officials in Rochester disputed this victory claim, asserting that the final plan would have been much the same without FIGHT's intervention. Neither Florence nor the other FIGHT leaders believed that for a moment.

As for other issues, FIGHT negotiated with City Hall for a program to recruit and train ghetto youth for police jobs, but this was a short-lived failure. Then FIGHT went after the City Hall-controlled poverty program agency, A Better Chance (ABC), charging that it didn't really represent the poor. Chambers says, "We subjected them to constant harassment. Our first issue was that the public business can't be conducted in private. If their board went into private session, we would force our way in." Then FIGHT insisted it had the right to speak at ABC meetings. Then it demanded the right to name six members to the ABC board, and eventually got three. Chambers says, "They finally realized FIGHT was here to stay. They said to themselves, 'We'd better give those people something to shut them up.' So they gave us three people on their board and $65,000," money to enable FIGHT to recruit and train a hundred blacks to pass civil service examinations.

FIGHT was adept at using public forums to good advantage, increasing its visibility and reinforcing the message to white Rochesterians that the black community could no longer be ignored. FIGHT also made its presence known through its frequent, deliberate verbal battles with many of Rochester's civic leaders. Whenever someone attacked FIGHT, as when Public Safety Commissioner Harper Sibley, Jr., called FIGHT "a bully" for trying to intimidate the local anti-poverty agency, FIGHT counterattacked.

From the beginning, FIGHT's black leaders did not want whites playing prominent roles in the organization. Among delegates to FIGHT's first convention, only a small minority were white. At the convention, Florence spoke explicitly about FIGHT being a black organization, suggesting to the nine hundred sympathetic whites who filled the spectators' gallery that if they wanted to help, they should organize among themselves. And soon such an organizing process was underway, led by a few clergy such as Herb White and Paul Long, as well as lay activists and others. The white auxiliary that emerged, Friends of FIGHT, was embraced by Alinsky—indeed, he even suggested in speeches that it was an idea *he* dreamed up. This surprised his young California friend Mike Miller, who was deeply involved in the civil rights movement, for he remembered that Alinsky, only a short time before, had ridiculed a similar idea—a Friends of SNCC support group—that Miller and other whites had proposed when the black leaders of the Student Nonviolent Coordinating Committee no longer wanted white participation on the committee itself. As a fervent integrationist, Alinsky resented any arrangement that smacked of a "separate but not quite equal" mentality. Now, however, Alinsky provided a strategic rationale that served to tone down the specter of reverse racism. He told a Rochester audience in early 1966 after FIGHT had started making some progress: "Purely on numbers the movement can't go much further without allies. Suppose Rochester's 35,000 Negroes were all organized. This is still a very small minority group."

In truth, Alinsky had no detailed plan of how Friends of FIGHT might relate to its black counterpart; his immediate concern was to find some plausible scheme to keep liberal whites from becoming awkward, disenchanted bystanders. Making up a scenario as he went along, Alinsky attempted to portray Friends of FIGHT as a group that would "work shoulder to shoulder with FIGHT, and not just in terms of finance."

The behind-the-scenes relationship was, of course, very hard to work out. With coaching from Alinsky and Chambers, White and Long took the first steps to position Friends of FIGHT as an ecumenical group by recruiting the lay Catholics Louis Martin and George Jost, Estelle Wurth, a Jewish activist, and Benjamin Phelesof, a Jewish attorney and Paul Long's next-door neighbor. While Friends of FIGHT remained heavily Protestant, its membership grew to a well-educated, articulate corps of more than four hundred largely liberal lawyers, doctors, teachers, and housewives. Frustration over their limited, subservient role did not set in immediately.

The controversy that began to unfold in Rochester in late 1966 temporarily sidetracked a reevaluation of the white support group's role vis-à-vis FIGHT.

In September, discussions started between FIGHT and Eastman Kodak over a job-training program. If FIGHT's style was to turn issues into conflicts that could then be negotiated to FIGHT's benefit, it certainly wasn't Kodak's, whose moderate leadership had vast resources at its disposal to smooth over, if not solve, "community relations" problems. Furthermore, it was difficult to envision how a storefront operation like FIGHT could—in any meaningful sense of the word—*battle* Eastman Kodak, one of the world's premier corporations and a huge presence in Rochester's civic life.

Then, too, without much wrangling, FIGHT had already developed a working relationship on a job-training program with another Rochester corporation, Xerox, whose dynamic chairman, Joseph Wilson, had been instrumental in starting discussions with FIGHT. Alinsky and Chambers were eager to strike a deal with Xerox, an important, although much smaller company than Kodak, as a necessary prelude to approaching the city's dominant business. "These are the guys who are going to give us a credential," Chambers explained to Florence. "If we went to Kodak now, they'd say, 'Who are you? Who recognized you?' So our best credential is Xerox. Then, later, the liberals at Xerox can say, 'We worked out something with FIGHT—they're hard to deal with, but, you know, they're not crazy bomb throwers.' "

Chambers, knowing how important the first meeting with Xerox was, joined a delegation of four or five FIGHT leaders, including Florence, who met with Xerox president Peter McColough and other top executives, though normally he avoided this kind of public activity, not wanting to undercut Florence's authority. But, Chambers says, "I had to go because I had never seen Florence in that kind of action. I'm glad I did." No sooner had the FIGHT delegation walked into the meeting room than Chambers saw FIGHT's black leader intentionally walk past the outstretched hand of each white executive, including McColough. Chambers had forgotten that on general principle Florence did not shake white people's hands. After the meeting, Chambers exploded in anger. "Goddamnit, you pulled that Malcolm X Black Power crap. What the hell's wrong with you? You want to win or you want to lose?" Chambers proposed a compromise for the next meeting with Xerox: "When you come into the room, you make an announcement. You say, 'Gentlemen, I'll be glad to shake your hands but I'd like to do it at the end of the meeting after we've worked something out.'" And that is what happened. Eventually, Xerox agreed to hire and train about fifteen hard-core unemployed young blacks with limited skills and little work experience; FIGHT agreed, as Florence put it, "to prepare them for the world of work—getting up on time, making sure they had transportation, following them on Friday to make sure they didn't drink all weekend." The modest number was a disappointment, since FIGHT had hoped for a program for a hundred or more. But Xerox promised to expand the experimental program once they figured out the most effective training methods, and in any event the agreement itself represented a breakthrough.

The first big meeting between FIGHT and Kodak was held on September 2, and Kodak chairman Abraham Chapman, company president William Vaughn, and other executives and members of the board of directors all attended. This was unusual—not many corporations the size of Kodak would have had virtually all the top brass on hand to "discuss" (FIGHT preferred "negotiate") issues with the leading black militant in town. FIGHT proposed that Kodak initiate a training and remedial-education program for six hundred unemployed men and women over eighteen months, waiving the usual hiring requirements and providing special on-the-job training. Although placing its proposal on the table was a necessary opening move, the FIGHT delegation's main objective at the first meeting was to win a commitment from Kodak to a second meeting, thus snaring a reluctant adversary into a negotiating process. On September 14, there was such a meeting in Kodak's State Street offices, again with Kodak's senior management present, at which the company presented an outline for an expanded jobs program beyond what they said the company was already doing, with an emphasis on hiring minority members. Toward the end of the meeting, Vaughn suggested that the FIGHT leaders meet with the company's staff in industrial relations, personnel, and training to work out details of a cooperative program. Florence pinned down a time for the following day.

The tenor of the September 15 meeting, however, was quite different from the previous day's. Florence "clarified" the FIGHT proposal by insisting that FIGHT must be the exclusive referral agency for the proposed six hundred job trainees. Although he had mentioned this provision at the first meeting, it only now, apparently, became the central focus. Florence argued that not only was FIGHT best qualified to identify and recruit hard-core unemployed but it was also in a unique position to offer support and guidance, just as it was doing with the workers in the Xerox program. (It was also true, of course—and of prime importance to Alinsky—that by controlling six hundred jobs, FIGHT would achieve a new level of power and prestige in the black community—in all of Rochester, for that matter.) But for nonunion Kodak, FIGHT's demand for "exclusive referral" smacked of unionism. "Florence wanted to set up a hiring hall," as Vaughn saw it, "and tell us what people to hire."

The fourth and final September meeting ended on an angry note, and throughout October and November the growing conflict was played out in the public arena. Kodak's basic strategy was to appear reasonable and accommodating, stressing its willingness to expand existing training programs and work with FIGHT and other local groups to make such programs successful. In October, Kodak contracted with a private group, the Board of Fundamental Education, to train about a hundred undereducated persons—forty of whom already worked at Kodak—in basic skills. While Kodak was attempting to prove its goodwill, FIGHT counterattacked, Florence calling Kodak's BFE project, for example, "a trick" and "a fraud," emphasizing that Kodak filled all of the training slots without widely advertising them. Kodak was also using the BFE project, he charged, "to make FIGHT look unreasonable." At Alinsky's direction, Florence led a protest delegation to Kodak's offices and announced later that "[this] was just the beginning" as FIGHT members signed pledges that they would be "ready at a moment's notice" to take part in future protests. "Black leaders in every ghetto across the nation," warned Florence, were watching the FIGHT-Kodak conflict.

By early December, even with the chill of another upstate winter already in the air, the heated FIGHT-Kodak controversy was making a lot of Rochesterians uncomfortable. In a span of only three months, not only had FIGHT and Kodak become antagonists but, it seemed, many others in town were choosing up sides. Even Alinsky was affected when his longtime friend Happy Macy resigned from the IAF board. The Macys had recently sold their Westchester newspaper chain to the Gannett corporation, but their son was staying on in a top management position, making Happy's link to Alinsky, well, awkward. Regardless of what he might have thought privately, Alinsky was gracious—as he had been when Dutch Smith resigned over the University of Chicago controversy—telling Happy he understood and that he knew they would remain friends.

Then, still early in December, John Mulder, an assistant vice president at Kodak, met with Marvin Chandler, the black associate director of the Rochester Area Council of Churches and active in FIGHT, to discuss ways in which the impasse might be broken. Mulder was widely respected for his integrity, compassion, and competence; he was an elder at Paul Long's Third Presbyterian Church; and he was a leading candidate to become one day the head of Kodak Park, largest of Kodak's Rochester facilities. On December 16, a FIGHT negotiations team led by Chandler met with Kodak's top executives at the company's offices. Vaughn, who was about to replace Chapman as board chairman, was there, as well as Louis Eilers, soon to be Kodak's new president. Vaughn, who seemed optimistic about finding solutions, announced that he was turning the entire matter over to Mulder. On December 19 and 20, Mulder and others from Kodak met with a FIGHT delegation at a neutral site (the Downtowner Motor Inn), and by midday of the second day an agreement was reached.

The settlement, which obviously had national implications, provided that FIGHT would recruit and send to Kodak "six hundred employees, the bulk of which would be hard-core unemployed (unattached, uninvolved with traditional institutions)." Although Kodak was not unequivocally committed to hiring all six hundred referrals during the specified two-year period, Mulder explained, "that is definitely our goal—in fact, we're hoping for more."

Like the other FIGHT leaders, Florence was elated. Not only was the victory sweet but so too was the way it had been achieved—with a minimum of white help. As Florence had told a Friends of FIGHT steering committee meeting in November: "I bet that if Friends of FIGHT negotiated with Kodak and got six hundred jobs [for blacks], black folks would say, 'Forget it.' " In Chicago, Alinsky was thrilled, envisioning the agreement as a model that he could claim credit for and promote around the country.

The sudden resolution of the FIGHT-Kodak dispute surprised nearly everyone in Rochester. On December 22, an especially joyous Christmas party at Marvin Chandler's house included Franklin Florence and his wife, as well as other FIGHT leaders and their wives. It *was* a joyous occasion—until the phone rang and Chandler heard the voice of an obviously distraught John Mulder, who insisted that he needed to see Chandler immediately, even after Chandler explained that he had guests. When Mulder appeared at the door at ten-thirty, he looked badly shaken. Upstairs, Mulder showed Chandler a statement that Kodak's new president, Eilers, had just released to the media. Incredibly, he was completely renouncing the FIGHT-Kodak agreement. Moments later, everybody gathered in front of the television and listened in shocked silence as the Kodak renunciation—Mulder had been "unauthorized" to sign such an agreement, the company said—was reported on the eleven o'clock news.

The silence did not last for long. Franklin Florence was enraged, on the verge of losing control. His life experiences had taught him not to trust white people. For the past eighteen months, however, he had been persuaded—or had he been seduced?—to put aside the old, bitter feelings. It must have taken a considerable expenditure of psychic energy to hold in check a powerful assortment of suspicions and predispositions. Now, he felt total despair, as though the bottom had dropped out of his life and he had suddenly plunged into the depths. He felt betrayed and humiliated. He could hear the voices of so many in the black community who had warned him, "Don't let 'em trick you." And now it had happened. By the time the other FIGHT leaders drove him to Chambers's house a half hour later, Florence was not only ready to quit; he remembers thinking, If somebody comes along wanting to mount an insurrection, I'm ready to join in. He yelled at Chambers: "You told me you could trust these people, that if they signed something they would live up to it! You whites always lie!" Chambers conferred with Alinsky by phone, and by three in the morning they all agreed upon a couple of moves that, at least temporarily, kept Florence from bolting the organization.

The next day a FIGHT delegation met with Kodak's executive committee. It was still not totally clear why Kodak had reneged, but the specter of unionism was apparently a factor. Kodak's top executives still grumbled about having had their Canadian operations unionized; the full implications of working out a "deal" with FIGHT had not really sunk into their collective consciousness. "It was awful, I'll tell you that," Vaughn says now of the news that Mulder had signed on the dotted line with FIGHT. "I don't remember the exact words, but our counsel took one look at it and said, 'Bill, this is a hiring law we're agreeing to. We're involved with the National Labor Relations Board if we agree to this.'" While FIGHT was anxious to salvage at least a partial victory and save face, Kodak had left itself practically no room to maneuver. Having made a dramatic public announcement less than a day earlier that it could not engage in a special relationship with an outside group, let alone a relationship that was forced on the company, Kodak had no alternative but to hold to its uncompromising position.

At noon the following day at his church, Minister Florence preached to an overflow, nearly all-white audience of Rochester's clergy who had been rounded up by Herb White and other FIGHT supporters. Alinsky and Chambers wanted to avoid a mass rally of FIGHT members, fearful that Florence's own passions might ignite the kind of explosion that they had spent a year and a half trying to prevent. But there was a need to do something, to provide Florence with a platform to address the moral issues that had been raised—indeed, to turn the Kodak dispute into a moral issue. With the media barred from the church, Florence, still visibly angry and upset, was anything but gentle with his audience. He blamed the country's white clergy for the failings of the country's white leaders, and in Rochester he blamed the clergy for abdicating their prophetic role and responsibility. Too many of them, he charged, were on the sidelines, passive bystanders who, by their inaction, were in effect protecting the Vaughns, the Eilers, and the Paul Millers from moral accountability. Florence said that black leaders like himself were under terrible pressure trying to reassure an increasingly desperate constituency that there was hope and a chance for a better life. He portrayed himself and FIGHT as standing in the gap between anarchy and tranquillity in Rochester. Now, however, the burden was squarely on their shoulders, he said menacingly, because his role had become untenable in the face of Kodak's double cross. "I no longer have faith in a process that would force people to capitulate to [that kind of] hypocrisy."

As he spoke, Florence felt the tension and fear in the church. Suddenly, a white clergyman was on his feet, nearly trembling with his own rage. "My brother, I'll stand with you. I'm willing to lay my life down." It was the Reverend Lee Beynon, pastor of the First Baptist Church and a supporter of FIGHT, although not part of the core group that had brought Alinsky to Rochester. Ed Chambers, who had never seen Beynon before, was stunned by the intensity of his reaction. Minutes later, Beynon came up to Florence and shouted even more emotionally, "They can't do this, goddamnit! They can't do this to you!" Like other white clergy who supported FIGHT, he had been the recipient of nasty letters and threatening phone calls, some from his own parishioners. None of his colleagues, however, had ever seen him as disturbed as he was in Florence's church. Other, unrelated problems may also have been troubling him, for soon thereafter Beynon hanged himself in the basement of his own church.

Before long there were other casualties of varying degrees. By the spring of 1967, John Mulder was stripped of his title as assistant vice president by Kodak's board of directors, a promising career over. Ironically, the greatly heightened turmoil that suddenly engulfed Rochester was exactly what Alinsky would have preferred to avoid—he was deeply disappointed when the FIGHT-Kodak agreement could not be salvaged. But as he had so often lectured, a good, creative organizer must be able to turn a negative into a positive, which was the challenge now confronting him.

"THE ONLY CONTRIBUTION the Eastman Kodak company has ever made to race relations is the invention of color film," Alinsky cracked a few weeks later. "They run the town of Rochester like a Southern plantation." These remarks appeared in a long Washington *Post* feature written by none other than the *Post*'s new recruit from the Chicago *Daily News,* Nicholas von Hoffman, who himself had fun at Kodak's expense, concluding that if Rochester didn't find a way to include jobless blacks in the general prosperity, "Negroes may again be out on the streets shooting, and not with Brownie Instamatics." The *Post* story was only one in a small flood of national news accounts, many, if not most, critical of or at least unflattering to Kodak. In one, a public relations executive remarked that Kodak's actions "fell like a bombshell into the pro-civil rights milieu of contemporary America. A company dependent on goodwill went against the current social mores and folkways. It was a colossal public relations blunder that will go down in history."

Meanwhile, Rochester was polarized as never before. The president of its Council of Churches, as well as one of its directors, resigned, objecting to the Council's uncritical support of FIGHT. On the other hand, the newly arrived Roman Catholic bishop, Fulton J. Sheen, appointed one of FIGHT's few white members, David Finks, assistant pastor of an inner-city parish, to the new position of Vicar to the Poor, an action that many interpreted as implicit support of FIGHT. The polarization was not entirely along racial lines. For example, the black executive director of Rochester's Urban League, Laplois Ashford, probably spoke for a portion of the city's small black middle class when he criticized FIGHT's tactics as "dirty, mean, and low-down." There was also dissension within the "Kodak family." The wife of John Mulder was a Friends of FIGHT member, as were more than a few Kodak employees. Jack McCrory, also prominent in Friends of FIGHT, was a partner in the law firm that represented Kodak. Internally, Kodak had a potential morale problem, even a potentially explosive racial problem. "Feelings ran high among our employees," a Kodak manager says. "We especially didn't want our white and black employees getting into a conflict over the disagreement with FIGHT."

Thus, although Kodak was king in Rochester, top management moved cautiously, even meeting again with representatives of FIGHT. But on February 22 Kodak announced that it was breaking off negotiations. "We believe that there have been enough meetings about meetings and believe that employment referrals which result in jobs—though they receive less publicity—are of more benefit to the unemployed in the inner city and the community at large." Indeed, "publicity" is exactly what Kodak wanted to avoid—out of sight, out of the public's mind, was the strategy they were now trying to implement. Within hours of Kodak's statement, Florence sent a telegram to the company's president and simultaneously released it to the media, a provocative message that riled FIGHT's critics. It read in part:

> PLEASE BE ADVISED THAT THE NEGRO POOR OF ROCHESTER AND THE POOR THROUGHOUT THE COUNTRY FROM HARLEM TO WATTS ARE NOT SATISFIED WITH YOUR "SEE NO EVIL" AND "HEAR NO EVIL" ATTITUDE. INSTITUTIONAL RACISM AS EXEMPLIFIED AT KODAK IS AMORAL AND UN-CHRISTIAN. THE COLD OF FEBRUARY WILL GIVE WAY TO THE WARM OF SPRING AND EVENTUALLY TO THE LONG HOT SUMMER. WHAT HAPPENS IN ROCHESTER IN THE SUMMER OF '67 IS AT THE DOORSTEP OF EASTMAN KODAK.

Tough-sounding as it was, the statement was an obvious sign of FIGHT's weakness, perhaps even of its defeat on the jobs issue. In truth, FIGHT's chances for keeping the issue alive and in the public spotlight were not good. Picketing and demonstrations seemed futile, a boycott unrealistic because, as Alinsky later explained dryly, "you couldn't ask the country to stop taking pictures." The hard truth was that as long as the dispute was confined to Rochester, FIGHT didn't have the troops or leverage to win.

In March, however, FIGHT set forth a new tactic to expand the conflict beyond Rochester's borders. It announced that it had bought ten shares of Kodak stock so that its leaders could have access to Kodak's annual meeting on April 25 in Flemington, New Jersey, and, of even greater significance, that it was beginning to solicit proxy statements from other Kodak shareholders, especially from national church denominations. Suddenly, FIGHT had expanded both the playing field and the number of players eligible to take sides. Who dreamed up this clever plan? Not surprisingly, several claimed authorship. Herb White maintains that the idea came to him in a creative burst after a night of drinking with an old seminary classmate and that he then passed the idea on to Chambers. Chambers, however, insists that the idea originated with him and that he passed it along to his boss. Although Alinsky later acknowledged that the idea of buying stock originated with someone else, he took full credit for inventing the bigger and more dramatic scenario of a stock proxy campaign.

By the end of March, Alinsky's connections in the national offices of a number of mainline Protestant denominations began paying dividends. On March 31 the Reverend Roger A. Harless, executive director of the Interracial Council of the United Presbyterian Church, announced in Rochester that the United Church of Christ planned to vote its 11,000 shares of Kodak stock in support of FIGHT's position—and that pastors from Philadelphia, Washington, D.C., Camden, New Jersey, and New York City would be descending upon Flemington to protest Kodak's intransigence. A front-page story in *The New York Times* threw a national spotlight on this new phase of the battle. On April 7, under the headline "2 Churches Withhold Proxies to Fight Kodak Rights Policy," the *Times* reported that the presiding bishop of the Episcopal Church and the Board for Homeland Ministries of the United Church of Christ had decided to challenge Kodak's repudiation of the job-training program. "Officials of both church bodies," the *Times* story noted, "said it was the first time they had not signed over the votes on their holdings, which are worth almost $1 million." Indeed, in organizing the proxy campaign, Alinsky launched the first collective church effort to use stockholdings to influence corporate policy on social-justice issues. This was the forerunner and source of the "corporate responsibility" movement's increasingly ambitious campaigns in subsequent decades on such issues as corporate policies on South African apartheid. Since Alinsky had only six weeks or so to round up support, he was battling against time as well as against the reluctance of many church officials to break new ground on such a controversial issue. (Alinsky and FIGHT also tried to obtain a shareholders list from Kodak. When the company refused, FIGHT initiated a lawsuit, but the court ruled in Kodak's favor the day before the company's annual meeting.)

Alinsky himself went into action soliciting proxy support—traveling, for example, to a national meeting of Unitarians in Denver to make his pitch. His argument was straightforward: American corporations had a responsibility to help solve the problems of poverty and discrimination. Kodak, after implicitly agreeing that it had such a responsibility, abrogated a signed agreement with FIGHT. Therefore, it was the duty of all people of goodwill, but especially religious leaders and their institutions, to demonstrate their moral condemnation of Kodak's management. Alinsky made it clear—although it hardly needed to be said—that FIGHT was not interested in taking over Kodak or even winning a seat on its board of directors. FIGHT only wanted jobs for poor people—and the churches' moral support was a means to that end.

As Alinsky, Kodak, and others realized, however, moral support and political power were hard to separate. Kodak executives were very worried; the press coverage could lead to what every corporate executive feared— the intervention of the federal government, congressional hearings perhaps, or even Justice Department investigations into hiring policies and marketing practices. In fact, Kodak's top executives took the threat of mainline church opposition so seriously that they personally lobbied church officials. The chairman of the Board, Bill Vaughn, for example, went to New York City to talk to the Presbyterians—"to remedy false information," as he puts it. "We spoke with the chief secretary or moderator or whatever it is; he just plain wasn't interested in listening, frankly." Kodak's counsel, Harmar Brereton, an Episcopalian, went on a similar mission to see the Bishop of Boston, where the results were similar.

As the annual meeting drew near, the Unitarians and four major Protestant denominations voted to withhold their proxies—representing about 40,000 shares—from Kodak's management. (FIGHT also received support from a small number of individual Kodak stockholders.) While the proxies in support of FIGHT were a tiny fraction of the 80 million shares of Kodak stock outstanding, this was an unprecedented involvement of the clergy. FIGHT's general plan was to organize a large contingent that would travel in buses to Flemington and demonstrate outside the auditorium where the stockholders' meeting was held, while FIGHT's ten-person delegation—one person for each share of stock it owned—was inside. Kodak began to prepare Vaughn and its security personnel for a range of possibilities, including acts of civil disobedience or violence. Company officials were nearly frantic over the possibility that violence would turn their meeting into chaos and apparently pressed their concern with New York's Republican senator, Jacob Javits. A week before the meeting, Javits announced he had contacted the Justice Department's Community Relations Service, asking that it mediate the FIGHT-Kodak dispute, an offer FIGHT refused within hours of its appearing in Rochester's *Democrat & Chronicle*.

As for Vaughn, Kodak's lawyers organized a dress rehearsal at Kodak headquarters where they peppered him with the kind of hostile questions and insults he might expect at Flemington. For the tall, slender, mild-mannered chairman, it was not a confidence-boosting experience. "I wasn't used to that sort of thing," he says. "I just tried the best I could." Like his predecessors, Abe Chapman and Tom Hargraves, Vaughn came down from Rochester a few days ahead of time, spending the weekend at the nearby Princeton Inn to relax and study his script. But the weekend had hardly been relaxing, and his "script" anything but certain; he had been given a lot of contradictory advice from the hawks and doves in his circle of advisers. As he prepared to go to bed on the night of April 24, with the moment of truth drawing near—some twelve hours later he would be on stage in the auditorium of Hunterdon Central High School, opening the annual meeting of the world's largest photographic company—Vaughn felt acutely alone and vulnerable. "I'm not a praying man, normally, but I prayed the night before that meeting. I went down on my knees and said, 'I want to do a job on this thing tomorrow. And we've got to see it come out right.' I never told anybody else that, but I did." If Saul Alinsky had only known that he had, so to speak, brought Kodak to its knees, he would have been a very happy man.

Alinsky was in fine form in Flemington, boasting to reporters that virtually every room in his motel was filled with Kodak security men because "Kodak's afraid that if somebody knocks me off, they'll get blamed for it." When asked if he came to Flemington to direct FIGHT's strategy, Alinsky said he hadn't, "[but] I'm not an innocent bystander either." "I strongly believe that if Kodak doesn't say tomorrow it will honor the agreement, FIGHT will scrap the agreement, too," he warned. "Any future agreement will have to be right down to a 'T' on jobs, hours, and everything else Kodak didn't want to get into."

At noon on a cool, sunny day with a few white cloud puffs high in the sky, about seven hundred FIGHT members and supporters marched along Main Street displaying protest signs that read: "Kodak Snaps the Shutter on the Negro" and "Kodak Out of Focus." Police were everywhere—on the street along the march route and atop buildings with rifles drawn. "They really thought we were going to riot," Chambers says, recalling the tense scene. The FIGHT-Kodak confrontation, according to local historians, was the biggest event in town since the trial of Bruno Hauptmann for the Lindbergh kidnapping in 1935. In fact, when Chambers had checked into his hotel the day before, the police more or less insisted that he come right away to a meeting with their police chief to discuss FIGHT's plans.

While FIGHT's demonstrators waited outside, the ten-person FIGHT delegation, including Alinsky and Chambers, entered the auditorium, shareholder credentials in hand. The room was already packed—apparently Kodak had filled most of the approximately one thousand seats with employees and others bused down from Rochester. Press reports later said that the FIGHT delegation was greeted with chants of "Throw them out," though others heard more graphic whispers—"Throw the niggers out"—as the FIGHT delegation made its way in.

No sooner had Vaughn gaveled the meeting to order than Florence was on his feet. "Point of order! I'll be heard as long as I'm on the floor." As other shareholders shouted their disapproval, Florence yelled at Vaughn: "We will give you until two o'clock to honor that agreement." Then he, Alinsky, and the rest of the FIGHT delegation walked out, joined by twenty or so other sympathetic shareholders. Just moments earlier Alinsky had made the tactical decision to issue a quick challenge and then leave. He apparently sensed that the dynamics in the auditorium were not going to work to FIGHT's advantage—and, in any event, FIGHT's strength was outside with the rallying demonstrators and the television cameras and microphones. "From what I've seen of the ghettos from Harlem to Watts, the feeling is very bitter," Alinsky said as he stood in his rumpled beige raincoat before the network television cameras. "We are ready to move on a national scale and FIGHT is going to be the fountainhead for the resurrection of the civil rights movement." And Florence added: "This is war, Mr. Alinsky. We have given them until two o'clock. After that, we don't have any more agreement. You [Kodak] will honor the agreement or reap the harvest."

While Alinsky and Florence were addressing the rally, inside the auditorium Vaughn was employing a conciliatory approach when queried by clergy on Kodak's job policies. Noting that the company had expanded its job-training programs in the fall soon after talks began with FIGHT, Vaughn observed, "I think FIGHT deserves credit for this, for putting the pressure on us." But when Florence was back in the auditorium at two o'clock demanding the answer to his question: "Will you honor the agreement?" Vaughn replied without hesitation, "No."

Back outside, in front of the TV cameras, Alinsky promised a new, stepped-up national proxy campaign against Kodak. "We're going to ask churches to put their stocks where their sermons are."

Suddenly, however, it was Florence's inflammatory rhetoric that became the center of attention and controversy. Castigating Kodak for its hypocrisy and racism, Florence's emotional oratory ended with him threatening—much to Alinsky's surprise and dismay—a nationwide pilgrimage to Rochester and a huge demonstration ("a candlelight service") at Kodak's headquarters on July 25, the third anniversary of the city's riot. This specific provocative threat had not been in Alinsky's game plan. It was one thing for Florence to have said earlier, "This is war," a hyperbolic generality Alinsky often used himself to mean a nonviolent war of nerves— tough and bitter, perhaps, but nonviolent. Now, however, Florence was crossing the line, threatening a specific incendiary act, and Alinsky was angry about Florence's outburst. It was not a fatal mistake, but the Rochester press and others jumped on it, forcing the Rochester Area Council of Churches to issue a statement "expressing its disapproval of this strategy" and, without criticizing Florence by name, suggesting that "such a far-reaching decision should have been subject to full discussion and approval by the Delegates' Council of FIGHT."

The episode symbolized the continuing volatility of the racial climate in many Northern cities. With the summer only a couple of months away, Alinsky must have felt that time was running out in Rochester as he swung into action soon after the Flemington drama. A continuing FIGHT-Kodak stalemate was unacceptable—the frustration it was bound to breed would not be good for FIGHT or for the tranquillity of the city. Although details are murky, Alinsky apparently thought he had a chance to force Kodak to make concessions through a two-step process: mobilize massive church support, turn the FIGHT-Kodak dispute into the cause célèbre of the civil rights movement; and then leverage that support into a credible demand for a congressional investigation of Kodak. Alinsky recounted to friends that he had been in touch with Robert Kennedy, recently elected to the U.S. Senate from New York, who told him—or at least encouraged Alinsky to believe—that if church support was forthcoming on the scale Alinsky envisioned, then Kennedy would be amenable to orchestrating the kind of congressional pressure Alinsky wanted.

Alinsky, however, was not having spectacular success among the churches. Even at Flemington, some of the churches that withheld their proxies from management explained their actions in measured, qualified words. An Episcopal spokesman, for example, said that "the action of the Episcopal presiding bishop . . . is intended only to underscore the church's deep concern for a resolution of the issues involved"—and not, it was added pointedly, as support for a specific solution. The basic problem Alinsky was now encountering was not restricted to the churches' reluctance to charge ahead with the still new, controversial proxy tactic. Equally, perhaps even more important was that upon closer inspection the FIGHT-Kodak dispute struck many as a mixed bag rather than a clear case of good versus evil. National stories in business publications such as *Fortune* and *The Wall Street Journal* not unconvincingly attributed Kodak's plight to clumsy, inept negotiating rather than to corporate racism or malevolence. Moreover, there had been some progress on the jobs front in Rochester. On April 12, a sizable number of Rochester's industrial, religious, and civic leaders announced the formation of a corporation, Rochester Jobs, Inc., that would guarantee 1,500 jobs for unemployed blacks. About forty of the city's largest businesses—including Kodak—made commitments to fulfill the hiring goals. At the insistence of FIGHT, which also participated in the formation of Rochester Jobs, the new organization's leaders described its program as "separate and distinct" from the running dispute between FIGHT and Kodak. Obviously, however, it wasn't. RJI had been a response to the furor Alinsky and FIGHT had created, but, ironically, their very success in stirring the city's leadership—including Kodak—also made their attack on Kodak's intransigence and immorality sound less than compelling.

In short, quite a few church officials apparently felt that a full-throttle campaign against Kodak was out of proportion to the corporation's current sins. By early June, when he went to Boston for a meeting with church leaders and to see Irene, Alinsky was getting discouraged. Together they walked from her place over to the Public Garden, where they stretched out on the grass near a little lagoon, his head in her lap. Well into the night he talked, a wounded warrior hiding none of his pain and frustration.

Alinsky slept fitfully that night, Irene recalls, tossing and turning and mumbling a number of times, "No, that won't work." In the morning, as soon as he awoke, he said, "I'm going to settle it today." It was a Saturday, and Irene's first reaction was to say, "Hey, you haven't thought it through; how are you going to settle it today?" But Alinsky had thought it through, and shortly he was on the phone to a Boston acquaintance who was a friend of Daniel Patrick Moynihan. "Tell Moynihan I want to settle," Alinsky said. He had heard that Kodak, through Moynihan's good friend and Kodak lawyer Storey Zartman, had invited Moynihan to consult with the company's board of directors regarding the FIGHT dispute and minority hiring policies. Alinsky hardly knew Moynihan—their paths may have crossed briefly once or twice—but he knew of him as an Assistant Secretary of Labor in the Johnson administration. And, of course, Moynihan had also been the center of controversy early in 1965, when he wrote a report that cited the instability of black family life as a cause of continuing poverty and social disorganization. Many black leaders and white liberals bitterly accused Moynihan of "blaming the victim," although his report emphasized that slavery and white racism generally had taken a heavy toll on the black family. Indeed, Moynihan thinks that Alinsky first heard about his private meeting with Kodak's board after word of it had leaked out to several Episcopal ministers who, Moynihan recalls, quickly spread a message to the effect of: "Ah-ha, they have brought in that racist Moynihan, and it just shows what a terrible outfit Kodak is." Moynihan was now director of the Joint Center for Urban Studies at MIT and Harvard, and Alinsky wanted someone like him to help him move fast, not only because the summer was approaching, not only because the dispute had dragged on long enough, but also because once Kodak discovered that the grand strategy with the churches was unraveling, it would have no incentive to settle.

Moynihan, who lived in Cambridge, remembers Alinsky's phone call and visit. "We won't hold Kodak to a contract," Alinsky said right off. "They obviously can't live with it. But we want something." It took Moynihan four days, numerous phone conversations, and a trip to Rochester to convince Kodak officials that Alinsky was sincere—that this wasn't a trap.

At FIGHT's third convention on June 23, Florence announced that a settlement had been reached with Kodak—actually, FIGHT called it an "agreement," while Eilers referred to it as "an understanding." For Alinsky and FIGHT, the key passage in Eilers's statement was that "Kodak recognizes that FIGHT, as a broad-based community organization, speaks on behalf of the basic needs and aspirations of the Negro poor in the Rochester area." After this recognition of FIGHT, Eilers went on to say that the two organizations should work together to recruit and counsel Rochester's black unemployed. There was no mention of an exclusive jobs program, but "there now appears to be an opportunity to create better understanding and to work in mutual respect." Florence had little difficulty persuading most of his constituency that the settlement was an important victory. "Black men today can walk taller in this community," he proclaimed. In the black community, the increased pride, respect, and dignity that Florence stressed were no small achievements.

At a news conference Alinsky claimed victory in the classic manner of his mentor John L. Lewis by redefining and reinterpreting "victory." The big issue all along, he said, was "recognition—clear and unmistakable recognition; the door is now open for a cooperative relationship . . . that may well set the pattern for large industries across the nation." As for the other accusations and demands that FIGHT had made, Alinsky said softly, "You say some pretty tough things on both sides when you are in the crisis of negotiations. When it is settled and both sides are happy, you become more polite." He kidded the photographers: "Are you using Kodak film? If you're not, you're doing a great disservice to the community. The best film in the world is Kodak film and everybody should use it." (Kodak executives were totally baffled by Alinsky's exuberant endorsement of their product.)

Privately, Saul Alinsky was not satisfied. By not winning a jobs commitment from Kodak he had been forced to settle for a lesser prize—and he was determined to make one last, behind-the-scenes try at winning Kodak over.

"THEY'VE GOT to meet with me," an exasperated Saul Alinsky told Pat Moynihan, but Kodak's top management was still distrustful of him— they couldn't forgive or forget that only months earlier he had bragged: "When I get through with Eastman Kodak, there won't be enough toilet paper left in the world to wipe them clean." After some prodding by Moynihan, Kodak executives finally agreed to a meeting, although they insisted that it be billed as a "seminar," like one Alinsky had conducted for AT&T executives, not as something that could be construed as a "bargaining session." "They're crazy as hell," Alinsky said. "If they want to meet as a seminar, it'll cost them a thousand bucks a day plus expenses." But that's what Kodak preferred, and the two-day meeting took place in the privacy of the Episcopal Theological Seminary in Cambridge, Massachusetts, in early August 1967.

In sheer volume 1967 was the worst year of the decade for riots or "racial disorders"—there were more than 160 of them—but the most violent by far occurred in July, first in Newark and less than a week later in Detroit, where 43 people were killed, 7,000 arrested, and 1,300 buildings destroyed. For the first time, federal troops—4,700 paratroopers—had to be summoned before order was restored, at which point the mayor of Detroit said of the incredible devastation, "It looks like Berlin in 1945." Later, studies would show that there had been some differences between the riot in Newark, where white-owned businesses seemed to be special targets of looting and destruction, and the riot in Detroit, where the ghetto rampage was total. In retrospect, it seems amazing that the ghetto violence in so many cities that summer did not spread into white neighborhoods; at the time, white residents, fearing precisely this development, purchased handguns at record levels.

With no end to the violence in sight, a great fear also pervaded the upper echelons of the Johnson administration. When Detroit exploded, the administration's sense of desperation deepened. Willard Wirtz, then Secretary of Labor, recalls that his department and the White House were willing to embrace virtually any plan or scheme that might dampen these inflammable situations—including the plan Alinsky wanted to implement in Rochester with Kodak's help. Wirtz, who had spent many years teaching and practicing law in Chicago, knew Alinsky slightly and respected him. "I considered Alinsky a very helpful force in knowing where the fires were and doing something about them." At the Cambridge meeting, Alinsky invoked Wirtz's name, saying he could get the Labor Department's support for a project that would make Kodak look like "the number one corporate leader" in addressing the problems of urban violence and black despair. He outlined a plan whereby FIGHT would establish a corporation that would be a subcontractor for some item that Kodak would buy—and said that this joint effort would be announced at a Kodak-FIGHT news conference as soon as possible so that it would be interpreted as a positive response to the Detroit catastrophe, which had received worldwide attention. Alinsky even offered to write Kodak's statement, the theme of which he ad-libbed for the executives in Cambridge: "As a corporation, Eastman Kodak recognizes it has two sets of stockholders, its own stockholders who own stock and the people of the United States of

America. Kodak is concerned about the welfare of the nation and on this basis is going ahead with this joint project." There was no risk to the proposal, he argued. "You can write off the costs as a tax loss, and the Secretary of Labor will pick up the job-training costs. If you don't believe me, pick up the phone and call Wirtz." Apparently, some of the younger Kodak executives were enthusiastic, but Kodak's senior representative, their counsel, Harmar Brereton, would have no part of it and the "seminar" ended uneventfully. (Later, FIGHT and Xerox worked out a deal along the lines Alinsky had proposed, which led to a FIGHT-controlled subcontracting company called FIGHTON.)

Less than a year later, by the spring of 1968, Alinsky and his Industrial Areas Foundation withdrew from Rochester, his three-year commitment at an end. Originally, he had agreed to organize in Rochester even though only two years of funding was assured, which, as it turned out, meant that pro-Alinsky church leaders were forced to raise an additional $50,000 for a third year in the midst of the FIGHT-Kodak battle. As each denomination reconsidered its support, there were tense, difficult debates, perhaps none more so than at the Baptist Association meeting where Kodak's chairman, Bill Vaughn, a Baptist, spoke against refunding, while several black Baptist churches spoke for it. The Baptists' monetary contribution was small, but the political significance of their support was very large. Nobody was more surprised—and emotionally moved—than Herb White, who was helping to organize the pro-Alinsky forces and had all but written off the Baptists as a lost cause, when the Association voted in favor of funding a third year.

In fact, not a single denomination bailed out and, with very few exceptions, individual church leaders—both black and white—remained steadfast in their support. This often required a good deal of courage and commitment, not least of all among the most visibly involved white clergy who were subjected to threatening phone calls and letters and acts of vandalism against their homes and cars. Although no pastor or church executive was run out of town for supporting Alinsky and FIGHT, Paul Long for one knew it was time to leave by the fall of 1967, three years after he arrived at the Third Presbyterian Church. Long was continually impressed by the courage of a small number of his own parishioners and others involved in Friends of FIGHT, some of them ranking Kodak employees. But Long himself was in an extremely difficult, if not impossible situation. By his estimate, only about 10 percent of the congregation really supported FIGHT; most were troubled and upset by what was going on, and still others, a sizable cluster of establishment leaders like Paul Miller and Ed Harris, were angry. The church budget dropped precipitously, and when he left Third Presbyterian for a new church in Cincinnati, Long's going-away party was a small, cozy affair.

As Alinsky pulled out of Rochester, Friends of FIGHT changed its name to Metro-Act, broadened its agenda, and soon became a new, important force for social and political change while remaining broadly supportive of FIGHT. At FIGHT's fourth convention, where the Woodlawn Organization's Arthur Brazier was the keynote speaker, Franklin Florence gave a typically fiery oration which was, in effect, a testimonial to Alinsky and his right-hand man, Ed Chambers.

> I remember three years ago when our critics said, "You will never be able to organize the Negro community." Their wishful thinking soon gave way to "If you do get them organized, they won't stick together." When the critics, like Paul Miller and his Gannett press, saw their attacks and snipings melt like butter on a hot grill, they started the refrain "But they won't support themselves." But we have supported ourselves. We have been self-supporting and paying our own way for six months and we've got $25,000 in the bank for a rainy day and we are going to pay our own way until we get freedom, equality, and dignity. Those diehards like Miller and Kodak better put up or shut up. FIGHT stock is as sound as their stock.

Alinsky withdrew from Rochester having reached a new peak of national prominence, his well-publicized battle with Kodak adding considerably to his stature as someone uniquely able to build strong community organizations among poor Northern blacks. Ironically, it would be the last black ghetto that he'd organize.

26

New Career

The civil rights movement of the late 1950s and early 1960s, Southern-based and carried out by blacks and whites using nonviolent means to confront a violent, segregationist society, turned sour and fragmented long before the assassination of Martin Luther King in the spring of 1968. In spite of the passage of historic federal legislation in 1964 and 1965 striking down discriminatory public accommodations and voting laws, the underlying daily realities for most black people had not changed significantly—and most of these realities were tied to the old discriminatory arrangements that resulted in limited job opportunities, poverty, bad housing, and inferior schools. The "progress" of the civil rights movement that Northern liberals and opinion-makers applauded appeared more like a mirage to angry, impatient young blacks in the movement who began openly to challenge King's leadership over tactical and philosophical issues like nonviolence, the role of whites in the movement, and racial integration itself as a desirable goal. Reflecting on the black-white issue, King later wrote that "the paths of Negro-white unity that had been converging crossed at Selma and like a giant X began to diverge." But even before the internecine warfare surrounding the Selma marches in March 1965, there had been a major, divisive battle with lasting consequences at the Democratic National Convention in Atlantic City in August 1964 over the issue of which Mississippi delegation would be seated, the all-white regulars representing the old segregated political system or the sixty-eight mainly black delegates of the Mississippi Freedom Democratic Party. Fearful of a Southern walk-out, President Johnson pushed a "compromise," which would allow the Mississippi regulars to be seated while giving the MFDP two at-large seats and ensuring that four years hence no delegation could be seated if black voters were disenfranchised. It was a pragmatic proposal of a pro–civil rights President, and leading white liberals at the convention embraced it—and national black leaders, too, such as the NAACP's Roy Wilkins, Bayard Rustin, and King himself, who was under great pressure from Johnson's operatives and allies, especially the Automobile Workers' Walter Reuther, whose union was a financial supporter of King's SCLC. But the MFDP, which included many small farmers and the celebrated Fannie Lou Hamer—a sharecropper's wife who told a gripping story to the convention's credentials committee of having been beaten when she attempted to register to vote in Ruleville, Mississippi—had come to Atlantic City with high hopes that justice, not compromise, would prevail. Now they felt betrayed, and militant black leaders like SNCC's Robert Moses and Stokely Carmichael who accompanied the MFDP were outraged. "This proves that the liberal Democrats are just as racist as Goldwater," Carmichael sneered, contemptuous not only of white liberals but of the treasonous acts of King and other black leaders. (Ultimately the compromise satisfied none of the principals: the MDFP voted 64–4 to reject it, and the Mississippi regulars walked off the convention floor. In the fall election, which marked the beginning of the end of Democratic Party dominance in the Old Confederacy, Republican Barry Goldwater carried six states, his home state of Arizona and five in the Deep South, including Mississippi, where he won 87 percent of the vote.)

After Atlantic City, when King announced plans to begin a voter-registration drive in Selma, Alabama, territory SNCC had been working for two years, Carmichael and other SNCC leaders were once again furious. King and his aides led a series of demonstrations in January and February 1965, protesting the barriers to voter registration, but the most dramatic event, a landmark of the civil rights movement, was a planned march from Selma to the state capitol in Montgomery. Although the night before at a Selma meeting King had urged people to participate in spite of the possibility of violence, he himself returned to Atlanta before the marchers assembled on March 7 and began crossing the Pettus Bridge onto the old Jefferson Davis Highway. Then a brutal attack began, witnessed that night on television by a horrified nation, police wading into the peaceful assembly with clubs, electric cattle prods, and tear gas. Many of the marchers were seriously injured. There was moral outrage in Washington, enough to help pass the Voting Rights Act of 1965. But in Selma, the splintering of the movement worsened as Carmichael and other radical blacks doubted King's judgment, disapproved of his reliance on the federal government for protection, and, more than ever, were openly scornful of his philosophical adherence to passive resistance and nonviolence.

By the spring of 1966, when Carmichael was elected chairman of SNCC, replacing John Lewis, a proponent of nonviolence, he also became the leading advocate of "Black Power," a term that quickly became controversial and had different meanings for different people. Although Carmichael himself sometimes used the term in a way that suggested familiar ethnic and interest-group politics, Black Power was also an implicit rejection of King's philosophy of racial equality and nonviolence. At SNCC, for example, while whites were not officially expelled, they were ordered to work only in white communities. (As for violence, not much changed immediately, since many SNCC organizers had packed guns for self-protection long before the emergence of Black Power.)

The Black Power slogan triggered an immediate, vociferous national debate—indeed, part of its appeal among younger blacks was the consternation that the words caused among whites, just as Carmichael's use of a picture of a black panther as a symbol of SNCC's voter-registration campaign in Lowndes County, Alabama, had rattled whites there.

Saul Alinsky explained the white reaction to Black Power in terms of semantics—"black" was the color of evil, and "power" suggested coercion, even corruption; together they elicited a potent synergistic effect. When Black Power first surfaced, Alinsky spoke favorably about it. "I agree with the concept," he said in the fall of 1966. "We've always called it community power, and if the community is black, it's black power." But a year later he had turned critical, charging that Carmichael and others "have got to stop going around yelling 'Black Power!' and just addressing meetings. It's time they got trained to really go down and organize." He loved to talk about a Detroit meeting at which he and Carmichael shared the platform; when the audience pressed Carmichael to cite a real, concrete example of what he meant by Black Power, Carmichael was forced to name Alinsky's project in Rochester.

Nonetheless, with black chauvinism on the rise, Alinsky understood it would be virtually impossible for him to continue organizing in black ghettos. In fact, just as he left Rochester, a sign of the times was an attack on him by a black nationalist, one Maulana Ron Karenga, who in a speech in Dayton, Ohio, listed six categories of "exploiting liberals." Among political exploiters he named Abraham Lincoln and Senator Robert F. Kennedy, who had been assassinated only weeks before. Alinsky was an economic exploiter—an apparent reference to the fees required for Alinsky's organizing services. If Karenga's logic was hard to follow, so too were some of the details of the dispute that now erupted. Karenga was identified in news reports as a board member of the newly formed Interfaith Foundation for Community Organization, but he in fact was not a board member, though Alinsky had so identified him in an angry letter he sent to IFCO's executive director, Lucius Walker, a black, who was an advocate of what he termed "the Black consciousness movement," which apparently subscribed to a substantial part, if not all, of Karenga's sentiments. It was not clear at the time whether Walker took exception to one of Karenga's "insights," that "blacks are a country and if you support America then you are against my community." But it was a statement that Alinsky jumped on. "[I reject his statement] in its entirety and find it repugnant and nauseous," he wrote to Walker. "I and my staff associates not only plead guilty to supporting America, but we will go further and gladly admit that we love our country." Virtually no leftist dissenter— black or white—was using this kind of patriotic rhetoric in 1968, and Alinsky's public tongue-lashing of a black nationalist was equally rare.

On both accounts, Alinsky's remarks were treated as news, but his letter to IFCO also dealt with another matter, a grant proposal he had submitted to that foundation: $250,000 for partial funding of a new IAF training institute for organizers. Ironically, Alinsky had been a major inspiration of IFCO, which had been two years in the making. His Protestant church allies in New York and Jack Egan in Chicago had been trying to find a mechanism to institutionalize church support for community organizing, with Alinsky as a kind of first-among-equals beneficiary. (To some extent, a forerunner to IFCO was the Urban Training Center in Chicago. Established in 1963 by several national Protestant denominations, it was the first systematic effort to teach clergy about community change and organizing. Alinsky was a frequent lecturer there, and the Center became closely identified with his concepts, much to the displeasure of Walter Kloetzli, who served on the Center's board of directors.) But by the time IFCO was up and running, the racial climate had changed greatly. A bit earlier, when IFCO was still in the planning phase, a campaign was underway by Alinsky enthusiasts in the San Francisco Bay Area, led by Presbyterian and Episcopal clergy, to bring him to Oakland to start a community organization there. Eventually, Alinsky told them he was interested in Oakland only if a training institute could also be part of a package. So when IFCO opened its doors, William Grace, a young Presbyterian minister, and several others from the Bay Area met with an IFCO advisory committee to press the matter of funding an Alinsky training institute, and by mid-May 1968, Alinsky submitted a proposal. But just six weeks later he withdrew it after hearing about Karenga's speech in which, according to a transcript, the black nationalist contemptuously dismissed Alinsky's IFCO proposal, saying that a white man "has neither the ability nor the right to dictate to the [black] community, either through training

. . . or any other way, how it should organize, how it should run itself and what concepts it should advocate." This, of course, was not what Alinsky was about, but this was an era when black nationalists and too many others were not interested in making fine distinctions. Alinsky had little doubt that Karenga was speaking for Walker and other enemies at IFCO—and that a nasty debate was in the offing if the grant application was pursued.

At this point, Alinsky could have walked quietly away from the messy situation, sparing some of his white church friends a measure of discomfort. But he did not take kindly to attacks on his character and integrity, and he was also genuinely disgusted not only by the dangerous drivel of the black nationalists but also by the silence and acquiescence of too many white liberals. In his letter to IFCO announcing that he was withdrawing his request for funds, Alinsky charged that many liberals were accepting as "interesting approaches" to social problems statements by Black Power leaders which, if they were made by whites, would be grounds for sending them to lunatic asylums. This kind of double standard, he warned, created a situation where no real communication could take place between blacks and whites, a situation that he would not tolerate. "Believing in full equality and the full dignity of all races, neither I nor my associates can surrender their own dignity and be part of the masochistic cult which submits to outrageous and, in many cases, patently psychotic charges and attacks." It was vintage Alinsky, the kind of blunt, combative, and essentially honest statement that had endeared him to close friends and now to a new legion of admirers, not the least of whom were journalists. Indeed, sympathetic journalists tended to overlook his shortcomings and mistakes, of which several were especially important.

IRONICALLY, it was at this juncture that Saul Alinsky, himself a great seducer, was seduced and swept up by the call of history. It all started with his success in Woodlawn, a real if somewhat shaky success by the time Charles Silberman's laudatory book appeared in 1964, trumpeting Alinsky and his methods as exciting and of first-rank importance. The urban riots led to a small stampede to Alinsky's office of dedicated clergy, small groups from cities all over the country, properly reverential, promising to raise tens of thousands of dollars to underwrite Alinsky projects. Some of these overtures led nowhere but, in fairly rapid succession, Alinsky could not resist the blandishments of groups from Rochester, Kansas City, and Buffalo even though he did not have enough experienced organizers to do the jobs.

In a sense, this was an old story, a problem Alinsky had never resolved, in part because of his ambivalence about what, exactly, he wanted to do—to organize, or to write and lecture about organizing and be a social critic. In the early 1950s, he had wanted to hire a cadre of organizers for an ambitious, multi-city campaign to build People's Organizations, but the funding never materialized. By the close of that decade, he seemed more interested in promoting ideas, and was comfortable with a Chicago staff of two, Lester Hunt and Nick von Hoffman, who could do double duty as writer-researchers and—if and when the right project turned up—as organizers, too. But both of them had since left, von Hoffman for journalism and Hunt for teaching, after a brief job for Alinsky as an organizer-consultant in Butte, Montana. So Alinsky was forced to raid TWO for organizers. First Ed Chambers was pulled out and sent to Rochester; then Squire Lance was dispatched to head up the new project in Kansas City, barely two years after training under Chambers and serving briefly as Chambers's TWO replacement; Dick Harmon was next, rushed up to Buffalo when the funding came through there. Alinsky, whose energy and interest were largely expended on the lecture circuit and the Rochester project, gave precious little of either to Kansas City and Buffalo.

In Kansas City, Lance lasted only a year, replaced by Alinsky's talented young friend Mike Miller, who did not fare much better. By his own admission, Miller, who was white and barely twenty-five years old, was in over his head. When he first arrived on the job, Alinsky told him on the phone, "I don't care how wet the wood is, you can make a fire," but it was hard to be imaginative when the pressures were so great. Miller understood that in theory, his role was to listen, agitate, think an issue through with the people, and train them. In practice, while he felt he was a good listener, "I couldn't agitate . . . some of these fifty-five-year-old black ministers. I just didn't have the confidence to confront them—you know, get them to sit down and talk with me or build stuff underneath them to move them aside if they weren't involving enough people, if they were trying to keep it all in their own hip pockets. And on training I just didn't have enough experience myself to train people in a whole lot of things."

On a rare trip into Kansas City to meet with some of the black minister-leaders of the Council for United Action, Alinsky gave Miller a small but very impressive demonstration of a master organizer at work. Until then, Miller suspected that Alinsky had lost touch with the realities of organizing, had become sort of a philosopher of social change. But on this particular day, he was a patient teacher, drawing people out, asking questions, leading a Socratic dialogue, challenging them to find the answers themselves. Miller was as impressed with him as Alinsky's old friend

Sidney Hyman had been with a similar display in the Back of the Yards more than twenty years earlier.

Unfortunately for Miller and the Kansas City project, such personal appearances by Alinsky could be counted on the fingers of one hand, and the project soon ended, a rare instance when Alinsky admitted to a failure. Buffalo went much better. It was not the showy, national headline grabber that Rochester was, but a good effort by Dick Harmon produced a reasonably solid organization, BUILD, by the time Harmon's tour was up.

Both BUILD and FIGHT proved that Alinsky and his methods could be effective in black ghettos beyond Chicago, where, some critics suggested, he had had the financial backing of the Catholic archdiocese and other unique, home-court advantages. But these successes outside of Chicago came at a price—namely, the effect on TWO and the failure to pursue a strategy that Alinsky thought might produce revolutionary political change in Chicago and important side effects elsewhere.

As early as the fall of 1965, not many months after Chambers left TWO for Rochester, the keen, crotchety Doc Farrell, the pastor at Holy Cross who kept tugging at Alinsky's sleeve until he agreed to organize in Woodlawn, hoisted a warning flag. "It is a tough fight and things are not going well," he began in a pointed note to Alinsky.

> Time was when we could maybe blame you or your men—but now we are on our own. . . . Leadership is there. People are holding together but no real progress on the issues. . . . Crushing blow came tonight when it became known that you want Squire Lance in K.C. There is no one to replace him, with the exception of Harmon. I don't think you should take a man from a going organization that is in trouble to start another when you don't have manpower, Saul, old friend.

It was a simple yet critically important observation. Apparently, Alinsky had become a believer of his own romantic rhetoric, that after three years a People's Organization could—and must—stand on its own feet and no longer rely on his services. It was a tenet that satisfied a trio of needs: it was "evidence" of Alinsky's belief in the capacities of ordinary people; it freed him from a time-consuming, long-term involvement with these organizations; and it obviated the need to train and supervise junior organizers. But the truth of his own experience should have led him to a different conclusion. His most successful, stable, and enduring organization was the Back of the Yards Neighborhood Council, in which he remained active as a mentor-consultant to Joe Meegan for more than twenty years. Even in the 1960s, when he and Meegan saw much less of each other, Alinsky was still listed nostalgically on the Council's letterhead as the "technical consultant." And in California, throughout the 1950s his men Fred Ross and Cesar Chavez were indispensable in keeping alive the network of Community Service Organizations they set up in more than thirty cities. There was nothing inherently contradictory about believing in—and promoting—the capacity of ordinary people, even poor people, to determine their own destinies while at the same time keeping a skilled organizer on the scene. One of Alinsky's persistent critics in the mid-1960s, the sociologist Frank Riessman, argued persuasively that to withdraw abruptly, totally, as Alinsky did, "leads further to the possibility of a localist agenda, because it is the organizer-strategist-intellectual who should provide connections, the larger view that will lead to the development of a movement."

But something like that—masterminding a larger political organization, if not a movement per se—was what Alinsky had in mind in Chicago not long after Nick von Hoffman left Woodlawn and Alinsky's employ. Although by 1964 von Hoffman was working at the Chicago *Daily News,* the two of them continued to talk seriously about building on their TWO success, indeed about the necessity of doing so. "It was apparent to both of us that ultimately this thing in Woodlawn was stymied, that it couldn't get past where it was and that if we didn't do something, it would go down," von Hoffman says. The problem, essentially, was that TWO was a political island without enough of a power base—control of enough precincts, wards, and people—to grow and prosper. There were few natural allies of any consequence to hook up with. One possible strategy might have been to establish another community organization in nearby Englewood—to begin to create a critical mass. But of far greater interest to Alinsky was a more overtly political move: to challenge Richard J. Daley's Democratic machine—as well as his black ally, Congressman Bill Dawson—head-on in key elections on the South Side. Beyond Chicago, it was often not fully appreciated how critically important the black vote was to the machine—that, in fact, Daley's grip on some of the white ethnic vote, such as on the Polish Northwest Side, was less than firm. If Alinsky and TWO could crack the machine's hold on the South Side, the political map of Chicago would forever be changed. Not only would blacks have a claim on an unprecedented amount of power in Chicago but Daley's role as a kingmaker in national Democratic Party affairs would be vastly diminished—unless, of course, he found a way to make a deal, but even then, inevitably it would be much less to his liking than the arrangements he had with Dawson.

All of this was no mere pipe dream to Alinsky—he really believed that it could be pulled off. He thought it would be possible to ride to electoral victories on the same wave of enthusiasm that brought people into TWO. Alinsky's willingness to abandon a community-organizing approach when he saw a large electoral opening was perhaps another example of his tactical brilliance, just as he had earlier been able to see the import of taking a different approach in Woodlawn after learning about the community's reaction to the Freedom Riders. Von Hoffman says, "A lot of people, especially those who turned 'community organizing' into a kind of religion, now take it as gospel from Saul Alinsky—who sort of becomes the Walt Whitman of all of this—that one never gets directly involved in electoral politics. Well, he never thought that."

But to bake this new cake on the South Side, there were two essential ingredients: Art Brazier and Nick von Hoffman. Alinsky's plan was to run Brazier for Congress, beat the machine candidate, and move from there, beyond the precincts and wards of the 2nd Congressional District to the rest of the black South Side. But it wasn't clear whether the dynamic but cautious Brazier could be talked into running, and von Hoffman turned out to be an even larger stumbling block. Alinsky told him that he would only go ahead with this campaign if von Hoffman would leave the *Daily News* and come back to run it. Von Hoffman had not only done a spectacular job in Woodlawn but had near-encyclopedic knowledge of the South Side, which Alinsky did not. "Sometimes I think I made a great mistake," von Hoffman says about his decision not to leave journalism and rejoin his old mentor.

In the 1966 Democratic primary election, the machine-backed incumbent in the 2nd Congressional District, Barrett O'Hara, was challenged by a young, reform-minded state legislator, Abner Mikva, who was supported by liberal, independent forces and TWO. To avoid jeopardizing the organization's nonpartisan tax exemption, TWO staffers went on the Mikva campaign payroll, working Woodlawn's precincts in competition with the resourceful ward committeeman, Marshall Korshak, and his dedicated band of precinct captains, some of whom, it was said in Woodlawn, were not above buying votes if moral suasion fell on deaf ears. To check Korshak's men, TWO used the Blackstone Rangers, an increasingly notorious street gang, to plaster Woodlawn buildings with signs at two in the morning of election day that warned it was a violation of federal law to accept money in return for your vote. When Korshak's men saw the signs a few hours later, they were livid, not least because they couldn't remove them; the Rangers had used the same Super-Glue that the Chicago police used to affix virtually irremovable signs to abandoned cars. Nonetheless, when Mikva was defeated in a close election, Alinsky was furious, blaming

TWO's new staff director, Leon Finney, for allowing the machine to pull out a victory by stealing just enough votes in Woodlawn precincts. Alinsky, even without von Hoffman and Brazier, thought that a Mikva victory, made possible by TWO's political muscle, could have been a springboard to bigger things on the South Side.

TWO was not devastated by either the Mikva loss or the departure of organizers in rapid succession for Alinsky's other projects, but it was weakened. It faced a perpetual uphill existence, its universe a staggering array of deteriorating housing, high unemployment, and bad schools, surrounded by an unfriendly-to-hostile political atmosphere. TWO was often quite effective at coming to the help of tenants victimized by slum landlords, or consumers by dishonest merchants. But larger initiatives and issues required vast amounts of energy and perseverance—like TWO's job-training program and, perhaps most of all, the subsidized housing TWO fought for on a strip of land on Cottage Grove Avenue. Although the 502-unit project—a scaled-down version of the original—was still a proud achievement, one of the first housing developments in a black ghetto planned, owned, and managed by an indigenous community organization, some important goals had been sacrificed because of the delays and other factors.

TWO survived Alinsky's departure in the fall of 1966, but Woodlawn itself was soon racked by an unprecedented wave of gang violence as the Blackstone Rangers grew larger and more menacing, their turf battles with the East Side Disciples turning the community into a virtual war zone. The First Presbyterian Church's new pastor, John Fry, wanted to find ways to convert the Rangers' energy and organizational talent into socially useful endeavors—and to gain their trust, he allowed them to store their guns in the church basement, which outraged many in Woodlawn and elsewhere in Chicago when it became public. Others in Woodlawn, including many homeowners and those who had children in local schools increasingly plagued by gang violence, called for aggressive police action to crush the Rangers. To some extent, TWO was caught in the middle, finally opting for a highly controversial job-training program in which gang members themselves were employed to work with school dropouts and hard-core unemployed youth. At first, the federally funded program seemed to have broad if tenuous political support, including Mayor Daley's. But Police Superintendent O. W. Wilson was never sold on a training program for "criminal gangs," and rather quickly the program was in trouble, the Chicago *Tribune* contributing to the perhaps inevitable downfall in a series of sensationalized accounts of indicted gang members being paid with federal funds, other gang members receiving kickbacks from those em-

ployed in the program, and so forth. Families began moving out of Woodlawn in droves. And Saul Alinsky, whose career began on the West Side
of Chicago working with Italian street gangs, had no easy solutions either.

WITH HIS ORGANIZING projects almost finished and with Black
Power in full stride, Alinsky's interest in establishing a training institute
grew stronger. After the IFCO proposal fell apart, the next-best possibility
looked like the church-backed operation in the San Francisco Bay Area
that Bill Grace was still trying to put together. One of his co-conspirators
was a fascinating intellectual turned dress manufacturer, Alvin Duskin,
who first met Alinsky when he came to rent Alinsky's house in the Carmel
Highlands in the early 1960s. Duskin, who was then teaching, already knew
a little about Alinsky's work and was immediately impressed by his gruff
exterior and amused that there was this street-fighter kind of personality
living right in the middle of Brigadoon. Duskin went out and bought
Reveille for Radicals and became a devoted admirer and friend. In the
meantime, he switched careers, began manufacturing dresses—his parents
had been in the garment business in New York—and was a meteoric
success, one of the hottest things on Seventh Avenue by 1968. By then he
was also devoting considerable time to helping Grace and other clergy raise
money for Alinsky's school for organizers—Duskin had been part of the
ill-fated IFCO discussions—and thought the key was to raise $100,000
from individuals so that church leaders wouldn't be out on a limb by
themselves.

Unbeknownst to Duskin, in Chicago another intellectual-business-
man, Gordon Sherman, suddenly entered the picture. The forty-one-year-
old son of the Russian Jewish immigrant founder of the Midas Muffler
company, Sherman was no ordinary corporate president. He was also a
bagpipe-playing poet and keeper of exotic birds—indeed, he had turned the
Midas corporate headquarters on the top floor of a Loop office building
into something of an aviary, the sounds of chirping and wings flapping
everywhere as a visitor made his way from the reception area to Sherman's
office. By the spring of 1968, Sherman was already deeply involved in the
anti-Vietnam War movement—he picketed the White House with others
who belonged to Business Executives Move to End the War in Vietnam
and gave frequent antiwar speeches. Generally, the growing controversy
over U.S. foreign policy had the important subsidiary effect of draining
energy and attention away from the civil rights movement and urban
issues. But in Sherman's case, the opposite happened. His political radicali-

zation began with Vietnam, but he wanted to have an impact on something closer to home. A crystallizing moment came early in April 1968, when he and his wife, Kate, were at a near North Side party, high atop an apartment building from which Sherman could see smoke from the fires burning out of control on the West Side. That black ghetto, like many others around the country, had exploded in rage at the news of Dr. Martin Luther King's assassination. As the fires and violence continued, Mayor Daley issued a provocative order to his police department to "shoot to maim looters and shoot to kill arsonists." Sherman saw and heard enough to know that he wanted to do something about the conditions that spawned so much human misery and despair, and he quickly asked his corporate trouble-shooter to find out who was doing the best work on urban problems.

A series of phone calls led to Monsignor Jack Egan, who knew as much about Chicago politics and the poor as anybody in the city, Sherman was told. A dinner meeting was arranged at the Standard Club, the legendary German Jewish club. Sherman and his man were there, and John McKnight, Midwest director of the U.S. Civil Rights Commission and an acquaintance of Egan's. Sherman was struck by how small and fragile and pale Egan looked. Sherman had heard of Egan's heart trouble and of his political troubles, too—the new, autocratic John Cardinal Cody, ending a long tradition of progressive leadership in the archdiocese, had abolished Egan's office of urban affairs and banished the popular monsignor to Presentation parish in the old 24th Ward, not far from where Alinsky grew up. Now, as Egan sat down, he seemed impatient, out of sorts, and with a sigh and a gasp said to Sherman, "Well, what is it you'd like from me?" But when it quickly became apparent that Sherman wanted Egan's advice and was prepared to throw a couple of hundred thousand dollars in his direction, the color returned to his cheeks and the light to his eyes. "You must talk to Saul Alinsky" was Egan's recommendation.

And a week later, when he met Alinsky, Sherman was immediately captivated, swept off his feet. He loved everything about him—the acerbic-sounding name; the big, shapeless, bespectacled face, full of smiles and mischief and the improbability of it all; the promise of trouble if he backed him. "I was looking for something dramatic, something rich by its gesture and protest," Sherman says, "something that made a statement, something that bit the thumb against the ancient narrow-minded corporate mentality that is fatuously driving this globe to oblivion." Alinsky played hard to get but not too hard, saying that he needed $400,000 and that his Bay Area friends were on the verge of closing a deal out there for a training institute. But within several weeks, Sherman made a solid offer of $200,000 with the proviso that the institute be in Chicago.

When Egan heard that Sherman's money was going for the institute instead of a new organizing project, he felt double-crossed. Even though he had been badgering Alinsky for several years to set up a school of some sort, he thought a community organization on the West Side was more urgently needed. To mollify Egan, Alinsky promised that the first four trainees would be black and that he'd send them out to organize on the West Side, a promise Egan correctly believed Alinsky had no interest in keeping. And Egan wasn't the only one who was angry about the Chicago deal. Al Duskin was still beating the bushes for support on the West Coast when he heard secondhand about the Midas money. Feeling betrayed and humiliated, he dismissed Alinsky's explanations and never spoke to his hero again.

Gordon Sherman brought Alinsky to his house to meet his parents, especially his father, Nat, who had a say in dispensing the Midas money and who did not approve of his son's progressive inclinations. Indeed, the Alinsky project was the beginning of much deeper, bitter divisions between father and son, but on this night, one of the country's best-known agitators was soft-spoken, understated, and congenial.

The first public announcement of the Midas grant was made with little fanfare; there was a small ceremony in Gordon Sherman's office, which is what Alinsky preferred. That night he walked alone along the lakefront, a long walk until dawn, brooding over the transition, as if something had died instead of being born.

27

"Be Thou a Man"

"Alinsky emerges from the 1960s a man of enhanced stature," Daniel Patrick Moynihan wrote in a postmortem on the War on Poverty's Community Action Program, recalling that Alinsky's "near to perfect" prognosis should have been attended to but was not.

To his old friends, he was the same old Saul, except that he now drank Scotch instead of Bourbon and smoked Benson & Hedges deluxe instead of Dunhill's. And he had made some new friends, too. On a trip to Washington, he met the chairman of the Senate Foreign Relations Committee, J. William Fulbright of Arkansas, who had begun to oppose the Vietnam War policies of his former Senate colleague Lyndon Johnson. Alinsky approved heartily, both of Fulbright's criticism and of his courage in taking on the Democratic President. The two began meeting occasionally for lunch, and to his friends, Alinsky defended Fulbright's voting record on civil rights, which was typical for southern Senators of the period, explaining that in private Bill Fulbright had a progressive view but couldn't vote accordingly if he wanted to keep his Senate seat and continue his criticism of the war. (In a similar vein, Alinsky was privately critical of Martin Luther King when the civil-rights leader became a leading critic of the war; King, Alinsky argued, was diluting his effectiveness, and losing the support of the President, among others.)

Another new friend was Charles Merrill, a son of one of the founders of Merrill, Lynch, Pierce, Fenner & Smith. A thoughtful, quiet man, Charlie Merrill met Alinsky through the Presbyterian Church executive George Todd; Merrill supported liberal church causes and tried to persuade his fellow trustees on the Charles E. Merrill Trust to do the same, which was often not an easy task, since two of the five trustees were very

520 LET THEM CALL ME REBEL

conservative—Donald Regan, then chief executive at Merrill Lynch (later Secretary of the Treasury in the Reagan administration) and Robert McGowan, chief executive of the Safeway food chain and Merrill's brother-in-law. In fact, it took Merrill several years before he got his fellow trustees to contribute money to Alinsky's project in Kansas City—where the head of the local Merrill Lynch office was soon complaining to Regan about the trouble Alinsky was causing.

On one occasion in the summer of 1966, Alinsky took a short detour from the lecture and seminar circuit to Delano, California, where his former IAF associate, Cesar Chavez, was in the throes of his epic struggle to organize a farm workers union. For ten years, beginning in 1952 when Fred Ross knocked on Chavez's door in San Jose to see if he might be interested in attending a house meeting to discuss forming a new Community Service Organization chapter, the two men made a phenomenal team, endlessly crisscrossing the state to set up CSO chapters, which at their peak numbered more than thirty.

Chavez's rise to inspirational, legendary leader of Mexican-American farm workers had unlikely beginnings. He spent most of his childhood riding the California migrant circuit with his family, often living in tents or under bridges, going to school sporadically but dropping out for good before high school. At the time of his and Ross's first meeting he was twenty-five years old, married, and working in apricot groves, barely scratching out a living. But even as a young boy, Chavez had been unusually sensitive to the pain of racial discrimination and the immorality of the economic arrangements that had caused so much misery for his family and other Mexican-Americans. When he met Ross and discovered the CSO, a redress of these grievances suddenly became a possibility. Although Chavez initially had doubts about Ross as he would have had about any gringo, these were relatively brief; he was quickly won over not only by Ross's sincerity but by his vision of a method through which Chavez, his friends in San Jose, and Chicanos across California could gain the power to change their lives. "He did such a good job of explaining how poor people could build power that I could even taste it, I could feel it," Chavez recalled.

Soon he went on Alinsky's IAF payroll at $35 a week and became Ross's constant companion, watching and learning from his every move but still terrified when the time came for him to run his own first house meeting. For a long time, Chavez was known for his quiet, almost shy manner even as he gained confidence—and a growing reputation—as a CSO organizer. By the end of the 1950s, the CSO had chalked up a large number of significant accomplishments, exposing and fighting police brutality, school and job discrimination, inadequate housing. But in addition to protesting various forms of discrimination, the CSO became well known for its extraordinarily successful citizenship classes and voter registration campaigns—in 1960 alone, propelled in part by the appeal of John F. Kennedy's presidential campaign, the CSO registered an estimated 135,000 Mexican-Americans.

Perhaps no one has studied the work of the CSO more closely than Carl Tjerandsen, the long-time executive secretary of the Schwarzhaupt Foundation, who concludes that "for a period of fifteen years, the CSO did more to help the Mexican-American community to feel a sense of *being* something, as a prerequisite to *becoming* something more, than any other organization in California." That period came to an end, for all practical purposes, in March 1962, when Cesar Chavez announced he was quitting the CSO—and shortly thereafter announced his plans to begin a farm workers union.

Chavez had always hoped that the CSO would become a base from which to organize farm workers, but it hadn't turned out that way. Indeed, by the early 1960s, when the CSO had attained a certain stature within the Mexican-American community, the leaders of many CSO chapters were increasingly from the ranks of the middle class—small businessmen, teachers, politicians, some lawyers—and organizing farm workers and addressing issues of concern to poor Mexican-Americans were not among their highest priorities. The split along class lines, together with the CSO's long-standing financial problems, proved increasingly frustrating to Chavez (who by now was officially on the CSO payroll). Finally, at the annual CSO convention in Los Angeles, he shocked nearly everybody by resigning, walking away from what had been a historic movement, one that had become identified with him as much as with any other person, Ross included.

Up to a point, Chavez's decision to leave had Alinsky's approval, though the latter was still hopeful that the CSO could be reinvigorated. He was proud of both Chavez and Ross and what had been accomplished; indeed, during the mid-1950s, when his other work in New York and Chicago was limping along, the CSO was an exception. And it was during this period that the first woman, Dolores Huerta, joined the IAF staff. At Carl Tjerandsen's urging and a promise of more money from Schwarzhaupt, Alinsky agreed to set up "educationals"—reflective, analytical sessions for rank-and-file CSO members whose participation otherwise tended to be limited to the action program. Some of these sessions were led by the bright, energetic Huerta, who, along with Ross, would later join Chavez's quest to organize farm workers. Alinsky, however, considered that quest a quixotic one. He doubted that Chavez could organize a large mass of farm workers into a union—or, if somehow he did pull off a miracle, then the Teamsters would promptly move in to undercut him. (As subsequent events have shown, this latter surmise was not far off the mark.)

But now, in July 1966, one of Chavez's immediate problems was the word being spread by his enemies among the grape growers and the media that he was a communist, or had communist connections—and his association with Alinsky was sometimes cited as "evidence" to that effect. So, when a California State Senate fact-finding committee held a hearing in Delano to look into the farm workers' growing dispute with the Di Giorgio Corporation and other major growers, Chavez asked Alinsky to testify, to debunk not only the communist issue but also the rumors that Alinsky was the mysterious, behind-the-scenes mastermind of Chavez's United Farm Workers' Association.

Striking farm workers packed the local high school auditorium where the hearing was held, and they were on their feet cheering after Alinsky's opening barb. He had been preceded to the witness table by a local druggist who had made some wild accusations, which prompted Alinsky to tell the committee that "I'm flattered by the attention that's been given to me, as well as the statement by Mr. Marshall. I think you will understand why I would have some reservations in having a personal prescription filled in Marshall's Drug Store." He then went on to assure the committee that he had not been in contact with Chavez for a number of years, "but I have read about what he's been doing and I must admit that I have been extremely proud of him." Toward the end of the hearing, perhaps frustrated by Alinsky's ability to wrap himself in the protective moral covering provided by his Christian church support, one senator suddenly announced:

"This report has just been handed me, Mr. Alinsky. I don't know where it originated, [but it states that] several weeks ago you appeared on T.V., that you were asked if you had ever had any connection with the Communist Party and you answered, 'Yes.' Is that a correct report?"

To which Alinsky replied, with the properly sarcastic tone that primed the audience to erupt in thunderous applause, "I want to point out that I am not now, and never have had any connections with either the John Birch Society, the Ku Klux Klan, the Minute Men, the Communist Party, or the Di Giorgio Corporation."

BY THE end of the decade, Alinsky reveled in the role of sage, seer, and social critic as he crisscrossed the country lecturing on college campuses. In the spring of 1968, he correctly predicted that a confrontation between

Mayor Daley's police in Chicago and young anti-Vietnam War demonstrators would lead to a political disaster at the Democratic National Convention that summer. Later he said that the whole ugly episode would have been avoided had Robert Kennedy been the Democratic nominee—which he would have been, Alinsky thought, with Daley's backing. With the Kennedys in charge of the convention, he said, the demonstrators would have been brought into the process, negotiated with, perhaps given a forum and a measure of recognition and legitimacy, and a confrontation would have been avoided.

But Alinsky's own relationship with student activists was uneven. His popularity was highest among the sizable segment who were pro-civil rights, opposed to the war, and often involved in Student Power or campus-reform movements where they were able to express anti-establishment sentiments close to home through their own demonstrations and sit-ins. To these students, Alinsky was something of a folk hero, spinning wonderful, funny, yet instructive stories to packed auditoriums. His speech usually began in a serious vein with Alinsky, dressed conservatively in a dark suit and tie, sounding like a political science professor as he lectured on *The Federalist Papers* and the Founders' understanding of power and self-interest as they applied to the governing process. The American system, Alinsky continued to argue, functioned best when power was evenly distributed throughout society—and, conversely, was headed for trouble if some segments were relatively powerless. His analysis strongly implied that political stability and social justice were mutually consistent goals, a comforting thought to his largely middle-class audiences. But, of course, he also made it abundantly clear that there was no polite, painless way to change the prevailing power inequities, especially as they applied to black Americans. "Change means movement; movement means friction; friction means heat; and heat means controversy," an aphorism he delivered with appropriate emphasis on the last word. Only in the rarefied atmosphere of outer space or—he added with just the right amount of contempt—in a political science seminar on revolution, could there be movement without friction or conflict. Both the remainder of his set speech and the question-and-answer periods were peppered with stories and anecdotes to illustrate these principles and assumptions. The story about the Rochester symphony and the baked-bean dinner became a classic, and a generation later, many people who were then students recall Alinsky's telling it—only now, more often than not, their recollection is that he actually pulled the trick off rather than merely musing about it. Much the same is true with another story Alinsky invented after the fun he had with the baked-bean gambit. In its original version, he told how he had come up with a new, creative tactic for bringing a reluctant Mayor Daley to the bargaining table over a dispute with TWO. The mayor was especially proud of the newly built O'Hare International Airport, a modern symbol of Chicago's greatness. Alinsky envisioned a scene calculated to embarrass Daley. Late in the day when most airplanes were arriving and O'Hare was at its busiest, hundreds of TWO supporters would be bused to the airport, where they would proceed to tie up all of the pay toilets— to the surprise and discomfort of thousands of disembarking passengers. Of course, no such thing ever happened, although Alinsky eventually stretched the story into a version that ended up with Daley agreeing to meet and negotiate with TWO because he wanted to head off the airport demonstration.

With prudish exceptions here and there, student audiences loved these tales, and even if all of the outrageous stories about tactics were not literally true, they drove home many of Alinsky's salient points—that some of the best weapons an organizer used to fight the status quo were rudeness, ridicule, and imagination.

Alinsky's colorful tactics, irreverence, and championing of the underdog especially attracted these students, and many sought him out for advice, a task he thoroughly enjoyed. On many occasions, he would be up half the night talking and arguing, and his friend Leona Baumgartner, who was teaching at Harvard during this period, recalls a memorable night when a small group of students sat on the floor of her apartment talking with him until six in the morning, when he had to catch a plane. At Princeton, where his friend Paul Yilvasaker was teaching a seminar, Alinsky was the last to leave Yilvasaker's house at about 2 a.m., but on this occasion he had an additional reason for staying late. In the course of the evening, his cigarette had burned a hole in his host's lovely white couch and, embarrassed, he insisted that he be allowed to pay for the repairs. Yilvasaker replied, "Saul, I'm going to display that couch with pride and say, 'Saul Alinsky burned here.' "

But Alinsky was not a hero or role model to all student activists. He had virtually no influence on the most important leaders of the New Left, early leaders of Students for a Democratic Society, for example, like Tom Hayden, Todd Gitlin, Paul Booth, and Lee Webb. In many respects, they and Alinsky should have been kindred spirits, but they only occasionally even crossed paths. The early New Left emphasized the problems of apathy, indifference, and powerlessness, themes Alinsky had been expounding for twenty-five years. And by late 1963, some of SDS's best and brightest decided to switch from writing and research into action, specifically into community organizing among poor whites and blacks in Northern cities like Chicago, Cleveland, and Newark, to complement SNCC's work in the South. The new initiative was called the Economic Research and Action Project, ERAP (pronounced "EE-rap"). A generation later, Hayden, one of ERAP's prime architects, writes about the excitement of "the unprecedented event in the history of American students: the migration of hundreds, and ultimately thousands into organizing projects in impoverished communities. . . . The spirit of the effort . . . was one of transformation, from book-carrying students to American kibbutzniks dedicated to organizing the poor for power."

Sometime around the summer of 1964, Ralph Helstein, one of the few labor leaders who were interested in the emerging New Left, invited Hayden, Gitlin, and Webb to a backyard barbecue to meet Alinsky. Helstein had been very impressed with all three young men, with their intellect and commitment, and thought they and Alinsky had much in common and might even work together. Both Gitlin and Webb had read "Finding and Making Leaders," an article by Nick von Hoffman that summarized Alinsky's thoughts on indigenous neighborhood leaders. (And Webb, who had started organizing in Chicago on the North Side, spent hours of his spare time in the basement of the University of Chicago library reading the old dissertations and monographs about Chicago politics and sociology that Alinsky's professors had written in the 1920s.)

Much to Helstein's dismay, the backyard conclave did not go well, Alinsky quickly sliding into a familiar mode, dismissing their ideas and work as naïve and doomed to failure. Helstein was appalled, not because he thought Alinsky was wrong but because he was needlessly harsh. Part of what happened could be explained by Alinsky's contrariness: if Helstein thought these kids were so sharp, he'd show his friend differently. But there were real differences, too, of a kind that piqued Alinsky's ire. The young community organizers romanticized the poor and wanted to identify with them—Hayden and his cohorts in Newark not only lived in the ghetto but, for a time, lived on a welfare food budget of fifty cents a day, and Webb recalls existing on even less than that in Chicago. "Participatory democracy," a central concept of the SDS Port Huron Statement, meant something fundamentally different to Hayden and the others from what "citizen participation" meant to Alinsky. Theirs was something akin to the old town-meeting democracy, where everybody speaks his piece, consensus is the goal, and leadership and hierarchy are resisted, while Alinsky's "organization of organizations" approach put a premium on strong leadership, structure, and centralized decision-making. Apart from the serious differences over process, these New Left leaders were not content with the goal of merely enabling the outsiders to become insiders; they wanted a different quality to the inside. While Alinsky himself was a harsh critic of "our materialistic, sanitized, Madison Avenue-dominated society," he was also adamant that effective organizing had to begin with "the world as it is"—and in the here and now, he told the young radicals sarcastically, what the poor want is a share of the so-called decadent, bourgeois, middle-class life that the SDS kids were so eager to reject.

The backyard bust at the Helsteins' was, more or less, the beginning of Alinsky's ambivalent, off-and-on attempt to relate to—and court—the student generation of "1968." Even with the early SDS leaders, Alinsky was sometimes on the same side of a policy debate. Gitlin recalls one such time in April 1966 at Dartmouth College, where he and Alinsky appeared on a panel discussion about the future of the Peace Corps with Corps advocates like Frank Mankiewicz, Harris Wofford, and other liberals who tried to align themselves and the Corps with "participatory democracy," "justice," and the glory of "revolution." After a heavy round of rich rhetoric, Alinsky began a no-nonsense counterattack—"I suppose after all that I'll sound like a primitive slob"—arguing that the last thing in the world the Peace Corps was about was fomenting revolution, because it would never be allowed to meddle in the affairs, say, of the United Fruit Company in Central America. What was needed in Central America and other Third World countries was land reform, Alinsky argued, and perhaps the best that the American government could do toward that end was to clamp down at home on exploitative American-based multinational corporations.

ERAP's focus on community organizing and poverty was short-lived, for its efforts were soon diverted to the growing antiwar movement as American military involvement in Vietnam escalated. Of this shift, Hayden writes of a "missed opportunity, a road tragically not taken. . . . Had the nation been able to focus on its internal agenda, students might have triumphed as catalysts to channel the frustrations of poverty into constructive reform. Instead the cities, and soon the campuses, were lit by what James Baldwin forecast as 'the fire next time.' "

Chicago was one such city; the West Side ghetto riot after Martin Luther King's assassination was followed four months later by pitched battles along South Michigan Avenue near Alinsky's office as antiwar demonstrators and police clashed while the Democrats held their national convention at the International Amphitheatre in the old Back of the Yards neighborhood. The antiwar movement came to Chicago because it was Democratic President Lyndon Johnson's policies that had escalated the war—policies which had so divided his own party that Johnson decided not to seek renomination. And now Johnson could not even attend his farewell convention because his very appearance would be divisive. Even without Johnson's presence, local, state, and federal officials were bracing for the worst: on the eve of the convention National Guard and U.S. Army troops were placed on alert and soon moved into the city itself. The Amphitheatre was a virtual armed camp. Violence had not been inevitable, but Mayor Daley, determined not to give an inch of his city to the antiwar protesters, played into the hands of those who wanted to provoke a police overreaction. Leading up to convention week, he had refused to provide permits for rallies or to suspend the nightly curfew so that young protesters could camp out in Lincoln Park. And Chicago authorities were primed to believe the wildest rumors (one was that the city's water supply would be spiked with LSD) and the most inflated predictions (an anticipated 100,000 demonstrators turned out to be about a tenth the size, if that). The demonstrators who actually showed up were a varied lot, ranging from earnest, clean-cut college students who had worked in the presidential primary campaign of antiwar candidate Eugene McCarthy to the long-haired, sandaled hippies and Yippies. The Yippies—for Youth International Party— were essentially a put-on, a small band that "roared" into Chicago the week before the convention, led by guerrilla-theater mischief-makers Abbie Hoffman and Jerry Rubin, who brought with them Pigasus, a live hog they said was the Yippies' presidential nominee.

The battles between police and protesters began in Lincoln Park over the weekend before the convention, and grew in scope and intensity on Monday and Tuesday nights, police beating and chasing protesters on North Side streets, the protesters in turn taunting the police with chants of "Pigs!" and "Sieg Heil!" But the biggest, bloodiest confrontation occurred on Wednesday night, as Vice President Hubert Humphrey was about to become the Democratic presidential nominee, when demonstration leaders began to march south on Michigan Avenue. Their original plan was to march all the way to the Amphitheatre, but they got only as far as the intersection of Michigan and Balboa. There the police waded into the crowd, nightsticks flailing, running down their prey and beating them in full view of network television cameras sending out the violent images for the nation to see. Many of the police were out of control, clubbing anybody within reach, journalists and other observers, even invading the Conrad Hilton's Haymarket Lounge through a street-level window that was kicked in. After the convention, an independent investigation charged that a "police riot" had occurred, a judgment that played well among antiwar activists and liberals but not, of course, with Mayor Daley and— more importantly in terms of political consequences—not with white middle- and working-class Americans who made up an important part of the Democrats' New Deal coalition. If their choice was between Yippies taunting the police and chanting "Ho-Ho Ho Chi Minh" and Mayor Daley calling for law and order and defending the American flag, then there was really nothing to agonize over. When the civil rights movement—or at least the issue of racism in its many forms—moved to the North, the beginning of the end of the Democratic coalition was underway; by 1968, the New Left, with its simultaneous embrace of cultural rebellion and political protest, speeded up the process.

Saul Alinsky and Irene McInnis were on South Michigan Avenue on those tense, tumultuous nights of convention week, usually in front of the Conrad Hilton, where journalists and others gathered. One night, Alinsky and the writer Louis Lomax walked across the street into Grant Park to talk to the students, many of whom felt defeated and demoralized. They had worked for McCarthy—or Bobby Kennedy—but even though their efforts had helped knock Johnson out of the presidential race, here they were being tear-gassed and beaten while Johnson's Vice President, who supported his Vietnam policies, was being nominated in the Amphitheatre. Alinsky was sympathetic to a point, urging them to go back home and begin organizing so that next time *they* would be inside the convention hall wielding the power. But in the months that followed, he was also highly critical of many student activists who, he felt, "aren't interested in changing society. Not yet. They're concerned with doing their own thing, finding themselves. They want revelation, not revolution." He was not amused, either, by the street-theater antics of Yippies Hoffman and Rubin, whose attempt at humor and ridicule reminded some of Alinsky himself. When a television interviewer asked Alinsky to hazard a guess as to what the two Yippies would be doing ten years later, Alinsky shrugged and said, "They'll probably be in a vaudeville act someplace." And by 1970, after the newly notorious Weatherman faction of the SDS engaged in a series of violent street demonstrations and bombings, Alinsky was unsparing in his criticism, charging that violent acts were scaring and alienating the middle-class majority. "Any serious radical organization would have executed the Weatherman bombers as a matter of course. The worst form of social treason is to stir up a reaction that is more damaging to you than to your enemy. The Weathermen should be getting paid by the extreme right for the work they do."

For all his popularity among some student activists, Alinsky was clearly an outsider during the demonstrations in Chicago. And despite the immaturity, narcissism, and naïveté of so many young activists, there was also a great amount of idealism and energy that was impossible to ignore. Soon after the Democratic convention, Alinsky phoned Staughton Lynd, a gentle Quaker and prominent antiwar activist who had taught history at Yale but was now living in Chicago. Lynd had been active in the civil rights movement in the South and had become a controversial figure when he—and Tom Hayden and Herbert Aptheker—traveled to Hanoi in December 1965, met with North Vietnamese leaders, and reported that they were willing to pursue peace talks, contrary to the Johnson administration's portrayal of the North Vietnamese communists as intransigent and ruthless.

Alinsky, who envisioned Lynd as a bridge to the younger generation, now offered him a job at the new IAF training institute. (Coincidentally, in the mid-1940s Lynd's father Robert served briefly on the IAF board when he was a sociology professor at Columbia. He and his wife, Helen, were co-authors of *Middletown,* the classic study of the community power structure of Muncie, Indiana.) Lynd accepted Alinsky's offer, and he stayed at the institute for about a year as one of the three full-time "faculty," along with Ed Chambers and Dick Harmon. The institute was housed in a suite of offices on North Michigan Avenue, six blocks from Alinsky's. But Alinsky himself appeared only sporadically. Before Gordon Sherman gave him the start-up money, Alinsky warned him that he wouldn't be around much, that Chambers would be running the school on a day-to-day basis, all of which was fine with Sherman. He understood perfectly not only that Alinsky preferred the public stage to the classroom but that he had reached the point in his career where his most important contribution was in shaping the public dialogue and legitimizing his ideas and concepts.

Sherman's Midas Muffler grant was followed by another from the Rockefeller Foundation for $225,000. By the early 1970s, Alinsky was clearly attracting a new, "respectable" following—a two-page *Time* essay, "Radical Saul Alinsky: Prophet of Power to the People," was typical. "It is not too much to argue that American democracy is being altered by Alinsky's ideas," the *Time* essayist noted approvingly. Might all of this new establishment acclaim become a corrupting influence on him? a questioner kiddingly asked Alinsky after his Smithsonian Institution address on social protest in December 1970. "For one thing, I haven't been fashionable so very long," he began, warming up to the challenge of an appropriate retort. "But you know you're in trouble when they begin giving cocktail parties for you. You go in there and everyone comes up to you with a big smile, and you begin to smell something is wrong. What you have to do is piss on the floor. Then they throw you out and you can begin all over again somewhere else."

Alinsky viewed the training institute as a great experiment, in some respects no less so than the Back of the Yards Neighborhood Council was in the summer of 1939. Before Gordon Sherman walked into his life, somebody asked Alinsky what he would do with, say, $4 million if the churches decided to throw such a wad in his direction. Train organizers, was his answer, for he now believed that the biggest obstacle to creating a critical mass of popular participation was no longer money but the lack of skilled organizers. He also finally admitted, although he didn't advertise it widely, that he had been wrong about his career-long insistence that after three years local leaders should be able to make it on their own. In a notebook he kept of thoughts and observations about the new institute, he wrote, "This did not work out." Alinsky envisioned two kinds of students at the institute, those who would return to their own communities with enhanced skills and others, a smaller number, who might become professional organizers. "The reason for the training institute," he later wrote in a statement of purpose, "is because of the appalling dearth of persons who know how to organize in and for a free society."

The first trainees began arriving early in 1969—young men and women recently out of college; seminarians and other clergy who had been in the civil rights and antiwar movements; neighborhood activists and community organizers. Alinsky's plan was to have about forty full-time students who would take twelve to fifteen months of intensive training while others would stay for shorter periods ranging from two-week seminars to three or four months. A trainee's tuition was usually paid by his or her sponsoring organization. If anybody thought their stay at this school was going to be like their college experience, they were disabused of the notion quickly, usually during a series of admission interviews with, first, Alinsky, then Chambers and the next day Harmon.

One prospect, Susan Kellock, who had been sent by the National Student Association, remembers going into Alinsky's office for her first interview. "Why do you want to organize?" he asked innocently. Her earnest, lengthy reply was to the effect that she wanted to bring people together, work at the grass roots, create better living conditions. When she finished, Alinsky glared at her, his deep voice getting louder as he repeated: "Why do you want to organize, goddamnit?" She later discovered that the correct answer was one word: "power."

For those who survived the admissions test, what followed was no less tough, tense, and demanding. Alinsky half bragged that there would be many "washouts"—and there were. Generally, the training consisted of readings, discussion, and fieldwork that was similar to what von Hoffman and Lester Hunt had been exposed to. The trainees read Alinsky's biography of John L. Lewis and T. Harry Williams's study of Huey Long—and spent hours discussing how each had accumulated and used power. They read *The Federalist Papers,* H. L. Mencken, Mark Twain, Reinhold Niebuhr, and even Don Marquis's *archy and mehitabel,* and talked about the many faces and forms of self-interest. They studied Thucydides' *History of the Peloponnesian War,* especially Chapter 7, and role-played a negotiating session between the Athenians and the Melians. They were told to observe a meeting of the Chicago City Council and the way Mayor Daley ran it—Alinsky had a great deal of respect for Daley's organizational genius, if for little else about him. They were sent out to various neighborhoods to analyze how they worked—to discover the real leaders, power patterns, and issues—and every night they would phone in reports, which were tape-recorded and transcribed the next day. Several times a week each trainee would meet with Chambers, Harmon, or Lynd to discuss these reports—and Chambers, in particular, could be very rough in the manner of a Marine drill sergeant at boot camp, screaming about a trainees' dumb mistake or missed opportunity.

But since Alinsky believed that the best learning was accomplished by doing, most of the trainees' time was eventually spent in the field on real organizing projects. In Chicago, the biggest project soon centered on the issue of air pollution, which had its genesis in articles by Chicago *Daily News* columnist Mike Royko. In the summer of 1969, the city had been suffering through days of breath-choking inversions—a "blanket of floating filth," Royko called it. Although the poisonous air sent a number of older residents to the hospital, Mayor Daley denied there was a serious problem, to which Alinsky shot back: "What in the hell does he breathe with, his ears?" Royko wrote a column calling on Alinsky to organize a city-wide fight against pollution: "He is what this city needs to wrestle with the polluters and the politicians who let them get away with it." When Alinsky agreed to organize the anti-pollution drive, Royko printed a post office box number in his column, inviting all those who wished to join to send in their names and addresses.

And that is how the Campaign Against Pollution (CAP) began, with Alinsky's organizers and trainees fanning out over the city to contact the people who had written. (Interestingly, the first chairman of CAP was the talented Paul Booth, the former SDS leader, who was now living in Hyde Park.) Targeting steel companies and utilities, CAP was soon charging that the Cook County tax assessor's office had undervalued various corporate facilities, costing the county millions in revenues, and that environmental regulations were not being enforced. Eventually, the focus of CAP began to shift to an issue that had even greater organizing potential: the proposed billion-dollar Crosstown Expressway. Although it was a favorite project of

Mayor Daley and powerful labor unions and contractors, thousands of homeowners and hundreds of small businesses who were in the path of the project would be uprooted, and they were violently opposed. The Campaign Against Pollution became the Citizens Action Program to stop the Crosstown, a campaign which resulted in a great victory but one that Saul Alinsky was not there to savor.

"IF I'M LUCKY, I'll have ten good years left," Alinsky said when he turned sixty, not long before his new book was published in 1971. The book itself had been ten years in the making, the overly long gestation period being the result of his inability to shut himself off from virtually every other activity he found less distasteful than writing. For a number of years, the working title was *The Morality of Power.* Then he seized upon *Rules for Revolution,* and planned an opening line that read: "Machiavelli wrote *The Prince* as a handbook for the Haves on how to hold on to their power; my book is for the Have-Nots on how to take it away." Although that line made it into the final version nearly intact, the title became *Rules for Radicals,* with an intriguingly oxymoronic subtitle: *A Pragmatic Primer for Realistic Radicals.* The passage of time also had an effect on the focus and tone of the final manuscript: Alinsky now saw the young generation of activists as his primary audience and spoke to them as a teacher and friend, although not without some scolding.

> The revolutionary force today has two targets, moral as well as material. Its young protagonists are one moment reminiscent of the idealistic early Christians, yet they also urge violence and cry, "Burn the system down!" They have no illusions about the system, but plenty of illusions about the way to change our world. It is to this point that I have written this book. These words are written in desperation, partly because it is what they do and will do that will give meaning to what I and the radicals of my generation have done with our lives.

Alinsky saw *Rules for Radicals* as a historic book, in part as he had *Reveille for Radicals,* following in the great American tradition of Thomas Paine, Samuel Adams, and other early radicals. More specifically, he also saw this new work as, first, bridging a gap caused by "the Joe McCarthy holocaust." The young people who are now the vanguard, he wrote, "had to start almost from scratch. . . . Few of us [radicals] survived [McCarthyism] and of those there were even fewer whose understanding and insights had developed beyond the dialectical materialism of orthodox Marxism.

My fellow radicals who were supposed to pass the torch of experience and insights to a new generation just were not there." Second, the book was intended to spotlight the historic realities of power in postwar America: rather suddenly, in not much more than a generation, the United States had become predominantly middle-class and that meant a major share of political power was in the hands of the middle class: "[E]ven if all the low-income parts of our population were organized—all the blacks, Mexican-Americans, Puerto Ricans, and Appalachian poor whites—if through some genius of organization they were all united in a coalition, it would not be powerful enough to get significant, basic, needed changes." Without the help of the white middle class, Alinsky wrote, the FIGHT organization in Rochester wouldn't have gotten off the ground nor would it have been as successful. He also cited Cesar Chavez's successful grape boycott, which forced the growers to bargain with Chavez's new union, the United Farm Workers. Ironically, Alinsky thought the grape boycott was a bad idea when he first heard that his former student was going to organize it; he didn't think you could get enough middle-class Americans to stop eating grapes, picket supermarket chains, and pressure Congress, but Chavez did.

Alinsky's "discovery" of the middle class as the focal point of a new strategy for social change was, to a significant degree, a matter of some necessity. With the advent of Black Power, Alinsky didn't really have any other place to go. By 1970, he had even conceded publicly that "all whites should get out of the black ghettos. It's a stage we have to go through." But even if his new interest in a middle-class strategy was driven by necessity and convenience, he was able to make a pretty good case for it. Although he was still interested in training black and Hispanic organizers to work in minority communities, in *Rules for Radicals* he appealed to middle-class activists and radicals "on or off the campus" not to forsake the advantages of their cultural experience.

> [They] must make a complete turnabout. With rare exceptions, our activists and radicals are products of and rebels against our middle-class society. They have stigmatized it as materialistic . . . imperialistic, war-mongering, brutalized, and corrupt. They are right . . . but it is useless self-indulgence for an activist to put his past behind him. Instead, he should realize the priceless value of his middle-class experience. His middle-class identity, his familiarity with the values and problems, are invaluable for organization of "his own people."

He was not merely interested in organizing the middle class so that their organizations could form alliances with the poor. He now believed that much of the middle class felt an increasing sense of powerlessness, in spite of being relatively well-off materially. He was deeply concerned and troubled that the lower middle class, threatened and angered by the civil rights movement and the cultural rebellion of the privileged young, was being lost to the conservatives and the right wing. They must be worked with, he wrote, "as one would work with any other part of our population—with respect, understanding, and sympathy. . . . To reject them is to lose them by default. Even if you cannot win over the lower middle class, at least parts of them must be persuaded to where there is at least communication, then to a series of partial agreements and a willingness to abstain from hard opposition as changes take place." The rest of the middle class, Alinsky wrote, "with few exceptions, reside in suburbia, living in illusions of partial escape. Being more literate, they are even more lost. Nothing seems to make sense," as many of their children have rejected their values and the good life is no longer so clear.

Typically, Alinsky would not predict exactly what form and direction a new middle-class organization would take—he was too empirical for that. "The chance for organization for action on pollution, inflation, Vietnam, violence, race, taxes is all about us," he wrote, making it clear that he was thinking of new organizations based on a community of interests rather than on a geographical basis. For more than a decade, as people scattered to the suburbs, he had talked about the declining importance of the old geographical neighborhood where people had lived, worked, and played. He also speculated about tactics, intrigued with using stock proxies—"Proxies for People"—to raise issues of national importance, and he began to fantasize filling Yankee Stadium with 50,000 dissident shareholders who would shout down management's claim that it had enough "silent" proxies to win. All of this was to be done methodically, slowly, because "tactics must begin within the experience of the middle class, accepting their aversion to rudeness, vulgarity, and conflict." Nonetheless, one key to mobilizing this group was "to excite their imagination with tactics that can introduce drama and adventure into the tedium of middle-class life."

Rules for Radicals received much attention when it was published. Like *Reveille for Radicals,* the book had long-term appeal, and as with his first book, the reviews tended to be favorable among mainstream and liberal critics, while leftists were less enthusiastic. Writing in *The New York Review of Books,* Christopher Lasch acknowledged that Alinsky had invented "a new political type—the professional organizer whose constituents are not workers but citizens," and had developed methods so that "exploited people overcome the habit of deference and feelings of helplessness engendered by the vastness and impenetrability of modern society." But Lasch also questioned "Alinsky's habit of setting himself limited objec-

tives [that] causes him to overestimate the importance of his achievement,"
and cited as a case in point Alinsky's new interest in using stock proxies
as a means to democratize corporate America. A more "revolutionary"
strategy, Lasch observed, "would attempt to put the corporations under
the control of not the stockholders, but of those who work in them. The
community organizer thinks of his constituents almost automatically as
consumers. This is at once his strength and weakness." But perhaps
Lasch's most fundamental concern was over Alinsky's celebration of democracy as process—or as Alinsky had written twenty-five years earlier in
Reveille for Radicals: "The objective is never an end in itself." This analysis
led Lasch to conclude that Alinsky, "having divested his movement of any
suspicion of 'ideology,' having substituted 'citizens' for 'workers' and interests for classes, and having exalted process over objectives, was free to
define 'participation' itself as the objective of community organization—of
politics in general."

Harsher, even bitter criticism came from the New Leftist Todd Gitlin,
who attacked Alinsky for having "no transcendent vision of a society
worth living in," no ideology. In the absence of a truly revolutionary
critique "his approach, like the CIO's, can lead only to the integration of
insurgent groups into the lower reaches of the political system." By now
these were familiar criticisms that Alinsky had dealt with to his satisfaction
over the years, although he almost never took such criticism with equanim-
ity. But he flew into a rage over another passage in Gitlin's review in *The
Nation:* "The most remarkable revelation of this book is blunt enough:
Alinsky admits that his methods have engendered 'more failures than
successes.' " He fired off a letter of protest to *The Nation*'s editor, Carey
McWilliams, an old friend, who two months earlier had written a brief
bouquet of a review, noting that Alinsky was "this country's leading hell-
raiser—the polite term is community organizer—who has set down some
of the rules of the game. No one has had more experience or has been more
successful at it than Alinsky." Alinsky now protested to McWilliams that
one of his favorite periodicals "should provide the setting for a personal
smear job masquerading as a book review by one Todd Gitlin," zeroing in
on the passage about "more failures than successes," which Gitlin had
quoted, he said, out of context. In his book, Alinsky had used the phrase
to characterize his experience in training new organizers, not as an evaluation of his methods or projects. Alinsky continued: "The balance of [Git-
lin's] piece is corroborative evidence of one of the theses in *Rules for
Radicals* that one can only communicate within the experience of the
other, and since pragmatism is completely outside of Gitlin's experience
as evidenced by his record of complete failure as well as an 'ideology' fifty

years behind the times, it is clear that there was not and could not be any communication."

Alinsky was indebted to two people in particular for helping him finish his book before time ran out. His secretary, Georgia Harper, not only provided the usual support services when it came to refining and retyping the manuscript, no small task in itself, but for nine years also did the work of two or more people with exceptional competence and dedication—on one occasion she was in a hospital recovery room after surgery when she was handed a phone; it was the boss, calling from the airport about next week's schedule, urgent letters that had to be sent, and so forth. To Alinsky's closest friends and associates, Georgia was his savior; they doubted that Alinsky could have survived his frenetic schedule and trying personal life without her.

But perhaps her single most delicate duty was to act as a buffer between Alinsky and his mother, Sarah, probably the only person in the country who could strike fear into her son's heart. Sarah was very proud of her son, and although she knew he was famous, she wasn't quite sure why. For many years, she would call one of Saul's friends and ask him to explain what Saul did for a living, which was not an easy question to answer. When Sarah wasn't boasting about Saul to others, she was kvetching that he didn't spend enough time with her—the key word being "enough." For his part, Saul felt very protective about Sarah and knew how proud she was of him, but Sarah was much easier to love at a distance. So when she phoned his office, Georgia would sometimes lie that Saul wasn't in, but that, unfortunately for Georgia, was not the end of the conversation. One of Saul's stratagems in satisfying his mother's demands for his attention was to have Georgia address a batch of envelopes to Sarah, which he would fill with brief notes composed before he left on a business trip, mailing them back to her from his various stops around the country.

Rules for Radicals was dedicated to Irene, who helped Saul think through and reorganize parts of the book. In 1969, Saul and Jean went through an amicable divorce, but he felt guilty about it and talked to close friends constantly about his feelings. Even after he married Irene in 1971, he continued to arrange his schedule so that he was in Carmel as much as possible to look after Jean, whose multiple sclerosis had reached something of a plateau. But he was deeply in love with Irene, and their times together—she continued to live in Boston while he kept his Chicago apartment—were precious. They shared many weekends and took vacations to the rhythms of her teaching schedule—a winter holiday in a New Hampshire cabin; a spring trip to the Smokies, where Saul and Helene used to go; a summer stay on the Maine coast, just north of Boothbay Harbor, where they put the finishing touches on his book, away from the usual distractions. He valued her opinions about new ideas he was working into speeches, and she was touched by his tenderness and sweet surprises, like discovering one morning that he had drawn their initials and an infinity sign on the bathroom mirror. And they laughed together, even occasionally at Saul's expense. Irene, who had a wonderful sense of humor, teased him about being a magnificent failure when he grumbled about the deficiencies that had set in at FIGHT or some other project after promising starts. But more often the laughs centered on his stories or audacious one-liners or the periodic stunts he pulled in restaurants, which Irene often found more amusing after her initial embarrassment passed. (One evening at an intimate French restaurant on the East Side of New York, they were dining with friends of Jacques Maritain whom they had just met. Soon a very proper, tuxedoed waiter brought the wine, poured a small sample for Alinsky, and waited stiffly for his approval, having no reason to suspect that he had just served a real-life counterpart of the Three Stooges. Alinsky picked up the glass, sniffed the bouquet, took a sip, tilted his head back, and began to gargle.)

Saul and Irene's delayed honeymoon was a tour of Asia and the Philippines, thanks to George Todd, the director of urban programs for the United Presbyterian Church. Partly through Todd's efforts, Alinsky's ideas on social change and community organization had spread through church networks to a number of other countries, but they were most visible in South Korea and the Philippines. Herb White, the man who helped bring Alinsky to Rochester, had been active in both countries—first in South Korea, where, working with local Catholic and Protestant clergy, he trained organizers, setting the stage for an important new movement among the urban poor in the 1970s. After two years, White moved on to the Philippines, where he helped start a community organization in one of Asia's most notorious squatter districts, the Tondo Foreshoreland of Manila's North Harbor. Todd was excited about these new developments and had been trying for more than a year to persuade Alinsky to see them firsthand, but Alinsky wasn't particularly interested in movements beyond American shores, even ones influenced by his ideas. The lone exception was South Africa, where the garish evil of apartheid attracted his attention. (From time to time he dropped mysterious, somber hints to friends that something might be in the works there involving him, but nothing ever happened.) When Todd suggested that he and Irene make the Asian trip together, Alinsky agreed, and he met with clergy and young organizers in five countries, coming away very impressed with their courage, resourcefulness, and imagination in the face of police-state harassment, imprisonment, and torture. In a final summing-up session in the Philippines, he was very humble, encouraging them to carry on and learn from each other.

Before they married, Saul again raised the issue of their age difference, telling Irene that maybe he was being unfair because there was always the chance she'd suffer the pain and sadness of being a young widow. As for himself, he had talked about the prospect of dying with the same kind of swagger he affected when talking about the merely mortal enemies he had conquered. "Death has not been a stranger to me," he told Marion Sanders in the *Harper's* interviews.

> And I have learned one lesson, I learned it in my belly, the astonishing lesson that I wasn't going to live forever. Now this may sound like a very simple thing, but there are very few people who realize that they're going to die someday. Intellectually they know it, but they go on saving for their old age and so forth. After the full realization, on a gut basis, that I was going to die, my whole life changed. I was confronted with the question "What's the meaning of my life, since I'm here for just so long a period?" I don't ever expect to be able to answer it. But I know that once you reach that point of accepting your own death, you no longer care much whether you're important or not.

Earlier, when he shared these same "truths" with Ralph Helstein in a late-night bull session, it led to a big argument. Helstein, assuming one of his favorite roles as logician provocateur, challenged Alinsky to discuss death on a philosophical basis. "But all I'd get from Saul," he recalls, "is 'I'm not afraid of it because I know I'm going to die.' So I said, 'Saul, anybody with any sense accepts that; it's prima facie—you're born, you live, you die, and that's the way it works. Death is as much a part of life as being born is.' " And when Alinsky replied, "You've got to feel it in your gut," Helstein elicited a sizable explosion when he asked, with feigned curiosity, "Well, Saul, tell me how it feels in your gut."

It was not the certitude of death that most fascinated Alinsky. As with any good dramatist, his preoccupation was with how one died, and he had been working on an appropriate finish to his own story, a grand climax that would be in the American tradition, violent and heroic. In 1966, for example, he had accepted a speaking invitation in Shreveport, Louisiana, and soon there were death threats serious enough to alarm Irene. But he went anyway, later saying that it would not have surprised him if the Ku Klux Klan had bumped him off. On the basis of principle alone, any self-respecting Imperial Wizard should have been violently outraged by Alinsky's unforgivably contemptuous behavior. There was the time in 1968 when he arrived at a small North Carolina airport to lead a seminar at the nearby Johnson C. Smith Presbyterian seminary and was greeted by a phalanx of hooded Klan demonstrators—only none of them recognized Alinsky, who took advantage of his temporary anonymity, walking quietly behind one of the demonstrators and shouting in his ear, "Boo!" At the Houston airport, another Klan greeting party in full regalia picketed his arrival, and when a newspaper reporter on the scene asked Alinsky for his reaction, he said dryly, "It looks like a department store had a white sale." Klansmen followed him to his speech, where one of them hollered out that Alinsky was responsible for the decline of white power in the United States. Alinsky walked to the edge of the stage and, glaring at the man who had just spoken, explained to the audience that he had studied anthropology at college and was familiar with the physical characteristics of the various racial classifications, and he found it ironic that if you looked carefully at this man who had just spoken—if you looked at the structure of his head, especially the broad nose and wide nostrils—then you were certain to conclude he was a Negro.

Nor was Alinsky gunned down by the radical right-wing Minute Men, although the FBI warned him in San Francisco in the spring of 1968 that it would be prudent to stay out of Orange County, in southern California, where he had a speech scheduled.

Instead, death came quickly but nonviolently on June 12, 1972. Alinsky's stepsister, Kay Mann, was watching the network evening news in her Los Angeles apartment when she was stunned to see Saul's picture on the screen and hear the report: "Saul Alinsky, the social activist, died today of an apparent heart attack on a street corner in Carmel, California." This is not the way Saul would have preferred it, not the ending he would have written, not such a prosaic death. And in Carmel, of all places! That postcard-perfect oasis where not a speck of the world's troubles was to be found on the soft, white beaches caressed each day by gentle Pacific waters.

Jack Egan heard the news on a car radio as he was driving from Chicago to the University of Notre Dame campus. He pulled off the road and called Nick von Hoffman, and soon they were both crying. There wasn't much in the way of detail—Saul had been visiting Jean, had gone to a bank, and then collapsed outside.

There was no funeral—Saul's body was cremated—but Ralph Helstein organized a memorial service at KAM-Isaiah Israel, the Reform Jewish temple in the Kenwood section of Chicago where he had been a member and, in the mid-1950s, had persuaded Saul to join—for only a year, as it turned out—when the liberal rabbi, Jacob Weinstein, whom Alinsky respected, was under attack by a faction within the congregation. Although the eulogists—they included Helstein, Jack Egan, Nick von Hoffman—spoke the customary words of praise, their sincerity was also easily evident. "I say to myself, 'You have lost the best friend you have ever had,' " said George Shuster, former president of Hunter College, assistant to the president of the University of Notre Dame, and president of the IAF board. "There never has been anybody, anywhere, who was so deeply committed to the cause of democracy in the United States," he continued, and then added with a twinkle: "But I wonder, what happens to his vocabulary when he arrives at the gate of St. Peter? When I say to his family that I am going to pray for him, they may say that is totally ridiculous. Nevertheless, I am going to try." Joe Meegan, recalling how they first met in the Back of the Yards, said his Jewish friend had "made the Catholic Church more catholic—actually universal, which is what it is supposed to be." And Rabbi Weinstein eulogized that "Saul Alinsky was like a cactus pear: he was prickly outside but sweet within."

At the Chicago City Council, a motion was offered by one of the liberal, independent aldermen to name a park for Alinsky—somebody had already placed a homemade sign on a tree in a small vacant North Side lot that proclaimed it "The Saul Alinsky People's Park." But Mayor Daley exercised his power, and the motion was referred to a committee where other noble ideas were also buried.

In the mid-1960s, Alinsky had written the IAF board that in the event of his sudden death, he hoped they would appoint Ed Chambers as his successor, which the board did. Just before Alinsky died, Chambers and Dick Harmon had persuaded him to hold a retreat at the end of the summer at which the three of them, along with a number of young organizers, clergy, and citizen-leaders, could begin to develop a strategy for the future. They went ahead with the retreat, which Chambers and a new generation of organizers would later refer to as the beginning of the modern IAF, a new era in which Alinsky's methods and insights were refined and adapted to a changing social environment.

"THE EPITAPH for Saul Alinsky," Chicago columnist Irv Kupcinet offered, "should read: 'Here lies the man who antagonized more people than any contemporary American.' He would consider it high praise." Yes, he could have appreciated that, but in the final analysis, Saul David Alinsky was a serious man, a driven man, ferociously determined to establish his self-worth and dignity, the highest of democratic ideals. His friend Robert Maynard Hutchins once wrote that "the dignity of man is an ideal worth fighting for and dying for," and Alinsky intuitively knew the truth of that. His defiance of every power that robbed poor people of their dignity was ultimately an act of preserving his own. Where and how this all started is, of course, not easy to untangle, but the thread of a childhood story Alinsky recalled not long before he died is perhaps near to the spiritual core.

When he was twelve years old and living on the old West Side, one day a friend was jumped and beaten by three kids from the nearby Polish neighborhood west of Crawford Avenue. "So naturally we went on the hunt and found a couple of Poles," Alinsky remembered. "We were merrily beating them up when the police suddenly appeared and arrested all of us." The boys were taken to the police station, where their mothers soon appeared, screaming as to how the boys had disgraced their families and would be punished when they got home.

But Alinsky's mother first took her son to their rabbi, and the rabbi lectured him about how wrong he was. Young Sollie defended himself. " 'They beat my friend up,' I said. 'So we beat them up. That's the American way. It's also in the Old Testament: an eye for an eye, a tooth for a tooth. Beat the hell out of them. That's what everybody does.' The rabbi answered, 'You think you're a man because you do what everybody does. Now I want to tell you something the great Rabbi Hillel said: "Where there are no men, be thou a man." I want you to remember that.' "

"I've never forgotten it," Alinsky said, a lifetime later.

Epilogue

Saul Alinsky's legacy is alive and well nearly a generation after his death, but the health of American democracy is more problematic. "The death of democracy," Robert Maynard Hutchins warned during the somnambulent 1950s, "is not likely to come by assassination from ambush. It will be a slow extinction from indifference, ignorance, and apathy." Now, early in the third century of American democracy, Hutchins's old words have a disturbing freshness.

Unprecedented numbers of people—only by the narrowest of definitions can they be thought of as citizens—are disconnected, unengaged, and on the sidelines. Perhaps the simplest barometer of democracy's decline is the decline in voting—"the first duty of democracy," as President Lyndon Johnson called it in 1964 during the historic struggle for stronger voting-rights laws. But since the 1960s voter participation in the United States has been on a downward course, hitting a sixty-four-year low in the 1988 presidential election, when only half the eligible voters bothered to go to the polls.

Citizens who don't even vote are not likely to be participants in the other areas of community life Alinsky cared so much about—in deliberations about the quality of schools, the environment, housing, and health care. Decisions will continue to be made, of course, but, contrary to his passionate hopes, they reflect the participation of only a very limited segment of the population. As a nation, we are moving closer to a government of half the people, by half the people, and for half the people. And although voter participation has decreased among both white- and blue-collar Americans, the dropout rate is most pronounced among the less affluent. It is no wonder that federal government decisions in the 1980s—in the areas of taxes and social welfare policies, for example—were skewed in favor of the more affluent and to the disadvantage of lower-income Americans.

Although there is no consensus as to why millions of Americans have abandoned the democratic process at both the local and national levels, there is a familiar litany of possible causes ranging from cynicism and disillusionment associated with the Vietnam War and Watergate, to the rise of well-heeled special interests corrupting the electoral process with an endless flow of campaign contributions, and the pernicious influence of television which is turning us into a nation of couch potatoes. Cited less often but perhaps as important as any other factor is the decline in the mediating institutions about which Alinsky knew so much. It is no mere coincidence that the decline in participatory democracy parallels the atrophy of labor unions, political parties, and other voluntary organizations— organizations that once mobilized and educated their constituencies about political issues and candidates and, in the process, gave them a sense of cohesion and purpose. As these mediating institutions have weakened or disappeared altogether, more and more people find themselves adrift in an anonymous mass urban society.

It is inevitable, perhaps, in industrial and post-industrial society that intermediary groups organized and run on democratic principles should be in short supply. But even the most cursory calculation leads to the inescapable conclusion that the current democratic landscape is dangerously barren, that the democratic infrastructure is in need of repair and refurbishing. Indeed, comparable conditions in the late 1930s and '40s led Alinsky to argue for the need of "People's Organizations."

That is why the work of Alinsky's disciples and others doing similar work is especially important today. Alinsky more than anybody deserves credit for demonstrating that community organizing could be a lifelong career and profession. Countless organizers and activists are working to build democratic citizen organizations throughout the country—indeed, a trip to almost any good-sized American city can turn up one or more community or mass-based organizations that show Alinsky's influence. Some of these focus on housing or environmental concerns, while others have an Alinsky-like multi-issue agenda.

Beyond these local, ad hoc efforts (they vary tremendously in size and effectiveness) is a second generation of Alinsky-style professionals who have formed their own training centers and, in several cases, national networks of grass-roots organizations as well. Michael Miller, who organized for Alinsky in Kansas City in the 1960s, now directs the well-regarded ORGANIZE Training Center in San Francisco. Thomas Gaudette, who also directed an Alinsky project in the 1960s, founded the Mid-American Center more than a decade ago. Gale Cincotta, one of the citizen-leaders of a community organization Gaudette organized on Chicago's West Side in the late 1960s, eventually developed her own National Training and Information Center. From that base, she has welded together National People's Action, an alliance of senior-citizen, housing, and neighborhood groups around the country that deserves much credit for forcing Congress to take action against redlining practices by banks and other lending institutions. Heather Booth, who trained briefly at Alinsky's IAF in the early 1970s, went off to establish the Midwest Academy and, later, to organize Citizen Action, now a federation of statewide organizations operating in more than twenty states. Citizen Action, which has often lobbied on utility rate issues, energy matters, and other consumer concerns, has also experimented with some success with sophisticated door-to-door canvassing in strategically selected electoral districts. At its most effective, this canvassing raises a good part of the budget for Citizen Action programs, registers people to vote, and reassures progressive candidates that they have a constituency which can be mobilized at election time.

But in many ways the most exciting and important work is being carried out by Alinsky's successors at the Industrial Areas Foundation. Ed Chambers, who has served as head man since Alinsky's death in 1972, deserves much credit for addressing and overcoming Alinsky's own conceptual shortcomings. He has assembled a cadre of talented organizers—something Alinsky was never able to do. The "modern IAF," as Chambers and his senior colleagues call it in the post-Alinsky period, is anchored by Chambers and four organizers who have been with the organization for many years. The IAF "cabinet" of Chambers, Ernesto Cortes, Arnold Graf, Larry McNeil, and Michael Gecan comprises probably the most skilled and effective creators of broad-based citizen organizations in America. In addition to these veterans, the IAF has second and third tiers of some twenty-five other men and women who have been working there for five years or longer.

This sizable stable of organizers embodies another significant change that Chambers has instituted: the IAF now maintains an ongoing relationship with every community organization it has helped to set up. No longer is it "three years and out," that overly romantic notion which even Alinsky came to see as unrealistic. The network of IAF community organizations also allows for more opportunities for more IAF organizers—and, not incidentally, gives them a measure of stability, compared to the vagabond existence that Chambers himself experienced under Alinsky. The stability of the IAF's current community organizations is also in marked contrast to a goodly number of Alinsky's own projects. For example, in San Antonio, Citizens Organized for Public Service (COPS), often described as the

most impressive mass-based citizens organization in the country, celebrated its fifteenth anniversary last year, and similar IAF-spawned organizations in Houston, El Paso, Los Angeles, Brooklyn and Queens in New
York, and Baltimore are all going strong a decade after their inception.

In all, the IAF network now consists of twenty-three large-scale projects, including new ones in Memphis, Phoenix, and suburban Washington,
D.C. These projects typically begin in a way reminiscent of Alinsky's work
in the 1960s: local church leaders, usually an interfaith and interracial
coalition, initiate discussions with the IAF, form a sponsoring committee,
and begin the process of raising funds for a two- or three-year organizing
program. (In fact, the constituent parts of every IAF project consist almost
exclusively of church congregations.) Alinsky's ideas and concepts have
become widely accepted in both mainline Protestant denominations and
the American Roman Catholic Church. Virtually all the Protestant
churches' national programs include support for Alinsky-style community
organizing, although the funding levels are well below those of the late
1960s—reflecting the overall contraction of strength and membership
among these denominations.

As for the Roman Catholic Church, its commitment both in principle
and in funding is stronger than ever. Except within certain religious and
activist circles, it is not widely known that the Church's Campaign for
Human Development expends most of its $8 million annual budget in
grants to community organizing and related grass-roots empowerment
efforts. And many recipients of the CHD largesse are IAF-directed projects. The embrace of Alinsky's basic ideas by both the CHD and influential Catholic bishops has led Charles Curran, a leading Catholic
theologian, to credit Alinsky with having the most distinctive impact on
the American Catholic social justice movement over the last twenty years.

To be sure, Alinsky's ideas about self-interest and power remain controversial. And the ghost of Saul Alinsky can still inflame opposition
within a Catholic parish and elicit charges that he—and by implication his
followers—was a Red (as happened in El Paso, Texas, when the IAF was
invited there to organize). But, by and large, there is a fairly broad acceptance among mainline Protestant and Catholic clergy and lay leaders of
empowerment strategies for low-income and working-class people because
they see a clear moral dimension to such activities that can and should be
part of congregational life.

The IAF's current work expresses this moral dimension much more
explicitly than it did in the Alinsky era. IAF organizers keep the values
of family and church at the center of all discussions—values that are, as
they say repeatedly, the basic raison d'être for building a community

organization. In the hundreds of one-on-one conversations an IAF organizer has with pastors and laymen, the welfare of church and family is the focal point, and the questions are, what are the problems sapping a congregation's strength or jeopardizing a family's economic well-being—problems that can be turned into issues around which to organize. Personal relationships develop as people are brought together in small groups and as agendas and priorities begin to emerge, all tied to the values of family and church.

Although the modern IAF has had its share of organizational washouts, there have been many more successes over the last decade, even extraordinary successes. COPS in San Antonio has helped in "fundamentally altering the moral tone and the political and physical face of the city," declares San Antonio's Mayor Henry Cisneros, himself a beneficiary (as the first Hispanic mayor of a major American city) of COPS's success at redistributing local political power. COPS has become the linchpin of a growing network of IAF organizations in Houston, El Paso, Fort Worth, the Rio Grande Valley, and Austin. Texas Interfaith, as the IAF calls its Texas groups, now claims a base of nearly 300 churches and perhaps as many as 300,000 families, a critical mass of significance, and the IAF's state director, Ernesto Cortes, is already considered a powerful figure in Texas affairs.

There have been impressive results elsewhere, too. In the Los Angeles area, where Larry McNeil is the key IAF man, four organizations are in varying stages of development and recently helped to fashion a successful strategy to increase California's minimum wage. In New York, the IAF's East Brooklyn Congregations, under the direction of Michael Gecan, mobilized Protestant and Catholic support—both political and financial—pressured and lobbied city officials, and, with the help of a dedicated, creative housing consultant, achieved what few observers thought was possible: the construction of more than a thousand neat brick row houses in a formerly devastated area of Brownsville at a cost within reach of families of very modest incomes, some of whom had been living in nearby public housing. The Nehemiah Plan (named after the Biblical leader sent to rebuild Jerusalem) has attracted national attention, including federal laws that will encourage similar experiments elsewhere. In Baltimore, with guidance from the skillful Arnie Graf, BUILD (Baltimoreans United in Leadership Development) has negotiated an agreement between the public schools and business leaders that guarantees a job or a college education to high school graduates who fulfill certain attendance and performance requirements. During a recent mayoral election in Baltimore, both candidates traveled to New York at BUILD's request to inspect the Nehemiah project—and something comparable has now been endorsed by both the mayor and the governor of Maryland, a program that is part of BUILD's broad agenda for revitalizing Baltimore. In fact, Chambers and his colleagues have even begun talking about a new "urban agenda" that the IAF network would promote nationwide.

There is one overarching reason why, during an era when so much of the political tide has run against it, the modern IAF has been so stunningly successful in first mobilizing and then maintaining the active participation of thousands of working-class and poorer people, mostly black and Hispanic, who seek a better life for their families and communities. The *training* the IAF organizers provide is the key to their success, and they are committed to it as their highest priority. "The IAF is one of the only organizations I know of," Ernie Cortes says, "that's teaching people about what politics is really about—public discourse, negotiations, how to argue, when to compromise, not just the quadrennial electronic plebiscite we usually call politics." Three times each year, the IAF conducts "national training," intensive ten-day sessions for clergy and lay leaders of the IAF network. Although some of the discussions, lectures, and role-playing exercises date to Alinsky's own time, what is different is the current commitment to a systematic, ongoing training program rather than the seat-of-the-pants approach that was more typical of the 1960s. And the training is by no means limited to a small elite. Each national training session has up to a hundred people: the IAF aims to develop leadership collectives. "We're trying to build organizations with staying power, not a movement based on instant power and charisma," says Chambers. Back at home, leaders are trained to analyze and evaluate virtually every meeting and "action"—as, for example, when four or five hundred COPS members hold "an accountability session" with an elected official. For some of the bigger actions or events, the analysis may take several weeks and a number of meetings. As much time and energy is devoted to learning why and how something occurred as to the planning and actual action.

Other, related activities that Alinsky thought important have received less attention, such as articulating to a national audience an overall strategy for achieving a greater measure of social justice. To be sure, Alinsky could be at once enlightening, entertaining, and inspiring; and his voice and great spirit—"happiness is in the pursuit," as he was fond of saying—are sorely missed. But his disciples have a newly refined method and set of experiences that should and can be part of any serious debate about how to revitalize American democracy, and about how to encourage ordinary Americans to work out their own destiny—an ideal no less radical in its implications today than it was when Alinsky started fifty years ago, or when America's great experiment in democracy began two centuries ago.

NOTES

INTERVIEWS

The author gratefully acknowledges the following people for consenting to interviews in the preparation of this book:

Larry Adler, Jean Alinsky, Lee David Alinsky, Ira Bach, Lawrence P. Bachmann, Frank Barnard, Joe Berger, Herbert Blumer, Richard Boone, Heather Booth, Paul Booth, Georgia Boyer, Arthur Brazier, Herbert Bronstein, Marjorie Buckholz, Daniel Carpenter, Edward Chambers, Cesar Chavez, Robert Christ, Analoyce Clapp, Norman Clapp, Harrison Combs, Michael P. Connolly, Jack Conway, Vincent Cooke, Richard Cornuelle, Ernesto Cortes, Robert W. Craig, Len DeCaux, Marian Despres, Leon Despres, Bill Dodds, Bernard Doering, Ephraim Donor, Jim Drake, Robert Dunn, Alvin Duskin

Marian Edelman, Peter Edelman, Julius C. C. Edelstein, John J. Egan, Alex Elson, Miriam Elson, Elliot Epstein, Jason Epstein, William Fanning, Martin Farrell, Theodora Cogley Farrell, Carol Bernstein Ferry, Leon Finney, John Fish, Joseph L. Fisher, Joseph Fitzpatrick, Joseph Fletcher, Pat Flood, Franklin D. R. Florence, Walter Frank, Gaylord Freeman, J. W. Fulbright, Tom Gaudette, Michael Gecan, Elmer Gertz, Georgie Anne Geyer, Frances Gitelson, Todd Gitlin, Grace Goodell, William R. Grace, Arnie Graff, Katharine Graham, Andrew Greeley, Bertha Greenebaum

Robert Haas, Warren Haggstrom, Stan Hallet, Don Harris, T. George Harris, Wayne C. Hartmire, Phillip Hauser, Charles Hayes, Ed Heckelbeck, Francis Heisler, Freda Heisler, Nina Helstein, Rachel B. Helstein, Ralph Helstein, Loy Henderson, John Heyman, George Higgins, Adolph Hirsch, Meyer Hirst, Eric Hoffer, Edward Holmgren, Myles Horton, Lester C. Hunt, Sidney Hyman, Ivan Illich, Homer Jack, Miriam Jackson, Jane Jacobs, Agnes James, Sidney L. James, Morris Janowitz, A. L. Johnson, Earl Johnson, Roger Johnson, Walter Johnson, Harry Jones

Grace Kaplan, Stanley A. Kaplan, Richard Katzoff, Susan Kellock, Clarence Kelly, Fallon Kelly, Joseph Kelly, Walter Kloetzli, Erwin Knoll, Bill Koch, Herman Kogan, Saul Kolbrin, Maynard Krueger, Irv Kupcinet, Squire Lance, Joan Lancourt, Leona Baumgartner Langmuir, Charles Leber, Sidney Lens, Julian Levi, Jennifer Lewis, Sol Linowitz, Dorothy Liveright, Paul Long, Pare Lorenz, Clara Lustgarten, Staughton Lynd, Jack McClory, Irene McInnis, John McKnight, Larry McNeil, Florence Maniloff, Kay Mann, Herbert March, Jane March, Fran Martin, John Bartlow Martin, Peter Martinez, Dollie Martinson, Robert Martinson, Milton Mayer, Helen Meegan, Joseph Meegan, Jack Meltzer, Barry Menuez, Charles Merrill, Abner J. Mikva, Jerome Miller, Mike Miller, James Morton, Daniel Patrick Moynihan

Bernard Nath, Tommy Newman, Leo Nieto, James Norris, J. S. Oh, Leslie Orear, Seniel Ostrow, Evelyn Ostrowski, Donald O'Toole, Sidney Perlstadt, Edward Plawinski, Justine Wise Polier, Dorothy Levin Ponce, Donald Price, Ann Prosten, Jesse Prosten, David Ramage, James M. Reed, Thomas Rehorn, Irv Richter, Frank Riessman, Tony Rios, George Romney, Fred W. Ross, Sr., Edward Roybal, Mike Royko, Bruce Sagan, Tim Sampson, Berkley Sanders, Edith

Macy Schoenborn, Mike Sedlak, Robert Shayon, Gordon Sherman, Kate Sherman, Jay Shulman, Charles Silberman, Louis Silverman, Rose Silverman, Charles L. Simon, Jean Simon, Robert Slayton, Hermon Dunlop Smith, Anthony Sorrentino, Robert F. Squires, Victoria Starr, Mary Maize Stinson, Anthony Stompanata, Kenneth Stuart, Margery Tabankin, Felix Taccio, Nick Taccio, Studs Terkel, Carl Tjerandsen, Myrtle Tjerandsen, George Todd, Brian Urquhart, William Vaughn, Joseph Vilimas, Nicholas von Hoffman, Lucius Walker, Allan Wallis, J. Raymond Walsh, Lee Webb, Palmer Weber, Gerson Weinberg, Herbert White, Kathleen Wilson, Jules Witcover, Zigmund Wlodarczyk, Elizabeth Wood, Estelle Wurth, Marvin Wurth, Adam Yarmolinsky, Paul Ylvasaker

Much of the information in this book came from personal interviews with people listed above. In these Notes, the abbreviation "Int." designates such an interview. Citations of books generally supply only the author's last name, a (usually) shortened form of the book's title, and the page reference; in all such cases, complete bibliographical information will be found in the section "Major Works Cited" that follows the Notes. And for certain frequently cited institutional sources, the following abbreviations have been used:

AP	Alinsky Papers
CHS	Chicago Historical Society
IAF	Industrial Areas Foundation, Franklin Square, New York
SHSW	State Historical Society of Wisconsin
UIC	University of Illinois at Chicago

Introduction

xvii   *Harper's:* Marion K. Sanders, "The Professional Radical: Conversations with Saul Alinsky," June 1965, pp. 37–47, and "Conversations with Saul Alinsky," Part II, July 1965, pp. 52–59.

most interesting person: Int. Jules Witcover, March 9, 1989.

"great men of our century": Quoted in Curran, *Critical Concerns,* p. 192.

xix   *"an unchristian, prehistoric muttonhead":* Buffalo *Evening News,* August 27, 1965.

"invention of color film": Washington *Post,* January 9, 1967, p. 3.

xx   *"The KKK Supports Bush":* Int. Richard Katzoff, February 16, 1989.

1. Sarah's Son

3   *"Socrates is a lean":* Act 1, Scene 2, p. 32, IAF.

4   *"they began to trust me":* Playboy, March 1972, p. 68.

5   *"title of 'regular guys' ":* draft of "Gang Study," Chap. 1, p. 6, Stephan Bubacz papers, UIC.

"the truth imagined": Int. Eric Hoffer, May 10, 1981.

from 4,000 to 1.7 million: Berkow, *Maxwell Street,* p. 5.

263 Maxwell Street: Chicago City Directory, 1898.

before they separated: Int. Kay Mann, April 5, 1983.

6   *"I was born":* Harper's, June 1965, p. 38.

population of the Western Hemisphere: Berkow, *Maxwell Street,* p. 9.

moved to Douglas Park: Int. Kay Mann, April 5, 1983; City Directory of Chicago; also on the migration of Jews to Lawndale: Jones and Holli, ed., *Ethnic Chicago,* p. 64.

"sometimes there'd be fatalities": Playboy, March 1972, p. 62.

bigger guys hung out: Int. Joseph Berger, December 2, 1982.

7   *was able to buy:* Int. Kay Mann, April 5 1983.

    called him a shlub: Int. Joseph Berger, December 2, 1982. In other interviews on the same day, Rose Silverman, Florence Maniloff, and Clara Lustgarten provided similar recollections of Alinsky's father.

    Sarah was the third oldest: Int. Walter Frank, May 5, 1984.

    lived in Drogichan: Ibid. Also, I would like to express my appreciation to Karen Sherman, research assistant at the Kennan Institute for Advanced Russian Scholars, Washington, D.C., for identifying the location and spelling of the town based on Mr. Frank's information.

    "didn't think much of Sarah": Int. Walter Frank, May 5, 1984.

    outliving the other two: Based on accounts from several family members.

    Sarah's attacks and tirades: Int. Kay Mann, April 5, 1983.

8   *"Everybody hits my Sollie":* Int. Joseph Berger. December 2, 1982.

    affair between Sarah and a deliveryman: Ibid.

    morning and afternoon shifts: Marshall News, Marshall High School, September 19, 1922, p. 1.

    took the general course: Ibid.; Alinsky's high school transcripts.

    severely injured his hip: Int. Irene McInnis, June 2, 1982. Other family members recall Alinsky mentioning the injury, and he refers to it in an undated college term paper, possibly written in 1928, Ernest W. Burgess papers, University of Chicago.

    "as black, hopeless": Ibid., p. 2.

9   *"I didn't see much of my father": Harper's,* June 1965, p. 39.

    "I was shacked up": Ibid.

    "don't think I ever hated": Playboy, March 1972, p. 62.

    he left $50: Ibid. Confirmed by Los Angeles County court records.

    you knew the son: Int. Irene McInnis, June 2, 1982.

2. Helene and the University of Chicago

10   *father paid for Saul's tuition:* Int. Kay Mann, April 5, 1983.

11   *The Liberal Club:* Int. Leon Despres, December 5, 1982.

    on academic probation: Alinsky's transcript obtained from the University of Chicago, Office of the Registrar.

    on an interpersonal basis: Int. Mary Maize Stinson, July 10, 1981; Constance Weinberger, July 27, 1982.

    "the Park and Burgess text": Farris, *Chicago Sociology,* p. 37.

12   *"the most unobtrusive":* Int. Philip Hauser, October 11, 1982.

    larger interest in social reform: Farris, *Chicago Sociology,* pp. 130–31.

    during the height of the controversy: Int. Philip Hauser, October 11, 1982.

    "These natural areas": Quoted in Farris, *Chicago Sociology,* p. 60.

13   *"that the city is rooted":* Morris Janowitz, ed., *The City,* p. 4.

    a more radical program: See, for example, Snodgrass, *American Criminological Tradition,* esp. pp. 173–79.

14   *"The most striking change":* Alinsky's report dated January 30, 1929, in Ernest W. Burgess papers, University of Chicago,

    At the Merry Garden Ballroom: Ibid.

15   *the Simons moved:* Int. Charles Simon, March 28, 1982.

    sent her to Oaklane Country Day: Int. Bertha Heimerdinger Greenebaum, February 9, 1983.

    Helene's father suffered serious financial losses: Int. Mrs. Charles Simon, March 28, 1982.

    water sports were her specialty: Int. Bertha Heimerdinger Greenebaum, February 9, 198?

16   *"it was that kind of love affair":* Int. Mary Maize Stinson, July 10, 1981.

    "Ec-o-nom-ics": Ibid.

    "the most lovable, tenderhearted guy": Ibid.

17   *change his name to Saul Allen:* Mrs. Charles Simon, March 28, 1982.
      a better cup of coffee: Int. Charles Simon, March 28, 1982.
      admiration of labor-movement radicals: Int. Herbert March, August 13, 1982.

3. Prison Bug Ward and Other Stories

18   *an underworld orgy:* Wendt and Kogan, *Bosses,* pp. 282–90.
19   *"I didn't kill him":* Allsop, *Bootleggers,* p. 106.
      briefly to the Law School: University of Chicago transcript.
20   *"My reception was pretty chilly":* Playboy, March 1972, p. 66.
      "I became his student": Ibid.
21   *"Capone was the establishment":* Ibid.
      "when I was looking over their records": Ibid.
22   *"Saul was talking":* Int. Stanley Kaplan, September 15, 1983.
23   *" 'Who's this guy' ":* Int. Felix Taccio, October 13, 1982.
24   *"Saul knew everybody":* Int. Anthony Stompanata, October 13, 1982.
      he instructed them: Ibid. Also Nick and Felix Taccio, October 13, 1982.
      became a lifelong friend: Snodgrass, *American Criminological Tradition,* p. 141.
25   *jobs through Alinsky:* Int. Anthony Sorrentino, October 13, 1982.
      Companions in Crime: An unfinished draft is in the Chicago Area Project papers, CHS.
26   *"giving up the family ideologically":* Ibid., summary, p. 4.
      "Family traditions": Ibid., summary, pp. 5–6.
27   *Illinois became the first:* Jacobs, *Stateville,* p. 18.
      Washington's Birthday Massacre: Ibid., p. 25.
28   *"delinquent vocabularies":* Proceedings of the Sixty-fourth Annual Congress of the Ameri-
      can Prison Association, September 17–21, 1934, p. 176.
      "out here for whorehouses": Allsop, *Bootleggers,* p. 169.
29   *"blasted into her face":* Untitled, undated entry, pp. 1–2, IAF.
      "The difference between": Ibid., p. 3.
      "Alinsky, you're sending me": Ibid., p. 4.
30   *one of the themes in* Prison Bug Ward: February 1943, IAF.
31   *"You're all washed up":* Ibid., pp. 8–9.
      "The convict's side: Ibid., preface, p. 2.
      "Theoretically": Ibid., p. 17.
32   *drove with Saul:* Int. Frances Gitelson, April 23, 1982.
33   *"am deeply grateful":* Prison Bug Ward, preface, pp. 3–4, IAF.

4. A New Hero

34   *rigidly bureaucratic:* Jacobs, *Stateville,* p. 19.
      $105 a month: Int. Anthony Sorrentino, March 17, 1982.
35   *giving fifty bucks:* Int. Leon Despres, December 5, 1982.
      they had a sexual encounter: Int. Marian Despres, December 5, 1982.
      "The Big Boy told Cermak": Alinsky's journal, untitled, undated entry, p. 6, IAF.
36   *develop a friendly, useful relationship:* Int. Gerson S. Weinberg, June 2, 1982.
37   *Alinsky knew everybody:* Int. Saul Kolbrin, May 5, 1982.
38   *"fascist movement in the United States":* Quoted in Schlesinger, *The Politics,* p. 565.
39   *"hated with a passion":* Harper's, June 1965, p. 44.
      not been enthusiastic: Int. Sidney Hyman, September 16, 1983.
      "I don't think he ever": Int. Leon Despres, December 31, 1982.
      "The definition of myself": Alinsky's journal, "The Communist Party Goes Out," p. 3,
      IAF.
      "The Philosophical Implications": Proceedings of the Sixty-seventh Annual Congress of the
      American Prison Association, Philadelphia, Pennsylvania, October 10–15, 1937, pp. 156–71.

40 *"Prior to":* Ibid., p. 157.
    "keynote of a capitalistic society": Ibid., p. 168.
    "individualistic symphony": Ibid., p. 160.
    "Dr. Freud": Ibid., p. 162.
41 *"cannot be ignored":* Ibid., p. 167.
    "the present chaos": Ibid., p. 169.
42 *"the rubbish at labor's door":* Dubofsky and Van Tine, *Lewis,* p. 203.
    Lewis and his advisers: Ibid., Chap. 9.
    Lewis had won for his miners: Ibid., pp. 197–200.
43 *"exuberance of his own verbosity":* Ibid., p. 199.
    "the three times": De Caux, *Labor Radical,* p. 208.
44 *"with fire and sword":* Ibid., p. 183.
    "a new Lewis": Ibid., p. 209.
    "there is nothing there": Alinsky, *Lewis,* p. 216.
45 *"to the rostrum":* Dubofsky and Van Tine, *Lewis,* p. 220.
    might have ended in violent tragedy: Alinsky, *Lewis,* pp. 142–47.
    Lewis had privately and personally: For a good discussion of the motives involved on the part of each man, see Dubofsky and Van Tine, pp. 272–77.

5. The Area Project

47 *physically attacked a prison guard:* Int. Palmer Weber, May 11, 1983.
    "it was a [telling] commentary": Jacobs, *Stateville,* p. 19.
48 *"the social milieu":* Clifford R. Shaw and Jesse A. Jacobs, "The Chicago Area Project: An Experimental Community Program for the Prevention of Delinquency in Chicago," proceedings of the Sixty-ninth Annual Congress of the American Prison Association, New York City, October 16–20, 1939, p. 40.
49 *"report it to the authorities":* In the Chicago Area Project papers, a footnote to a verbatim life history, p. 9, box 11A, folder 76.
    "great experiment": Ibid., p. 44
50 *Shaw had dispatched another staff person:* Steven Schlossman and Michael Sedlak, *The Chicago Area Project Revisited,* A Rand Note, January 1983, p. 8.
    "curbstone counselors": Ibid., p. 61.
    worked with one Russell Square gang: Several of Alinsky's reports on his work with the University Juniors between November 1932 and May 1933 are in the Stephen Bubacz papers, UIC.
51 *"fight the devil with fire":* Quoted in Sorrentino, *Organizing Against Crime,* p. 89.
    the Russell Square Area: Schlossman and Sedlak, p. 3.
    organizational breakthrough: Ibid., p. 11.
    "activities for the children": Ibid.
52 *"superimposed upon the community":* Ibid., p. 13.
53 *Shaw's staff encouraged:* Ibid., pp. 42–43.
    "becoming a Frankenstein": Ibid., p. 106.
54 *"role of agitators":* Ibid., p. 108.
    "reorganization of community life in specific areas": Shaw and Jacobs, p. 52.

6. Life in the Jungle

57 *popped on the surface:* Slayton, *Back of the Yards,* p. 15.
58 *Shaw first started:* Chicago Area Project papers, "Back of the Yards Survey," p. 1, CHS.
    Shaw sent John Brown: Ibid.
    Brown first drew a profile: Ibid., pp. 1–14.
59 *families survived:* Slayton, *Back of the Yards,* pp. 190–91.
    a precocious fifteen-year-old: Int. Herb March, November 16, 1970, SHSW.

60   *save the streetcar fare:* Int. Herb March, August 13, 1982.
      appreciated Alinsky's pragmatic approach: Ibid.
61   *Poles accounted for about 40 percent:* From John Brown's profile.
      cleavages and a pecking order: Slayton, *Back of the Yards,* p. 23.
      tried to Americanize: Int. Joseph Kelly, January 18, 1983. Father Kelly served at St. Rose
      of Lima Church in the Back of the Yards in the late 1930s. Also Shanabruch, *Chicago's
      Catholics,* especially Chap. 9, pp. 199–225.
      priests had been there years before: Slayton, *Back of the Yards,* pp. 22–23.
62   *old tried-and-true support system:* Ibid., pp. 189–92.
      small group of women: Int. Jane March, August 13, 1982.
63   *young women would explain:* Int. Vicki Starr, December 31, 1982.
      "turned us down": Ibid.
      but never speaking: Ibid.
64   *at the Meegan house:* Int. Slayton, *Back of the Yards,* p. 193. Also Slayton, . . . *Our Own
      Destiny: The Development of Community in Back of the Yards,* diss., 1982, p. 309.
      go to jail or go to the seminary: Anonymous.
65   *"How are you today, mother?":* Int. Evelyn Ostrowski, July 13, 1982.

7. Organizing the Back of the Yards

67   *"like a great battleship":* Chicago *Daily Times,* July 20, 1939, p. 1.
      March was driving: Int. Herb March, November 16, 1970, SHSW.
      "among the workers": Ibid.
68   *a brief account:* Town of Lake Journal, March 15, 1939, p. 1.
69   *theological tradition and the politics of the 1930s:* Int. Joseph Kelly, January 18, 1983. Also
      Slayton, *Back of the Yards,* p. 201.
70   *Through Joe:* Int. Joseph Meegan, November 11, 1981.
      the senior pastors: Int. Edward Plawinski, October 13, 1982.
      tried to raid: Anonymous.
71   *playing rivals off:* A tactic mentioned by several priests friendly with Alinsky, and by
      Alinsky himself when recounting his approach.
      announced in the neighborhood newspaper: Town of Lake Journal, July 6, 1939, p. 1.
72   *"Either by accident or design":* Chicago *Daily News,* July 14, 1939, p. 5.
      "Red C.I.O. revolutions": Chicago *Tribune,* July 22, 1939, p. 10.
73   *more than indifference:* Int. Herb March, August 13, 1982.
      "has enlisted churchmen": Chicago *Daily News,* July 14, 1939, p. 5.
      engineered by Alinsky: Int. Don Harris, November 10, 1983.
74   *"Our organization here":* Town of Lake Journal, June 29, 1939, p. 1.
      bring out 350 people: Slayton, *Back of the Yards,* p. 203.
      March heard the shot: Int. Herb March, November 16, 1970, SHSW.
75   *"Sheil defies threats":* Chicago *Daily Times,* July 16, 1939, p. 3.
      "marked a departure": Chicago *Tribune,* July 17, 1939, p. 7.
      admirer of Sheil's: Int. Sidney James, August 12, 1982.
      "but U.S. history": Time, July 24, 1939, p. 12.

8. New Friends in High Places

77   *"For fifty years":* Robert Slayton, ". . . Our Own Destiny: The Development of Community
      in Back of the Yards," diss., 1982, p. 202.
      never saw him as a CIO man: Int. Herb March, August 13, 1982.
78   *"made a beeline":* Alinsky's journal, "Communist Party Goes Out," p. 6, IAF.
      "At the time": Ibid.
      "from two to four": Ibid., p. 7.
      "Alinsky said to me": Int. Herb March, August 13, 1982.

79   *"I told Alinsky":* Ibid.
     "This organization": Although Slayton writes (*Back of the Yards,* pp. 202–3) that Alinsky
     and Meegan "sat down together" to craft the statement, the rhetorical style is reminiscent
     of Alinsky's.
     "half-dizzy liberal": Alinsky's journal, "Communist Party Goes Out," p. 2.
80   *being a Jew:* Int. Ralph Helstein, October 10, 1982.
     "Bill, the Council": Int. Joseph Meegan, December 2, 1982.
81   *"A hundred bucks!":* Alinsky's journal, "Mr. Lewis Contributes," p. 1J, IAF.
     "I'll go up from": Ibid., p. 3J.
82   *they did want two things:* Int. Joseph Meegan, December 2, 1982.
83   *Meyer Bros. bought:* Int. Sidney Lens, July 15, 1982.
84   *"must have a letter":* Back of the Yards Journal, November 21, 1939, p. 1.
     conspicuous by its absence: Chicago Area Project papers, CHS.
85   *not particularly happy:* Int. Joseph Meegan, November 11, 1981.
     more reflective, research-oriented: Int. Herbert Blumer, April 23, 1982; Int. Anthony Sor-
     rentino, March 17, 1982.
     Sheil told Marshall Field: Becker, Marshall Field, p. 359.
     "a traitor to his class": Ibid., book jacket.
86   *grossly exaggerated:* Ibid., pp. 134–38.
     at the Waldorf: Ibid., p. 359.
87   *talked about money:* Ibid.
     By February 1940: Ibid., p. 360.

9. The Great John L. and Presidential Politics

88   *officially resigned:* Clifford Shaw memo, Chicago Area Project papers, January 22, 1940,
     CHS.
     "ignominious defeat": Quoted in Dubofsky and Van Tine, *Lewis,* p. 342.
89   *"Lewis, prior to departing":* Alinsky, *Lewis,* p. 130.
     "It ill behooves": Ibid., p. 168.
     "gutted the New Freedom": Dubofsky and Van Tine, *Lewis,* p. 343.
90   *"To the coal miner":* Alinsky, *Lewis,* p. 172.
     "a strong labor man": Quoted in Dubofsky and Van Tine, *Lewis,* p. 340.
91   *veracity of Alinsky's account:* Ibid., p. 355.
     apple of her father's eye: Int. Len De Caux, August 15, 1982.
     "the great smiler": Int. Sidney Hyman, September 16, 1983.
92   *"his people would follow":* Alinsky, *Lewis,* p. 174.
     "The Communist Party at that time": Ibid.
93   *"my idols":* Vintage edition, p. ix.
     "An arrangement was devised": Alinsky, *Lewis,* p. 176.
     The White House Ushers' Diary: Correspondence to the author from the supervisory
     archivist of the Franklin D. Roosevelt Library, Hyde Park, New York, March 17, 1982.
     "the Catholic Church was important to Lewis": Int. Len De Caux, August 15, 1982.
     "Bishop Sheil not only supervised": Alinsky, *Lewis,* p. 176.
94   *"until the end":* Ibid., p. 180.
95   *"Roosevelt and I are done":* Ibid., p. 187.
     "together again": Ibid.
     Alinsky met Dutch Smith: Int. Hermon Dunlop Smith, March 3, 1982.
96   *"He was different":* Ibid.
     "only Republican I know": Ibid.
     "an extra contribution": Ibid.
97   *"reign of President Roosevelt":* Quoted in Alinsky, *Lewis,* p. 190.
98   *could not deliver:* Josephson, *Hillman,* p. 488.
     Alinsky and Kathryn together: Int. Don Harris, November 10, 1983.

98 *in the incinerator:* Dubofsky and Van Tine, *Lewis*, p. 159.
99 *"stopped me from voting for Roosevelt":* Int. Len DeCaux, August 15, 1982.
    "uncomfortable for him": Int. Sidney Hyman, September 16, 1983.
    "unite the CIO and the AF of L": Alinsky, *Lewis*, p. 208.
100 *"knife in your back":* Alinsky's journal, untitled, undated entry, p. 1C, IAF.
    "against ruthless evils": Ibid., pp. 2C–3C.
101 *"that urinates backwards":* Int. Sidney Hyman, September 16, 1983.
    "the great American Tragedy": Alinsky, *Lewis*, p. 212.

10. "Miracle of Democracy"

102 *"salvation of our way of life":* New York *Herald Tribune,* August 21, 1940, p. 14.
103 *the first IAF board:* IAF files.
    was familiar with the work: See the Chicago Area Project papers at the CHS for correspondence between Clifford Shaw and G. Howland Shaw that predates the latter's relationship with Alinsky.
    "the American way of life": Reprint of articles, mostly between December 1940 and February 1941, IAF.
104 *"Fundamentally . . . our purpose":* "Statement," p. 8, IAF.
    "threaten the very foundations": Ibid., p. 1.
105 *"shaping of their own destinies":* Ibid., pp. 6–7.
    "miracle of democracy": Herb Graffis, Chicago *Daily Times,* undated reprint, IAF.
    "Fifteen months ago": Time, September 2, 1940, p. 12.
106 *"get to know each other":* Alinsky's journal, "A Human Philosophy," p. 1, IAF.
107 *"ardent follower of Father Coughlin":* Ibid.
    "stand or all fall together": "Statement," p. 5, IAF.
108 *"plight of the area":* Ibid., p. 6.
    "pro or con": Ibid.
109 *"you made it":* Int. Sidney Hyman, September 16, 1983.
    "free citizens in a democracy": "Statement," p. 8, IAF.
    "evolution of American democracy": New York *Herald Tribune,* August 21, 1940, p. 14.
110 *people's special interests:* Alinsky's journal, "Sketches of Kansas City," August 5–9, 1941, p. 2A, IAF.
111 *"they were talking with":* Ibid., p. 3A.
    "the heart of democracy": Kansas City *Times,* undated reprint, IAF.
    "an Armourdale rat": Int. Dollie Martinson, June 27, 1983.
112 *"between good and evil":* Alinsky's journal, draft of a letter to Shaw, September 23, 1941, IAF.
    "two young leaders": Ibid.
113 *"got two horses":* Int. Dollie Martinson, June 27, 1983.
    acted so aggressively: Ibid.
114 *"turn a lot of people off":* Ibid., also Int. Robert Martinson.
    "communistically controlled": FBI, file no. 100-3731, October 21, 1940.
    "or subversive group": FBI, file no. 100-3731, November 20, 1940.
    was not a communist: FBI, file no. 100-522, January 13, 1941; FBI, file no. 100-891, February 24, 1941.
115 *"the character and the objectives":* Alinsky's journal, "Place: Hotel Lowry," p. 1, IAF.
    "on the right track": Ibid., pp. 1–2.
115 *"communists by going along":* Alinsky's journal, "The Packers Start 'Packing,' " p. 1F, IAF.
    "those kind of words": Int. Fallon Kelly, July 31, 1981.
116 *"fire Burnley":* Alinsky's journal, "Packers Start 'Packing,' " p. 2F.
    "a participating agency": Alinsky's journal, "The Packer," p. 1, IAF.
    "something of a panic": Ibid., p. 2.

117   *"My wire from"*: Alinsky's journal, draft of a letter to Howland Shaw, September 23, 1941, p. 1K, IAF.

       "behavior of the technical consultant": Alinsky's journal, "Inside Track," p. 1G, IAF.

       "This tree": Draft of a letter to Howland Shaw, September 23, 1941, pp. 1K–2K, IAF.

118   *"carbon to one"*: Ibid., p. 3K.

       "as a Jew in the Gestapo": Ibid.

       "started South St. Paul": South St. Paul *Daily Reporter,* May 1, 1941.

11. War Years

120   *"Mr. Alinsky is rendering"*: October 4, 1941; letter courtesy of David Alinsky.

121   *"about concentration camps"*: Alinsky's journal, draft of a letter to Howland Shaw, September 23, 1941, p. 7K, IAF.

       his good friend: Int. Jean Alinsky, April 27, 1982. Saul's friendship with Johnson was also mentioned by Herb March and several others.

       cost the white neighbor his life: Stephen Brier, "Labor, Politics, and Race: A Black Worker's Life," *Labor History,* Summer 1982, p. 419.

122   *blacks made up 25 percent:* Int. Herb March, August 13, 1982.

123   *"we had some black guys"*: Ibid.

       a rumor: Washington *Post,* June 7, 1945, p. 9.

124   *mesmerize an audience:* Int. Jean Alinsky, April 27, 1982.

       conspicuous by his absence: Int. Herb March, August 13, 1982.

       "implicit faith in Johnson": Ibid.

125   *shot and killed him:* Int. Edward Heckelbeck, November 11, 1983.

       "considered Johnson a traitor": Int. Herb March, August 13, 1982.

       "I have written [Kathryn]": January 22, 1945, AP, UIC.

       "nor prejudice toward each other": October 17, 1942, AP, UIC.

126   *was adamantly opposed:* Int. Helen Meegan, July 13, 1982.

       into the man's face: Int. Sidney Hyman, September 16, 1983.

       "How does he survive?": Ibid.

127   *"the Hull-House idea"*: Ibid.

       "nationality or race": July 25, 1944, letter to Happy Macy, AP, UIC.

128   *"for our services"*: August 18, 1944, AP, UIC.

       "considerable growing reputation": Int. Jack Conway, June 19, 1983.

129   *"a nonunion environment"*: Ibid.

       "wasn't ready to organize like that": Int. August 31, 1983.

       "terribly fatherly": Int. Frances Gitelson, April 23, 1982.

130   *"the FBI National Academy:* FBI, file no. 100-3731, August 23, 1944.

131   *invited Alinsky to serve:* Letter from Glueck, January 30, 1942, AP, UIC.

       share a platform: The paper Alinsky presented, under the general heading of "Youth and Morale," appears in *American Journal of Orthopsychiatry,* October 1942, pp. 598–601.

       "twelve people on it": July 8, 1942, AP, UIC.

132   *"get to know you"*: June 1, 1943, AP, UIC.

       "irresponsible power": Horowitz, *Mills,* p. 65.

       "by the root": December 18, 1943, AP, UIC.

133   *"pagan in soul"*: September 28, 1942; text of speech in AP, UIC.

134   *"courage to say it"*: October 15, 1942, AP, UIC.

12. Battle for Survival

135   *"preliminary" report:* "General Principles of Community Organization and a Statement on the Back of the Yards Neighborhood Council," February 16, 1943, Welfare Council of Metropolitan Chicago papers, CHS.

136   *"central factors"*: Ibid., p. 8.

136   *"If the labor group":* Ibid., p. 9.
      "our personal friendship": Letter and response to Byron, April 12, 1943, CHS.
137   *"reason it was conceived":* Ibid., p. 5.
      "turn-over of leadership": Ibid., p. 6.
138   *"he is all milk":* Ibid., p. 5.
139   *Grudzinski's early evaluation:* Slayton, *Back of the Yards,* p. 177.
140   *Before the meeting had ended:* Untitled report of meeting held August 30, 1944, between Saul Alinsky and other representatives of the BYNC and representatives of the Settlement House, Welfare Council of Metropolitan Chicago papers, CHS.
      drive them out: Ibid.
141   *elect at least half:* Statement by the board of directors of the University of Chicago Settlement House, September 1945, p. 5; courtesy of the University of Chicago Press, where this summary of the dispute was filed among other papers and correspondence having to do with the publication of Alinsky's first book in 1945.
      "ends justify the means": Ibid., p. 6.
      "admittedly prejudiced": Ibid., p. 5.
142   *"from the inside":* Ibid., p. 6.
      "wholly unfit": Ibid., p. 15.
      "tragic waste of time": P. 12, as quoted from *Back of the Yards Journal,* June 14, 1945.
143   *"morally bankrupt civilization":* Washington *Post,* June 7, 1945, p. 7.
      "Confederate money": Letter to Charles A. Nelson, June 4, 1956, UIC.
144   *Irish leadership and domination:* See Slayton, *Back of the Yards,* pp. 152–54.
      Judge knew a lot: Ibid.
      the 25th Precinct: Robert Slayton, ". . . Our Own Destiny," p. 261.
145   *every 14th Ward alderman:* Slayton, *Back of the Yards,* p. 156.
146   *"financially and every other way":* Ibid., p. 169.
147   *"100 percent regular Democrats":* Ibid., p. 171.
148   *"I'll fix it for you":* Int. Sidney Hyman, September 16, 1983.
      "What's your draft status?": Int. Joseph Meegan, July 13, 1982.
149   *"Children Pray":* Chicago *Sun,* January 3, 1944.
150   *he lived there:* Int. Joseph Meegan, July 13, 1982.
      "his park duties": Chicago *Sun,* January 4, 1944, p. 1.
151   *one of the powers:* Chicago *Sun-Times,* February 4, 1948.
      "Sixty-day reprieve?": Chicago *Sun,* January 4, 1944, p. 5.
      "bankers versus babies": Ibid.
      "only welfare agency": Ibid., p. 1.
152   *"at the noon hour":* Chicago *Sun,* January 5, 1944, p. 1.
      "Milk in Park": Chicago *Sun,* January 8, 1944, p. 1.
      "Kelly machine": January 11, 1944, AP, UIC.
      "heart has always": Chicago *Sun,* January 8, 1944, p. 5.
153   *"removed from the payroll":* Chicago *Sun,* January 15, 1944, p. 5.
      collegiate coats: Int. Joseph Meegan, July 13, 1982.
154   *"Don't worry":* Int. Helen Meegan, July 13, 1982.
      three Catholic priests: Chicago *Sun,* January 5, 1944, p. 1.
      " 'very little brain indeed' ": Chicago *Sun,* January 14, 1944, p. 1.
      "consummate stupidity": Chicago *Sun,* January 17, 1944. p. 5.
155   *"stop fighting our people":* Chicago *Sun,* January 19, 1944, p. 7.
      "a fair investigation": *Back of the Yards Journal,* February 17, 1944, p. 1.
      "the role of Saul Alinsky": Chicago *Daily Tribune,* February 9, 1944, p. 7.
156   *"Reputed Head":* Chicago *Daily Tribune,* February 11, 1944, p. 13.
      " 'What's the pitch, bud?' ": Ibid.
      In rebuttal: Chicago *Sun,* February 13, 1944, p. 5.

157   *"Saul Alinsky got busy"*: Chicago *Daily Tribune*, February 11, 1944, p, 130.
     source of political kickbacks: Chicago *Daily News*, February 25 and 29, 1944; *Back of the Yards Journal*, March 2, 1944.
158   *"evenhandedness"*: Chicago *Sun*, March 11, 1944, p. 5.
     Sheil's integrity: Back of the Yards Journal, February 17, 1944, p. 1.
     "As a bishop": Ibid.
159   *"arrogant 'big shots' "*: *Back of the Yards Journal*, March 9, 1944, p. 1.
160   *"deeply regrettable"*: Chicago *Sun*, March 10, 1949, p. 1.
     "DUNHAM GIVES IN": Ibid.
     "have won again": Ibid., p. 11.
     reason to be ecstatic: Int. Helen and Joe Meegan, July 13, 1982.
     "bishop pushed him": Int. Joseph Meegan, July 13, 1982.
161   *"cease using the park"*: Chicago *Daily Tribune*, March 10, 1945, p. 7.
     strategy committee would not: Chicago *Daily News*, March 10, 1944, p. 1.
162   *"defeated both of them"*: Washington *Post*, June 4, 1945, p. 7.

13. Reveille for Radicals!

163   *"Wanted: American Radicals"*: May 1943, pp. 41–45.
164   *"tools of production"*: Ibid., p. 42.
     "American 'reactionaries' ": Ibid.
     "present picture": Ibid.
     "fanatic believer in equality": Ibid., p. 43.
165   *" 'Does it work?' "*: Ibid.
     "worry 'em some": Ibid., p. 44.
     "just what I wanted": Letter to Alinsky, June 12, 1944; courtesy of the University of Chicago Press.
166   *"starting with selfish interests"*: Maritain's draft of a review of *Reveille for Radicals* that he sent to Alinsky, October 9, 1945, AP, UIC.
     "loved to be secretive": Int. Walter Johnson, July 31, 1981.
167   *"epoch making"*: Chicago *Tribune*, January 13, 1946, p. 9.
     "with Patrick Henry": *Reveille*, p. 21.
168   *"Liberals give and take"*: Ibid., pp. 27–28.
     "hard-boiled" rhetoric: Lasch, *New Radicalism*, p. 289.
     "Only a fool": *Reveille*, p. 115.
169   *"disagreeing with the tactics"*: Ibid., p. 29.
     "shifts his position": Ibid., p. 24.
     "in danger of foundering": Ibid., p. 34.
170   *"jungle of laissez-faire capitalism"*: Ibid., pp. 33–34.
     "more promising system": Hodgson, *America*, p. 77.
171   *"welfare of its constituents"*: *Reveille*, p. 60.
     "complete change in the philosophy": Ibid., pp. 60–61.
172   *"job of building People's Organizations"*: Ibid., p. 172.
     "faith in the people": Ibid., p. 80.
     "most difficult job": Ibid., p. 94.
     "inwardly feel superior": Ibid., p. 123.
     "local taboos": Ibid., p. 100.
173   *"the Poop"*: Lawyer's memorandum to University of Chicago Press, July 23, 1945, p. 2; courtesy of the press.
     "the tremendous speed": *Reveille*, p. 73.
174   *"quarter of a million"*: Ibid., p. 74.
175   *"part of none"*: Ibid., p. 204.
176   *"so much decency and dignity"*: Ibid., p. 114.

177   *"amazing movements of our time"*: New York *Herald Tribune*, January 20, 1946.
       "great importance": April 1946.
       " 'a life-saving handbook' ": February 25, 1946.
       "own social salvation": Chicago *Tribune*, January 13, 1946, p. 14.
       "real leaders can emerge": Ibid., p. 9.
178   *"Mrs. Meyer arrived on schedule"*: Alinsky's letter to Hyman, May 23, 1945, AP, UIC.
       "an orderly revolution": Washington *Post*, June 4–9, 1945.
179   *"powerful upsurge"*: Washington *Post*, June 4, p. 7.
       "What a gathering!": Washington *Post*, June 6, p. 9.
       "mutual enrichment": Washington *Post*, June 8, p. 9.
       "like wildfire": Washington *Post*, June 4, 1945, p. 7.
       5 to 7 percent: Reveille, p. 201.
180   *"he is a robust saint"*: Washington *Post*, June 9, p. 5.
       "live in hell and like it": Washington *Post*, June 5, p. 7.
       "ordered 100 reprints": Memo, July 2, 1945; courtesy of the University of Chicago Press.
       at the Meyers' home: Alinsky letter to the director of the University of Chicago Press,
       February 27, 1946; courtesy of the press.
181   *"wait around for two hours"*: Int. Sidney Hyman, September 16, 1983.
       "bloody passages": University of Chicago Press memo, September 4, 1945; courtesy of the
       press.
       "promote a blood bath": August 31, 1945; courtesy of the press.
182   *"don't know of two other titles"*: February 11, 1946; courtesy of the press.
       "cannot afford to ignore": Reprint of a sermon, January 27, 1946, p. 7, IAF.
183   *"the end justifies the means"*: Ibid., p. 6.
       "developing away *from the democracy"*: Horace Cayton, *The New Republic*, January 21,
       1946.
       "this sort of 'radical' talk": Ralph Bates, *The Nation*, April 20, 1946.
184   *"is just never developed"*: Daniel Bell, *Commentary*, March 1946, p. 93.
       "if I have been harsh": Ibid., p. 92.
185   *"sense of wonderful possibilities"*: Goldman, *Crucial Decade*, p. 13.

14. The Cruelest Summer

186   *Henry Holt & Co.*: Alinsky letter to Paul Hollister, February 13, 1946, AP, UIC.
187   *"100 more of you"*: Handwritten, undated note, spring 1944, AP, UIC.
       The family holdings: Int. William Fanning, February, 9, 1985, and Edith Macy Schoen-
       born, July 15, 1985.
       had been a Democrat: Int. William Fanning, February 9, 1985.
188   *"excellent addition to our staff"*: May 9, 1944, AP, UIC.
       "They live in Bel Air": Handwritten, undated note, spring 1944, AP, UIC.
189   *"whatever else runs into money"*: July 25, 1944, AP, UIC.
190   *"went into* REVOLUTION"*: June 13, 1945, AP, UIC.
       "he is hard up": May 23, 1947, AP, UIC.
       " 'rugged' for their tastes": August 27, 1945, AP, UIC.
       "What really gripes me": Handwritten, undated note, probably spring 1947, AP, UIC.
       "your obedient servant": Telegram, December 9, 1946, AP, UIC.
       between pictures of: January 11, 1946, AP, UIC.
191   *"reputation of being hard-boiled"*: December 23, 1946, AP, UIC.
       " 'pissy-eyed Park Avenue bastards' ": July 27, 1945, AP, UIC.
       " 'OK, Bud' ": Ibid.
       "P. 33, last sentence": Handwritten, undated note, December 1945, AP, UIC.
192   *"if I hadn't swung a few punches"*: December 27, 1945, AP, UIC.

193 *"chuckle out of it":* June 17, 1946, AP, UIC.
" *'I'll be God damned' ":* June 17, 1946, AP, UIC.
"most pronounced talent": Letter to Happy Macy, June 7, 1945, AP, UIC.
194 *"I'll be staying with":* February 25, 1946, AP, UIC.
"even he didn't believe": Int. Ralph Helstein, May 12, 1981.
195 " *'with my fountain pen' ":* Ibid.; also letter to Happy Macy, February 21, 1946, AP, UIC.
"get away with anything": Int. Ralph Helstein, May 12, 1981.
"the kosher Cardinal": Letter of June 11, 1947, AP, UIC.
"corn beef and cabbage": Letter of April 11, 1946, AP, UIC.
196 *"lonesome without it":* March 27, 1947, AP, UIC.
"Sheil vs. Spellman": Handwritten, undated letter by Alinsky to Mrs. Meyer, probably spring 1947, Agnes Meyer papers, Library of Congress.
"carve bowling pins": April 11, 1946, AP, UIC.
"wouldn't hurt you a bit": Handwritten, undated note to Alinsky, probably 1946, IAF.
197 *"just hammed it up":* Int. Frances Gitelson, April 23, 1982.
"do nothing but moan": Letter of May 2, 1946, AP, UIC.
"tremendous impression on me": Ibid.
198 *"Will I be accused":* Letter of April 19, 1947, AP, UIC.
"this philosophical contradiction": April 23, 1947, AP, UIC.
199 *"Don't be silly":* Ibid.
Mrs. Meyer warned Alinsky: Letter to Alinsky, December 21, 1945, IAF.
200 *"You're going to be chairman":* Int. Walter Johnson, July 31, 1981.
"picture of the year?": January 4, 1946, AP, UIC.
201 *applauded and encouraged:* Cited in *The Nation,* February 9, 1946, p. 159.
During the strike: Slayton, *Back of the Yards,* p. 222.
"lengthened shadow of one Saul Alinsky": The Nation, February 9, 1946, p. 160.
"I just got a flash": January 4, 1946, AP, UIC.
202 *"therefore I am where I am":* Alinsky's letter to Paul Hollister, January 3, 1946, AP, UIC.
"puts me over a barrel": January 4, 1946, AP, UIC.
by his boss, Pare Lorentz: Int. Pare Lorentz, April 28, 1985.
203 *"splendid film it would make":* Correspondence to the author from Lawrence Bachmann, March 21, 1982.
"humor about himself": Ibid.
"Kaffee mit Schlag": Ibid.
204 *Patterson himself had informed her:* Mrs. Meyer sent Alinsky a copy of Patterson's letter of March 28, 1947, AP, UIC.
"into the postwar years": Int. Robert Shayon, March 8, 1983.
205 *"a totally depressing experience":* Ibid.
"saw a vision of hope": Ibid.
206 *"drive and boundless enthusiasm":* Transcript of "The Eagles Brood," p. 24, SHSW. Originally broadcast on March 5, 1947.
"CBS is being deluged": March 8, 1947, AP, UIC.
"some negative feelings about Saul": Int. Frances Gitelson, April 23, 1982.
207 *"might lose some of the drive":* Ibid.
"didn't try to outshine Saul": Ibid.
"wouldn't accept direction very well": Int. Leon Despres, December 5, 1982.
208 " *'any future Alinskys' ":* Letter to Gretta Palmer, September 6, 1946, AP, UIC.
"All of the crawling insect life": Ibid.
209 *Helene was dead:* Int. Dorothy Liveright, August 6, 1982.
210 *it was too late:* Int. Ralph Helstein, May 12, 1981; Int. Dorothy Liveright; Chicago *Sun,* September 4, 1947.
left on horseback: Int. Frances Gitelson, April 23, 1982.
211 *in the darkness, called out:* Int. Dorothy Ponce, October 11, 1982.

15. Good Fortune, Bad Luck

212   *didn't want to go on:* Int. Kay Mann, April 5, 1983.
      "absolutely helpless": Int. Frances Gitelson, April 23, 1982.
213   *"in the car until four in the morning":* Int. Ralph Helstein, November 11, 1981:
      "and loving it": Ibid.
      " 'One more cigarette' ": Int. Nina Helstein, November 10, 1981.
214   *"alone with your thoughts":* November 26, 1947, AP, UIC.
      "pressing it affectionately." Ibid.
      recognized the futility: Author's notes, July 19–29, 1966, Asilomar, California.
215   *"$20,000 a year short":* November 26, 1947, AP, UIC.
      "redeem" his contribution: Mentioned by Alinsky in letter to Val Macy, September 7, 1948,
      AP, UIC.
      arranged for a loan: Ibid.
      "must be a better way": Letter to Alinsky, October 26, 1947, AP, UIC.
216   *Knopf's proposal:* Dubofsky and Van Tine, *Lewis,* p. 598.
      Lewis was not interested: Int. Sidney James, August 12, 1982.
      a romantic motive: Int. Grace Kaplan, June 11, 1985.
      "put his arm through mine": Alinsky, *Lewis,* Vintage edition, p. 388.
      "a national ogre": Dubofsky and Van Tine, *Lewis,* p. 476.
217   *"encouraged the old man":* Int. Len De Caux, August 15, 1982.
      "sounds somewhat unlikely": Letter, September 13, 1950, AP, UIC.
      excerpted in Look: "The Hates of John L. Lewis," November 22, 1949, pp. 38–45.
218   *"important historical material":* Alinsky, *Lewis,* p. 233.
219   " *'here that I leave it!'* ": Ibid., p. 237.
      "Nothing in the surviving Lewis papers": Dubofsky and Van Tine, *Lewis,* p. 598.
220   *attending a lunch in Chicago:* Int. Ralph Helstein, November 10, 1981. Also Myles Horton,
      November 10, 1981, who recalls being with Lewis and Alinsky in Washington, D.C.
      "we divided up his social life": Int. Julius C. C. Edelstein, June 30, 1982.
      "at ease with Saul": Int. Palmer Weber, May 11, 1983.
221   " *'something of a man'* ": P. 372.
      a day Saul Alinsky never forgot: Int. Sidney Hyman, September 16, 1983.
      information critical of Lewis: Int. Sidney Lens, June 15, 1982.
      great intake of both food and drink: Int. Carol Bernstein Ferry, June 7, 1983. One of
      Alinsky's favorite anecdotes about Lewis; he told it to many others over the years.
222   *"going over materials with him":* Int. Ralph Helstein, May 26, 1982.
      asked for Ross's address: Int. Fred Ross, April 24, 1982.
223   *violent sucks on the straw:* Ibid.
      "a natural for our work": Letter to Agnes Meyer, June 11, 1947, AP, UIC.
224   *"I was an organizer":* Int. Fred Ross, April 24, 1982.
      "from symptom to cause": Ross's recollections to Alinsky, IAF.
225   *different from Alinsky's approach:* Int. Fred Ross, April 24, 1982.
226   *"into the mainstream":* Ibid.
      "with a deadpan delivery": Ibid.
227   *"sit and listen":* Int. Seniel Ostrow, April 29, 1982.
      "self-interest point of view": Int. Fred Ross, April 24, 1982.
228   *"telegram from Saul Alinsky":* Int. Edward Roybal, August 4, 1983.
      " *'but so am I'* ": Ibid.
      changed to CSO: Anonymous.
      "seventeen thousand people": Int. Edward Roybal, August 4, 1983.
229   *"It was a terrific strain":* Ross's recollections to Alinsky, IAF.
230   *"turn out to be mine":* Ibid.
231   *"haven't thought much about these things":* Ibid.
      Ross was "tireless": Int. Edward Roybal, August 4, 1983.
232   *"I had no time":* Int. Fred Ross, April 24, 1982.

233 *"tied into real experiences":* Quoted in Tjerandsen, *Education,* p. 96.
     "getting him to listen": Int. Fred Ross, April 24, 1982.
234 *"walked out without a contribution":* Letter of June 11, 1947, AP, UIC.
     "don't have the tact": Ibid.
235 *15,000 had Spanish surnames:* Int. Edward Roybal, August 4, 1983.
     "withdrew the picket line": Ibid.
236 *"brought up right?":* Letter of August 23, 1949, AP, UIC.
     "Saul talked me into going": Int. Ralph Helstein, May 12, 1981.
237 *"tricks they have":* Alinsky's letter to Sidney Hyman, July 21, 1947, AP, UIC.
     "a keen understanding": Int. Ed Holmgren, May 16, 1983.
238 *Before the month was out:* Int. Ralph Helstein, May 26, 1982.

16. An Anti-Anti-Communist

240 *"one hell of a situation":* Letter to Happy Macy, April 22, 1947, AP, UIC.
     a combination of reasons: Int. Walter Johnson, July 31, 1981.
241 *"didn't have anything on him":* Int. Herb March, August 13, 1982.
     "do something about this": Letter to Agnes Meyer, March 28, 1951, AP, UIC; also Int.
     Walter Johnson, July 31, 1981.
     "stand up and slug back": Letter to Agnes Meyer, March 28, 1951, AP, UIC.
242 *"investigated more than any other union":* Int. Ralph Helstein, May 12, 1981.
     "weren't about to conform": Ibid.
     fired off protests: Letter to Agnes Meyer, March 21, 1947, AP, UIC.
243 *from the communist newspaper:* Philip Graham's letter to Alinsky, May 5, 1947; courtesy
     of Katharine Graham.
     "write-up is a distortion": Letter to Philip Graham, May 27, 1947; courtesy of Katharine
     Graham.
     "can't believe that it's progressive": Graham letter to Alinsky, June 2, 1947; courtesy of
     Katharine Graham.
244 *"don't think that I am being facetious!":* June 12, 1947; courtesy of Katharine Graham.
245 *"this one is going to be on you":* Int. Herb March, August 13, 1982.
     "that was a serious mistake": Ibid.
     "heartsick about his situation": January 9, 1950, AP, UIC.
246 *"Give me the fucking phone":* Int. Walter Johnson, July 31, 1981.
     " 'should have never been listed' ": Int. Robert Shayon, March 8, 1983.
247 *"drove my wife crazy":* Ibid.
     "for the racy dialogue": Ibid.
248 *"didn't break our friendship":* Int. Sidney Hyman, September 16, 1983.
     Gallup polls: Crosby, *God, Church, and Flag,* p. 148.
249 *"blow up the damn paper":* Letter to Agnes Meyer, October 29, 1953, AP, UIC.
250 *widely interpreted:* Crosby, *God, Church, and Flag,* pp. 158–62.
     "over-emphasis of the Communist danger": May 26, 1945; courtesy of Judge Justine Wise
     Polier.
251 *"beleaguered spokesman":* Ibid., pp. 161–62.
     against "McCarty": Ibid., p. 164; see also John Cogley's memoir, *A Canterbury Tale,*
     p. 46.
     "Sheil's name the most celebrated": "The Bishop and the Senator," *The Progressive,* July
     1954, p. 4.
     "perversion of morality": Bernard J. Sheil, "The Immorality of McCarthyism," *The Pro-
     gressive,* May 1954, p. 12.
252 *"21,763 letters and telegrams":* "The Bishop and the Senator," p. 6.
     "handle the public relations": Letter to Miriam Jackson, April 15, 1954, AP, UIC.
     "bitterest, dirtiest fight": Letter to Miriam Jackson, April 25, 1954.
253 *"how vulnerable he is":* Letter to Alinsky, August 2, 1948, IAF.

253   *"typical of the cold hostility":* Letter to Spellman, November 16, 1946, IAF.
254   *"sense of loyalty":* Int. Ralph Helstein, March 15, 1983.
255   *"not accorded the hearing":* Letter to Agnes Meyer, November 10, 1954, AP, UIC.
      "break with the establishment": Int. Milton Mayer, April 10, 1983.
      Sheil had resigned: Minutes of IAF board meeting, October 20, 1954, United Packinghouse
      Workers of America papers, SHSW.

17. Pennies from Heaven

256   *"Her antecedents":* Letter to Milton Mayer, January 5, 1953, IAF.
      "a happy-go-lucky babe": Ibid.
257   *" 'thought you would never ask' ":* Int. Jean Alinsky, April 27, 1982.
      "perfectly wonderful": January 5, 1953, IAF.
258   *"a great relief":* Ibid.
      wash the windows: Int. Helen Meegan, July 13, 1982.
      "furnishing the house": January 5, 1953, IAF.
      "took part in the community": Int. Leon Despres, December 5, 1982
      "eat, shed and shit": Alinsky's letter to Happy Macy, June 23, 1953, AP, UIC.
259   *"the Fifth Amendment":* Letter of August 10, 1954, AP, UIC.
      "not your man": Letter to Alfred A. Knopf, December 24, 1954, IAF.
260   *saw each other occasionally:* Int. Eric Hoffer, April 26, 1982.
      books and magazines underlined: Int. Dorothy Ponce, October 11, 1982.
      cosmic brotherhood: Int. Nicholas von Hoffman, June 22, 1982.
261   *"Church was corrupt":* Int. Palmer Weber, May 11, 1983.
      a humanitarian Catholicism: See, for example, Alinsky's letter to Lowell Mellett, June 14,
      1954, IAF.
      "turning to grass roots organization": From Alinsky's unfinished manuscript of his
      O'Grady biography, IAF.
262   *O'Grady was reluctant:* Alinsky's letter to Lowell Mellett, June 14, 1954, IAF.
      Catholic social case work: Letter from Howland Shaw to Alinsky, June 18, 1954, IAF.
      "Money was dirty stuff": Int. Fred Ross, April 24, 1982.
263   *"knew that the freight":* Ibid.
      "can't let that happen": Ibid.
      "experimental demonstrations": Alinsky's letter to the National Information Bureau, No-
      vember 21, 1952, AP, UIC.
      "not a holding company": Letter of September 10, 1946, AP, UIC.
264   *three-year program:* Minutes of the IAF board meeting, December 12, 1950, pp. 1–3, IAF.
      "could name others": Letter of July 9, 1951, AP, UIC.
265   *"ought to get him":* Letter of October 24, 1951, AP, UIC.
      "saw a good deal of me": Alinsky's letter to Maritain, October 29, 1951, IAF.
      "important democratic initiative": Maritain letter to Hutchins, May 27, 1952, IAF.
      "breaking through of this climate": January 5, 1953, AP, UIC.
266   *less than $30,000 a year:* IAF audit, November 7, 1951, IAF. Also, Alinsky mentions his
      deferred salary increase in a letter to Happy Macy, December 20, 1951, AP, UIC.
      pioneering tax attorney: Int. Adolph Hirsch, September 13, 1983.
267   *big financial killing:* Ibid.
      " 'I would write it out' ": Ibid.
      within twenty-five years: Ibid.
268   *"giving us more trouble with Alinsky":* Ibid.
      "the things that Emil wanted": Ibid.
      three-year grant of $150,000: Tjerandsen, *Education,* p. 81.
269   *"better ecumenical spirit":* Int. Jack Egan, April 17, 1981.
      "asks Cardinal Spellman for something": Ibid.

270   *"needs of poor people":* Ibid.
       "warm and so human": Ibid.
       get his advice: Ibid.
       "There were eight or ten women": Int. Louis Silverman, April 15, 1983.
271   *"what Christ had in mind":* Ibid.
       "a fellow named Nicholas von Hoffman": Ibid.
272   *"The guy's a genius":* Ibid.
273   *"if the lamb pissed on the carpet":* Ibid.
       "you're over the hill": Int. Nicholas von Hoffman, June 22, 1982.
       "There was shouting and yelling": Int. Jack Egan, April 17, 1981.
274   *"a lot of money in those days":* Ibid.
       "a decent suit": Int. Nicholas von Hoffman, June 22, 1982.

18. The Big Eight Ball

275   *"ever want to see you again":* Int. Nicholas von Hoffman, March 25, 1982.
276   *"I learned more":* Ibid.
       "didn't have anything else": Ibid.
277   *met with Stritch:* Minutes of IAF board meeting, October 20, 1954, IAF.
       the first non-Catholic: Int. Lester Hunt, November 13, 1981.
278   *absorbed all this:* Von Hoffman's work was the basis for Alinsky's memorandum to
       Cardinal Stritch of June 24, 1955, AP, UIC.
       just under $150,000: "Revised Application of the Industrial Areas Foundation," December
       21, 1955.
279   *"segregated pattern is mutually detrimental":* Ibid., p. 2.
       Alinsky and the CPHA: Int. Elmer Gertz, January 21, 1983.
280   *" 'out to your belt buckle' ":* Int. Nicholas von Hoffman, March 25, 1983.
       "because he was Jewish": Int. Julius C. C. Edelstein, June 30, 1982.
       "all fascinated by it": Int. Leona Baumgartner, April 2, 1982.
281   *"agreed entirely with me":* Ibid.
       "time to talk about Saul": Ibid.
282   *Moses who put New York City:* Caro, *Power Broker,* p. 12.
283   *"when Dr. Alinsky got to New York":* November 12, 1953; courtesy of the New York
       Foundation.
       "help people help themselves": Ibid.
284   *"discuss things with me?":* Alinsky's letter to McGhee, June 27, 1955, IAF.
       "we can try to sell": McGhee's note to Alinsky, June 28, 1955, IAF.
285   *"Does that surprise you?":* Alinsky's memo to McGhee, also dated June 27, 1955 (see
       above), IAF.
       that he would be turned down: Int. Ralph Helstein, March 15, 1983.
286   *"the Helen Harris bloc":* Letter to O'Grady, October 12, 1955, AP, UIC.
       "responsibility for themselves": Letter to McGhee, October 27, 1955; courtesy of the New
       York Foundation.
       Sulzberger endorsed: Letter to David Heyman from Arthur Hays Sulzberger, October 26,
       1955, in the Chelsea file at the New York Foundation.
287   *might be combined with Alinsky's:* Notes made by Maxwell Hahn, executive director of the
       Field Foundation, of his telephone conversation with Dan Carpenter, March 3, 1955;
       courtesy of the Field Foundation, where the notes are filed under "Industrial Areas
       Foundation."
       blind carbon copy: Alinsky's letter to Hermon Dunlop Smith, March 7, 1955, IAF.
288   *"better than none at all":* Minutes of IAF board meeting, October 20, 1956, p. 6, IAF.
       "standards of professional social work: Ibid.
       "anxious to influence social work": Int. Lester Hunt, March 18, 1982.

288   *reassuring on this issue*": Minutes of IAF board meeting, October 20, 1956, p. 6, IAF.
289   "*but not to hire*": Int. Nicholas von Hoffman, June 22, 1982.
       "*difficult to do with a woman*": Alinsky's letter to Carl Tjerandsen, March 4, 1959, IAF.
       "*God pissing on him*": Int. Nicholas von Hoffman, June 22, 1982.
290   "*feel much more optimistic*": Letter of October 23, 1956, IAF.
291   "*could bomb this social workers' meeting*": Int. Marjorie Buckholz, November 9, 1984.
       "*all we had to do about it*": Ibid.
       "*mean as hell*": Ibid.
       "*tying balloons on telephone polls*": Ibid.
292   *more than fifty organizations:* Tjerandsen, *Education,* p. 292.
       "*from that day forth*": Int. Marjorie Buckholz, November 9, 1984.
       "*than one of Dunn's puppets*": Ibid.
293   "*as a Catholic priest*": Int. Robert Dunn, January 13, 1984.
       force Dunn to reexamine: Ibid.
       never occurred to Dunn: Int. Marjorie Buckholz, November 9, 1984.
294   "*actual lodestar*": Alinsky's letter to Carpenter, July 15, 1957, IAF.
       modest victories were few: Tjerandsen, *Education,* pp. 297–99.
295   *sold not one:* Letter to Leonard Rieser, November 17, 1958.
       Carpenter crowd found appalling: Int. Marjorie Buckholz, November 9, 1984.
       for financial independence: Tjerandsen, *Education,* p. 299.
296   "*not formed for the sake of the Puerto Ricans*": Int. Robert Dunn, January 13, 1984.
       "*didn't want those little men*": Int. Marjorie Buckholz, November 9, 1984.
       drain on Church resources: Cooney, *American Pope,* p. 322.
       Illich met Alinsky: Int. Ivan Illich, March 8, 1984.
297   "*threw a fit*": Int. Marjorie Buckholz, November 9, 1984.
       "*a great idea*": Int. Lester Hunt, March 18, 1982.
298   "*wasn't much to work with*": Ibid.
       "*education of Father Kane*": Memo from Lester Hunt to Alinsky, June 9–15, 1957, pp. 3–4.
       "*advantage to the church in all of this*": Letter to Dunn from Lester Hunt, February 18, 1958.
300   *no conflict on the night of June 20, 1956:* As described in Tjerandsen, *Education,* p. 287.
       "*how far down the road [Penn Station South] was*": Int. Marjorie Buckholz, November 9, 1984.
301   "*with a person like Carpenter*": Letter to Carl Tjerandsen from Alinsky, February 10, 1959, IAF.
       "*How Chelsea Was Torn Apart*": C. Everett Parker, *Christian Century,* February 3, 1960, pp. 130–33.
       into Chelsea rather than into the South Bronx: Int. Joseph Fitzpatrick, August 7, 1985.
       not very creative or inspiring: Alinsky's letter to Carl Tjerandsen, March 4, 1959.
302   "*as much art as there is science*": Letter from J. Donald Kingsley to D. John Heyman, October 25, 1955; courtesy of the New York Foundation.
       "*New York is not Chicago*": Int. Nicholas von Hoffman, March 25, 1983.

19. Race

304   *A yearly average:* Hodgson, *America,* p. 58.
       "*Colored? Cheap it out*": Int. Jerome Watson, November 25, 1982.
305   "*one of the outstanding priests*": Minutes of IAF board meeting, December 15, 1957.
       "*to stop it*": Int. Jack Egan, April 17, 1981.
306   "*Is God in today?*": Int. Dorothy Ponce, October 11, 1982.
307   "*show the damn movie*": Int. Nicholas von Hoffman, June 22, 1982.
308   "*in the Bartenders Union*": Alinsky's letter to Leonard Rieser, November 17, 1958, IAF.
       "*never wanted to be inconvenienced*": Int. Jack Egan, April 17, 1981.

309   " '*chastity on us* ' ": Ibid.
       was not amused: Int. Lester Hunt, November 13, 1981.
       "never-ending furor": Int. Nicholas von Hoffman, June 22, 1982.
310   *"can't do that, John":* Ibid.
       "go in the men's room": Ibid.
311   *"unofficial go-between":* Ibid.
       "Alinsky's effect on me": Int. T. George Harris, September 22, 1982.
       "locked him up in a car": Ibid.
       "muscle and minds and people": Ibid.
312   *paper that he presented:* "The Urban Immigrant," February 13, 1959, AP, UIC.
313   *"ugly word":* Ibid.
314   *"Many Negro leaders":* Ibid.
       short of highly doubtful: Int. Nicholas von Hoffman, June 22, 1982.

20. Church's Last Stand

315   *"the crucial history":* Int. Nicholas von Hoffman, June 22, 1982.
316   *unaware of the community's position on race:* Int. Jane Jacobs, August 13, 1984.
       "It wasn't integration": Int. Elizabeth Wood, March 13, 1984.
317   *4,000 houses:* Chicago *Sun-Times,* February 15, 1958, p. 17.
318   *"a record unsurpassed":* Ibid.
       Nobody who was at the dinner: Both Helen and Joseph Meegan (Int. July 13, 1982) and Jack
       Egan (Int. June 16, 1982) provided similar accounts of the after-dinner discussion.
320   *"Saul was really asking for a lot".* Int. Mike Royko, April 26, 1984.
       "He would have been done": Ibid.
       "pushed and shoved": Int. Jack Egan, March 3, 1982.
321   *"white people would move away":* Report from Egan to Alinsky, December 4, 1957, AP,
       UIC.
322   *"didn't want to get bogged down":* Int. Lester Hunt, March 18, 1982.
       "minds by rhetoric": Ibid.
323   *"for the common good":* Quoted in Fish et al., *Edge of the Ghetto,* pp. 41–42.
       money from the parish treasury: Int. Jack Egan, April 17, 1981.
324   *"liberal nudniks":* Int. Nicholas von Hoffman, June 22, 1982.
       "allowed us to do it": Int. Jack Egan, April 17, 1981.
325   *"only worried about blacks":* Int. Jack Egan, March 3, 1982.
326   *"six dollars a month":* Int. Ed Chambers, June 30, 1982.
       "guy I'd like to know": Ibid.
327   *"scratch around":* Ibid.
       "they wouldn't understand": Ibid.
328   *"off to a good start":* Ibid.
329   *"took on the mob":* Int. Joseph Vilimas, November 18, 1985.
       "a very big operation": Int. Nicholas von Hoffman, June 22, 1982.
330   *left the spiritual duty:* Allsop, *Bootleggers,* p. 85.
       similar tales: Both von Hoffman and Chambers had heard such stories.
       "plunk of horsehide": Int. Nicholas von Hoffman: June 22, 1982.
       shooing away a black: Ibid.
332   *"that night was tough":* Int. Ed Chambers, June 30, 1982.
       pastor wanted to distance: Int. Andrew Greeley, December 6, 1982.
       "don't ever do it!": Int. Nicholas von Hoffman, June 22, 1982.
       "because of Maritain": Int. Robert Christ, December 2, 1982.
333   *"turned me toward theology":* Ibid.
       "no more enlightened": Ibid.
       "hungry to make our mark": Ibid.

334   *"did a couple of things right":* Ibid.
335   *"no hanky-panky":* Int. Ed Chambers, June 30, 1982.
336   *lore of real estate:* Int. Donald O'Toole, May 4, 1984.
        "undesirables move in": Ibid.
337   *"pressure on the blacks":* Ibid.
        next instructive experience: Ibid.
        "wholesale fear of the man": Ibid.
338   *"matter of confessing":* Ibid.
        Alinsky was very guarded: Ibid.
339   *Nick von Hoffman had written:* Letter from von Hoffman's and Hunt's secretary to Hunt,
        who was in Butte, Montana, May 11, 1959, AP, UIC.
        "boundaries of the racial ghetto": Chicago *Daily News,* May 6, 1959, p. 1.
        "a sizeable mental laxative": Alinsky's letter to Gordon Clapp, May 20, 1959, IAF.
        "with 'Amen!' ": Ibid.
340   *"hand over your heart":* Int. Ed Chambers, June 30, 1982.
341   *"things you have to think of":* Alinsky's letter to Clapp, May 28, 1959, IAF.
        "is the plan of Saul Alinsky": Quoted in *Southtown Economist,* October 25, 1959, p. 1.
        "Even my mother": Int. Joe Vilimas, November 18, 1985.
342   *"You name the place":* Int. Ed Chambers, June 30, 1982.
343   *"all wired":* Ibid.
        "give them something concrete": Int. Nicholas von Hoffman, June 22, 1982.
344   *"begun to soft-pedal":* Von Hoffman's memo to Alinsky, August 18, 1959, IAF.
345   *"jackals in the night":* Alinsky's memo to von Hoffman, August 18, 1959, IAF.
        "bandwagon psychology": Von Hoffman's memo to Alinsky, August 18, 1959, IAF.
346   *"Daley put him off":* Ibid.
        " 'God rest his soul' ": Int. Donald O'Toole, May 5, 1984.
347   *"less than a communication problem?":* Int. Nicholas von Hoffman, June 22, 1982.
        " 'interested in real estate' ": Von Hoffman's memo to Alinsky, August 18, 1959, IAF.
348   *"nobody recognizes more than I":* Alinsky's memo to von Hoffman, August 18, 1959, IAF.

        21. Tears of Joy

349   *"We don't talk that way":* Int. Ed Chambers, September 23, 1982.
350   *"constant balancing act":* Ibid.
        "Catholic steamrolling": Von Hoffman's memo to Alinsky, August 18, 1959, IAF.
        wanted to approach Meyer carefully: Alinsky's memo to von Hoffman, August 18, 1959,
        IAF.
        advance the general relationship: Ibid.
351   *"jugulars ought to be nicely sliced":* Alinsky's memo to von Hoffman, September 8, 1959,
        IAF.
        "not at all surprised": Ibid.
352   *"how we can lose":* Von Hoffman's memo to Alinsky, September 2, 1959, IAF.
        articles on blockbusting: See, for example, Chicago *Daily News,* October 14, 15, 17, and 24,
        1959.
354   *a white cake:* Alinsky's letter to Gordon Clapp, May 20, 1959, IAF.
        "no burr heads": Anonymous.
        a panicky pastor: Int. Ed Chambers, June 30, 1982.
355   *"Negro church afterward?":* Ibid.
        "convention without us": Ibid.
        "move we admit them": Ibid.
356   *scanned 104 delegations:* Chicago *Daily News,* October 26, 1959, p. 12.
        fell ominously silent: Int. Ed Chambers, June 30, 1982.
357   *"thrills of my life":* Int. Jack Egan, April 17, 1981.

358 *"man like Norris"*: Int. Ed Chambers, June 30, 1982.
    immediate, tangible enemies: Int. James Norris, December 4, 1982.
359 *Norris was spending:* Ibid.
    "Norris got the idea": Int. Ed Chambers, June 30, 1982.
    "impregnated everything": Int. James Reed, October 12, 1982.
360 *"immediately convincing"*: Ibid.
    "he's a communist": Ibid.
    "send my salary": Ibid.
    talked to Rickey about it: Ibid.
361 *"let your enemies"*: Ibid.
362 *"can be defrocked"*: Int. Bob Christ, December 2, 1982.

22. Civil Rights in Chicago

363 *food through a straw:* Int. David Alinsky, April 4, 1982.
364 *recommended to Saul:* Int. Friedy Hiesler, April 29, 1982.
    "the course will be": September 11, 1956, IAF.
    on the car seat: Int. Jean Alinsky, April 27, 1982.
    "two analysts on one's back": Letter to Leonard Rieser, November 30, 1958, IAF.
365 *of a typical day:* Int. Dorothy Ponce, October 11, 1982.
    "get them into the Church": Int. Martin Farrell, March 16, 1982.
366 *"American and Alinsky principles"*: Farrell's letter, February 22, 1958, IAF.
    "until you organize blacks": Int. Martin Farrell, March 16, 1982.
    "didn't know what I was doing": Ibid.
367 *"bucket of steam to me"*: Int. Vincent Cooke, April 22, 1982.
    "not sure you could separate it": Int. Ralph Helstein, March 15, 1983.
    " 'keep them out' basis": Alinsky's memo to von Hoffman, September 25, 1959, AP, UIC.
368 *"start right now, today"*: Ibid.
    "it had to be Woodlawn": Int. Nicholas von Hoffman, June 22, 1982.
369 *"made a marvelous boss"*: Ibid.
    had grown up in the neighborhood: Int. Julian Levi, April 8, 1983.
    to nearly 75,000: Rossi and Dentler, *Politics of Urban Renewal,* p. 26.
370 *"threatened him with legal action"*: Ibid., pp. 82–83.
371 *"a great program"*: Chicago *Tribune,* July 9, 1958, p. 19.
    "a national test": Chicago *Sun-Times,* March 2, 1958, p. 3.
372 *"do something about this"*: Int. Jack Egan, June 16, 1982.
    "so oppose it": Ibid.
    "sort of a gray person": Ibid.
373 *"you assholes?"*: Int. Louis Silverman, September 15, 1983.
    "with Hyde Park, not much": Int. Nicholas von Hoffman, June 22, 1982.
374 *behind Levi:* Rossi and Dentler, *Politics of Urban Renewal,* p. 236.
    "miscalculated the reaction": Int. Louis Silverman, September 15, 1983.
    "never felt more lonely": Int. Jack Egan, June 16, 1982.
375 *"against the lower classes"*: Hyde Park *Herald,* September 17, 1958.
    "you have your troops": Int. Jack Egan, June 16, 1982.
376 *troublesome interloper:* In a letter to Happy Macy, Alinsky told her that Levi was spreading
    stories to the effect that both he and the Catholic Church were cooking up "a horrendous
    Jim Crow scheme," and Alinsky was prepared to use his connections on the university's
    board of trustees to confront Levi at an audience with university president Lawrence
    Kimpton. June 23, 1953, AP, UIC.
377 *"to permit further exploration"*: June 1960, IAF file; courtesy of the Field Foundation.
    mutually satisfying solution: Int. Hermon Dunlop Smith, March 18, 1982.
378 *"to cause a little scandal"*: Von Hoffman's memo to Alinsky, May 28, 1960, AP, UIC.

378   *"not be sucked out":* Ibid.
379   *it was a news conference:* Fish, *Black Power/White Control,* p. 19.
      "against everything I wanted": Ibid.
      disliked this on principle: Ibid.
      meeting did not go well: Int. Vincent Cooke, April 22, 1982.
380   *"game of power politics?":* November 11, 1959, p. 1308.
      "in the user": Alinsky, "From Citizen Apathy to Participation," reprint of a speech given
      in Chicago, October 19, 1957, IAF.
      "altered by power": Ibid.
      wanted to work with churches: Int. Douglas Still, February 22, 1982.
381   *"real world was about":* Ibid.
      "an enemy out there": Int. Chris Hartmire, April 30, 1982.
      "not going to save yourself": Int. Douglas Still, February 22, 1982.
382   *"was senseless":* Ibid.
      exchange between Moses and God: An unabridged version appears in several sources,
      including Alinsky's *Rules for Radicals,* pp. 89–91.
383   *"then we'll have reconciliation":* Douglas Still and author's notes, July 19–29, 1966, Asilo-
      mar, California.
      "assertion of personal value: Int. Douglas Still, February 22, 1982.
384   *"not that they were deviants":* Int. David Ramage, December 12, 1981.
      "my eyes just went like that": Ibid.
385   *"Negro organizations to cooperate with":* February 9, 1960, p. 2, AP, UIC.
      "white horses to ride": Int. David Ramage, December 12, 1981.
386   *"finger in the dike":* Int. Robert Christ, December 2, 1982.
      "started that night": Int. David Ramage, December 12, 1981.
387   *" 'committee will not be threatened' ":* Int. Charles Leber, September 23, 1982.
      "Alinsky's prestige has lessened": Field Foundation memo of spring 1960; Smith's letter to
      foundation executive, May 19, 1960, and return letter to Smith, May 23, 1960; courtesy of
      Mr. Smith.
388   *"meet at the summit":* Alinsky's letter to Ruth Field, June 3, 1960, IAF.
      "I must beg": Ruth Field's letter to Alinsky, June 2, 1960; courtesy of Mrs. Field and in
      IAF files.
      more than $700,000: Tjerandsen, *Education,* Appendix B.
389   *"a man on a cross":* Int. Jack Egan, April 17, 1981.

23. *Woodlawn*

390   *"what I had in mind":* Alinsky's memo to von Hoffman, August 1, 1960, AP, UIC.
391   *"if Daley thought":* Ibid.
      "being the university's friend": Ibid.
392   *an "offer" of money:* Fish, *Black Power/White Control,* p. 19.
      phoned von Hoffman: Ibid., p. 30.
      "thought we had five hundred": Int. Charles Leber, September 23, 1982.
393   *"might as well say a thousand":* quoted in Fish, *Black Power/White Control,* p. 31.
      "as a white person": Int. Charles Leber, September 23, 1982.
      "he was marvelous!": Int. Nicholas von Hoffman, June 22, 1982.
394   *"won't have any time to organize":* Int. Robert Squires, October 13, 1982.
      might be more humaneness: Ibid.
395   *"salmon faces":* Int. Nicholas von Hoffman, June 22, 1982.
      "emotionally this was too much": Von Hoffman's memo to Alinsky, October 14, 1958, AP,
      UIC.
      a very strong stereotype: Sanders, "Professional Radical," *Harper's,* June 1965, p. 44.
396   *communist insurgents democratically:* Int. Douglas Still, February 22, 1982.

carefully rehearsed: According to von Hoffman, all such public meetings were scripted and planned so that there would be no unexpected outcomes.

"Saul had no objections": Int. Nicholas von Hoffman, June 22, 1982.

"We were outnumbered": Int. Ann Prosten, November 22, 1982.

397 *"not bring in too many a priori maps":* Int. Nicholas von Hoffman, June 22, 1982.

"None of them will work": Von Hoffman's memo to Alinsky, October 14, 1958, AP, UIC.

398 *"feel it and hear it":* Int. Robert Squires, October 13, 1982.

"Harmon just kind of turned up": Int. Nicholas von Hoffman, June 22, 1982.

399 *"Saul said many, many times":* Ibid.

"wipe you out": Int. Robert Squires, October 13, 1982.

400 *"We shall teach it to you":* Int. Nicholas von Hoffman, June 22, 1982.

401 *"Get on it tomorrow":* Ibid.

"never put up any money": Ibid.

402 *"larger than a crap game":* Ibid.

"most satisfying scene": Ibid.

403 *to cover the emerging TWO:* Int. Georgie Anne Geyer, June 21, 1982.

averting still another: Int. Nicholas von Hoffman, June 22, 1982.

Egan had heard a rumor: Int. Jack Egan, March 22, 1989.

"even the nuns": Int. Nicholas von Hoffman, June 22, 1982.

404 *"Miller had so little clout":* Int. Nicholas von Hoffman, March 25, 1983.

to win their rent strikes: Ibid.

405 *"double talk public relations":* Quoted in Fish, *Black Power/White Control,* p. 52.

only two of the three: Int. Robert Squires, October 13, 1982.

406 *"more than Saul".* Int. Nicholas von Hoffman, June 22, 1982.

Carnegie students stayed away: Fish, *Black Power/White Control,* p. 55.

ever come to quitting: Int. Nicholas von Hoffman, July 18, 1987.

407 *"is a slum landlord":* Fish, *Black Power/White Control,* p. 59.

"the darkest Negroes": Author's notes, July 19–29, 1966, Asilomar, California.

"flip the coin": Ibid.

408 *"where those slum landlords":* Int. Charles Leber, September 23, 1982.

"war over urban renewal": Chicago *Daily News,* April 12, 1962.

409 *"foreign domination":* Fish, *Black Power/White Control,* p. 36.

"not going to move again": Int. Charles Leber, September 23, 1982.

410 *"elected to decide":* Chicago *Daily News,* April 12, 1962, p. 42.

" 'private regarding' ": James Q. Wilson, "Planning and Politics," *Journal of the American Institute of Planners,* November 1963, p. 246.

411 *"don't even know who to fire":* Int. Nicholas von Hoffman, March 25, 1983.

"only first-rate thing": Int. Charles Silberman, June 29, 1982.

a measure of disapproval: Int. Ralph Helstein, March 19, 1983.

"this kind of dog": Int. Nicholas von Hoffman, July 18, 1987.

412 *"making things very difficult":* Int. Hermon Dunlop Smith, March 18, 1982.

"didn't know what he might do": Int. Hermon Dunlop Smith, June 26, 1982.

"to a substantial degree": March 15, 1961, IAF.

to arrange a meeting: Int. Hermon Dunlop Smith, March 18, 1982.

413 *"Permit me to suggest":* Alinsky's letter to Beadle, November 20, 1961, IAF.

Helstein feared: Int. Ralph Helstein, March 19, 1983.

"agreeing 100 percent": Int. Hermon Dunlop Smith, March 18, 1982.

414 *"between the University of Chicago and TWO":* December 5, 1961, IAF.

415 *"they create them":* Chicago *Daily News,* April 7, 1962, p. 5.

"I was calm": Alinsky's letter, June 2, 1961, AP, UIC.

"they do not understand": Farrell's memo to von Hoffman, April 10, 1961, AP, UIC.

416 *"to Saul early in life":* Int. Charles Leber, September 23, 1982.

"sake of a new ministry": Ibid.

417   *four thousand jobs:* Int. Nicholas von Hoffman, June 22, 1982.
      "patronage and money": Int. Lester Hunt, March 18, 1982.
418   *"received severe criticism":* Int. Arthur Brazier, July 5, 1983.
      "You dumb jerk": Int. Nicholas von Hoffman, July 18, 1987.
      one-word cutline: Chicago *Daily News,* April 7, 1962.
419   *"how the city worked":* Int. Arthur Brazier, July 5, 1983.
      "betterment of the entire city": Chicago *Daily News,* April 7, 1962, p. 1.
      memo for the mayor: Signed by Arthur Brazier, February 20, 1962, AP, UIC.
420   *a shot rang out:* Int. Robert Squires, October 13, 1982.
421   *"You cannot believe":* Int. Nicholas von Hoffman, March 25, 1983.
      "wildest nights": Int. Charles Leber, September 23, 1982.
      "never understand it": Int. Nicholas von Hoffman, March 25, 1983.
422   *"always wanted to believe that":* Ibid.
423   *"every eye":* Ibid.
      supported TWO financially: Ibid.
      "stuck with turkeys": Ibid.
424   *"your house by nine":* Int. Charles Leber, September 23, 1982.
      "salt-laden tears": Int. Nicholas von Hoffman, March 25, 1983.

24. Black and White

425   *in the Chicago* Daily News: April 7–13, 1962.
426   *slowed white flight:* Int. Ed Chambers, June 30, 1982.
427   *omitted any mention:* Fish et al., *Edge of the Ghetto.*
      "Alinsky's a wild man": Int. Barry Menuez, June 2, 1982.
      " 'or you're through' ": Ibid.
428   *"like a doctor":* Ibid.
      "do him a favor": Ibid.
429   *"stole the election":* Int. Ed Chambers, June 30, 1982.
      "housing opportunities": Fish et al., *Edge of the Ghetto,* p. 22.
430   *two distinct "parties":* Ibid., p. 23.
431   *left the OSC for good:* Ibid., p. 25.
      first to leave: Int. Ed Chambers, June 30, 1982.
      "great Mississippi flood": Int. Nicholas von Hoffman, June 22, 1982.
432   *economic considerations became salient:* Int. Ed Chambers, September 23, 1982.
      if not originated: Jackson, *Crabgrass Frontier,* p. 198.
433   *"to sort them out":* Ibid.
      "couldn't rent these places to whites": Int. Nicholas von Hoffman, June 22, 1982.
      often felt overwhelmed: Int. James Norris, December 4, 1982.
      had to steal time: Int. Barry Menuez, June 2, 1982.
      "a terrible risk": Int. Bruce Sagan, December 2, 1982.
434   *"whole gang":* Int. Donald O'Toole, May 4, 1984.
      "getting up and fighting": Ibid.
      special accounts: Ibid.
      "With certain notable exceptions": Von Hoffman's memo to Alinsky, June 21, 1963, AP, UIC.
435   *"big issue, which is race":* Ibid.
436   *by one of his cousins:* Int. Donald O'Toole, May 4, 1984.
      "sapped the strength": Ibid.
      appointment of school principals: Int. Peter Martinez, March 4, 1983.
      battled successfully: Ibid.
437   *begin a new career:* Int. Thomas Gaudette, May 26, 1982.
      "not only consolidate them": Alinsky's letter to Ross, November 16, 1962, IAF.

438   *verge of quitting:* Int. Ed Chambers, September 23, 1982.
    "You're out": Ibid.
    "from central casting": Ibid. and Int. November 15, 1982.

439   *"hell of a good party":* Int. Ed Chambers, September 23, 1982.
    "stand on its own feet": Von Hoffman's memo to TWO's staff and steering committee, June 1, 1962, AP, UIC.
    TWO had $14,500: Int. Ed Chambers, September 23, 1982.

440   *highly excessive:* Ibid.
    "one of the first": Chicago *Daily News,* July 11, 1963, p. 1.

441   *by Jane Jacobs:* Fish, *Black Power/White Control,* p. 69.
    to initiate a second move: Ibid., p. 70.
    alternative had to be invented: Int. Ed Chambers, September 23, 1982.
    "hear it here": Chicago *Daily News,* July 11, 1963, p. 1.

442   *signs that read:* Ibid.
    Brazier froze: Int. Ed Chambers, September 23, 1982.
    "all over you": Int. Arthur Brazier, July 5, 1983.

443   *"that a black man":* Int. Ed Chambers, September 23, 1982.
    "majority of the people": Fish, *Black Power/White Control,* pp. 71–72.

445   *tactic was recalled:* Chicago *Sun-Times,* July 29, 1982, p. 2.
    "the problem of race": Int. Charles Silberman, June 29, 1982.
    the most important piece: Ibid.

446   *"even to admit":* Silberman, *Crisis in Black and White,* p. 3.
    "their business interrupted": Ibid., p. 10.

447   *"prison we have all made":* Ibid., p. 11.
    somewhat accidentally: Int. Charles Silberman, June 29, 1982.
    "rang all sorts of bells": Ibid.
    saw the draft and called: Ibid.

448   *"evidence of Saul's corruption":* Ibid.
    "beads for trade": Transcript of a radio interview on KPFA, Berkeley, California, October 31, 1965, IAF.

449   *"TWO's greatest contribution":* Silberman, *Crisis in Black and White,* p. 348.
    "the most impressive experiment": Ibid., p. 318.

25. Smugtown and Stardom

450   *"two for one":* Int. Lester Hunt, November 13, 1981.
    changed direction: Int. Seniel Ostrow, April 29, 1982.

451   *elevator escapades:* Int. Dorothy Ponce, October 11, 1982.

452   *"radicalized by the experience":* Int. Jack McCrory, July 21, 1987.
    "concept of power": Ibid.

453   *like a war zone:* Based on a twenty-page special report in the Rochester *Times-Union,* on the twentieth anniversary of the riot, July 25, 1984.

454   *tripled from 7,600:* Ibid., p. 2.

455   *"or twenty-eight families":* Ibid.
    "critics paint": Ibid., p. 3.
    "sat around on the side": Int. Jack McCrory, July 21, 1987.

456   *some black clergy:* Int. Herbert White, March 30, 1985.
    "guilt feelings": Ibid.

457   *"There's a tactic":* Ibid. and Rochester *Times-Union,* July 25, 1984, p. 18.
    called his friend: Int. Allen Wallis, December 7, 1985.
    getting similar calls: Int. Gaylord Freeman, December 5, 1982.
    "I'm not Mahatma Gandhi": Rochester *Times-Union,* March 17, 1965, p. 1A.

458   *"faucets are being turned off":* Rochester *Times-Union,* January 29, 1965, p. 1B.

458   *"the support of Alinsky"*: Rochester *Times-Union,* February 25, 1965, p. 1B.
       "This is your problem": Rochester *Times-Union,* July 25, 1984, p. 18.
459   *"could not now break faith"*: White's letter to Alinsky, February 9, 1965, IAF; courtesy
       of Mr. White.
       "We're going into Rochester": Int. Ed Chambers, November 15, 1982.
460   *"free staff assistant"*: Int. Barry Menuez, September 21, 1982.
       "like an advance man": Ibid.
       "want your word of honor": Ibid.
461   *"thought Chambers was black"*: Int. Herb White, March 30, 1985.
       "Then call it FIGHT": Int. Franklin Florence, October 28, 1987.
       "God is in": Int. Ed Chambers, November 15, 1982.
       "Because Rochester": Rochester *Democrat & Chronicle,* March 26, 1965, p. 1A.
462   *"WORK or LOVE or DEED"*: Rochester *Times-Union,* January 14, 1967, p. 6A.
       schedules did not permit: Alinsky's letter to Happy Macy, March 10, 1965, and her response
       of June 4, IAF.
463   *"didn't say the words"*: Int. Sol Linowitz, July 23, 1984.
       "very patient with us": Alinsky's interview with Lawrence Bachmann, November 11, 1971;
       courtesy of Mr. Bachmann.
       "Alinsky is smart and mean": Jones memo to Miller, April 1, 1965; courtesy of Mr. Jones.
464   *Alinsky knew more about:* Rochester *Times-Union,* July 25, 1984, p. 18.
       "Saul was at his best": Int. Franklin Florence, October 28, 1987.
       "How do I know": Int. Ed Chambers, November 15, 1982, and November 9, 1983.
465   *" 'someday in heaven' "*: Int. Herb White, March 30, 1985.
       "getting connections": Int. Ed Chambers, November 15, 1982.
       four out of five: Rochester *Democrat & Chronicle,* May 23, 1965, p. 1A.
466   *"white media were astounded"*: Int. Ed Chambers, November 15, 1982.
       "dangerous situation": James Ridgeway, "Saul Alinsky in Smugtown," *The New Republic,*
       June 26, 1965.
       "the most controversial figure": Jules Witcover, "Rochester Braces for Another July, *The
       Reporter,* July 15, 1965, p. 34.
467   *"my wilderness"*: Sanders, "Professional Radical," *Harper's,* June 1965, p. 46.
468   *"Imprisonment not only"*: "Law school lecture" notes, IAF.
470   *"His way of dealing"*: Int. Ralph Helstein, November 10, 1981.
       "can't compete with the Lord": Int. Ed Chambers, January 12, 1984.
471   *"before the thing blew"*: Transcript of a radio interview on KPFA, Berkeley, California,
       October 31, 1965, IAF.
       "When [the riot started]": Ibid.
       "through their own efforts": Author's notes, July 19–29, 1966, Asilomar, California.
472   *"derail our political progress"*: Ibid.
473   *"the archetypal liberal"*: Hodgson, *America,* p. 270.
       dispense funds: Matusow, *The Unraveling,* esp. pp. 108–12.
       "no matter how liberal": See Silberman, *Crisis in Black and White,* pp. 250–52.
474   *"even radical implications"*: Matusow, *The Unraveling,* p. 112.
       lack of understanding: Ibid., p. 120.
475   *"the very war itself"*: Ibid., p. 123.
       "Two interesting things": Int. Richard Boone, June 1, 1982.
476   *"to their field"*: Ibid.
       "it becomes part of the program": Matusow, *The Unraveling,* p. 124.
477   *"few and far between"*: Int. Richard Boone, June 1, 1982.
478   *impressed Kravitz:* Int. Warren Haggstrom, August 14, 1982.
       "about $10,000 for a year": Ibid.
       "that anything would happen": Ibid.
       "to near-hysteria": Erwin Knoll and Jules Witcover, "Fighting Poverty and City Hall,"

The Reporter, June 3, 1965, p. 21.
Ross used house meetings: Int. Fred Ross, July 19, 1987.

479 *"it could be decisive":* Knoll and Witcover, p. 20.
"tenants will permit": Ibid.

480 *"on a moral dynamism":* "War on Poverty—Political Pornography," *Journal of Social Issues,* January 1965, p. 46.
"blue chip investment": Ibid., p. 45.

481 *"Not only lacking money":* Ibid., p. 47.
"not be looking through": Ibid., pp. 46–47.

483 *"I'll answer":* Int. Irene McInnis, January 17, 1982.

484 *"a friend he could count on":* Int. Jack Egan, March 3, 1982.

485 *"zookeeper mentality":* Rochester *Democrat & Chronicle,* January 14, 1966, p. 3.
"right people so miserable": Ibid.
"leave him alone": Chambers's memo to Alinsky, March 31, 1966, IAF.

486 *"the signed statements":* Ibid.
"exclusive apartments": Rochester *Times-Union,* May 19, 1966, p. 5B.
"constant harassment": Patrick Anderson, "Making Trouble Is Alinsky's Business," *New York Times Magazine,* October 9, 1966. p. 32.

487 *ridiculed a similar idea:* Int. Mike Miller, April 25, 1982.
"shoulder to shoulder with FIGHT": Rochester *Times-Union,* January 14, 1966, p. 2B.

488 *"Black Power crap":* Int. Ed Chambers, November 9, 1983.

489 *"prepare them for":* Int. Franklin Florence, October 28, 1987.

490 *"what people to hire":* Int. William Vaughn, August 14, 1984.
"in every ghetto": Rochester *Democrat & Chronicle,* October 26, 1966, p. 3B.

491 *"hoping for more":* Rochester *Democrat & Chronicle,* December 21, 1966, p. 1A.
" 'Forget it' ": Alexander Hawryluk, *Friends of FIGHT: A Study of a Militant Civil Rights Organization,* diss., 1967, p. 205.

492 *"Don't let 'em trick you":* Int. Franklin Florence, October 14, 1987.
"whites always lie!": As recalled by Ed Chambers, January 12, 1984.
Canadian operations unionized: Int. William Vaughn, August 14, 1984.
"It was awful": Ibid.

493 *"[that kind of] hypocrisy":* As recalled by Franklin Florence, October 28, 1987.
"lay my life down": Ibid.
"can't do this, goddamnit!": Int. Ed Chambers, January 12, 1984.
stripped of his title: Rochester *Times-Union,* July 25, 1987, p. 19.
"Southern plantation": Washington *Post,* January 9, 1967, p. 3.

494 *"will go down in history":* Quoted in *The Wall Street Journal,* June 30, 1967, p. 1.
"low-down": Rochester *Democrat & Chronicle,* February 1, 1967, p. 1B.
"benefit to the unemployed": Rochester *Democrat & Chronicle,* February 22, 1967, p. 4B.

495 *"Please be advised":* February 22, 1967, IAF.
"stop taking pictures": Int. Ed Chambers, January 12, 1984.
Herb White maintains: Int. Herb White, March 30, 1985.
originated with him: Int. Ed Chambers, January 12, 1984.
11,000 shares: Rochester *Democrat & Chronicle,* March 31, 1967, p. 8D.

496 *ruled in Kodak's favor:* Rochester *Democrat & Chronicle,* April 25, 1967, 1B.
meeting of Unitarians: Int. Joseph L. Fisher, September 5, 1987.

497 *"false information":* Int. William Vaughn, August 14, 1984.
"prayed the night before": Ibid.

498 *"they'll get blamed":* Int. Ed Chambers, January 12, 1984.
"right down to a 'T' ": Rochester *Times-Union,* April 25, 1967, p. 1A.
when Chambers had checked in: Int. Ed Chambers, January 12, 1984.
"Point of order!": New York Times, April 26, 1967.

499   *"resurrection of the civil rights movement"*: Ibid.
       "where their sermons are": Chicago *Daily News*, April 25, 1967, p. 33.
       "a candlelight service": *New York Times*, April 26, 1967.
       "such a far-reaching decision": Text of Church Council resolution, May 11, 1967, IAF.
500   *in touch with Robert Kennedy*: Int. Ed Chambers, January 12, 1984.
       "only to underscore": Rochester *Democrat & Chronicle*, April 8, 1967.
501   *"I'm going to settle it today"*: Int. Irene McInnis, December 20, 1984.
       "terrible outfit Kodak is": Int. Daniel Patrick Moynihan, February 25, 1984.
       "won't hold Kodak": Ibid.
502   *"Kodak recognizes that FIGHT"*: Rochester *Democrat & Chronicle*, June 24, 1967, p. 3A.
       "Black men today": Ibid., p. 1A.
       "clear and unmistakable recognition": Ibid. Regarding Alinsky's remarks about Kodak
       film: Int. Daniel Patrick Moynihan, February 25, 1984.
       "They've got to meet with me": Alinsky interview with Lawrence Bachmann, November
       11, 1971; courtesy of Mr. Bachmann.
       "to wipe them clean": Ibid.
503   *"crazy as hell"*: Ibid.
       "Berlin in 1945": Quoted in Matusow, *The Unraveling*, p. 363.
       "very helpful force": Int. Willard Wirtz, July 15, 1984.
       "has two sets of stockholders": Alinsky interview with Lawrence Bachmann, November 11,
       1971; courtesy of Mr. Bachmann.
504   *as a lost cause*: Int. Herb White, March 30, 1985.
       courage of a small number: Int. Paul Long, September 29, 1987.
505   *"I remember three years ago"*: Text of the speech, IAF.

26. New Career

506   *"like a giant X"*: Quoted in Hodgson, *America*, p. 218.
507   *"racist as Goldwater"*: Quoted in Gitlin, *The Sixties*, p. 159.
508   *color of evil*: Author's notes, July 19–29, 1966, Asilomar, California.
       "exploiting liberals": Los Angeles *Times*, July 7, 1968, p. 13.
509   *"repugnant and nauseous"*: Ibid.
       major inspiration of IFCO: Int. David Ramage, February 23, 1989.
       displeasure of Walter Kloetzli: Int. James Morton, February 23, 1987; Int. Walter Kloetzli,
       November 13, 1986.
510   *"Believing in full equality"*: Los Angeles *Times*, July 7, 1968, p. 14.
511   *"I couldn't agitate"*: Int. Mike Miller, April 9, 1983.
512   *"Saul, old friend"*: Farrell's note to Alinsky, September 13, 1965, IAF.
513   *"localist agenda"*: Frank Riessman, "The Myth of Saul Alinsky," *Dissent*, July 1965, p.
       474.
       "would go down": Int. Nicholas von Hoffman, July 18, 1987.
514   *"he never thought that"*: Ibid.
       "made a great mistake": Ibid.
       used the Blackstone Rangers: Int. Elliot Epstein, December 6, 1987.
516   *admirer and friend*: Int. Alvin Duskin, August 21, 1982.
       By the spring of 1968: Int. Gordon Sherman, April 26, 1982.
517   *"must talk to Saul Alinsky"*: Ibid.; also Int. Jack Egan, April 17, 1981.
       "driving this globe to oblivion": Int. Gordon Sherman, April 26, 1982.

27. "Be Thou a Man"

519   *"Alinsky emerges"*: Moynihan, *Maximum Feasible*, p. 187.
520   *the trouble Alinsky was causing*: Int. Charles Merrill, April 2, 1982.

barely scratching out a living: Matthiessen, *Sal Si Puedes,* pp. 43–44.
"I could feel it": Ibid.; Int. Cesar Chavez, April 28, 1982.

521 *135,000 Mexican-Americans:* Tjerandsen, *Education,* p. 113.
"a prerequisite to becoming": Ibid., p. 112.

522 *not far off the mark:* Int. Cesar Chavez, April 28, 1982.
"I'm flattered by the attention": Author's transcript of Alinsky's testimony before the California Senate Fact-Finding Committee of Agriculture, Delano, California, July 19, 1966.
"never had any connections with": Ibid.

523 *"Change means movement":* Author's notes, July 19–29, 1966, Asilomar, California.

524 *the airport demonstration:* Alinsky told several similar versions of the story, and Warren Haggstrom believes he was the first to hear it on a visit to Chicago in the mid-1960s.
" 'Alinsky burned here' ": Int. Paul Yilvasaker, May 6, 1984.

525 *"the unprecedented event":* Hayden, *Reunion,* p. 124.

526 *"a primitive slob":* Based on excerpts of a letter written by Todd Gitlin on April 7, 1966; courtesy of Mr. Gitlin.

528 *and the writer Louis Lomax:* Int. Annaloyce Clapp, July 9, 1982.
"in a vaudeville act": I remember this response to journalist Mike Royko's question when Alinsky appeared on a Chicago television news program, probably in 1970. Another put-down that proved memorable was Alinsky's observation in a *Rolling Stone* interview (March 4, 1971) that "Jerry and Abbie couldn't organize a luncheon, much less a revolution."
phoned Staughton Lynd: Int. Staughton Lynd, June 4, 1988.

529 *legitimizing his ideas and concepts:* Int. Gordon Sherman, April 26, 1982.
"by Alinsky's ideas": March 2, 1970, p. 56.
"know you're in trouble": Boston *Globe,* December 8, 1970.

530 *"in and for a free society":* Undated entry, IAF.
one word: "power": Int. Susan Kellock, September 23, 1985.

532 *"The revolutionary force today":* Rules for Radicals, p. xiii.

533 *"Even if all":* Ibid., p. xiv.
" 'his own people' ": Ibid., p. 185.

534 *"To reject them is to lose":* Ibid., p. 189.
"tactics must begin within": Ibid., p. 195.
"a new political type": Christopher Lasch, "Can the Left Rise Again?," *New York Review of Books,* October 21, 1971.

535 *"personal smear job":* Alinsky's letter to McWilliams, October 25, 1971, IAF.

536 *in a hospital recovery room:* Int. Georgia Harper Boyer, March 20, 1983.
what Saul did for a living: Int. Sidney Hyman, September 16, 1983.
a batch of envelopes: Int. Georgia Harper Boyer, March 20, 1983.

537 *began to gargle:* Int. Irene McInnis, December 20, 1984.
impressed with their courage: Ibid.

538 *"learned it in my belly":* Sanders, *Professional Radical,* p. 47.
"tell me how it feels": Int. Ralph Helstein, March 15, 1983.
to alarm Irene: Int. Irene McInnis, June 2, 1982.

539 *in his ear, "Boo!":* Int. Bill Grace, September 2, 1981.
FBI warned him: Int. Irene McInnis, June 2, 1982.
the network evening news: Int. Kay Mann, April 5, 1983.
Egan heard the news: Int. Jack Egan, March 3, 1982.

540 *sincerity was also evident:* Int. Ralph Helstein, Jack Egan, Nicholas von Hoffman, Irene McInnis, Joseph Meegan.
went ahead with the retreat: Int. Ed Chambers, November 9, 1983.

MAJOR WORKS CITED IN NOTES

Alinsky, Saul. *Reveille for Radicals.* University of Chicago Press, 1945.
————. *John L. Lewis: An Unauthorized Biography.* G. P. Putnam's Sons, 1949.
————. *Rules for Radicals.* Random House, 1971.
Allsop, Kenneth. *The Bootleggers.* Arlington House, 1968.
Becker, Stephan. *Marshall Field III.* Simon and Schuster, 1964.
Berkow, Ira. *Maxwell Street.* Doubleday & Company, 1977.
Caro, Robert. *The Power Broker.* Vintage, 1975.
Cogley, John. *A Canterbury Tale.* Seabury, 1976.
Cooney, John. *The American Pope.* Times Books, 1984.
Crosby, Donald F. *God, Church, and Flag.* University of North Carolina Press, 1978.
Curran, Charles E. *Critical Concerns in Moral Theology.* University of Notre Dame Press, 1984.
De Caux, Len. *Labor Radical.* Beacon Press, 1970.
Dubofsky, Melvyn, and Warren Van Tine. *John L. Lewis.* Quadrangle/New York Times Book Co., 1977.
Farris, Robert E. L. *Chicago Sociology, 1920–1932.* University of Chicago Press, 1979.
Fish, John Hall. *Black Power/White Control.* Princeton University Press, 1973.
Fish, John, Gordon Nelson, Walter Stuhr, and Lawrence Witmer. *The Edge of the Ghetto.* University of Chicago Divinity School, 1966.
Gitlin, Todd. *The Sixties: Years of Hope, Days of Rage.* Bantam Books, 1987.
Goldman, Eric F. *The Crucial Decade—and After: America, 1945–1960.* Vintage, 1960.
Hayden, Tom. *Reunion.* Random House, 1988.
Hodgson, Godfrey. *America in Our Time.* Vintage, 1976.
Horowitz, Irving Louis. *C. Wright Mills: An American Utopian.* The Free Press, 1983.
Howe, Irving. *World of Our Fathers.* Touchstone, 1976.
Jackson, Kenneth T. *Crabgrass Frontier.* Oxford University Press, 1985.
Jacobs, James B. *Stateville.* University of Chicago Press, 1977.
Jacobs, Jane. *The Death and Life of Great American Cities.* Vintage, 1961.
Janowitz, Morris, ed. *The City.* University of Chicago Press, 1967.
Jones, Peter d'A., and Melvin G. Holli, eds. *Ethnic Chicago.* Wm. B. Eerdmans Publishing Company, 1981.
Josephson, Matthew. *Sidney Hillman: Statesman of American Labor.* Doubleday & Company, 1952.
Lasch, Christopher. *The New Radicalism in America, 1889–1963.* Vintage, 1967.
Matthiessen, Peter. *Sal Si Puedes.* Random House, 1969.
Matusow, Allen J. *The Unraveling of America.* Harper & Row, 1984.
Moynihan, Daniel P. *Maximum Feasible Misunderstanding.* The Free Press, 1969.
Rossi, Peter H., and Robert A. Dentler. *Politics of Urban Renewal.* The Free Press of Glencoe, 1961.
Sanders, Marion K. *The Professional Radical: Conversations with Saul Alinsky.* Harper & Row, 1970.

Schlesinger, Arthur M., Jr. *The Politics of Upheaval.* Houghton Mifflin Company, 1966.

Shanabruch, Charles. *Chicago's Catholics.* University of Notre Dame Press, 1981.

Silberman, Charles E. *Crisis in Black and White.* Vintage, 1964.

Slayton, Robert A. *Back of the Yards: The Making of a Local Democracy.* University of Chicago Press, 1986.

Snodgrass, Jon Dundee. *The American Criminological Tradition: Portraits of the Men and Ideology in a Discipline.* Diss., University of Pennsylvania, 1972.

Sorrentino, Anthony. *Organizing Against Crime.* Human Sciences Press, 1977.

Tjerandsen, Carl. *Education for Citizenship.* Emil Schwarzhaupt Foundation, 1980.

Wendt, Lloyd, and Herman Kogan. *Bosses in Lusty Chicago.* Indiana University Press, 1967.

Permissions Acknowledgments

Grateful acknowledgment is made to the following for permission to reprint previously published material:

The Atlantic: Excerpts from "Wanted: American Radicals" by James Bryant Conant, *Atlantic Monthly* (May 1943). Reprinted by permission of *The Atlantic,* 745 Boylston Street, Boston, MA 02116.

Harper's Magazine: Excerpts from Marion K. Sanders' "The Professional Radical" and "Conversations with Saul Alinsky." Copyright © 1965 by *Harper's Magazine.* All rights reserved. Reprinted from the June/July issue by special permission.

The New York Review of Books: Excerpts from Christopher Lasch's "Can the Left Rise Again," October 21, 1971. Copyright © 1971 by Nyrev, Inc. Reprinted by permission of *The New York Review of Books.*

Random House, Inc.: Excerpts from *Crisis in Black and White* by Charles Silberman. Copyright © 1964 by Random House, Inc. Rights in the British Commonwealth administered by Jonathan Cape Ltd. Reprinted by permission of Random House, Inc., and Jonathan Cape Ltd. Excerpt from *John L. Lewis: An Unauthorized Biography* by Saul Alinsky. Copyright 1949, renewed 1970 by Saul Alinsky. Reprinted by permission of Random House, Inc.

The Washington Post: Excerpts from "Orderly Revolution," a six-part series by Agnes Meyer (June 1945). Copyright 1945 by *The Washington Post.* Reprinted by permission of *The Washington Post.*

Grateful acknowledgment is made to The University Library, University of Illinois at Chicago, for permission to reprint previously unpublished material from the Saul Alinsky/Industrial Areas Foundation Records, Special Collections, and the Stephen Bubacz Papers, Special Collections.